Frommer's®
Washington, D.C.

My Washington, D.C.

by Elise Hartman Ford

"FOUR SCORE AND SEVEN YEARS AGO, OUR FATHERS BROUGHT FORTH on this continent, a new nation, conceived in Liberty . . ." Reading these words from Lincoln's Gettysburg Address, etched on the walls of the Lincoln Memorial, is just one of the many experiences in D.C. that evokes the inspiring idealism on which America was founded.

Grand monuments, historic structures, and memorials mark the U.S. capital like stars in a constellation. You can look up and search for the tip of the Washington Monument, point to the Capitol dome lit up at night, or spy the Washington National Cathedral's spires in the distance. From Capitol Hill to Georgetown's cobblestone streets to the stately embassies on Massachusetts Avenue, past, present, and future collide in this city. Basketball fans cheer at the Verizon Center while music lovers applaud at the Kennedy Center. A jazz club is in the Smithsonian's National Museum of Natural History and an Irish pub is in Chinatown.

Tourism officials have dubbed Washington, D.C., "The American Experience," which makes it sound like a static historical diorama. Of course, the city's history is formidable, but D.C. continues to thrive and evolve, nourished by diverse communities bursting with political and cultural energy. And the photos on these pages show the city at its best.

© Chuck Pefley/Alamy

Lots of people think the best time to visit the **LINCOLN MEMORIAL (left)** is at night, when it's lit up and dramatic. Romantic, too. But I like visiting during the day—swallowed up in the crush of chattering international travelers and curious school children—and feeling oh-so-proud of being linked by nationality to this remarkable American, considered by many to be the country's greatest president.

On September 21, 2004, 25,000 Native Americans representing 400 tribes from all over the Western Hemisphere marched and danced down the National Mall—to the beat of drums and thunderous applause from more than 55,000 spectators—to herald the opening of the **NATIONAL MUSEUM OF THE AMERICAN INDIAN (above)**. When you visit, be sure to admire every detail—from the windswept-look exterior to the Indian fry bread served in the museum cafe.

These are the words of my husband Jim, a veteran of the Vietnam War, to those who visit the **VIETNAM VETERANS MEMORIAL (left):** Run your fingers over the names of the lost inscribed here. Observe the reflections of others tracing a particular name. Notice the impromptu memorials left along the wall—flowers, a set of dog tags, an old photo, a faded combat badge. And listen to the murmurs of other visitors in the procession past the wall, ongoing since November 13, 1982, when the memorial was dedicated.

Of all the war memorials, the **KOREAN WAR VETERANS MEMORIAL (above),** dedicated in 1995, moves me the most on a visceral level. The lifelike statues of 19 men, weighed down by their gear, appear to be trudging through a field. Surrounded by juniper bushes (symbolic of Korea's rugged terrain) and covered in ponchos (a reminder of the foul weather they endured), they convey in their wary poses both cold fear and courage.

It can be hard to get through the doors of the Library of Congress, thanks to security procedures, but once you're in, patient volunteer docents treat you like you're the first one to ask how to get to the **READING ROOM OVERLOOK (left),** where to find the Gutenberg Bible, and how one registers to use the Reading Room. The best-kept secret is the lineup of engaging lectures, concerts, and films the Library hosts, mostly in the evenings; see the list on www.loc.gov.

"Meet you at the elephant." Translation: Meet you in the Rotunda of the **NATIONAL MUSEUM OF NATURAL HISTORY (below).** Washingtonians and visitors alike love these hard-to-miss museum landmarks as places to rendezvous and opportunities to marvel. This natural history museum is the largest in the world, with more than 126 million artifacts—including the legendary Hope Diamond—and yet it's only one of the Smithsonian Institution's 19 museums.

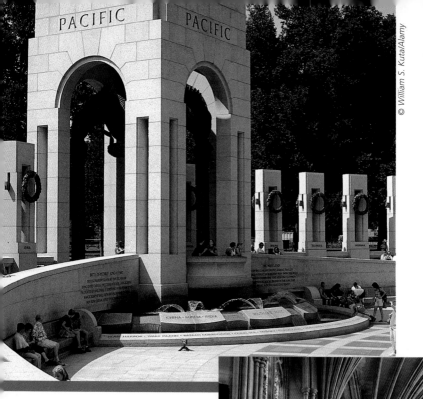

I would have preferred a museum that honored our soldiers by telling their stories, the way my dad recalls his time as a POW after being captured at the Battle of the Bulge. But the still powerful **NATIONAL WORLD WAR II MEMORIAL** (above) honors those who fought and died in the war with a pavilion of 56 granite pillars (one for each state and territory); 24 bas-relief panels illustrating scenes from the Atlantic and Pacific theaters; and a wall of 4,000 gold stars—one for each 100 soldiers who perished.

At the **WASHINGTON NATIONAL CATHEDRAL** (right), you can enjoy a picnic and get comfortable on the lawn of the Bishop's Garden. Inside this sixth largest cathedral in the world, you can admire the stained glass windows, stare up at the parade of state flags arrayed high up along the walls, and listen to an organ practice (every Mon and Wed 12:30–1pm).

At **TRYST CAFÉ (above)** in Adams Morgan—an eclectic, comfy coffeehouse/lounge—patrons hook up to laptops, cellphones, and lattes during the day, and connect with each other, over cocktails, at night. Tryst features free live jazz performances Monday through Wednesday evenings.

Ballets grace the stage at the **KENNEDY CENTER (right),** along with the best opera, orchestra, and theater performances. You'll also find free concerts, affordable family events, and $25-per-person jazz shows. Above all, I love the center's festivals, which range from Chinese culture to American country music.

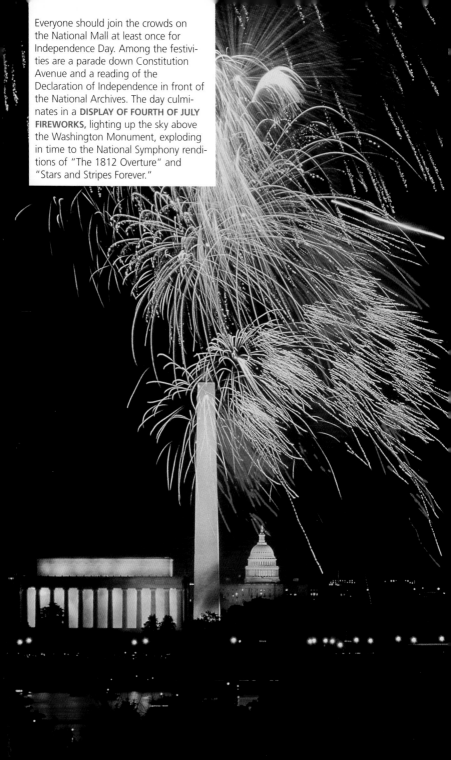

Everyone should join the crowds on the National Mall at least once for Independence Day. Among the festivities are a parade down Constitution Avenue and a reading of the Declaration of Independence in front of the National Archives. The day culminates in a **DISPLAY OF FOURTH OF JULY FIREWORKS,** lighting up the sky above the Washington Monument, exploding in time to the National Symphony renditions of "The 1812 Overture" and "Stars and Stripes Forever."

After dining at one of **GEORGETOWN**'s (left) great restaurants or browsing in one of its well-known shops, I like to stroll though the neighborhood's quiet back streets—where dollhouse-ish dwellings and grande-dame mansions line up behind brick sidewalks. Who lives here, I wonder as I stroll by, and who lived here 200 years ago? And how ever do they fit furniture through those narrow doors?

Traveling through **ROCK CREEK PARK** (above)—whether on foot, bike, or by car—one can reach the National Zoo, the Kennedy Center, and neighborhoods from Foggy Bottom and Georgetown all the way to Cleveland Park and Chevy Chase. It's a haven, beautiful in every season, and it's the one place you'll see Washingtonians of all stripes, unplugged and relaxed.

Historic Houses in Georgetown

President Ulysses S. Grant's summer White House in the 1870s

John and Jacqueline Kennedy lived in this brick townhouse while he was a U.S. Senator

Area of Detail

VIRGINIA

ARLINGTON

Union Station
The White House
The Capitol

Potomac River

0 1 mi
0 1 km

1 Dumbarton House
2 Evermay
3 Tudor Place
4 Dumbarton Oaks
5 3238 R Street NW
6 3307 N Street NW
7 Cox's Row
8 Halcyon House
9 Prospect House

0 100 meters
0 1/8 mile

Frommer's®

Washington, D.C.

2009

by Elise Hartman Ford

Here's what the critics say about Frommer's:

"Amazingly easy to use. Very portable, very complete."
—*Booklist*

"Detailed, accurate, and easy-to-read information for all price ranges."
—*Glamour Magazine*

"Hotel information is close to encyclopedic."
—*Des Moines Sunday Register*

"Frommer's Guides have a way of giving you a real feel for a place."
—*Knight Ridder Newspapers*

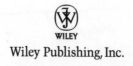

WILEY

Wiley Publishing, Inc.

About the Author

Elise Hartman Ford has been a freelance writer in the Washington, D.C., area since 1985. Her writing has appeared in the *Washington Post, Washingtonian* magazine, the London-based *Bradman's North America Guide, The Essential Guide to Business Travel, Ladies' Home Journal,* and other national, regional, and trade publications. In addition to this guide, she is the author of *Frommer's Washington, D.C., from $80 a Day, Frommer's Memorable Walks in Washington, D.C.,* and *Unique Meeting, Wedding, and Party Places in Greater Washington.*

Published by:

Wiley Publishing, Inc.

111 River St.
Hoboken, NJ 07030-5774

ISBN 978-0-470-28788-0

Editor: Christina Summers
with Ian Skinnari
Production Editor: Jonathan Scott
Cartographer: Roberta Stockwell
Photo Editor: Richard Fox
Production by Wiley Indianapolis Composition Services

Front cover photo: Thomas Jefferson Memorial
Back cover photo: Cyclist on sidewalk along old C&O Canal in Georgetown

For information on our other products and services or to obtain technical support, please contact our Customer Care Department within the U.S. at 800/762-2974, outside the U.S. at 317/572-3993 or fax 317/572-4002.

Wiley also publishes its books in a variety of electronic formats. Some content that appears in print may not be available in electronic formats.

Manufactured in the United States of America

5 4 3

Contents

List of Maps

An Invitation to the Reader

In researching this book, we discovered many wonderful places—hotels, restaurants, shops, and more. We're sure you'll find others. Please tell us about them, so we can share the information with your fellow travelers in upcoming editions. If you were disappointed with a recommendation, we'd love to know that, too. Please write to:

Frommer's Washington, D.C. 2009
Wiley Publishing, Inc. • 111 River St. • Hoboken, NJ 07030-5774

An Additional Note

Please be advised that travel information is subject to change at any time—and this is especially true of prices. We therefore suggest that you write or call ahead for confirmation when making your travel plans. The authors, editors, and publisher cannot be held responsible for the experiences of readers while traveling. Your safety is important to us, however, so we encourage you to stay alert and be aware of your surroundings. Keep a close eye on cameras, purses, and wallets, all favorite targets of thieves and pickpockets.

Other Great Guides for Your Trip:

Washington, D.C. Day by Day
Frommer's Portable Washington, D.C.
Frommer's Washington, D.C. with Kids
The Unofficial Guide to Washington, D.C.

Frommer's Star Ratings, Icons & Abbreviations

Every hotel, restaurant, and attraction listing in this guide has been ranked for quality, value, service, amenities, and special features using a **star-rating system.** In country, state, and regional guides, we also rate towns and regions to help you narrow down your choices and budget your time accordingly. Hotels and restaurants are rated on a scale of zero (recommended) to three stars (exceptional). Attractions, shopping, nightlife, towns, and regions are rated according to the following scale: zero stars (recommended), one star (highly recommended), two stars (very highly recommended), and three stars (must-see).

In addition to the star-rating system, we also use **seven feature icons** that point you to the great deals, in-the-know advice, and unique experiences that separate travelers from tourists. Throughout the book, look for:

Finds	Special finds—those places only insiders know about
Fun Fact	Fun facts—details that make travelers more informed and their trips more fun
Kids	Best bets for kids and advice for the whole family
Moments	Special moments—those experiences that memories are made of
Overrated	Places or experiences not worth your time or money
Tips	Insider tips—great ways to save time and money
Value	Great values—where to get the best deals

The following **abbreviations** are used for credit cards:

AE	American Express	DISC	Discover	V	Visa
DC	Diners Club	MC	MasterCard		

Frommers.com

Now that you have this guidebook to help you plan a great trip, visit our website at **www.frommers.com** for additional travel information on more than 4,000 destinations. We update features regularly to give you instant access to the most current trip-planning information available. At Frommers.com, you'll find scoops on the best airfares, lodging rates, and car rental bargains. You can even book your travel online through our reliable travel booking partners. Other popular features include:

- Online updates of our most popular guidebooks
- Vacation sweepstakes and contest giveaways
- Newsletters highlighting the hottest travel trends
- Podcasts, interactive maps, and up-to-the-minute events listings
- Opinionated blog entries by Arthur Frommer himself
- Online travel message boards with featured travel discussions

What's New in Washington, D.C.

Wassup D.C.? It's 2009 and change is breaking out all over. A new president is in the White House. The shaken-not-stirred Congress is full of new faces. As the administration turns over, so do our neighborhoods, where people from the old political guard depart to their home states and new politicos arrive to take their place.

On a personal level, I would say that hope is in the air. Even locals, like me, who have lived here for decades and witnessed many shifts in administration, look with eagerness toward our newly elected officials, ready to believe that these people surely will strive to represent our country's best interests as well as our own. You might think that Washingtonians would be the most jaded of Americans, having experienced, often firsthand, the ruthlessness of politics. I think, instead, we may be some of the most positive-thinking individuals in the country. Maybe it's a criterion for living here, this belief in the essential goodness of people and in our democratic institutions. The discouraged move away.

Thankfully, politics is not the only game in town. How about them **Washington Nationals**? Hmm. It's true that so far the capital's baseball team has not excelled in its Eastern Division of Major League Baseball, but once again, hope springs eternal. As of April 2008, the team has its own stadium, **Nationals Ballpark** (p. 256), whose worst seats, in nosebleed territory, offer the best view of city landmarks—some consolation, I guess, if yours is only a bird's-eye view of the game.

The other good news about the ballpark is the fact that local-favorite restaurants are the food vendors. Vendors include **Gifford's** ice cream; **Red, Hot & Blue** barbecue; and the Washington institution, **Ben's Chili Bowl.**

Feed Washingtonians well and we're yours. We love to eat, and we have a booming restaurant scene to show for it. Apparently, word has seeped out to the culinary world at large, for suddenly several celebrity chefs are setting up shop here. (Just to make sure you understand they are celebrities, these VIP chefs always use their own names in the restaurant titles.) So now look for the **Westend Bistro by Eric Ripert** (p. 131), in the Ritz-Carlton Washington, and the **Source by Wolfgang Puck** (p. 126) inside the Newseum (see below). By the time you read this, another big name restaurant will have debuted, **Adour Alain Ducasse,** in the lavishly renovated **St. Regis Hotel** (p. 93). Honestly, though, you're in for a treat if you dine at any of these restaurants. (Try the dumplings at the Source.)

Long before Eric, Wolfgang, and Alain graced us with their presence, we had our own resident bon vivant Frenchman, chef extraordinaire Michel Richard. Richard, who fell in love with Washington, D.C., ages ago, is renowned for his award-winning **Michel Richard Citronelle** (p. 152). In 2007, Richard opened his more casual bistro, **Central** (p. 128), which promptly won the James Beard

Foundation's 2008 "Best new restaurant in America" award. Central, which is located at 10th Street and Pennsylvania Avenue NW, in the Penn Quarter, is currently our hardest restaurant to get in to.

Other new restaurants are wowing locals and food critics, alike, including the wine-centric **Proof** (p. 130) in the Penn Quarter and **Tackle Box** (p. 157) in Georgetown, a very inexpensive place to enjoy fresh fish, obtained in ecofriendly fashion, and delicious sides, like mac and cheese and french fries.

So what else is there besides food, sports, and politics going on in the nation's capital? Culture, of course. Making headline news in its own right is the humongous **Newseum** (p. 209), which debuted on Pennsylvania Avenue in April 2008, billing itself as "the most interactive museum in the world." You can watch 4-D movies on heroic journalists, like Nellie Bly, and tape your own news broadcast. Folks from National Public Radio and other TV and radio stations sometimes broadcast their programs from the Newseum's studio.

Not far from the Newseum, the **National Museum of Crime and Punishment,** which opened in May 2008, presents a sort-of Hollywoodish take on crime, displaying the car used by Warren Beatty and Faye Dunaway in the 1967 *Bonnie and Clyde* movie, for instance, rather than the actual car used by the criminals.

Up on Capitol Hill, the **Capitol Visitor Center** (p. 168) is now open—for real, this time. The center lies beneath the Capitol and can fit as many as 4,000 (!) people. This is where you go to queue for a tour of the Capitol, and to learn a bit about the building and its history, too. The center holds exhibits, a restaurant, and 26 restrooms.

In Smithsonian news, the **National Museum of Natural History** (p. 193) pulled back the curtains on its grand new **Ocean Hall** in September 2008; and the **National Museum of American History** (p. 192) reopened its doors in the fall of 2008, ready to show off its **Star-Spangled Banner Gallery.**

On September 11, 2008, the Pentagon dedicated its outdoor **Pentagon 9/11 Memorial** to the 125 Pentagon workers and 58 passenger victims killed in the terrorist plane attack of the Pentagon on September 11, 2001. The Pentagon has taken pains to allow the public 24-hour access to the memorial while restricting parking and walkways. In other words, whether you take the subway, drive, or take the Tourmobile to the memorial, you're going to have a bit of a walk to reach it. As has been true since September 11, 2001, only Pentagon employees are allowed to enter the Pentagon building.

The conclusion of 2009 will see the dedication of the National Mall's newest memorial, the **Martin Luther King, Jr., National Memorial** (p. 175).

The Best of Washington, D.C.

I'm standing on the steps of the **Lincoln Memorial,** where the wind is having its way with my hair. "It's often breezy here," I overhear a park ranger say, just as another gust lifts the cap off the head of the T-shirted tourist next to me. I reach for it, and then it's gone. I scan the landscape, across to the **Reflecting Pool** and beyond that to the **World War II Memorial** and then to the **Washington Monument,** presiding on its own hill nearly a mile away. Snaking my way left across the crowded steps, around the Buddhist monk in saffron robes aiming his digital camera at the marvelous view, through a throng of German visitors listening intently to their interpreter guide, I am able to spy the **Capitol,** lined up in the distance behind the Washington Monument.

A noisy commotion has broken out on a nearby street, and I observe a stream of black sedans and limos sweeping through an intersection cleared by police. "The President, out on an official visit," says someone behind me. It's my capless tourist, who thanks me for trying to catch his hat. He's from Louisiana, it turns out, which compels me to recommend a favorite restaurant, **Johnny's Half Shell** on Capitol Hill, for authentic tastes of New Orleans' gumbo, but also of our regional cuisine—crab imperial, crab cakes. He in turn enthuses about the free nightly concerts at the **Kennedy Center;** a zydeco band played there the night before, it seems.

"You know, you can see the Kennedy Center from here," I say. And together we stroll to the back platform of the Lincoln Memorial to admire the gorgeous sight of the **Memorial Bridge** and the Potomac River, which swerves gracefully past the Kennedy Center and on to **Georgetown.** A handful of other tourists have migrated to this choice location, including a sunburned British family, whose patriarch is attempting to pose his brood for a family portrait.

In another few minutes my little band of tourists will rejoin the hordes of other sightseers visiting the **National Museum of American History,** boarding a tour bus, standing in line at the Capitol. And by day's end, back at the hotel, they will be regretting that they didn't wear sunscreen, or resolving to rise earlier tomorrow to secure a ticket to tour the **Newseum.**

I wish I could gather them around me before they go. I would tell them that Washington is a place of grand images, but also of remarkable words. They should note them everywhere, starting with the inscription of Lincoln's Gettysburg Address, right there in the memorial: "Four score and seven years ago, our fathers brought forth on this continent, a new nation, conceived in Liberty, and dedicated to the proposition that all men are created equal."

I would direct them to make time for visiting my favorite museum, the **Smithsonian American Art Museum,** as well as the **National Portrait Gallery**—in my favorite part of town—the Penn Quarter, to view the masterpieces like Howard Finster's folk art, William H. Johnson's scenes of African-American life, Louise Nevelson's sculptures, and portraits of national figures, Pocahontas to George Washington, Samuel

Clemens (Mark Twain) to Katherine Hepburn. I would recommend that they enjoy a drink in the museum's second-floor portico overlooking the bustling downtown scene. And follow up that experience with dinner at the nearby joyful Mexican restaurant **Oyamel,** or at a beloved Washington haunt, the **Tabard Inn,** in Dupont Circle. And top off the night at **Twins Jazz,** on U Street, for sounds of top-notch, cool performances by jazz legends.

Finally, I would say, "Leave room for the chance encounter." In this city, whose population is as culturally diverse as those who tour here, you may find yourself forging connections with people from halfway around the world, or from your own hometown, and these experiences may prove your fondest memories of the city. As the nation's capital and the home of our democratic government, Washington, D.C., like no other city, holds a certain place in the world, as it represents all the freedoms and ideals that Americans hold dear. Against the backdrop of the **White House,** the Capitol, and the **Supreme Court;** in the corners of our national memorials and museums; within the shared experience of the music and food and theater and shops and parks and sights and sounds of our Washington neighborhoods, a little small talk between strangers creates opportunities for understanding differences.

But of course, I won't say all this, and maybe it's better that way. For right now, I can see that my erstwhile Washingtonians are thrilling in the moment, and the view, and the possibilities of this monumental day in the nation's capital. And really, that's the best of what Washington's all about.

1 The Most Unforgettable Travel Experiences

- **Watch the Supreme Court in Action:** Only in Washington can one watch and listen to the country's nine foremost legal experts nimbly and intensely dissect the merits of both sides of an argument, whose decisions can affect profoundly both a person and the nation. Think of the Supreme Court justices as a team representing the U.S. Constitution, and only in their chamber do you get to see them play. See p. 169.

- **View Washington Landmarks by Moonlight:** A must. There is nothing as spectacular as seeing the Lincoln Memorial illuminated at night, unless it's the sight of the White House, the Capitol, or the Washington Monument lit up after dark. Go by bus on Tourmobile or by bike via the Bike the Sites service; both operations offer narrated day- and nighttime tours. See p. 176.

- **Visit Your Senator or Member of Congress:** Take advantage of your constituent status and stop by your senator's and/or representative's office in the Capitol to offer your two cents on current issues. Pick up passes to the Capitol's Senate and House chambers and attend a session to observe your elected politicians at work. Try to tour the Capitol while you're here. See p. 163.

- **Bicycle past the Potomac River and Around the Tidal Basin:** Rent a bike and ride the paved bike/walking path that extends 11 miles from the Lincoln Memorial to the Maryland border (through Rock Creek Park). Or head the other direction from the Lincoln Memorial, following the combination of street, sidewalk, and pathway that encircles the cherry tree–rimmed Tidal Basin. The Potomac River, Rock Creek, and spectacular Washington sites are on either side of you as you make your way. For a really long bike ride, follow the pathway past the Lincoln

Memorial, cross the Arlington Memorial Bridge to the trail on the other side, and pedal the 19 miles to Mount Vernon. See p. 228 and 282.

2 The Best Splurge Hotels

- **Mandarin Oriental,** 1330 Maryland Ave. SW, near National Mall (☎ 202/554-8588; www.mandarinoriental.com/washington): This is the capital's prettiest and most luxurious hotel. You're away from it all but still within walking distance of Smithsonian museums. Its spa and restaurant are the crème de la crème, and guestroom designs follow the principles of Feng shui to attract good fortune. See p. 84.

- **Four Seasons,** 2800 Pennsylvania Ave. NW, Georgetown (☎ 202/342-0444; www.fourseasons.com/washington): It's so nice to be loved, isn't it? And the Four Seasons staff make you feel that way, pampering you relentlessly and greeting you by name, remembering your likes and dislikes. Thanks to its second multi-million-dollar renovation in 3 years, hotel guest rooms are 50% larger and twice as inviting, suites are redone, and the lobby and restaurant are completely transformed. See p. 108.

- **Willard InterContinental,** 1401 Pennsylvania Ave. NW, Penn Quarter (☎ 202/628-9100; www.washington.interconti.com): The Willard provided a temporary home for a president or two and continues to be a major gathering spot for capital powermongers. This homegrown, but world-class, hotel has a fine restaurant, a historic bar, a spa, and a just-opened courtyard cafe. You'd be missing something if you didn't at least step inside, even if you're not staying here. See p. 90.

3 The Best Moderately Priced Hotels

- **Four Points by Sheraton Washington, D.C. Downtown,** 1201 K St. NW, Midtown (☎ 202/289-7600; www.fourpoints.com/washingtondcdowntown): Plenty of attractions are within walking distance of this central downtown hotel: the Verizon Center, convention center, museums, restaurants, and clubs. But you have good reason to stay put, too: comfortable rooms, a fitness center, a restaurant, and a rooftop pool—all for rates that can be as low as $109 (though usually start at $195). See p. 96.

- **Georgetown Suites,** 1111 30th St. NW, Georgetown (☎ 202/298-1600; www.georgetownsuites.com): The suites are large, light-filled, and cheery and the service welcoming in this great-value hotel. All sorts of lodging are available, from studio to penthouse, but all units have a full kitchen. And while hotels throughout the city increase their rates from year to year, Georgetown Suites' rates remain fairly constant, in the range of $155 for a studio to $425 for a town house. See p. 109.

- **Hampton Inn Washington, D.C. Convention Center,** 901 6th St. NW, Penn Quarter (☎ 202/842-2500; www.washingtondc.hamptoninn.com): Close to the convention center and the heart of the Penn Quarter, this hotel, which opened in 2005, still has a fresh feeling about it. Rates start as low as $129 on weekends, $201 weekdays. Included in rates are use of the hotel's exercise room and pool, and the daily hot breakfast. See p. 92.

4 The Most Unforgettable Dining Experiences

- **Michel Richard Citronelle,** in the Latham Hotel in Georgetown, 3000 M St. NW (© **202/625-2150**): Richard ebulliently works in his open kitchen creating sumptuous, constantly changing dishes, from fricassee of escargots to squab leg confit with macaroni gratin and black truffles. Each presentation is a work of art, with swirls of colorful sauce surrounding the main event. See p. 152.

- **Komi,** 1509 17th St. NW, Dupont Circle (© **202/332-9200**): A dinner at Komi restores one, thanks to creative—but not too creative—dishes (grilled asparagus with watercress and feta, squab stuffed with foie gras and figs), polished service, and a remarkably relaxed atmosphere. And then there's the chef, the unassuming Johnny Monis, who somehow has figured this all out at the tender age of 20-something. See p. 146.

- **CityZen,** 1330 Maryland Ave. SW, in the Mandarin Oriental Hotel, near National Mall (© **202/787-6868**): Eric Ziebold is the chef here, having previously served at the renowned French Laundry, in Napa Valley. Washingtonians don't quite know what they've done to deserve the culinary gifts he bestows upon them: North Carolina rainbow trout served with petite red Russian kale and smoked salmon roe emulsion, for example. Bring a full wallet. See p. 118.

- **1789,** 1226 36th St. NW, Georgetown (© **202/965-1789**): Isn't it romantic? Washingtonians think so, and you will too—especially if you're seated near one of the warming fireplaces on a wintry night, slurping up the restaurant's signature oyster and champagne stew with Smithfield ham and walnuts. So put on your best duds and be prepared for a relaxing meal with only your food and your dinner companion to distract you. See p. 153.

- **Restaurant Eve,** 110 S. Pitt St., Old Town Alexandria (© **703/706-0450**): It's as hard to book a table here as at CityZen in the District. Exotic drinks, entrees such as bouillabaisse and butter-poached halibut with lobster, and service that includes ironing tablecloths between seatings, have drawn people here from all over the area. Birthday or not, order the "birthday cake" for dessert: delicious white cake layered and iced with pink frosting and sprinkles. Yum. See p. 286.

5 The Best Things to Do for Free

- **Peruse the Constitution:** Only in Washington and only at the National Archives will you ever be able to read the original documents that so well grounded this nation in liberty. Here, you'll find the Declaration of Independence, the Constitution of the United States, and the Bill of Rights—all on display behind glass. See p. 199.

- **People-Watch at Dupont Circle:** This traffic circle is also a park, an all-weather hangout for mondo-bizarre biker-couriers, chess players, street musicians, and lovers. Sit on a bench and watch the scenes around you. See p. 69.

- **Attend a Millennium Stage Performance at the Kennedy Center:** Every evening at 6pm, the Kennedy Center presents a free 1-hour concert performed by local, up-and-coming, national, or international musicians. This is a winner. After the performance, head through the glass doors to the terrace for a view of the Potomac River. See p. 211.

- **Groove to the Sounds of Live Jazz in the Sculpture Garden:** On summer's Friday evenings at the National Gallery of Art Sculpture Garden, you can dip your toes in the fountain pool and chill, as live jazz groups serenade you from 5 to 8pm. The jazz is free; the tapas and wine and beer served in the garden's Pavilion Café are not. See p. 187.
- **Pick a Museum (Just About), Any Museum:** That's the thing about Washington—because this is the U.S. capital, many of its museums are federal institutions, which means admission is free. The National Gallery of Art, the U.S. Botanic Garden, and the Smithsonian's 17 Washington museums, from National Air and Space to the Freer Gallery, are among the many spectacular free places to visit. See chapter 7.

6 The Best Outdoor Activities

- **Ice-Skate at the National Gallery:** The National Gallery of Art Sculpture Garden pool turns into an ice-skating rink in winter. So visit the Gallery, finishing up at the Sculpture Garden, where you can rent skates and twirl around on the ice, admiring sculptures as you go. Treat yourself to hot chocolate and sandwiches at the Pavilion Café in the garden. See p. 229.
- **Attend an Event on the Mall:** Think of the National Mall as the nation's public square, where something is always going on, whether it's a book festival in the fall, the splendid Independence Day celebration every Fourth of July, or soccer, baseball, even cricket games year-round. Pack a picnic and hold your own little party. See p. 30 for a calendar of annual events.
- **View Washington from the Water:** Rent a paddle boat to skim the surface of the Tidal Basin for an hour, or cruise the Potomac River aboard one of several sightseeing vessels to relax from foot-weary travels. The paddle boats give you a remarkable view of the Jefferson Memorial; river cruises offer a pleasant interval for catching a second wind, as they treat you to a marvelous perspective of the city. See chapter 7.
- **Sit at an Outdoor Cafe and Watch the Washington World Go By:** The capital has plenty of places that offer front-row seats, from the Penn Quarter's Les Halles, with views up and down Pennsylvania Avenue, to Hank's Oyster Bar, whose Dupont Circle perch is the perfect spot for watching a passing parade of live entertainment. See chapter 6.

7 The Best Neighborhoods for Getting Lost

- **Go Behind the Scenes in Georgetown:** The truth is, you *want* to get lost in Georgetown because it's the side streets that hold the history and centuries-old houses of this one-time Colonial tobacco port. And not to worry, Georgetown is so compact, you're never very far from the main drags of M Street and Wisconsin Avenue. For a back-streets tour of Georgetown, see p. 232.
- **Spend the Day in Alexandria:** Just a short distance (by Metro, car, boat, or bike) from the District is George Washington's Virginia hometown. On and off the beaten track are quaint cobblestone streets, charming boutiques and antiques stores, 18th-century houses and other historic attractions, and fine restaurants. See p. 275.

Site Seeing: The Best Washington, D.C., Websites

- **www.bnbaccom.com:** For those who prefer to stay in a private home, guesthouse, inn, or furnished apartment, this service offers more than 30 for you to consider.
- **www.bwiairport.com:** Ground transport, terminal maps, flight status, and airport facilities for Baltimore–Washington International Airport.
- **www.culturaltourismdc.org:** Cultural Tourism DC is a grass-roots, non-profit coalition of more than 200 arts, heritage, community, and cultural organizations collaborating to promote the less-known stories and attractions of Washington. The website lists tours, itineraries, calendars, and plenty of background information about historic and cultural sites that you won't find anywhere else.
- **www.dc.gov:** This is the city of Washington's website, full of details about both federal and local D.C., including history and tourism. Every day, the site lists a calendar of what's going on around town.
- **www.dcaccommodations.com:** This nicely designed site recommends hotels suited for families, women, sightseers, or business travelers.
- **www.destinationdc.org:** Destination DC is the new name for the Washington, D.C. Convention and Tourism Corporation. This website leads you through various screens of information on what to see and do in D.C. and provides travel updates on security issues. You have to play around with the site a little to find all the information you need. Start by clicking on "Visiting" and take it from there, for tips on where to stay, dine, shop, and sightsee.
- **www.fly2dc.com:** In addition to its extensive information about airline travel in and out of Washington (and ground transportation from each airport), this site also offers fun articles about restaurants and things to do in D.C. The monthly print magazine version, *Washington Flyer,* is available free at Washington National and Dulles airports.
- **www.house.gov:** Once you're in the U.S. House of Representatives site, click on "Visiting D.C." to learn more about touring the Capitol building. The site allows you to take a virtual tour of the chamber where the House meets and to learn whether the House is in session. The site also connects you with the websites for each of the representatives; you can use this site to e-mail your representative.
- **www.kennedy-center.org:** Find out what's playing at the Kennedy Center and listen to live broadcasts through the Net.
- **www.metwashairports.com:** Ground transport, terminal maps, flight status, and airport facilities for Washington Dulles International and Ronald Reagan Washington National airports.
- **www.mountvernon.org:** Click on "Visit" for daily attractions at Mount Vernon and a calendar of events, as well as information on dining, shopping,

- **Stroll Embassy Row:** Explore the neighborhood of Dupont Circle to view smaller embassies, then head northwest on Massachusetts Avenue to admire the larger ones. You'll walk along gorgeous tree-shaded streets

and school programs. For a sneak preview, click on "Virtual Mansion Tour" to see images of the master bedroom, dining room, slave memorial, and the Washingtons' tomb.

- **www.nps.gov:** This National Park Service site includes links to some dozen memorials and monuments. When you click "DC" on the map, a listing of the capital's National Park sites appears, including the National World War II Memorial, Washington Monument, Jefferson Memorial, National Mall, Ford's Theatre, FDR Memorial, Lincoln Memorial, and Vietnam Veterans Memorial.
- **www.opentable.com:** This site allows you to make reservations at some of the capital's finest restaurants.
- **www.senate.gov:** In the U.S. Senate site, click on "Visitors" for an online virtual tour of the Capitol building and information about touring the actual Senate Gallery. It takes a few seconds for the images to download, but it's worth the wait to enjoy the panoramic video tour. Also, find out when the Senate is in session. The site connects you with the websites for each of the senators; you can use this site to e-mail your senator.
- **www.si.edu:** This is the Smithsonian Institution's home page, which provides information about visiting Washington and leads you to the individual websites for each Smithsonian museum.
- **www.washingtondchotelsonline.com:** Capitol Reservations, a 25-year-old company, represents more than 100 hotels in the Washington area, each of which has been screened for cleanliness, safety, and other factors. You can book your room online.
- **www.washingtonian.com:** The print magazine of the same name posts some of its articles here, including "What's Happening," a monthly guide to what's on at museums, theaters, and other cultural showplaces around town, and a directory of reviews of Washington restaurants. The magazine really wants you to buy the print edition, though—for sale at bookstores, drugstores, and grocery stores throughout the area.
- **www.washingtonpost.com:** The *Washington Post*'s site is an extremely helpful source for up-to-date information on restaurants, attractions, shopping, and nightlife (as well as world news).
- **www.whitehouse.gov:** Click on "History & Tours" to learn about visiting the White House and upcoming public events. You'll find all sorts of links here, from a history of the White House, to archived White House documents, to an e-mail page you can use to contact the president or vice president.
- **www.wmata.com:** Timetables, maps, fares, and more for the Metro buses and subways that serve the Washington, D.C., metro area.

lined with Beaux Arts mansions, many built by fabulously wealthy magnates during the Gilded Age. See p. 259 for information about how to see the interiors of some of these embassies.

8 The Best Places to Hang with the Locals

- **Shop at Eastern Market:** Capitol Hill is home to more than government buildings; it's a community of old town houses, antiques shops, and the veritable institution Eastern Market. (Although a fire in spring 2007 destroyed much of the historic interior, the market should be up and running by the time you read this.) Here, the locals barter and shop every Saturday and Sunday for fresh produce, baked goods, and flea-market bargains. See p. 241.
- **Pub- and Club-It in D.C.'s Hot Spots:** Join Washington's footloose and fancy-free any night of the week, but especially Thursday through Saturday, along U Street between 9th and 16th streets; in Adams-Morgan; and in the Penn Quarter as they start out or end up (mostly end up—clubs and bars are open late in these neighborhoods). See chapter 9 for bar and club suggestions.
- **Go for a Jog on the National Mall:** Lace up your running shoes and race down the Mall at your own pace, dodging tourists and admiring famous sites as you go. Your fellow runners will be buff military staff who've zoomed over from the Pentagon, speed-walking members of Congress, and a cross section of downtown workers doing their best to stave off the telltale pencil pusher's paunch. Distance from the foot of the Capitol to the Lincoln Memorial: 2 miles. See p. 175.
- **Take Tea at the Top of Washington National Cathedral:** Join a certain segment of Washington society (mostly women friends and moms and daughters) for tea and a tour. Tuesday and Wednesday afternoons at 1:30pm you can tour the world's sixth-largest cathedral, then indulge in tea, scones, and lemon tarts served on the seventh floor of the West tower, whose arched windows overlook the city and beyond to Sugarloaf Mountain in Maryland. See p. 215.

9 The Best Offbeat Experiences

- **Listen to "Help Me Fake It to the Right" and "Campaign and Suffering":** The Capitol Steps, a musical political satire troupe, performs these and other irreverent original tunes in skits that skewer politicians on both sides of the aisle. You can see them every weekend at the Ronald Reagan Building. See p. 257.
- **Salsa Up a Storm:** At Habana Village in Adams-Morgan, Lucky Bar near Dupont Circle, and other clubs and bars, you can take salsa and tango lessons, and then put your steps to the test on the dance floor. See p. 263.
- **Explore Washington from a Different Angle:** Sign up for a tour of Washington that follows a certain theme, such as Civil War landmarks, theater trails, places where Dickens stopped, or scandal-laced sites, to name just a few. Several companies offer offbeat kinds of tours. See p. 225.
- **Sample Offbeat but World-Class Cuisine:** At the **minibar** inside Café Atlantico, chef José Andrés concocts whimsical little tastes—like foie gras in a cocoon of cotton candy. Thirty or more tastes make an unforgettable meal for 12 lucky people (2 seatings of 6 people each) per night. See p. 127.

Washington, D.C., in Depth

Allow me to introduce you to Washington, D.C. You may well have made her earlier acquaintance—so many people have. The city, after all, is the nation's capital, the seat of power for the world's most enlightened democracy, the home of the president of the United States, and to every embassy with whom our government maintains diplomatic relations.

So it's quite possible that you've been here before, and toured the Capitol, visited your representative in Congress, or watched the Supreme Court justices argue a momentous case. Perhaps you strolled the perimeter of the White House or even arranged a group tour of the interior. You might have peered at the original Declaration of Independence on view in the National Archives or taken a walking tour through Georgetown's historic streets.

No? History and politics leave you cold, you say? Well then, you must have visited Washington to bask in its beauty—we *are* known for that, you know. No doubt you arrived in spring, to gaze at our famous blossoming cherry trees bordering the Tidal Basin. Or in autumn perhaps, when you probably rode a bike through the woodlands of Rock Creek Park, the National Park Service's oldest and largest urban park. In summer, I'm certain you would have found time to cruise the placid Potomac, the perfect, coolest vantage spot for admiring Washington's elegant cityscape. And in winter, surely, you went ice-skating on the rink in the National Gallery's Sculpture Garden, surrounded by remarkable sculptures close up, and famous landmarks in the landscape beyond.

And if you arrived in D.C. wanting none of that, or only some of that, you must have been here for arts and culture—our museums, performing arts centers, and restaurants are world-renowned, as I'm sure you are well aware. I can imagine you would have attempted to tackle every one of D.C.'s 16 Smithsonian museums, from the Freer Gallery to the American History Museum, or made sure to take in a ballet at the Kennedy Center. You may have stopped to enjoy a champagne cocktail at Proof, in the Penn Quarter, and a juicy steak at the Palm, near Dupont Circle.

You may have done all of these things and been to Washington many times, but still, I am sorry—or rather, overjoyed—to have to tell you, that no, you really don't know Washington. You couldn't possibly. You are not here right now, in this particular moment.

For never has there been a more exciting time to visit the nation's capital. A charismatic new president is in the White House and a debonair young mayor is in charge of the city. The city's Penn Quarter, Dupont Circle, and Georgetown neighborhoods bustle with activity day and night. The U.S. Capitol Visitor Center is open on the Hill and the blockbuster Newseum has debuted on Pennsylvania Avenue. Celebrity chefs Alain Ducasse, Wolfgang Puck, and Eric Ripert now have their own restaurants in Washington, dubbed "one of the most exciting restaurant cities on the East Coast," by *Travel + Leisure.*

Thrilling change and a renewed sense of purpose, both political and cultural, are in the air. Come, come to Washington, to re-visit places of old with fresh eyes, and to celebrate what's new.

1 Looking Back at Washington, D.C.

Like most cities, Washington, D.C.'s history is written in its landscape. Behold the lustrous Potomac River, whose discovery by Captain John Smith in 1608 led to settlement of the area, getting the story going. Notice the lay of the land: the 160-foot-wide avenues radiating from squares and circles, the sweeping vistas, the abundant parkland, very much as Pierre Charles L'Enfant intended when he planned the "Federal District" in 1791. Look around and you will see the Washington Monument, the U.S. Capitol, the Lincoln Memorial, the White House, and other landmarks, their very prominence in the flat, central cityscape attesting to their significance in the formation of our nation's capital.

But Washington's history is very much a tale of two cities. Beyond the National Mall, the memorials, and our federal government buildings lies "D.C.," the municipality. Politicians speak critically of "Washington," shorthand, we understand, for all that is wrong with our current government. They should be more precise. With that snide dismissal, politicians dismiss, as well, the particular locale in which the capital resides. It is a place of vibrant neighborhoods and vivid personalities, a vaunted arts-and-culture scene, international diversity, rich African-American heritage, uniquely D.C. attractions and people—the very citizens who built the capital in the first place and have kept it running ever since.

EARLY DAYS

In the beginning, there were Indians. Of course. Captain John Smith may have been the first European to discover this waterfront property of lush greenery and woodlands, but the Nacotchtank and Piscataway Indians were way ahead of him. As Smith and company settled the area, they disrupted the Indian ways of life and introduced European diseases. The Indians gradually moved away.

By 1751, Irish and Scottish immigrants had founded "George Town," named for the king of England and soon established as an important tobacco shipping port. Several houses from those days still exist in Georgetown: the Old Stone House (on M St. NW), originally a woodworker's home from around the 1760s, operated by the National Park Service and open to the public; and a few magnificent ship merchants' mansions on N and Prospect streets, which, at the time, overlooked the Potomac River. (These are privately owned and not open to the public.)

BIRTH OF THE CAPITAL

After colonists in George Town and elsewhere in America rebelled against British rule, defeating the British in the American Revolution (1775–83), Congress, in quick succession, unanimously elected General George Washington as the first president of the United States, ratified a U.S. Constitution, and proposed that a city be designed and built to house the seat of government for the new nation and to function fully in commercial and cultural capacities. Much squabbling ensued. The North wanted the capital, the South wanted the capital. President Washington huddled with his secretary of state, Thomas Jefferson, and devised a solution that Congress approved in 1790: The nation's capital would be "a site not exceeding 10 miles square" located on the Potomac. The South was happy, for this area was nominally in their region; Northern states were appeased by the

Scandals

What is it about politicians and scandal? Examples throughout Washington's history suggest a mutual attraction. Consider these:

DNA tests have proven the sexual misconduct of our third president, Thomas Jefferson, who fathered a child with his slave, Sally Hemings; and about 200 years later, of our 42nd president, when the stain on the blue dress of White House intern Monica Lewinsky was indeed determined to be the remains of the president's semen.

In the famous Teapot Dome case of the early 1920s, our 29th president, Warren Harding, presided over a corrupt administration, several of whose members accepted bribes in return for helping private developers obtain federal oil fields. Other scandals surfaced after Harding's death, including the fact that the president had carried on several affairs while he was in the White House.

In 1979, John Jenrette, the Democratic congressman from South Carolina, was arrested on charges of corruption, but most people more readily remember him as the politician discovered having sex on the Capitol steps with his wife, Rita.

stipulation that the South pay off the North's Revolutionary War debt, and by the city's location, on the North-South border. Washington, District of Columbia, made her debut.

The only problem was that she was not exactly presentable. The brave new country's capital proved to be a tract of undeveloped wilderness, where pigs, goats, and cows roamed free, and habitable houses were few and far between. Thankfully, the city did have the masterful 1791 plan of the gifted but temperamental French-born engineer, Pierre Charles L'Enfant. Slaves, free blacks, and immigrants from Ireland, Scotland, and other countries strove to fulfill L'Enfant's remarkable vision, erecting first the White House (the city's oldest federal structure), then the Capitol, and other buildings. Gradually, the capital began to take shape, though too slowly perhaps for some. The writer Anthony Trollope, visiting in 1860, declared Washington "as melancholy and miserable a town as the mind of man can conceive."

WASHINGTON GROWS UP

During the Civil War the capital became an armed camp and headquarters for the Union Army, overflowing with thousands of followers. Parks became campgrounds; churches, schools, and federal buildings, including the Capitol and the Patent Office (now the National Portrait Gallery), became hospitals; and forts ringed the town. The population grew from 60,000 to 200,000, as soldiers, former slaves, merchants, and laborers converged on the scene. The streets were filled with the wounded, nursed by the likes of Walt Whitman, one of many making the rounds to aid ailing soldiers. In spite of everything, President Lincoln insisted that work on the Capitol continue. "If people see the Capitol going on, it is a sign we intend the Union shall go on," he said.

In the wake of the Civil War and President Lincoln's assassination, Congress took stock of the capital and saw a town worn out by years of war and awash in people, but still lacking the most fundamental facilities. The place was a mess. Members proposed moving the capital city elsewhere, perhaps to St. Louis or some other more centrally located city. A bilateral rescue of sorts arrived in the capital: in the development of a streetcar system that allowed the District's

On this Spot . . .

① Built in 1912, directly two miles west of the Capitol, the **Lincoln Memorial ①ⓐ** honors our most inspiring president. Among the inspired was the Rev. Dr. Martin Luther King. Find the marked spot, 18 steps down from the chamber and you will be standing exactly where King stood on Aug. 28, 1963, when he delivered his remarkable "I Have a Dream" speech to the crowd of 200,000 people who had gathered here after "Marching on Washington" with King to pressure Congress to pass the Civil Rights Act.

The Lincoln Memorial was the site of another significant moment in civil rights history, on Easter Sunday, 1939, when contralto Marian Anderson sang to a crowd of 75,000 people on the memorial steps, after the Daughters of the American Revolution refused to allow the African-American to perform at their **Constitution Hall ①ⓑ**. First Lady Eleanor Roosevelt resigned her DAR membership over the incident. Eventually, Anderson did sing at Constitution Hall (in 1943 and again in 1952), and at the Lincoln Memorial a second time, in 1952.

② **The Watergate Building** looks harmless enough these days, despite the fact that the very word "Watergate" calls up its scandalous history. In June 1972, members of President Nixon's re-election staff broke into the Democratic National Committee's offices here, an act that eventually forced Nixon to resign. Two decades later, Pres. Clinton carried on an affair at the White House with a 20-something intern, who just happened to live at the Watergate.

③ **The Hilton Washington** was the scene of the attempted assassination of Pres. Reagan on March 30, 1981, when John Hinkley shot Pres. Reagan, his press secretary James Brady, a DC police officer, and a Secret Service agent. All survived.

④ President Lincoln was not so lucky. On April 14, 1865, John Wilkes Booth fatally shot Abraham Lincoln as the president sat in the "State Box" in **Ford's Theatre** watching a performance of "Our American Cousin." (Upon completion of theater's renovation, visitors can view Lincoln's seat, but not sit there.)

⑤ In the early to mid-20th century, U Street was known as the Black Broadway and the general area between 11th and 15th streets was the epicenter of a black cultural renaissance. At places like the **Lincoln Theatre ⑤ⓐ** and the **Club Caverns ⑤ⓑ** (now Bohemian Caverns), African-Americans came to hear the music of Ella Fitzgerald, Cab Calloway, and most of all, DC native son Duke Ellington. Visit the re-born neighborhood today and you can follow in their footsteps, as you walk by **1212 T St. NW ⑤ⓒ**, where the Duke grew up; or take in a set at the Lincoln Theatre (p. 257), Bohemian Caverns (p. 261), or newer venues, like Twins Jazz (p. 262), always ending the night with a half-smoke at the decades-old Ben's Chili Bowl (p. 143).

⑥ Since its beginnings in 1850, and continuing on through its current incarnation (built on the site of the original in 1901), **The Willard Hotel** has always played a special role in the life of the capital. At least six presidents, Zachary Taylor to Abraham Lincoln, lived at the Willard for a while. Julia Ward Howe composed "The Battle Hymn of the Republic" in it in 1861, and the Rev. Dr. Martin Luther King composed his "I Have a Dream" speech here in 1963. Stop in at the hotel to admire the ornate lobby and exquisite architecture, but don't leave without visiting the bar, the city's historic center of activity. Sip a mint julep, introduced here by statesman Henry Clay in 1850, and consider the tradition you're upholding: It was here that Washington Irving brought Charles Dickens for a brandy, Samuel Clemens (Mark Twain) imbibed bourbon with his pal, Nevada Sen. Stewart., and Nathaniel Hawthorne set up his base for covering the Civil War for the Atlantic Monthly magazine, writing ". . . for the conviviality of Washington sets in at an early hour, and, so far as I have had the opportunity to observe, never terminates at any hour."

Kenyon St.
Irving St.
Columbia Rd.
Harvard St.
Girard St.
Fairmont St.
Euclid St.

Howard University

Barry Pl.

13th St.
12th St.
11th St.
10th St.
9th St.
8th St.

U STREET CORRIDOR
French St.

Rhode Island Ave.
7th St.

13th St.
12th St.
11th St.
10th St.
9th St.
8th St.

(29)

DOWNTOWN

Mt. Vernon Square
New York Ave.
CHINA-TOWN

PENN QUARTER
Pennsylvania Ave.

MALL

Presidential Quotes

I greatly fear that my countrymen will expect too much from me.

—George Washington

I'm the decider and I decide what is best.

—George W. Bush

I have an irrepressible desire to live till I can be assured that the world is a little better for my having lived in it.

—Abraham Lincoln

overflowing population to move beyond city limits, and in the persons of public works leaders, especially an official named Alexander "Boss" Shepherd, whose "comprehensive plan of improvement" at last incorporated the infrastructure so necessary to a functioning metropolis. Shepherd established parks, constructed streets and bridges, installed water and sewer systems and gas lighting, and just generally nudged the nation's capital closer to showplace design. Notable accomplishments included the completion of the Washington Monument finally in 1884 (only took 36 years) and the opening on the Mall of the first Smithsonian museum, in 1881.

WASHINGTON BLOSSOMS

With the streets paved and illuminated, the water running, streetcars and rail transportation operating, and other practical matters well in place, Washington, D.C., was ready to address its appearance. In 1900, as if on cue, a senator from Michigan, James McMillan, persuaded his colleagues to appoint an advisory committee to create "the city beautiful." This retired railroad mogul, with architectural and engineering knowledge, determined to complete the job that L'Enfant had started a century earlier. Using his own money, McMillan sent a committee that included landscapist Frederick Law Olmsted (designer of New York's Central Park), sculptor Augustus Saint-Gaudens, and noted architects Daniel Burnham and Charles McKim, to

Europe for 7 weeks to study the landscaping and architecture of that continent's great capitals.

"Make no little plans," Burnham counseled fellow members. "They have no magic to stir men's blood, and probably themselves will not be realized. Make big plans, aim high in hope and work, remembering that a noble and logical diagram once recorded will never die, but long after we are gone will be a living thing, asserting itself with ever growing insistency."

The committee implemented a beautification program that continued well into the 20th century, further enhanced by the efforts of a presidential Commission of Fine Arts, which positioned monuments and fountains throughout the city, and President Franklin Delano Roosevelt's Works Progress Administration, whose workers erected public buildings embellished by artists. The legacy of these programs is on view today, in the cherry trees along the Tidal Basin, the Lincoln Memorial at the west end of the Mall, the Arlington Memorial Bridge, the Library of Congress, Union Station, the Corcoran Gallery, and so many other sights, each in its perfect place in the city.

The American capital was coming into its own on the world stage, as well, emerging from the Great Depression, two world wars, and technological advancements in air and automobile travel, as a strong, respected, global power. More and more countries established their embassies here

and the city's international population increased exponentially.

As did Washington's black population, which by 1950 was about 60% of the total. The capital became known as a hub of black culture, education, and identity, centered on a stretch of U Street NW, called "Black Broadway," where Cab Calloway, Duke Ellington, and Pearl Bailey often performed in speak-easies and theaters. (The reincarnated "U Street Corridor" or "New U" is now a diverse neighborhood of blacks, whites, Asians, and Latinos, and a major restaurant-and-nightlife destination.) Nearby, Howard University, created in 1867, distinguished itself as the nation's most comprehensive center for higher education for blacks.

On August 28, 1963, black and white Washingtonians were among the 200,000 who "Marched on Washington" and listened to an impassioned Rev. Dr. Martin Luther King, Jr., deliver his stirring "I Have a Dream" speech on the steps of the Lincoln Memorial, where 41 years earlier, during the memorial's dedication ceremony, black officials were required to stand and watch from across the road.

During the final decades of the 20th century, Washington experienced riots following the assassination of Dr. King, protests of the Vietnam War, and one political scandal after another, from Pres. Nixon's Watergate political debacle to D.C. Mayor Barry's drug and corruption problems, to Pres. Clinton's sexual shenanigans. And still, the city flourished. A world-class subway system opened, the Verizon Center debuted and transformed its aged downtown neighborhood into the immensely popular Penn Quarter, and the city's Kennedy

Little-Known Facts

- Many, including Washington, District of Columbia, residents, wonder how the city wound up with such an unwieldy name. Here's how: President Washington referred to the newly created capital as "the Federal City." City commissioners then chose the names "Washington" to honor the president and "Territory of Columbia" to designate the federal nature of the area. Columbia was the feminine form of Columbus, synonymous in those days with "America" and all she stood for, namely liberty. The capital was incorporated in 1871, when it officially became known as Washington, District of Columbia.

- The distance between the Capitol, at one end of the National Mall, and the Lincoln Memorial at the other, is 2 miles. The circumference of the White House property, from Pennsylvania Avenue to Constitution Avenue and 15th Street to 17th Street is about 1½ miles.

- Seventy percent of Washington, D.C., is national parkland, which makes the capital one of the "greenest" cities in the country. The biggest chunk is the 2,000-acre Rock Creek Park, the National Park Service's oldest urban park, founded in 1890.

- Every country that maintains diplomatic relations with the United States has an embassy in the nation's capital. Currently, the number of embassies comes to 178, located along Massachusetts Avenue, known as Embassy Row, and other streets in the Dupont Circle neighborhood.

Center, Shakespeare theaters, and other arts-and-culture venues came to world attention, receiving much acclaim.

Having begun the 20th century a backwater town, Washington finished the century a sophisticated city, profoundly shaken but not paralyzed by the September 11, 2001, terrorist attacks. Peace and prosperity have returned in the years since. The year 2009 glimmers with an "all things are possible" perspective, as a new president arrives to occupy the White House and as the District's young mayor, Adrian Fenty, continues to do his energetic best for his hometown.

History informs one's outlook, but so does the present. Look again at the Potomac River and think of Captain John Smith, but observe the Georgetown University crew teams rowing in unison across the surface of the water, and tour boats traveling between Georgetown and Old Town Alexandria. As you traverse the city, admire L'Enfant's visionary design, but also enjoy the sight of the wonks and office workers, artists and students, and people of every possible ethnic and national background, making their way around town. Tour the impressive landmarks and remember their namesakes, but make time for D.C.'s homegrown attractions, whether a meal at a sidewalk cafe in Dupont Circle, jazz along U Street, a walking tour past Capitol Hill's old town houses, or a visit to an old church where those original immigrants once worshiped.

2 Washington, D.C., Today

Washington, D.C., is the capital of our country and a city unto itself, and therein lies its charms, but also a host of complications, control of the city being the main issue. The District is a free-standing jurisdiction, but because it is a city with a federal overseer, and not a state, it has never been entitled to the same governmental powers as the states. For instance, Congress today, as it has from the beginning, supervises the District's budget and legislation. Originally, Congress granted the city the authority to elect its own governance, but rescinded that right in the late 1800s when the District overspent its budget in attempting to improve its services and appearance after the Civil War. The White House then appointed three commissioners, who ran D.C.'s affairs for nearly 100 years.

In 1972, the city regained the right to elect its own mayor and city council, but Congress retains control of the budget and the courts, and can veto municipal legislation. District residents can vote in presidential primaries and elections and they can elect a delegate to Congress, who introduces legislation and votes in committees, but who cannot vote on the House floor. This unique situation, in which residents of the District pay federal income taxes but don't have a vote in Congress, is a matter of great local concern. Among the ways that D.C. residents publicly protest the situation is by displaying license plates bearing the inscription "Taxation without Representation."

Another wrinkle in this uncommon relationship is the fact that Washington's economy relies heavily upon the presence of the federal government, which employs about 28% of D.C. residents, making it the city's single largest employer, and upon the tourism business that Washington, as the capital, attracts. Even as the city struggles toward political independence, it recognizes the economic benefits of the situation.

Does any of this affect you, as you tour the city this year? In a way, yes.

In 2009, you will find Washington, D.C., to be a remarkably vibrant city. But it wasn't always this way, and you should know a little bit of background. Fifteen, even 10 years ago, Washington wasn't so attractive. Tourists wanted to visit federal

What Was That? An Abridged Dictionary of Political Lingo

Washington politicos have their own vernacular, most words relating to Capitol Hill business. Here are choice examples and their definitions, for you to recognize while you're in town, and to bandy about in conversation when you return home.

- **Boondoggle:** Also known as a junket: a trip by congressional members and/or staff in which leisure is more of a focus than business.
- **Call up a Bill:** To raise up a bill on the floor for immediate consideration.
- **Caucus:** An informal group of members sharing an interest in the same policy issues.
- **Filibuster:** A tactic used to extend the debate on a proposal in order to block its vote in Congress.
- **Gerrymander:** To manipulate the geographic shape of a congressional district for political purposes.
- **Log Rolling:** The process in which two dissimilar interests join to help pass pieces of legislation that on their own, neither interest could pass.
- **Mark-up:** The meeting of a congressional committee to review and amend the text of a bill before sending the bill for review by the full House or Senate.
- **PAC:** The name for special interest groups that are legally permitted to give money to candidates running for political office.
- **Platform:** A formal, written statement of the principles, objectives, and policies of a political party.
- **Whip:** As a verb, whip means to gather votes. As a noun, whip refers to the officers, one Republican, one Democrat in the House, and one Republican and one Democrat in the Senate, responsible for counting potential votes and for promoting party unity in voting. The political party in the majority determines whether the whip is the Majority Whip or the Minority Whip in the House and Senate.

buildings, like the Capitol, the White House, and the Smithsonian museums, but stayed away from the dingy downtown and other off-the-Mall neighborhoods. The city had the potential for being so much more, and certain people, heroes, in my book, helped inspire action and brought about change themselves: Delegate Eleanor Holmes Norton, now in her ninth term in office, steadfastly fighting for state's rights and economic revival for the District; former Mayor Anthony Williams, who rescued the District's budget when his predecessor, the notorious, mismanaging Mayor Marion Barry brought the city to the brink of financial ruin; and the community-minded developers Abe and Irene Pollin, who used their own funds to finance the $200-million MCI sports center (now called the "Verizon Center") in the heart of town. Entrepreneurs started trickling in. Today, the wildly successful Verizon arena anchors the Penn Quarter neighborhood, utterly transformed and now one of the liveliest city centers in the country.

Revitalization continues to take root throughout the city, from southeast D.C., where a spanking-new baseball stadium, Nationals Ballpark, opened in March 2008, to the Columbia Heights enclave in upper northwest D.C., now a mélange of Latino culture, loft condominiums, and ethnic eateries. The city's evergreens, that is, the memorials and monuments, the historic neighborhoods, and the Smithsonian museums are unflaggingly popular. (Perhaps too much so: The National Mall is in dire need of re-landscaping and the Jefferson Memorial's base is disintegrating.)

But D.C. has its share of problems, some in fact deriving from the gentrification effort, like the displacement of residents from homes they can no longer afford in a newly improved but expensive neighborhood. Other problems are those that every municipality struggles with, namely how to provide healthcare, good schools, safe neighborhoods, adequate housing, and basic social services to all citizens.

Enter the dashing young Adrian Fenty, the city's new mayor, who seems more than up to the task of improving the city and carrying it forward. In office since January 2007, Fenty has shown himself to be a hands-on, can-do administrator, and he'll need that attitude as he governs this metropolis of 581,530 people.

The city he's inherited has a diverse population: 55% African American and 8% Latino, with 12% being foreign-born, and 15% speaking a language other than English at home. There are slightly more female than male residents and the median age for the population is 35. The citizenry is well educated: 46% of D.C. residents have a bachelor's degree, while 19% have advanced degrees. Women residents stand out: 43.9% have a bachelor's degree or higher, the highest percentage in the nation.

As the son of a white mother and black father, native son Fenty is in tune with the city's diversity. But mostly, it's clear that he loves his city.

And so, it seems, do visitors, as statistics and surveys bear out: The latest figures show that D.C. welcomes 15 million visitors a year, 1.2 million of whom are international tourists. The 2007 *Places Rated Almanac* ranks Washington seventh on its list of "best places" in the country to live and work, a measure of the quality and abundance of such features as arts, jobs, recreation, and transportation.

In a *Travel + Leisure–CNN Headline News* poll that asked travelers to rate 25 domestic urban destinations in various categories, the respondents named D.C. residents tops for worldliness and fourth for diversity and for intelligence, and the city itself best in the nation for historical sites and monuments, for museums and galleries, and for beautiful architecture, and sixth-best as a sophisticated getaway. Yes, Washington today is all that—and as you'll discover for yourself, a whole lot more.

3 Washington, D.C., in Popular Culture: Books, Film & Music

BOOKS

You can put yourself in the mood for a visit to Washington by reading a few of the great novels set in the capital, memoirs and histories by some of the city's more famous residents, and other guidebooks, whose topics supplement what you learn in these pages.

By far the most popular kind of Washington book being published these days is the insider's tell-all memoir, a genre unto itself. If you are a political junkie you've got a lot to choose from, including former Bush press secretary Scott McClellan's *What Happened: Inside the Bush White House and Washington's Culture of*

Deception; former CIA director George Tenet's *At the Center of the Storm: My Years at the CIA;* and former Pentagon official Douglas Feith's *War and Decision: Inside the Pentagon at the Dawn of the War on Terrorism.*

Two memoir musts that offer real insight into how the powerful operate in Washington are these two pre-Bush administration tales: *Personal History,* by the late Katharine Graham, who for many years was publisher of the *Washington Post;* and *Washington,* by Graham's close friend and colleague, Meg Greenfield, a columnist and editor at the *Washington Post* for more than 30 years.

Fiction lovers might pick up books by Ward Just, including his short-story collection, *The Congressman Who Loved Flaubert;* Ann Berne's *A Crime in the Neighborhood;* Marita Golden's *The Edge of Heaven;* Allen Drury's *Advise and Consent;* or one of the growing number of mysteries whose plot revolves around the capital, such as Margaret Truman's *Murder at the Smithsonian* or George Pelicanos's hard-core thrillers that take you to parts of the city you'll never see as a tourist: *Hell to Pay* and *King Suckerman,* to name just two.

If you're keen on learning more about the history of the nation's capital, you might try Arthur Schlesinger's *The Birth of the Nation,* F. Cary's *Urban Odyssey,* David Brinkley's *Washington at War,* and Douglas E. Evelyn and Paul Dickson's *On This Spot,* which traces the history of the city by revealing exactly what took place at specific locations—"on this spot"—in years gone by, neighborhood by neighborhood.

And for hilarious takes on the capital, read Christopher Buckley's *Washington Schlepped Here: Walking in the Nation's Capital,* an irreverent sendup of the city's most famous attractions and characters, its anecdotes all true. And don't miss Buckley's equally humorous Washington-based novels, *The White House Mess, No Way to Treat a First Lady,* and *Thank You for Smoking.*

FILMS

Hollywood has long used Washington as a setting and politicians as actors, so much so that some refer to D.C. as "Hollywood on the Potomac." Starting in 1915 with *Birth of a Nation,* the lineup includes *Mr. Smith Goes to Washington* (1939), *All the King's Men* (1949), *Advise and Consent* (1962), *All the President's Men* (1972), and *Wag the Dog* (1998). These represent only a fraction of the films based in Washington, whose popularity as a subject and location only grows and grows. Currently in production or recent releases are the following:

State of Play, an adaptation of the BBC miniseries by the same name and starring Russell Crowe, Ben Affleck, and Helen Mirren in a plot that involves investigative reporters trying to solve the murder of a congressman's mistress.

W, Oliver Stone's biopic, examines the life of George W. Bush.

Night at the Museum 2: Escape from the Smithsonian, which is a sequel to the blockbuster starring Ben Stiller.

Burn After Reading is a Coen Brothers production, which explains why it's described as a "dark comedy-thriller." George Clooney, Brad Pitt, and Frances McDormand star.

Get Smart, the Steve Carrell and Anne Hathaway comedy based on the classic television series.

Next time you're taking in a movie, note whether the film involves Washington at all, then look for shots of famous landmarks (that really is the Smithsonian's National Air and Space Museum seen in *Night at the Museum 2*). And when you're in Washington visiting, keep your eyes peeled for film crews as you tour the city, and who knows? Maybe you'll end up in the film as an extra.

Finds Ethnic Eating

Locals and visitors both benefit from the capital's multicultural population and the resulting abundance of restaurants serving cuisine from around the world. If you want to taste the most authentic food available in the capital for a particular country, seek out one of the restaurants on the following list. Though hardly comprehensive, the list, at least, names reliable "real deals" for ethnic eats. If you don't see a mention of your favorite cuisine, for instance, Chinese, it's probably because the restaurants best representing that country have fled to the suburbs.

Indian: This turns out to be a controversial category—everyone seems to have her own favorite Indian restaurant. I consulted the Indian Embassy, which declined to weigh in. So let's go with *Washingtonian* magazine's selection of **Heritage India** (p. 158), which the food critic describes as "Best for diners, including vegetarians, who savor the subtlety and elegance of refined Indian cooking."

Spanish: No controversy here: **Jaleo** (p. 133), with its long list of classic tapas, is the hands-down best for casual Spanish fare, while the ornate **Taberna del Alabardero** (p. 139) is easily the top choice for upscale Spanish dining. (This is where King Juan Carlos and Queen Sophia dine when in Washington.)

Salvadoran: Salvadorans make up the largest immigrant population in the capital, and yet a good Salvadoran restaurant is hard to find. **El Tamarindo,** in Adams-Morgan, 1785 Florida Ave. NW (© **202/328-3660;** www.el tamarindodc.com) is your best bet for great pupusas, tamales, and other Salvadoran favorites. Plus, the place is open until 5am Friday and Saturday.

Ethiopian: Washington is said to have more Ethiopian restaurants than any other American city. The preponderance of Ethiopian restaurants in the U Street Corridor has even lent the name "Little Ethiopia" to the area. **Etete,**

MUSIC

Washington's musical heritage is steeped in jazz and the legendary performances and compositions of native son Duke Ellington, who started his career playing in clubs along historic U St. NW. "Black Broadway" was the name given to this section of U Street, for Washingtonians Pearl Bailey, Jelly Roll Morton, and Shirley Horn, all performed here as well. The jazz scene lives on, along U Street, but also at venues throughout town, including, most notably, Blues Alley in Georgetown, where the biggest names in jazz take the stage, continuing the capital's most famous musical tradition.

More recently, a Washingtonian named Chuck Brown pioneered the birth of another music form, "go-go," a forerunner of rap; go-go blends African percussion with funk, jazz, and verbal interplay. Heard the tune "Bustin' Loose"? That's a Chuck Brown original, his first hit.

Other famous local musicians include big names on the rock scene, the Foo Fighter's Dave Grohl and members of the band O.A.R.; and on the opera front, the world-famous mezzo soprano, Denyce Graves, who returns to perform here from time to time.

And Washington offers a distinctly American musical experience in its military

1942 9th St. NW (© **202/232-7600**; www.eteterestaurant.com), is recommended for its spicy stews and lentil-filled pastries *(sambusas)*, to name just two good examples.

Belgian: How is it that Belgian cuisine has become such a hot commodity in the nation's capital? (There are at least four Belgian restaurants.) I have no idea. But for yummy tastes of lamb sausage, beef carbonade, and Belgian beers, and for a super fun time, try **Brasserie Beck** (p. 144).

Mexican: Its owner chef is Spanish and the place is only a couple years old, but Jose Andres's **Oyamel** (p. 136) is the uncontested place for true regional tastes of Mexico, from ceviche to avocado soup to chipotle-sauced meatballs.

Peruvian: Las Canteras (p. 144), in Adams-Morgan, is a pretty restaurant serving pleasurable, traditional Peruvian dishes, such as the seco de carne (a slow-cooked beef stew) and causa (a cake of yellowed potatoes layered with corned and shredded chicken).

Lebanese: Our **Lebanese Taverna** (p. 160) might be considered a national treasure, nearly 2 decades old and still going strong. For the best, most authentic tastes of Lebanon, choose from the mezze dishes: hummus, baba ghanouj, taboulleh, and so on.

Japanese: The city's oldest sushi restaurant is still the best: go to **Sushi-Ko** (p. 158), in Glover Park, for superb sushi and sashimi, but also for shrimp in tempura and other non-sushi, Japanese tastes.

Greek: Washington has a few Greek restaurants now, but, as good as they are, I wouldn't call their food "traditional Greek." **Zorba's Café**, 1612 20th St. NW (© 202/387-8555), in downtown D.C., is nothing if not classic Greek, from its bouzouki music to its grilled Greek sausages and ground beef and onion pie. Inexpensive, too.

bands, each representing the Air Force, Army, Navy, and Marine Corps, who play for free during the summer at designated locations throughout the city, and are known for their highly professional, wide-ranging performances.

This covers just the tip of the city's fabulous musical scene. For more information, see chapter 9.

4 Eating & Drinking in Washington, D.C.

Food writers outside the city like to talk about Washington's culinary scene as if it has newly come into its own. They're out of touch. The truth is that the capital has been cultivating an enviable stable of truly excellent restaurants gradually for about the last 10 years—and by "excellent," I don't necessarily mean fine dining/expensive. For example, old-timer **Jaleo** (p. 133) specialty is its small plates of authentic Spanish tapas, priced at $5 to $10, while newcomer **Tackle Box** (p. 157) offers a full dinner of wood-grilled fresh fish and two delicious sides for a flat $13.

It *is* true that our restaurants keep getting better and better. In its 23rd annual "Best New Restaurants in America" feature, *Esquire* magazine recognized Brasserie Beck and Oyamel in its list of the top 20 new eateries. As mentioned earlier, *Travel + Leisure* recently named D.C. "one of the most exciting cities on the East Coast." And our restaurants consistently receive AAA five diamond and James Beard Award Foundation distinctions. The 2008 James Beard Awards recognized Michel Richard Central as the best new restaurant in America.

All of this attention has encouraged several of the world's most esteemed chefs to establish restaurants in the capital, including Wolfgang Puck, whose the **Source** (p. 126), is in the Newseum; Eric Ripert and his **Westend Bistro** (p. 131), in the Ritz-Carlton Washington, and Alain Ducasse, whose Adour is the **St. Regis Hotel Washington**'s resident restaurant (p. 93).

Washingtonians are in the catbird's seat, licking their lips. Eating out is a way of life here, whether simply for the pleasure of it, or for business—the city's movers and shakers meet over breakfast, lunch, and dinner. When Congress passed a ban prohibiting members of Congress and their staffs from accepting gifts of any value, including meals, restaurateurs feared that their clientele would stop going out to eat. But business is flourishing, it turns out, with congressional members and staff paying for themselves, if need be, and with corporate executives, lobbyists, and other professionals taking each other, but not elected politicians, out for a meal.

One other thing to note here: When Congress is in town, that is, not out on recess, restaurants are full and reservations are an absolute must. When Congress is on recess, in August, mid-December to January, and at other times,

many restaurants, especially those close to Capitol Hill and in the downtown, are so empty, it's creepy.

We have quite a number of restaurants to choose from: 1,727 delis to showplace dining rooms, according to the Restaurant Association of Metropolitan Washington. An immense variety of cuisines is on hand, representing the international population of the capital, including the diplomatic staffs of 178 foreign embassies and our immigrant communities from Ethiopia and El Salvador, especially, but from scores of other countries, as well (see the "Ethnic Eating" box, below). A strong African-American presence means that the District has some delicious soul food eateries and our location in the Mid-Atlantic region near the Chesapeake Bay means that crabs are a favorite item here, served in soft-shell, hard-shell, soup, or cake form.

Currently, the capital is witnessing a variety of culinary trends, with wine bars (see chapter 9) and chocolate lounges (see chapter 6) proliferating and vegetarian options on the rise. Exotic drinks, such as fruit-infused martinis, are increasingly a draw at popular restaurants, many of which now include a bar lounge for those who want to unwind with a cocktail before dinner, or sip a nightcap afterward.

A growing concern about the environment is inspiring restaurants to pursue ecologically friendly practices, like the sustainable seafood restaurant **Hook** (p. 155), which serves only those varieties of fish that can reproduce at the rate they're being caught; or **Poste** brasserie (p. 129), which despite its downtown location, grows and harvests its own herbs, vegetables, and greens on-site for immediate use.

All in all, Washington's eating and drinking culture, already hot, keeps getting hotter.

Planning Your Trip to Washington, D.C.

Get excited. You're going to visit the nation's capital and you've got your itinerary all lined up: a tour of the Capitol, dining at the hot restaurants in the Penn Quarter, a bus tour of the memorials by moonlight, viewing American cultural artifacts at the National Museum of American History. Sounds like a plan, right? Now let's get real: A plan without proper preparation is just a wish list.

What kind of weather can you expect? What kind of clothes should you bring? When you visit the Capitol, do you want to drop by your representatives' offices? If the answer is yes, you'd better make sure Congress is going to be in session during your stay. Do you hope to visit the White House? (Then you'd better contact your congressperson or senator right away to get the admittance process going.) If you're driving here, do you know how expensive parking rates are? If you're flying, do you know which of the three airports is most convenient for you? Do you know the best way to get into the city from the airport? Which hot restaurants do you want to try? (Whichever, better make your reservations now.) Has the National Museum of American History reopened after its renovation (it's been closed for renovation since the fall of 2006)? Are any other sites closed that you'd hoped to visit?

You catch my drift. Something wonderful this way lies, but the wonderfulness of the experience increases exponentially according to how well you organize yourself in advance. The purpose of this book, but especially this chapter, is to help you do just that. So look over the following pages, create a to-do list, and start crossing off items as you go. And, last but not least: Get excited!

For additional help in planning your trip and for more on-the-ground resources in Washington, D.C., see the "Fast Facts, Toll-Free Numbers & Websites" appendix on p. 289.

1 Visitor Information

BEFORE YOU LEAVE

Contact **Destination D.C.,** the official tourism and convention corporation for Washington, D.C., 901 7th St. NW, 4th Floor, Washington, DC 20001-3719 (© **800/422-8644** or 202/789-7000; www.destinationdc.org), and ask for a free copy of the *Washington, D.C. Visitors Guide,* which covers hotels, restaurants, sights, shops, and more and is updated twice yearly. At the © **202/789-7000** number, you can speak directly to a staff "visitor services specialist" and get answers to your specific questions about the city.

Be sure to consult Destination D.C.'s website, where you can read and download the visitors guide, along with the latest travel information, including upcoming exhibits at the museums and

anticipated closings of tourist attractions. The website is also an excellent source for maps, which you can download and print from the site or order for delivery by mail. Once in D.C., you can stop by Destination D.C.'s offices on 7th Street NW (Metro: Gallery Place/Chinatown, H St. exit), to pick up the visitors guide and maps, and to talk to visitors services specialists. Office hours are Monday to Friday, 9am to 4:30pm.

AT THE AIRPORTS AND TRAIN STATION

If you're arriving by plane or train, you can think of your airport or the train station as visitor information centers; all three Washington-area airports and Union Station offer all sorts of visitor services. See section 4 of this chapter, "Getting There & Getting Around," for specific information about Union Station's and each airport's services, location, flights/train routes, and transportation options into town.

AROUND TOWN

The **D.C. Chamber of Commerce Visitor Information Center** (© 866/324-7386 or 202/289-8317; www.dcchamber.org; click on "Tourism," then "Visitor Information Center") is a small bureau inside the immense Ronald Reagan International Trade Center Building, at 1300 Pennsylvania Ave. NW. To enter the federal building, you need to show a picture ID. The visitor center lies on the ground floor of the building, a little to your right as you enter from the Wilson Plaza, near the Federal Triangle Metro. From March 15 to Labor Day, the center is open Monday through Friday, 8:30am to 5:30pm, and on Saturday from 9am to 4pm; from Labor Day to March 14, the center is open Monday through Friday 9am to 4:30pm.

Also look for business improvement district (BID) offices and their patrolling "ambassadors," who dispense information,

directions, and other assistance in their individual neighborhoods. Among the most established are:

Downtown D.C. Business Improvement District (Downtown D.C. BID), 1250 H St. NW (© 202/638-3232; www.downtowndc.org), which covers the territory between Union Station and the White House (Constitution to Massachusetts aves., and btw. 16th and 1st sts.). Red-uniformed "SAMS" (for "safety and maintenance") are on hand to help. In spring and summer, the Downtown D.C. BID also has special information kiosks shaded by red-and-white umbrellas, stationed near Metro stops and throughout the downtown.

Golden Triangle Business Improvement District (Golden Triangle BID), 1120 Connecticut Ave. NW (© 202/463-3400; www.gtbid.com), encompassing the area between the White House and Dupont Circle (bounded by 16th and 21st sts. NW and Pennsylvania Ave. and Dupont Circle). Hospitality ambassadors are outfitted in black and gold.

Capitol Hill Business Improvement District (Capitol Hill BID), 30 Massachusetts Ave. NE, inside Union Station's garage (© 202/842-3333; www.capitolhillbid.org), which covers the streets around the U.S. Capitol and Union Station. Blue-and-gold-attired "STARS" roam Capitol Hill.

National Park Service information kiosks are located inside or near the Jefferson, Lincoln, FDR, Vietnam Veterans, Korean War, and World War II memorials and at the Washington Monument (© 202/426-6841 or 619-7222; www.nps.gov/state/dc for all national parklands in D.C. or www.nps.gov/nama for National Mall and Memorials Park sites).

The **White House Visitor Center,** on the first floor of the Herbert Hoover Building, Department of Commerce, 1450 Pennsylvania Ave. NW (btw. 14th and 15th sts.; © 202/208-1631, or

456-7041 for recorded information), is open daily (except for Christmas Day, Thanksgiving, and New Year's Day) from 7:30am to 4pm.

The **Smithsonian Information Center,** in the "Castle," 1000 Jefferson Dr. SW (© **202/633-1000,** or TTY 633-5285; www.si.edu), is open every day but Christmas from 8:30am to 5:30pm; knowledgeable staff answer questions and dispense maps and brochures.

The **American Automobile Association (AAA)** has a new office near the White House, at 1405 G St. NW, between 14th and 15th streets, (© **202/481-6811**). Hours are 9am to 5:30pm Monday through Friday. Maps and travel advice are available to members.

OTHER HELPFUL WEBSITES

Take a look at the D.C. government's website, **www.dc.gov**, and that of the nonprofit organization Cultural Tourism D.C., **www.culturaltourismdc.org**, for more information about the city. The Cultural Tourism D.C. site, in particular, provides helpful and interesting background knowledge of D.C.'s historic and cultural landmarks, especially in neighborhoods, or in parts of neighborhoods, not usually visited by tourists.

Also helpful is the *Washington Post* site, **www.washingtonpost.com**, which gives you up-to-the-minute news, weather, visitor information, restaurant reviews, and nightlife insights; its online City Guide, a must-read for locals and tourists alike, features a "Going Out Gurus" blog, covering daily entertainment happenings, as well as a "For Visitors" section, which you might find of use.

Washington Flyer magazine, which you can obtain free at the airports, or browse online in advance (at **www.fly2dc.com**) often covers airport and airline news and profiles upcoming events in Washington—things you might want to know before you travel.

Finally, check out the websites and blogs of dcist.com and ontaponline.com for the latest commentary and information about Washington happenings, especially those geared toward 20- and 30-somethings.

2 Entry Requirements

PASSPORTS

New regulations issued by the Department of Homeland Security now require virtually every air traveler entering the U.S. to show a passport. As of January 23, 2007, all persons, including U.S. citizens, traveling by air between the United States and Canada, Mexico, Central and South America, the Caribbean, and Bermuda are required to present a valid passport. As of January 31, 2008, U.S. and Canadian citizens entering the U. S. at land and sea ports of entry from within the Western Hemisphere will need to present government-issued proof of citizenship, such as a birth certificate, along with a government-issued photo ID, such as a driver's license. U.S. or Canadian citizens entering by land or sea are not required to present a passport but they are highly encouraged to carry one.

For information on how to obtain a passport, see **"Passports"** in the **"Fast Facts, Toll-Free Numbers & Websites"** appendix (p. 293).

VISAS

The U.S. State Department has a **Visa Waiver Program (VWP)** allowing citizens of the following countries to enter the United States without a visa for stays of up to 90 days: Andorra, Australia, Austria, Belgium, Brunei, Denmark, Finland, France, Germany, Iceland, Ireland, Italy, Japan, Liechtenstein, Luxembourg, Monaco, the Netherlands, New Zealand, Norway, Portugal, San Marino, Singapore, Slovenia, Spain, Sweden, Switzerland, and

the United Kingdom. (*Note:* This list was accurate at press time; for the most up-to-date list of countries in the VWP, consult www.travel.state.gov/visa.) Canadian citizens may enter the United States without visas; they will need to show passports (if traveling by air) and proof of residence, however. *Note:* Any passport issued on or after October 26, 2006, by a VWP country must be an **e-Passport** for VWP travelers to be eligible to enter the U.S. without a visa. Citizens of these nations also need to present a round-trip air or cruise ticket upon arrival. E-Passports contain computer chips capable of storing biometric information, such as the required digital photograph of the holder. (You can identify an e-Passport by the symbol on the bottom center cover of your passport.) If your passport doesn't have this feature, you can still travel without a visa if it is a valid passport issued before October 26, 2005, and includes a machine-readable zone, or between October 26, 2005, and October 25, 2006, and includes a digital photograph. For more information, go to **www.travel.state.gov/visa**.

Citizens of all other countries must have (1) a valid passport that expires at least 6 months later than the scheduled end of their visit to the U.S., and (2) a tourist visa, which may be obtained without charge from any U.S. consulate.

As of January 2004, many international visitors traveling on visas to the United States will be photographed and fingerprinted on arrival at Customs in airports and on cruise ships in a program created by the Department of Homeland Security called **US-VISIT.** Exempt from the extra scrutiny are visitors entering by land or those (mostly in Europe; see p. 295) that don't require a visa for short-term visits. For more information, go to the Homeland Security website at **www.dhs.gov/dhspublic**.

For specifics on how to get a visa, see **"Visas"** in the **"Fast Facts, Toll-Free Numbers & Websites"** appendix (p. 295).

MEDICAL REQUIREMENTS

Unless you're arriving from an area known to be experiencing an epidemic (particularly cholera or yellow fever), inoculations or vaccinations are not required for entry into the United States.

CUSTOMS
WHAT YOU CAN BRING INTO THE U.S.

Every visitor 21 and older may bring in, free of duty, the following: (1) 1 liter of wine or hard liquor; (2) 200 cigarettes, 100 cigars (but not from Cuba), or 3 pounds of smoking tobacco; and (3) $100 worth of gifts. These exemptions are offered to travelers who spend at least 72 hours in the United States and who have not claimed them within the preceding 6 months. It is forbidden to bring into the country almost any meat products (including canned, fresh, and dried meat products such as bullion, soup mixes, and so on). Generally, condiments including vinegars, oils, spices, coffee, tea, and some cheeses and baked goods are permitted. Avoid rice products, as rice can often harbor insects. Bringing fruits and vegetables is not advised, though not prohibited. Customs will allow produce depending on where you got it and where you're going after you arrive in the U.S. Foreign tourists may carry in or out up to $10,000 in U.S. or foreign currency with no formalities; larger sums must be declared to U.S. Customs on entering or leaving, which includes filing form CM 4790. For details regarding U.S. Customs and Border Protection, consult your nearest U.S. embassy or consulate, or **U.S. Customs** (www.customs.ustreas.gov).

WHAT YOU CAN TAKE HOME FROM WASHINGTON, D.C.:

Canadian Citizens: For a clear summary of Canadian rules, write for the booklet *I Declare*, issued by the Canada Border Services Agency (© **800/461-9999** in Canada, or 204/983-3500; www.cbsa-asfc.gc.ca).

U.K. Citizens: For information, contact **HM Customs & Excise** at © **0845/ 010-9000** (from outside the U.K., 020/ 8929-0152), or consult their website at **www.hmce.gov.uk**.

Australian Citizens: A helpful brochure available from Australian consulates or Customs offices is *Know Before You Go.* For more information, call the **Australian Customs Service** at © **1300/ 363-263,** or log on to **www.customs. gov.au**.

New Zealand Citizens: Most questions are answered in a free pamphlet available at New Zealand consulates and Customs offices: *New Zealand Customs Guide for Travellers, Notice no. 4.* For more information, contact **New Zealand Customs,** The Customhouse, 17–21 Whitmore St., Box 2218, Wellington (© **04/473-6099** or 0800/428-786; **www.customs.govt.nz**).

3 When to Go

The city's peak seasons generally coincide with two activities: the sessions of Congress and springtime—starting with the appearance of the cherry blossoms along the Potomac. Specifically, from about the second week in September until Thanksgiving, and again from about mid-January to June (when Congress is "in"), hotels are full with guests whose business takes them to Capitol Hill or to conferences. And mid-March through June traditionally is the most frenzied season, when families and school groups descend upon the city to see the cherry blossoms and enjoy Washington's sensational spring. This is also a popular season for protest marches. Hotel rooms are at a premium and airfares tend to be higher.

If crowds turn you off, consider visiting Washington at the end of August/ early September, when Congress is still "out" and families return home to get their children back to school, or between Thanksgiving and mid-January, when Congress leaves again and many people are ensconced in their own holiday-at-home celebrations. Hotel rates are cheapest at this time, too, and many hotels offer attractive packages. The year 2009 is an election year, which means that Washington during the normally quiet month of January will be rocking out with visitors here to pay tribute and party before,

during, and a little bit after inauguration day, January 20.

If you're thinking of visiting in July and August, be forewarned: The weather is very hot and humid. Summer is also the season for outdoor concerts, festivals, parades, and other events (see chapter 9 for details about performing arts schedules). And, of course, Independence Day (July 4th) in the capital is a spectacular celebration.

THE WEATHER

Check the *Washington Post*'s website (**www.washingtonpost.com**) or the Destination D.C. website (**www.destination dc.org**) for current and projected weather forecasts.

Season by season, here's what you can expect of the weather in Washington:

Fall: This is my favorite season. The weather is often warm during the day—in fact, if you're here in early fall, it may seem entirely *too* warm. But it cools off, even getting a bit crisp, at night. Washington trades its famous greenery for the brilliant colors of fall foliage, and the stream of tourists tapers off.

Winter: People like to say that Washington winters are mild—and sure, if you're from Minnesota, you'll find Washington warmer, no doubt. But D.C. winters can be unpredictable: bitter cold one

day, an ice storm the next, followed by a couple of days of sun and higher temperatures. Pack for all possibilities.

Spring: Early spring weather tends to be colder than most people expect. Cherry blossom season, late March to early April, can be iffy—and very often rainy and windy. Then, as April slips into May, the weather usually mellows, and people's moods with it. Late spring is especially lovely, with mild temperatures and intermittent days of sunshine, flowers, and trees colorfully erupting in gardens and parks all over town. Washingtonians, restless after having been cooped inside for months, sweep outdoors to stroll the National Mall, sit on a park bench, or laze away an afternoon at an outdoor cafe. Spring is a great time to enjoy D.C.'s outdoor attractions. But during this season, the city is also at its most crowded with visitors and school groups, here to view the blooming cherry blossoms or take advantage of spring breaks.

Summer: Anyone who's ever spent July and August in D.C. will tell you how hot and steamy it can be. Though the buildings are air-conditioned, many of Washington's attractions, like the memorials, monuments, and organized tours, are outdoors and unshaded, and the heat can quickly get to you. Make sure you stop frequently for drinks (vendors are everywhere), and wear a hat, sunglasses, and sunscreen. But if you can deal with all that, this is a good time to visit. Locals often go elsewhere on vacation, so the roads and attractions are somewhat less crowded. Best of all, hotels tend to offer their best rates in July and August.

Average Temperatures (°F/°C) & Rainfall (in inches) in Washington, D.C.

	Jan	Feb	Mar	Apr	May	June	July	Aug	Sept	Oct	Nov	Dec
Avg. High	43/6	47/8	55/13	66/19	76/24	84/29	89/32	87/31	80/27	69/21	58/14	48/9
Avg. Low	24/-4	26/-3	33/0	42/6	52/11	62/17	67/19	65/18	57/14	44/7	36/2	28/-2
Rainfall	3.6	2.8	3.9	3.3	4.3	3.6	4.2	3.9	4.1	3.4	3.3	3.3

WASHINGTON, D.C., CALENDAR OF EVENTS

Washington's most popular annual events are the Cherry Blossom Festival in spring, the Fourth of July celebration in summer, and the lighting of the National Christmas Tree in winter. But some sort of special event occurs almost daily. For the latest schedules, check **www.destination dc.org**, **www.nps.gov/ncro** (click on "Calendar of Events"), **www.culturaltourismdc.org**, **www.dc.gov**, and **www.washingtonpost. com**.

For an exhaustive list of events beyond those listed here, check http://events.frommers.com, where you'll find a searchable, up-to-the-minute roster of what's happening in Washington (and other cities all over the world).

In the calendar below, I've done my best to accurately list phone numbers for more information, but they seem to change constantly. If the number you try doesn't get you the details you need, call **Destination D.C.** at C 202/789-7000.

When you're in town, grab a copy of the *Washington Post*, especially the Friday "Weekend" section, or a copy of the monthly magazine, *Washingtonian*, whose "Where and When" section features recommended goings-on around town.

For annual events in Alexandria, see p. 275.

January

Martin Luther King, Jr.'s Birthday. Events include speeches by prominent leaders and politicians, readings, dance, theater, concerts and choral performances, and prayer vigils. On the Friday preceding the national holiday (third Mon in Jan), the National Park Service holds a ceremony at the Department of Interior Building at 1849 C St. NW, attended by schoolchildren and open to the public; park rangers then transfer the wreath used during the ceremony to the Lincoln

Memorial. (The entire ceremony used to take place at the Memorial but was switched indoors because of the cold.) Call ✆ **202/619-7222.** Many events take place at the Martin Luther King, Jr., Memorial Library, 901 G St. NW (✆ **202/727-0321**). Third Monday in January.

February

Black History Month. Numerous events, museum exhibits, and cultural programs celebrate the contributions of African Americans to American life, including a celebration of abolitionist Frederick Douglass's birthday. For details, check the *Washington Post* or call the National Park Service at ✆ **202/619-7222.**

Chinese New Year Celebration. A friendship archway, topped by 300 painted dragons and lighted at night, marks Chinatown's entrance at 7th and H streets NW. The celebration begins the day of the Chinese New Year and continues for 10 or more days, with traditional firecrackers, dragon dancers, and colorful street parades. Some area restaurants offer special menus. For details, call ✆ **202/789-7000.** Early February.

Abraham Lincoln's Birthday. This day is marked by a wreath-laying and reading of the Gettysburg Address at noon at the Lincoln Memorial. The year 2009 marks the 200th anniversary of Lincoln's birthday, so expect a grand celebration. Call ✆ **202/619-7222.** February 12.

George Washington's Birthday. Celebratory events similar to Lincoln's birthday, centered on the Washington Monument. Call ✆ **202/619-7222** for details. The Washington Monument is open, with new security barriers placed in concentric circles around the obelisk. See the review in chapter 7 of the Washington Monument for more information. Both presidents' birthdays also bring annual citywide sales. February 22. (See chapter 10, "Side Trips from Washington, D.C.," for information about the bigger celebrations held at Mount Vernon and in Old Town Alexandria on the third Mon in Feb.)

March

Women's History Month. Various institutions throughout the city stage celebrations of women's lives and achievements. For the schedule of National Park Service events, check the calendar at www.nps.gov/ncro; for Smithsonian events, call ✆ **202/633-1000** or go online at www.si.edu; for other events, check the websites listed in the intro to this section.

St. Patrick's Day Parade. A big parade on Constitution Avenue NW, from 7th to 17th streets, with floats, bagpipes, marching bands, and the wearin' o' the green. For parade information, call ✆ **202/789-7000** or go online at www.dcstpatsparade.com. The Sunday before March 17.

Smithsonian Kite Festival. This event is delightful if the weather cooperates—an occasion for a trip in itself. Throngs of kite enthusiasts fly their unique creations on the grounds of the Washington Monument, and compete for ribbons and prizes. Now in its 43rd year, the kite festival even has its own website: **www.kitefestival.org**. Visit the website or call ✆ **202/633-1000** or 633-3030 for details. To compete, just show up at the designated spot with your kite between 10am and noon and register. A Saturday in mid- or late March, or early April, but always at the start of the Cherry Blossom Festival.

April

National Cherry Blossom Festival. Washington's best-known annual event:

a 2-week festival coinciding with the blossoming of more than 3,700 Japanese cherry trees by the Tidal Basin, on Hains Point, and on the grounds of the Washington Monument. Events take place all over town, including fireworks, concerts, special art exhibits, park ranger–guided talks and tours past the cherry blossom trees, and sports competitions. A grand parade caps the festival, complete with floats, marching bands, dancers, celebrity guests, and more. For information, call © 877/44BLOOM (442-5666) or go to www.nationalcherryblossomfestival.org. Also see "Potomac Park" on p. 219 for more information about the cherry blossoms. March 28 to April 12, 2009. National and local news programs monitor the budding.

White House Easter Egg Roll. The biggie for little kids. The annual White House Easter Egg Roll continues a practice begun in 1878. Entertainment on the White House South Lawn and the Ellipse traditionally includes appearances by costumed cartoon characters, clowns, egg-decorating exhibitions, puppet and magic shows, military drill teams, an egg-rolling contest, and a hunt for 1,000 or so wooden eggs, many of them signed by celebrities, astronauts, or the president. *Note:* Children of all ages are welcome, as long as a child age 7 or younger, and no more than two adults, are in your group. You may obtain a maximum of five tickets. The hourly timed tickets are issued at the National Parks Service Ellipse Visitors Pavilion just behind the White House at 15th and E streets NW beginning at 7:30am on the Saturday before Easter and again on Easter Monday. Call © 202/208-1631 for details. Easter Monday between 8am and 2pm, enter at the southeast gate on East Executive Avenue. Arrive early to make

sure you get in and to allow for increased security procedures.

African-American Family Day at the National Zoo. This tradition extends back to 1889, when the zoo opened. The National Zoo, 3001 Connecticut Ave. NW, celebrates African-American families the day after Easter with music, dance, Easter egg rolls, and other activities. Free. Call © 202/633-1000 for details. Easter Monday.

Thomas Jefferson's Birthday. Celebrated at the Jefferson Memorial with wreaths, speeches, and a military ceremony. Call © 202/619-7222 for time and details. April 13.

White House Spring Garden Tour. These beautifully landscaped creations are open to the public for free tours, 2 days only. Tickets are required. Call © 202/208-1631 for details. Two days in mid-April.

Shakespeare's Birthday Celebration. Music, theater, children's events, food, and exhibits are all part of the afternoon's hail to the Bard at the Folger Shakespeare Library. Call © 202/544-4600, or go to www.folger.edu. Free admission. Mid- to late April.

Filmfest D.C. This annual film festival presents more than 100 works by filmmakers from around the globe. Screenings take place primarily in movie theaters. Tickets are usually $10 per movie and go fast; some events are free. Call © 202/628-FILM (3456) or check the website, www.filmfestdc.org. Two weeks in April.

Smithsonian Craft Show. Held in the National Building Museum, 401 F St. NW, this juried show features one-of-a-kind limited-edition crafts by more than 120 noted artists from all over the country. There's an entrance fee of about $15 per adult each day, free for children 12 and under. No strollers.

For details, call © 888/832-9554 or 202/633-5006, or check the website, www.smithsoniancraftshow.com. Four days in late April.

May

Washington National Cathedral Annual Flower Mart. Now in its 70th year, the flower mart takes place on cathedral grounds, featuring displays of flowering plants and herbs, decorating demonstrations, ethnic food booths, children's rides and activities (including an antique carousel), costumed characters, puppet shows, and other entertainment. Admission is free. Call © 202/537-3185 or go to www.cathedral.org (click on "All Hallows Guild") for details. First Friday and Saturday in May, rain or shine.

Georgetown Garden Tour. View remarkable private gardens in one of the city's loveliest neighborhoods. Admission ($30–$35) includes light refreshments. Some years there are related events such as a flower show at a historic home. Call © 202/789-7000 or browse the website www.georgetowngardentour.com for details. Early to mid-May.

Shakespeare Theatre Free for All. This free theater festival presents a different Shakespeare play each year for a 2-week run at the Carter Barron Amphitheatre in upper-northwest Washington, D.C. Tickets are required, but they're free. Call © 202/334-4790, or check the website, www.shakespearetheatre.org. Evenings, end of May through early June.

Memorial Day. At 11am, a wreath-laying ceremony takes place at the Tomb of the Unknowns in Arlington National Cemetery, followed by military band music, a service, and an address by a high-ranking government official (sometimes the president); call

© 703/607-8000 for details. A National Memorial Day Parade marches from the Capitol, down Constitution Avenue, to the White House. Ceremonies are held at the National World War II and Vietnam Veterans Memorial (© 202/619-7222 for details), and other activities take place at the U.S. Navy Memorial (© 202/737-2300). On the Sunday before Memorial Day, the National Symphony Orchestra performs a free concert at 8pm on the West Lawn of the Capitol to honor the sacrifices of American servicemen and servicewomen; call © 202/619-7222 for details.

June

Dupont-Kalorama Museum Walk Day. This 26th annual celebration welcomes visitors to eight museums and historic houses located in several charming, off-the-Mall neighborhoods. Free food, music, tours, and crafts demonstrations are on offer. Shuttle buses travel to each location. Call © 202/667-0441, ext. 35, or access the website, www.dkmuseums.com. First full weekend in June.

Smithsonian Folklife Festival. A major event reveling in both national and international traditions in music, crafts, foods, games, concerts, and exhibits, staged the length of the National Mall. Each Folklife Festival showcases three or four cultures or themes; 2008 introduced those of Bhutan, NASA, and the state of Texas to festivalgoers. All events are free; most events take place outdoors. Call © 202/633-6440, or check the website, www.folklife.si.edu, or the listings in the *Washington Post,* for details. For 10 days in late June and early July, always including July 4.

July

Independence Day. There's no better place to be on the Fourth of July than

in Washington, D.C. The festivities include a massive National Independence Day Parade down Constitution Avenue, complete with lavish floats, princesses, marching groups, and military bands. A morning program in front of the National Archives includes military demonstrations, period music, and a reading of the Declaration of Independence. In the evening, the National Symphony Orchestra plays on the west steps of the Capitol with guest artists (for example, Leontyne Price). And big-name entertainment precedes the fabulous fireworks display behind the Washington Monument. You can also attend a free 11am organ recital at Washington's National Cathedral. Consult the *Washington Post* or call © **202/619-7222** for details. July 4, all day.

Bastille Day. This Washington tradition honors the French Independence Day with live entertainment and a block-long race by tray-balancing waiters and waitresses, along the stretch of Pennsylvania Avenue in front of Brasserie Les Halles. Free, *mais bien sûr.* At 12th Street and Pennsylvania Avenue NW. Call © **202/347-6848.** July 14.

Capital Fringe Festival. This event debuted in 2006 and celebrates experimental theater in the tradition of the original fringe festival held annually in Edinburgh, Scotland. With 120 separate productions taking place at more than 20 venues daily for 18 days, it adds up to about 600 individual performances in all. Local and visiting artists perform in theater, dance, music, and other disciplines. Ticket prices are $10 to $35 each and the action centers around the Penn Quarter. Check the website, www.capfringe.org, for more information. The end of the month.

September

Labor Day Concert. The National Symphony Orchestra closes its summer season with a free performance at 8pm on the West Lawn of the Capitol; call © **202/619-7222** for details. Sunday before Labor Day. (Rain date: Same day and time at Constitution Hall or the Kennedy Center.)

Kennedy Center Open House Arts Festival. A daylong festival of the performing arts, featuring local and national artists on the front plaza and river terrace (which overlooks the Potomac), and throughout the stage halls of the Kennedy Center. Past festivals have featured the varied performances of the Suzanne Farrell Ballet Co., the Cirque de Soleil, pop rocker Ben Kweller, and Washington Opera soloists. Kids' activities usually include a National Symphony Orchestra "petting zoo," where children get to bow, blow, drum, or strum a favorite instrument. Admission is free, although you may have to stand in a long line for the inside performances. For details, check the *Washington Post,* call © **800/444-1324** or 202/467-4600, or access the website, www.kennedy-center.org. A Saturday or Sunday in early to mid-September, 11:30am to 7:30pm.

Black Family Reunion. Performances, food, and fun are part of this 2-day celebration of the African-American family and culture, held on the Mall. Free. Check the website, www.ncnw.org/events/reunion.htm. Early to mid-September.

Adams-Morgan Day. Thousands turn out along 18th Street NW, Columbia Road NW, and other streets in this small neighborhood to revel in the music, art, dance, and cuisines representing the international roots of the residents. Check the website, adamsmorgandayfestival.com. Second Sunday in September.

Library of Congress National Book Festival. Co-sponsored by the Library of Congress and the First Lady, this festival welcomes at least 80 established authors and their many fans to the National Mall for readings, author signings, and general hoopla surrounding the love of books. Check www.loc.gov/bookfest, or call ✆ **888/714-4696** for more information. A Saturday in late September.

October

Marine Corps Marathon. Thirty thousand runners compete in this 26.2-mile race (the fifth-largest marathon in the United States). It begins at the Marine Corps Memorial (the Iwo Jima statue) and passes major monuments. Call ✆ **703/432-1159** for details. Anyone can enter; register online at www.marinemarathon.com. Last Sunday in October.

Halloween. There's no official celebration, but costumed shenanigans seem to get bigger every year. Giant block parties take place in the Dupont Circle and Georgetown neighborhoods. Check the *Washington Post* for special parties and activities. October 31.

November

Veterans Day. The nation's war dead are honored with a wreath-laying ceremony at 11am at the Tomb of the Unknowns in Arlington National Cemetery followed by a memorial service. The president of the United States or his stand-in officiates, as a military band performs. Wreath-laying ceremonies also take place at other war memorials in the city. Call ✆ **703/607-8000** for more information about Arlington Cemetery events and **202/619-7222** for information about events elsewhere. November 11.

December

Christmas Pageant of Peace/National Tree Lighting. At the northern end of the Ellipse, the president lights the national Christmas tree to the accompaniment of orchestral and choral music. The lighting inaugurates the 4-week Pageant of Peace, a tremendous holiday celebration full of free activities, including musical performances, mostly of local school and church choruses, nightly on the Ellipse. (Brrrr!) Call ✆ **202/208-1631,** or check the website, **www.nps.gov/whho/pageant. htm**, for details; tickets are free but required to attend the tree-lighting ceremony. The tree-lighting ceremony takes place at 5pm on a day in early December, and the Pageant of Peace continues every night throughout the month.

4 Getting There & Getting Around

GETTING TO WASHINGTON, D.C. BY PLANE

Three airports serve the Washington, D.C., area. General information follows that should help you determine which airport is your best bet. See the appendix at the back of this book for the listing of airline 800 numbers and websites.

Ronald Reagan Washington National Airport (DCA) lies 4 miles south of D.C., across the Potomac River in Virginia, a trip of only a few minutes by car, 15 to 20 minutes by Metro in non-rush-hour traffic. Its proximity to the District and its direct access to the Metro rail system are reasons why you might want to fly into National.

Approximately 12 airlines serve this airport, which has nonstop flights to 69 U.S. cities, plus Nassau, Bermuda, Montreal, and Toronto. Nearly all nonstop flights are to and from cities located within 1,250 miles from Washington.

The exceptions are flights between National and Phoenix, Denver, Las Vegas, Seattle, Los Angeles, and Salt Lake City. Among the airlines serving National Airport are **Air Canada, American, Continental, Delta, Northwest, United,** and **US Airways,** and discount airlines **Frontier** and **AirTran.** Delta and US Airways shuttles, together, offer hourly or nearly hourly flights between National and Boston's Logan Airport, and National and New York's LaGuardia Airport.

National Airport's traveler-friendly services include ticket counters that provide access to passengers with disabilities, about 36 eateries, 33 shops, one currency-exchange station, 13 ATMs, commissioned artwork displayed throughout the terminals (go on a tour if your flight's been delayed), and climate-controlled pedestrian bridges that connect the terminal directly to the Metro station, whose Blue and Yellow lines stop here. The Metropolitan Washington Airports Authority oversees both National and Dulles airports, so the website is the same for the two facilities: www.mwaa.com. Check there for airport information, or call © 703/417-8000. For Metro information, call © 202/637-7000.

Washington Dulles International Airport (IAD) is 26 miles outside the capital, in Chantilly, Virginia, a 35- to 45-minute ride to downtown in non-rush-hour traffic. Of the three airports, Dulles handles more daily flights, with about 30 airlines flying nonstop to 127 destinations, including 40 foreign cities. And though the airport is not as convenient to the heart of Washington as National, it's more convenient than BWI, thanks to an uncongested airport access road that travels half the distance toward Washington.

Dulles is closing in on the completion of a decades-long expansion. In 2009, the airport plans to debut its underground airport train system and station, replacing the cumbersome mobile lounges that until now have transported most travelers to and from the main and midfield terminals. Other recent improvements include the addition of a fourth runway, new concourses, a parking garage, and a pedestrian walkway between the main terminal and concourses A and B. Eventually, the airport will add a fifth runway and more than triple its annual passenger traffic to 55 million.

Among Dulles's major domestic airlines are **American, Continental, Delta, Northwest, United,** and **US Airways,** and discount airlines **AirTran, JetBlue, Southwest, Ted,** and **Virgin America.** The airport's major international airlines include **Aeroflot, Air Canada, British Airways, Aer Lingus, Air France, Lufthansa, Virgin Atlantic, ANA Airways,** and **Saudi Arabian Airlines.**

Dulles has 45 eateries, 37 shops, 4 currency exchange stations, 1 bank branch, 12 ATMs, and 7 public computer terminals with Internet access.

The airport's website is www.mwaa.com, and its information line is © 703/572-2700.

Last but not least is **Baltimore–Washington International Thurgood Marshall Airport (BWI),** which is located about 45 minutes from downtown, a few miles outside of Baltimore. A vast expansion has added 11 gates to a newly improved concourse, skywalks from parking garages to terminals, and triple the number of parking spaces. One factor especially accounts for this tremendous growth, the same that recommends BWI to travelers: the major presence of **Southwest Airlines,** whose bargain fares and flights to nearly 40 cities seem to offer something for everyone. (Southwest also serves Dulles Airport, but in a much smaller capacity.)

In all, 16 airlines serve BWI, flying nonstop to 70 destinations, including 8 foreign cities. Major domestic airlines

include **American, Continental, Delta, Northwest, United,** and **US Airways** and discount airlines **AirTran, Southwest, America West,** and **USA 3000.** Major international airlines include **British Airways, Air Greenland,** and **Air Canada.**

Among BWI's on-site attractions are 43 eateries, 28 shops, 3 currency exchange stations, and 1 bank branch.

Call © **800/435-9294** for airport information, or point your browser to www.bwiairport.com.

Arriving at the Airport

IMMIGRATION & CUSTOMS CLEARANCE International visitors arriving by air, no matter what the port of entry, should cultivate patience and resignation before setting foot on U.S. soil. U.S. airports have considerably beefed up security clearances in the years since the terrorist attacks of September 11, 2001, and clearing Customs and Immigration can take as long as 2 hours.

Getting into Town from the Airport

Each of the three airports offers similar options for getting into the city. Follow the signs to "ground transportation" and look for the banners or a staff representative of the service you desire. All three airports could really use better signage, especially because their ground transportation desks always seem to be located quite a distance from the gate at which you arrive. Keep trudging, and follow baggage claim signs, too, since ground transportation operations are always situated near baggage carousels.

TAXI SERVICE For a trip to downtown D.C., you can expect a taxi to cost anywhere from $10 to $20 for the 10- to 20-minute ride from National Airport; $50 to $60 for the 30- to 45-minute ride from Dulles Airport; and $79 for the 45-minute ride from BWI.

SUPERSHUTTLE Vans (© **800/258-3826;** www.supershuttle.com) offer shared-ride, door-to-door service between the airport and your destination, whether in the District or in a suburban location. You make a reservation by phone or online and then proceed to the Super-Shuttle desk in your airport to check in and be assigned to your bus. The only drawback to this service is the round-about way the driver must follow, as he or she drops off or picks up other passengers en route. If you arrive after the Super-Shuttle desk has closed, you can summon a van by calling customer service at © **888/888-6025.** The 24-hour service bases its fares on zip code, so to reach downtown, expect to pay about $12, plus $10 for each additional person from National; $27, plus $10 per additional person from Dulles; and $35, plus $12 per additional person from BWI. If you're calling the SuperShuttle for a ride from a D.C. area location to one of the airports, you must reserve a spot at least 24 hours in advance.

LIMOUSINES Limousine service is the most costly of all options, with prices starting at $40 at National, $75 at Dulles, and $120 at BWI, for private car transportation to downtown D.C. For pickup from BWI, reserve passage by calling © **800/878-7743** or 301/912-0000. For pickup from National or Dulles, try **Red Top Executive Sedan** (© **800/296-3300;** www.redtopcab.com), or choose a limousine service from the list posted on Destination D.C.'s website, www.destinationdc.com. (Click on "Visiting," then "Browse DC," and then scroll to the categories window, and choose "Limousine/Sedan Service.")

Free hotel/motel shuttles operate from all three airports to certain nearby properties. Best to inquire about such transportation when you book a room at your hotel.

Individual transportation options at each airport are as follows:

FROM RONALD REAGAN WASHINGTON NATIONAL AIRPORT If you are not too encumbered with luggage, you should take **Metrorail** (© 202/637-7000) into the city. Metro's Yellow and Blue lines stop at the airport and connect via an enclosed walkway to level two, the concourse level, of the main terminal, adjacent to terminals B and C. If yours is one of the airlines that still uses the "old" terminal A (Spirit, AirTran, Midwest, Northwest), you will have a longer walk to reach the Metro station. Signs pointing the way can be confusing, so ask an airport employee if you're headed in the right direction; or, better yet, head out to the curb and hop a shuttle bus to the station, but be sure to ask the driver to let you know when you've reached the Metro (it may not be obvious, and drivers don't always announce the stops). **Metrobuses** (© 202/637-7000) also serve the area, should you be going somewhere off the Metro route. But Metrorail is fastest, a 15- to 20-minute non-rush-hour ride to downtown. It is safe, convenient, and cheap, costing $1.35 base fare and going up from there, depending on when (fares increase during rush hours) and where you're going.

If you're renting a car from an on-site **car-rental agency, Alamo** (© 888/215-0010), **Avis** (© 703/419-5815), **Budget** (© 703/419-1021), **Dollar** (© 800/800-4000), **Hertz** (© 703/419-6300), **National** (© 703/419-1032), or **Thrifty** (© 877/283-0898), go to level two, the concourse level, follow the pedestrian walkway to the parking garage, find garage A, and descend one flight. You can also take the complimentary Airport Shuttle (look for the sign posted at the curb outside the terminal) to parking garage A. If you've rented from off-premises agency **Enterprise** (© 703/553-7744), head outside the baggage claim area of your terminal, and catch the Enterprise shuttle bus.

To get downtown by car, follow the signs out of the airport for the George Washington Parkway, headed north toward Washington. Stay on the GW Parkway until you see signs for I-395 north to Washington. Take the I-395 north exit, which takes you across the 14th Street Bridge. Stay in the left lane crossing the bridge and follow the signs for Route 1, which will put you on 14th Street NW. (You'll see the Washington Monument off to your left.) Ask your hotel for directions from 14th Street and Constitution Avenue NW. Or take the more scenic route, always staying to the left on the GW Parkway as you follow the signs for Memorial Bridge. You'll be driving alongside the Potomac River, with the monuments in view across the river; then, as you cross over Memorial Bridge, you're greeted by the Lincoln Memorial. Stay left coming over the bridge, swoop around to the left of the Memorial, take a left on 23rd Street NW, a right on Constitution Avenue, and then, if you want to be in the heart of downtown, left again on 15th Street NW (the Washington Monument will be to your right).

FROM WASHINGTON DULLES INTERNATIONAL AIRPORT The **Washington Flyer Express Bus** (© 888/927-4359; www.washfly.com) runs between Dulles and the West Falls Church Metro station, where you can board a train for D.C. In the airport, look for signs for the DULLES AIRPORT SHUTTLE, which leaves from Door 4 on the arrivals level. Buses to the West Falls Church Metro station run daily, every 30 minutes, and cost $9 one-way. (By the way, **"Washington Flyer"** is also the name under which the taxi service operates at Dulles.)

More convenient is the **Metrobus** service (no. 5A) that runs between Dulles (buses depart from curb 2E, outside the

Ground Transportation area) and the L'Enfant Plaza Metro station, located near Capitol Hill and within walking distance of the National Mall and Smithsonian museums. The bus departs every 40 minutes weekdays, hourly on weekends; costs only $3; and takes about an hour.

If you are renting a car at Dulles, head down the ramp near your baggage claim area, and walk outside to the curb to look for your rental car's shuttle-bus stop. The buses come by every 5 minutes or so en route to nearby rental lots. These include **Alamo** (🕾 703/260-0182), **Avis** (🕾 703/661-3505), **Budget** (🕾 703/437-9373), **Dollar** (🕾 866/434-2226), **Enterprise** (🕾 703/661-8800), **Hertz** (🕾 703/471-6020), **National** (🕾 703/260-0182), and **Thrifty** (🕾 877/283-0898).

To reach downtown Washington from Dulles by car, exit the airport and stay on the Dulles Access Road, which leads right into I-66 east. Follow I-66 east, which takes you across the Theodore Roosevelt Memorial Bridge; be sure to stay in the center lane as you cross the bridge, and this will put you on Constitution Avenue (Rte. 29). Ask your hotel for directions from this point.

FROM BALTIMORE–WASHING-TON INTERNATIONAL AIRPORT
Washington's Metro service runs an Express Metro Bus ("B30") between its Metrorail Green Line Greenbelt station and BWI Airport. In the airport, head to the lower level and look for PUBLIC TRANSIT signs to find the bus, which operates daily, departs every 40 minutes, takes about 30 minutes to reach the station, and costs $3. At the Greenbelt Metro station, you purchase a Metro fare card and board a Metro train, which will take you into the city. Depending on where you want to go, you can either stay on the Green Line train to your designated stop or get off at the Fort Totten Station to

transfer to a Red Line train, whose stops include Union Station (near Capitol Hill) and various downtown locations. Transfers can be tricky, so you may want to ask a fellow passenger or a Metro attendant to make sure you're headed in the right direction.

You also have the choice of taking either an **Amtrak** (🕾 **800/872-7245**) or a **Maryland Rural Commuter** (**MARC;** 🕾 **800/325-7245**) train into the city. Both trains travel between the BWI Railway Station (🕾 **410/672-6169**) and Washington's Union Station (🕾 **202/484-7540**), about a 30-minute ride. Amtrak's service is daily (ticket prices range from $12 to $38 per person, one-way, depending on time and train type), while MARC's is weekdays only ($6 per person, one-way). A courtesy shuttle runs every 10 minutes or so between the airport and the train station; stop at the desk near the baggage-claim area to check for the next departure time of both the shuttle bus and the train. Trains depart about once per hour.

BWI operates a large off-site car-rental facility. From the ground transportation area, you board a shuttle bus that transports you to the lot. Rental agencies include **Alamo** (🕾 410/859-8092), **Avis** (🕾 410/859-1680), **Budget** (🕾 410/859-0850), **Dollar** (🕾 800/800-4000), **Hertz** (🕾 410/850-7400), **National** (🕾 410/859-8860), and **Thrifty** (🕾 410/850-7139).

Here's how you reach Washington: Look for signs for I-195 and follow I-195 west until you see signs for Washington and the Baltimore–Washington Parkway (I-295); head south on I-295. Get off I-295 when you see the signs for Route 50/New York Avenue, which leads into the District, via New York Avenue. Ask your hotel for specific directions from New York Avenue NE.

Long-Haul Flights: How to Stay Comfortable

- Your choice of airline and airplane will definitely affect your legroom. Find more details about U.S. airlines at **www.seatguru.com**. For international airlines, the research firm Skytrax has posted a list of average seat pitches at **www.airlinequality.com**.
- Emergency exit seats and bulkhead seats typically have the most legroom. Emergency exit seats are usually left unassigned until the day of a flight (to ensure that someone able-bodied fills the seats); it's worth checking in online at home (if the airline offers that option) or getting to the ticket counter early to snag one of these spots for a long flight. Many passengers find that bulkhead seating offers more legroom, but keep in mind that bulkhead seats have no storage space on the floor in front of you.
- To have two seats for yourself in a three-seat row, try for an aisle seat in a center section toward the back of coach. If you're traveling with a companion, book an aisle and a window seat. Middle seats are usually booked last, so chances are good you'll end up with three seats to yourselves. And in the event that a third passenger is assigned the middle seat, he or she will probably be more than happy to trade for a window or an aisle.
- To sleep, avoid the last row of any section or the row in front of an emergency exit, as these seats are the least likely to recline. Avoid seats near highly trafficked toilet areas. Avoid seats in the back of many jets—these can be narrower than those in the rest of coach. Or reserve a window seat so you can rest your head and avoid being bumped in the aisle.
- Get up, walk around, and stretch every 60 to 90 minutes to keep your blood flowing. This helps avoid **deep vein thrombosis,** or "economy-class syndrome."
- Drink water before, during, and after your flight to combat the lack of humidity in airplane cabins. Avoid caffeine and alcohol, which will dehydrate you.

BY CAR

About one-fifth of leisure visitors to Washington arrive by plane, and if that's you, don't worry about renting a car. In fact, it's better if you don't, since the traffic in the city and throughout the region is absolutely abysmal, parking spaces are hard to find, garage and lot charges are exorbitant, and hotel overnight rates are even worse. Furthermore, Washington is amazingly easy to traverse on foot—so easy, in fact, that the Brookings Institution recently named it the most walkable city in the country. Our public transportation and taxi systems are accessible and comprehensive, as well.

But if you are like most visitors, you're planning on driving here, traveling on one of the following major highways: I-70 and I-270, I-95, and I-295 from the north; I-95 and I-395, Route 1, and Route 301 from the south; Route 50/301 and Route 450 from the east; and Route 7, Route 50, I-66, and Route 29/211 from the west.

No matter which road you take, there's a good chance you will have to navigate some portion of the **Capital Beltway** (I-495 and I-95) to gain entry to D.C. The Beltway girds the city, about 66 miles around, with more than 56 interchanges or exits, and is nearly always congested (especially during weekday morning and evening rush hours, roughly btw. 5:30–9:30am and 3–7pm). Commuter traffic on the Beltway rivals, maybe surpasses, that of major L.A. freeways, and drivers can get a little crazy, weaving in and out of traffic.

Get yourself a good map before you do anything else. As mentioned earlier, **Destination D.C.'s** website, www.destination dc.com, posts downloadable maps that are quite helpful. Another great source is the **American Automobile Association (AAA; ℂ 800/763-9900** for emergency road service and for connection to the mid-Atlantic office; www.aaa.com), which provides its members with maps and detailed Trip-Tiks that give precise directions to a destination, including up-to-date information about areas of construction. AAA also provides towing services should you have car trouble during your trip.

If you are driving to a hotel in D.C. or its suburbs, contact the establishment to find out the best route to the hotel's address and other crucial details concerning parking availability and rates.

The District is 240 miles from New York City, 40 miles from Baltimore, 700 miles from Chicago, 500 miles from Boston, and about 630 miles from Atlanta.

CAR RENTALS

If you need to rent a car while you're here, you have several options.

Residents and tourists alike seem to be turning to car-rental clubs that allow you more flexible car-use arrangements, whether you need a car for an hour or for a month, with parking and other services included. One such company in Washington is **Zipcars** (**ℂ 866/494-7227;** www.zipcar.com), which has a downtown office at 403 8th St. NW, entrance on 8th Street (ℂ **202/737-4900**).

Here's how it works: You apply and pay a membership fee or application fee ahead of time online, order the car online or by phone using a credit card, and establish exactly when and where you need a car. You receive a special card in the mail, which you use to activate the specific car you've reserved at the specific location, time, and day you've pre-arranged. The idea is that this special card unlocks the reserved car and you climb inside to retrieve the keys, following instructions you're given ahead of time. Zipcar's rates start at $7.65 an hour and this fee covers gas, insurance, and parking.

Or, you can go the usual route and rent a car from one of the major car-rental companies.

Car-rental rates can vary even more than airfares. Check out **Breezenet.com,** which offers domestic car-rental discounts with some of the most competitive rates around. Also worth visiting are Orbitz, Hotwire.com, Travelocity, and Priceline.com, all of which offer competitive online car-rental rates.

If you're visiting from abroad and plan to rent a car in the United States, keep in mind that foreign driver's licenses are usually recognized in the U.S., but you should get an international one if your home license is not in English.

For listings of the major car-rental agencies in Washington, please see the preceding section on airport car rentals, as well as the "Fast Facts, Toll-Free Numbers & Websites" appendix (p. 289).

It helps to do your homework: Take the time to shop around and ask a few key questions and you might save hundreds of dollars:

- Are weekend rates lower than weekday rates? Ask if the rate is the same for pickup Friday morning, for instance, as it is for Thursday night.
- Is the weekly rate cheaper than the daily rate? Even if you need the car for only 4 days, it may be cheaper to keep it for 5.
- Does the agency assess a drop-off charge if you don't return the car to the same location where you picked it up? Is it cheaper to pick up the car at the airport or at a downtown location?
- Are special promotional rates available? If you see an advertised price in

your local newspaper, be sure to ask for that specific rate; otherwise, you may be charged the standard cost. Terms change constantly.

- Are discounts available for members of AARP, AAA, frequent-flier programs, or trade unions?
- How much tax will be added to the rental bill? Local tax? State use tax? Local taxes and surcharges can vary from location to location, even within the same car company, which can add quite a bit to your costs.
- What is the cost of adding an additional driver's name to the contract?
- How many free miles are included in the price? Free mileage is often negotiable, depending on the length of your rental.
- Are there extra charges if you're under 25? For instance, Avis tacks on an additional $25 for those 21 to 25. *Note:* All car rental agencies require drivers be at least 21.

Some companies offer "refueling packages," in which you pay for an entire tank of gas upfront. The price is usually fairly competitive with local gas prices, but you don't get credit for any gas remaining in the tank. If a stop at a gas station on the way to the airport will make you miss your plane, then by all means take advantage of the fuel purchase option. Otherwise, skip it.

For information on insurance, review your own car insurance policy and contact the **American Automobile Association** (AAA; © 800/763-9900) for advice and helpful information.

BY TRAIN

Amtrak (© 800/USA-RAIL; www. amtrak.com) offers daily service to Washington from New York, Boston, and Chicago. Amtrak also travels daily between Washington and points south, including Raleigh, Charlotte, Atlanta, cities in Florida, and New Orleans.

Amtrak's **Acela Express** trains offer the quickest service along the "Northeast Corridor," linking Boston, New York, Philadelphia, and Washington. The trains travel as fast as 150 mph, making the trip between New York and Washington in about 3 hours and 30 minutes and between Boston and Washington in about 7 hours. Amtrak runs fewer Acela trains on weekends, and honors passenger discounts, such as those for seniors and AAA members, only on weekend Acela travel.

Amtrak offers a smorgasbord of good-deal rail passes and discounted fares; although not all are based on advance purchase, you may have more discount options by reserving early. The bargain fares can be used only on certain days and hours of the day; be sure to find out exactly what restrictions apply. Tickets for children ages 2 to 15 cost half the price of a regular coach fare when the children are accompanied by a fare-paying adult. For more information, go to **www.amtrak. com** and click on the website's "Hot Deals" section, where you'll find assorted discount possibilities. *Note:* Amtrak requires reserved seating on its regional trains running between Boston and Newport News, Virginia, which means that every traveler is guaranteed a seat.

International visitors who plan to travel to other places in the country can buy a **USA Rail Pass,** good for 15 or 30 days of unlimited travel on **Amtrak** (© 800/USA-RAIL; www.amtrak.com). The pass is available online or through many overseas travel agents. See Amtrak's website for the cost of travel within the western, eastern, or northwestern United States. Reservations are generally required and should be made as early as possible. Other rail passes are also available.

Amtrak trains arrive at historic **Union Station,** 50 Massachusetts Ave. NE (© 202/371-9441; www.unionstation dc.com), a short walk from the Capitol,

across the circle from several hotels, and a short cab or Metro ride from downtown. Union Station is a turn-of-the-20th-century Beaux Arts masterpiece that was magnificently restored in the late 1980s. Offering a three-level marketplace of shops and restaurants, this stunning depot is conveniently located and connects with Metro service. Taxis are almost always available. (For more on Union Station, see chapters 7 and 8.)

GETTING AROUND

Washington is one of the easiest U.S. cities to navigate, thanks to its comprehensive public transportation system of trains and buses. Ours is the second-largest rail transit network and the fifth-largest bus network in the country. But because Washington is of manageable size and marvelous beauty, you may find yourself shunning transportation and choosing to walk.

CITY LAYOUT

Washington's appearance today pays homage to the 1792 vision of French engineer Pierre Charles L'Enfant, who created the capital's grand design of sweeping avenues intersected by spacious circles, directed that the Capitol and the White House be placed on prominent hilltops at either end of a wide stretch of avenue, and superimposed this overall plan upon a traditional street grid. The city's quadrants, grand avenues named after states, alphabetically ordered streets crossed by chronologically ordered streets, and parks integrated with urban features are all ideas that started with L'Enfant. President George Washington, who had hired L'Enfant, was forced to dismiss the temperamental genius after L'Enfant apparently offended quite a number of people. But Washington recognized the brilliance of the city plan and hired surveyors Benjamin Banneker and Andrew Ellicott, who had worked with L'Enfant, to continue to implement L'Enfant's design.

The U.S. Capitol marks the center of the city, which is divided into **northwest (NW), northeast (NE), southwest (SW), and southeast (SE) quadrants.** Most, but not all, areas of interest to tourists are in the northwest. The boundary demarcations are often seamless; for instance, you are in the northwest quadrant when you visit the National Museum of Natural History, but by crossing the National Mall to the other side to visit the Freer Gallery, you put yourself in the southwest quadrant. Pay attention to the quadrant's geographic suffix; as you'll notice when you look on a map, some addresses—for instance, the corner of G and 7th streets—appear in all quadrants.

MAIN ARTERIES & STREETS From the Capitol, North Capitol Street and South Capitol Street run north and south, respectively. East Capitol Street divides the city north and south. The area west of the Capitol is not a street at all, but the National Mall, which is bounded on the north by Constitution Avenue and on the south by Independence Avenue.

The primary artery of Washington is **Pennsylvania Avenue,** which is the scene of parades, inaugurations, and other splashy events. Pennsylvania runs northwest in a direct line between the Capitol and the White House—if it weren't for the Treasury Building, the president would have a clear view of the Capitol—before continuing on a northwest angle to Georgetown, where it becomes M Street.

Pennsylvania Avenue in front of the White House—between 15th and 17th streets NW—remains closed to cars for security reasons but has been remade into an attractive pedestrian plaza, lined with 88 Princeton American Elm trees.

Constitution Avenue, paralleled to the south most of the way by Independence Avenue, runs east-west, flanking the Capitol and the Mall. If you hear Washingtonians talk about the "House" side of the

Hill, they're referring to the southern half of the Capitol, the side closest to Independence Avenue, and home to Congressional House offices and the House Chamber. Conversely, the Senate side is the northern half of the Capitol, where Senate offices and the Senate Chamber are found, closer to Constitution Avenue.

Washington's longest avenue, **Massachusetts Avenue,** runs parallel to Pennsylvania (a few avenues north). Along the way, you'll find Union Station and then Dupont Circle, which is central to the area known as Embassy Row. Farther out are the Naval Observatory (the vice president's residence is on the premises), Washington National Cathedral, American University, and, eventually, Maryland.

Connecticut Avenue, which runs more directly north (the other avenues run southeast to northwest), starts at Lafayette Square, intersects Dupont Circle, and eventually takes you to the National Zoo, on to the charming residential neighborhood known as Cleveland Park, and into Chevy Chase, Maryland, where you can pick up the Beltway to head out of town. Downtown Connecticut Avenue, with its posh shops and clusters of restaurants, is a good street to stroll.

Wisconsin Avenue originates in Georgetown; its intersection with M Street forms Georgetown's hub. Antiques shops, trendy boutiques, nightclubs, restaurants, and pubs all vie for attention. Wisconsin Avenue basically parallels Connecticut Avenue; one of the few irritating things about the city's transportation system is that the Metro does not connect these two major arteries in the heart of the city. (Buses do, and, of course, you can always walk or take a taxi from one avenue to the other; read about two supplemental bus systems, the Georgetown Metro Connection shuttle and the D.C. Circulator, below.) Metrorail's first stop on Wisconsin Avenue is in Tenleytown, a residential area. Follow the avenue north and you land in the affluent Maryland cities of Chevy Chase and Bethesda.

FINDING AN ADDRESS If you understand the city's layout, it's easy to find your way around. As you read this, have a map handy.

Each of the four corners of the District of Columbia is exactly the same distance from the Capitol dome. The White House and most government buildings and important monuments are west of the Capitol (in the northwest and southwest quadrants), as are major hotels and tourist facilities.

Numbered streets run north-south, beginning on either side of the Capitol with 1st Street. Lettered streets run east-west and are named alphabetically, beginning with A Street. (Don't look for a B, a J, an X, a Y, or a Z St., however.) After W Street, street names of two syllables continue in alphabetical order, followed by street names of three syllables; the more syllables in a name, the farther the street is from the Capitol.

Avenues, named for U.S. states, run at angles across the grid pattern and often intersect at traffic circles. For example, New Hampshire, Connecticut, and Massachusetts avenues intersect at Dupont Circle.

With this in mind, you can easily find an address. On lettered streets, the address tells you exactly where to go. For instance, 1776 K St. NW is between 17th and 18th streets (the first two digits of 1776 tell you that) in the northwest quadrant (NW). *Note:* I Street is often written as "Eye" Street to prevent confusion with 1st Street.

To find an address on numbered streets, you'll probably have to use your fingers. For instance, 623 8th St. SE is between F and G streets (the sixth and seventh letters of the alphabet; the first digit of 623 tells you that) in the southeast

D.C. Metropolitan Area

quadrant (SE). One thing to remember: You count B as the second letter of the alphabet even though no B Street exists today (Constitution and Independence aves. were the original B sts.), but because there's no J Street, K becomes the 10th letter, L the 11th, and so on. To be honest, though, I don't know anyone who actually uses this method for figuring out an exact location.

BY PUBLIC TRANSPORTATION
Metrorail

Metrorail is a wonderful way to get around, but if you travel Metrorail during rush hour (Mon–Fri 5–9:30am and 3–7pm), you may not be so smitten with the system, since delays can be frequent, lines at farecard machines long, trains overcrowded, and Washingtonians at their rudest. An increasing ridership is

overloading the system, maintenance problems are cropping up, and the **Washington Metropolitan Area Transit Authority (WMATA; ℂ 202/637-7000; www.wmata.com)** is struggling just to keep pace, much less prevent future crises. Among the solutions are the addition of new trains and the installation of passenger information display boxes on station platforms reporting the number of minutes before the arrival of the next train and any delays or irregularities.

Though it's true that service has deteriorated, Washingtonians were spoiled to begin with. Stations are cool, clean, and attractive. Rides are quiet, and cars are air-conditioned and fitted with comfortable upholstered seats. You can expect to get a seat during off-peak hours (basically weekdays 10am–3pm, weeknights after 7pm, and all day weekends).

Metrorail's system of 86 stations and 106 miles of track includes locations at or near almost every sightseeing attraction; it also extends to suburban Maryland and northern Virginia. There are five lines in operation—Red, Blue, Orange, Yellow, and Green. The lines connect at several points, making transfers easy. All but Yellow and Green Line trains stop at Metro Center; all except Red Line trains stop at L'Enfant Plaza; all but Blue and Orange Line trains stop at Gallery Place/Chinatown. See the color map inside the back cover of this book.

Metro stations are indicated by discreet brown columns bearing the station's name and topped by the letter M. Below the M is a colored stripe or stripes indicating the line or lines that stop there.

When entering a Metro station for the first time, go to the kiosk and ask the station manager for a free *Metro System Pocket Guide.* It contains a map of the system, explains how it works, and lists the closest Metro stops to points of interest. The station manager can also answer questions about routing or purchase of farecards. You can download a copy of the pocket guide and loads of information, including schedules, from Metro's website (www.wmata.com). The pocket guide is available in 11 languages, from Arabic to Vietnamese.

To enter or exit a Metro station, you need a computerized **farecard,** available at vending machines near the entrance. The machines take nickels, dimes, quarters, and bills from $1 to $20; they can return up to $4.95 in change (coins only). The vending machines labeled PASSES/FARECARDS accept both cash and credit cards. At this time, the minimum fare to enter the system is $1.35, which pays for rides to and from any point within 7 miles of boarding during non-peak hours; during peak hours (Mon–Fri 5–9:30am and 3–7pm), $1.35 takes you only 3 miles. The maximum you will pay to the farthest destination is $4.50. Metro Authority is always contemplating a fare hike, though.

Once you're on the platform, you'll figure out your correct side of the track by finding your desired station stop on the list of upcoming stops posted on the brown pylon for trains headed in your direction. A display board overhead flashes the number of minutes anticipated before the next train pulls into the

Tips **Metro Maps**

D.C.'s most important Metro stops are highlighted on the "Washington, D.C., Major Metro Stops" map in the color insert at the front of this book. The insert also features a list of D.C.'s major attractions and their corresponding Metro lines. For a basic Metro map, refer to the back cover.

> **Tips Metro Etiquette 101**
>
> To avoid risking the ire of commuters, be sure to follow these guidelines: Stand to the right on the escalator so that people in a hurry can get past you on the left. And when you reach the train level, don't puddle at the bottom of the escalator, blocking the path of those coming behind you; move down the platform. Eating, drinking, and smoking are strictly prohibited on the Metro and in stations.

station. Lights embedded in the platform floor pulsate to alert you to the train's impending arrival. The only tricky part of traveling on Metro concerns transferring to a different line. Metro has eight transfer hubs, and probably the busiest hub is at Metro Center, where tracks crisscross on upper and lower levels and passengers can switch to a red, blue, or orange line train; read and follow the signs carefully, or ask someone for help, to make sure you get to the right track.

If you plan to take several Metrorail trips during your stay, put more value on the farecard to avoid having to purchase a new card each time you ride. For stays of more than a few days, your best value would be the **7-Day Fast Pass,** for $39 per person, which allows you unlimited travel; **1-Day Rail Passes** are available for $7.80 per person, allowing you unlimited passage for the day after 9:30am weekdays, or all day on Saturday, Sunday, and holidays. You can buy these passes online or at the Passes/Farecards machines in the stations. You can also purchase them at WMATA headquarters (weekdays only), 600 5th St. NW (© **202/637-7000;** www. wmata.com), its sales office at Metro Center (weekdays only), 12th and F streets NW, or one of the retail stores, like Giant or Safeway grocery stores, where farecards are sold.

Other passes are available—check out the website or call the main number for further information. Up to two children ages 4 and under can ride free with a paying passenger. Seniors (65 and older) and people with disabilities (with valid proof) ride Metrorail and Metrobus for a reduced fare.

When you insert your card in the entrance gate, the time and location are recorded on its magnetic tape, and your card is returned. Don't forget to snatch it up and keep it handy; *you have to reinsert your farecard in the exit gate at your destination,* where the fare will automatically be deducted. The card will be returned if there's any value left on it. If you arrive at a destination and your farecard doesn't have enough value, add what's necessary at the Exitfare machines near the exit gate.

Most Metro stations have more than one exit. To save yourself time and confusion, try to figure out ahead of time which exit gets you closer to where you're going. In this book, I include the specific exit you should use for every venue mentioned, including hotels, restaurants, and attractions. For instance, if you ride the Blue and Orange lines to the Smithsonian stop, you'll want to exit at the Mall to visit the museums, but exit at 12th St. and Independence Ave. SW if you're headed to the Mandarin Oriental Hotel.

Metrorail opens at 5am weekdays and 7am Saturday and Sunday, operating until midnight Sunday through Thursday, and until 3am Friday and Saturday. *Note:* The one exception is the stretch of the Yellow line between Mt. Vernon Square/7th Street–Convention Center, which does not operate during weekday rush hours, 5–9:30am and 3–7pm, but otherwise

Tips Getting to Georgetown

Metrorail doesn't go to Georgetown, and though Metro buses do (the no. 30 line), the public transportation I'd recommend is that provided by two other bus systems, the D.C. Circulator (see p. 49 for more information about its services and the Georgetown route) and the Georgetown Metro Connection shuttle, which travels between the Rosslyn, Virginia, and Dupont Circle Metro stations, stopping at designated points in Georgetown along the way. The shuttle runs every 10 minutes from 7am to midnight Monday through Thursday, 7am to 2am Friday, 8am to 2am Saturday, and 8am to midnight Sunday. One-way fares cost $1.50, or 35¢ with a Metrorail transfer. Look for the pretty blue school buses, stamped "Georgetown Metro Connection." See www.georgetowndc.com/getting-here for more information.

follows the same schedule as the rest of the system. Call ✆ **202/637-7000,** or visit www.wmata.com, for holiday hours and for information on Metro routes.

Metrobus

The **Metrobus** system encompasses 12,301 stops on its 338 routes (it operates on all major D.C. arteries as well as in the Virginia and Maryland suburbs). You'll know the stops by their red, white, and blue signs. However, the signs tell you only what buses pull into a given stop, not where they go. Furthermore, don't rely on the bus schedules posted at bus stops, which are sometimes out-of-date. Instead, for routing information, call ✆ **202/637-7000.** Calls are taken Monday through Thursday from 6am to 10:30pm, Friday 6am to 11:30pm, Saturday 7am to 11:30pm, and Sunday 7am to 10:30pm. Call this same number to request a free map and time schedule, and information about parking in Metrobus fringe lots, as well as for locations and hours of the places where you can purchase bus tokens.

Base fare in the District is $1.35, $3.10 on express routes; bus transfers are free and valid for 2 hours from boarding. There may be additional charges for travel into the Maryland and Virginia suburbs. Bus drivers are not equipped to make change, so be sure to carry exact change or tokens. If you'll be in Washington for a while and plan to use the buses a lot, consider buying a 1-week pass ($11), available online and also at the Metro Center station and other outlets. Buy tokens at the Metro Center Sales Office located at 12th and F streets. (Use the 12th St. entrance.)

Most buses operate daily almost round-the-clock. Service is quite frequent on weekdays, especially during peak hours. On weekends and late at night, service is less frequent.

Tips Transit Tip

If you're on the subway and plan to continue your travel via Metrobus, pick up a free transfer at the station when you enter the system (not your destination station). Transfer machines are on the mezzanine levels of most stations. With the transfer, you pay a reduced fare, usually 45¢, when you board a bus upon exiting your Metrorail station. There are no bus-to-subway transfers.

Tips D.C. Circulator

In addition to the Georgetown Metro Connection shuttle bus (p. 48), D.C. offers another fantastic supplemental bus system that is efficient, inexpensive, and convenient. The D.C. Circulator's fleet of air-conditioned red-and-gray buses travel three circumscribed routes in the city: the north-south route between the D.C. Convention Center and the waterfront, the east-west route between upper Georgetown and Union Station, and the Smithsonian/National Gallery route, which simply loops around the Mall, from 4th Street to Independence Avenue, to 17th Street, to Constitution Avenue, and back around. Buses stop at designated points on their routes (look for the distinctive red-and-gold sign, often topping a regular Metro bus-stop sign) every 10 minutes, and operate daily between 7am and 9pm, except for the Smithsonian/National Gallery route, which operates from 10am to 6pm weekends only. In addition, the system accommodates nightlifers by offering a special service between upper Georgetown and the intersection of 17th and I streets NW, from 9pm to midnight Sunday to Thursday, 9pm to 2am Friday and Saturday. The fare at all times is $1 (35¢ with the use of a Metrorail transfer) and you can order passes online, or pay upon boarding with exact change or with the use of a SmarTrip Metro card, or a D.C. Circulator bus ticket purchased at a street meter near the bus stop. For easy and fast transportation in the busiest parts of town, you can't beat it. Call ℂ 202/962-1423 or go to www.dccirculator.com.

Up to two children 4 and under ride free with a paying passenger on Metrobus, and there are reduced fares for seniors (ℂ 202/637-7000) and people with disabilities (ℂ 202/962-1245 or 962-1100; see "Travelers with Disabilities" later in this chapter for transit information). If you leave something on a bus, on a train, or in a station, call Lost and Found Tuesday through Friday, 11am to 6pm, at ℂ 202/962-1195.

BY CAR

Nearly 75% of all leisure visitors to the District arrive by car; but when you get here, my advice is to park your car and use your own feet, Metrorail, the Georgetown Shuttle, and the D.C. Circulator to get around.

If you must drive, be aware that traffic is always thick during the week, parking spaces are often hard to find, and parking lots are ruinously expensive. You can expect to pay overnight rates of at least $25 at hotels, hourly rates of $8 at downtown parking lots and garages, and flat rates starting at $20 in the most popular parts of town, like Georgetown and the Penn Quarter when there is an event at the Verizon Center. If you're hoping to snag a metered space, better set out with a pocketful of quarters, since 25¢ buys you 15, sometimes 20, minutes.

Gasoline, as you're well aware, is expensive everywhere. In the District, I can tell you of one centrally located service station that offers some of the best rates: the Sunoco White House, at 1442 U St. NW (at 15th St. NW). You'll know you've found it when you see the number of cabbies pulling up to the pumps—always a good sign that the gas price is probably a better deal here than elsewhere. For a listing of other D.C. stations selling the cheapest gas, access the AAA website, www.aaa.com, and click on "Fuel Price Finder," under "Find It," on the home

page. From there, enter the zip code of your hotel, say "20004," and you'll turn up names and locations of area service stations listed in order of gas prices, cheapest to most expensive. You don't have to be a member to use this service.

Tip: The Brookings Institution in late 2006 named Washington, D.C., the country's most walkable city.

Watch out for **traffic circles.** The law states that traffic already in the circle has the right of way. No one pays any attention to this rule, however, which can be frightening (cars zoom into the circle without a glance at the cars already there). The other thing you'll notice is that while some circles are easy to figure out (Dupont Circle, for example), others are nerve-rackingly confusing (Thomas Circle, where 14th St. NW, Vermont Ave. NW, and Massachusetts Ave. NW come together, is to be avoided at all costs).

Sections of certain streets in Washington become **one-way** during rush hour: Rock Creek Parkway, Canal Road, and 17th Street NW are three examples. Other streets change the direction of some of their traffic lanes during rush hour: Connecticut Avenue NW is the main one. In the morning, traffic in four of its six lanes travels south to downtown, and in late afternoon/early evening, downtown traffic in four of its six lanes heads north; between the hours of 9am and 3:30pm, traffic in both directions keeps to the normally correct side of the yellow line. Lit-up traffic signs alert you to what's going on, but pay attention. Unless a sign is posted prohibiting it, a right-on-red law is in effect. The speed limit within city boundaries is usually 25 mph, up to 35 mph on some streets.

To keep up with street closings and construction information, go online to the *Washington Post*'s home page, at www.washingtonpost.com, and click on "Traffic," to learn about current traffic and routing problems in the District and suburban Maryland and Virginia. Another helpful source is a page on the D.C. government's website, www.dc.gov/closures, which identifies major street closures, traffic alerts, and construction in the city, though this info is not always current.

BY TAXI

In May 2008, the D.C. taxicab system switched from charging passengers by geographical zones to charging passengers according to time- and distance-based meters. Fares begin at $3, plus 25¢ per each additional ⅙ mile, 25¢ per minute of wait time, and $1.50 per additional passenger. Other charges might apply, for instance, if you telephone for a cab, rather than hail one in the street, or for extra luggage or services. *Note:* Generally speaking, taxis accept only cash for payment, not credit cards.

Try **Diamond Cab Company** (© 202/387-6200) or **Yellow Cab** (© 202/544-1212).

Call © **202/645-6018** to inquire about fares within the District and © **202/331-1671** to find out the rate between any point in D.C. and an address in Virginia or Maryland. For more information about D.C. taxicabs than you could ever even guess was available, check out the D.C. Taxicab Commission's website, www.dctaxi.dc.gov.

5 Money & Costs

Anyone who travels to the nation's capital expecting bargains is in for a rude awakening, especially when it comes to lodging. Less expensive than New York and London, Washington, D.C.'s average daily hotel rates range from $157 per room per night in August, traditionally, D.C.'s slowest month, to a hefty $252 per room per night in October, reflecting the city's popularity as a top destination among

U.S. travelers. D.C.'s restaurant scene is rather more egalitarian: heavy on the fine, top-dollar establishments, where you can easily spend $100 per person, but with plenty of excellent bistros and small restaurants offering great eats at lower prices. When it comes to attractions, though, the nation's capital has the rest of the world beat, since most of its museums and tourist sites offer free admission.

ATMs

Nationwide, the easiest and best way to get cash away from home is from an ATM (automated teller machine), sometimes referred to as a "cash machine" or "cashpoint." In Washington, D.C., ATMs are ubiquitous, in locations ranging from the National Gallery of Art's gift shop, to Union Station, to grocery stores. The **Cirrus** (© 800/424-7787; www.mastercard. com) and **PLUS** (© 800/843-7587; www.visa.com) networks operate in D.C., as they do across the country. Go to your bank card's website or call one of your branches to find ATM locations in Washington. Be sure you know your personal identification number (PIN) and daily withdrawal limit before you depart. If your PIN is five or six digits, you should obtain a four-digit PIN from your local bank before you leave home, since the four-digit PINs are what most ATMs in Washington accept.

Note: Many banks impose a fee every time you use a card at another bank's ATM, and that fee is often higher for international transactions (up to $5 or more) than for domestic ones (where they're rarely more than $2). In addition, the bank from which you withdraw cash may charge its own fee. Visitors from outside the U.S. should also find out whether their bank assesses a 1% to 3% fee on charges incurred abroad.

CREDIT CARDS & DEBIT CARDS

Credit cards are the most widely used form of payment in the United States: **Visa** (Barclaycard in Britain), **MasterCard** (Eurocard in Europe, Access in Britain, Chargex in Canada), **American Express, Diners Club,** and **Discover.** They also provide a convenient record of all your expenses, and offer relatively good exchange rates. You can withdraw cash advances from your credit cards at banks or ATMs, but high fees make credit-card cash advances a pricey way to get cash.

It's highly recommended that you travel with at least one major credit card. You must have a credit card to rent a car, and hotels and airlines usually require a credit card imprint as a deposit against expenses.

ATM cards with major credit card backing, known as **"debit cards,"** are now a commonly acceptable form of payment in most stores and restaurants. Debit cards draw money directly from your checking account. Some stores enable you to receive cash back on your debit-card purchases as well. The same is true at most U.S. post offices.

TRAVELER'S CHECKS

Travelers increasingly prefer to use credit cards and debit cards over traveler's checks, though traveler's checks are still accepted here. Foreign visitors should make sure that traveler's checks are denominated in U.S. dollars; foreign-currency checks are often difficult to exchange.

You can buy traveler's checks at most banks. Most are offered in denominations of $20, $50, $100, $500, and sometimes $1,000. Generally, you'll pay a service charge ranging from 1% to 4%.

The most popular traveler's checks are offered by **American Express** (© 800/221-7282 for cardholders—this number accepts collect calls, offers service in several foreign languages, and exempts Amex cardholders from the service fee); and **Visa** (© 800/732-1322). Be sure to keep a copy of the traveler's checks' serial numbers separate from your checks in the event that they are stolen or lost. You'll get a refund faster if you know the numbers.

What Things Cost in Washington, D.C.	US$	UK£*
Cup of coffee	1.80	0.93
Movie ticket	9.75	5.01
Taxi from Dulles	60.00	30.82
Subway fare	1.65	0.85
Moderate hotel rate	200.00	102.74

* Assuming a US$ to UK£ conversion rate of $1 = .513712 UK£.

PREPAID TRAVEL CARDS

As traveler's checks go out of fashion, **prepaid traveler's check cards** are quickly taking their place. These are reloadable cards that work much like debit cards but aren't linked to your checking account.

AAA, which stopped selling traveler's checks in December 2007, now sells its own version of the prepaid travel card, called the **Visa Travel Money Card.** Members can order the card online (www. aaa.com) or over the phone (© **866/674-9622**) for $4.95, or at a participating AAA office and retail location for up to $14.95. The pin-based card may be used at any ATM or for any purchase throughout the world, where Visa credit is accepted. A card can hold from $100 to $9,999 and AAA applies a $1.50 fee for U.S. transactions, a $3 fee for all others. Unlike banks, AAA does not stipulate a minimum age for a card user, which means a parent can purchase a card for a child who will be traveling.

AAA's downtown Washington office, open weekdays 9am to 5:30pm, at 1405 G St. NW, between 14th and 15th streets, (© **202/481-6811**), sells these cards to members.

International travelers should know that U.S. money comes in paper bills, most commonly in $1 (a "buck"), $5, $10, and $20 denominations. There are also $2 bills (seldom encountered), $50 bills, and $100 bills (the last two are usually not welcome as payment for small purchases).

Coins come in seven denominations: 1¢ (1 cent, or a penny); 5¢ (5 cents, or a nickel); 10¢ (10 cents, or a dime); 25¢ (25 cents, or a quarter); 50¢ (50 cents, or a half dollar); the gold-colored Sacagawea coin, worth $1; and the rare silver dollar.

6 Health

BEFORE YOU GO

Although it's not required of travelers, health insurance is highly recommended. Most health insurance policies cover you if you get sick away from home—but check your coverage before you leave.

International visitors should note that unlike many European countries, the United States does not usually offer free or low-cost medical care to its citizens or visitors. Doctors and hospitals are expensive, and in most cases will require advance payment or proof of coverage before they render their services. So, it's worth investing in a good travel and health insurance policy to make sure you're able to cover the costs of an accident, illness, or repatriation. Packages such as **Europ Assistance's "Worldwide Healthcare Plan"** are sold by European automobile clubs and travel agencies at attractive rates. **Worldwide Assistance Services, Inc.** (© **800/777-8710;** www.worldwide assistance.com) is the agent for Europ Assistance in the United States.

Though lack of health insurance may prevent you from being admitted to a hospital in nonemergencies, don't worry about being left on a street corner to die: The American way is to treat you, and then bill you for it.

If you suffer from a chronic illness, consult your doctor before your departure. Pack **prescription medications** in your carry-on luggage, and carry them in their original containers with the pharmacy labels—otherwise they won't make it through airport security. Visitors from outside the U.S. should carry generic names of prescription drugs, if possible.

WHAT TO DO IF YOU GET SICK AWAY FROM HOME

Before you leave, you should talk to your local physician and ask for a referral in the D.C. area, should you need one. If your doctor isn't able to help, talk to the concierge or general manager at your hotel. Most hotels are prepared for just such medical emergencies and work with local doctors, who are able to see ill or injured hotel guests. You can also try the emergency room of any D.C. hospital, all of which have walk-in clinics for emergency cases that are not life-threatening. (See "Insurance" in the "Fast Facts, Toll-Free Numbers & Websites" appendix to make sure your insurance policy covers you in any of these circumstances.) For a list of **hot lines, hospitals,** and **emergency numbers,** see the appendix at the back of this book, and look under "Fast Facts: Washington, D.C.," p. 289.

7 Safety

STAYING SAFE

The first thing you want to do is get on the Internet and access Destination D.C.'s website, **www.destinationdc.org**, which publishes travel updates, sometimes on a daily basis. The travel updates alert you to the general state of affairs in D.C. and to new security and touring procedures around town, and refers you to other sections of its website for information about restaurants, hotels, and attractions.

In the years following the September 11, 2001, terrorist attack on the Pentagon, the federal and D.C. governments, along with agencies such as the National Park Service, have continued to work together to increase security, not just at airports, but around the city, including government buildings, tourist attractions, and the subway. The most noticeable and, honestly, most irksome aspect of increased security at tourist attractions can be summed up in three little words: **waiting in line.** Although visitors have always had to queue to enter the Capitol,

the Supreme Court, and other federal buildings, now it can take more time to get through because of more intense scrutiny when you finally reach the door.

Besides lines, you may notice vehicle barriers in place at a wider radius around the Capitol building and new vehicle barriers and better lighting installed at the Washington Monument and at the Lincoln and Jefferson memorials. Self-guided tours of the Capitol are no longer possible, and public guided tours are less comprehensive than they used to be. (A new, tightly secured underground visitor center at the Capitol, which opened in late 2008, should help streamline the process.) Greater numbers of police and security officers are on duty around and inside government buildings, the monuments, and the Metro.

Just because so many police are around, you shouldn't let your guard down. Washington, like any urban area, has a criminal element, so it's important to stay alert and take normal safety precautions.

Ask your hotel front-desk staff or the city's tourist office if you're in doubt about which neighborhoods are safe. Read the section "The Neighborhoods in Brief," at the beginning of this chapter, to get a better idea of where you might feel most comfortable.

Avoid deserted areas, especially at night, and don't go into public parks at night unless there's a concert or similar occasion that will attract a crowd.

Avoid carrying valuables with you on the street, and don't display expensive cameras or electronic equipment. If you're using a map, consult it inconspicuously—or better yet, try to study it before you leave your room. In general, the more you look like a tourist, the more likely someone will try to take advantage of you. If you're walking, pay attention to who is near you as you walk. If you're attending a convention or event where you wear a name tag, remove it before venturing outside. Hold on to your purse, and place your billfold in an inside pocket. In theaters, restaurants, and other public places, keep your possessions in sight.

Remember also that hotels are open to the public, and in a large hotel, security may not be able to screen everyone entering. Always lock your room door.

Be careful crossing streets, especially in the downtown area, and be even more cautious at rush hour. Though this may seem like obvious advice, it's worth a mention here, as there's been an alarming increase lately in the number of pedestrians being hit by cars and buses. Drivers in a hurry run red lights, turn corners too quickly, and so on, so be sure to take your time and check for oncoming traffic when crossing streets, and to use the crosswalks. If you're from Great Britain or Australia, remember to look to your left first, rather than to your right, on two-way streets.

8 Specialized Travel Resources

TRAVELERS WITH DISABILITIES

Washington, D.C., is one of the most accessible cities in the world for travelers with disabilities. The best overall source of information about accessibility at specific Washington hotels, restaurants, shopping malls, and attractions is available from the nonprofit organization **Access Information.** You can read the information (including restaurant reviews) online at **www.disabilityguide.org**, or order a free copy of the *Washington, DC Access Guide* by calling *C* **301/528-8664,** or by writing to Access Information, 21618 Slidell Rd., Boyds, MD 20841.

The **Washington Metropolitan Transit Authority** publishes accessibility information on its website **www.wmata.com**, or you can call *C* **202/962-1245** with questions about Metro services for travelers with disabilities, including how to obtain an ID card that entitles you to discounted fares. (Make sure that you call at least 3 weeks ahead to allow enough time to obtain an ID card.) For up-to-date information about how Metro is operating on the day you're using it—to verify that the elevators are operating at the stations you'll be traveling to, for instance—call *C* **202/962-1212.**

Each Metro station is equipped with an elevator (complete with Braille number plates) to train platforms and extra-wide fare gates for wheelchair users; rail cars are fully accessible. Metro has installed punctuated rubber tiles leading up to the granite-lined platform edge to warn visually impaired Metro riders that they're nearing the tracks; barriers between rail cars prevent the blind from mistaking the gap for entry to a car. For the hearing-impaired, flashing lights indicate arriving trains; for the visually impaired, door chimes let you know when the train doors are closing.

Train operators make station and onboard announcements of train destinations and stops, although the noise of the train and a less-than-perfect audio system often make these announcements unintelligible. Nearly all of the District's Metrobuses have wheelchair lifts and kneel at the curb, though they aren't always operating. The TTY number for Metro information is *© 202/638-3780.*

Regular **Tourmobile** trams (p. 226) are accessible to visitors with disabilities. The company also operates special vans for immobile travelers, complete with wheelchair lifts. Tourmobile recommends that you call a day ahead to ensure that the van is available for you when you arrive. For information, call *© 703/979-0690,* or go to www.tourmobile.com.

Major Washington museums, including all **Smithsonian museum buildings,** are accessible to wheelchair visitors. The Smithsonian has in place an accessibility program, the details of which you can learn about by calling *© 202/633-2921* or TTY 202/633-4353. Go online at www.si.edu/visit/visitors_with_disabilities.htm for more information, including downloadable maps that identify accessibility points throughout all Smithsonian buildings.

Likewise, all of the memorials, including the **Lincoln, Jefferson, Franklin Delano Roosevelt, Vietnam, Korea,** and **World War II memorials** and the **Washington Monument** are each equipped to accommodate visitors with disabilities and keep wheelchairs on the premises. There's limited parking for visitors with disabilities at some of these locations. Call ahead to other sightseeing attractions for accessibility information and special services.

Washington theaters are handily equipped. Among the most accessible are these two:

The **John F. Kennedy Center for the Performing Arts** is fully accessible. The center provides headphones to hearing-impaired patrons at no charge. A wireless, infrared listening-enhancement system is available in all theaters. Some performances offer sign language and audio description. A public TTY is located at the Information Center in the Hall of States as well as on parking lot level A. Large-print programs are available at every performance; a limited number of Braille programs are available from the house manager. All theaters in the complex are wheelchair accessible. To reserve a wheelchair, call *© 202/416-8340.* For other questions regarding patrons with disabilities, including information about half-price tickets (you will need to submit a letter from your doctor stating that your disability is permanent), access the center's website, www.kennedy-center.org, or call the Office for Accessibility (*© 202/416-8727*). The TTY number is *© 202/416-8728.*

The **National Theatre** is wheelchair accessible and features special performances of its shows for visually and hearing-impaired theatergoers. To obtain amplified-sound earphones for narration, simply ask an usher before the performance (you'll need to provide an ID). The National also offers a limited number of half-price tickets to patrons with disabilities who have obtained a Special Patron card from the theater, or who can provide a letter from a doctor certifying disability; you may receive no more than two half-price tickets. For details, call *© 202/628-6161,* or go the website, www.nationaltheatre.org.

For more on organizations that offer resources to travelers with disabilities, go to Frommers.com.

GAY & LESBIAN TRAVELERS

Washington, D.C., has a large and vibrant gay and lesbian community and clearly welcomes gay and lesbian visitors, as

evidenced by the fact that the city's convention and tourism bureau, Destination D.C., includes on its website, **www.destinationdc.org**, a link to information for the GLBT crowd: On the home page, click on "Visiting," then "Experience DC," then scroll to and click on "Pride in D.C." This special section covers the history of the gay rights movement in the capital; a calendar of noteworthy events, like the annual, weeklong Capital Pride Celebration held in June, complete with a street fair and a parade; and favorite-place recommendations made by local gays and lesbians. Better yet is the WCTC's *GLBT Traveler's Guide,* which covers just about every aspect of the not-straight life in D.C. You can order the 68-page guide by calling Destination D.C.'s main number, © **202/789-7000,** or download it from the website.

When in Washington, you'll want to get your hands on the *Washington Blade* (© **202/797-7000;** www.washingtonblade.com), a comprehensive weekly newspaper distributed free at Metro stations and hundreds of other places throughout the city, including Olsson's Books/Records, 1307 19th St. NW; Borders, 18th and L streets; and Kramerbooks, 1517 Connecticut Ave. NW. Every issue provides an extensive events calendar and a list of hundreds of resources, such as crisis centers, health facilities, switchboards, political groups, religious organizations, social clubs, and student activities; it puts you in touch with everything from groups of lesbian bird-watchers to the Asian Gay Men's Network. Gay restaurants and clubs are also listed and advertised.

Washington's gay bookstore, **Lambda Rising,** 1625 Connecticut Ave. NW (© **202/462-6969;** www.lambdarising.com), informally serves as an information source and gathering place for the gay community, which centers on the Dupont Circle neighborhood.

For more gay and lesbian travel resources visit frommers.com.

SENIOR TRAVEL

Members of **AARP,** 601 E St. NW, Washington, DC 20049 (© **888/687-2277;** www.aarp.org), get discounts on hotels, airfares, and car rentals. AARP offers members a wide range of benefits, including *AARP The Magazine* and a monthly newsletter. Anyone over 50 can join.

With or without AARP membership, seniors often find that discounts are available to them at hotels, especially chain hotels such as the Hilton, so be sure to inquire when you book your reservation.

Venues in Washington that grant discounts to seniors include the Metro; certain theaters, such as the Shakespeare Theatre; and those few museums, like the Phillips Collection, that charge for entry. Each place has its own eligibility rules, including designated "senior" ages: The Shakespeare Theatre's is 60 and older, the Phillips Collection's is 62 and older, and the Metro discounts seniors 65 and older. Check the websites for these and other venues to learn the specifics of individual discount programs.

Many reliable agencies and organizations target the 50-plus market. **Elderhostel** (© **800/454-5768;** www.elderhostel.org) arranges worldwide study programs for those age 55 and over. In 2008, Elderhostel hosted more than 20 programs in Washington, D.C., ranging from 1 to 5 days in length and covering diverse topics—from espionage to historic neighborhoods.

Frommers.com offers more information and resources on travel for seniors.

FAMILY TRAVEL

To locate accommodations, restaurants, and attractions that are particularly kid-friendly, see the "Kids" icon throughout this guide. Also be sure to see the "Especially for Kids" section on p. 223 of chapter 7.

Field trips during the school year and family vacations during the summer keep Washington, D.C., crawling with kids all year long. More than any other city, perhaps, Washington is crammed with historic buildings, arts and science museums, parks, and recreational sites to interest young and old alike. The Smithsonian Institution's family of 16 D.C. museums is a stellar example. First of all, the National Zoo is a Smithsonian entity. Enough said. But even the Smithsonian's grandiose museums on and off the National Mall are utterly kid-oriented. You can show up and be entertained, or check things out the calendar ahead of time on the website: www.si.edu. Click on "Events" at the top of the page, and then "Events for Kids" displayed on the left-hand side of the screen. A long menu of options appears, from Indian dance performances at the National Museum of the American Indian, to Family Day activities scheduled at the National Postal Museum.

It's worth calling or checking websites in advance for the schedules of other attractions you're thinking of visiting. The fact that so many attractions are free is a boon to the family budget.

Hotels, more and more, are doing their part to make family trips affordable, too. At many lodgings, children under a certain age (usually 12) sleep free in the same room with their parents. (I've noted these policies in all the listings in chapter 5.) Hotel weekend packages often offer special family rates. See the "Family-Friendly Hotels" box on p. 91 for a rundown of the hotels that are most welcoming to young travelers.

Restaurants throughout the Washington area are growing increasingly family-friendly. Many provide kids' menus or charge less for children's portions. The best news, though, is that families are welcome at all sorts of restaurants these days and need no longer stick only to burger joints. See the "Family-Friendly Restaurants" box on p. 134 for a list of places kids will especially love.

Washington, D.C., is easy to navigate with children. The Metro covers the city, and it's safe. Children 4 and under ride free.

The *Washington Post* publishes a "Weekend" section every Friday that covers all possible happenings in the city, including family-friendly activities. If you arrive on a Friday, be sure to pick up a copy of the paper; otherwise, you can go online to www.washingtonpost.com, click on the "City Guide" section, and then click on "This Weekend" in the browsing window to read what's up, entertainment-wise, in Washington.

Also look for *Frommer's Washington, D.C., with Kids,* which makes an excellent companion piece to this book, providing in-depth coverage of sightseeing with children in Washington.

For a list of more family-friendly travel resources, turn to the experts at frommers.com.

AFRICAN-AMERICAN TRAVELERS

African Americans currently compose about 55% of the District's population, but have long made their home in the nation's capital, richly contributing to the District's history, culture, personality, and identity. African-American museums, monuments, memorials, musical venues, and other landmarks all over town herald their achievements, individually or as a group. Naturally, all of this makes D.C. a compelling destination for African Americans or anyone interested in their culture. From the **Smithsonian Anacostia Neighborhood Museum and Center for African American History and Culture;** to Benjamin Banneker Park; to the **jazz clubs along U Street,** where Duke Ellington and Cab Calloway once catted; to the **African-American Civil War Memorial and Museum;** to the **Mary**

McLeod Bethune House, Washington's black-American heritage is here to discover. Check out Destination D.C.'s website, www.destinationdc.org, and peruse its calendar for annual events, like the **Black Family Reunion** in September and the **Black History Month** activities in February. Browse the Cultural Tourism D.C. website, www.culturaltourismdc.org, to review its database of 98 sites on the **African American Heritage Trail.** (You can also order a copy of the booklet or find out where in Washington you can pick one up for free.) The Cultural Tourism D.C. site lists guided tours that follow an African-American theme, for instance the "Before Harlem, There Was U St. Tour," but you can also create your own tour with the information provided. Coming in 2009: the dedication of the **Dr. Martin Luther King, Jr., Memorial** on the National Mall.

STUDENT TRAVEL

When it comes to admission discounts in Washington, students rule. The one caveat: You must have a valid ID, although your current school ID should be good enough. For benefits that extend beyond reduced admission to D.C. attractions, you may want to consider obtaining an **International Student Identity Card (ISIC),** from the **International Student Travel Confederation** (**ISTC;** www.istc.org). ISTC was formed in 1949 to make travel around the world more affordable for students. Check out its website for comprehensive travel services information and details on how to get the ISIC, which qualifies students for substantial savings on rail passes, plane tickets, entrance fees, and more. It also provides students with basic health and life insurance and a 24-hour help line. The card is valid for a maximum of 18 months. You can apply for the card online or in person at **STA Travel** (✆ **800/ 781-4040** in North America; www.sta travel.com), the biggest student travel agency in the world. STA has a Washington location, on the George Washington University campus, in the Marvin Center, at 800 21st St. NW (✆ **202/994-7800**). If you're no longer a student but are still under 26, you can get an **International Youth Travel Card (IYTC)** from the same people, which entitles you to some discounts.

9 Sustainable Tourism

Sustainable tourism is conscientious travel. It means being careful with the environments you explore, and respecting the communities you visit. Two overlapping components of sustainable travel are **eco-tourism** and **ethical tourism.** The **International Eco-tourism Society** (**TIES**) defines eco-tourism as responsible travel to natural areas that conserves the environment and improves the well-being of local people. TIES suggests that eco-tourists follow these principles:

- Minimize environmental impact.
- Build environmental and cultural awareness and respect.
- Provide positive experiences for both visitors and hosts.

- Provide direct financial benefits for conservation and for local people.
- Raise sensitivity to host countries' political, environmental, and social climates.
- Support international human rights and labor agreements.

You can find some eco-friendly travel tips and statistics, as well as touring companies and associations—listed by destination under "Travel Choice"—at the **TIES** website, www.eco-tourism.org. Also check out **Ecotravel.com**, which lets you search for sustainable touring companies in several categories (water-based, land-based, spiritually oriented, and so on).

Frommers.com: The Complete Travel Resource

Planning a trip or just returned? Head to **Frommers.com,** voted Best Travel Site by *PC Magazine*. We think you'll find our site indispensable before, during, and after your travels—with expert advice and tips; independent reviews of hotels, restaurants, attractions, and preferred shopping and nightlife venues; vacation giveaways; and an online booking tool. We publish the complete contents of over 135 travel guides in our **Destinations** section, covering over 4,000 places worldwide. Each weekday, we publish original articles that report on **Deals and News** via our free **Frommers.com Newsletters.** What's more, **Arthur Frommer** himself blogs 5 days a week, with cutting opinions about the state of travel in the modern world. We're betting you'll find our **Events** listings an invaluable resource; it's an up-to-the-minute roster of what's happening in cities everywhere—including concerts, festivals, lectures, and more. We've also added weekly **podcasts, interactive maps,** and hundreds of new images across the site. Finally, don't forget to visit our **Message Boards,** where you can join in conversations with thousands of fellow Frommer's travelers and post your trip report once you return.

While much of the focus of ecotourism is about reducing impacts on the natural environment, ethical tourism concentrates on ways to preserve and enhance local economies and communities, regardless of location. You can embrace ethical tourism by staying at a locally owned hotel or shopping at a store that employs local workers and sells locally produced goods.

Responsible Travel (www.responsible travel.com) is a great source of sustainable travel ideas; the site is run by a spokesperson for ethical tourism in the travel industry. **Sustainable Travel International** (www.sustainabletravelinternational.org) promotes ethical tourism practices, and manages an extensive directory of sustainable properties and tour operators around the world.

In the U.K., **Tourism Concern** (www.tourismconcern.org.uk) works to reduce social and environmental problems connected to tourism. The **Association of Independent Tour Operators** (AITO; www.aito.co.uk) is a group of specialist operators leading the field in making holidays sustainable.

Volunteer travel has become increasingly popular among those who want to venture beyond the standard group-tour experience to learn languages, interact with locals, and make a positive difference while on vacation. Volunteer travel usually doesn't require special skills—just a willingness to work hard—and programs vary in length from a few days to a number of weeks. Some programs provide free housing and food, but many require volunteers to pay for travel expenses, which can add up quickly.

For general info on volunteer travel, visit **www.volunteerabroad.org** and **www.idealist.org**.

Before you commit to a volunteer program, it's important to make sure any money you're giving is truly going back to the local community, and that the work you'll be doing will be a good fit for you. **Volunteer International** (www.volunteer international.org) has a helpful list of questions to ask to determine the intentions and the nature of a volunteer program.

Tips It's Easy Being Green

Here are a few simple ways you can help conserve fuel and energy when you travel:

- If possible, leave your car at home when coming to Washington, D.C., or, if you must drive here, keep your car parked. The capital is made for walking, despite the traffic-clogged roads you'll notice while you're here. You'll produce zero emissions and stay fit and healthy on your travels. Or use public transport—trains, buses, and even taxis are more energy-efficient forms of transport than driving.

- If renting a car is necessary, ask the rental agent for a hybrid, or rent the most fuel-efficient car available. You'll use less gas and save money at the pump.

- Each time you take a flight or drive a car, greenhouse gases release into the atmosphere. You can help neutralize this danger to the planet through "carbon offsetting"—paying someone to invest your money in programs that reduce your greenhouse gas emissions by the same amount you've added. Before buying carbon offset credits, just make sure that you're using a reputable company, one with a proven program that invests in renewable energy. Reliable carbon offset companies include **Carbonfund** (www.carbonfund.org), **TerraPass** (www.terrapass.org), and **Carbon Neutral** (www.carbonneutral.org).

- Whenever possible, choose nonstop flights; they generally require less fuel than indirect flights that stop and take off again. Try to fly during the day—some scientists estimate that nighttime flights are twice as harmful

10 Packages for the Independent Traveler

Package tours are simply a way to buy the airfare, accommodations, and other elements of your trip (such as car rentals, airport transfers, and sometimes even activities) at the same time and often at discounted prices.

One good source of package deals is the airlines themselves. Most major airlines offer air/land packages, including **Southwest Airlines Vacations** (☎ 800/243-8372; www.southwestvacations.com), **Continental Airlines Vacations** (☎ 800/301-3800; www.covacations.com), and **United Vacations** (☎ 888/854-3899; www.unitedvacations.com). For example, on the Southwest Airlines

vacation packages page, I plugged in mid-July dates and round-trip flights for two people from Cleveland, Ohio, to Baltimore–Washington International Airport, and selected the Kimpton Hotel Helix from a diverse list of hotel options. The result was excellent: a total of $788 covering round-trip flights for two and lodging for 3 nights.

Amtrak Vacations (☎ 800/268-7252; www.amtrakvacations.com) offers similar great-value trips, with travel by train. Also check out **Cosmos** (☎ 800/276-1241; www.cosmos.com), a longtime specialist in budget travel planning. Cosmos trips to D.C. tend to be part of

to the environment. And pack light—each 15 pounds of luggage on a 5,000-mile flight adds up to 50 pounds of carbon dioxide emitted.

- Where you stay during your travels can have a major environmental impact. To determine the green credentials of a property, ask about trash disposal and recycling, water conservation, and energy use; also question if sustainable materials were used in the construction of the property. The website **www.greenhotels.com** recommends green-rated member hotels around the world that fulfill the company's stringent environmental requirements. Also consult **www.environmentallyfriendlyhotels.com** for more green accommodations ratings. See p. 83 in chapter 5 for examples of green-leaning hotels in D.C., and their eco-friendly policies.

- At hotels, request that your sheets and towels not be changed daily. (Many hotels already have programs like this in place.) Turn off the lights and air conditioner (or heater) when you leave your room.

- Eat at locally owned and operated restaurants that use produce grown in the area. This contributes to the local economy and cuts down on greenhouse gas emissions by supporting restaurants where the food is not flown or trucked in across long distances. Visit **Sustain Lane** (www.sustainlane.org) to find sustainable eating and drinking choices around the U.S.; also check out **www.eatwellguide.org** for tips on eating sustainably in the U.S. and Canada.

- See more recommendations for Washington's eco-friendly hotels, restaurants, attractions, and stores within individual chapters.

multi-city tours that take groups and individuals in private air-conditioned motorcoach to their various destinations along the East Coast.

Travel packages are also listed in the travel section of your local Sunday newspaper. Or check ads in the national travel magazines such as *Arthur Frommer's Budget Travel Magazine, Travel + Leisure, National Geographic Traveler,* and *Condé Nast Traveler.*

For more information on package tours and for tips on booking your trip, see Frommers.com.

11 Special-Interest Trips

Escorted tours are structured group tours, with a group leader. The price usually includes everything from airfare to hotels, meals, tours, admission costs, and local transportation. Often, operators and agencies offer tours embracing a special interest. In Washington, the majority of special-interest tours are educational, organized for students. Heritage and culture themes are also big. (See examples below.)

If you're interested in exploring escorted tour packages and special-interest trips, you might start by accessing the websites of two major trade organizations, the **U.S. Tour Operators Association** (© 212/599-6599; www.ustoa.com) and the **National Tourism Association**

(© 800/682-8886; www.ntaonline.com). Tour companies and other travel professionals must satisfy certain requirements to become members, which means that you can count on finding dependable professionals in each association's roster. Both associations list their members online and offer a destination-search feature, which brings up names of companies that offer trips in that particular place. (I recommend the organizations, which are reputable, but the search engines for both websites are, frankly, maddeningly inadequate. Still, the listings give you a place to start.)

HISTORY AND CULTURE

Fancy a behind-the-scenes tour of the Smithsonian's renowned American art museums and rare access to exhibitors at the institution's fabled annual juried craft show? Or maybe a trip that focuses on politics in the nation's capital is more appealing. **Smithsonian Journeys** (© 877/338-8687; www.smithsonian journeys.com) offers a round of options at different times throughout the year, each package designed to satisfy the intellectually curious. Expert "study leaders" give lectures and share their insights.

ACADEMIC TRIPS

Julian Tours (© 703/379-2300; www. juliantours.com) organizes day and overnight trips for student groups. The 26-year-old, family-owned company is based in Alexandria, Virginia, so is on first-name terms with the capital. (Other trips go to Boston, New York, Quebec/Montreal, and Philadelphia.) Julian customizes each tour to accommodate the group's needs and desires.

12 Staying Connected

TELEPHONES AND CELLPHONES

If you are American and own a **cellphone,** bring your phone with you to D.C., making sure first, of course, that your cellphone service does not charge excessively—or at all—for long-distance calls. In fact, if you are from outside the country and own an international cellphone with service that covers the Washington area, bring that phone along. The point is, that hotels often charge outrageous fees for each long-distance or local call you make using the phone in your hotel room.

Just because your cellphone works at home doesn't mean it'll work everywhere in the U.S. (thanks to our nation's fragmented cellphone system). If you're not from the U.S., you'll be appalled at the poor reach of the **GSM (Global System for Mobile Communications) wireless network,** which is used by much of the rest of the world. To see where GSM phones work in the U.S., check out www.t-mobile.com/coverage. You may or may not be able to send SMS (text messaging) home.

It's a good bet that your phone will work here in Washington—except, possibly on the subway. Verizon is the sole provider of wireless service in Washington's Metro.

At any rate, take a look at your wireless company's coverage map on its website before heading out. If you know your phone won't work here, or if you don't have a cellphone, you have several options:

You can **rent** a phone before you leave home from **InTouch USA** (© 800/872-7626 in the U.S., or 703/222-7161 outside the U.S.).

You can use a **public pay telephone,** although these are increasingly hard to find. Many public pay phones at airports now accept American Express, MasterCard, and Visa credit cards. **Local calls** made from pay phones in most locales cost 35¢. (No pennies, please.)

You can **buy** a phone once you arrive. All three Washington-area airports sell cellphones and SIM cards. Look for the **Airport Wireless** shops at Dulles International Airport (© 703/661-0411), National Airport (© 703/417-3983), and BWI Airport (© 410/691-0262).

You can purchase a pay-as-you-go phone from all sorts of places, from Amazon.com to any Verizon store. In D.C., Verizon has a store at Union Station (© 202/682-9475) and another at 1314 F St. NW (© 202/624-0072), to name just two convenient locations.

Your final option is to buy **prepaid calling cards,** which are sold at convenience and grocery stores, post offices and pharmacies, in denominations up to $50. These calling cards can be useful to anyone, but they come in handy especially if you're a traveler from abroad; the cards can be the least expensive way to call home.

Most long-distance and international calls can be dialed directly from any phone. **For calls within the United States and to Canada,** dial 1 followed by the area code and the seven-digit number. **For other international calls,** dial 011 followed by the country code, the city code, and the number you are calling.

Calls to area codes **800, 888, 877,** and **866** are toll-free. However, calls to area codes **700** and **900** (chat lines, bulletin boards, "dating" services, and so on) can be very expensive—usually a charge of 95¢ to $3 or more per minute, and they sometimes have minimum charges that can run as high as $15 or more.

For **reversed-charge or collect calls,** and for person-to-person calls, dial the number 0 and then the area code and number; an operator will come on the line, and you should specify whether you are calling collect, person-to-person, or both. If your operator-assisted call is international, ask for the overseas operator.

For **local directory assistance** ("information"), dial 411; for long-distance information, dial 1, then the appropriate area code and 555-1212.

VOICE-OVER INTERNET PROTOCOL (VOIP)

If you have Web access while traveling, consider a broadband-based telephone service (in technical terms, **Voice-over Internet protocol,** or **VoIP**) such as Skype (www.skype.com) or Vonage (www.vonage.com), which allow you to make free international calls from your laptop or in a cybercafe. Neither service requires the people you're calling to also have that service (though there are fees if they do not). Check the websites for details.

INTERNET & E-MAIL
WITH YOUR OWN COMPUTER

More and more hotels, resorts, airports, cafes, and retailers are going Wi-Fi (wireless fidelity), becoming "hot spots" that offer free high-speed Wi-Fi access or charge a small fee for usage. Most laptops sold today have built-in wireless capability. To find public Wi-Fi hot spots in Washington, go to **www.jiwire.com**; its Hotspot Finder holds the world's largest directory of public wireless hot spots (465 in the center of Washington, last time I checked). Or, you could just head to your corner Starbucks, which has offered up free Wi-Fi service with its lattes for quite some time.

All of the D.C. hotels listed in chapter 5 offer Internet access, mostly high-speed or Wi-Fi, but some still furnishing dial-up service.

Wherever you go, bring a **connection kit** of the right power and phone adapters, a spare phone cord, and a spare Ethernet network cable—or find out whether your hotel supplies them to guests.

WITHOUT YOUR OWN COMPUTER

Increasingly, hotels provide guests computer and Internet access on one or more computers in the hotel business center,

Ways to Get Ahead

Popularity has its price, and in Washington that equals a lengthy wait in a long line for admission to its famous sites. Doesn't have to be that way, though: When you know generally the dates of your trip to Washington, call or e-mail in advance for desired tickets, passes, or reservations, and you might be able to visit places off-limits to the walk-up tourist and waltz through the door of A-list attractions, leaving the queues behind you. Follow this timeline to make sure you obtain tickets and reservations to those venues you most want to visit. Turn to the page numbers listed for specific information on how to proceed.

- **Washington National Cathedral Tour and Tea:** 5 months ahead of the desired date, p. 214.
- **White House Tours:** At least 2 months and as much as 6 months in advance, p. 174.
- **Washington Monument:** At least 1 day prior, as much as 6 months in advance, p. 177.
- **United States Holocaust Memorial Museum:** Two weeks ahead in spring and summer; the day before, otherwise, p. 201
- **Theater Performances, Concerts, and Special Museum Exhibits:** As soon as you can.
- **Restaurant Reservations:** Two weeks ahead.

often as a complimentary service. Both of D.C.'s **Embassy Suites Hotels,** the **Downtown** location and the **Convention Center** property (p. 103 and 90), are two examples.

Of D.C.'s three airports, only Dulles has public computer terminals with Internet access. BWI and National airports offer Wi-Fi, but travelers at BWI and some at National have to pay for it.

Check out copy shops like **Kinko's** (FedEx Kinko's), which offers computer stations with fully loaded software (as well as Wi-Fi).

For help locating cybercafes and other establishments where you can go for Internet access, please see "Internet Access" in the **"Fast Facts, Toll-Free Numbers & Websites"** appendix (p. 289).

Suggested Washington, D.C., Itineraries

Nothing is more thrilling to a traveler than that very first moment of arrival in a new place, unless it's a return to a favorite spot. When that place is Washington, D.C., both the wide-eyed ingénue and the repeat customer arrive and look about in wonder and anticipation. For Washington is a beautiful city, whose famous landmarks—the stunning Capitol, the patiently waiting Lincoln in his memorial—are living, breathing monuments to the American ideals of freedom and equality. And it's a hustling, bustling town, poised to amuse any and all with an endless menu of dining, theatrical, cultural, recreational, and shopping possibilities.

So now you've arrived, and you're standing on the threshold of an enthralling experience. How do you ensure you capture it? Simple. The following three itineraries will help guide you to it. But first, read the brief descriptions of D.C.'s neighborhoods to help you get an overall sense of the city. Consider the individual appeal and attractions of each.

Then, look over all three itineraries to see which one fits your personal agenda and schedule, allowing you the amount of time you'd like at each site. Call ahead and make sure the places on your desired itinerary are open. Be calm and flexible: Lines to enter public buildings are longer than ever, thanks to security clearance procedures and the capital's continuing popularity. Reserve spots on tours to avoid some of those waits, and book advance reservations at recommended restaurants, to make sure you get a table. Most important, don't be afraid to ask questions: The police on Capitol Hill, the National Park Service rangers on duty at the memorials, and the staff at all the museums know an awful lot—take advantage of their expertise.

1 The Neighborhoods in Brief

Adams-Morgan Though this ever-trendy, multiethnic neighborhood is about the size of a postage stamp, it's crammed with boutiques, bars, clubs, and restaurants. Everything is located on either 18th Street NW or Columbia Road NW. You won't find any hotels here, but there are several nearby in the Dupont Circle and Woodley Park neighborhoods (see below). Parking during the day is okay, but difficult at night, especially weekends (a parking garage on Champlain St., just off 18th St., helps things a little). Luckily, you can easily walk (be alert—the neighborhood is edgy) to Adams-Morgan from the Dupont Circle or Woodley Park Metro stops, bus it, or take a taxi there. The weekend begins Thursday nights in the nightlife land of Adams-Morgan.

Washington, D.C., at a Glance

0 1/2 mi
0 0.5 km

Georgia Ave.

Michigan Ave.

McMillan Reservoir

Howard University

U STREET CORRIDOR

Rhode Island Ave.

Vermont Ave.

West Virginia Ave.

50

Gallaudet University

New York Ave.

New York Ave.

New Jersey Ave.

North Capitol St.

7th St.

DOWNTOWN

K St.

CHINATOWN

Massachusetts Ave.

H St.

Maryland Ave.

PENN QUARTER

Union Station

Louisiana Ave.

Constitution Ave.

NW **NE**

NATIONAL MALL

U.S. Capitol

East Capitol St.

Tennessee Ave.

Independence Ave.

CAPITOL HILL

North Carolina Ave.

SW **SE**

South Carolina Ave.

Pennsylvania Ave. SE

Maine Ave.

Southeast Fwy.

395

John Phillip Sousa Bridge

Washington Channel

South Capitol St.

Washington Navy Yard

River

11th St. Bridge

Anacostia Fwy.

EAST POTOMAC PARK

Fort McNair

Frederick Douglass Mem. Bridge

Anacostia

Minnesota Ave.

ANACOSTIA

Atlas District The Atlas District, no more than a section of H Street NE, really, between 12th and 14th streets northeast of Union Station, is increasingly a nightlife and live music destination. A hardscrabble part of town by day, the Atlas District turns into a music and bar playground at night, especially Thursday through Saturday, as the city's thirsty scenemakers hit the street. There are no hotels, for now.

Barracks Row Barracks Row, likewise, refers mainly to a single stretch of 8th Street SE, south of Pennsylvania Avenue, SE, but also to side streets occupied by Marine Corps Barracks since 1801, hence the name. Known for its lineup of shops, casual bistros, and pubs, Barracks Row's attractions have been rapidly multiplying, ever since the Nationals baseball team's stadium, Nationals Park, opened in April 2008. The closest hotel, Capitol Hill Suites, is 6 blocks away, at C and 2nd Street SE. Expect more hotels to blossom as part of Nationals Park development.

Capitol Hill Everyone's heard of "the Hill," the area crowned by the Capitol. The term, in fact, refers to a large section of town, extending from the western side of the Capitol to the D.C. Armory going east, bounded by H Street to the north and the Southwest Freeway to the south. It contains not only the chief symbol of the nation's capital, but the Supreme Court building, the Library of Congress, the Folger Shakespeare Library, Union Station, and Eastern Market. Much of it is a quiet residential neighborhood of tree-lined streets and Victorian homes. There are a number of restaurants in the vicinity and a smattering of hotels, mostly close to Union Station. Keep to the well-lit, well-traveled streets at night, and don't walk alone—crime occurs more frequently in this neighborhood than in some other parts of town.

Cleveland Park Cleveland Park, just north of Woodley Park, is an enclave of beautiful old houses with wraparound porches, found on picturesque streets extending off the main artery, Connecticut Avenue. With its own stop on the Red Line Metro system and a respectable number of excellent restaurants, Cleveland Park is worth visiting when you're near the zoo (just up the street) or in the mood for some fine cuisine and a sense of affluent D.C. neighborliness. Most hotels lie a short walk away in Woodley Park, and farther south into the city.

Downtown The area roughly between 6th and 21st streets NW going east to west, and M Street and Pennsylvania Avenue going north to south, is a mix of the Federal Triangle's government office buildings; K Street, ground zero for the city's countless law and lobbying firms; Connecticut Avenue restaurants and shopping; historic hotels; the city's poshest small hotels; **Chinatown;** the huge convention center; and the White House. You'll also find the historic **Penn Quarter,** now D.C.'s hottest area, which has continued to flourish ever since the 1997 opening of the Verizon Center (venue for Washington Wizards and Mystics basketball games and rock concerts). A number of off-the-Mall museums, like the mammoth Newseum, the International Spy Museum and the Smithsonian's National Portrait Gallery and American Art Museum, are here. This is also where you'll find the hippest restaurants, boutique hotels, and nightclubs. The total downtown area takes in so many blocks and attractions that I've divided discussions of accommodations (chapter 5) and dining (chapter 6) into two sections: "**Midtown,**" roughly the area west of 15th Street to 21st Street, and north of Pennsylvania Avenue to M Street; and "**Penn Quarter,**" roughly east of 15th Street to 6th Street, and Pennsylvania Avenue north to New York Avenue.

Dupont Circle One of my favorite parts of town, Dupont Circle, is fun day or night. It takes its name from the traffic circle minipark, where Massachusetts, New Hampshire, and Connecticut avenues collide. Washington's famous **Embassy Row** centers on Dupont Circle, and refers to the parade of grand embassy mansions lining Massachusetts Avenue and its side streets. The streets extending out from the circle are lively, with all-night bookstores, good restaurants, wonderful art galleries and art museums, nightspots, and Washingtonians at their loosest. It is also the hub of D.C.'s gay community. There are plenty of hotels.

Foggy Bottom/West End The area west of the White House, south of Dupont Circle, and east of Georgetown encompasses both Foggy Bottom and the West End. Foggy Bottom, located below, or south, of Pennsylvania Avenue, was Washington's early industrial center. Its name comes from the foul fumes emitted in those days by a coal depot and gasworks, but its original name, Funkstown (for owner Jacob Funk), is perhaps even worse. There's nothing foul (and not much funky) about the area today. The West End edges north of Pennsylvania Avenue, booming with the latest big-name restaurants and new office buildings. Together, the overlapping Foggy Bottom and West End neighborhoods present a mix of town-house residences, George Washington University campus buildings, small- and medium-size hotels, several fine eateries, student bars, and the Kennedy Center, lining either side of Pennsylvania Avenue and its side streets, beyond.

Georgetown This historic community dates from Colonial times. It was a thriving tobacco port long before the District of Columbia was formed, and one of its attractions, the Old Stone House, dates from pre-Revolutionary days. Georgetown action centers on M Street and Wisconsin Avenue NW, where you'll find the luxury Four Seasons hotel (and less expensive digs—see chapter 5), numerous boutiques (see chapter 8), chic restaurants, and popular pubs. Expect lots of nightlife here. But detour from the main drags to relish the quiet, tree-lined streets of restored Colonial row houses, stroll the beautiful gardens of Dumbarton Oaks, and check out the C&O Canal. Georgetown is also home to Georgetown University. Note that the neighborhood gets pretty raucous on the weekends, which won't appeal to everyone.

Glover Park Mostly a residential neighborhood, this section of town, just above Georgetown and just south of the Washington National Cathedral, is worth mentioning because of several good restaurants and bars located along its main stretch, Wisconsin Avenue NW. Glover Park sits between the campuses of Georgetown and American Universities, so there's a large student presence here.

The Mall This lovely, tree-lined stretch of open space between Constitution and Independence avenues, extending for 2½ miles from the Capitol to the Lincoln Memorial, is the hub of tourist attractions. It includes most of the Smithsonian Institution museums and several other notable sites. Tourists as well as natives—joggers, food vendors, kite flyers, and picnickers among them—traipse the 300-foot-wide Mall. Most hotels and restaurants are located beyond the Mall to the north, with a few located south of the Mall, across Independence Avenue.

U Street Corridor D.C.'s avant-garde nightlife neighborhood radiates out from 14th Street to include U Street between 9th and 18th streets NW. The quarter continues to rise from the ashes of the nightclubs and theaters located here decades ago when the performances of jazz and blues legends Duke Ellington, Louis Armstrong, and Cab Calloway gave the area the name "Black Broadway." Today, clubs like Twins Jazz and HR-57

honor that legacy, drawing a diverse mix of jazz lovers, while the corridor's many clubs fill nightly with the city's young and restless. New restaurants (see chapter 6) and little shops (see chapter 8) proliferate. Go here to party, not to sleep—there are no hotels along this stretch.

Woodley Park Home to Washington's largest hotel (the Marriott Wardman Park), Woodley Park boasts the National Zoo, many good restaurants, and some antiques stores. Washingtonians are used to seeing conventioneers wandering the neighborhood's pretty residential streets with their name tags still on.

2 The Best of Washington in 1 Day

Note: For this itinerary, you should call in advance to reserve tickets for a moonlight tour and to book a table at Johnny's Half-Shell (see information below).

The first two stops on this tour are the Capitol, which is open to visitors Monday through Saturday, and the Supreme Court, open only on weekdays. If you're here on a weekend, plan accordingly. If you're here on a weekday, let's be honest: When both the Supreme Court and Congress are in session, and you're hoping to attend both, and to tour the Capitol, you can expect those activities alone to take up the better part of a day. So I'm offering you some choices: Visit the Supreme Court *or* the Capitol, and continue with the itinerary as laid out; *or* hope for the best, attempt to take in both the Court *and* the Capitol, and work in other stops on this itinerary as you're able. It's possible, with everything working in your favor, to experience this itinerary in its entirety. But many factors will come into play: ebbs and flows of tourist seasons, interest in a particular case being argued in the Supreme Court, legislation up for a vote in the Senate or House, even the weather. And if you're traveling with children age 12 and under, that's another factor: Visit the Capitol and, if you want, do a tour of the Supreme Court, but do not try to attend a Supreme Court argument with young children. Rule of thumb: To be sure of attending a Supreme Court argument or of obtaining a ticket to tour the Capitol, line up at either place by 7:30am. *Start: Metro on the Blue Line to Capitol South, or on the Red Line to Union Station.*

❶ The Capitol ✸✸✸

The story of the design and construction of the Capitol is a tumultuous one, full of strong personalities and brave compromises—kind of like the history of the United States, actually. Startling truths abound, beginning with the fact that the most important U.S. building was designed in 1792 by a Scottish-trained physician from the British West Indies. William Thornton, the first architect of the Capitol, explained himself, "I lamented not having studied architecture and resolved to attempt that grand undertaking and study at the same time." Seventy years and three architects later,

the Capitol completed its most notable feature, a 287-foot-high dome, made of two enormous cast-iron shells, one inside the other, with all the exterior trim, cornices, and columns painted to look like marble. Tilt your head all the way back to see the 19-foot-statue, *Freedom*, which was set in place atop the dome in December 1863, at the height of the Civil War—the same year that Abraham Lincoln issued his Emancipation Proclamation. See p. 163.

❷ Supreme Court ✸✸✸

You don't have to be aware of the Supreme Court's schedule to know when

1 Capitol
2 Supreme Court
3 Library of Congress
4 Le Bon Café
5 Folger Shakespeare Library and Garden
6 U. S. Botanic Garden
7 National Gallery of Art
8 Johnny's Half Shell
9 Union Station
10 Moonlight Tour

a controversial case is up—you'll observe the line of hopeful visitors stretching across the Court's front plaza. You'll spot media types, too. The southwest corner of the plaza is a favorite location for TV correspondents to deliver on-camera reports; with the right angle, the shot captures the newsperson and the crowds of people in endless queues, framed against the backdrop of the Court's stately columned edifice and elaborate pediment inscribed with the words EQUAL JUSTICE UNDER LAW. See p. 169.

3 Library of Congress 🞳
As the world's largest library, the Library of Congress commands an inventory of nearly 140 million items. In an enduring

effort to share its wealth, the Library reaches into its pockets, so to speak, to pull out wondrous objects from one of its particular collections, and then mounts an exhibition to show them off. One example: An ongoing exhibit titled "Creating the United States," displays an assortment of artifacts that inform our understanding of the birth of our democracy, from an "original Rough Draught" of Thomas Jefferson's much marked-up Declaration of Independence, to early-18th-century hand-colored etchings conveying political satire, to a 1797 manuscript in George Washington's hand, outlining a plan of government for Virginia. The Library of Congress: not just for bibliophiles. See p. 212.

🍴 LE BON CAFÉ

Order a sandwich and try to snag a seat at one of the outside tables. Or better yet, get it to go, and proceed to your next destination, where an Elizabethan garden awaits you. ✆ 202/547-7200. See p. 123.

❺ Folger Shakespeare Library and Garden

If your timing is right (try before noon or after 1pm), you'll have the garden to yourself—to sit on a bench; munch on a picnic lunch; and relax amid the English ivy, rosemary, and lavender, all plantings true to Shakespeare's day. Positioned throughout the garden are statues of characters from eight of the Bard's plays. Stop inside to see "what's on" in the paneled, Tudor-style Great Hall, and check the calendar for plays being staged in the re-created Elizabethan Theatre. Attend an evening production, if you can; they're always a treat. See p. 203.

Note: If you're running out of time, skip the next stop and head straight to #7—unless you love flora, in which case, continue on to:

❻ U.S. Botanic Garden 🌸

At the foot of the Capitol grounds on the Independence Avenue side is this other garden—well, several gardens and plant collections, in fact—contained within a large greenhouse. Not much is asked of you here—you don't have to be a gardener to appreciate the beauty of orchids or the wonder of the "Musa Praying Hands" (it's in the banana family). Be sure to climb all the way up the stairs in the tallest part of the conservatory and look out: You'll have views of the Capitol and the neighborhood that I'll bet even most locals haven't discovered. See p. 219.

❼ National Gallery of Art and Sculpture Garden 🌸🌸🌸

The National Gallery's special exhibits are always amazing, so if there's one being staged, go, no matter who the artist. But first, head to the East Wing and go straight to the tower at the top to take a look at the Matisse cutouts. They get less traffic than other artwork in the museum, mostly because not everyone's hip to them. Here's the tricky part, though: You should be here by 1:30pm (or 2:30pm on Sun) at the latest, for this exhibit is open only between 10am and 2pm Monday through Saturday, 11am to 3pm Sunday, to protect the pigments and paper of the cutouts. From here, you'll want to high-tail it over to the West Wing, to view as much of the grand sculpture galleries, European paintings from the 13th to the 19th century, and modern artworks in the Sculpture Garden, as time allows. See p. 199.

If you're short on time or energy, take a taxi; otherwise walk the half-mile or so to Johnny's Half Shell.

🍴 JOHNNY'S HALF SHELL 🌸🌸

Sit on the terrace in view of the Capitol or head inside to enjoy Johnny's particular conviviality and "Seafood Specialties, Strong Drinks," as the restaurant puts it. Never sampled a soft-shell crab? This is the place to try it, if in season. Non-seafood items are also available. Arrive weekdays 4:30 to 7:30pm and you'll be in time for happy hour, or Monday to Saturday 5 to 7pm, to enjoy the good value pretheater menu. From here, it's just a couple of blocks to Union Station, your next destination. ✆ 202/737-0400, p.121.

❾ Union Station 🌸

This handsome structure is a major thoroughfare for commuters rushing for Metro and Amtrak trains, so watch out. The ticket kiosks for the various tour operations are at the front of the Main Hall, making them hard to miss; whether you've reserved space in advance (recommended) online or by phone, or you're just now purchasing your tickets, you'll

need to stop by the booths to obtain the actual tour tickets. See p. 213.

⑩ Moonlight Tour ✹✹✹

Tourmobile and Old Town Trolley offer nighttime tours of the memorials and the Washington Monument. Some consider this the most dramatic way to view the historic sites. After a full day of sightseeing, it is certainly the easiest and most relaxing way to get around. Both operations offer narrated tours, with stops (for 20 min. or so) at the Lincoln, FDR, Vietnam Veterans, and Jefferson memorials. But their specific fares, routes, and schedules differ (Tourmobile's twilight tour, for instance, is a seasonal operation.) Hop aboard and enjoy the ride. See p. 176.

3 The Best of Washington in 2 Days

Note: For this itinerary, you should call in advance for restaurant and ticket reservations (see information below).

Your second day takes you to three powerhouse museums just off the National Mall, in the hopping Penn Quarter, as well as to several Smithsonian museums. (You will have passed some of these edifices the night before on your moonlight tour.) If you're here between March and September, when the National Archives stays open until 7pm, make that your last stop; afterward or otherwise, cross Pennsylvania Avenue to return to the Penn Quarter for cocktails and dinner. *Suggestion:* Purchase advance tickets to tour the Newseum to guarantee entry for the day and time you desire and to bypass lines. *Start: Metro on the Green or Yellow Line to Archive/Navy Memorial or Penn Quarter station; or on the Red Line to the Judiciary Square stop, using the 4th Street exit.*

❶ Newseum ✹✹

This mammoth museum debuted April 11, 2008, and the word is "Wow!" Its glass-fronted, seven-story, block-long-and-wide building grabs your attention, vying with nearby notables, like the Capitol just up the avenue. Is it truly "the world's most interactive museum," as it proclaims? Maybe so: Fourteen galleries, 15 theaters, 2 broadcast studios, and 130 interactive stations invite visitors to explore 5 centuries of news history. You can put yourself in the reporter's seat in an interactive newsroom, play the NewsMania game to test your knowledge of news events, or be "on the scene" at a dramatic moment in history, through an amazing 4-D theater experience that puts you virtually back in that moment. Awesome. See p. 209.

❷ National Portrait Gallery &
❸ American Art Museum ✹✹✹

Before this building was even finished, in 1867, it had already served as a Civil War hospital and as the site of Abraham Lincoln's second inaugural ball. Upon completion, the building housed patent offices, whose clerks eventually issued patents to Alexander Graham Bell, Thomas Edison, and 500,000 other inventors. The Smithsonian took over the Patent Office Building and remodeled it before opening two-museums-in-one in 1968.

Fast-forward to 2006, after an even more intense renovation to the museums, which just happened to coincide with the remarkable renewal taking place in the museums' surrounding Penn Quarter neighborhood. The reopening of the National Portrait Gallery and the American Art Museum in July 2006 signified nothing less than a rebirth, and the city staged a celebration to herald this much-improved bastion of "American Originals." The museums and their vast displays do America proud, representing the nation's spirit and people at their best

in every artistic genre, including presidential portraits, folk art, photographs, Latino art, African-American art, and paintings by the masters, from Gilbert Stuart to Georgia O'Keeffe to modernist Aaron Douglas. Go. See p. 197.

> **④ ZOLA** ⚔
> In the same building as the Spy Museum and across the street from the Smithsonian museums, Zola plays upon a sleuth theme in its decor. The food's for real, though, and highly recommended. ✆ **202/654-0999.** See p. 132.

⑤ National Air and Space Museum ⚔⚔

Nothing attests to human ingenuity better than this vast display of the machines we've created to fly through air and space. And yet, one of this museum's enduring attractions is something that puts those human accomplishments in perspective: The Albert Einstein Planetarium (you'll need a ticket to enter). It coaxes you to wonder about the dimensions of the universe and where it leads. See p. 188.

⑥ Freer Gallery ⚔

This handsome building, with its Italian Renaissance architecture and arched courtyard, is devoted to Asian art, with one major exception: its Whistler holdings. Visit the spectacular Peacock Room, so called for the golden peacock feathers that Whistler painted upon the walls of the room, which was once part of a friend's London town house. The friend was most displeased, but today's gallerygoers are generally intrigued. Continue through other chambers of the gallery to admire ancient jade objects, early Buddhist sculpture, Islamic art, and a wealth of Asian works. See p. 186.

⑦ National Museum of American History ⚔⚔⚔

Across the Mall from the Freer lies this ponderous museum, newly reopened after a much-needed renovation. You won't have time to view everything on display in this fascinating tribute to American culture and history. But certain things you shouldn't miss: the magnificent, original Star-Spangled Banner, now on display in its own multistory, glass-paneled gallery; 10-foot-high, glass-paned artifact walls showcasing choice items from the museum's three-million-piece collection, from an 1815 tavern sign to Helen Keller's watch; and a favorite, Julia Child's kitchen, moved from the famous chef's home in Cambridge, Massachusetts, to its permanent niche here. See p. 192.

⑧ National Museum of Natural History ⚔⚔

This is yet another so-much-to-see, so-little-time venue, especially given the fact that this is the largest natural-history museum in the world. Do take a gander at the Hope Diamond and other gems and minerals, and don't miss the fossil collection and the dinosaur hall. But if your time is limited, visit the museum's two newest exhibits. The 23,000-square-foot Ocean Hall, the museum's largest permanent exhibit, aims to explain the essential connection between oceans and all life. Displays include a life-size replica of a North Atlantic whale and an 1,800-gallon-tank display of coral reef. Butterflies + Plants: Partners in Evolution is two exhibits in one. Partners in Evolution explores the relationship between plants and insects and animals, while the Butterfly Pavilion is aflutter with live and colorful butterflies, allowing visitors to walk in their midst, observing them straight on, not through glass. The Butterfly Pavilion is the Smithsonian's rare exhibit that

1 Newseum
2 National Portrait Gallery
3 Smithsonian American Art Museum
4 Zola
5 National Air and Space Museum
6 Freer Gallery
7 National Museum of American History
8 National Museum of Natural History
9 National Archives
10 Central Michel Richard

charges admission. Tickets cost $5 for children, $6 for adults, every day but Tuesday, when admission is free but a timed ticket still necessary. See p. 193.

9 National Archives

Area residents are slow to catch on, but the National Archives has gradually been transforming itself into a multimedia complex, mounting major exhibitions, screening documentaries, and hosting talks by contemporary authors. Its finest feature, however, will always be its display of the original Declaration of Independence, U.S. Constitution, and Bill of Rights. See p. 199.

10 CENTRAL MICHEL RICHARD ✸✸✸

You've been on your feet all day! Treat yourself to a lobster burger, cassoulet, or steak au poivre, accompanied by an apricot sour or a glass of fine wine. Congratulate yourself if you've succeeded in booking a reservation (and reservations are a must) at perhaps the hottest restaurant in the city. As you'll discover, its popularity has as much to do with the party atmosphere as with the top-notch cuisine. ℂ 202/626-0015. See p. 128.

4 The Best of Washington in 3 Days

Especially if you're traveling with children ages 11 and under, you might start Day 3 with a lively visit to the National Zoo. Otherwise, consider visiting the U.S. Holocaust Memorial Museum in the morning and then spend the afternoon taking a restorative stroll through some of D.C.'s loveliest quarters. Obtain admission tickets ahead of time for the museum, if possible; if not, you should plan to arrive early to wait in line. *Start: Metro on the Red Line to National Zoo to go to the zoo; Metro on the Blue Line to Smithsonian, exiting at Independence Avenue and 12th Street SW, to visit the Holocaust Museum.*

① National Zoological Park ★★ **or ② U.S. Holocaust Memorial Museum** ★★

If you (or your children) want to get an early start on the day, the National Zoological Park, an off-the-Mall Smithsonian complex, opens at 6am, year-round. Make your way to the Asia Trail, whose winding path presents close-up sights of sloth bears sucking up termites, giant pandas frolicking in a waterfall, fishing cats caught in the act, and the assorted activities of clouded leopards and Japanese salamanders. Those three giant pandas remain the zoo's top draws. See p. 195.

Fifteen years after its debut, crowds continue to tour the U.S. Memorial Holocaust Museum, especially its heart-tearing main exhibit. Some people also come here to do research: Open to the public without appointment is a library on the fifth floor, where you can look up information on a name, a town, or any subject to do with the Holocaust. The museum, meanwhile, is expanding its mission to include special exhibits on related events—firsthand accounts and photographs depicting the persecution and torture of the people of Darfur, Sudan, for instance. See p. 201.

From the Metro's Red Line National Zoo stop, take the Metro south one stop to the Dupont Circle station. From the Metro's Blue Line Smithsonian station, take the Metro to Metro Center and switch to the Red Line, going toward Shady Grove. Debark at Dupont Circle.

③ Phillips Collection ★★

This beautiful museum-mansion was expanded in 2006 to include a sculpture garden, a new cafe, an auditorium, a gallery devoted to the works of Mark Rothko, and a larger exhibit space for postwar contemporary art. Always keep an eye out for visitors' favorite pieces: Renoir's *Luncheon of the Boating Party;* numerous Bonnards; and, on display from time to time, a painting executed by founder Duncan Phillips's wife, Marjorie Phillips: *Night Baseball.* See p. 211.

> ◢ **PIZZERIA PARADISO** ★
> Open daily from lunch straight through to 10pm (Sun), 11pm (Mon–Thurs), or midnight (Fri–Sat), this cherished pizzeria expanded in 2008 to satisfy its steady stream of customers, who come for the pies that are several cuts above the average: cooked in an oak-burning oven and topped with your choice of 31 fresh ingredients, from pancetta to eggplant. ✆ **202/223-1245.** See p. 148.

⑤ Embassy Row and Dupont Circle

Stop in shops along Connecticut Avenue, and then follow side streets to discover boutiques, little art galleries, and quaint century-old town houses. If you look carefully, you'll start to notice that some of these buildings are actually embassies or historic homes. The most awesome embassies lie on Massachusetts Avenue,

Map labels (reading across the map):

Woodley Rd. · Devonshire Pl. · Klingle Rd. · Cortland Pl. · Hawthorne St. · Lamont St. · Kilbourne Pl. · Park Rd. · Park Rd.

NATIONAL ZOOLOGICAL PARK

Cathedral Ave. · Garfield St. · Garfield Terr. · Woodland Dr. · 35th St. · 34th St. · 34th Pl. · 33rd St. · 31 St. Pl. · Cleveland Ave. · 29th Pl. · 28th St. · 27th St. · Woodley Pl. · Kenyon St. · Irving St. · Hobart St. · Harvard St. · Hiatt Pl. · Mt. Pleasant St. · Adams Mill Rd.

Columbia Heights
Green Line

① National Zoo

Woodley Park-Zoo/Adams Morgan
Red Line

Observatory Circle · Massachusetts Ave. · McGill Terr. · Calvert St. · Connecticut Ave. · 24th St. · Ontario Rd. Pl. · Lanier Pl. · Columbia Rd. · Ontario Rd. · Champlain St. · Euclid St.

U.S. Naval Observatory

EMBASSY ROW

ROCK CREEK PARK

ADAMS-MORGAN

Belmont St. · Florida Ave. · W St. · V St. · U St.

Rock Creek · Belmont Rd. · Kalorama Rd. · Wyoming Ave. · Tracy Pl. · California St. · Bancroft Pl. · S St. · Belmont · Kalorama · Wyoming Ave. · California Ave. · Vernon St. · Florida Ave. · Swann St.

DUMBARTON OAKS PARK

MONTROSE PARK

⑤ Embassy Row/Dupont Circle Neighborhood

Decatur Pl. · R St. · **③** Riggs St. · New Hampshire Ave. · 17th St. · 16th St. · 15th St. · T St. · S St. · R St. · Q St.

Dent Pl. · Q St. · Volta Pl. · P St. · O St. · 32nd St. · Wisconsin Ave. · Dumbarton St. · 28th St. · 26th St.

Dupont Circle
Red Line

④ Pizzeria Paradiso

DUPONT CIRCLE

Dupont Circle · Church St. · P St. · Logan Circle

Scott Circle

GEORGETOWN

Prospect St. · M St. · **⑦** Georgetown

Rock Creek and Potomac Pkwy · 24th St. · 23rd St. · 22nd St.

Washington Circle · (29) · L St. · K St. · Pennsylvania Ave. · I St.

Farragut North
Red Line

Farragut West
Blue & Orange Lines

Farragut Square

Thomas Circle · 14th St. · 15th St.

McPherson Square
Blue & Orange Lines

Whitehurst Fwy. · 25th St.

Foggy Bottom-GWU
Blue & Orange Lines

George Washington University · H St. · G St. · F St. · Virginia Ave. · E St. · 18th St. · 17th St.

White House

THE ELLIPSE · 15th St.

Theodore Roosevelt Island

Little River · Georgetown Channel · Rock Creek and Potomac Pkwy · **⑥** Kennedy Center

FOGGY BOTTOM

C St.

(1) (50)

Constitution Ave.

Vietnam Veterans Memorial ■

WWII Memorial ■

Washington Monument ②

Lincoln Memorial

Arlington Mem. Bridge

Reflecting Pool

WEST POTOMAC PARK

(50) Independence Ave.

Potomac River · Ohio Dr. · W. Basin Dr.

FDR Memorial ■

Tidal Basin

Legend:

① National Zoo
② U.S. Holocaust Memorial Museum
③ Phillips Collection
④ Pizzeria Paradiso
⑤ Embassy Row/Dupont Circle Neighborhood
⑥ Kennedy Center
⑦ Georgetown

west of Dupont Circle. Flags and plaques clearly identify them. Turn onto S Street NW and look for no. 2340 to see where President Woodrow Wilson lived after he left the White House. Right next door is a cool little museum, the Textile Museum, which opened a second location in 2008, on 7th Street NW in the heart of the Penn Quarter. Both the Woodrow Wilson House and the Textile Museum are worth touring if you have time. Embassies are rarely open to the public. See p. 259 and 233.

Walk, if you feel up to it, or take a taxi to the Kennedy Center.

⑥ Kennedy Center

Head to the Kennedy Center for the 6pm nightly free concert in the Grand Foyer (part of the center's Millennium Stage program). At concert's end, proceed through the glass doors to the terrace overlooking Rock Creek Parkway and the Potomac River, and enjoy the view. See p. 211.

⑦ Georgetown

Finish up the day with dinner and shopping in Georgetown, where stores and restaurants tend to stay open later than those in other parts of town. See p. 152 and 234.

Where to Stay

If you have a favorite brand of hotel chain, you're likely to find it represented in Washington, D.C. The Hilton family of Doubletree, Embassy Suites, Hampton Inn, and Hilton Garden Inn properties offers good value for both business and leisure guests; the Marriott dynasty of 16 D.C. hotels includes upscale Renaissances, extended-stay Residence Inns, business-traveler mainstay Courtyard by Marriott, and the high-end traveler option, the JW Marriott; and our all-American Hyatt, Sheraton, and Omni brands offer a range, from the luxurious Park Hyatt to the more practical Four Points Sheraton.

International chains, like Ireland's gracious Jurys and France's chic Sofitel, are here. So is Kimpton Group Hotels, the un-chainlike chain, that now counts 10 hotels in the D.C. area and continues to up the ante on chicly whimsical lodging. One of the new brands to debut here in 2008 was the hip Thompson Hotels Collection, in the form of Donovan House, whose description is found in the "Midtown" section of this edition.

Luxury lodging is big business in D.C. The Four Seasons, two Ritz-Carltons, and the Mandarin Oriental vie with each other—and with three exquisite smaller establishments, the Hay-Adams, the St. Regis, and the Jefferson hotels—for the patronage of the wealthy. (The Jefferson has been closed for an immense renovation, which precludes its inclusion in this edition; the hotel [www.thejefferson-washingtondc.com] should be open for business by the time you read this.)

Washington also has quite a number of beloved, homegrown accommodations, from the romantic Swann House in the Dupont Circle neighborhood to the Georgetown Suites, always a remarkable deal given its buzzing locale.

You'll find descriptions of 50 hotels and inns within this chapter, along with tips on choosing a neighborhood, getting the best rate, landing the best room, and finding a place to stay when the whole city seems booked.

CHOOSING A NEIGHBORHOOD

Most of Washington's hotels lie downtown, near Dupont Circle, and in the West End/Foggy Bottom areas, with a handful scattered in Georgetown, on Capitol Hill, and northward on Connecticut Avenue. Each of these communities has its own character, as detailed in the section "The Neighborhoods in Brief," in chapter 4.

If proximity to Capitol Hill is important to you, consider the cluster of hotels on the north side of the Hill, close to Union Station and just off North Capitol Street. If you want to be within a short walk of the National Mall, think about staying in either the lah-di-dah Mandarin Oriental or the family-friendly Residence Inn, each just a couple of blocks from the Smithsonian-lined Mall. They are convenient for sightseeing and in the thick of things during the day. Both areas, especially the neighborhood

closest to the Mall, can feel isolated at night, when tourist sites and offices close and Hill staff, government office workers, and museumgoers go home. The hotels are not near residential areas, and restaurants and shops are few.

To take the pulse of the city as it goes about its business, stay in a downtown hotel. This is also where you should stay if you want to be able to walk to good restaurants, bars, and nightclubs. Divided into two sections here, Penn Quarter (btw. 6th and 15th sts. NW) and Midtown (btw. 15th and 21st sts. NW), Washington's downtown is bustling day and night all week long. Hotels in the downtown segment east of 15th Street are close to theaters and several museums; properties on or near Pennsylvania Avenue, like the Willard or the JW Marriott, are within walking distance of the National Mall and the White House. The Hotel Monaco, between 7th and 8th streets, is just a few blocks north of Pennsylvania Avenue, the Newseum, and the National Gallery. Downtown hotels west of 15th Street are also within a stroll of the White House, as well as some smaller museums, like Decatur House and the Renwick and Corcoran galleries.

If you prefer the feel of a residential neighborhood, look to hotels in Dupont Circle and Woodley Park. For a taste of campus life, you might choose lodging in Foggy Bottom; the accommodations near Pennsylvania Avenue and Washington Circle border George Washington University's widening campus. And if you're a serious shopper, Georgetown should be your top choice, with Dupont Circle as your second pick.

Within each neighborhood heading, this chapter further organizes hotels by rate categories, based on their lowest high-season rates for double rooms: **Very Expensive** (from about $350 and up); **Expensive** (from about $250); **Moderate** (from about $175); and **Inexpensive** (anything under $175). But these categories are intended as a general guideline only—rates can rise and fall dramatically, depending on how busy the hotel is. In 2008, the rise in D.C. hotel rates also reflected increased energy prices and property values, for which hotels were having to pay substantially higher taxes than in the past; that may still be true. Nevertheless, it's often possible to obtain a special package or a better rate than the first rate quoted, as the next section explains.

SAVING ON YOUR HOTEL ROOM

The **rack rate** is the maximum rate that a hotel charges for a room. Hardly anybody pays this price, however, except during peak season. Every hotel usually offers ways for customers to pay a lower rate than the published rate. These general guidelines can help lower the cost of your room:

- **Ask about special rates or other discounts.** Always ask whether a room less expensive than the first one quoted is available, or whether any special rates apply to you. You may qualify for corporate, government, student, military, senior, or other discounts, and these can be substantial. Mention membership in AAA, AARP, frequent-flier programs, or trade unions, which may entitle you to special deals as well.

- **Dial direct.** When booking a room in a chain hotel, you'll often get a better deal by calling the individual hotel's reservation desk rather than the chain's main number. *Warning:* You'll want to confirm that you are talking to someone on-site at the hotel, even if you've dialed a local "202" phone number. Increasingly, chain hotels are outsourcing the bulk of their reservation bookings to regional offices, whose staff are simply not informed enough to answer basic questions about a particular hotel.

- **Book online.** Many hotels offer Internet-only discounts or supply rooms to Priceline, Travelocity, or Expedia at rates lower than the ones you can get through the hotel itself.

- **Remember the law of supply and demand.** Washington's downtown hotels are busiest during the week and when Congress is in session, so you can expect the best discounts over the weekend and on holidays, when Congress heads out of town. Most hotels have high-season and low-season prices, and booking the day after high season ends can mean good deals.

- **Look into group or long-stay discounts.** If you come as part of a large group, you should be able to negotiate a bargain rate, because the hotel can then guarantee occupancy in a number of rooms. Likewise, if you're planning a long stay (at least 5 days), you might qualify for a discount. As a general rule, expect 1 night free after a 7-night stay.

- **Avoid excess charges and hidden costs.** D.C. hotels charge unbelievable rates for overnight parking—usually more than $25 a night—plus tax! So if you can avoid driving to D.C., you can save yourself parking expenses. Use your own cellphone, pay phones, or prepaid phone cards instead of dialing direct from hotel phones, which usually have exorbitant rates, as do the room's minibar offerings. Finally, ask about local taxes and service charges. The D.C. hotel sales tax is a whopping 14.5%, merchandise sales tax is 5.75%, and restaurant tax is 10%, all of which can rapidly increase the cost of a room.

- **Book an efficiency room.** A room with a kitchenette allows you to shop for groceries and cook your own meals—a big money saver, especially for families on long stays.

- **Consider enrolling in hotel "frequent-stay" programs,** which aim to win the loyalty of repeat customers. Frequent guests can now accumulate points or credits to earn free hotel nights, airline miles, in-room amenities, merchandise, tickets to concerts and events, and discounts on sporting facilities. Perks are awarded not only by many chain hotels and motels (Hilton HHonors and Marriott Rewards, to name two), but also by individual inns and B&Bs. Many chain hotels partner with other hotel chains, car-rental firms, airlines, and credit card companies to give consumers additional incentive to do repeat business.

LANDING THE BEST ROOM

Somebody has to get the best room in the house; it might as well be you. You can start by joining the hotel's frequent-guest program, which may make you eligible for upgrades. A hotel-branded credit card usually gives its owner "silver" or "gold" status in frequent-guest programs for free. Always ask about a corner room. They're often larger and quieter, with more windows and light; and they often cost the same as standard rooms. When you make your reservation, ask if the hotel is renovating; if it is, request a room away from the construction. Ask about nonsmoking rooms, rooms with views, rooms with twin, queen- or king-size beds. If you're a light sleeper, request a quiet room away from vending machines, elevators, restaurants, bars, and discos. Ask for one of the rooms that have been most recently renovated or redecorated. If you aren't happy with your room when you arrive, say so; most properties will try to accommodate you.

USING A LOCAL RESERVATIONS SERVICE

If you suffer from information overload and would rather someone else do the research and bargaining, you can always turn to one of the following reputable—and free!—local reservations services:

- **Capitol Reservations** (© 800/VISIT-DC [847-4832] or 202/452-1270; www.visitdc.com) will find you a hotel that meets your specific requirements and is within your price range. The 25-year-old service works with about 100 area hotels that have been screened for cleanliness, safe locations, and other desirability factors; you can check rates and book online.
- **Washington D.C. Accommodations** (© 800/503-3330 or 202/289-2220; www.dcaccommodations.com) has been in business for 24 years and, in addition to finding lodgings, can advise you about transportation and general tourist information and even work out itineraries.
- **Bed & Breakfast Accommodations, Ltd.** (© 877/893-3233 or 413/582-9888; www.bedandbreakfastdc.com), in business since 1978, works with more than 30 homes, inns, guesthouses, and unhosted furnished apartments to find lodging for visitors.

1 Best Hotel Bets

- **Best Historic Hotel:** The **Willard InterContinental** celebrated its 100th anniversary in 2006, as the "new" 12-story Willard, replacing the original, smaller "City Hotel" that existed here between 1816 and 1906. Whether known as the City or the Willard, the hotel has hosted nearly every U.S. president since Franklin Pierce in 1853, including two presidents who lived here for a time—Lincoln in 1861 and Calvin Coolidge in 1923. President Ulysses S. Grant liked to unwind with cigar and brandy in the Willard lobby after a hard day in the Oval Office, and literary luminaries like Mark Twain and Charles Dickens used to hang out in the Round Robin bar. The hotel continues to draw political, society, business, and cultural icons today. See p. 90.
- **Best Location:** Three contenders in three different locations win this category: For a true heart-of-the-city experience, the **Hotel Monaco** (p. 89) can't be beat. The hotel lies halfway between the White House and Capitol Hill, across the street from the Verizon Center and two Smithsonian museums, and in the middle of a neighborhood known for its many restaurants, shops, and clubs. If you desire proximity to the White House, no hotel gets closer than the **Hay-Adams** (p. 92), right across Lafayette Square from the Executive Mansion. And if you'd like to be within walking distance of both Capitol Hill and the National Mall, the **Residence Inn Capitol** (p. 88) is a good choice.
- **Best Trendy Hotel:** With the arrival of **Donovan House** (p. 94) in March 2008, Washington's gang of seven hip Kimpton hotels faces some competition in this category. With its cocoon spiral showers and leather-wrapped beds, rooftop bar, and big-name chef (Todd English, of Olives), Donovan House may just come out on top. But do consider Kimpton's fun **Hotel Helix** (p. 96), effervescent **Hotel Monaco** (p. 89), funky **Hotel Rouge** (p. 97), New Age-y **Topaz Hotel** (p. 105), the hot **Hotel George** (p. 85), tree-hugging **Hotel Madera** (p. 103), and the artsy **Hotel Palomar** (p. 101).

ⓘ Tips Staying Green in D.C.

D.C. hotels are taking the green cause to heart, though with varying degrees of fervor. The W hotel chain is building a luxury, thoroughly organic, "green-minded" hotel in the West End even as we speak. Upon completion, the hotel will surely be included in these pages. Until then, you have several eco-conscious lodging options from which to choose. The following list, though not comprehensive, is a good starting point for assessing the level of ecological commitment at some D.C. hotels.

- **Four Seasons** (p. 108) has a behind-the-scenes program that directs various departments toward practices that conserve energy and reduce, reuse, and recycle, whenever possible. The hotel's "It Is Easy Being Green" program allows guests the option of keeping the same bed linens and towels during their stay.

- **All Kimpton Hotels in D.C.** participate in the chain's EarthCare program, which uses low-flow toilets, sinks, and shower heads; non-toxic cleaning agents; in-room recycle bins; and a service that allows guests to keep the same linens and towels during their stay, saving on water and energy use. Individual properties go a bit further; for instance, the Hotel Madera has an on-site hybrid car available for guest use and provides free parking to guests whose own cars are hybrids.

- **The Willard InterContinental** (p. 90) buys all of its electricity from such renewable energy sources as wind power. A hybrid car is available for guest transport. All of the hotel's light bulbs are now low-impact fluorescents. The hotel invests in local environmental causes, such as the cleanup of the much-polluted Anacostia River.

- **Phoenix Park Hotel** (p. 85), has a green procurement program, "Irish Green Goes Extreme," which includes recycling goods and purchasing recycled goods as much as possible; using energy-efficient light bulbs and sensors, timers, and non-toxic cleaning supplies; and installing low-flow shower heads, sinks, and toilets. The hotel also offers guests the option of keeping the same linens and towels during their stay to conserve water and energy, and reduce the use of detergents.

- **All Marriott properties,** in D.C. and elsewhere, have low-flow toilets and shower heads. The chain is moving toward replacing all standard light bulbs with fluorescent lighting and is partnering with Conservation International to determine ways to reduce its carbon footprint.

- **Best Place for a Romantic Getaway:** The posh **Ritz-Carlton Georgetown** (p. 108) in the heart of Georgetown is just enough off the beaten track to make you feel like you've really escaped; its small size, only 86 rooms, adds an air of intimacy. While the Ritz's spa, sexy bar, lovely rooms, and solicitous service may tempt you to stay put, it would be a shame to pass up the chance to stroll hand in hand along Georgetown's quaint streets to dine close by at one of the city's most romantic restaurants—1789 (p. 153), Citronelle (p. 152), and La Chaumiere (p. 156) among them.

- **Best Washington Insider Hotel:** The **Willard** wins again. This is where the term "lobbyists" came into popular use, after all. When President Ulysses S. Grant enjoyed a brandy in the Willard lobby, he was often besieged by politicians and businessmen clamoring for his attention. "Lobbyists," Grant called them, making famous a term someone else had coined. Lobbyists still come and go here, as do high-ranking government officials, television news anchors, and visiting heads of state. Be sure to duck your head into the Round Robin bar, as well as the Willard dining room. See p. 90.

- **Best Inexpensive Hotel:** The boutique **Jurys Normandy Inn** charges $89 to $239 for personable service and rooms that are small but charming. Extras like an exercise room and pool are available at its sister hotel around the corner. A multitude of restaurants, bars, art galleries, and shops lie within walkable reach in the Dupont Circle and Adams-Morgan neighborhoods. See p. 100.

- **Best Service:** The **Four Seasons** (p. 108) staff pampers you relentlessly and greets you by name. The hotel also offers an "I Need It Now" program that delivers any of 100 or more left-at-home essentials (tweezers, batteries, cuff links, electric hair curlers, and so on) to you in 3 minutes, at no cost. And then there's the **Mandarin Oriental** (p. 84), where staffers speak in hushed tones, almost bowing; the spa features something called an amethyst steam room; and the very design of the hotel follows the principles of Feng shui, the better to attract good fortune.

- **Best Health Club:** The **Ritz-Carlton, Washington, D.C.'s** is still the best fitness center in the city. Its two-level, 100,000-square-foot Sports Club/LA boasts state-of-the-art weight-training equipment and free weights, two regulation-size basketball courts and four squash courts, an indoor heated swimming pool and aquatics pool with sun deck, exercise classes, personal trainers, the full-service Splash Spa and Roche Salon, and its own restaurant and cafe. See p. 106.

- **Best Views:** The **Hay-Adams** has such a great, unobstructed view of the White House that the Secret Service comes over regularly to do security sweeps of the place. Ask for a room on the H Street side of the hotel, on floors six through eight. See p. 92. For a coveted overlook of Washington's famous cherry blossoms in spring or of the Tidal Basin and Jefferson Memorial year-round, stay at the **Mandarin Oriental,** specifying a room offering that particular view. See p. 84.

- **Best for Travelers with Disabilities:** The **Omni Shoreham Hotel** has 41 specially equipped rooms for guests with disabilities, about half with roll-in showers, and vibrating door knockers and pillows, TTYs, and flashing lights to alert guests when fire alarms are sounding (all of these devices are available, but you must ask for them). The hotel carries copies of disabilityguide.org's *Access Entertainment* guide, which offers detailed information about how to travel around and enjoy D.C., if you have limited mobility. See p. 110.

2 Capitol Hill/The Mall

VERY EXPENSIVE

Mandarin Oriental, Washington, D.C. ✦✦✦ The location of this fabulously posh hotel is in a government-building neighborhood, a few blocks from the National Mall. By day, the location is convenient; at night, not at all. These streets are dark, not meant for strolling; and there's nothing to do.

Never mind. Once you're ensconced inside the Mandarin, you may have no inclination to leave. Hotel decor richly combines Asian and American traditions. Each guest room is laid out in accordance with the principles of Feng shui, and furnishings include replica pieces from the Smithsonian's collections and handmade silk tapestries. Sensuously beautiful Fili D'Oro linens rest on the thick-mattressed beds. The service is sublime.

Rather than roam the neighborhood, you may enjoy rambling around the hotel's terraces of landscaped gardens, taking in views of the Tidal Basin and marina, the Jefferson Memorial, and the Virginia skyline. Guest rooms offer these same views. The hotel's renowned CityZen restaurant (p. 118), world-class spa, fitness center, and indoor pool offer more reasons to stay put.

1330 Maryland Ave. SW (at 12th St.), Washington, DC 20024. ⓒ 888/888-1778 or 202/554-8588. Fax 202/554-8999. www.mandarinoriental.com/washington. 400 units. $495–$695 double; $1,150–$8,000 suite. Children age 12 and under stay free in parent's room. For information about special packages, call the hotel directly or check the website. AE, DC, DISC, MC, V. Parking $34. Metro: Smithsonian (Independence Ave. & 12th St. SW exit). Dogs under 40 lb. accepted, with certain restrictions. **Amenities:** 2 restaurants (Modern American, Asian-influenced cafe cuisine); 2 bars; heated indoor pool in spa; fully equipped fitness center; 10,400-sq.-ft. full-service spa; 24-hr. concierge; business center w/full Internet access; 24-hr. room service; same-day laundry service; dry cleaning; 20 rooms for those w/limited mobility. *In room:* A/C, TV w/cable, DVD/CD player, 3-line phone w/dataports, Wi-Fi ($15/day), minibar, hair dryer, iron, safe, robes.

EXPENSIVE

The Hotel George ★★ Behind a facade of stainless steel, limestone, and glass is one of Washington's hippest places to stay, and one within easy reach of the Capitol. Clientele leans toward powerbrokers and celebrities, who often meet with Washington's version of the same in the hotel's Bistro Bis restaurant (p. 119). Decor in the oversize guest rooms is minimalist, all creamy white and modern, with 32-inch plasma-screen television, and shades (not fussy drapes) nestled perfectly within the window frame. Fluffy vanilla-colored comforters rest on over-large beds; an ergonomically designed chair draws up to the black granite-topped desk. Spacious bathrooms feature black granite and marble, and a speaker that broadcasts TV sounds from the other room. Like all Kimpton hotels, the George offers in-room spa services, reservable when you book your room. The smoke-free hotel has three one-bedroom suites.

15 E St. NW (at N. Capitol St.), Washington, DC 20001. ⓒ 800/576-8331 or 202/347-4200. Fax 202/347-4213. www.hotelgeorge.com. 139 units. Weekdays $289–$659 double; weekends $169–$349 double. Year-round $750–$1,050 suite. Ask about seasonal and corporate rates, and the "Hot Dates, Great Rates" deal. Extra person $25. Children 17 and under stay free in parent's room. AE, DC, DISC, MC, V. Parking $36 plus tax overnight. Metro: Union Station (Massachusetts Ave. NW exit). Pets accepted. **Amenities:** Restaurant (French bistro); small 24-hr. fitness center w/steam rooms; 24-hr. concierge; business services; room service (7am–11pm); same-day laundry service; dry cleaning; VCR rentals; 4 rooms for those w/limited mobility. *In room:* A/C, TV w/pay movies, DVD player, 2-line phone w/dataport, free wireless high-speed Internet access, minibar, hair dryer, iron, safe, robes, umbrella.

Phoenix Park Hotel ★ The Phoenix Park is one in a cluster of hotels across from Union Station and 2 blocks from the Capitol. It's distinguished by its popular and authentic Irish pub, the **Dubliner** (p. 104), which helps set the tone of Irish hospitality for the entire property. Guest rooms are in sage, gold, or dusky rose hues and feature pretty patterned wallpaper and drapes of the same design enclosing a toile-printed sheer curtain. All rooms include a pillow-topped mattress and 32-inch, high-definition, flatscreen TV. Best rooms are on the top floors (the hotel has nine) facing Massachusetts Avenue, toward the North Capitol Street end, with views of the National Postal

Washington, D.C., Accommodations

AKA White House District **25**
Beacon Hotel **32**
Capital Hilton **34**
Courtyard by Marriott Northwest **6**
Donovan House **42**
Doubletree Washington **30**
Embassy Circle Inn **9**
Embassy Suites Hotel Convention Center **44**
Embassy Suites Hotel Downtown **15**
Four Points by Sheraton **43**
Four Seasons **18**
George Washington University Inn **22**
Georgetown Inn **20**
Georgetown Suites **19**
Grand Hyatt Washington **45**
Hamilton Crown Plaza **41**
Hampton Inn Convention Center **47**
Hay-Adams Hotel **36**
Hilton Garden Inn **40**
Hilton Washington **7**
Hotel George **48**
Hotel Helix **31**
Hotel Madera **13**
Hotel Monaco **46**
Hotel Palomar **11**

Hotel Rouge **29**
Hotel Tabard Inn **27**
Jurys Normandy Inn **5**
Jurys Washington Hotel **10**
JW Marriott **39**
Kalorama Guest House Adams-Morgan **1b** Woodley-Park **1a**
Mandarin Oriental **51**
Mansion on O St. **12**
Omni Shoreham Hotel **4**
One Washington Circle **24**
Park Hyatt Washington **17**
Phoenix Park Hotel **49**
The Quincy **26**
Renaissance Mayflower **33**
Residence Inn Capitol **50**
Ritz-Carlton Georgetown **21**
Ritz-Carlton Washington DC **16**
The River Inn **23**
Sofitel Lafayette Square **37**
St. Gregory Luxury Hotel and Suites **14**
St. Regis Hotel **35**
Swann House **8**
Topaz Hotel **28**
Wardman Park Marriott **3**
Willard InterContinental **38**
Woodley Park Guest House **2**

Tips When All Else Fails

If your luck and time are running out and you still haven't found a place to stay, these ideas are worth a try:

- **Call one of the free reservations services** at the beginning of this chapter, including the Bed & Breakfast Accommodations service. Talk to someone "on location" who can work with you to find a place.
- **Check out the Vacation Rental by Owner website, www.vrbo.com,** and enter "Washington" as your city to read about furnished apartments for rent around the city.
- **Consider house swapping.** Try **HomeLink International** (Homelink.org), the largest and oldest home-swapping organization, founded in 1953, with more than 13,000 listings worldwide ($110 for a yearly membership). **www.homexchangevacation.com** and **InterVac.com** are also reliable.
- **Call the Washington Convention and Tourism Corporation's local number** ((ℂ) 202/789-7000) and ask the tourist rep for the names and numbers of any **new or about-to-open hotels.** If the rep isn't sure, ask her to check with the marketing director. Up-and-coming hotels may have available rooms, for the simple reason that few people know about them.
- **Consider lodging outside the city.** See separate box in this chapter, "Inside and Outside the Beltway, Beyond-D.C. Hotel Options," p. 112

Museum and a smidgen of Union Station. Or book a one- or two-story suite with kitchenette, working fireplace, and spiral staircase. Irish decorative accents include linens and artwork. Call direct to the hotel or check the website for packages.

520 N. Capitol St. NW (at Massachusetts Ave.), Washington, DC 20001. (ℂ) **800/824-5419** or 202/638-6900. Fax 202/393-3236. www.phoenixparkhotel.com. 149 units. Weekdays $149–$489 double; weekends $99–$299 double; year-round $699–$1,899 suite. Extra person $30. Children 15 and under stay free in parent's room. AE, DC, DISC, MC, V. Valet parking $30 plus tax. Metro: Union Station (Massachusetts Ave. NW exit). No pets. **Amenities:** Irish pub; complimentary use of small exercise room; room service (7am–11pm); same-day dry cleaning; 7 rooms for those w/limited mobility. *In room:* A/C, TV w/pay movies, 2-line phone w/dataport, complimentary wired Internet access and Wi-Fi, minibar, coffeemaker, hair dryer, iron, safe.

MODERATE

Residence Inn Capitol Four Native American tribes are 49% owners of this hotel, which makes this the first multitribal partnership with nontribal partners on land off a reservation. During the day, you can easily walk to the Smithsonian National Museum of the American Indian and other Mall museums, as well as to Capitol Hill; at night, however, this part of town shuts down.

Hotel features mimic the look of the Indian Museum. Guest rooms evince a Native American cultural motif through the use of etched wood headboards, artwork, and other design elements. The roomy suites all have fully equipped kitchens. Rates include a generous breakfast, social-hour buffets Monday through Wednesday, and grocery-delivery service. The property has an indoor pool and exercise room and a gift shop, which sells tour tickets.

000

333 E St. SW (at 4th St.), Washington, DC 20024. © **800/331-3131** or 202/484-8280. Fax 202/554-0484. www. marriott.com/wascp. 233 suites. $189–$359 studio; $199–$379 1-bedroom suite; $259–$399 2-bedroom suite. Weekend and long-term rates available. Rates include hot breakfast daily and "social hour" weeknights. AE, DC, DISC, MC, V. Parking $30. Metro: Federal Center Southwest. Pets accepted for a fee. **Amenities:** Indoor pool, whirlpool, and sun deck; exercise room; business center; copy/fax service; laundry valet and self-serve laundry; grocery-shopping service; Wi-Fi in public space. *In room:* A/C, TV w/pay movies, 2-line phones, free wired Internet access, full kitchen, coffeemaker, hair dryer, iron, safe.

3 Penn Quarter

VERY EXPENSIVE

Hotel Monaco Washington D.C. ✿✿ Museum-like in appearance, the Monaco occupies a four-story, all marble mid-19th-century building, half of which was designed by Robert Mills, the architect for the Washington Monument. The other half was designed by Thomas Walter, one of the architects for the U.S. Capitol. The halves connect seamlessly, enclosing a landscaped courtyard.

Spacious guest rooms feature vaulted ceilings and long windows hung with charcoal-and-white patterned drapes. Eclectic furnishings include neoclassical armoires and three-legged desks. (The hotel's historic status precludes it from installing closets; hence, the armoires, which some guests say are too small.) A color scheme successfully marries creamy yellow walls with periwinkle-blue lounge chairs and orangey-red damask pillows. (Plans to refresh the decor were being contemplated as we went to press.)

Interior rooms overlook the courtyard and the restaurant, **Poste** (p. 129); exterior rooms view city sights on floors two through four. The first floor is nearly subterranean (a window close to the ceiling lets in some light). When you stay at the Monaco, you're not just downtown, you're part of the scene.

700 F St. NW (at 7th St.), Washington, DC 20004. © **800/649-1202** or 202/628-7177. Fax 202/628-7277. www.monaco-dc.com. 184 units. Weekdays $369–$609 double, $509–$1,200 suite; weekends $169–$369 double, $269–$800 suite. Extra person $20. Children 17 and under stay free in parent's room. Rates include complimentary organic coffee in morning and a hosted evening wine hour. AE, DC, DISC, MC, V. Parking $30 plus tax. Nonsmoking property. Metro: Gallery Place (7th and F sts. NW exit). Pets welcomed—they get VIP treatment, with their own registration cards at check-in, maps of neighborhood fire hydrants and parks, and gourmet puppy and kitty treats. **Amenities:** Restaurant (modern American); bar; spacious fitness center w/flatscreen TVs; 24-hr. concierge; full-service business center; 24-hr. room service; same-day laundry service; dry cleaning; 9 rooms for those w/limited mobility, 4 w/roll-in showers. *In room:* A/C, TV w/pay movies and Nintendo, Web TV access ($10/day), CD/DVD player, 2-line phones w/dataports, free Internet access, minibar, hair dryer, iron, safe, robes.

JW Marriott Hotel on Pennsylvania Avenue ✿ You're in a prime location here—on Pennsylvania Avenue, adjacent to the National Theatre, 1 block from the Warner Theater, 2 blocks from the White House, and within walking distance of the Washington Monument, the Smithsonian museums, and lots of stores and restaurants.

A recently completed $40-million overhaul thoroughly transformed the lobby and jazzed up guest rooms, replacing beds and adding thick mattresses, top-of-the-line linens, seven big pillows, and white duvet comforters, laundered afresh after every guest. Decor now features earth-tone fabrics, cherry furnishings, and chrome-and-glass bathroom fixtures. Each room has a state-of-the-art, 32-inch, LCD HDTV, able to connect with a guest's laptop or iPod. Ask for a room on floors 3 through 15 facing Pennsylvania Avenue for views of the avenue and of the Washington Monument beyond. Floors 7 and 12 on the Pennsylvania Avenue side have balconies; floors 14 and 15 are the concierge level.

1331 Pennsylvania Ave. NW (at E St.), Washington, DC 20004. © **800/228-9290** or 202/393-2000. Fax 202/626-6991. www.experiencejw.com. 772 units. Weekdays $299–$529 double; weekends $159–$259 double; year-round $749–$3,100 suites. Extra person free. AE, DC, DISC, MC, V. Valet parking $35. Metro: Metro Center (13th St. NW exit). **Amenities:** 2 restaurants (both upscale American); Starbucks; complete health club (w/indoor swimming pool and whirlpool); concierge (morning and evening hours, weekdays only); business center; 24-hr. room service; same-day laundry service; dry cleaning; concierge-level rooms; 15 rooms for those w/limited mobility, 6 w/roll-in shower. *In room:* A/C, TV w/pay movies, 2-line phones w/dataports, high-speed Internet access ($9.95/day), minibar, coffeemaker, hair dryer, iron, safe.

Willard InterContinental Washington ★★★ This is one of D.C.'s finest hotels, and certainly its most famous. From its magnificent lobby and grand **Willard Room** restaurant (p. 126), favorite settings for movie directors, to its illustrious history, which includes the fact that two presidents (Lincoln in 1861, Coolidge in 1923) lived here for a while, the Willard warrants visiting, even if you don't stay here. But if you do stay here, you'll find you're perfectly situated near the White House, Smithsonian museums, excellent restaurants, and theaters.

Guest rooms present a handsome decor, heavy on reproduction Federal- and Edwardian-style furnishings. The rooms with the best views are the oval suites overlooking Pennsylvania Avenue to the Capitol and the rooms fronting Pennsylvania Avenue. Rooms facing the courtyard are the quietest.

The Willard's designation as a National Historic Landmark in 1974 and magnificent restoration in the 1980s helped revitalize Pennsylvania Avenue and this part of town. Stop in at the Round Robin Bar for a mint julep (introduced here), and listen to barman Jim Hewes spin tales about all the people who have stopped or stayed here, from Mark Twain to Bill Clinton.

The hotel's I Spa, charming **Café du Parc** (p. 132), and schedule of seasonal festivities (Christmas caroling, a cherry blossom-themed afternoon tea in spring) offer further inducement to stop by.

1401 Pennsylvania Ave. NW (at 14th St.), Washington, DC 20004. © **800/827-1747** or 202/628-9100. Fax 202/637-7326. www.washington.interconti.com. 332 units. $349–$1,149 double; $699–$4,199 suite. Ask about special promotions and packages. AE, DC, DISC, MC, V. Parking $35 per 24 hr. Metro: Metro Center (13th St. NW exit). Small pets accepted. **Amenities:** Restaurant (modern French-American); cafe; seasonal terrace; bar; thoroughly equipped fitness center and health spa; children's programs; concierge; 24-hr. business center; 24-hr. room service; babysitting; same-day laundry service; same-day dry cleaning; currency exchange; airline/train ticketing. *In room:* A/C, TV, CD player, 2-line phone w/dataport, Wi-Fi ($11/day), minibar, hair dryer, iron, safe, robes.

EXPENSIVE

Embassy Suites Hotel Convention Center ★ *Kids* Business is booming in Washington; and this hotel is booming along with it, thanks to its clever location a short walk from both the convention center and the heart of the Penn Quarter. The hotel often sells out—with families during extended school breaks, and with conventioneers at other times. Every suite offers a separate living room and bedroom, with a bathroom serving as the divider. Decor is fresh and upbeat, employing light woods, earth tones, and glass accents. Each living room has a pullout sofa. Common areas in the hotel are also attractive, from the glass- and wood-paneled, six-story-high atrium, to the popular Finn & Porter restaurant, in whose sunroom a stunning complimentary breakfast is served daily. The hotel hosts a nightly, complimentary cocktail reception in the two-level bar. The hotel's exercise room and pool are on the second floor, where wide windows overlook D.C.'s downtown.

(Kids) Family-Friendly Hotels

Embassy Suites Hotel Downtown (p. 103) Close to both a Red line and a Blue line Metro station (the zoo is on the Red line; the Smithsonian museums are on the Blue line) and within walking distance of Georgetown, this hotel lets your kids sleep on the pullout sofa in the separate living room. Rooms have some kitchen facilities, but the complimentary breakfast in the atrium is unbelievable. There are also an indoor pool and a free game room. For all of the same reasons, but a different location (within walking distance of Penn Quarter attractions), also consider the **Embassy Suites Hotel Convention Center** (p. 90).

Hilton Washington (p. 98) A large heated outdoor pool, three tennis courts, and a goodie bag at check-in—what more does a kid need?

Omni Shoreham Hotel (p. 110) Adjacent to Rock Creek Park, the Omni is within walking distance of the zoo and Metro and is equipped with a large outdoor pool and kiddie pool. Children receive a goodie bag at check-in, and the concierge has a supply of board games (no charge to borrow, just remember to return).

900 10th St. NW (btw. New York Ave. and K St. NW), Washington, DC 20001. © **800/EMBASSY** (362-2779) or 202/739-2001. Fax 202/739-2099. www.washingtonconventioncenter.embassysuites.com. 384 units. Peak weekdays $279–$399, weekends $199–$279 double; off-peak weekdays $229–$329, weekends $159–$209 double. Extra person $20. Children 17 and under stay free in parent's room. Book online or call direct for best rates. AE, DC, DISC, MC, V. Valet parking $29. Metro: Metro Center (11th St. NW exit). **Amenities:** Restaurant (steak, sushi, and seafood); bar; indoor pool; whirlpool; fitness center; concierge; 24-hr. business center w/free use of computers, printer, Internet access; gift shop; room service (at lunch and dinner); coin-op laundry; same-day laundry and dry cleaning; 12 rooms for those w/limited mobility, all w/roll-in showers. *In room:* A/C, TV w/pay movies, 2-line phone w/dataports, high-speed Internet access ($9.95/day), fridge, microwave, coffeemaker, hair dryer, iron, safe.

Grand Hyatt Washington 🏵 With its room count of 888, the Grand Hyatt is the largest hotel near the convention center, 3 blocks away. The hotel lies between Capitol Hill and the White House, 2 blocks from the Verizon Center.

Guest rooms feature a contemporary look of dark hardwood furniture and hues of brown and gold. Every guest room has a "Grand Bed," a 13-inch-thick pillow-top mattress, triple-sheeted and covered with a fluffy white duvet instead of a bedspread. The Regency Club (12th) floor is the VIP level; guests here pay an extra $60 for premium services, including access to the fitness and health club and to the 12th-floor lounge, where food and beverages are available. The fitness club is state-of-the-art, offering cardio and weight equipment; spa treatment rooms; Pilates, yoga, and jazzercise classes; and massages. With total fitness in mind, this hotel is entirely smoke free, including its guest rooms.

1000 H St. NW (at 10th St. NW), Washington, DC 20001. © **800/233-1234** or 202/582-1234. Fax 202/637-4781. www.grandhyattwashington.com. 888 units. Weekdays $199–$429 double; weekends $129–$199 double; $450–$2,500 suite. Extra person $25. Children 17 and under stay free in parent's room. Ask about special promotions and packages. AE, DC, DISC, MC, V. Valet parking $30; self-parking $20. Metro: Metro Center (11th St. NW exit). **Amenities:** 4 restaurants (bistro, traditional American, contemporary American, deli); 3 bars; Starbucks; health club, lap pool, steam and sauna rooms, aerobics, and spa services (hotel guests pay $10 per room per day for club use);

concierge; business center; room service (6am–1am); in-room and health-club massage; same-day dry cleaning; concierge-level rooms; 26 rooms for those w/limited mobility, some w/roll-in showers. *In room:* A/C, TV w/pay movies, 2-line phone w/dataports, Wi-Fi ($10/day or $5/hr.), minibar, coffeemaker, hair dryer, iron.

MODERATE

Hampton Inn Washington, D.C., Convention Center ✦ This 13-story hotel is 2 blocks from the convention center, within walking distance of Penn Quarter restaurants and attractions. (Though not technically "in" the Penn Quarter, the hotel lies close enough to be included.) From the saltwater aquarium on display in the airy lobby to guest rooms that feature a charcoal and chocolate-brown color scheme, fluffy duvets, ergonomic chairs, and lapboard bed trays, this Hampton Inn is a cut above the standard for this particular Hilton brand. Other amenities include an exercise room, an indoor pool and spa, and a Hampton Inn signature perk, the "On the House Hot Breakfast Buffet." Ask for a corner room on the Massachusetts Avenue side, high up, for best city views. In addition to standard king- and queen-size-bed rooms, the hotel has 10 studio suites, 11 two-room suites, and 20 king study suites (the suite holds both a king-size bed and a sofa bed).

901 6th St. NW (at Massachusetts Ave.), Washington, DC 20001. © **800/HAMPTON** (426-7866) or 202/842-2500. Fax 202/842-4100. www.washingtondc.hamptoninn.com. 228 units. Weekdays $201–$349 double; weekends $129–$199 double; $249–$329 suite. Extra person $10. Children 17 and under stay free in parent's room. AE, DC, DISC, MC, V. Parking $25 plus tax, in and out service. Metro: Gallery Place/Chinatown (7th and H sts. NW exit) or Mount Vernon Square/Convention Center. No pets. **Amenities:** Cardio fitness center w/indoor pool and spa; 24-hr. free business center; same-day laundry service; dry cleaning; on-site washer/dryer; 20 rooms for those w/limited mobility, some w/roll-in showers. *In room:* A/C, TV w/pay movies, 2-line phone w/dataports, free wired Internet access, fridge, microwave, coffeemaker, hair dryer, iron, safe.

Hilton Garden Inn, Washington, D.C., Franklin Square The Hilton Garden Inn is across the street from Metro's Blue Line McPherson Square station (and three stops from the Smithsonian museums station), within a short walk of the White House. Rooms are spacious with either king-size or double beds and are designed for comfort. Each room has a cushiony chair with an ottoman and a large desk with an ergonomic chair and adjustable lighting; a dial on the side of the mattress allows guests to adjust its firmness. Each room has a 32-inch, flatscreen LCD HDTV set, capable of connecting with a guest's personal laptop or iPod. The hotel's 24-hour pantry sells essentials; the 24-hour business center allows free use of computer, faxing, and copying services. All but 14th-floor guest rooms are smoke free. Each of the hotel's 20 suites holds a small pullout sofa in the living room.

815 14th St. NW (btw. H and I sts.), Washington, DC 20005. © **877/782-9444** or 202/783-7800. Fax 202/783-7801. www.washingtondcdowntown.stayhgi.com. 300 units. Weekdays $209–$349 double, $409 suite; weekends $129–$149 double, $179 suite. Extra person $10. No more than 4 people per room. Children 17 and under stay free in parent's room. AE, DC, DISC, MC, V. Parking $28. Metro: McPherson Square (Franklin Sq./14th St. NW exit). No pets. **Amenities:** Restaurant (American); bar w/fireplace; 24-hr. fitness center w/indoor pool; 24-hr. business center; limited room service; same-day laundry service; dry cleaning; on-site washer/dryer; 16 rooms for those w/limited mobility, 3 w/roll-in showers. *In room:* A/C, TV w/pay movies, 2-line phone w/dataports, free Wi-Fi and wired Internet access, fridge, microwave, coffeemaker, hair dryer, iron.

4 Midtown

VERY EXPENSIVE

Hay-Adams ✦✦✦ This classic D.C. hotel is boutique in size and grand in sophisticated ambience. It consistently wins awards such as its "Most Excellent Service in the

Americas" rating by *Condé Nast Johansens* in 2008. Famous for its great views and proximity to the White House, the hotel's first-floor dining room and guest rooms on the sixth through eighth floors on the H Street side of the hotel overlook Lafayette Square, the White House, and the Washington Monument. Rooms facing 16th Street overlook the 1815 St. John's Episcopal Church, known as the "church of the presidents."

Built in the 1920s, the hotel's original, ornate plaster moldings, ornamental fireplaces, walnut-paneled lobby, and high-ceilings are still in place. Guest rooms present an elegant decor of sage green, off-white, beige, and gold toile fabrics; custom European linens; and marble bathrooms with brass fixtures.

The hotel has about 14 one-bedroom suites and seven junior suites. Stop in at the Off the Record bar for a drink and the chance of spying a big name in the media or administration.

One Lafayette Square (at 16th and H sts. NW), Washington, DC 20006. © 800/853-6807 or 202/638-6600. Fax 202/638-2716. www.hayadams.com. 145 units. Weekdays $415–$1,000 double; weekends $329–$789 double; from $799 junior suite; from $1,099 1-bedroom suite. 3rd person $30. Children 17 and under stay free in parent's room. AE, DC, DISC, MC, V. Valet parking $40. Metro: Farragut West (17th St. NW exit). Pets under 25 lb. accepted. **Amenities:** Restaurant (American); bar; access to local health club ($15 per day); 24-hr. concierge; complimentary morning car service; secretarial and business services; complimentary 24-hr. business center; 24-hr. room service; same-day laundry service; dry cleaning; 9 rooms for those w/limited mobility, 3 w/roll-in showers. *In room:* A/C, TV w/pay movies, 2-line phone w/dataports, free Wi-Fi, Bose CD player, minibar, hair dryer, iron, safe, robes, slippers, umbrella.

St. Regis Hotel Washington 🏵🏵

A glance to the right as you enter or leftward as you exit the St. Regis confirms that you can only be in Washington, D.C.: That's the White House, all right, staring back at you from the end of 16th Street. Inside the hotel, the ornate lobby and the charming paneled Library bar have been touched up, but are otherwise, thankfully, unchanged by the recent 16-month, multimillion-dollar renovation. Already-elegant guest rooms are more so now, with built-in, handcrafted armoires hiding the 32-inch LCD TV, minibar, wine fridge, drawers, and closets. Add plumped-up beds and sofas; golden sienna, sage, and rust tones; and antiqued desks and tables, and you've got an especially lovely place to stay the night. Don't miss ultra-cool amenities, like the television embedded behind the bathroom mirror—the picture appears within the glass. The hotel's 25 suites offer individually designed, ultra-deluxe rooms, one-bedrooms, and junior suites. The cherries on top are the new restaurant, Alain Ducasse's Adour, and the 5,000-square-foot designer spa, scheduled to debut by early 2009.

926 16th and K St. NW, Washington, DC 20006. © 202/638-2626 or 866/716-8116. Fax 202/638-4231. www.stregis. com. 175 units. In season $375–$795 double; junior suite $575–$1,495; specialty suite from $3,400; 1-bedroom suite $635–$3,200. Call for holiday, off-peak, and promotional rates. 3rd person $75. Children 12 and under stay free in parent's room. AE, DC, DISC, MC, V. Valet parking $40. Metro: Farragut West (17th St. NW exit) or Farragut North (K St. NW exit). Pets under 25 pounds allowed for $100 nonrefundable fee, plus $25 per day. **Amenities:** Restaurant (French); Library bar; 24-hr. fitness center w/spa; concierge; complimentary morning car service; complimentary 24-hr. business center; 24-hr. "butler" service; 24-hr. room service; same-day laundry service; dry cleaning; 5 rooms for those w/limited mobility, all w/roll-in showers. *In room:* A/C, TV w/pay movies, 2-line phone w/dataports, Wi-Fi ($13 per 24 hr.), Bose radio, iPod docking station, DVD/CD player, minibar, hair dryer, iron, safe, robes, slippers, umbrella.

Sofitel Lafayette Square, Washington, D.C. 🏵🏵

The Sofitel, like the Hay-Adams Hotel, borders Lafayette Square and is just minutes from the White House.

This early-20th-century building's distinctive facade includes decorative bronze corner panels, bas-relief sculptural panels at ground-floor level, and a decorative 12th-floor balcony. Inside, hotel staff dressed in designer uniforms greet you with

"Bonjour!"—a hint that the French company Accor Hotels owns the Sofitel. Noted French designer Pierre-Yves Rochon styled the interior; the hotel's restaurant, Ici, serves French bistro fare.

Because of the corner location and exceptionally large windows, guest rooms are bright with natural light, and second- and third-floor rooms facing 15th or H street boast windows that extend nearly from floor to ceiling. Each room sports elegantly modern decor that includes a long desk, plasma-screen TV, creamy duvet on a king-size bed (about 17 rooms have two double beds), a much-marbled bathroom, fresh flowers, and original artwork.

806 15th St. NW (at H St.), Washington, DC 20005. (© 800/763-4835 or 202/737-8800. Fax 202/730-8500. www. sofitelwashingtondc.com. 237 units. Weekdays $300–$500 double; weekends $250–$400 double; from $495 suite. For lowest rates at any time, call directly to the hotel and ask about specials or packages; also check out the web-site. Extra person $20. Children 12 and under stay free in parent's room. AE, DC, DISC, MC, V. Parking $34. Metro: McPherson Square (Vermont Ave. NW/White House exit). Pets accepted with prior approval. **Amenities:** Restaurant (bistro chic); bar; 24-hr. state-of-the-art fitness center; 24-hr. concierge; 24-hr. business services; 24-hr. room service; same-day laundry service; dry cleaning; library w/books about D.C. and Paris; 8 rooms for those w/limited mobility, all w/roll-in showers. *In room:* A/C, TV w/pay movies, 2-line phones w/dataports, high-speed Internet access ($9.95/day), CD player, minibar, hair dryer, iron, safe, robes, slippers.

EXPENSIVE

Capital Hilton ☆ This longtime Washington hotel attracts locals as well as hotel guests to its fitness center and full-service day spa. The club fronts on K Street, so you can work your buns off while watching the downtown Washington scene. Use of the club is free to certain Hilton HHonors guests and $10 per day ($25 maximum, for stays 3 days or longer) for others.

Located just 2 blocks from the White House, the hotel has hosted 13 presidents since it opened in 1943. Guest rooms don't offer much in the way of character; service is rather unremarkable. Corner rooms on the 16th Street side are the most spacious and offer the best city views. Business travelers appreciate the Executive concierge floors (10, 11, 12, and 14) and extensive facilities. A number of suites are available, including three with outdoor patios.

1001 16th St. NW (btw. K and L sts.), Washington, DC 20036. (© 800/HILTONS (445-8667) or 202/393-1000. Fax 202/ 639-5784. www.capital.hilton.com. 544 units. Weekdays and weekends $159–$399 double, $45 more for Executive units; $219–$459 minisuite. Extra person $25. Children 18 and under stay free in parent's room. Weekend packages and other discounts available. AE, DC, DISC, MC, V. Parking $35. Metro: Farragut North (K St. NW exit) or McPherson Square (Vermont Ave./White House exit). **Amenities:** Restaurant (American); bar; 10,000-sq.-ft. health club and spa; concierge (6:30am–11pm); tour and ticket desk; business center; room service (until 1am); massage; same-day laundry service; dry cleaning; concierge floors; ATM w/foreign currency; 13 rooms for those w/limited mobility. *In room:* A/C, TV w/pay movies, 2-line phone w/dataport, high-speed Internet access ($13/day), coffeemaker, hair dryer, iron.

Donovan House ☆☆ Managed by trendy Thompson Hotels, Donovan House gets high marks for hipness, starting with the lobby: an arty chandelier/sculpture, buzzing bar scene, Italian leather chairs, and a banquette nook set in the wall endow a night-club vibe. Ditto the guest rooms; the same ergonomic designer chairs in coffee, plum, and olive contrast with snow-white dressers and walls. A brown leather strip head-boards the bed, extending up to and across the ceiling. The pristine bathroom features a snail-like shower stall, whose cylindrical shape protrudes into the guest room—its opaque walls ensure the shower-er is not on show. "People are art" is the theme, so mirrors take the place of artwork. Floor-to-ceiling windows overlook Thomas Circle, nearby landmark churches, and cityscapes. The best spot for great views, though, is the seasonal rooftop pool and bar. Todd English, of Olives, chefs the Asian-themed

restaurant. Seventeen one-bedroom suites are available. Complimentary Wi-Fi is available everywhere.

1155 14th St. NW (at Thomas Circle NW), Washington, DC 20005. © 800/383-6900 or 202/737-1200. Fax 202/521-1410. www.donovanhousedc.com. 193 units. Weekdays $279–$499 double; weekends $229–$459 double; from $449 suite. 3rd person $30. Children 17 and under stay free in parent's room. AE, DC, DISC, MC, V. Valet parking $35. Metro: McPherson Sq. (Franklin Sq./14th St. NW exit). No pets accepted. **Amenities:** Restaurant (Asian-themed); 2 bars (lobby and seasonal rooftop); 24-hr. state-of-the-art fitness center; rooftop pool; 24-hr. concierge; complimentary 24-hr. business center; 24-hr. room service; same-day laundry service; dry cleaning; 10 rooms for those w/limited mobility, all w/roll-in showers. *In room:* A/C, TV w/pay movies, 2-line phone w/dataports, free Wi-Fi, iPod docking station, minibar, hair dryer, iron, safe, robes, umbrella.

Hamilton Crowne Plaza 𝓡

This well-placed hotel is situated midway between the two sections of downtown: the K Street side and the revitalized Penn Quarter neighborhood surrounding the Verizon Center. The hotel's restaurant is especially popular with office workers at weekday lunch, thanks to a generous buffet of soups, salads, and rotisserie items for $19. Guest rooms feature CD players, handsome royal blue robes, dark-wood armoires and headboards, and comfortable accommodations like the seven-layer bed. Rooms are rather small; so those with king-size beds feel a bit tight, those with two double beds a little roomier. K Street–side rooms overlook Franklin Park, and those on the upper floors offer views of the city skyline. In keeping with the times, the hotel has a designated "women's floor," accessible only to those with a special elevator key. The newly upgraded fitness center offers cardiovascular machines with built-in televisions, treadmills, and elliptical equipment.

1001 14th St. NW (at K St.), Washington, DC 20005. © 800/2-CROWNE (227-6963) or 202/682-0111. Fax 202/682-9525. www.hamiltonhoteldc.com. 318 units. Weekdays $119–$325 double; suites $300–$800; look for much lower rates on weekends. Extra person $20. Children 17 and under stay free in parent's room. AE, DC, DISC, MC, V. Parking $28. Metro: McPherson Square (Franklin Sq./14th St. NW exit). Pets accepted. **Amenities:** Restaurant (American); bar; 24-hr. fitness room; concierge; 24-hr. business center; room service (6am–midnight); same-day laundry service; dry cleaning; club level (weekdays only). *In room:* A/C, TV w/pay movies, 2-line speaker phone w/dataport, Wi-Fi ($9.95/day), CD player/clock radio, coffeemaker, hair dryer, iron, safe, robes.

Renaissance Mayflower 𝓡𝓡

The Mayflower is steeped in history: When it opened in 1925, it was the site of Calvin Coolidge's inaugural ball. President-elect FDR and family lived in room nos. 776 and 781 while waiting to move into the White House; this is where he penned the words, "The only thing we have to fear is fear itself."

Guest rooms feature silvery-green bed coverings, embroidered drapes, silk wall coverings, pillow-topped mattresses, and sink-into armchairs. Each guest room has its own marble foyer, high ceiling, combination of reproduction and contemporary furnishings, and Italian marble bathroom. The Mayflower has a club level on the eighth floor, as well as 74 executive suites.

In the hotel's lovely Café Promenade, lawyers and lobbyists continue to gather for weekday power breakfasts. At cocktail time, the clubby, mahogany-paneled Town and Country Lounge is a favorite spot for locals, thanks to complimentary hors d'oeuvres and bartender Sambonn Lek's magical martinis.

1127 Connecticut Ave. NW (btw. L and M sts.), Washington, DC 20036. © 800/228-7697 or 202/347-3000. Fax 202/776-9182. www.renaissancemayflower.com. 657 units. Weekdays $299–$519 double, $499–$599 suites; weekends $179–$299 double, $499–$599 suites. Rates include complimentary coffee service in Town and Country. No charge for extra person in room. AE, DC, DISC, MC, V. Parking $35. Metro: Farragut North (L St. NW exit). **Amenities:** Restaurant (Mediterranean); lobby lounge; bar; 24-hr. fitness center; concierge; 24-hr. business center; 24-hr. room service; same-day laundry service; dry cleaning; club level; 15 rooms for those w/limited mobility. *In room:* A/C, TV w/pay movies, 2-line phone w/dataport, wireless high-speed Internet access ($9.95/day), hair dryer, iron, robes.

MODERATE

Doubletree Washington Hotel ⊛ The Doubletree, though thoroughly urban, has beautifully landscaped terraces front and back that act as buffers between the hotel and the city. The flow of the public spaces leading back to the garden courtyard accentuate the hotel's theme of "bringing the outdoors in." This theme resonates in the guest rooms, where windows larger than the hotel norm deliver lots of natural light. Ask for a room at the front of the hotel for a view of Scott Circle, the park across the street, and the city; request a room at the back for a view of the garden terrace. A complete renovation of guest rooms will have replaced paint, fabrics, wallpapers, and furnishings, and installed flatscreen plasma televisions by the end of 2008. Every guest room has a "Sweet Dreams by Hilton" pillow-top mattress and a large desk with ergonomic chair.

1515 Rhode Island Ave. NW (at Scott Circle), Washington, DC 20005. ✆ 800/492-5195 or 202/232-7000. Fax 202/521-7103. www.doubletreewashington.com. 220 units. Weekdays $209–$499 double; weekends $139–$189 double; rates for suites usually run $50 higher than doubles. Extra person $30. Children 16 and under stay free in parent's room. AE, DC, DISC, MC, V. Parking $26. Metro: Dupont Circle South/19th St. NW exit) or McPherson Square (Franklin Sq./14th St. NW exit). **Amenities:** Restaurant (contemporary American); bar; 24-hr. fitness center; 24-hr. concierge; 24-hr. business center (complimentary use of computers, copier, and fax services); room service (6:30am–midnight); same-day laundry service; dry cleaning; 10 rooms for those w/limited mobility, 2 w/roll-in showers. *In room:* A/C, TV w/pay movies, 2-line phones w/dataport, high-speed Internet access ($9.95), fridge, hair dryer, iron, safe, robes.

Four Points by Sheraton, Washington, D.C. Downtown ⊛ This contemporary property offers complimentary wired Internet access, a 650-square-foot fitness center, and an unbeatable location close to both the convention center and the Verizon Center. Add in reasonable rates and fine hotel amenities and you've got a good choice for both business and leisure visitors.

A recent refurbishment gives a stylish, retro look to the guest rooms, with the help of lots of earth tones, leather, tweeds, and modern furniture. Bedding is new, too, and now features the "Four Points" custom-designed, multilayered, pillow-top mattress. Guests have a choice of rooms with two double beds or one king-size bed. Corner rooms (there are only about 10) are a little more spacious than others. *Be forewarned:* These book first, so they are seldom available. While guest rooms offer city views, the rooftop pool and lounge present a wider vista of the city.

1201 K St. NW (at 12th St.), Washington, DC 20005. ✆ 888/481-7191 or 202/289-7600. Fax 202/349-2215. www. fourpoints.com/washingtondcdowntown. 265 units. In season $195–$450 double; off season $109–$265 double. Extra person $20. Children 12 and under stay free in parent's room. AE, DC, DISC, MC, V. Parking $35. Metro: McPherson Square (Franklin Sq./14th St. NW exit). **Amenities:** Restaurant (seasonal American); bar; indoor heated pool on rooftop; 24-hr. fitness center; complimentary Internet service in lobby; gift shop; room service (during restaurant hours); same-day laundry service; dry cleaning; executive-level rooms; 5 rooms for those w/limited mobility, 2 w/roll-in showers. *In room:* A/C, TV w/pay movies, 2-line phone w/dataport, free high-speed wired Internet access, cooler, coffeemaker, hair dryer, iron, safe, robes.

Hotel Helix ⊛ A sprucing up will have refreshed decor throughout the hotel by 2009, but you can still expect to see eye-popping patterns and bright colors. Guest rooms have a minimalist feel; the platform bed is placed behind sheer drapes in an alcove (in the king deluxe rooms), leaving the two-person settee, a triangular desk, and the flatscreen TV out in the open. Roomiest are the 18 suites, each with a separate bedroom and slate-blue sectional sofas in the living room. Specialty rooms include "Eats" rooms, which have Italian cafe tables, bar stools, and a fully equipped kitchenette; kid-friendly "Bunk" rooms that have a separate bunk bed area with TV/DVD player combo; and "Zone" rooms equipped with a plasma-screen TV, high-tech stereo

system, lava lamp, and lounge chair. The Helix Lounge is popular with locals, especially from May to October, when its outdoor patio is open.

1430 Rhode Island Ave. NW (btw. 14th and 15th sts.), Washington, DC 20005. ✆ **800/706-1202** or 202/462-9001. Fax 202/332-3519. www.hotelhelix.com. 178 units. Weekdays and weekends $149–$329 double; specialty rooms: add $30 to double rate; suites: add $100 to double rate. Best rates usually Fri–Sun. Extra person $20. Children 17 and under stay free in parent's room. Rates include hosted evening "bubbly hour" (champagne). AE, DC, DISC, MC, V. Parking $30 plus tax. Nonsmoking property. Metro: McPherson Square (Vermont St. NW/White House exit). Pets welcome. **Amenities:** Bar/cafe; exercise room; room service (during breakfast and dinner hours); same-day laundry service; dry cleaning; 9 rooms for those w/limited mobility, some w/roll-in showers. *In room:* A/C, TV w/pay movies, Web TV access (for a fee), 2-line phones w/dataports, free Wi-Fi, CD/DVD player, Nintendo, minibar, hair dryer, iron.

Hotel Rouge ⚜ Shades of red are everywhere: in the staff's red-striped shirts, in the accent pillows on the retro furniture, and in the artwork. Rouge guest rooms have deep crimson drapes at the window and a floor-to-ceiling red "pleather" headboard for your comfortable, white-with-red-piping duvet-covered bed. The dressing room holds an Orange Crush–colored dresser, where the built-in minibar holds such red goodies as Hot Tamales candies, red wax lips, and Red Bull. Rooms are spacious enough to easily accommodate several armchairs and a large ottoman (in shades of red and gold), a number of funky little lamps, a huge mahogany-framed mirror leaning against a wall, and a 10-foot-long mahogany desk. Fifteen specialty guest rooms include "Chill Rooms," which have a chaise longue and a little sitting-room area, DVD player, and PlayStation and Wii; "Chat Rooms," which have computer/printers; and "Chow Rooms," which have a microwave and refrigerator.

1315 16th St. NW (at Massachusetts Ave. NW and Scott Circle), Washington, DC 20036. ✆ **800/738-1202** or 202/ 232-8000. Fax 202/667-9827. www.rougehotel.com. 137 units. Weekdays and weekends $149–$359 double; add $40 to reserve a specialty room. Best rates available on the website and by calling the 800 number and asking for promotional price. Extra person $20. Rates include complimentary bloody marys and cold pizza weekend mornings 10–11am and hosted evening wine hour weeknights 5–6pm. Children 17 and under stay free in parent's room. AE, DC, DISC, MC, V. Parking $30. Nonsmoking property. Metro: Dupont Circle (South, 19th St. NW exit). Pets welcomed and pampered. **Amenities:** Bar/restaurant (American, w/French twist); modest-size fitness center; business center; room service (7am–11pm); same-day laundry service; dry cleaning; 6 rooms for those w/limited mobility, 3 w/roll-in shower. *In room:* A/C, 27-in. flatscreen TV w/pay movies, 2-line cordless phones w/dataport, free Wi-Fi, CD/DVD player, minibar, hair dryer, iron, robes.

The Quincy ⚜ *Value* The Quincy has gone upscale in a renovation completed in 2007, adding pillow-top mattresses, sectional sofas, flatscreen TVs, complimentary high-speed Internet access, and double-paned windows to all rooms. It remains a good value for all that it offers. The top-to-bottom transformation evinces a "conservative contemporary" decor, so that the overall design is brighter and very 21st century. Suites are large and comfortable; about 28 are equipped with full kitchens, while the rest have wet bars (minifridge, microwave, and coffeemaker). The Quincy has direct access to **Mackey's,** an Irish pub right next door, and to **Recessions,** a lounge on the lower level serving American/Mediterranean cuisine.

Lots of extended-stay guests and repeat customers bunk here and are often rewarded for it with goodies in the room or complimentary room upgrades.

1823 L St. NW, Washington, DC 20036. ✆ **800/424-2970** or 202/223-4320. Fax 202/293-4977. www.thequincy.com. 99 suites. Weekdays $169–$269; weekends $99–$189 year-round. Discounts available for long-term stays. Children 17 and under stay free in parent's room. AE, DC, DISC, MC, V. Parking $28 (in adjoining garage). Metro: Farragut North (L St. NW exit). Pets under 25 lb. accepted for $150 nonrefundable deposit. **Amenities:** Restaurant (American/Mediterranean); bar (Irish); free passes to the well-equipped Bally's Fitness Center nearby; 24-hr. front desk; room service (11am–10pm); coinop washer/dryers; Mon–Sat same-day laundry service; dry cleaning; 2 rooms for those w/limited mobility, 1 w/roll-in shower. *In room:* A/C, TV w/pay movies, free hard-wired Internet access, fridge, microwave, coffeemaker, hair dryer, iron.

5 Adams-Morgan

Note: The hotels listed here are situated just north of Dupont Circle, more at the mouth of Adams-Morgan than within its actual boundaries.

EXPENSIVE

Hilton Washington ✦ *Kids* This sprawling hotel, built in 1965, occupies 7 acres and calls itself a "resort"—mostly on the basis of having landscaped gardens, tennis courts, and an Olympic-style pool on its premises (unusual amenities for a D.C. hotel). Embassies, great restaurants, and museums are just a stroll away.

The Hilton caters to corporate groups, some with families in tow (during the summer, the reception desk gives families a complimentary gift and lends them board games—ask for the "Vacation Station" perk), and is accustomed to coordinating meetings for thousands of attendees. Its vast conference facilities include one of the largest hotel ballrooms on the East Coast (it accommodates nearly 4,000). By contrast, guest rooms are on the small side. From the fifth floor up, poolside, you'll have panoramic views of Washington. A multimillion-dollar, top-to-bottom renovation should be complete by the end of 2009. (The hotel will stay open throughout.)

1919 Connecticut Ave. NW (at T St.), Washington, DC 20009. ✆ **800/HILTONS** (445-8667) or 202/483-3000. Fax 202/232-0438. www.washington.hilton.com. 1,119 units. Weekdays and weekends $119–$319 double; $30 more for Towers rooms. Look for deals on the website or by calling Hilton's 800 number. Extra person $25. Children 18 and under stay free in parent's room. AE, DC, DISC, MC, V. Self-parking $23. Metro: Dupont Circle (North, Q St. NW exit). **Amenities:** 2 restaurants (both American); deli; 2 bars (a pub and lobby bar); Olympic-style heated outdoor pool; extensive health-club facilities; concierge; transportation/sightseeing desk; comprehensive business center; lobby shops; room service (until 12:45am); same-day laundry service; dry cleaning; concierge-level rooms; 28 rooms for those w/limited mobility, some w/roll-in showers. *In room:* A/C, TV w/pay movies, 2-line phone w/dataport, high-speed Internet access ($12/day), coffeemaker, hair dryer, iron.

MODERATE

Courtyard by Marriott Northwest This hotel's nondescript exterior contrasts with its interior, which has a European feel and a well-heeled appearance. Crystal chandeliers hang in the lobby and in the restaurant, and you may hear an Irish lilt from time to time (the hotel is one of three in Washington owned by Jurys Doyle Hotel Group, an Irish management company). Guests tend to linger in the comfortable lounge off the lobby, where coffee is available all day.

A complete refurbishment in 2004 replaced nearly everything in the guest rooms, which now present a comfortable and bright decor that includes cherry furniture, plush carpeting, and 25-inch TVs. Accommodations facing the street on the sixth to ninth floors now have floor-to-ceiling windows, providing panoramic views. Especially nice are the 16 "executive king" rooms, which are a little larger and are equipped with marble bathrooms, trouser presses, and robes.

For the best deals, call direct to the hotel or go to the website.

1900 Connecticut Ave. NW (at Leroy Place), Washington, DC 20009. ✆ **888/236-2427** or 202/332-9300. Fax 202/319-1793. www.marriott.com. 147 units. $99–$349 double. Extra person $15. Children 17 and under stay free in parent's room. Ask about discount packages. AE, DC, DISC, MC, V. Parking $20. Metro: Dupont Circle (North, Q St. NW exit). **Amenities:** Restaurant (American, open for breakfast and dinner); bar; outdoor pool (seasonal); small exercise room; business center; room service (5–10pm); coin-operated laundry; same-day laundry service; dry cleaning; 2 rooms for those w/limited mobility, both w/roll-in showers. *In room:* A/C, TV w/pay movies, 2-line phone w/dataport, free Internet access, coffeemaker, hair dryer, iron, safe.

Adams-Morgan, Dupont Circle & West End Accommodations

Beacon Hotel **22**
Courtyard by Marriott Northwest **6**
Donovan House **26**
Doubletree Washington **24**
Embassy Circle Inn **8**
Embassy Suites Hotel Downtown **14**
Hilton Washington **7**
Hotel Helix **25**
Hotel Madera **13**

Hotel Palomar **11**
Hotel Rouge **23**
Hotel Tabard Inn **20**
Jurys Normandy Inn **5**
Jurys Washington Hotel **10**
Kalorama Guest House **1**
Mansion on O St. **12**
Omni Shoreham Hotel **4**
Park Hyatt Washington **15**

The Quincy **18**
Renaissance Mayflower **19**
Ritz-Carlton Washington **16**
St. Gregory Luxury Hotel
 and Suites **17**
Swann House **9**
Topaz Hotel **21**
Wardman Park Marriott **3**
Woodley Park Guest House **2**

INEXPENSIVE

Jurys Normandy Inn ⭐ *Finds* This gracious hotel is a gem—a small gem, but a gem nonetheless. Situated in a neighborhood of architecturally impressive embassies, the hotel hosts many embassy-bound guests. You may discover this for yourself on a Tuesday evening, when guests gather in the charming Tea Room to enjoy complimentary wine and cheese served from the antique oak sideboard. Here you'll also find daily continental breakfast (for about $9), complimentary coffee and tea after 10am, and cookies after 3pm. You can lounge or watch TV in the conservatory; or, in nice weather, you can move outside to the garden patio.

The six-floor Normandy has small but pretty twin and queen guest rooms, all recently remodeled and sporting a bright, contemporary look with cherry-wood furnishings and fabrics in colors of light blues and greens. Rooms facing Wyoming Avenue overlook the tree-lined street, while other rooms mostly offer views of apartment buildings. The Normandy is an easy walk from the restaurants and shops in both Adams-Morgan and Dupont Circle.

2118 Wyoming Ave. NW (at Connecticut Ave.), Washington, DC 20008. © **800/424-3729** or 202/483-1350. Fax 202/387-8241. www.jurysdoyle.com. 75 units. $89–$239 double. Extra person $10. Children 12 and under stay free in parent's room. AE, DC, DISC, MC, V. Parking $15 plus tax. Metro: Dupont Circle (North, Q St. NW exit). **Amenities:** Access to the neighboring Courtyard by Marriott Northwest's pool and exercise room; room service at breakfast; coin-op washer/dryers; same-day laundry service; dry cleaning (Mon–Sat); 4 rooms for those w/limited mobility, 1 w/roll-in shower. *In room:* A/C, TV, 2-line phone w/dataport, free Internet access, minifridge, coffeemaker, hair dryer, iron, safe.

Kalorama Guest House This San Francisco–style B&B has two locations: a set of Victorian town houses in Adams-Morgan and two houses in nearby Woodley Park (see "Woodley Park," later in this chapter). As of 2007, all of the guest rooms at both locations have new beds.

The cozy common areas and homey guest rooms are furnished with finds from antiques stores, flea markets, and auctions. Rooms offer either double or queen-size beds. The Mintwood Place town house also has an efficiency apartment with a kitchen, telephone, and TV; one small two-room apartment with a kitchen, cable TV, and telephone; and four suites (two, two-bedroom and two "executive" suites, in which the living room and bedroom are together). Each location serves an expansive complimentary breakfast. Guests have access to laundry and ironing facilities, a refrigerator, a TV, and a phone. Free Wi-Fi access is available in all of the rooms.

1854 Mintwood Place NW (btw. 19th St. and Columbia Rd.), Washington, DC 20009. © **800/974-6450** or 202/667-6369. Fax 202/319-1262. www.kaloramaguesthouse.com. 29 units, 15 with private bathroom. $140 double with shared bathroom; $155–$185 double with private bathroom. Extra person $10. Rates include expansive breakfast. AE, DISC, MC, V. Very limited parking $15 plus tax. Metro, Woodley Park location: Woodley Park–Zoo. Adams-Morgan location: Dupont Circle (North, Q St. NW exit). Kids 6 and older only. **Amenities:** Washer/dryer; common fridge; common TV. *In room:* A/C, free Wi-Fi access.

6 Dupont Circle

VERY EXPENSIVE

The Mansion on O Street ⭐⭐ *Finds* A legend in her own time, H. H. Leonards Spero operates this Victorian property, made up of five interconnecting four- and five-story town houses. It's a museum, an event space, a private club, and a hotel.

Guest rooms will blow you away. Most breathtaking is the two-level Log Cabin loft suite, with Remington sculptures, a bed whose headboard encases an aquarium, and an eco-friendly bathroom with sauna. The Art Deco–style penthouse takes up an

entire floor, with large living room, two bathrooms, a bedroom, and a kitchen; it has its own security cameras and elevator. The mansion also has conference spaces; 32 far-out bathrooms; 18 fireplaces; and art, antiques, and books everywhere (everything is for sale). Be sure to look for the electric guitars displayed throughout the mansion; each is signed by a famous musician guest, from Sean Ono Lennon to Eric Clapton. It's possible to rent the entire mansion or a portion of it. Full business services are available. Don't miss the mansion's Sunday brunch featuring jazz or gospel music, or regularly scheduled evening performances by big names on the local music scene.

2020 O St. NW (btw. 20th and 21st sts.), Washington, DC 20036. ℂ **202/496-2000.** Fax 202/833-8333. www. omansion.com. 23 units, all with private bathrooms. $350–$850 double; $550–$2,000 suites. Nonprofit, group, government, and long-term rates available. Rates include continental breakfast. AE, DC, DISC, MC, V. Parking $25 by reservation. Metro: Dupont Circle (South, 19th St. NW exit). **Amenities:** Free passes to Sports Club/LA health club at the nearby Ritz-Carlton; concierge; state-of-the-art business center; laundry service. *In room:* A/C, TV, 2-line phone w/dataport, free Wi-Fi, iron, robes.

EXPENSIVE

Beacon Hotel and Corporate Quarters ⋇

Opened in 2005, the Beacon attracts a lively local gathering in its bar and grill, right off the lobby, which adds to the overall genial ambience of the hotel. All rooms are furnished with flatscreen TVs and contemporary touches, like down-filled duvets and large leathery-looking headboards. The best rooms are in the "turret": the one-bedroom suites, one per floor, that perch in the corner of the building. But the New York–style junior suites offer a great deal: Each suite's compact kitchen includes a dishwasher, fridge, stovetop, microwave, and cabinets. Add the roomy living room with a sleep sofa and you've got a good home base—for both corporate folks on business and families on holiday. The hotel's seasonal 10th-floor bar is open Wednesday to Saturday and offers views of the Dupont Circle neighborhood, the boulevards of the city, and—come the Fourth of July—the fireworks on the Mall.

1615 Rhode Island Ave. NW (at 17th St.), Washington, DC 20036. ℂ **800/821-4367** or 202/296-2100. Fax 202/331-0227. www.beaconhotelwdc.com. 199 units. Peak season: $329–$529 weekdays, $129–$309 weekends; off peak: $199–$289 weekdays, $109–$189 weekends. Ask for AAA or AARP discounts or check the website for best rates; always ask for promotional rates. Extra person $20, up to 3 adults maximum per room. Children 13 and under stay free in parent's room. AE, DC, DISC, MC, V. Parking $25 weekdays, discounted on weekends; no oversize SUVs, buses, conversion vans. Metro: Dupont Circle (South, 19th St. NW exit). **Amenities:** Restaurant (modern and classic American); bar w/indoor atrium and outdoor patio; seasonal rooftop bar; in-house cardio fitness center, plus free access to nearby, fully equipped YMCA w/indoor pool; tour bus stop; 24-hr. business center; room service (6:30am–11pm); same-day laundry service; dry cleaning; 8 rooms for those w/limited mobility, 2 w/roll-in showers. *In room:* A/C, TV w/pay movies, 2-line phone w/dataport, Internet access ($11/day), CD player, coffeemaker, hair dryer, iron, robes.

Hotel Palomar Washington, D.C. ⋇⋇

If you prefer a hotel to be more than simply a place to sleep, you'll love the Palomar. This Kimpton hotel lies in the heart of the fun Dupont Circle neighborhood, full of art galleries, boutiques, and excellent restaurants; and it regularly invites local artists to pop in for the evening wine hour. The Palomar fancies itself a kind of art gallery, from its displays of handcrafted decorative arts in the lobby, to the splashes of mulberry and magenta, zebrawood, and faux-leather finishes in the guest rooms. These are spacious rooms and comfortably appointed, with a maneuverable, oversize elliptical desk, an ergonomic mesh chair, and an undulating chaise longue. The bathrooms hold granite-topped vanities and L'Occitane bath products. Specialty rooms include 18 "Tall" rooms (the beds are 90-in. kings) and 8 "Motion" rooms (each comes with your choice of available in-room exercise equipment).

2121 P St. NW (at 21st St.), Washington, DC 20037. ℂ **877/866-3070** or 202/448-1800. Fax 202/448-1801. www. hotelpalomar-dc.com. 335 units. $189–$469 double; from $500 suite. Book online for best rates. Extra person $25. Children 17 and under stay free in parent's room. Rates include hosted evening wine reception and morning coffee (in lobby). AE, DC, DISC, MC, V. Parking $36. Nonsmoking property. Metro: Dupont Circle (South, 19th St. NW exit). Pets welcome. **Amenities:** Restaurant (Italian/Mediterranean); bar/lounge; outdoor (seasonal) lap pool w/sun deck and private cabanas; 24-hr. fitness center; 24-hr. concierge; 24-hr. business center; 24-hr. room service; same-day laundry and dry cleaning; 10 rooms for those w/limited mobility, all w/roll-in showers; In room: A/C, flatscreen TV w/pay movies, multiline cordless phone w/dataports, free Wi-Fi, CD/DVD players, minibar, hair dryer, iron, safe, robes, umbrella.

St. Gregory Luxury Hotel and Suites ⭑⭑

Open since June 2000, the St. Gregory is an affordable luxury property, whose $3-million sprucing-up in 2006–07 pushed decor toward a comfortably contemporary and sexy look. Wingback chairs, soft benches in place of coffee tables, high-backed sofas, oversize silk-fabric-covered slipper chairs, and multilayered mattresses are just some of the fresh appointments. Flatscreen TVs are in the rooms; flat-panel TVs are in the suites.

Most of the rooms are one-bedroom suites with separate living room and bedroom. For privacy and views, choose one of the 16 "sky" suites on the top three floors, each with terrace and city overlooks. Of the 100 suites, 85 have pantry kitchens, including microwaves, ovens, and full-size refrigerators.

The St. Gregory offers special rates to long-term and government guests, and to those from the diplomatic community. If you don't fall into one of those categories, check the hotel's website for great deals.

2033 M St. NW (at 21st St.), Washington, DC 20036. ℂ **800/829-5034** or 202/530-3600. Fax 202/466-6770. www. stgregoryhotelwdc.com. 154 units. Weekdays $329–$489 double or suite; weekends $139–$309 double or suite. Extra person $20. Children 13 and under stay free in parent's room. Ask about discounts, long-term stays, AAA and AARP rates, and packages. AE, DC, DISC, MC, V. Parking $25 weekdays, discounted price on weekends (garage has maximum 6-ft. clearance). Metro: Dupont Circle (South, 19th St. NW exit). No pets. **Amenities:** Restaurant (contemporary American); coffee bar; bar/lounge; state-of-the-art fitness center, as well as access (for $20 fee) to the nearby and larger Sports Club/LA health club at the Ritz-Carlton; concierge; tour desk; self-serve 24-hr. business center; room service (6:30am–10:30pm); massage; babysitting; coin-op laundry room; same-day laundry service; dry cleaning; concierge-level rooms; 6 rooms for those w/limited mobility, 2 w/roll-in showers. In room: A/C, TV w/pay movies, 2-line phone w/dataport, Internet access ($11/day), CD player, fridge, coffeemaker, hair dryer, iron.

Swann House ⭑ Finds

This stunning 1883 mansion, poised prominently on a corner 4 blocks north of Dupont Circle, has nine exquisite guest rooms. Hard to say which is the prettiest, but I do love the Blue Sky Suite, covered in blue-and-white toile, with the original rose-tiled working fireplace, a queen-size bed and daybed, a sitting room, and a gabled ceiling. The most romantic room might be Il Duomo, with Gothic windows, a cathedral ceiling, a working fireplace, and a turreted bathroom with angel murals, a claw-foot tub, and a rain shower head. There are three suites. You'll want to spend some time on the main floor of the mansion, which has 12-foot ceilings, fluted woodwork, inlaid wood floors, a turreted living room, a columned sitting room, and a sunroom leading through three sets of French doors to the garden and pool. Check the inn's website for rate specials. No smoking.

1808 New Hampshire Ave. NW (btw. S and Swann sts.), Washington, DC 20009. ℂ **202/265-4414.** Fax 202/265-6755. www.swannhouse.com. 9 units, all with private bathroom (3 with shower only). $150–$365 depending on unit and season. 2-night minimum weekends, 3-night minimum holiday weekends. Extended-stay and government rates available. Extra person $35. Rates include expanded continental breakfast. AE, DISC, MC, V. Limited off-street parking $14. Metro: Dupont Circle (North, Q St. NW exit). No children 12 and under. **Amenities:** Outdoor pool; free Wi-Fi; business services; in-room massage; same-day dry cleaning. In room: A/C, TV, phone w/voice mail and dataport, free Wi-Fi, hair dryer, iron, robes.

MODERATE

Embassy Circle Guest House ⭐ This delightful, turn-of-the-20th-century mansion, whose owners also own the lovely Woodley Park Guest House (p. 111), is a rather more upscale and sophisticated inn than its sister. First of all, you're in the thick of Embassy Row, surrounded by enchanting chancelleries and embassies, a brief walk from Dupont Circle cafes, bars, and galleries. Guests are welcome to enjoy complimentary wine and snacks each evening and breakfast in the elegantly furnished parlor and dining room, respectively. Guest rooms take their decorative cues and their names from the antique Persian carpet displayed in each. So room no. 124, the Pearl Gazvin, presents the carpet of that name and a creamy, tranquil space to complement it. The Red Kashan carpet adds vivid color to its namesake, room no. 111, further enhanced by the room's colorful paintings and furnishings. As at the Woodley Park Guest House, all of the Embassy Circle's artworks are original pieces created by artists who have stayed there.

2224 R St. NW (at Massachusetts Ave. NW), Washington, DC 20008. ℂ **877/232-7744** or 202/232-7744. www. dcinns.com. 10 units, each with private bathroom. $180–$275 double. Rates include continental breakfast and wine and snacks. AE, MC, V. Limited parking; call for specific dates and information. Metro: Dupont Circle (North, Q St. NW exit). (Well-behaved) children 12 and older. **Amenities:** Laundry and ironing service; impromptu dinner parties, at the whim of the owner or even guests. *In room:* A/C, phone w/voice mail and dataports, free high-speed Internet access.

Embassy Suites Hotel Downtown ⭐ *Kids* This well-placed hotel offers great value within walking distance of Georgetown and Dupont Circle. A tropical eight-story atrium is the setting for an ample complimentary breakfast every morning and complimentary cocktails and light snacks every evening.

Every unit is a two-room suite. The living room holds a queen-size sofa bed, 32-inch plasma TV, easy chair, and table and chairs. The bedroom lies at the back of the suite, overlooking a quiet courtyard or the street. A king-size bed or two queen-size beds, TV, armchair, and bureau furnish this space. Between the living room and the bedroom are the bathroom, a small closet, and a kitchenette. Request a room on the eighth or ninth floor for views of Georgetown and beyond; request an "executive corner suite" for a slightly larger unit.

Another plus: free Internet use available at nine mobile kiosks throughout the public area and at three business center computers.

1250 22nd St. NW (btw. M and N sts.), Washington, DC 20037. ℂ **800/EMBASSY** (362-2779) or 202/857-3388. Fax 202/293-3173. www.washingtondc.embassysuites.com. 318 suites. $159–$369 double. Rates include full breakfast and evening reception. Ask for AAA discounts or check the website for best rates. Extra person $20 weekdays, $25 weekends. Children 18 and under stay free in parent's room. AE, DC, DISC, MC, V. Parking $24. Metro: Foggy Bottom. **Amenities:** Restaurant (rustic Italian); state-of-the-art fitness center w/indoor pool, whirlpool, and sauna; game room; concierge; 24-hr. business center w/free use of computers and printer; mobile and free Internet kiosks in public area; room service (11am–11pm); coin-op washer/dryers; same-day laundry service; dry cleaning; 8 rooms for those w/limited mobility, 4 w/roll-in showers. *In room:* A/C, TV w/pay movies and PlayStation, 2-line phone w/dataport, high-speed Internet access and Wi-Fi ($9.95/day), kitchenette w/fridge and microwave, coffeemaker, hair dryer, iron.

Hotel Madera ⭐ The Hotel Madera fancies itself a kind of eco-conscious *pied-à-terre* for travelers. Guest rooms are large, with those on the New Hampshire Avenue side offering balconies and city views. If you have trouble sleeping, ask for a higher-up room on this side, because you're directly over the entrance to the restaurant, **Fire-fly**. Rooms at the back of the house on floors 6 through 10 have views of Rock Creek Park and the Washington National Cathedral. All rooms are comfortable and furnished with beds whose headboards are giant dark-wood panels inset with a patch of

vibrant blue padded mohair. Other distinct touches: pillows covered in animal print or satiny fabrics, grass cloth–like wall coverings, and black granite with chrome bathroom vanities. This Kimpton hotel's "specialty" rooms include "Snack" rooms (studio with kitchenette and grocery shopping service), "Flash" rooms (with personal computer and printer), "Cardio" rooms (with treadmill, exercise bike, or elliptical steps), and "Entertainment" rooms (with a second TV and DVD player).

1310 New Hampshire Ave. NW (btw. N and O sts.), Washington, DC 20036. © **800/430-1202** or 202/296-7600. Fax 202/293-2476. www.hotelmadera.com. 82 units. Weekdays and weekends $169–$409 double; add $40 to the going rate for a specialty room. For best rates, call direct to the hotel or go to its website. Extra person $20. Children 17 and under stay free in parent's room. Rates include hosted evening wine hour. AE, DC, DISC, MC, V. Parking $30 plus tax. Nonsmoking property. Metro: Dupont Circle (South, 19th St. NW exit). Pets welcome. **Amenities:** Bar/restaurant (American bistro); access to the posh Sports Club/LA health club at the nearby Ritz-Carlton ($15 per guest per day); 24-hr. concierge; business center; room service (during restaurant hours); same-day laundry service; dry cleaning; 4 rooms for those w/limited mobility, 2 w/roll-in showers. *In room:* A/C, TV w/pay movies, 2-line cordless phones w/dataports, free Wi-Fi, CD/DVD player, minibar, coffeemaker w/organic coffee, hair dryer, iron, safe, robes, umbrella.

Hotel Tabard Inn If you favor the offbeat and personal over cookie-cutter chains, try the Tabard. Named for the hostelry in Chaucer's *Canterbury Tales,* the Tabard is three Victorian town houses that were joined in 1914 and have operated as an inn ever since.

The heart of the ground floor is the dark-paneled lounge, with worn furniture, fireplace, the original beamed ceiling, and bookcases. Washingtonians come here for drinks, jazz on Sundays, or to linger before or after dining in the charming **Tabard Inn** restaurant (p. 147).

From the lounge, the inn leads you up and down stairs, along dim corridors, and through nooks and crannies to guest rooms furnished with antiques and flea-market finds. Perhaps the most eccentric room is the spacious top-floor "penthouse," which has skylights, exposed brick walls, an ample living room, and the feel of a New York City loft. The inn is not easily accessible to guests with disabilities.

Moments **All That Jazz**

For a pleasurable evening's entertainment, you need look no further than the bar/lounge or in-house restaurant of your own or a nearby hotel. The genre is usually jazz, the performers are top-notch, and the admission is free. So if it's a Sunday night, you might want to plant yourself in the paneled parlor of the **Hotel Tabard Inn** (p. 104) to listen to bassist Victor Dvoskin play world-class jazz, often accompanied by a guitarist. Weeknights, locals crowd into the **Renaissance Mayflower** hotel's (p. 95) fabled Town & Country Lounge for happy hour to imbibe bartender Sambonn Lek's legendary cocktails, gobble complimentary hors d'oeuvres, and enjoy the jazz and other standards turned out by the resident pianist. And every single night, starting at 9pm, the **Phoenix Park Hotel's** (p. 85) Dubliner restaurant is the place to be if you enjoy hoisting a pint to the tune of "Danny Boy" and rowdier Irish ballads, performed live by musicians with such names as "Conor Malone" and "Andy O'Driscoll."

1739 N St. NW (btw. 17th and 18th sts.), Washington, DC 20036. ⒞ **202/785-1277.** Fax 202/785-6173. www.tabardinn.com. 40 units, 27 with private bathroom (6 with shower only). $113–$160 double with shared bathroom; $158–$218 double with private bathroom. Extra person $15. Rates include continental breakfast. AE, DC, DISC, MC, V. Limited street parking, plus 2 parking garages on N St. Metro: Dupont Circle (South, 19th St. exit). Small and confined pets accepted for a $20 fee. **Amenities:** Restaurant (regional American) w/lounge (free live jazz Sun evenings); free access to nearby YMCA (w/extensive facilities that include indoor pool, indoor track, and racquetball/basketball courts); laundry service; fax, hair dryer, iron, and safe available at front desk; free computer access in lobby. *In room:* A/C, dataport, free Wi-Fi.

Jurys Washington Hotel ⭐ 🄥alue

This hotel gets high marks for convenience (it's right on Dupont Circle), service, and comfort. A thorough renovation in 2008 put an urban-chic spin on guest room appearance and amenities. Expect spa-style bathrooms with heated marble floors and Kohler rain shower heads equipped with body massage features; luxurious pillow-top mattresses with down comforters, duvet covers, and bolster pillows; and LG flatscreen televisions. Each of the large rooms is furnished with either a king-size bed or two double beds with firm mattresses, a desk, and a wet-bar alcove. Despite its prime location in a sometimes-raucous neighborhood, the hotel's rooms are insulated from the noise. The hotel's restaurant, dupont**grille,** provides a perfect spot to slurp a cosmo and dine on seared red snapper, while watching an entertaining cast of Dupont Circle characters pass by. Check the hotel's website for lowest rates.

1500 New Hampshire Ave. NW (across from Dupont Circle), Washington, DC 20036. ⒞ **877/587-9787** or 202/483-6000. Fax 202/328-3265. www.jurysdoyle.com. 314 units. $99–$349 double; from $600 suite (there are only 5). Extra person $15. Children 17 and under stay free in parent's room. AE, DC, DISC, MC, V. Parking $20. Metro: Dupont Circle (either exit). **Amenities:** Restaurant (American); bar; exercise room; 24-hr. concierge; business center; room service (6:30am–midnight); same-day laundry service; dry cleaning; 11 rooms for those w/limited mobility, 4 w/roll-in showers. *In room:* A/C, TV w/pay movies, 2-line phone w/dataport, free Wi-Fi, minibar, coffeemaker, hair dryer, iron, safe.

Topaz Hotel ⭐

A whimsical decor rules in the guest rooms, where a refurbishment completed in 2007 transformed rooms with splashes of emerald, sapphire, ruby, and other jewel tones on wallpaper, down comforter, armoire, and armchair. The rooms are unusually large; half have an alcove with a desk and a separate dressing room. The Topaz pursues a sort of New Age wellness motif; note the smooth "energy" stones and horoscope placed upon your pillow. You have the option to book a specialty room: either an "Energy" guest room, which includes a piece of exercise equipment (an elliptical or a stationary bike), fitness magazines, and TV with VCR and CD player; or a "Yoga" room, which comes with an exercise mat, an instructional tape, padded pillows, special towels, and yoga magazines.

The Topaz lies on a quiet residential street whose front-of-the-house windows overlook picturesque town houses.

1733 N St. NW (right next to the Tabard Inn [see above] btw. 17th and 18th sts.), Washington, DC 20036. ⒞ **800/775-1202** or 202/393-3000. Fax 202/785-9581. www.topazhotel.com. 99 units. Weekdays and weekends $149–$369 double; add $40 to rate for specialty rooms. It is very likely that you can get a much lower rate by calling direct to the hotel or by booking a reservation online. Extra person $25. Children 17 and under stay free in parent's room. Rates include complimentary morning Power Hour, serving energy potions. AE, DC, DISC, MC, V. Parking $30 plus tax. Nonsmoking property. Metro: Dupont Circle (North, Q St. NW exit). Pets welcome. **Amenities:** Bar/restaurant (innovative American w/Asian influence); access to nearby health club ($5 per guest); 24-hr. concierge; 24-hr. business center; room service (7am–11pm); same-day laundry service; dry cleaning; 5 rooms for those w/limited mobility, 3 w/roll-in showers. *In room:* A/C, TV w/pay movies, 2-line cordless phones w/dataports, free Wi-Fi, CD/DVD player, minibar, hair dryer, iron, safe, robes, teapot w/exotic teas.

7 Foggy Bottom/West End

VERY EXPENSIVE

Park Hyatt, Washington, D.C. ✿✿ This luxury hotel features spacious lodging, from the "Park" room, at 408 square feet, to the "Park Deluxe" room, which measures 618 square feet. Wood-slat blinds are on the windows, puffy down duvets cover the beds, and decorative features include coffee-table books on American culture, like Annie Leibowitz's photo portraits of American musicians. The flatscreen television in the Park Deluxe rooms pivots in the wall to present an antique chessboard on its reverse side (decorative, not functional). Creamy yellow leather chairs are actually rockers. Bathrooms are spa-like, with floor, ceiling, and walls of dark gray limestone. Everything is out in the open, from the deep soaking marble tub to its adjoining shower.

Don't miss the hotel's tea cellar, complete with a tea humidor for storing the cellar's collection of rare and single estate teas, and the restaurant, the **Blue Duck Tavern** (see p. 150), which serves food that's out of this world.

2400 M St. NW (at 24th St.), Washington, DC 20037. ✆ **800/778-7477** or 202/789-1234. Fax 202/419-6795. www. parkhyattwashington.com. 215 units. From $350 Park Room double; from $450 Park Deluxe double; from $750 suites. For best rates, go to the hotel's website or call the main reservation number. Extra person $60. Children 17 and under stay free in parent's room. Families should ask about the family plan. AE, DC, DISC, MC, V. Parking $35. Metro: Foggy Bottom. Pets welcome, with $100 fee per stay. **Amenities:** Restaurant (regional American); lounge; tea cellar; indoor pool (daytime hours); 24-hr. fitness center; 24-hr. concierge; complimentary Audi sedan service upon availability, Mon–Fri 7–11am; 24-hr. business center; 24-hr. room service; in-room massage; same-day laundry and dry cleaning, w/pressing; children's welcome gifts at check-in; 12 rooms for those w/limited mobility, all w/roll-in showers. *In room:* A/C, flatscreen HDTV, cordless phone w/2 lines and dataports, complimentary wired Internet access, Wi-Fi ($9.95/day), minibar/fridge, hair dryer, safe, robes.

The Ritz-Carlton, Washington, D.C. ✿✿✿ Doormen greet you effusively when you arrive, and poised young women in the bar swan around, gracefully serving you your cocktail. The Ritz staff is always looking after you.

Some guest rooms overlook the hotel's peaceful landscaped courtyard; rooms on the outside perimeter view the West End's cityscape. The recently renovated deluxe rooms are spacious and richly furnished with decorative inlaid wooden furniture, a comfy armchair and ottoman, and pretty artwork. Large marble bathrooms offer ample counter space, separate bathtub and shower stall, and the toilet in its own room behind a louvered door. The clock radio doubles as a CD player, and the phone features a button for summoning the "technology butler" (a complimentary, 24/7 service for guests with computer questions). For a $15 fee, guests may use the two-level, 100,000-square-foot **Sports Club/LA,** the best hotel health club in the city. The hotel's **Westend Bistro by Eric Ripert** (see p. 131) is one of the hottest restaurants in town.

1150 22nd St. NW (at M St.), Washington, DC 20037. ✆ **800/241-3333** or 202/835-0500. Fax 202/835-1588. www. ritzcarlton.com/hotels/washington_dc. 300 units. Weekday from $649 double, from $749 suite; weekend from $349 (on occasion, $249) double, from $449 suite. No charge for extra person in the room. Ask about discount packages. AE, DC, DISC, MC, V. Valet parking $28. Metro: Foggy Bottom. Pets accepted and pampered (no fee). **Amenities:** Restaurant (American); lounge; health club and spa (the best in the city; see above); 24-hr. concierge; business center (open weekdays); 24-hr. fax and currency-exchange services; salon; 24-hr. room service; in-room massage; same-day laundry; dry cleaning w/1-hr. pressing; club level w/5 complimentary food presentations throughout the day (including a chef station each morning to prepare individual requests); 10 rooms for those w/limited mobility, 6 w/roll-in showers. *In room:* A/C, TV w/pay movies, 2-line phone, Wi-Fi ($10/day), CD player, minibar/fridge, hair dryer, iron, safe, robes, umbrella.

MODERATE

George Washington University Inn Kennedy Center performers, corporate folks, visiting professors, and parents of GW students are frequent guests at this hotel owned by George Washington University.

Rooms are a little larger and corridors are a tad narrower than those in a typical hotel, and each room includes a roomy dressing chamber. More than one-third of the units are one-bedroom suites. These are especially spacious, with living rooms that hold a sleeper sofa and a TV hidden in an armoire (there's another in the bedroom). The suites, plus the 16 efficiencies, have kitchens. The spaciousness and the kitchen facilities make this a popular choice for families and for long-term guests.

The hotel is located in a lovely neighborhood, close to Georgetown, the Kennedy Center, and downtown. Mention your affiliation with George Washington University, if you have one, and you may receive a special "GWU" rate.

824 New Hampshire Ave. NW (btw. H and I sts.), Washington, DC 20037. ℭ **800/426-4455** or 202/337-6620. Fax 202/298-7499. www.gwuinn.com. 95 units. Weekdays $159–$269 double, $179–$289 efficiency, $199–$309 1-bedroom suite; weekends $139–$209 double, $159–$229 efficiency, $179–$249 1-bedroom suite. Children 12 and under stay free in parent's room. AE, DC, DISC, MC, V. Limited parking $22. Metro: Foggy Bottom. **Amenities:** Restaurant (Italian trattoria); complimentary passes to nearby fitness center; room service; coin-op washer/dryers; same-day laundry service; dry cleaning; 5 rooms for those w/limited mobility, 1 w/roll-in shower. *In room:* A/C, TV w/pay movies and Nintendo, 2-line phone w/dataport, free Internet access, CD player, fridge, microwave, coffeemaker, hair dryer, iron, safe, robes, slippers, umbrella.

One Washington Circle Hotel The George Washington University owns this hotel, whose corporate and family clientele like the outdoor pool, in-house restaurant, prime location near Georgetown and the Metro, and the full kitchen with oven, microwave, and refrigerator (about 10% of rooms have kitchenettes). Five types of suites are available, ranging in size from 390 to 710 square feet. The one-bedroom suites have a sofa bed and dining area; all rooms are spacious, evince a contemporary look, and have walkout balconies, some overlooking the Circle and its statue of George Washington. Keep in mind that across the Circle is George Washington University Hospital's emergency-room entrance, busy with ambulance traffic. Even though rooms have double-paned windows, sirens are still audible, so ask to stay on the L Street side for a quieter room.

Call the hotel directly for best rates; mention a GWU affiliation if you have one and you may receive a discount.

One Washington Circle NW (btw. 22nd and 23rd sts. NW), Washington, DC 20037. ℭ **800/424-9671** or 202/872-1680. Fax 202/887-4989. www.thecirclehotel.com. 151 units. Weekdays $159–$299 smallest suites, $199–$339 largest suites; weekends $139–$199 smallest suites, $179–$239 largest suites. Call hotel to get best rates. Extra person $20. Children 12 and under stay free in parent's room. AE, DC, MC, V. Parking $25. Metro: Foggy Bottom. **Amenities:** Restaurant (traditional bistro w/Mediterranean flair); bar; outdoor pool; on-site fitness center; concierge; room service (7am–midnight weekends, 7am–11pm weekdays); coin-op washer/dryers; same-day laundry service; dry cleaning; 5 rooms for those w/limited mobility, 1 w/roll-in shower. *In room:* A/C, TV w/pay movies and Nintendo, 2-line cordless phones, free Internet access, CD player, full kitchens (in 90% of suites, w/oven, fridge, microwave), coffeemaker, hair dryer, iron, robes.

The River Inn ℛ *Finds* The River Inn is a sweet little secret that lies on a quiet residential street of town houses near both the Kennedy Center and Georgetown. Guest rooms feature pillow-top mattresses on beds; comfortable armchairs with soft leather footstools; ebony armoires; coppery gold, rust, and brown tones; and a cool chaise longue that unfolds into a sofa bed. Suites have all this, plus a dressing room and a

separate, well-equipped kitchen. All but 31 suites combine the bedroom and living-room areas, and include an oversize desk that doubles as workspace and dining table in a corner off the kitchen. Those 31 suites are roomy one-bedrooms, with an expansive living room (with sleep sofa) and a separate bedroom that holds a king-size bed and a second TV. Best are the suites on the upper floors, offering views of the Potomac River and from some (no. 804, for example) the Washington Monument.

924 25th St. NW (btw. K and I sts.), Washington, DC 20037. ✆ 800/424-2741 or 202/337-7600. Fax 202/337-6520. www.theriverinn.com. 125 units. Peak season weekdays $219–$299 double, $269–$349 1-bedroom suite; off-peak season weekdays $159–$199 double, $209–$249 1-bedroom suite; peak-season weekends $149–$199 double, $199–$249 1-bedroom suite; off-peak-season weekends $99–$149 double, $149–$199 1-bedroom suite. Extra person $20. Children 17 and under stay free in parent's room. AE, DC, DISC, MC, V. Parking $20. Metro: Foggy Bottom. **Amenities:** Restaurant (American); bar; small fitness center w/treadmill, stair climber, stationary bike, and other equipment; room service during restaurant hours; coin-op laundry; same-day laundry/dry cleaning; 2 rooms for those w/limited mobility. *In room:* A/C, flat-panel LCD-HD TV w/pay movies, 2-line phone w/dataport, free Internet access, fridge, microwave, coffeemaker, hair dryer, iron, safe, robes, slippers, umbrella, iHome (alarm clock/iPod docking station).

8 Georgetown

VERY EXPENSIVE

Four Seasons ★★★ No sooner did the Four Seasons complete an immense renovation in autumn 2005 than it embarked on another to the tune of $35 million in spring 2008. Changes include renovations of suites in the hotel's "west wing," the addition of a fifth presidential suite, a complete transformation of the lobby and the restaurant, and the introduction of ENO, a wine, charcuterie, and chocolate bar. Located at the mouth of Georgetown, the hotel's original (east) wing holds spacious guest rooms (500–700 sq. ft.) designed by Pierre-Yves Rochon (also tapped for the west wing's re-do), with custom-crafted furniture and color schemes of either celadon or purple. Most rooms have sleeper sofas, and all have 32-inch plasma-screen televisions. Bathrooms are prettily turned out in pear- and maple-wood accents, with a deep soaking tub separate from the shower.

Expect the very best in service, for Four Seasons staff are trained to know the names, preferences, and even allergies of guests.

2800 Pennsylvania Ave. NW (which becomes M St. a block farther along), Washington, DC 20007. ✆ 800/332-3442 or 202/342-0444. Fax 202/944-2076. www.fourseasons.com/washington. 222 units. Weekdays $595–$750 double, $895–$6,500 suite; weekends from $395 double, from $565 suite. Extra person $50. Children 17 and under stay free in parent's room. AE, DC, DISC, MC, V. Parking $42. Metro: Foggy Bottom. Pets accepted, up to 15 lb. **Amenities:** 2 restaurants (formal regional American, breakfast cafe); wine/chocolate/charcuterie bar; extensive state-of-the-art fitness club and spa w/personal trainers, lap pool, Vichy shower, hydrotherapy, facials, and synchronized massage (2 people work on you at the same time); children's program (various goodies provided but no organized activities); 24-hr. concierge; complimentary sedan service daily within the District; 24-hr. business center; salon; 24-hr. room service; in-room massage; babysitting; same-day laundry service; dry cleaning; 7 rooms for those w/limited mobility, some w/roll-in showers. *In room:* A/C, TV w/pay movies and Web access, Wi-Fi ($12/day), high-tech CD player, minibar, coffeemaker, hair dryer, iron, safe, robes.

The Ritz-Carlton Georgetown ★★★ This Ritz is exclusively small, designed like a sophisticated refuge in the middle of wild and woolly Georgetown. It's especially favored by privacy-seeking celebrities and romancing couples. Look for the 130-foot-high smokestack to guide you to the hotel, which is built on the site of a historic incinerator and incorporates the smokestack into the design and overall theme. The lobby's front brick wall is original to the incinerator, the restaurant's name is "Fahrenheit," the

bar's is "Degrees," and the signature drink is the "Fahrenheit 5 Martini." Guest rooms lie one level below the lobby, accessible by an elevator that requires a key card to operate, so anyone visiting you must either be escorted by you or a staff person. Rooms are very large, decorated in shades of moss green, gold, and a burnt red, with lots of dark-wood furniture and accents. The bathroom, like those at all Ritz-Carltons, is sublime: spacious, with marble vanity, separate tub and shower, fancy wood shelving. More than one-third of the rooms are one-bedroom suites.

3100 South St. NW (at 31st St., btw. K and M sts.), Washington, DC 20007. © 800/241-3333 or 202/912-4100. Fax 202/912-4199. www.ritzcarlton.com/hotels/georgetown. 86 units. Weekdays from $699 double, from $799 suite; weekends from $499 double ($399 on occasion), from $599 suite. No charge for extra person in the room. Check website or 800 number for weekend packages and specials. AE, DC, DISC, MC, V. Valet parking $32. Metro: Foggy Bottom. Small (under 30 lb.) pets accepted (no fee). **Amenities:** Restaurant (seasonal American); bar; lobby lounge; fitness room (complimentary) and spa; 24-hr. concierge; fax and some currency-exchange services; 24-hr. room service; in-room massage; same-day laundry service; dry cleaning; 1-hr. pressing; 3 rooms for those w/limited mobility, all w/roll-in showers. *In room:* A/C, TV w/pay movies and Web access, 2-line phone, Wi-Fi ($10/day), CD player, minibar, hair dryer, iron, safe, robes, umbrella.

EXPENSIVE

Georgetown Inn This hotel is in the thick of Georgetown. Come the third weekend in May, the hotel is full of the proud parents of students graduating from blocks-away Georgetown University. (The hotel books up 2 years in advance for graduation weekend.) Its location is what best recommends the hotel, so if you're a shopper, visiting the university, or conducting business in Georgetown, this is a good pick.

A million-dollar renovation completed in 2006 refurbished the hotel without changing its general style: traditional American, heavy on the dark woods with pretty sage-green accents. About one-third of the rooms hold two beds, the others have a king- or queen-size bed. Ask for an "executive room" if you'd like a sitting area with pullout sofa. Best are the 10 one-bedroom suites, in which bedroom and large living room are separate. The bathrooms have only showers (some also have bidets), no tub.

1310 Wisconsin Ave. NW (btw. N and O sts.), Washington, DC 20007. © 800/368-5922 or 202/333-8900. Fax 202/333-8308. www.georgetowninn.com. 90 units. Peak season $239–$499 double weekdays, $199–$409 double weekends; off season from $159 double weekdays, from $149 double weekends; suites from $299. Ask about promotional rates. Extra person $20. Children 12 and under stay free in parent's room. AE, DC, DISC, MC, V. Valet parking $32 plus tax. Metro: Foggy Bottom. **Amenities:** Restaurant (American); bar; exercise room; complimentary shoeshine; room service during restaurant hours; same-day laundry service; dry cleaning; 4 rooms for those w/limited mobility, all w/roll-in showers. *In room:* A/C, TV w/pay movies and Nintendo, 2-line phones w/dataport, Wi-Fi ($11/day), hair dryer, iron.

MODERATE

Georgetown Suites ✦ (Value) This hotel was designed to meet the needs of business travelers on extended visits, but its casual atmosphere and kitchen suites work well for families, too. The hotel offers a good deal: friendly service; clean, bright, and spacious lodging; and up-to-date amenities. It has two locations within a block of each other. The main building is on quiet, residential 30th Street, steps away from Georgetown's action. The Harbor Building, on 29th Street, is situated next to Whitehurst Freeway and across from the Washington Harbor complex, so is a bit noisier.

Accommodations at both locations have living rooms, dining areas, and fully equipped kitchens, bedding with fluffy duvets, and HDTV flatscreen televisions. Half are studios, half are one-bedroom suites. The biggest and best suites are the three two-level, two-bedroom town houses attached to the main building. Also recommended are two penthouse suites, which have their own terraces overlooking Georgetown rooftops.

1111 30th St. NW (just below M St.) and 1000 29th St. NW (at K St.), Washington, DC 20007. ✆ **800/348-7203** or 202/298-1600. Fax 202/333-2019. www.georgetownsuites.com. 220 units. Weekdays $155 studio, $215 1-bedroom suite; weekends $155 studio, $185 1-bedroom suite. Penthouse suites from $350; town houses from $425. Rollaway or sleeper sofa $10 extra. Rates include continental breakfast. AE, DC, DISC, MC, V. Limited parking $15. Metro: Foggy Bottom. **Amenities:** Small exercise room; business center w/computers and free Wi-Fi; coin-op laundry; same-day laundry service; dry cleaning; 2 rooms for those w/limited mobility, both w/roll-in showers. *In room:* A/C, TV, 2-line phone w/dataport, free Wi-Fi, full kitchen (w/fridge, coffeemaker, microwave, and dishwasher), hair dryer, iron, safe.

9 Woodley Park

EXPENSIVE

Omni Shoreham Hotel ⭐ *Kids* This is Woodley Park's *other* really big hotel, although with 834 rooms, the Omni Shoreham is still about 500 short of the behemoth Marriott Wardman Park. And it's all the more appealing for it, since it's not quite so overwhelming as the Marriott. Its design—wide corridors, vaulted ceilings and archways, and arrangements of pretty sofas and armchairs in the lobby and public spaces—endows the Shoreham with the air of a grand hotel. The Omni rightfully boasts its status as the city's largest AAA four-diamond hotel, as well as its membership in Historic Hotels of America. Guest rooms evince a certain elegance and are twice the size of your average hotel room. The hotel sits on 11 acres overlooking Rock Creek Park and beyond—you can spot the Washington Monument from some rooms.

Built in 1930, the Shoreham has been the scene of inaugural balls for every president since FDR. Do you believe in ghosts? Ask about room no. 870, the haunted suite (available for $3,000 a night).

2500 Calvert St. NW (near Connecticut Ave.), Washington, DC 20008. ✆ **800/843-6664** or 202/234-0700. Fax 202/265-7972. www.omnishorehamhotel.com. 834 units. $199–$359 double; suites from $350 and way up. Call the hotel directly for best rates. Extra person $30. Children 17 and under stay free in parent's room. AE, DC, DISC, MC, V. Valet parking $30; self-parking $23. Metro: Woodley Park–Zoo. Pets allowed, $50 cleaning fee. **Amenities:** Restaurant (Continental; terrace overlooks Rock Creek Park); gourmet carryout; bar/lounge (serves light fare); fitness center and spa w/heated outdoor pool, separate kids' pool, and whirlpool; concierge; travel/sightseeing desk; ATM; business center; shops; 24-hr. room service; massage; same-day laundry service; dry cleaning; children's gifts; 41 rooms for those w/limited mobility, half w/roll-in showers. *In room:* A/C, TV w/pay movies and Nintendo, 2-line phone w/dataport, Wi-Fi ($9.95/day), coffeemaker, hair dryer, iron, robes.

Wardman Park Marriott Hotel ⭐ This is Washington's biggest hotel, resting on 16 acres just down the street from the National Zoo and several good restaurants. Its size and location (the Woodley Park–Zoo Metro station is literally at its doorstep) make it a good choice for conventions, tour groups, and individual travelers.

The hotel's oldest section, built in 1918, houses about 100 rooms, each with high ceilings, ornate crown moldings, and an assortment of antique French and English furnishings. The main building has just undergone a major renovation of all guest rooms and public spaces, adding multilayered, Marriott-brand bedding, flatscreen TVs, and long desks with high-backed chairs. The Wardman Park now has one fine restaurant, the Stone's Throw, as well as Harry's Bar and Starbucks. Also brand-new is the state-of-the-art fitness center. Wireless Internet access is available in the Lobby Lounge, Starbucks, and the atrium.

2660 Woodley Rd. NW (at Connecticut Ave. NW), Washington, DC 20008. ✆ **800/228-9290** or 202/328-2000. Fax 202/234-0015. www.marriotthotels.com/wasdt. About 1,300 units. Weekdays $309 double; weekends $119–$289 double; $350–$2,500 suite. Children 17 and under stay free in parent's room. AE, DC, DISC, MC, V. Valet parking $24; self-parking $19. Metro: Woodley Park–Zoo. Pets under 20 lb. accepted, but charges may apply; call for details.

Finds **Extended Stays in the Heart of the City**

Travelers to Washington, D.C., who plan to visit for a week or longer should know about the centrally located **AKA White House District** apartment/hotel (1710 H St. NW; ℭ **202/904-2500; www.stayaka.com**). The D.C. location is one of 10 AKA properties (most are in NYC), all of which offer luxuriously furnished one- and two-bedroom apartments that are available for per-night rates (a minimum of 4–7 nights is generally required) or negotiated lease terms for extended stays. Federal employees will be happy to learn that AKA accepts the government's per-diem rate. Check out the website to see for yourself some of the property's fine appointments and amenities, including fully equipped kitchens, stylish decor, free Wi-Fi, on-site fitness center, washer/dryer (in each apartment), and complimentary continental breakfast. K Street law offices, the White House, the Smithsonian's Renwick Gallery, and excellent restaurants, like the Taberna del Alabardero, are just some of the property's notable neighbors.

Amenities: Restaurant (American); pub (serves meals); deli/pastry shop; lobby bar; Starbucks; outdoor heated pool w/sun deck; well-equipped fitness center; concierge; business center; salon; room service (6am–1am); in-room massage; babysitting; coin-op washer/dryers; same-day laundry service; dry cleaning; concierge-level rooms; 32 rooms for those w/limited mobility, 10 w/roll-in showers. *In room:* A/C, TV w/pay movies, 2-line phone w/dataport, Internet access ($9.95/day), coffeemaker, hair dryer, iron, safe.

INEXPENSIVE

In addition to the Woodley Park Guest House, listed below, you might consider the Woodley Park location of the **Kalorama Guest House,** at 2700 Cathedral Ave. NW (entrance on 27th St.; ℭ **800/974-9101** or 202/328-0860; fax 202/328-8730; www.kaloramaguesthouse.com), which has 18 units, 12 with private bathrooms. Rates are $140 for a double with a shared bathroom, $155 to $185 for a double with private bathroom, and include an expansive breakfast. A communal television and telephone are available in the parlor; individual guest rooms do not provide TV or telephone at this location. Free Wi-Fi access is available in all the rooms of the main house. Very limited parking (only two spots) is available for $15 plus tax, and the Woodley Park–Zoo Metro stop is nearby. See p. 100 for the full listing for the main location of the Kalorama Guest House in Adams-Morgan for more information.

Woodley Park Guest House This charming, 18-room B&B offers clean, comfortable, and cozy lodging; inexpensive rates; a super location; and a personable staff. Guests hail from around the globe, a fact which inspired the owners to add a globe to the breakfast room; people sitting across the table from each other in the morning often go over to the globe and point out exactly where they live: the Arctic Circle, Brazil, Seattle.

Special features of the guesthouse include a wicker-furnished, tree-shaded front porch; exposed, century-old brick walls; beautiful antiques; and original art. (The innkeepers buy works only from artists who have stayed at the guesthouse.) Rooms have either one or two twins, one double, or one queen-size bed. The guesthouse benefits from its proximity to the Marriott Wardman Park Hotel, where airport shuttles and taxis are on hand. The Woodley Park–Zoo Metro stop, good restaurants, Rock

Tips **Inside and Outside the Beltway, Beyond-D.C. Hotel Options**

Normally, I don't like to recommend hotel options outside the capital, since I believe that to get a real sense of a place, you need to wake up in it. Circumstances sometimes dictate otherwise, however. If you're having a hard time finding available and/or affordable rooms at D.C. hotels, first look to northern Virginia. Route 1, also known as "Jefferson Davis Highway" within Crystal City limits, is lined with hotels for every budget, though most are aimed at the high-end traveler. Crystal City and its Northern Virginia neighbors are also prime locations if you want to stay near Ronald Reagan Washington National Airport, which is less than a mile away. (National Airport, by the way, is only 4 miles from downtown Washington.) So, whether you're looking for vacancies or affordable lodging, or simply want to guarantee a free shuttle and a quick trip between your hotel and National Airport, go to the Metropolitan Washington Airports Authority website (www.mwaa.com), click on "Travel Tips," under the National Airport section, and then click on "Local Hotels," in the Local Tourism section on that page to discover a long listing of hotels. One of the closest to the airport is the **Crystal City Marriott** (1999 Jefferson Davis Hwy.; ☏ **703/920-3230**).

Likewise, if you want to stay as close as possible to Washington Dulles International Airport, refer to the same website, but click on the Travel Tips line in the Dulles box, then the Local Hotels line within Local Tourism. Of the hotels listed, one is actually located on airport property: the **Washington Dulles Marriott** (45020 Aviation Dr.; ☏ **703/471-9500**).

Finally, the Baltimore–Washington International Thurgood Marshall Airport's website, www.bwiairport.com, directs you to its list of nearby hotels: Click on "Around Town," and then "Accommodations." As at Dulles Airport, only one of the many hotels listed is located on BWI airport property: the **Four Points by Sheraton** (7032 Elm Rd.; ☏ **410/859-3300**).

Creek Park, and the National Zoo are all a short walk away. See the Dupont Circle section to read about the owners' other property, the **Embassy Circle Guest House** (p. 103).

2647 Woodley Rd. NW (at Connecticut Ave. NW), Washington, DC 20008. ☏ **866/667-0218** or 202/667-0218. Fax 202/667-1080. www.dcinns.com. 16 units, 12 with private bathroom (shower only), 4 singles, with shared bathroom. $115–$155 single with shared bathroom; $150–$225 double with private bathroom. Rates include continental breakfast. AE, MC, V. On-site parking $18, plus tax. Metro: Woodley Park–Zoo. (Well-behaved) children 12 and over. **Amenities:** Laundry and ironing service. *In room:* A/C, phone w/voice mail and dataports, free high-speed Internet access.

Where to Dine

A world capital should have world-class restaurants, and so we do. Washington restaurants include award winners from Michel Richard's **Central,** which landed the James Beard Foundation's 2008 award for "best new restaurant," to **Ben's Chili Bowl,** a 50-year-old hometown joint serving half-smokes and chili dogs recognized by the James Beard Foundation as an "American Classic."

A world capital should offer international cuisine, and so we do. In a city whose population includes more than 150 embassies and international cultural centers, 74,000 foreign-born residents, and hundreds of international associations and companies, Washington restaurants span the globe in terms of tastes, from ethnic Ethiopian (try **Meskerem,** p. 146), to haute cuisine French (**Citronelle,** p. 152).

A world capital's eateries should accommodate all budgets, and so ours do. From **On the Fly** (p. 194), an eco-friendly street vendor, to Georgetown's **Tackle Box** (grilled seafood and two sides: $13) (p. 157), D.C.'s dining options demonstrate that one can eat well at a quite reasonable price.

And a world capital's culinary scene should be forward-thinking (our restaurants are increasingly "green-oriented") and trendsetting (look over the list of wine bars, p. 270, and chocolate lounges, p. 161).

Washington, D.C.: not just a center of political power, but of sensational dining.

This chapter presents you with choices from as many different tastes, budgets, and styles as our pages allow, about 100 restaurants in all.

Read through the descriptions; if a place beckons, call ahead for **reservations,** especially for Saturday night. More and more restaurants are affiliated with an online reservation service called **www.opentable.com**, so you can also reserve your table online.

If you wait until the last minute to make a reservation, expect to dine really early, say 5:30 or 6pm, or after 9:30pm. Or you can sit at the bar and eat, which can be more of a culinary treat than you might imagine; some of the best restaurants, including Palena, Citronelle, and PS7's, offer a reasonably priced bar menu. See "A Seat at the Bar," p. 159.

Better yet, consider a restaurant that doesn't take reservations. At places like Pesce and Lauriol Plaza, where the atmosphere is casual, the wait can become part of the experience. The food is worth standing in line for.

Few places require men to wear a jacket and tie; I've made a special note in the listings for those places that do. If you're driving, call ahead to inquire about valet parking, complimentary or otherwise—on Washington's crowded streets, this service can be a true bonus.

I've listed the closest Metro station to each restaurant only when it's within walking distance of that restaurant. The closest Metro stop to Georgetown is the Blue Line's Foggy Bottom station; from there you can walk or catch the D.C. Circulator bus on Pennsylvania Avenue, up the street from the Metro station.

ABOUT THE PRICES

I've selected a range of menus and prices in the major "restaurant" neighborhoods of Washington. Restaurant groupings are first by location, then alphabetically in each price category. Keep in mind that the price categories refer to dinner prices, but some very expensive restaurants offer affordable lunches, early-bird dinners, tapas, or bar meals. The prices within each review refer to the cost of individual entrees, not the entire meal. I've used the following price categories: **Very Expensive** (entrees at dinner average more than $30); **Expensive** ($20–$30); **Moderate** ($10–$19); and **Inexpensive** ($10 and under).

1 Best Dining Bets

- **Best for Romance:** The **1789** (p. 153) is renowned for its romantic ambience; this is where Nicole Kidman brought husband Keith Urban on his 38th birthday. The five dining rooms are cozy dens—complete with historical prints on the walls, silk-shaded brass oil lamps on tables, and, come winter, fires crackling in the fireplaces. You'll want to dress up; but don't worry, the 1789 isn't at all stuffy. And if the oyster and champagne stew with Smithfield ham and walnuts doesn't put your date in the mood for love, nothing will. Other worthy contenders: **Taberna del Alabardero** (p. 139) and **Palena** (p. 160).

- **Best for Business:** **Charlie Palmer Steak** (p. 118), conveniently located within a walk of the Capitol, is a favorite spot for expense-account lobbyists and lawyers. They enjoy its great bar, fine cuts of steak, private rooms, and cleverly laid out seating that allows for discreet conversations. And then there's the **Caucus Room** (p. 123), where there's always a whole lot of handshaking going on.

- **Best for Regional Cuisine:** The **Blue Duck Tavern** (p. 150) pays homage to the tastes of various American regional cuisines by stating the provenance of each dish on the menu. The seasonal farm vegetables might hail from the Tuscarora Co-op in Pennsylvania, the duck from Crescent Farms in New York. **Johnny's Half Shell** (p. 121), meanwhile, is the place to go for superb Eastern Shore delicacies: crab cakes, crab imperial, and soft-shell crab. While Washington doesn't have its own cuisine, per se, its central location within the Mid-Atlantic/Chesapeake Bay region gives it license to lay claim to these local favorite foods. And nobody does 'em better than Johnny's.

- **Best Decor:** The **Willard Room,** in the historic Willard Hotel, stands out for its elegance. Its expansive dining room has a two-story-high ceiling, oak-paneled walls, enormous windows hung with shimmery drapes, green marble columns, beautifully upholstered chairs, and tables placed well apart from each other. The service and the food match the decor. See p. 126.

- **Best Haute Cuisine:** Two restaurants vie for this title: **CityZen** (p. 118) and **Michel Richard Citronelle** (p. 152). Chef Eric Ziebold came to CityZen from the renowned French Laundry in Napa Valley; his culinary skills can take a simple mushroom and transform it (fry it, add truffles) into a spiritual experience. Likewise, Michel Richard is an artist in the kitchen, creating heavenly foods using cuttlefish, pigs' feet, foie gras—or really, any ingredient he chooses.

- **Best All-Around for Fun and Food:** Two obvious choices: José Andrés's **Oyamel,** where the festivities on display through the windowed storefront reel in passersby.

Everyone's slurping foam-topped margaritas and savoring ceviches and the table-side-churned guacamole made to requested specifications of spiciness (p. 136). A few blocks away, **Central** (p. 128) is making everybody happy with its convivial atmosphere and Michel Richard's take on French bistro and American classics, from mussels in white wine to fried chicken. And if the ebullient Michel Richard is in the house, the place rocks.

- **Best French Cuisine:** You can go in two directions here. For exquisite, upscale French cuisine, consider Michel Richard's upscale restaurant, **Citronelle** (p. 152), as well as Robert Wiedemaier's **Marcel's** (p. 151) and Frank Ruta's **Palena** (p. 160). Not only are these the best French restaurants, but they are among the top 10 restaurants in the city, period. For French classics with Moulin Rouge ambience, check out **La Chaumiere** (p. 156), whose nightly specials and rustic decor have been attracting regulars for more than 30 years.

- **Best Italian Cuisine: Tosca** (p. 126) is a winner, serving fine and unusual dishes derived from the chef's northern Italian upbringing. At **Obelisk** (p. 146), chef/owner Peter Pastan continues to do what he's always done, craft elegantly simple and delicious food in a pleasantly sparse room.

- **Best Pizza:** At **Pizzeria Paradiso,** peerless chewy-crusted pies are baked in an oak-burning oven and crowned with delicious toppings; you'll find great salads and sandwiches on fresh-baked focaccia here, too. See p. 148.

- **Best for "Taste of Washington" Experience:** Eat lunch at the **Monocle** (p. 122) and you're bound to see a Supreme Court justice, congressman, or senator dining here, too. For some down-home and delicious Washington fun, sit at the counter at **Ben's Chili Bowl** (p. 143), and chat with the owners and your neighbor over a chili dog or plate of blueberry pancakes. The place is an institution, and you can stop by anytime—it's open for breakfast, lunch, and dinner.

2 Restaurants by Cuisine

AMERICAN/NEW AMERICAN

Acadiana ⚜ (Penn Quarter, $$$, p. 127)

Ben's Chili Bowl (U Street Corridor, $, p. 143)

Blue Duck Tavern ⚜⚜ (West End, $$$$, p. 150)

Café Saint-Ex ⚜ (U St. Corridor, $$, p. 142)

Cashion's Eat Place ⚜⚜ (Adams-Morgan, $$$, p. 144)

CityZen ⚜⚜⚜ (Capitol Hill, $$$$, p. 118)

Clyde's of Georgetown (Georgetown, $$, p. 156)

Corduroy ⚜⚜ (Midtown, $$$, p. 140)

Creme Café ⚜ (U St. Corridor, $$, p. 143)

DC Coast ⚜ (Midtown, $$$, p. 140)

Equinox ⚜⚜ (Midtown, $$$$, p. 138)

Hank's Oyster Bar ⚜ (Dupont Circle, $$, p. 148)

Hook ⚜ (Georgetown, $$$, p. 155)

Johnny's Half Shell ⚜⚜ (Capitol Hill, $$$, p. 121)

Kinkead's ⚜⚜ (Foggy Bottom, $$$$, p. 150)

Komi ⚜⚜⚜ (Dupont Circle, $$$$, p. 146)

Le Bon Café (Capitol Hill, $, p. 123)

Lobby Café ⚜⚜ (West End, $$, p. 135)

Mendocino Grille and Wine Bar ⚜ (Georgetown, $$$, p. 155)

The Monocle (Capitol Hill, $$$, p. 122)

Key to Abbreviations: $$$$ = Very Expensive $$$ = Expensive $$ = Moderate $ = Inexpensive

Old Ebbitt Grill (Penn Quarter, $$, p. 135)

The Oval Room ✪ (Midtown, $$$, p. 140)

Palena ✪✪✪ (Cleveland Park, $$$$, p. 160)

Poste ✪ (Penn Quarter, $$$, p. 129)

Proof ✪✪ (Penn Quarter, $$$, p. 130)

PS7's ✪✪ (Penn Quarter, $$$, p. 130)

1789 ✪✪✪ (Georgetown, $$$$, p. 153)

Sonoma ✪ (Capitol Hill, $$, p. 122)

Tabard Inn ✪✪ (Dupont Circle, $$$, p. 147)

Vidalia ✪✪ (Midtown, $$$$, p. 139)

Westend Bistro by Eric Ripert ✪ (West End, $$$, p. 131)

Willard Room ✪ (Penn Quarter, $$$$, p. 126)

Zola ✪✪ (Penn Quarter, $$$, p. 132)

ASIAN FUSION

Café Asia (Midtown, $, p. 141)

Teaism (Dupont Circle, $, p. 149)

TenPenh ✪ (Penn Quarter, $$$, p. 131)

The Source ✪✪ (Penn Quarter, $$$$, p. 126)

Zengo ✪ (Penn Quarter, $$$, p. 131)

AUSTRIAN

Leopold's Kafe & Konditorei ✪ (Georgetown, $$, p. 156)

BARBECUE

Old Glory Barbecue (Georgetown, $$, p. 157)

BELGIAN

Brasserie Beck ✪✪ (Midtown, $$, p. 141)

Belga Café ✪ (Capitol Hill, $$$, p. 119)

CHINESE

Ching Ching Cha (Georgetown, $, p. 157)

City Lights of China (Dupont Circle, $$, p. 148)

Tony Cheng's Seafood Restaurant ✪ (Penn Quarter, $, p. 137)

ETHIOPIAN

Meskerem (Adams-Morgan, $, p. 146)

Zed's (Georgetown, $, p. 157)

FRENCH

Bistro Bis ✪✪ (Capitol Hill, $$$, p. 119)

Bistro D'Oc ✪ (Penn Quarter, $$, p. 132)

Bistrot Lepic ✪ (Georgetown, $$$, p. 154)

Café du Parc ✪ (Penn Quarter, $$, p. 132)

Central Michel Richards✪✪✪ (Penn Quarter, $$$, p. 128)

La Chaumiere ✪✪ (Georgetown, $$, p. 156)

Les Halles ✪ (Penn Quarter, $$, p. 134)

Lobby Café ✪✪ (West End, $$, p. 135)

Marcel's ✪✪ (Foggy Bottom, $$$$, p. 151)

Michel Richard Citronelle ✪✪✪ (Georgetown, $$$$, p. 152)

Montmartre ✪ (Capitol Hill, $$, p. 122)

Palena ✪✪✪ (Cleveland Park, $$$$, p. 160)

Westend Bistro by Eric Ripert ✪ (West End, $$$, p. 131)

Willard Room ✪ (Penn Quarter, $$$$, p. 126)

GREEK

Komi ✪✪✪ (Dupont Circle, $$$$, p. 146)

Zaytinya ✪✪ (Penn Quarter, $$, p. 137)

INDIAN

Bombay Club ✪ (Midtown, $$, p. 141)

Indique ✿ (Cleveland Park, $$,
 p. 160)
Heritage India ✿ (Glover Park,
 Dupont Circle, $$, p. 158)
Rasika ✿✿ (Penn Quarter, $$,
 p. 136)

ITALIAN

Cafe Milano ✿ (Georgetown, $$$,
 p. 154)
D'Acqua ✿ (Penn Quarter, $$$,
 p. 129)
Matchbox ✿ (Penn Quarter, $$,
 p. 135)
Obelisk ✿✿✿ (Dupont Circle, $$$$,
 p. 146)
Palena ✿✿✿ (Cleveland Park, $$$$,
 p. 160)
Pizzeria Paradiso ✿ (Dupont Circle,
 $, p. 148)
Tosca ✿✿✿ (Penn Quarter, $$$$,
 p. 126)

JAPANESE

Ching Ching Cha (Georgetown, $,
 p. 157)
Kaz Sushi Bistro ✿ (Foggy Bottom,
 $$$, p. 152)
Sushi-Ko ✿ (Glover Park, $$, p. 158)

LATIN AMERICAN

Café Atlantico ✿✿ (Penn Quarter,
 $$$, p. 127)
Ceiba ✿ (Penn Quarter, $$$, p. 128)
Las Canteras ✿ (Adams-Morgan, $$,
 p. 144)
Lauriol Plaza ✿ (Adams-Morgan, $$,
 p. 144)
Oyamel ✿✿✿ (Penn Quarter, $$,
 p. 136)
Zengo ✿ (Penn Quarter, $$$, p. 131)

MEXICAN

Lauriol Plaza ✿ (Adams-Morgan, $$,
 p. 144)
Oyamel ✿✿✿ (Penn Quarter, $$,
 p. 136)
Rosa Mexicano ✿ (Penn Quarter,
 $$$, p. 131)

MIDDLE EASTERN

Bistro Tabaq ✿ (U St. Corridor, $$,
 p. 142)
Lebanese Taverna (Woodley Park, $$,
 p. 160)
Zaytinya ✿✿ (Penn Quarter, $$,
 p. 137)

PERUVIAN

Las Canteras ✿ (Adams-Morgan, $$,
 p. 144)

PIZZA

Matchbox ✿ (Penn Quarter, $$,
 p. 135)
Pizzeria Paradiso ✿ (Dupont Circle, $,
 p. 148)

SEAFOOD

D'Acqua ✿ (Penn Quarter, $$$,
 p. 129)
Hank's Oyster Bar ✿ (Dupont Circle,
 $$, p. 148)
Hook ✿ (Georgetown, $$$, p. 155)
Johnny's Half Shell ✿✿ (Capitol Hill,
 $$$, p. 121)
Legal Sea Foods ✿ (Midtown, $$,
 p. 133)
Kinkead's ✿✿ (Foggy Bottom, $$$$,
 p. 150)
Oceanaire Seafood Room ✿ (Penn
 Quarter, $$$, p. 129)
Pesce ✿ (Dupont Circle, $$$, p. 147)
The Prime Rib ✿✿ (Midtown, $$$$,
 p. 138)
Tackle Box ✿ (Georgetown, $,
 p. 157)
Tony Cheng's Seafood Restaurant ✿
 (Penn Quarter, $, p. 137)

SOUTHERN/SOUTHWESTERN

Acadiana ✿ (Penn Quarter, $$$,
 p. 127)
Creme Café ✿ (U St. Corridor, $$,
 p. 143)
Vidalia ✿✿ (Midtown, $$$$, p. 139)

SPANISH

Jaleo ✦ (Penn Quarter, $$, p. 133)

Lauriol Plaza ✦ (Adams-Morgan, $$, p. 144)

Taberna del Alabardero ✦✦ (Midtown, $$$$, p. 139)

STEAK

BLT Steak ✦ (Midtown, $$$$, p. 137)

The Caucus Room ✦✦ (Penn Quarter, $$$$, p. 123)

Charlie Palmer Steak ✦✦ (Capitol Hill, $$$$, below)

Les Halles ✦ (Penn Quarter, $$, p. 134)

The Palm ✦ (Midtown, $$$$, p. 138)

The Prime Rib ✦✦ (Midtown, $$$$, p. 138)

THAI

Sala Thai (Dupont Circle, $, p. 149)

TURKISH

Zaytinya ✦✦ (Penn Quarter, $$, p. 137)

3 Capitol Hill

For information on eating at the Capitol and other government buildings, see the box titled "Views with a Meal," on p. 120.

VERY EXPENSIVE

Charlie Palmer Steak ✦✦ STEAK Washington restaurant critics continue to give Charlie Palmer Steak high marks, both for its steaks and for its seafood entrees, like the Maine lobster poached in butter fondue. Beef predominates, from the excellent wagyu sirloin to the rib-eye "cowboy cut," with "progressive American" veal, pork, fish, and fowl dishes splitting the rest of the list. The only steakhouse on Capitol Hill, CP Steak is more elegant than one might expect. Its dining room has three fireplaces, deep-cushioned couches, and intimate seating areas. The ceilings are high, the rooms expansive. It's a place to see and be seen—in big groups, preferably. The bar and lounge are made for circulating. The most provocative feature is the glass-walled wine storage "cube," which appears to float upon a shallow pool of water; the inventory stocks 10,000 bottles of exclusively American wines representing every state. Guests survey the wine list via the eWinebook, a kind of Palm Pilot that allows you to scroll through the selections, while a sommelier is on hand for consultation. The restaurant advertises that it overlooks the Capitol, but views are seasonal: In winter, you'll see more of the Capitol than you do in summer, when only the Capitol dome and the grounds are visible.

101 Constitution Ave. NW (at Louisiana Ave.). ✆ 202/547-8100. www.charliepalmer.com. Reservations recommended. Lunch entrees $17–$38; prix-fixe lunch $25; dinner entrees $23–$84. AE, MC, V. Mon–Fri 11:30am–2:30pm and 5:30–10pm; Sat 5–10pm. Metro: Union Station (Massachusetts Ave. exit).

CityZen ✦✦✦ MODERN AMERICAN Chef Eric Ziebold, winner of the 2008 James Beard Foundation's "Best Chef for the Mid-Atlantic Region" award, continues to fill tables nightly at CityZen and garner AAA five-diamond ratings annually. Located in the deluxe Mandarin Oriental Hotel, CityZen's dining room is temple-like: cathedral ceiling, dimly lit, with a coterie of acolytes flitting back and forth between tables and kitchen. You choose among three prix-fixe menus: three courses for $75, a six-course vegetarian tasting menu for $80, or a six-course $110 tasting menu. Starting with an *amuse-bouche* of fried mushroom with truffle butter; moving on to a grilled pork jowl with marinated French green lentils, micro watercress, and shaved foie gras confit; and further on to the crispy skin filet of Atlantic black bass served with

Rancho Gordo shelling beans, CityZen chorizo, and baby leeks—every taste is exquisite and out of the ordinary. Waitstaff bring intermittent refreshments, such as olive oil custard topped with infused butter or ginger sorbet in homemade root beer. Only a food artist would think to create sensations like the cardamom-dusted orange cruller with kumquat marmalade and African amber tea sorbet. The restaurant's 800-bottle wine selection concentrates on bordeaux, burgundy, and California cabernet.

As mentioned in the review of the Mandarin Oriental Hotel (p. 84), the hotel is in an odd neighborhood, off by itself in a sea of government buildings and construction. But it's worth finding your way here. Enjoy a drink first in the hotel lounge overlooking a landscaped terrace or in CityZen's handsome lounge and bar (with its amazing "wall of fire"). *Note:* You can also dine fabulously and less expensively at the bar (p. 159). Dress nicely (no denim, shorts, or sneakers).

In the Mandarin Oriental Hotel, 1330 Maryland Ave. SW (at 12th St.). © 202/787-6868. www.mandarinoriental. com/washington (then click on "Dining"). Reservations recommended. Prix-fixe $75 for 3-course menu; 6-course tasting menus $80 (vegetarian) and $110. AE, DC, DISC, MC, V. Tues–Thurs 6–9:30pm; Fri–Sat 5:30–9:30pm. Metro: Smithsonian (12th St./Independence Ave. exit).

EXPENSIVE

Belga Café ✪ BELGIAN Belga Café is located on a street called "Barracks Row," named for the Marine Corps barracks bordering the street to the east. This is one of those D.C. neighborhoods that's been here forever—the Marine Barracks and the Navy Yard, just blocks away, sprouted 200 years ago—but now is being revitalized by merchants and the city. New bars, restaurants, and shops are opening all the time along 8th Street, and this trend will continue as the newly completed Nationals Ballpark, the Washington Nationals baseball stadium, draws more and more people to this part of town.

But back to the Belga: When it opened in late 2004, the cafe was almost too popular for its own good. Things have quieted down somewhat, service has improved, and you can probably now snag a table without a wait. Enjoy sitting at the outdoor cafe on a fine spring day or inside the bustling, noisy, European-ish dining room. Everything's a waffle at brunch and lunch, meaning many of the sandwiches—croque-monsieur to hamburger—are served on *wafel* (waffled) bread. The menu might look gimmicky, since every item gets its Flemish name first, followed by the translation: *dagsoep* (soup of the day), *waterzooi* (free-range chicken with vegetables). I recommend the Belgian fries; the Belgian beers (several on tap, another 30 or so in bottles); the mussels, accompanied by one of five sauces; and the *eendenborst,* which is duck breast à l'orange with duck confit, salsify, and orange cacao sauce. Order the Belgian waffles, not the French toast, at brunch.

514 8th St. SE (at Pennsylvania Ave.). © 202/544-0100. www.belgacafe.com. Reservations accepted. Brunch $8.75–$23; lunch entrees $8.75–$23; dinner entrees $8.50–$27. AE, DC, DISC, MC, V. Lunch Mon–Thurs 11:30am–3pm, Fri 11:30am–5:30pm; brunch Sat 10am–5:30pm, Sun 10am–5pm; dinner Sun 5–9:30pm, Mon–Thurs 5:30–10pm, Fri–Sat 5:30–11pm. Metro: Eastern Market.

Bistro Bis ✪✪ FRENCH BISTRO The chic Hotel George is the home of this inconsistent, though mostly fine, French restaurant. The chef/owner, Jeff Buben, and his wife, Sallie, also run **Vidalia** (p. 139). You can sit at tables in the bar area (which always seems loud, even when it's not that crowded), on the balcony overlooking the bar, or at leather banquettes in the main dining room. In warm weather, there's a sidewalk cafe. The menu covers French classics like bouillabaisse, boeuf bourguignon, and

Views with a Meal

Is there anything more wonderful than discovering that the attraction you are currently visiting also offers an excellent repast? Most tourist sites provide sustenance of some sort, generally humdrum in taste and high in price. Very few establishments proffer a delightful setting and food that's a real pleasure to eat. At the pinnacle of my list in Washington, D.C., are the **National Gallery of Art**'s restaurants, and in particular the **Sculpture Garden Pavilion Café** (© 202/289-3360). You can sip a glass of wine and savor Cuban panini (roasted pork with crinkle-cut pickles, mustard, ham, cheese, and onions on Cuban bread), sitting inside in the glass pavilion in winter or on the terrace in warm weather, in view of sculpture, the landscaped garden, and grand sights of Washington, D.C. The gallery's **Cascades** and the **Garden Café** (© 202/712-7460) are worthy second choices, offering a wide range of appetite-pleasers and really lovely surroundings.

Four other eateries are worth special mention: The **National Museum of the American Indian's Mitsitam Café** (© 202/633-1000) seeks to educate as well as please the palate, since its menu represents traditional dishes from various Native American regions. Examples include cedar-planked juniper salmon from the Pacific Northwest, buffalo burgers from the Great Plains, and, a favorite, fry bread from all over. The **International Spy Museum's Spy City Café** (© 202/654-0995) is one of the rare museum eateries to open early—8am weekdays and 9am weekends—and is rightly famous for its cleverly named hot dogs, like the Red Square Dog. The petite **Café** (© 202/387-2151, ext. 351), in the **Phillips Collection,** is operated by a local bakery chain, Firehook Bakery, which Washingtonians love for its sandwiches on thick breads and for its selection of delicious desserts. (Firehook also operates the cafe at the **National Building Museum.**) The **Newseum's** separately owned, but in-house restaurant is the exceptional the **Source** (© 202/637-6100), Wolfgang Puck's three-level, glass-fronted, crowd-attracting eatery serving Asian-influenced cuisine.

Finally, you just can't beat the atmosphere (political) and value (cheap) of the all-American food served in certain dining rooms on Capitol Hill. Keep

steak frites. But Buben gives the traditional his own twist: Seared scallops Provençal comes with the anticipated tomatoes, garlic, and olives, but also an eggplant custard. A spring appetizer might be a crab fritter Provençal: soft-shell crab tempura lightly fried with olives and roasted garlic. The beet salad arrives with goat cheese, walnuts, and arugula and is dressed with a citron olive oil vinaigrette. Many items, including the sea scallops and the steak frites, appear on both the lunch and dinner menus but are considerably cheaper at lunch. The wine list is mostly French and American. Look around the dining room for nightly news types, since Bis's proximity to the Capitol, lovely setting, and scrumptious cuisine make it a must-stop for movers and shakers.

15 E St. NW. © 202/661-2700. www.bistrobis.com. Reservations recommended. Breakfast $9–$14; brunch entrees $12–$18; lunch entrees $15–$24; dinner entrees $23–$33. AE, DC, DISC, MC, V. Daily 7–10:30am, 11:30am–2:30pm, and 5:30–10:30pm. Metro: Union Station.

these places in mind while touring the Hill; but always call ahead, since these restaurants sometimes close to the public.

For a most exclusive experience, try to dine in the **House of Representatives Restaurant** (also called the "Members' Dining Room") in Room H118, at the south end of the Capitol (② 202/225-6300). You are always welcome (after you've gone through security, of course) in the eateries located in the Capitol office buildings across the street from the Capitol. These are quite affordable—your meal isn't taxed, for one thing. You'll be surrounded by Hill staffers, who head to places like the immense, full-service **Rayburn House Office Building Cafeteria** (② 202/225-7109), which is in Room B357, in the basement of the building, at 1st Street and Independence Avenue SW. Adjoining the cafeteria is a carryout that sells pizza and sandwiches. In the basement-level **Longworth Building Cafeteria**, Independence Avenue and South Capitol Street SE (② 202/225-0878), you can grab a bite from a fairly nice food court. Other options include the Russell Carryout and the Cannon Carryout, both in the basement of the Cannon Building. All of these eateries are open weekdays only. The carryouts stay open until late afternoon, while the other dining rooms close at 2:30pm.

The opening of the **Capitol Visitors Center** in late 2008 introduced another option: a large dining hall accommodating 600 people. At this writing, the center hadn't opened, so that's all I can tell you. Check it out if you're planning to tour the Capitol in 2009.

Right across the street from the Capitol are two other institutions offering inexpensive dining and fair views (of famous sights or people) at weekday breakfast and lunch: the **Library of Congress's Cafeteria** and its more formal **Montpelier Room** (② 202/707-5000), where the options usually cost under $10 per person and the views are of Capitol Hill; and the **Supreme Court's Cafeteria** (② 202/479-3246), where you may spy a famous lawyer or member of the press, but not any of the justices, who have their own dining room.

Johnny's Half Shell ★★ *Finds* AMERICAN/SEAFOOD Until September 2006, Johnny's was a neighborhood joint in Dupont Circle. Having outgrown its small space, Johnny's moved into this much larger Capitol Hill location but maintains the same warm vibes and welcoming atmosphere, with the help of many of its faithful P Street staff. This Johnny's also mimics the decor of the original, by featuring an aquarium behind the long bar, booths along one paneled wall, a tile floor, and a partly open kitchen. One thing's for sure: The regional cuisine remains unbeatable.

The menu continues to offer its reliably good, farm-raised chicken with old-fashioned Eastern Shore slippery dumplings, garden peas, and button mushrooms; the crabmeat imperial with a salad of *haricots verts* (young green beans), tomatoes, and shallots; the delicious fried oyster po' boy sandwich (at lunch only); and Maryland crab cakes with coleslaw and french fries. If the sautéed soft-shell crabs with Old Bay

and basil beurre blanc and corn pudding are on the menu, get them; this is one of the best places in town to enjoy them. Oysters and Wellfleet clams on the half shell are always available, of course. The short wine list includes a few selections by the glass; there are four beers on tap. Desserts are simply perfect, including homemade ice cream, a choice of apple or Meyer lemon tart, chocolate angel food cake with caramel sauce, and coconut passion-fruit layer cake.

Johnny's also runs a *Taqueria Nacional* ((C) **202/737-7070**), which serves breakfast tacos, scrambled eggs, and waffles 7 to 11am, and five varieties of soft tacos priced at no more than $2.50 each, plus a daily special at $5.50, 11am to 3pm. The *taqueria* is a takeout operation open weekdays only and is located just behind Johnny's main entrance.

400 N. Capitol St. NW (at E St.). (C) 202/737-0400. www.johnnyshalfshell.net. Reservations recommended. Breakfast $7–$13; lunch entrees $8.25–$33; dinner entrees $18–$33. AE, MC, V. Mon–Fri 7–9:30am (*taqueria* 7–11am) and 11:30am–2:30pm (*taqueria* 11am–3pm); Mon–Sat 5–10pm; happy hour Mon–Fri 4:30–7:30pm. Metro: Union Station (Massachusetts Ave. exit).

The Monocle (Finds) AMERICAN A Capitol Hill institution, the Monocle has been around since 1960. At this men-in-suits place, the litter of briefcases resting against the too-close-together tables can make for treacherous navigating. But you might want to take a look at whose briefcase it is you're stumbling over, for its proximity to both the Supreme Court and the Capitol guarantees that the Monocle is the haunt of Supreme Court justices and members of Congress. At lunch you'll want to order the hamburger, which is excellent; the tasty federal salad (field greens and tomatoes tossed with balsamic vinaigrette); or the white-bean soup when it's on the menu. At dinner, consider the roasted oysters, the pork-rib chop with Pommery mustard sauce, or "Crab Conrad," a lump crab dish that owner John Valanos created to honor his father, Conrad Valanos, who opened the Monocle in 1960.

107 D St. NE. (C) 202/546-4488. www.themonocle.com. Reservations recommended. Lunch entrees $9.95–$26; dinner entrees $17–$35. AE, DC, DISC, MC, V. Mon–Fri 11:30am–10pm; Sat 5pm–midnight. Closed 2 weeks preceding Labor Day. Metro: Union Station (Massachusetts Ave. exit).

MODERATE

Montmartre (*) FRENCH Montmartre's ambience is warmed by its decor—pale yellow-orange walls, exposed-wood ceiling, cozy bar, and old wooden tables, all fronted by a sidewalk cafe open in warm weather. The owners here are French, and Montmartre is their little French restaurant offering big French pleasures: chicory salad tossed with goat cheese and croutons, chestnut soup, pistou, potato gratin, flatiron beef with Jerusalem artichokes, seared monkfish wrapped in smoked bacon, and calves' liver sautéed with smothered onions, bok choy, potato purée, and a balsamic vinegar sauce. Desserts, like the Alsatian apple tart, don't disappoint.

327 7th St. SE. (C) 202/544-1244. Reservations recommended. Brunch $8.95–$17; lunch and dinner entrees $14–$20. AE, DC, MC, V. Tues–Sun 11:30am–2:30pm; Sun 5:30–9pm; Tues–Thurs 5:30–10pm; Fri–Sat 5:30–10:30pm. Metro: Eastern Market.

Sonoma (*) AMERICAN Oenophiles and lounge lovers have equal reason to visit Sonoma, since the restaurant offers 40 wines by the glass from its inventory of 200 Californian wines, as well as a lively lounge scene on the second floor. And though 20- and 30-something Hill staffers quickly made this place their own after Sonoma opened in summer 2005, lots of people are happy to meet up here. (Families with small children should look elsewhere.) Plates of charcuterie and cheeses are for sharing, while a menu

of "firsts" offers pastas and "seconds" lists meat and seafood dishes. Do try a small plate of the charcuterie, then follow it up with a house-made goat cheese ravioli and the coffee-glazed Duroc baby back ribs. A variety of salads and pizzas are also available. The smart-looking Sonoma stands out on this stretch of Pennsylvania Avenue, where most of its neighbors are coffeehouses and bars. The long, narrow dining room often fills up with a drinking crowd waiting for a table in the evening. That's when you'll want to head upstairs and check out the lounge, which has a fireplace and overlooks Pennsylvania Avenue. As the night progresses, the tables turn and the second floor gets crowded; at that point, it's time to move on.

223 Pennsylvania Ave. SE (at 2nd St. SE). (*) 202/544-8088. www.sonomadc.com. Reservations recommended. Lunch and dinner entrees $11–$34. AE, DC, DISC, MC, V. Mon–Fri 11:30am–2:30pm; Mon–Thurs 5:30–10pm; Fri–Sat 5:30–11pm. Metro: Capitol South.

INEXPENSIVE

Le Bon Café *Finds* AMERICAN Pennsylvania Avenue on Capitol Hill is a stretch of been-around-a-while pubs, as well as newer coffeehouses, bakeries, and the occasional fine-dining establishment. The Capitol looms over the neighborhood, whose other big buildings hold the Library of Congress and Senate and House offices. Government edifices aside, this part of town is actually mostly residential. Pennsylvania Avenue and its town house–lined side streets compose a village, enlivened by the presence of young staffers who swarm here for lunch, dinner, coffee, or a drink. The local chains Firehook Bakery and Burrito Brothers have outposts here, as do national chains Starbucks and Cosi. Those are all fine places, but my favorite is the tiny Le Bon Café, whose menu is short but sweet: homemade pumpkin gingerbread and scones, smoked turkey club sandwich on farm bread, grilled salmon Niçoise salad, and the like. And it's cheap: The most expensive single item is that salmon salad for $9.85. Seating inside is minimal, with most people grabbing food to go; in pleasant weather, you can sit at outdoor tables. *FYI:* Pete's Diner and Carryout, right next door, also attracts a loyal Hill following with its low prices and burgers-and-fried-chicken menu; so stop there if you've got a greasy spoon kind of appetite.

210 2nd St. SE (at Pennsylvania Ave. SE). (*) 202/547-7200. Breakfast items $2.25–$5; salads/sandwiches/soups $3.85–$9.85. AE, DISC, MC, V. Mon–Fri 7am–3:30pm; Sat–Sun 8am–2pm. Metro: Capitol South.

4 Downtown, Penn Quarter

VERY EXPENSIVE

The Caucus Room ★★ STEAK Washington's powerful people like steakhouses. Since the Caucus Room is owned by a bipartisan bunch of heavy-hitting politicos and entrepreneurs (Democratic lobbyist Tommy Boggs and former Republican National Committee chairman Haley Barbour, to name but 2 of the 70 investors), the Caucus Room was almost a guaranteed success even before it opened in August 2000. At lunch and dinner, it's a true Washington scene, with all that this entails: a sprinkling of congressmen and -women, television newscasters, and corporate VIPs throughout the main dining room; lots of backslapping and shaking of hands; and private meetings taking place behind closed doors (the restaurant has a number of private dining rooms).

But they wouldn't keep coming back if the food weren't so good. Enduring favorites are the steaks and certain nonmeat entrees, such as the crab cakes (the pass/fail test for a D.C. restaurant) and seared fish. A recent preparation was seared rockfish, sesame

Capitol Hill, Downtown & Foggy Bottom Dining

FOGGY BOTTOM

Acadiana **23**
Belga Café **55**
Bistro Bis **48**
Bistro D'Oc **39**
BLT Steak **16**
Blue Duck Tavern **6**
Bombay Club **15**
Brasserie Beck **21**
Café Asia **12**
Café Atlantico **44**
Café du Parc **19**
Caucus Room **36**
Ceiba **20**
Central Michel Richard **34**
Charlie Palmer Steak **51**
CityZen **56**
CoCo. Sala **30**
Corduroy **22**
D'Acqua **37**
DC Coast **17**
Equinox **13**
Jaleo **43**
Johnny's Half Shell **49**
Kaz Sushi Bistro **9**
Kinkead's **8**
Le Bon Café **53**
Legal Sea Food **28**
Les Halles **33**
Lobby Café **5**
Marcel's **7**
Matchbox **25**

The Monocle **50**
Montmartre **54**
Oceanaire Seafood
 Room **31**
Old Ebbitt Grill **18**
The Oval Room **14**
Oyamel **45**
The Palm **2**
Poste **41**
The Prime Rib **10**
Proof **28**
PS7's **24**
Rasika **46**
Rosa Mexicano **42**
Sonoma **52**
The Source **47**
Tabard Inn **1**
Taberna del Alabardero **11**
Teaism Penn Quarter **38**
TenPenh **35**
Tony Cheng's Seafood
 Restaurant **26**
Tosca **32**
Vidalia **3**
Westend Bistro
 by Eric Ripert **4**
Willard Room **19**
Zaytinya **29**
Zengo **27**
Zola **40**

Rhode Island Ave.

13th St.

DOWNTOWN
29

12th St.
11th St.
10th St.
9th St.
8th St.
7th St.
6th St.
5th St.
4th St.
3rd St.

29
1

New Jersey Ave.

N St.

M St.

22

Mt. VernonSq./
Convention Ctr.
Green &
Yellow Lines

L St.
50

21

23

New York Ave.

Mt. Vernon
Square

1
50

US 1

24

25

Massachusetts Ave.

26

K St.

I St.

H St.

395

N. Capitol St.

1st St.

Metro Center
Red, Blue &
Orange Lines

29

28

27

G St.

Union
Station
Red Line

Union
Station

2nd St.

32

30

40 41

7th St.

42

Judiciary
Square
Red Line

3rd St.

2nd St.

1st St.

F St.

E St.

48

39

E St.

43

33

34

35 36

38 44

37

45

46

Indiana
Ave.

D St.

C St.

49

50

Pennsylvania Ave.

47

Louisiana Ave.

Delaware Ave.

51

Constitution Ave.

CAPITOL-
HILL

Federal
Triangle
Blue &
Orange Lines

Archives-
Navy Mem'l
Green &
Yellow Lines

Madison Dr.

NW

U.S. Capitol

NE

Smithsonian
Blue &
Orange Lines

Jefferson Dr.

Independence Ave.

SW

SE

52 →

53 →

Canal St.

54 →

55 →

56

L'Enfant Plaza
Yellow, Green,
Orange &
Blue Lines

395

Federal
Center SW
Blue &
Orange Lines

New Jersey Ave.

Capitol
South
Blue &
Orange Lines

Area of detail

GEORGETOWN

ARLINGTON

VIRGINIA

The White
House

Potomac River

Union
Station

U.S. Capitol

0 1 mi

0 1 km

crusted and served with Asian vegetables. Even side dishes, like the creamed spinach and the horseradish-spiked mashed potatoes, are winners.

After you finish your main course, lean back against the leather banquette and discreetly search for famous faces as you enjoy dessert, maybe a chocolate mousse or pecan pie. *Tip:* Make sure you sit in the main dining room when Congress is in session; otherwise, you'll find the Caucus Room fairly deserted.

401 9th St. NW (at D St.). ℂ 202/393-1300. www.thecaucusroom.com. Reservations recommended. Lunch items $16–$59; dinner entrees $24–$59. AE, DISC, MC, V. Mon–Fri 11:30am–2:30pm; Mon–Sat 5:30–10pm. Metro: Navy/Archives or Gallery Place (9th St. exit).

The Source 🐸🐸 ASIAN-INFLUENCED AMERICAN Even if you didn't know the Source was a Wolfgang Puck establishment, you would have to register its L.A.-cool vibe. Like the Newseum, in which the Source resides, the two-level restaurant is glass-fronted, attracting all who happen by. Background music veers from David Bowie to Indian trance. Hostesses look like models in their sexy black dresses and heels. And the place is extremely loud, whether in the downstairs lounge, where a young hip crowd gathers day and night, or up that long marble staircase to the main dining room, where the lighting is dim and the mood vibrant. The big news here is the food is really, really good. Though Puck himself is not in the kitchen, his inspiration is apparent in every dish. Do try the "tiny dumplings," my favorite item on the menu. Go on from there to stir-fried lamb, lacquered duck, or the short ribs, and end with the chocolate purse for dessert.

575 Pennsylvania Ave. NW (in the Newseum). ℂ 202/637-6100. www.wolfgangpuck.com/restaurants. Reservations recommended. Lounge entrees $12–$16; lunch entrees $14–$29; dinner entrees $26–$60. AE, DC, DISC, MC, V. Mon–Fri 11:30am–2pm; Mon–Thurs 5:30–9:30pm; Fri–Sat 5:30–10:30pm.

Tosca 🐸🐸🐸 NORTHERN ITALIAN Washington, which probably has more Italian restaurants than any other kind of ethnic eatery, saw the opening of several more in 2007, including the excellent D'Acqua (p. 129). Nevertheless, Tosca has nothing to worry about. Tosca remains the city's standout fine *ristorante italiano*.

Tosca's interior design of pale pastels in the thick carpeting and heavy drapes creates a hushed atmosphere, a suitable foil to the rich food. The menu, meanwhile, emphasizes the cooking of the Lake Como region of Italy. Recommended dishes include a grilled rack of veal with a mix of wild mushrooms and a roasted Mediterranean sea bass with balsamic vinegar sabayon and sautéed spinach with pine nuts and raisins. Tosca has something for everyone, including simply grilled fish accompanied by organic vegetables for the health-conscious, and desserts such as tiramisu or ricotta-and-goat-cheese fritters for those with a sweet tooth. No wonder the restaurant is always full. But even when there's a crowd, Tosca doesn't get too noisy—the restaurant's designers kept acoustics in mind. *Tip:* By the time you read this, Tosca will have opened a casual Italian restaurant, **Posto**, at 14th and P streets.

1112 F St. NW. ℂ 202/367-1990. www.toscadc.com. Reservations recommended. Lunch entrees $12–$24; dinner entrees $19–$42; pretheater menu $35; tasting menus $70–$95. AE, DISC, MC, V. Mon–Fri 11:30am–2:30pm; Mon–Thurs 5:30–10:30pm; Fri–Sat 5:30–11pm. Metro: Metro Center (12th and F sts. exit).

Willard Room 🐸 AMERICAN/FRENCH For the ultimate Washington experience: Take a taxi (better yet, a limo) to the Willard Hotel, and stroll through the lobby, heading right, to find the Round Robin bar. Enjoy a mint julep, old-fashioned, or gin rickey and listen to the tales told by the seasoned bartenders about Charles Dickens, Nathaniel Hawthorne, and others who frequented this hotel in earlier days. Proceed

to the Willard Room, which has to be the most elegant dining room in the capital: two-story-high ceiling, walnut-paneled walls, green marble columns, sumptuous fabrics, tables placed far from each other throughout the room. Enjoy a repast of classic dishes: Caesar salad, Maine lobster poached with onion-ginger ravioli, or rack of lamb with herbs Provençal. Discreetly observe the presence of the royal family from Denmark or the former prime minister from Israel. Ask for your bill, add a healthy tip, and then wander out to Peacock Alley and peruse the information on display about the history of the Willard (2006 marked the centenary of the "new" Willard). Return to the Round Robin for a nightcap.

1401 Pennsylvania Ave. NW. © 202/637-7440. Reservations recommended. Breakfast entrees $9–$25; lunch entrees $24–$29; dinner entrees $34–$39; Sun brunch $65. AE, DC, DISC, MC, V. Mon–Fri 7:30–10am and 11:30am–2pm; Sat 8am–noon; Sun 11am–2pm; Mon–Sat 6–10pm. Metro: Metro Center (13th St. exit).

EXPENSIVE

Acadiana ☆ AMERICAN/SOUTHERN This glass-walled triangle-shaped restaurant lies close to the convention center. If you're in need of a Sazerac or mint julep pick-me-up in the middle of your meetings, the bar stays open straight through from lunch to dinner and offers a menu of appetizers. The restaurant's high ceilings, ornate chandeliers, and oversize urns and other features fit with the over-the-top atmosphere that prevails. This is New Orleans central, right here. New Orleanians say the cuisine's the real thing, starting with the biscuits, served with a pepper jelly and cream cheese condiment; continuing on to deviled eggs, charbroiled oysters, and crabmeat and artichoke gratin starters; and even further to jambalaya, étouffée, red snapper in an almondine sauce, and barbecue shrimp. Service is excellent.

901 New York Ave. NW (at 9th St.). © 202/408-8848. www.acadianarestaurant.com. Reservations recommended. Lunch entrees $12–$28; dinner entrees $21–$29. AE, DISC, MC, V. Mon–Fri 11:30am–2:30pm; Mon–Thurs 5:30–10:15pm; Fri–Sat 5:30–10:30pm; Sun 11am–2:30pm and 5:30–9:30pm. Metro: Mount Vernon Sq./7th St. Convention Center.

Café Atlantico ☆☆ Finds LATIN AMERICAN Chef José Andrés is associated with seven restaurants in the Washington area; was inducted in 2007 into the James Beard Foundation's "Who's Who of Food and Beverage in America" (one of only 191 members); has been called the "boy wonder of culinary Washington" by the *New York Times;* hosts a daily television show about food that airs in Spain; has just launched a 26-episode national cooking show here in the U.S. in 2008; serves on the board of D.C.'s largest food-for-the-homeless operation, D.C. Central Kitchen; and has authored two cookbooks, the latest of which, *Passport to Spain,* has just been published—all before his 40th birthday.

It all started here. Well no, it all started in the farm town of Mieres, in northern Spain, where Andrés was born. But his success in America began 16 years ago when he was hired as the chef at nearby Jaleo, and then at Café Atlantico. He wears several toques now: He remains connected to Jaleo and is the chef behind one of the city's newest sensations, Oyamel, as well as the ever-popular Zaytinya, too. Still, you'll find Andrés in residence at the **minibar** ☆☆☆, upstairs at Café Atlantico, working with Café Atlantico chef Katsuya Fukushima to create 30 to 40 small concoctions, from foie gras in a cocoon of cotton candy to pineapple raviolis, for six people per seating, Tuesday to Saturday, at 6 and 8:30pm. The gourmet adventure costs $120 per person, not including wine, tax, and tip, and requires a reservation that's best made a month in advance.

The main restaurant of Café Atlantico, meanwhile, rocks on. All week long, but especially on weekend nights, this is a favorite hot spot in Washington's hottest neighborhood. The colorful three-tiered restaurant throbs with Latin, calypso, and reggae music; and everyone is having a fiesta—including, it seems, the waiters. If the place is packed, try to snag a seat at the second-level bar, where you can watch the genial bartender mix the potent drinks for which Café Atlantico is famous: the *caipirinha,* made of limes, sugar, and *Cachaça* (sugar-cane liqueur), or the *mojito,* a rum and crushed-mint cocktail.

Seated at the bar or table, you'll watch as your waiter makes fresh guacamole to your specified degree of spiciness. As for the main dishes, you can't get a more elaborate meal for the price. Check out the ceviche, Cornish hen wrapped in bacon served with deconstructed mole sauce, and seared scallops with coconut crispy rice and ginger, squid, and squid-ink oil; though the menu changes, you're sure to find these or their equivalent listed. Tropical side dishes and pungent sauces produce a burst of color on the plate. Feel free to ask your friendly waiter for guidance.

405 8th St. NW (at D St. NW). ℂ 202/393-0812. www.cafeatlantico.com. Reservations recommended. Lunch entrees $13–$15; dinner entrees $20–$28; pretheater menu $30 (nightly 5–6:30pm); Latino dim sum brunch (Sat–Sun): you can choose a la carte items ($2–$8 each), pay $25 for a vegetarian all-you-can-eat meal, or $35 for a deluxe version. AE, DC, DISC, MC, V. Tues–Fri 11:30am–2:30pm; Sat–Sun brunch 11:30am–2:30pm; Sun and Tues–Thurs 5–10pm; Fri–Sat 5–11pm. Bar stays open late on weekends. Metro: Archives–Navy Memorial or Gallery Place/Verizon Center (7th and F sts. exit).

Ceiba ⭐ CONTEMPORARY LATIN AMERICAN Ceiba is the creation of Jeff Tunks, the chef maestro behind TenPenh, DC Coast, and Acadiana (p. 131, 140, and 127). Here at Ceiba, Tunks works his magic on ceviches, offering four variations—grouper, shrimp, tuna, and striped bass—which you may order individually or as a sampler, as well as on other authentic Latin dishes, like the Veracruz-style red snapper, topped with tomatoes, capers, olives, and jalapeños. As is true at all Tunks establishments, fulsome drinks are integral to the experience. The ones offered here go down nicely: mojitos, mango margaritas, and pisco sours, as well as fine wines from Argentina and Chile. If you're stopping in for a quick fix, the bar menu complements those cocktails with tastes of octopus salad, beef empanadas, ceviches, and assorted others; each item is reasonably priced from $9 to $16. If you like to be where the action is, try for a table in the main dining room; it's to your right as you walk in.

701 14th St. NW. ℂ 202/393-3983. www.ceibarestaurant.com. Reservations recommended. Lunch entrees $13–$16; dinner entrees $14–$29. AE, DC, DISC, MC, V. Mon–Fri 11:30am–2:30pm; Mon–Thurs 5:30–10:30pm; Fri–Sat 5:30–11pm. Bar weekdays 2:30pm–closing; Sat 5:30pm–closing. Metro: Metro Center (13th and G sts. exit).

Central Michel Richard ⭐⭐⭐ FRENCH BISTRO It's official: Central is one of the best restaurants in the country. So says the James Beard Foundation, which in 2008 named Central "best new restaurant."

This place makes you feel good as soon as you walk through the door. It's a French-American brasserie with a *joie de vivre* ambience and a menu full of precociously re-created American and French classics. A lobster burger is layered with scallop mousse, macaroni and cheese is creamy with sour cream as well as cheeses, the fried chicken is an ungreasy version lightly dusted with bread crumbs. On and on it goes, the names of French dishes ping-ponging with American, hanger steak and onion soup to apple pan dowdy and banana split. The french fries, a country unto themselves, are perfection. Michel Richard is the chef of Citronelle (p. 152), the city's best restaurant, and he opened Central in early 2007 to entice younger diners with smaller budgets. The

Frenchman, who has lived in the U.S. for more than 30 years, has a special fondness for his adopted country; and it shows—and not just in the menu. The bistro is half dining room, half bar and exhibition kitchen; and there's an actual television in the bar. Richard wants you to have fun and, from all appearances, Central's succeeding on that score.

1001 Pennsylvania Ave. NW (at 11th St.). © 202/626-0015. www.centralmichelrichard.com. Reservations recommended. Lunch entrees $14–$33; dinner entrees $16–$33. AE, DC, DISC, MC, V. Mon–Fri 11:45am–2:30pm; Mon–Thurs 5–10:30pm; Fri–Sat 5–11pm; Sun 5–9:30pm. Metro: Metro Center (12th and F sts. exit).

D'Acqua ✪ ITALIAN/SEAFOOD D'Acqua's window-fronted dining room overlooks the Navy Memorial and courtyard, as well as a slice of Pennsylvania Avenue; its seasonal sidewalk seating allows you to feel a part of the capital's bustling scene—during the day, especially. Decorative elements inside convey an Italian coastal feel: Murano glass, wallpaper insets, glazed walls, and stucco columns, and a colorful palette of Tuscan gold and Mediterranean blue. The expansive L-shaped bar terminates at one end in a display of that day's fresh fish options, usually a dozen. You can select your fish and then request that it be grilled, oven-roasted, or salt-crust baked. But the menu also offers a variety of its own meat, fish, and pasta preparations, like the delicious *triangoli di pesce,* which is seafood and porcini ravioli with lemon and marjoram sauce. D'Acqua's opening in late 2006 means the nearby, inestimable Tosca (p. 126) now has some competition for excellent Italian cuisine in this part of town. Tosca's is still best, but D'Acqua might be a better fit for you if the combination of an Italian accent, fresh fish, and a less formal atmosphere seem more appealing.

801 Pennsylvania Ave. NW (at 8th St.). © 202/783-7717. www.dacquadc.com. Reservations accepted. Lunch entrees $11–$19; dinner entrees $16–$26. AE, DC, MC, V. Mon–Fri 11:30am–11pm; Sat–Sun 5–11pm. Metro: Gallery Place/Chinatown (7th and F sts. exit) or Archives/Navy Memorial.

Oceanaire Seafood Room ✪ SEAFOOD The Oceanaire is a good spot for a lively party, with its red-leather booths, Art Deco decor, long bar, and festive atmosphere. It would be hard to get romantic or serious about business here—there's just too much to distract you, like the sight of mile-high desserts en route to another table. Oceanaire serves big portions of everything (including cocktails, another reason to bring a bunch of friends here). On a menu that proclaims, "Fresh fish flown in daily from around the world!", you'll read intriguing names of fish on offer that day: grilled Hawaiian opah moonfish, Tasmanian steelhead trout, Ecuadorian mahimahi, and so on. These are usually served simply grilled or broiled. The waitstaff excel at explaining the tastes and textures of everything on the menu, so don't hesitate to ask. Two of the best entrees are the crab cakes, which are almost all lump crabmeat, and the fisherman's platter, a fresh, fried selection of oysters, scallops, shrimp, and other seafood, with hot matchstick fries alongside it all. The dozen varieties of oysters are fresh and plump. If you want to start with a salad, consider the BLT, which is just like eating a bacon-lettuce-tomato sandwich without the toast.

1201 F St. NW. © 202/347-2277. www.theoceanaire.com. Reservations recommended. Lunch entrees $20–$30; dinner entrees $20–$50. AE, DISC, MC, V. Mon–Thurs 11:30am–10pm; Fri 11:30am–11pm; Sat 5–11pm; Sun 5–9pm. Metro: Metro Center (12th and F sts.).

Poste ✪ MODERN AMERICAN This lovely brasserie lies within one of Washington's coolest hotels, the Monaco. You find its separate entrance via an arched carriageway that leads to a stone-paved courtyard, where the restaurant sets up tables in warm weather. Inside, past a small bar-lounge, is the dining area, which includes an

exhibition kitchen, banquettes, and a quieter back room. Poste chef Robert Weland has established himself well, settling into a pleasant culinary groove that wins praise from local critics and diners. Weland uses seasonal local ingredients to create modern American fare heavily influenced by traditional French cuisine. At lunch that means a croque-monsieur is made with Virginia ham and Gruyère on brioche; at dinner, your selections may include French onion soup, herbed fresh ricotta ravioli, red wine–braised rabbit, steak frites, and cassoulet. Desserts, too, blend French and American tastes; try the chocolate *pot de crème* (custard), which lists chili (!) as an ingredient. A wine list of 100 California and French bottles offers nearly 30 wines by the glass.

555 8th St. NW, in the Hotel Monaco. ℭ 202/783-6060. www.postebrasserie.com. Reservations recommended. Breakfast $8–$15; brunch $11–$20; lunch entrees $13–$26; dinner entrees $23–$30; pretheater menu $30. AE, DC, DISC, MC, V. Mon–Fri 7–10am and 11:30am–2:30pm; Sat–Sun 8am–2pm; Mon–Thurs 5–10pm; Fri–Sat 5–10:30pm; Sun 5–9pm. Bar daily 11:30am–closing. Metro: Gallery Place/Verizon Center (7th and F sts. exit).

Proof ✹✹ MODERN AMERICAN Proof plays up its superb location in the Penn Quarter, directly across the street from the Smithsonian American Art Museum/National Portrait Gallery. The restaurant's windowed front overlooks the stately building, while inside Proof, monitors over the bar flash images of works of art displayed in the museum. Message: Visit the museum, if you haven't already.

Meanwhile, you're in for a food and drink treat in the wine-centric Proof. Put yourself in your waiter's hands, as we did, and you will likely end up happy. We enjoyed rabbit terrine, pork rillettes, salmon flatbread (a little like small pizzas), heirloom tomatoes, wild king salmon, topped off with toffee pudding cake and a trio of sorbets for dessert. Portions are manageable, the dishes delicious. And absolutely put yourself in sommelier Sebastian Zutant's capable hands. Zutant, who is charmingly, graciously cool, knows his stuff and directs diners to those wines that will suit individual budgets and tastes.

775 G St. NW. ℭ 202/737-7663. www.proofdc.com. Reservations recommended. Lunch entrees $13–$23; dinner entrees $21–$24. AE, DC, DISC, MC, V. Mon–Fri 11:30am–2pm; Mon–Wed 5:30–10pm; Thurs–Sat 5:30–11pm; Sun 5–9:30pm. Metro: Gallery Place/Chinatown (9th and G sts. exit).

PS7's ✹✹ MODERN AMERICAN Chef Peter Smith opened PS7's in 2006 after many years working the kitchen at the award-winning Vidalia (p. 139). His culinary artistry is on excellent display here, but first you must navigate the fey menu, which organizes foods in categories of "Cool" (salads and such), "Hot" (soups and pastas), "Aqua" (fish), and "Terra" (meats). An Aqua entree might be sautéed sea scallops with Jerusalem artichokes; a Terra entree could be olive-and-garlic braised lamb shoulder. And though the portions are small, the food is rich . . . and delicious. We liked the short ribs, tuna sliders (bites of tuna tartare on Parker dinner rolls), fried oysters, and spring rolls. The dining room is elegantly modern, with floor-to-ceiling windows, lots of dark wood, and hues of charcoal, brown, and blue. The restaurant also has an expansive bar/lounge, whose menu features several items from the main menu— including those tuna sliders and fried oysters, each priced at $7 during the popular happy hour. But the lounge seating can make noshing problematic, so stand for a drink and then head to the dining room for a proper tuck-in.

777 I St. NW (at 8th St.). ℭ 202/742-8550. www.ps7restaurant.com. Reservations accepted. Lunch entrees $13–$19; dinner entrees $11–$30; 5-course tasting menu $65–$75. AE, DC, MC, V. Mon–Fri 11:30am–2:30pm; Mon–Thurs 5:30–9:45pm; Fri–Sat 5:30–10:45pm; lounge menu available Mon–Fri all day, Fri–Sat 5:30pm–closing. Metro: Gallery Place/Chinatown (H and 7th sts. exit).

Rosa Mexicano ☆ MEXICAN It's a chain, but hey, so what? Most of its other locations are in the Big Apple. This one stands out in the nation's capital for its sensational decor: a beautiful blue glass-tiled wall, over which flows a veil of water; 14-foot-high ceilings; and full-wall windows overlooking the hottest crossroads in town, at 7th and F streets, across from the Verizon Center. The place is popular. *Washington Flyer* magazine reports that Rosa serves "13,000 margaritas and 4,500 orders of guacamole every month." Trust those numbers, because both the guacamole and the margs are super. Other tasty items include quesadillas, grilled beef short ribs, and the *queso fundido* (melted cheese). Like a growing number of restaurants throughout the city, Rosa Mexicano's bar stays open from lunch until closing, even when the dining room shuts down. So if you're hungry or thirsty between lunch and dinner, stop in at the bar to consume your share of this month's quota of 13,000 margaritas and 4,500 orders of guacamole.

575 7th St. NW (at F St.). ✆ 202/783-5522. rosamexicano.com. Reservations recommended. Lunch entrees $10–$19; dinner entrees $17–$28. AE, DC, DISC, MC, V. Mon–Fri 11:30am–3pm; Sat–Sun noon–3pm; Sun–Thurs 5–10:30pm; Fri–Sat 5–11:30pm. Bar daily 11:30am–closing. Metro: Gallery Place/Verizon Center (7th and F sts. exit).

TenPenh ☆ ASIAN FUSION The atmosphere is lively, and the food here stellar. TenPenh has a separate, loungey, hard-to-leave bar; but the dining room itself is inviting, with soft lighting, comfortable booths, and an open kitchen. Jeff Tunks, the man also behind DC Coast, Ceiba, and Acadiana, presents translations of dishes he's discovered in travels throughout Asia: crispy whole fish; five-spice-chili-tea-rubbed beef tenderloin; Chinese-style smoked lobster (also available at DC Coast); wok-seared calamari; and dumplings filled with steamed shrimp and chives. In spring, look for soft-shell crab on the menu. Spring is when the sidewalk tables open up, too; and you can sit outside on a warm day and take in the sights of the capital as you finish your meal with ginger citrus crème brûlée.

1001 Pennsylvania Ave. NW (at 10th St.). ✆ 202/393-4500. www.tenpenh.com. Reservations recommended. Lunch entrees $13–$18; dinner entrees $15–$28. AE, DISC, MC, V. Mon–Fri 11:30am–2:30pm; Mon–Thurs 5:30–10:30pm; Fri–Sat 5:30–11pm. Bar weekdays 2:30pm–closing; Sat 5:30pm–closing. Metro: Archives–Navy Memorial.

Westend Bistro by Eric Ripert ☆ FRENCH-AMERICAN If you're going to use your name as part of your restaurant's name, you'd better be great. Apparently, Eric Ripert's (of New York City's esteemed Le Bernardin) name was enough to create a stampede of curious foodies when the bistro opened in November 2007. Its success continues. Me? I don't think the bistro is all that. The short menu ranges from a classic burger to fish stew to pasta Bolognese. We were fairly satisfied but not overwhelmed by our burger, macaroni and cheese, flatiron steak, and arugula salad. So maybe we were expecting too much. Perhaps we should have chosen Ripert's signature dishes of salmon rillettes and the Chesapeake seafood stew. Expect crowds weeknights and Saturdays; it's much quieter Sundays. The bistro bar is always hopping.

1190 22nd St. NW (in the Ritz-Carlton Washington Hotel). ✆ 202/974-4900. www.westendbistrodc.com. Reservations recommended. Lunch entrees $14–$29; dinner entrees $18–$36. AE, DC, DISC, MC, V. Mon–Fri 11:30am–2:30pm; Sun–Thurs 5:30–10pm; Fri–Sat 5:30–11pm. Bar Mon–Fri 11am–11pm; Sat–Sun 5–11pm (bar menu available). Metro: Foggy Bottom/West End.

Zengo ★ LATIN/ASIAN FUSION Downstairs is the lounge, a pulsing after-work destination for a multiethnic cross section of Washington professionals. Men and women in suits balance small plates of tapas on their laps or lean back upon the puffy, low-slung sofas and ottomans to drink Zengo's signature mojitos and margaritas. Up

two intimidating flights of wide, marble steps lies the dining room, which is just as popular; and it features a ceviche bar, a glass-enclosed private dining room, and tables scattered throughout the large room, with some overlooking 7th Street. Latin-Asian cuisine might be a new concept, but D.C. diners are nothing if not intrepid. And it turns out that bravery isn't necessary anyway, since ceviches, sushi rolls, and dim sum appetizers marry Asian and Latin tastes quite nicely, whether in a Thai chicken empanada or a won ton taco. Entrees, like the adobo-grilled mahimahi, prove the same.

781 7th St. NW (at H St.). © 202/393-2929. www.modernmexican.com. Reservations recommended. Lunch entrees $14–$33; dinner entrees $23–$29. AE, MC, V. Mon–Fri 11:30am–3pm; Sun–Thurs 5–10pm; Fri–Sat 5–11:30pm. Metro: Gallery Place/Verizon Center (either exit).

Zola ★★ AMERICAN Zola acquired a new chef in spring 2007. Bryan Moscatello is committed to continuing his predecessor's bent for "straight ahead American" cuisine, while adding his own creative twists. Not sure how that translates exactly, but count on deliciousness: a simple mushroom crepe or grilled lamb sandwich at lunch; delicately roasted sea scallops with creamy parsnip purée, and an artichoke-and-goat-cheese tart or lobster "mac and cheese" at dinner, with such sweets as lemon chiffon pudding with raspberries for dessert. Zola is a cleverly designed restaurant, trading on its location next to the International Spy Museum for a decor that includes red-velvet booths, backlit panels of coded KGB documents, and a center-pivoted swinging wall/door that's like something straight out of the TV show *Get Smart.* Zola, in its superb downtown location, has become a popular place for the young and single to hang. Servers are friendly. A $30 pretheater menu, available nightly 5 to 7pm, offers great value.

800 F St. NW (at 8th St.). © 202/654-0999. www.zoladc.com. Reservations recommended. Lunch entrees $11–$21; dinner entrees $16–$25; pretheater prix-fixe menu $30. AE, DC, DISC, MC, V. Mon–Fri 11:30am–midnight; Sat 5pm–midnight; Sun 5–10pm. Metro: Gallery Place/Chinatown (7th and F sts. exit).

MODERATE

Bistro D'Oc ★ FRENCH Grab your best girl or guy and duck in here at lunch to sit at a table set against the storefront window. Watch busloads of tourists waiting in line to enter Ford's Theater across the street before turning your attention to the meal: croque-monsieur, the *potage parisien* (potato and leek soup with Gruyère and croutons), or perhaps a salad of avocado, beets, and celeriac rémoulade. As you sup, the chef might emerge from the kitchen to chat in French with regulars, or to greet friends stopping in to say hello. From time to time, the place may erupt in more French, much commotion, and many kisses. You and your companion enjoy each other's company and the French-ness of the restaurant, with its orangey red-washed walls and Provençal tablecloths. If you're here at dinner, choose the hanger steak and *pommes frites,* mussels in cream sauce, bouillabaisse, or just about anything representing the tastes of Languedoc, in southwestern France. An extensive wine list includes selections from the Languedoc region.

518 10th St. NW (btw. E and F sts. NW). © 202/393-5444. www.bistrodoc.com. Reservations recommended. Lunch and brunch entrees $12–$19; dinner entrees $14–$22; daily pretheater (5:30–7pm) and post-theater (9–10pm) menu $22. AE, DC, DISC, MC, V. Mon–Sat 11:30am–2:30pm; Sun 11:30am–4pm (brunch); Mon–Thurs 5:30–10pm; Fri–Sat 5:30–11pm; Sun 4–8:30pm. Metro: Metro Center (12th and F sts. exit).

Café du Parc ★ FRENCH BRASSERIE Although Washington has only recently come into its own as a great restaurant destination, the city has always been known for its excellent French establishments. That tradition continues as more French eateries come on board, including the delightful Café du Parc next to the Willard Hotel. The

sunny two-level bistro overlooks Pershing Park and offers courtyard seating during clement weather; this is the best spot in the house. Renowned Michelin-starred chef Antoine Westermann oversees the menu and has dispatched his own assistants to staff the cafe; you can watch them at work in the open kitchen on the second floor. The dishes are redolent of Paris—*les tomates farcies aux legumes* (tomatoes stuffed with vegetables) and *choucroute alsacienne* (sauerkraut with pork and sausages). Francophiles find it a must, though most dine here at lunch, when the ambience is decidedly livelier than later in the day. (The lunch menu is a shortened version of the dinner menu.) You can carry out certain items daily until 5pm.

1401 Pennsylvania Ave. NW, part of the Willard InterContinental Washington Hotel (at 14th St.). ✆ 202/942-7000. www.cafeduparc.com. Reservations accepted. Breakfast $9.95–$23; lunch entrees $20–$27; dinner entrees $19–$29. AE, DC, DISC, MC, V. Mon–Fri 6:30–10:30am and 11:30am–2pm; Sat–Sun 7–11am and noon–2:30pm; daily 6–10pm; limited menu daily 2:30–6pm; carryout daily until 5pm. Metro: Metro Center (13th St. exit) or Federal Triangle.

Jaleo ⭐ *Finds* SPANISH In theater season, Jaleo's dining room fills and empties each evening according to the performance schedule of the Shakespeare Theater next door. Lunchtime always draws a crowd from nearby office buildings and the Hill. This restaurant and executive chef/partner José Andrés (see Café Atlantico for more about Andrés) may be credited with initiating the tapas craze in Washington, where it remains popular 16 years after Jaleo debuted. Though the menu offers a handful of entrees (available only after 5pm), you really want to consider those tapas—60 at last count, but more are always being added. These include a very simple but not-to-be-missed grilled bread layered with a paste of fresh tomatoes and topped with anchovies; date and bacon fritters; *torta es pagnola* (a layered omelet); savory warm goat cheese served with toast points; a skewer of grilled chorizo sausage atop garlic mashed potatoes; a delicious mushroom tart served with roasted red-pepper sauce; and gazpacho. Paella is among the few heartier entrees (it feeds two to four). Spanish wines, sangrias, and sherries are available by the glass. Finish with a rum-and-butter–soaked apple charlotte in bread pastry or a plate of Spanish cheeses. The casual-chic interior focuses on a large mural of a flamenco dancer inspired by John Singer Sargent's painting *Jaleo.*

Jaleo has two suburban locations, at 7271 Woodmont Ave., Bethesda, Maryland (✆ 301/913-0003), and 2250-A Crystal Drive, Arlington, Virginia (✆ 703/413-8181).

480 7th St. NW (at E St.). ✆ 202/628-7949. www.jaleo.com. Reservations accepted at lunch and for dinner until 6:30pm. Lunch entrees $8.50–$17; dinner entrees $15–$19; tapas $5–$13. AE, DC, DISC, MC, V. Sun–Mon 11:30am–10pm; Tues–Thurs 11:30am–11:30pm; Fri–Sat 11:30am–midnight. Metro: Archives or Gallery Place (7th and F sts. exit).

Legal Sea Foods ⭐ *Kids* SEAFOOD This famous family-run Boston-based seafood empire made its Washington debut in 1995. This location's expansive dining room features exposed brick and beams, booths, and an oyster bar. Sporting events, especially Boston games, are aired on a TV over the handsome bar. You're right across the street from the Verizon Center, where the city's basketball and hockey teams play. The motto here is "If it's not fresh, it's not Legal"; not only is everything fresh, but it's all from certified-safe waters.

Legal's buttery-rich clam chowder is a classic. Other worthy appetizers include garlicky golden-brown farm-raised mussels and fluffy pan-fried Maryland lump crab cakes served with mustard sauce and salad. You can have one of eight or so varieties of fresh fish grilled or opt for one of Legal's specialty dishes, like the baked Boston scrod or the New England fried clams. Top it off with a slice of Boston cream pie. Diners with allergies to wheat and gluten will be happy to know that Legal has a special

Kids Family-Friendly Restaurants

Nearly every restaurant welcomes families these days, starting, most likely, with the one in your hotel. What you need to know, mom and dad, is that many Washington restaurants are playgrounds for the city's vast population of young professionals. For example, I would love to recommend Matchbox, which serves an excellent pizza and other items kids love; but its reservations-only-for-six-or-more policy means that you and your little darlings are going to be waiting for your table (and there's almost always a wait) either in the jumping-all-day bar or out on the street in the middle of Chinatown. So read over this chapter and choose a place that sounds like its food, fun, and flexibility factors suit your family. Also consider dining early and getting a table away from the bar scene. Chinese restaurants and museum cafes are always a safe bet, and so are these:

Lebanese Taverna (p. 160) Its location down the hill from the National Zoo and its voluminous menu (including items marked for "the little ones") make the Taverna attractive to mom, dad, and the whole caboodle. Around for nearly 2 decades, the Taverna has fallen off the radar of food critics pursuing the latest greatest craze. But locals continue to favor the place, and the result is that the owners keep opening new locations—there are five now.

Legal Sea Foods (p. 133) Believe it or not, this seafood restaurant has won awards for its kids' menu. It features the usual macaroni and cheese and hot dogs, but it also offers kids' portions of steamed lobster; fried popcorn shrimp; a small fisherman's platter of shrimp, scallops, and clams; and other items, each of which comes with fresh fruit, fresh vegetables, and a choice of rice, mashed potatoes, or french fries. Prices range from $1.95 to $17.

Old Glory Barbecue (p. 157) A boisterous, laid-back place where the waiters are friendly without being patronizing. Go early, since this is one of those restaurants that becomes a bar mob scene as the evening progresses. There is a children's menu, but you may not need it—the barbecue, burgers, muffins, fries, and desserts are so good that everyone can order from the main menu.

gluten-free menu. Legal's award-winning kids' menu offers not just macaroni and cheese, but steamed lobster, popcorn shrimp, and other items, each of which comes with fresh fruit and vegetable, plus a choice of rice, mashed potatoes, or french fries. At lunch, the lobster roll is a real treat.

You'll find another Legal Sea Foods at National Airport (© **703/413-9810**).

704 7th St. NW (btw. G and H sts.). © 202/347-0007. www.legalseafoods.com. Reservations recommended, especially at lunch. Lunch entrees $12–$22; sandwiches $7.95–$19; dinner entrees $16–$43. AE, DC, DISC, MC, V. Mon–Thurs 11am–11pm; Fri–Sat 11am–midnight; Sun noon–10pm. Metro: Gallery Place/Chinatown (either exit).

Les Halles ✦ FRENCH/STEAK You will be happiest here ordering something steakish, whether *onglet,* a boneless French-cut hanger steak, steak au poivre, steak tartare, New York sirloin, or some other cut. All come with frites, which are a must. The menu isn't all beef; but it is classic French, featuring cassoulet, *confit de canard*

(duck leg slow-cooked in its own fat to crispness), escargots, onion soup, *choucroute garnie* (mélange of smoked pork, sausages, and sauerkraut), and an irresistible *frisée aux lardons* (a savory salad of chicory studded with hunks of bacon and toast, smeared thickly with Roquefort). If you spy something on the menu that's not Gallic, ignore it. Les Halles, bowing to Washingtonians' ghastly work schedules, started serving breakfast Monday through Friday, opening at 7am; choices range from a simple French croissant to a big American plate of steak and eggs and home fries.

Les Halles is big but charmingly French. The banquettes, pressed-tin ceiling, mirrors, wooden floor, and side bar capture the feel of a brasserie. A vast window front overlooks Pennsylvania Avenue and the awning-covered sidewalk cafe. Every July, from the 4th to the 14th, Les Halles hosts its Liberty Festival to celebrate America's Independence Day and France's Bastille Day (July 14). The celebration culminates in the annual Bastille Day races, for which the city actually closes a stretch of Pennsylvania Avenue that serves as the racetrack. The event turns into a wild block party.

1201 Pennsylvania Ave. NW. ✆ 202/347-6848. www.leshalles.net. Reservations recommended. Breakfast entrees $2–$13; lunch and dinner entrees $11–$28; pretheater menu Mon–Sat $18. AE, DC, DISC, MC, V. Mon–Fri 7:30–11:30am; daily 11:30am–midnight. Metro: Metro Center (12th and F sts. exit) or Federal Triangle.

Lobby Café ★★ FRENCH-AMERICAN The Ritz-Carlton Washington is home to a second restaurant, the more casual Lobby Café. Frenchman David Serrus is in the kitchen, and he is creating fabulous versions of tuna Niçoise salad, steamed asparagus with shallots vinaigrette, chicken panzanella, crispy skin steelhead trout, and for dessert, brioche bread pudding and a trio of pots de crème. (Just to name a few—and I've tried them all.) The bar/cafe has been recently renovated into a very pretty, very intimate space of banquettes and clusters of tables with cushioned chairs, all done up in shades of mossy green and gray. The bar lies at the back of the room.

1190 22nd St. NW (in the Ritz-Carlton Washington Hotel). ✆ 202/974-5556. www.ritzcarlton.com/en/properties/ WashingtonDC/Dining/TheLobbyLounge/Default.htm. Breakfast entrees $5–$26; lunch/dinner entrees $9–$28. AE, DC, DISC, MC, V. Daily 6:30am–11pm. Metro: Foggy Bottom.

Matchbox ★ PIZZA/ITALIAN This restaurant started out in 2003 as a skinny, three-level town house in Chinatown. It's an odd place to find a pizzeria, maybe, but welcome, nonetheless. By 2006, Matchbox had grown so popular that it expanded into an L-shaped structure that nearly triples its capacity and includes a patio. The key things here are the wood-fired brick ovens, which bake the thin pizza crust at temperatures as high as 900°F. You can choose a regularly featured pizza, like the "prosciutto white," which is topped with prosciutto, kalamata olives, fresh garlic, ricotta cheese, fresh mozzarella, and extra-virgin olive oil; or you can request your own set of toppings, from smoked bacon to artichoke hearts. Matchbox is actually a cut above a pizzeria, for it also serves super salads (the chopped salad is my favorite: diced tomatoes, crispy bacon, hair-thin "pasta ringlets," and greens in a creamy herb vinaigrette), appetizers, sandwiches, and entrees (the honey-glazed pecan-crusted chicken is a keeper). Its full bar on the first floor is quite the social scene. Matchbox now has a second location in the Barracks Row section of Capitol Hill, 521 8th St. SE.

713 H St. NW. ✆ 202/289-4441. www.matchboxdc.com. Pizzas and sandwiches $11–$21; lunch and dinner entrees $10–$26. AE, DC, DISC, MC, V. Sun–Thurs 11am–10:30pm; Fri–Sat 11am–1am. Metro: Gallery Place/Chinatown (H and 7th sts. exit).

Old Ebbitt Grill AMERICAN You won't find this place listed among the city's best culinary establishments, but you can bet it's included in every tour book. It's an

institution. The original Old Ebbitt was established in 1856, around the corner at 14th and F streets. The Grill moved to this location in 1980, bringing much of the old place with it. Among its artifacts are animal trophies bagged by Teddy Roosevelt, and Alexander Hamilton's wooden bears—one with a secret compartment in which it's said he hid whiskey bottles from his wife. The Old Ebbitt is attractive in a fusty sort of way, with Persian rugs strewn upon worn oak floors, beveled mirrors, flickering gaslights, etched-glass panels, and paintings of Washington scenes. The long, dark mahogany Old Bar area emphasizes the men's saloon ambience.

Tourists and office people fill the Ebbitt during the day, but flirting singles take it over at night. You'll generally have to wait for a table if you don't reserve ahead. The waiters are friendly and professional in a programmed sort of way; service could be faster. Menus change daily but always include certain favorites: burgers, trout Parmesan (Virginia trout dipped in egg batter and Parmesan cheese, flash fried), crab cakes, and oysters—Old Ebbitt's raw bar is its saving grace when all else fails. Aside from the fresh oysters, the tastiest dishes are usually the seasonal ones; fresh ingredients make all the difference.

675 15th St. NW (btw. F and G sts.). ℂ 202/347-4800. www.ebbitt.com. Reservations recommended. Breakfast $9.95–$14; brunch $5.95–$27; lunch and dinner entrees $13–$27; raw bar $8.95–$21. AE, DC, DISC, MC, V. Mon–Fri 7:30am–1am; Sat–Sun 8:30am–1am. Bar open until 2am Sun–Thurs, 3am Fri–Sat. Metro: Metro Center (13th and F sts. exit).

Oyamel ⭐⭐⭐ LATIN AMERICAN/MEXICAN José Andrés, the 30-something Spaniard who has wowed us repeatedly as chef at Jaleo, Café Atlantico, Zaytinya, and minibar, does it again, even better, at Oyamel. With its limited reservations policy meant to encourage passersby and spontaneous walk-ins, open-all-day hours, menu of antojitos priced below $10 each (the menu lists a few entrees, but it's these small plates that you'll want to order), hearty cocktails, and exuberant atmosphere, Oyamel serves as the ultimate chill pill for the capital's hungry and stressed-out wonks at their most wound-up. Order the Oyamel margarita, which is topped with salt-air foam, and the table-made guacamole (ask for the spiciest version, which is still not that spicy). Try something from the specials, like the beer-battered soft-shell crab (only $10!) served with a mango-roasted corn salsa that I gobbled up. The menu features items you won't see on offer at any other of D.C.'s Mexican cantinas, like the *"cochinita pibil con cebolla en escabeche"* (Yucatan-style pit-barbecued pork with pickled red onion and Mexican sour orange); try the taco version at only $3.50. With its lively bar scene and prime corner location in the heart of the Penn Quarter, Oyamel is always hopping.

401 7th St. NW (at D St.). ℂ 202/628-1005. www.oyamel.com. Limited reservations. Small plates and tacos $3–$12; lunch entrees $11–$15; dinner entrees $19–$25. AE, DC, DISC, MC, V. Sun–Mon 11:30am–10pm; Tues–Thurs 11:30am–11:30pm; Fri–Sat 11:30am–midnight. Metro: Gallery Place/Chinatown (7th and F sts. exit) or Archives/Navy Memorial.

Rasika ⭐⭐ INDIAN This sexy-cool restaurant opened in December 2005 and immediately started to attract the Washington glitterati, including not only Bill and Hil Clinton, but also daughter Chelsea and her pals. Soft lighting, cinnamon-and-spice tones, silk panels, and dangling glass beads contribute a rich and sensuously attractive feeling to the dining room and its adjoining lounge. Everyone's drinking martinis, usually the clove or the pomegranate. As for the food, it's divine. Try the crispy spinach, ginger scallops, tandoori salmon, black cod, or lobster masala.

633 D St. NW (at 7th St.). ℂ 202/637-1222. www.rasikarestaurant.com. Reservations recommended. Lunch entrees $14–$28; dinner entrees $15–$28; pretheater menu $28. AE, DC, DISC, MC, V. Mon–Fri 11:30am–2:30pm; Mon–Thurs

5:30–10:30pm; Fri–Sat 5:30–11pm. Lounge stays open throughout the day serving light meals. Metro: Archives/Navy Memorial or Gallery Place/Verizon Center (7th and F sts. exit).

Zaytinya 🐫🐫 GREEK/TURKISH/MIDDLE EASTERN How popular is Zaytinya? Well, the restaurant serves, on average, 750 people per night during the week and 1,000 per night on weekends. It's big and it's busy and it always has been. Executive Chef José Andrés is behind it all. (See reviews of Jaleo, where he continues as the executive chef/partner, and of Café Atlantico, where he is the creative director.)

The place takes reservations only at lunch and for pretheater dinners, 5 to 6:30pm. If you have to wait for a table, join the rollicking bar scene, where 20- and 30-somethings can be counted on to provide nightly entertainment. Once seated, you receive a basket of hot and billowy-thin shells of pita bread, along with a saucer of olive oil swirled with pomegranate syrup. Your waiter will guide you through the menu; explain that the wine list, like the meze dishes, are a mixture of Greek, Turkish, and Lebanese specialties; and inform you that the word "Zaytinya" is Turkish for "olive oil." Although the dinner menu lists several entrees, what you want to do here is order lots of little dishes: zucchini-cheese cakes, which come with a caper and yogurt sauce; the carrot-apricot-pine nut fritters served with pistachio sauce; sardines; a marinated salmon; *fattoush,* or salad of tomatoes and cucumbers mixed with pomegranate reduction, sumac, and olive oil, with crispy pita-bread croutons; and shrimp with tomatoes, onions, ouzo, and kefalograviera cheese. For dessert, try a Turkish coffee chocolate cake or the seductive apples in saffron cream.

701 9th St. NW (at G St.). ℂ 202/638-0800. www.zaytinya.com. Reservations at lunch and pretheater dinner 5–6:30pm. Mezze items $5.50–$12; dinner entrees $13–$25. AE, DC, DISC, MC, V. Sun–Mon 11:30am–10pm; Tues–Thurs 11:30am–11:30pm; Fri–Sat 11:30am–midnight. Metro: Gallery Place/Chinatown (9th St. exit).

INEXPENSIVE

Tony Cheng's Seafood Restaurant 🐫 CHINESE/SEAFOOD Most of the restaurants in Chinatown look seedy, no matter how good the food might be. Tony Cheng's is the most presentable of Chinatown's eateries, and it's also a good choice if you like Cantonese specialties and spicy Szechuan and Hunan cuisine. Downstairs is the Mongolian Barbecue eatery, where you have a choice of dipping your own vegetables, seafood, and meats in a "hot pot" of boiling broth or ordering a $18-per-person, all-you-can-eat spread of foods you select for the chef to barbecue over a huge grill. The second-floor Tony Cheng's Seafood Restaurant has been here for decades. It has earned a reputation for its Cantonese roast duck (see it for yourself before ordering, since it is displayed in a case at the back of the restaurant); lobster or Dungeness crab, stir-fried and served with either ginger and scallions or black-bean sauce; and Szechuan crispy beef, to name just a few. Dim sum is available at lunch daily, but during the week you order items off the menu, rather than from rolling carts.

619 H St. NW (btw. 6th and 7th sts.). ℂ 202/842-8669 (Mongolian Barbecue) and 202/371-8669 (Seafood Restaurant). www.tonychengrestaurant.com. Reservations recommended. Mongolian Barbecue entrees $18 all-you-can-eat, or $11–$20. Seafood restaurant lunch entrees $10–$15; dinner entrees $13–$19. AE, MC, V. Sun–Thurs 11am–11pm; Fri–Sat 11am–midnight. Metro: Gallery Place/Chinatown (7th and H sts. exit).

5 Midtown

VERY EXPENSIVE

BLT Steak 🐫 STEAK Are steakhouses passé? Not this one, that's for sure. The arrival of BLT Steak in late 2006 introduced D.C. to a younger, hipper cut of beeferie than the city's used to. The restaurant, with its expansive bar, suede seats, large and

airy room, and soul-music sound system, is a popular stamping ground for young professionals on weeknights and sees a steady stream of power brokers at all times. (BLT lies on a street btw. the White House and the K Street corridor of law firm and lobbyist offices.) The BLT stands not for bacon, lettuce, and tomato, but for Bistro Laurent Tourondel, the chef, whose other BLTs are located in New York City, San Juan, and assorted other hot spots. A meal begins with a basket of enormous, complimentary Gruyère popovers and a little pot of country pâté. Menu recommendations include the raw bar offerings, hanger steak, the American wagyu rib-eye (if you don't mind paying $92 for your entree!), blue cheese Tater Tots, onion rings, any of the salads, and the souffléd crepe with ricotta cheese for dessert.

1625 I St. NW (at 17th St.). ☎ 202/689-8999. www.bltsteak.com. Reservations accepted. Lunch entrees $16–$45; dinner entrees $24–$45 (prices go as high as $92 for wagyu beef). AE, DC, DISC, MC, V. Mon–Fri 11:30am–2:30pm; Mon–Thurs 5:30–11pm; Fri–Sat 5:30–11:30pm. Metro: Farragut West (17th St. exit) or Farragut North (K St. exit).

Equinox ★★ NEW AMERICAN Everyone seems to love Equinox, whose proximity to the White House guarantees a high-and-mighty clientele. Regulars appreciate that Equinox is not splashy in any way—it's just a pretty, comfortable restaurant serving creatively delicious American food. You'll eat all your vegetables here, because as much care is taken with these garnishes as with the entree itself. And every entree comes with a garnish or two, like creamed spinach or forest mushrooms with applewood bacon, or white-bean ragout. You can order additional side dishes; consider the macaroni and cheese: Gruyère and black truffle reduction. The home runs, of course, are the entrees. You order a la carte for lunch, and either a la carte or one of three tasting menus for dinner: $57 for three courses, $70 for four courses, and $85 for six courses. Standouts have included pan-roasted Alaska halibut with artichoke ragout; crab cakes made with lump crab mixed with capers, brioche bread crumbs, mayonnaise, and lemon-butter sauce; and veal strip loin with crispy sweetbreads and potato mousseline. The menu identifies dishes made from animals raised in accordance with Humane Farm Animal Care guidelines.

818 Connecticut Ave. NW. ☎ 202/331-8118. www.equinoxrestaurant.com. Reservations recommended. Lunch entrees $19–$30; dinner entrees $29–$35; dinner tasting menus $57, $70, and $85. AE, DC, DISC, MC, V. Mon–Fri 11:30am–2pm; Mon–Thurs 5:30–10pm; Fri–Sat 5:30–10:30pm; Sun 5–9pm. Metro: Farragut West (17th St. exit).

The Palm ★ *Finds* STEAK The Palm is one in a chain of 25 locations that started 83 years ago in New York—but here in D.C., it feels like an original. The Washington Palm is 37 years old; though recently renovated and expanded to include a glass-enclosed veranda, its walls are still covered with the caricatures of regulars, the famous and the not-so-famous. If you think you see Chris Matthews at a table, you're probably right. You can't go wrong with steak, whether it's the 36-ounce dry-aged New York strip or sliced in a steak salad. Oversize lobsters are a specialty, and certain side dishes are a must: creamed spinach, onion rings, palm fries (something akin to deep-fried potato chips), and hash browns. You can order half-portions of these, so you have no excuse but to order at least one. Several of the longtime waiters like to kid with you a bit, but the service is always fast.

1225 19th St. NW. ☎ 202/293-9091. www.thepalm.com. Reservations recommended. Lunch entrees $13–$20; dinner entrees $15–$64 (most items are in the neighborhood of $30–$39). AE, DC, MC, V. Mon–Fri 11:45am–10pm; Sat 5:30–10pm; Sun 5:30–9:30pm. Metro: Dupont Circle (19th St./South exit).

The Prime Rib ★★ STEAK/SEAFOOD The 33-year-old Prime Rib has plenty of competition in D.C., but it makes no difference. Beef lovers still consider this The

Place. Male beef lovers, anyway: The Prime Rib has a definite men's club feel about it, with brass-trimmed black walls, leopard-skin carpeting, and comfortable black-leather chairs and banquettes. Waiters are in black tie, and a pianist at the baby grand plays show tunes and Irving Berlin classics at lunch; at dinner, a bass player joins the pianist.

The meat is from the best grain-fed steers and has been aged for 4 to 5 weeks. Steaks and cuts of roast beef are thick, tender, and juicy. In case you had any doubt, the Prime Rib's prime rib is the best item on the menu—juicy, thick, top-quality meat. For less carnivorous diners, there are about a dozen seafood entrees, including an excellent crab imperial. Mashed potatoes are done right, as are the fried potato skins; but I recommend the hot cottage fries.

2020 K St. NW. ℂ 202/466-8811. www.theprimerib.com. Reservations recommended. Jacket and tie required for men. Lunch entrees $13–$28; dinner entrees $22–$45. AE, DC, MC, V. Mon–Thurs 11:30am–3pm and 5–10:30pm; Fri 11:30am–3pm and 5–11pm; Sat 5–11pm. Metro: Farragut West (18th St. exit).

Taberna del Alabardero ★★ *Finds* SPANISH Dress up to visit this truly elegant restaurant. You'll receive royal treatment from the Spanish staff, who are accustomed to attending to the real thing—Spain's King Juan Carlos and Queen Sofia have dined here. The Taberna is also a favorite of dignitaries attending meetings at the nearby World Bank and International Monetary Fund. The Spanish government recognized the Taberna as "the best Spanish restaurant outside Spain."

The dining room is ornate, with red tufted banquettes, green satin stretched across chairs, and gilded cherubs placed at ceiling corners. Order a plate of tapas to start: lightly fried calamari, shrimp in garlic and olive oil, artichokes sautéed with thin smoky serrano ham, and marinated mushrooms. Although the a la carte menu changes with the seasons (look for the duck breast with sweet vinegar sauce in spring), several paellas are always available, including the rich and flavorful seafood paella served on saffron rice. Other signature dishes are the stuffed squid sauced in its own ink and the traditional salted cod *(bacalao)*. The Taberna also offers vegetarian lunch and dinner menus. The wine list features a selection of 315 wines, some American, but mostly Spanish. Good deal: Weekdays 3 to 7pm, tapas are half-price at the bar.

1776 I St. NW (entrance on 18th St. NW). ℂ 202/429-2200. www.alabardero.com. Reservations recommended. Jacket and tie for men suggested. Tapas $6–$16; lunch entrees $19–$29; dinner entrees $30–$39. AE, DC, DISC, MC, V. Mon–Fri 11:30am–2:30pm; Mon–Sat 5:30–10:30pm. Metro: Farragut West (18th St. exit).

Vidalia ★★ REGIONAL AMERICAN/SOUTHERN Chef R. J. Cooper tied with Palena (p. 160) chef Frank Ruta for the James Beard Foundation's 2007 award as the best chef for the Mid-Atlantic region, and both the restaurant and its chefs frequently win prestigious culinary awards. You'll understand why when you dine here. Vidalia's cuisine marries tastes of various regions of the South, with an emphasis on New Orleans. Featured dishes might include a roasted young pig with braised savoy cabbage or rockfish filé with succotash and turnip greens. A signature entree is scrumptious sautéed shrimp on a mound of creamed grits and caramelized onions with tasso ham in a cilantro butter sauce. Corn bread and biscuits with apple butter are served at every meal. Vidalia is known for its lemon chess pie and pecan pie, but always check out alternatives, which might be an apple napoleon or caramel cake. Vidalia offers an extensive wine list; at least 30 are offered by the glass, in both 3-ounce and 6-ounce pours.

If you're hesitant to dine at a restaurant that's down a flight of steps from the street, your doubts will vanish as soon as you enter Vidalia's tiered dining room. There's a party going on down here. Arrive between 5 and 7pm weeknights and you'll get in on

the extremely popular wine tastings in the cozy wine bar. The chef sends out little canapés, like miniature BLTs; and both the wine tastings and the hors d'oeuvres are complimentary!

1990 M St. NW. ✆ 202/659-1990. www.vidaliadc.com. Reservations recommended. Lunch entrees $15–$19; dinner entrees $23–$34. AE, DC, DISC, MC, V. Mon–Fri 11:30am–2:30pm; Mon–Thurs 5:30–10pm; Fri–Sat 5:30–10:30pm; Sun 5:30–9:30pm. Metro: Dupont Circle (19th St. exit)

EXPENSIVE

Corduroy ✿✿ AMERICAN In March 2008, Corduroy, with chef Tom Power steady at the helm, moved from its perch inside the Four Points Sheraton Hotel to its own place in the up-and-coming convention center neighborhood. Cheffing at Corduroy since 2000, Power has built a following in this food-mad city, where diners can tell you exactly how many stars the best restaurants have been awarded by local food critics. Corduroy received three stars and came in at #17 out of 100, in the *Washingtonian* magazine's 2008 ranking of the city's top restaurants. Pretty amazing. Fans have followed Power to his new digs in a historic town house, where the rooms are cozy and the kitchen is on display. Winning dishes here include prime rib-eye with lyonnaise potatoes, red snapper bisque, duck egg and leg salad, and strawberry tart with strawberry creamsicle. Corduroy was serving only dinner at the time of this writing, but expected to be adding lunch service soon.

1122 9th St. NW. ✆ 202/589-0699. www.corduroydc.com. Reservations recommended. Dinner entrees $20–$38. AE, DC, DISC, MC, V. Mon–Sat 5:30–10:30pm. Metro: Mt. Vernon Sq./7th St./Convention Center.

DC Coast ✿ AMERICAN The dining room is sensational: two stories high, with glass-walled balcony, immense oval mirrors hanging over the bar, and a full-bodied stone mermaid poised to greet you at the entrance. Gather at the bar first to feel a part of the loud and trendy scene; while you're there, why not nosh on something from the bar menu, perhaps the crispy fried calamari or a luscious flatbread pizza? This continues to be one of the city's most popular restaurants, so call ahead to book a reservation. Chef Jeff Tunks, the chef behind TenPenh, Ceiba, and Acadiana (p. 131, 128, and 127), started his dynasty with DC Coast, which opened in 1998. Here, Tunks fuses the coastal cuisines of the Mid-Atlantic, Gulf, and West Coast. Almost always on the menu are his Chinese-style smoked lobster with crispy fried spinach, pan-roasted sea scallops, and the crispy whole striped bass, as well as the fish filet encrusted with portobello paste and served with truffled potatoes and porcini broth. Seafood is a big part of the menu, but there are a handful of meat dishes too; try the pork chop with sweet potato purée.

1401 K St. NW. ✆ 202/216-5988. www.dccoast.com. Reservations recommended. Lunch entrees $13–$29; dinner entrees $22–$29. AE, DC, DISC, MC, V. Mon–Fri 11:30am–2:30pm; Mon–Thurs 5:30–10:30pm; Fri–Sat 5:30–11pm; Sun 5:30–9:30pm. Bar weekdays 2:30pm–closing; Sat 5:30pm–closing. Metro: McPherson Square (14th St./Franklin Sq. exit).

The Oval Room ✿ MODERN AMERICAN The Oval Room is a local favorite, another winner for owner Ashok Bajaj, who also owns the Bombay Club (p. 141) right across the street and Rasika (p. 136) in the Penn Quarter. Current chef Tony Conti previously served as executive sous chef for Jean-Georges Vongerichten in New York. His reasonably priced modern American cuisine offers ricotta gnocchi, caramelized beef tenderloin, crispy snapper, and the like. The Oval Room is a handsome restaurant, with contemporary art hanging on its pale green walls. Its atmosphere is congenial, not stuffy, no doubt because the bar area separating the restaurant

into two distinct rooms sends cheerful sounds in either direction. In case you haven't made the connection, the Oval Room is a short walk from the White House.

800 Connecticut Ave. NW (at Lafayette Sq.). ℂ 202/463-8700. www.ovalroom.com. Reservations recommended. Lunch entrees $7–$24; dinner entrees $16–$30; pretheater dinner (5:30–6:30pm) $29. AE, DISC, MC, V. Mon–Fri 11:30am–3pm; Fri–Sat 5:30am–10:30pm. Metro: Farragut West (17th St. exit).

MODERATE

Bombay Club *Finds* INDIAN The delightful Bombay Club pleases patrons who know their Indian food as well as those who've never tried it. Dishes present an easy introduction to Indian food for the uninitiated and are sensitive to varying tolerances for spiciness.

The spiciest item on the menu is the fiery green chili chicken ("not for the faint-hearted," the menu warns). You can't go wrong ordering a tandoori entree (a food that has been marinated, then grilled and baked in a clay oven). Most popular are the tandoori salmon; the chicken tandoori, which is marinated in an almond, cashew, yogurt, ginger, and garlic dressing; and the delicately prepared lobster Lababdar. The Bombay Club is known for its vegetarian offerings (try the black lentils cooked overnight on a slow fire) and for its Sunday champagne brunch, which offers a buffet of fresh juices, fresh baked breads, and assorted Indian dishes. Patrons are as fond of the service as the cuisine; waiters seem straight out of *Jewel in the Crown,* attending to your every whim. This is one place where you can linger over a meal as long as you like. Slow-moving ceiling fans and wicker furniture accentuate the colonial British ambience. A pianist plays nightly.

815 Connecticut Ave. NW. ℂ 202/659-3727. www.bombayclubdc.com. Reservations recommended. Entrees $7.50–$32; Sun brunch $20. AE, DC, MC, V. Mon–Fri and Sun brunch 11:30am–2:30pm; Mon–Thurs 6–10:30pm; Fri–Sat 6–11pm; Sun 5:30–9pm. Metro: Farragut West (17th St. exit).

Brasserie Beck BELGIAN The place started rocking when the doors opened in April 2007, and it hasn't stopped. *Esquire* magazine placed Beck (along with another D.C. favorite, Oyamel, p. 136) on its top-20 list of "Best New Restaurants in America." Chef Robert Wiedmaier's West End restaurant, Marcel's (p. 151), is one of the best fine-dining establishments in the District. Beck's, which, like Marcel's, is named for one of Wiedmaier's young sons, has immediately taken off as one of the city's best bistros and hot spots. The bar scene is a crucial element of both ambience and popularity; and Beck's beckons, seating 21 people at its huge marble-and-walnut bar and handling many more beyond that. Restaurant design also plays its part; Beck's features an attractive open kitchen of glass, steel, and cobalt-blue tiles, and the overall feel of a large train station, with large round clocks on display beneath 22-foot-high ceilings. But in the end it comes down to the food, and here, Beck's pegs it: Belgian tastes of in-house cured salmon, beef carbonnade, steamed mussels served three ways, frites, duck confit, lamb sausage, and the list goes on. Beer-lover's bonus: a large assortment of Belgian beers on tap and by the bottle.

1101 K St. NW (at 11th St.). ℂ 202/408-1717. www.beckdc.com. Reservations recommended. Lunch and dinner entrees $16–$24. AE, DC, MC, V. Mon–Thurs 11:30am–11:30pm; Fri 11:30am–1am; Sat 5pm–1am; Sun 11:30am–8pm. Metro: Metro Center (11th and G sts. exit, with a few blocks' walk from there).

INEXPENSIVE

Café Asia ASIAN FUSION It's easy to miss Café Asia, nestled as it is between hair salons and offices on I Street right near the White House. Inside is a different story. The decor and menu both stand out in really interesting ways. The restaurant has

three levels to it, set within an atrium. From street level, walk downstairs to the main dining room. The furniture here looks like it was made for child's play; it comes in circular and rectangular shapes and colors of orange, yellow, and white, and these pieces are set closer to the ground than normal. Upstairs is more of a lounge area, overlooking the lower level; one more flight up is reserved mostly for private parties.

The menu here is Pan-Asian: Chinese, Indonesian, Japanese, Thai. If your waitress steers you to something "interesting," you can take that to mean "spicy," like the Indonesian fried rice, which is "more interesting than Chinese." (Yeah—it's got chilies in it, for one thing.) So if you like Americanized, or tamed down, Asian food, you might be happy with the teriyaki and satays. You have many more choices if you want to sample exotic food. Have a glass of water handy, but do try the *nasi uduk,* which is a tasty Indonesian coconut rice platter with spicy beef, crispy anchovies, pickled vegetables, *emping* (acorn chips), chicken satay, and spicy prawn sauce. Another winner is the *ikan pepes,* which is Indonesian grilled fish filet with spicy turmeric sauce, fresh basil, and lemon grass, wrapped in banana leaves. Café Asia also serves delicious sushi. Young professionals throng Café Asia's happy hour, Monday through Saturday from 4 to 7:30pm, when nigiri sushi is available for $1.25 per piece and select draft beers are sold for $2.50.

1720 I St. NW. ⓒ 202/659-2696. www.cafeasia.com. Reservations accepted. Lunch and dinner entrees $9–$16. AE, DC, DISC, MC, V. Mon–Thurs 11:30am–11pm; Fri 11:30am–midnight; Sat noon–midnight; Sun noon–11pm. Metro: Farragut West (17th St. exit) or Farragut North (K St. exit).

6 U Street Corridor

MODERATE

Bistro Tabaq ⭐ MIDDLE EASTERN Tabaq resides in a four-story building, but its restaurant levels are on the first and fourth floor. The fourth floor is the place to be; you'll be on the roof with a glorious view of the city, including the far-off Capitol and Washington Monument. A glass ceiling and glass doors open and close to accommodate the weather, so you can dine here year-round. The terrace is very dimly lit, making this a favorite spot for couples but a frustrating experience for anyone trying to decipher the menu in the almost-dark. And a word about those four flights to the top: Women might want to don longer skirts, so as not to reveal too much to the ones following in their wake, and to opt for lower heels, rather than trying to teeter their way up. Tabaq does try to keep to a dress code, though, so forget the athletic look. It's all about tapas here, with about 40 from which to choose. Winners include hummus, the tabaq salad, and *manti,* a Turkish-style beef ravioli, served with red pepper, garlic, and yogurt. From the small list of entrees, the Mediterranean sea bass, served with almond and currant rice, is your best choice. If the wait's too long for the terrace, you can always dine in the first-floor Red Room, quite romantic in its own way.

1336 U St. NW (at 13th St.). ⓒ 202/265-0965. www.tabaqdc.com. Reservations accepted. Entrees $11–$20; small plates $14–$22. AE, DC, DISC, MC, V. Sun–Thurs 5–11pm; Fri–Sat 5pm–midnight; Sat–Sun 11am–4pm. Metro: U St.–Cardozo (13th St. exit).

Café Saint-Ex ⭐ AMERICAN There goes the neighborhood, some say, only we're talking gentrification here. Some longtime residents are not so crazy about the fact that this precious restaurant/bar attracts legions, including food critics, who are

awarding the place several stars. And you know what that means: double-parked cars, lines out the door, and rowdy customers into the wee hours. This part of D.C. is changing, no doubt about it; if you're intrigued, Café Saint-Ex is worth investigating. Named for author/aviator Antoine de Saint-Exupéry, the dining room builds on the flight idea with black-and-white photos of pilots and aviation memorabilia. The critics are crowing about the charming atmosphere and certain items on the menu, like the roast chicken; the grilled mahimahi; and the beets, grapefruit, and feta cheese salad. Personally, I love the fried green tomato BLT. D.C. hipsters stay on or arrive later to get in on Saint's nightlife scene, which features a DJ spinning hip-hop or indie tunes downstairs at Gate 54.

1847 14th St. NW, btw. S and T sts. ℰ 202/265-7839. www.saint-ex.com. No reservations (this policy may change). Lunch and brunch entrees $8–$11; dinner entrees $10–$24; pretheater menu $32. AE, MC, V. Lunch Tues–Fri 11am–5pm; brunch Sat–Sun 11am–4pm; dinner daily 5pm–1:30am (until 2:30am Fri–Sat). Metro: U St.–Cardozo (13th St. exit).

Creme Café and Lounge ✦ AMERICAN/SOUTHERN All sorts of restaurants are opening in this U Street neighborhood, and all sorts of people are flocking to dine here. But the streets remain urban and edgy in appearance; in fact, no matter how upscale their eateries, crime occurs more often here than in most other parts of town. Creme, meanwhile, is a cross between upscale and down-home. First off, it's Creme, as in *cream,* not crème, as in *them.* On the menu are fare like shrimp and grits, pork and beans. But these are a twist on your grandmother's versions—hearty and delicious, but more sophisticated. The beans are no ordinary canned baked beans, but a mélange of cannellini and fava beans. Like everyplace else on U Street, Creme gets noisy and crowded as the night goes on, but try to stick around long enough for dessert. The coconut cake's my favorite—and everyone else's, too, it seems.

1322 U St. NW (at 14th St.). ℰ 202/234-1884. Reservations suggested. www.cremedc.com. Dinner entrees $9–$22. AE, DC, DISC, MC, V. Sun–Thurs 6–10:30pm; Fri–Sat 6–11:30pm; Sat 11am–3pm; Sun 10am–4pm. Metro: U St.–Cardozo.

INEXPENSIVE

Ben's Chili Bowl *Finds* AMERICAN Ben's is a veritable institution, a mom-and-pop place where everything looks, tastes, and probably even costs pretty much the same as when the restaurant opened in 1958. Ben's has won national recognition, too, including an award granted by the prestigious James Beard Foundation in 2004 for being an "America's Classic," one of four restaurants in the country so named for being "renowned for their timeless appeal."

The most expensive item on the menu is the veggie-burger sub for $8.15. Formica counters, red bar stools, and a jukebox that plays Motown and reggae tunes—that's Ben's. Ben's continues as a gathering place for black Washington and visitors like Bill Cosby, who's a longtime customer (a chili half-smoke is named after him). Everyone's welcome, though, even the late-nighters who come streaming out of nearby nightclubs at 2 or 3am on the weekend. Of course, the chili, cheese fries, and half-smokes are great, but so are the breakfast items. Try the salmon cakes, grits, scrapple, or blueberry pancakes (available during breakfast hours only).

1213 U St. NW. ℰ 202/667-0909. www.benschilibowl.com. Reservations not accepted. Entrees $2.50–$8.15. No credit cards. Mon–Thurs 6am–2am; Fri 6am–4am; Sat 7am–4am; Sun 11am–8pm. Metro: U St.–Cardozo (13th St. exit).

7 Adams-Morgan

EXPENSIVE

Cashion's Eat Place ⚶⚶ *(Finds* AMERICAN The name remains, even though original chef/owner Ann Cashion is no longer in residence, having sold her restaurant to her longtime sous chef, John Manalatos. Cashion has turned her full attention to Johnny's Half Shell (p. 121), which she owns with Johnny Fulchino. Fans of this award-winning restaurant are glad to find that so far it hasn't changed. Cashion's Eat Place is still very much a neighborhood restaurant—easy, warm, comfortable—that also just happens to serve out-of-this-world cuisine. Manalatos is putting his own stamp upon the cooking and changing the menu daily. A recent menu listed eight appetizers, including a Pennsylvania-raised goose egg, with arugula, Parmesan, truffled peaches, and bread crumbs, as well as seven entrees, including an Ecofriendly Foods pork leg with parsnip purée and sautéed local asparagus. An "after dark" menu is served Friday and Saturday nights from midnight to 2am at the bar; items include pork carnitas and wild mushroom risotto, ranging in price from $4 to $14 each. Sunday brunch is popular, too; you can choose from breakfast fare (challah French toast, spinach-and-Gruyère omelets) or heartier items (grilled rainbow trout, croque-monsieurs).

The charming dining room curves around the slightly raised bar. In warm weather, the glass-fronted Cashion's opens invitingly to the sidewalk and its tables. Tables at the back offer a view of the small kitchen. In winter, ask for a table away from the front door, which lets in a blast of cold air with each new arrival.

1819 Columbia Rd. NW. ℭ 202/797-1819. www.cashionseatplace.com. Reservations recommended. Brunch $8.95–$12; dinner entrees $19–$30. MC, V. Tues 5:30–10pm; Wed–Sat 5:30–11pm; Sun 11:30am–2:30pm and 5:30–10pm. Metro: Woodley Park/Adams-Morgan, with a walk.

MODERATE

Las Canteras ⚶ LATIN AMERICAN/PERUVIAN Traditional and contemporary Peruvian dishes are on the menu at this affordable new restaurant in the heart of Adams-Morgan, including three versions of *ceviche* (fish marinated in lime juice); *causa* (a dish made with mashed potatoes stuffed with chicken); and quinoa salad, which tosses the quinoa (grain) with chickpeas, tahini, and lime juice. Las Canteras is a pretty restaurant, decorated with colorful Peruvian fabrics, handcrafted wrought-iron chandeliers, and photographs of Machu Picchu and other Andean landmarks. Head here Tuesday through Thursday night at 5pm for the early-bird special, a three-course meal for $24.

2307 18th St. NW (at Kalorama St.). ℭ 202/265-1780. www.lascanterasdc.com. Lunch and dinner entrees $11–$18. AE, DC, MC, V. Tues–Sun 11am–3pm; Tues–Thurs and Sun 5–10pm; Fri–Sat 5–11pm. Metro: Woodley Park/Adams-Morgan, with a walk.

Lauriol Plaza ⚶ MEXICAN/SPANISH/LATIN AMERICAN This place is large (it seats 330) but immensely popular; so despite its size, you may still have to wait for a table. Lauriol Plaza looks like a factory from the outside, but inside it's stunning. You have a choice of sitting at sidewalk tables, on the rooftop deck, or in the two-tiered dining room with its large mural of a Spanish fiesta on one wall and windows covering another. Try the margaritas, *carne asada* (grilled meat) fajitas, and tasty *camarones diablo* (six broiled jumbo shrimp seasoned with spices). Anything mesquite grilled is sure to please. Servings seem as large as the restaurant. Sunday brunch, also recommended, is served from 11am to 3pm. With so many diners here, Lauriol Plaza is a good place to people-watch.

Adams-Morgan & Dupont Circle Dining

ACKC Cocoa Gallery **16**	Indique **2**	Palena **1**
Ben's Chili Bowl **8**	Komi **17**	The Palm **23**
Bistro Tabaq **10**	Las Canteras **6**	Pesce **21**
Blue Duck Tavern **26**	Lauriol Plaza **12**	Pizzeria Paradiso **18**
Café Saint-Ex **11**	Lebanese Taverna **3**	Sala Thai **18**
Cashion's Eat Place **4**	Lobby Café **25**	Tabard Inn **22**
City Lights of China **13**	Locolat Café **7**	Teaism Dupont Circle **14**
Crème Café **9**	Meskerem **5**	Vidalia **24**
Hank's Oyster Bar **15**	Obelisk **19**	Westend Bistro by Eric Ripert **25**

1835 18th St. NW. ℰ 202/387-0035. www.lauriolplaza.com. Reservations not accepted. Entrees $6.50–$18. AE, DC, DISC, MC, V. Sun–Thurs 11:30am–11pm; Fri–Sat 11:30am–midnight. Metro: Dupont Circle.

INEXPENSIVE

Meskerem ETHIOPIAN In the past few years, Washington has seen an explosion of Ethiopian restaurants, notably in the 9th and U streets area, where you will find at least 10 cafes offering authentic Ethiopian cuisine backed up by traditional or contemporary musical entertainment. But Meskerem in Adams-Morgan was one of the first Ethiopian restaurants to open in Washington and remains among the best, especially for newcomers to the food. It's attractive; the three-level, high-ceilinged dining room has an oval skylight girded by a painted sunburst and yellow-washed walls hung with African art and musical instruments. On the mezzanine level, you sit at *messobs* (basket tables) on low, carved Ethiopian chairs or upholstered leather poufs.

Diners share large platters of food, which they scoop up with a sourdough crepe-like pancake called *injera* (no silverware here). You'll notice a lot of *watt* dishes, which refers to the traditional Ethiopian stew, made with your choice of beef, chicken, lamb, or vegetables, in varying degrees of hot and spicy; the *alicha watts* are milder and more delicately flavored. You might share an entree—perhaps *yegeb kay watt* (succulent lamb in thick, hot *berbere* sauce)—along with a sampler platter of five vegetarian dishes, served with tomato and potato salads. Some combination platters comprise an array of beef, chicken, lamb, and vegetables. There's a full bar, and the wine list includes Ethiopian honey wine and beer.

2434 18th St. NW. ℰ 202/462-4100. www.ethiopianrestaurant.com. Reservations recommended. Lunch and dinner entrees $6.50–$15. AE, DC, MC, V. Sun–Thurs noon–11pm; Fri–Sat noon–midnight. Bar stays open later Fri–Sat.

8 · Dupont Circle

VERY EXPENSIVE

Komi ★★★ *Finds* NEW AMERICAN/GREEK Thirty-year-old chef/owner Johnny Monis looks like Johnny Depp and cooks like nobody's business. You may see him at the back of the restaurant in the half-exposed kitchen. As young as he is, Monis knows what he wants and continues to fiddle with his menu and dining room to achieve it. A slight renovation in 2006 created a Mediterranean feel, removed tables to make more room, and added tablecloths to buffer the sounds of the nightly full house. In 2007, Monis went completely to a five-course prix-fixe menu. Komi remains an intimate, comfortably attractive shotgun-length dining room where you can enjoy really superb Greek-influenced dishes. These include the *mezethakia* first course (crispy artichoke, smoked prosciutto, fava beans, and aged pecorino cheese); the *macaronia* second course, which offers a choice of six or so pasta dishes, like the ravioli of local beets with feta or Gorgonzola raviolini with pears and almonds; and the third-course entrees, which might include a *bronzini* (Mediterranean sea bass) roasted in the oven in parchment paper, or the slow-roasted local Iberian pig. Greek-style doughnuts are always an option for dessert. Servers are some of the most efficient but charming staff in the city.

1509 17th St. NW (near P St.). ℰ 202/332-9200. www.komirestaurant.com. Reservations recommended. Tues–Sat $84–$104 per person for the tasting menu. AE, MC, V. Tues–Sat 5:30–9:45pm. Metro: Dupont Circle (Q St. exit).

Obelisk ★★★ ITALIAN Obelisk is the most consistently excellent restaurant in the city. Service and food are simply the best. In this pleasantly spare room that seats only 36, the walls are decorated with 19th-century French botanical prints and Italian

lithographs. Here, owner Peter Pastan and chef Jerry Corso present small fixed-price menus of sophisticated Italian cuisine using the freshest-possible ingredients. Each night, diners are offered two or three choices for each of five courses. Dinner might begin with an antipasti misti of zucchini fritters, deep-fried risotto croquettes, and garbanzo beans with tuna in olive oil; followed by sweetbread and porcini ravioli with sage butter; and then an artfully arranged dish of grilled stuffed quail and duck sausage with spinach, or black bass with peppers, fennel and green sauce . . . or whatever the chef has been inspired to create. A cheese course is next, and the meal concludes with dessert, perhaps pear spice cake, rose-petal panna cotta, or some other heavenly concoction. Divine breads and desserts are all baked in-house. Pastan's carefully crafted wine list represents varied regions of Italy, as well as California vintages. The fixed-price menu is a good value, but the cost of wine and coffees can easily double the price per person.

2029 P St. NW. © 202/872-1180. Reservations recommended. Fixed-price 5-course dinner $65. DC, MC, V. Tues–Sat 6–10pm. Metro: Dupont Circle.

EXPENSIVE

Pesce ✴ SEAFOOD Tables are close together and every table is full—that's Pesce, where a no-reservations policy and a reliably pleasing menu means that there's usually a line. A large blackboard displays a long list of daily specials: monkfish roasted with celery, apples, and duck jus; lobster risotto; grilled whole flounder; scallops; and softshell crabs were among recent options. These days, Pesce's kitchen is looking back to its beginnings 16 years ago, when the late, renowned chef Jean-Louis Palladin and the equally famous Roberto Donna opened the restaurant, focusing on Mediterranean tastes. Pesce draws a wide swath of Washingtonians, from the secretary of state to NPR correspondents to locals from the neighborhood, everyone ready for a convivial time and good eats.

2016 P St. NW (near 20th St.). © 202/466-3474. www.pescebistro.com. Reservations accepted at lunch and for parties of 6 or more at dinner. Lunch $13–$19; dinner entrees $19–$29. AE, DC, DISC, MC, V. Mon–Fri 11:30am–2:30pm; Mon–Thurs 5:30–10pm; Fri–Sat 5:30–10:30pm; Sun 5–9:30pm. Metro: Dupont Circle (19th St./South exit).

Tabard Inn ✴✴ AMERICAN In spite of the fact that this restaurant lies inside the Hotel Tabard Inn (see description in chapter 5), the Tabard Inn is largely a beloved local spot. Saturday and Sunday brunch is a tradition for bunches of friends and families, weekday lunch pulls in the staff from surrounding embassies and association offices, and dinner seats couples, business partners, and Washingtonians meeting pals in town for meetings. The fetchingly homey main dining room holds wooden tables, hanging plants, a black-and-white tile floor, and windows overlooking a brick-walled garden. The kitchen smokes its own salmon (as it has for 26 years); cures its own pastrami, tasso ham, and prosciutto; and bakes its own bread and pastries, so these items are awfully good. Everything's good, though; and everything's fresh, from the oysters delivered straight from the coast of Maine to the grilled Hereford rib-eye steak, served with Gorgonzola new gold potatoes, broccolini, and bordelaise sauce. Desserts, with names like strawberry rhubarb Linzer crusted cobbler and chocolate mousse pudding cake, are as delicious as they sound.

1739 N St. NW (at 17th St., in the Hotel Tabard Inn). © 202/331-8528. www.tabardinn.com. Reservations recommended. Lunch and brunch entrees $10–$17; dinner entrees $23–$30. AE, DC, DISC, MC, V. Mon–Fri 7–10am and 11:30am–2:30pm; Sat 8–9:45am; Sun 8–9:15am; Sat brunch 11am–2:30pm; Sun brunch 10:30am–2:30pm; Sun–Thurs 6–9:30pm; Fri–Sat 6–10pm. Metro: Dupont Circle (19th St./South exit).

MODERATE

City Lights of China CHINESE The best of the Washington area's Chinese restaurants are not in the city at all, but in the suburbs. The increasingly shrinking Chinatown still has several, including **Tony Cheng's Seafood Restaurant** (p. 137). City Lights, meanwhile, has done quite well for itself in its Dupont Circle location since 1987, feeding the office and after-work crowd hungry for dumplings and fried rice. You can join the fray and dine in. If you are staying at a nearby hotel, you might consider ordering food to go; takeout prices are cheaper for some items. Some of the most popular dishes include crisp fried Cornish hen appetizer prepared in a cinnamon-soy marinade and served with a tasty dipping sauce, Chinese eggplant in garlic sauce, stir-fried spinach, crisp fried shredded beef, and Peking duck. The unpretentious setting is a three-tiered dining room with much of the seating in comfortable leather booths and banquettes. Neat white-linen tablecloths, cloth flower arrangements in lighted niches, and green neon track lighting complete the picture. The one hitch here is the inattentive service. There's a full bar.

1731 Connecticut Ave. NW (btw. R and S sts.). ⓒ **202/265-6688.** www.citylightsofchina.com. Reservations recommended. Lunch entrees $12–$24 (most are about $13); dinner entrees $11–$35 (most are about $15). AE, DC, DISC, MC, V. Mon–Fri 11:30am–10:30pm; Sat noon–11pm; Sun noon–10:30pm (dinner from 3pm daily). Metro: Dupont Circle (Q St. exit).

Hank's Oyster Bar ✹ AMERICAN/SEAFOOD Deep in the heart of Dupont Circle is this lively, laid-back hangout, fronted by a sidewalk cafe in warm weather. Decor inside is cozy and casual, with exposed brick walls and pipes and a mix of seating at the bar, tall round tables, and the usual wooden rectangles. You want to order the specials at Hank's, which on a recent night included a sautéed soft-shell crab in citrus butter, and pan-roasted halibut with tomato-lemon relish. Signature dishes feature classics like popcorn shrimp and calamari, and, of course, fresh oysters served on the half shell, fried, or in a po' boy. Hank's easy atmosphere puts you in a good mood and gives you a merry send-off when you've got a fun night on the town planned. Hank's now has a second location, in Old Town Alexandria, at 1026 King St. (ⓒ **703/739-4265**).

1624 Q St. NW (at 17th St.). ⓒ **202/462-4265.** www.hanksdc.com. No reservations. Dinner entrees $14–$25; brunch entrees $7–$23. AE, MC, V. Sun–Tues 5:30–10pm; Wed–Sat 5:30–11pm; Sat–Sun 11am–3pm. Metro: Dupont Circle (Q St. exit).

INEXPENSIVE

Pizzeria Paradiso ✹ PIZZA/ITALIAN In spite of awesome competition, this is still the best pizza place in the city. Situated on the second floor of a town house, this cool, 10-table-plus-counter-seating pizzeria often overflows with discriminating pizza fans. An oak-burning oven at one end of the charming room produces exceptionally doughy but light pizza crusts. The no-reservations policy means you'll have a wait if you arrive at peak times. It's worth the wait, though. Pizzas range from the plain Paradiso, which offers chunks of tomatoes covered in melted mozzarella, to the robust Siciliana, a blend of nine ingredients including eggplant and red onion. Or you can choose your own toppings from a list of 31. As popular as the pizzas are the panini (sandwiches) of homemade focaccia stuffed with marinated roasted lamb and vegetables and other fillings, and the salads, such as the panzanella (thick crusts of bread with chopped zucchini and peppers tossed with balsamic vinegar and olive oil). Paradiso serves beer and wine and good desserts. Pizzeria Paradiso has another location,

at 3282 M St. NW (© **202/337-1245**), in Georgetown, right next door to Dean & Deluca. This location is larger, has a full bar, a private party room, and the popular Birerria Paradiso, "one of the best pubs in the region," according to *Washingtonian* magazine.

2029 P St. NW. © 202/223-1245. www.eatyourpizza.com. Pizzas $9.50–$17; sandwiches and salads $4.95–$7.95. DC, MC, V. Mon–Thurs 11:30am–11pm; Fri–Sat 11:30am–midnight; Sun noon–10pm. Metro: Dupont Circle (19th St./South exit).

Sala Thai THAI At lunch, you'll see a lot of diners sitting alone and reading newspapers, happy to escape the office. At dinner, the restaurant is filled with groups and couples, plus the occasional family. Among the 82 items on the menu, look for *nua kra ting tone,* which is spicy beef with onion, garlic, and parsley sauce, and *ka prow,* which is an even spicier dish of beef, chicken, or pork sautéed with basil leaves and chili. The restaurant is downstairs from the street, with no windows to watch what's happening on P Street; but you're really here for the food, which is excellent and cheap. Even conventional Pad Thai doesn't disappoint. Pay attention if your waiter cautions you about the level of spiciness of a dish you order—for some dishes (like the stir-fried sliced pork in red curry sauce with peppers), you'll need an asbestos tongue. Sala Thai has several locations throughout the D.C. area, including one at 1301 U St. (© **202/462-1333**); if you like jazz, make sure you dine at this location Thursday to Saturday 7 to 10:30pm, when a trio or quartet performs.

2016 P St. NW. © 202/872-1144. www.salathaidc.com. Reservations accepted for 5 or more. Lunch entrees $8–$15; dinner entrees $10–$20. AE, DC, DISC, MC, V. Mon–Thurs 11:30am–10:30pm; Fri–Sat 11:30am–11pm; Sun noon–10:30pm. Metro: Dupont Circle (19th St./South exit).

Teaism Dupont Circle *Finds* ASIAN FUSION Occupying a turn-of-the-20th-century neoclassical building on a tree-lined street, Teaism has a lovely rustic interior. A display kitchen and tandoor oven dominate the sunny downstairs room, which offers counter seating along a wall of French windows that open in warm weather. Upstairs seating is on banquettes and small Asian stools at handcrafted mahogany tables.

The impressive tea list comprises close to 30 aromatic blends, most of them from India, China, and Japan. On the menu is light Asian fare served on stainless-steel plates or in lacquer lunchboxes (one Japanese bento box holds teriyaki salmon, cucumber-ginger salad, a scoop of rice with seasoning, and fresh fruit—all for $8.75). Dishes include Thai chicken curry with sticky rice, buffalo burger with Asian slaw, and a portobello and goat cheese sandwich. Baked jasmine crème brûlée and salty oat cookies are among desserts. At breakfast, you might try ginger scones or cilantro eggs and sausage with fresh tandoor-baked onion nan bread. Everything's available for takeout. Teapots, cups, and other gift items are for sale. *Note:* Teaism has two other locations, both convenient for sightseeing. **Teaism Lafayette Square,** 800 Connecticut Ave. NW (© **202/835-2233**), is across from the White House; it's open weekdays from 7:30am to 5:30pm and serves afternoon tea. **Teaism Penn Quarter** *Finds*, 400 8th St. NW (© **202/638-6010**), which is near the Verizon Center, the National Gallery, and nightspots, is the only branch that serves beer, wine, and cocktails. Teaism Penn Quarter is open daily, serving all three meals and afternoon tea, and brunch on Saturday and Sunday.

2009 R St. NW (btw. Connecticut and 21st sts.). © 202/667-3827. www.teaism.com. All menu items $1.50–$10. DC, DISC, MC, V. Mon–Thurs 8am–10pm; Fri 8am–11pm; Sat 9am–11pm; Sun 9am–10pm. Metro: Dupont Circle (Q St. exit).

9 Foggy Bottom/West End

VERY EXPENSIVE

Blue Duck Tavern ✿✿ CONTEMPORARY AMERICAN And now for something completely different. At the Park Hyatt Washington hotel's (p. 106) Blue Duck Tavern, award-winning executive chef Brian McBride presides over its open kitchen. Forget any preconceptions of "open kitchen." Here, no walls separate the cooking area from the dining room. McBride and his crew dance in and around counters, the wood-burning oven, and the immense Molteni commercial oven range in full view. Designer Tony Chi, who transformed the look of the entire hotel in 2006, also molded this light-filled space, which mixes modern American materials, like stainless steel and polished glass, with classic features, like dark oak and blue burlap. McBride does the same in his cuisine, choosing the freshest produce, meats, and seafood from local and regional artisans and purveyors. He uses a combination of traditional and state-of-the-art cooking methods and equipment to prepare exquisite, one-of-a-kind dishes right in front of you. The menu identifies the farm or other source of the prime ingredients for each dish. Then it's up to you to choose from three columns of categories that cover nearly every food grouping, from soup and salad, to meat and charcuterie, to fish and shellfish. Among the home runs so far are the baked Rhode Island clams with smoked bacon, peppers, and garlic; the galantine of duck and mushrooms with cherry preserve; jumbo lump crab cakes with rémoulade sauce; and the barbecued casserole of rice beans. The house-made steak fries are in a class of their own, so be sure to order those. And absolutely save room for dessert, like the chocolate cake flamed in bourbon, accompanied by a scoop of ice cream that you'll see hand-cranked minutes before it's delivered to your table. The wine list features 60 American wines and 300 from around the world. The Blue Duck Tavern was the only D.C. restaurant to make *Conde Nast Traveler*'s 2007 "Hot List" of the world's 95 top restaurants and came in at #12 on *Washingtonian* magazine's 2008 list of top 100 D.C. restaurants.

1201 24th St. NW (at M St. NW), in the Park Hyatt Washington Hotel. ✆ 202/419-6755. www.blueducktavern.com. Reservations recommended. Breakfast $5–$16; brunch entrees $14–$28; lunch entrees $19–$28; dinner entrees $18–$42. AE, DC, DISC, MC, V. Daily 6:30–10:30am, 11:30am–2:30pm, and 5:30–10:30pm. Metro: Foggy Bottom or Dupont Circle (19th St./South exit).

Kinkead's ✿✿ AMERICAN/SEAFOOD It's been open since 1983, but Kinkead's has a young spirit. This three-tier, 220-seat town-house restaurant is a reliable place to go for great food and festive atmosphere. Award-winning chef/owner Bob Kinkead orchestrates his kitchen staff in full view of the upstairs dining room, where booths and tables neatly fill nooks and alcoves. At street level is a scattering of tables overlooking the restaurant's lower level, the more casual 40-seat bar and cafe. A jazz pianist performs Tuesday through Sunday evenings from 7 to 10pm. When friends and I recently were seated too close to the pianist, we asked for a different table and were rewarded with what I consider the best seat in the house: the booth named after the irreplaceable master journalist, R. W. Apple, who used to dine here. The booth is tucked into a corner of the lively bar area and bears a plaque commemorating Apple. The worst seat in the house: anywhere in the "atrium," the area that extends outside the doors of the restaurant into an indoor mall.

Kinkead's menu (which changes daily) features primarily seafood, but always includes at least one beef and one poultry entree. Among the favorite dishes are the fried Ipswich clams; cod topped with crab imperial; clam chowder; and pepita-crusted

salmon with shrimp, crab, and chilies. Chef Kinkead piles on appetizing garnishes—that crab-crowned cod, for instance, comes with sweet potato purée and ham-laced spoon bread. The wine list comprises more than 300 selections. You can't go wrong with the desserts, like the chocolate dacquoise with cappuccino sauce. If you're hungry but not ravenous on a late weekday afternoon, stop in for some delicious light fare: fish and chips, lobster roll, soups, and salads.

2000 Pennsylvania Ave. NW. (C) **202/296-7700.** www.kinkead.com. Reservations recommended. Lunch and dinner entrees $22–$37; light fare $9–$27. AE, DC, DISC, MC, V. Mon–Fri 11:30am–2:30pm; daily 5:30–10pm (light fare served weekdays 2:30–5:30pm). Metro: Foggy Bottom.

Marcel's *FF* FRENCH When you walk through the front door, look straight ahead into the exhibition kitchen. Chances are you'll be staring directly into the eyes of chef Robert Wiedmaier (or his chef de cuisine, if Wiedmaier should be performing in his exhibition kitchen at Beck's). In any case, Wiedmaier's vivid style and cuisine are firmly on display here, with French dishes that include nods to his Belgian training: duck breast with baby turnips, rose lentils, and Calvados sauce, or venison with ragout of winter mushrooms and Madeira sauce. Wiedmaier's *boudin blanc* sausage is said to be out of this world. Desserts usually include such seasonal tarts as spring pear tart with raspberry coulis. Marcel's offers three tasting menus, four courses for $75, five courses for $90, and seven courses for $125, but you may choose any item listed on a tasting menu and order it as appetizer or entree.

Marcel's, named after Wiedmaier's young son, hews to a country French decor that includes panels of rough stone framed by rustic shutters and antique hutches displaying Provençal pottery. Drapes and carpeting help buffer the conversational buzz that otherwise would ricochet off the stone walls and floors. To the right of the exhibition kitchen is a spacious wine bar with its own menu (the full dinner menu is also available at some

(Value) Pretheater Dinners = Great Deals

Some of Washington's finest restaurants make you an offer you shouldn't refuse: a three-course dinner for just a little bit more than the cost of a typical entree. It's the pretheater dinner, available in the early evening on certain nights at certain restaurants; and while your choices may be limited, your meal will undoubtedly be delicious.

At one end of the spectrum is **Marcel's** *FF* (p. 151), whose $52 fixed-price includes a starter, such as an arugula salad with caramelized shallots; an entree, like pan-seared Norwegian salmon; and a dessert, perhaps crème brûlée or chocolate terrine. Marcel's offers this menu nightly from 5:30 to 7pm and throws in complimentary limo service to get you to the Kennedy Center, returning you to the restaurant after the show for the dessert portion, if you haven't already consumed it.

Café Atlantico's *FF* (p. 127) pretheater menu allows you three courses for $30; soup or salad to start, perhaps duck confit with pine nuts and apples or salmon with a Veracruz sauce for the main course, and sorbet or warm chocolate cake to finish. The restaurant's pretheater menu is available nightly between 5 and 6:30pm.

Other restaurants in this chapter that offer a pretheater menu are **Zola** *FF* (p. 132), **Rasika** *FF* (p. 136), **1789** *FFF* (p. 153), and **Café Saint-Ex** *F* (p. 142).

tables) and lovely live jazz Tuesday through Saturday year-round. Marcel's offers seating on the patio—right on Pennsylvania Avenue—in warm weather. Widely successful from the start is Marcel's sibling, **Brasserie Beck** (p. 141), which opened in 2007; Beck's is named after Wiedmaier's second-born son.

2401 Pennsylvania Ave. NW. ℂ 202/296-1166. www.marcelsdc.com. Reservations recommended. Tasting menus: 4-course $75, 5-course $90, 7-course $125 (any dish on the menu may be ordered individually); pretheater dinner 5:30–7pm (including round-trip limo to/from Kennedy Center) $52. AE, MC, V. Sun 5:30–9:30pm; Mon–Thurs 5:30–10pm; Fri–Sat 5:30–11pm. Metro: Foggy Bottom.

EXPENSIVE
Kaz Sushi Bistro ✹ JAPANESE Amiable chef/owner Kazuhiro ("Kaz") Okochi introduced Washington to sushi long ago, at a restaurant called Sushi-Ko (p. 158). Since 1999, Kaz has run his sushi bistro in this handsome town house. Aficionados vie for one of the six chairs at the bar to watch Kaz and his staff do their thing, especially at lunch, when fellow diners are likely to be Japanese men in Washington on business and young Washingtonians. Besides sushi, Kaz is known for his briny lobster with wasabi mayo, sea trout napoleon, and for his bento boxes, offering exquisite tastings of pan-seared salmon, spicy broiled mussels, and the like. This is also the place for premium sakes and a large selection of teas.

1915 I St. NW. ℂ 202/530-5500. Reservations recommended. www.kazsushibistro.com. Sushi a la carte $4–$9; lunch entrees $13–$20; dinner entrees $19–$27. AE, DC, DISC, MC, V. Mon–Fri 11:30am–2pm; Mon–Sat 6–10pm. Metro: Farragut West.

10 Georgetown

VERY EXPENSIVE
Michel Richard Citronelle ✹✹✹ INNOVATIVE FRENCH I consider this Washington's best restaurant—and so does *Washingtonian* magazine, which named it #1 in its 2008 listing of top D.C. restaurants. You can chalk its success up to ebullient chef/owner Michel Richard. Look for him in the kitchen (and you know when he is, since the dining room views the open kitchen), and then decline the menu and ask simply for whatever it is he wants to make. Whether you go that route, or choose from the fixed-price or tasting menus, you're in for a (very expensive) treat. Emerging from the bustling kitchen are appetizers like the fricassee of escargots, an eggshell filled with caviar, sweetbreads, porcinis, and crunchy pistachios, as well as entrees like the crispy lentil-coated salmon or squab leg confit with macaroni gratin and black truffles. Each presentation is a work of art, with swirls of colorful sauce surrounding the main event. If you're passionate about food, you may want to consider dining at the chef's table in the kitchen, so you can watch Richard at work. This will cost you: $295 per person, with a minimum of six people and maximum of eight, is the stated price, but that's to give you a ballpark idea; call for more exact information. One less expensive option is available at Citronelle: You can dine in the restaurant's bar and lounge (see "A Seat at the Bar," p. 159).

Citronelle's decor is also breathtaking and includes a wall that changes colors, a state-of-the-art wine cellar (a glass-enclosed room that encircles the dining room, displaying its 8,000 bottles and a collection of 18th- and 19th-c. corkscrews), and a Provençal color scheme of mellow yellow and raspberry red.

Michel Richard's richly layered chocolate "bar" with sauce noisette (hazelnut sauce) is recommended for dessert, if available. Citronelle's extensive wine list offers about 20 premium by-the-glass selections, but with all those bottles staring out at you from the

Bistrot Lepic **3**	Hook **6**	Old Glory Barbecue **11**
Café Milano **9**	La Chaumiere **14**	1789 **4**
Ching Ching Cha **10**	Leopold's Kafe & Konditorei **5**	Sushi-Ko **1**
Clyde's of Georgetown **8**	Mendocino Grille and Wine Bar **13**	Tackle Box **7**
Heritage India **2**	Michel Richard Citronelle **12**	Zed's **15**

wine cellar, you may want to spring for one. Also consider dining at Richard's French/American bistro, **Central** (p. 128), 2008 winner of the James Beard Award for "Best New Restaurant." Central offers a less expensive, less elaborate, but every bit as delicious meal.

In the Latham Hotel, 3000 M St. NW. ℂ **202/625-2150.** www.citronelledc.com. Reservations required. Jacket required, tie optional for men at dinner. Open for dinner only. Fixed-price 3-course dinner $95; 9-course tasting menu $175; 15-course tasting menu $225; bar/lounge entrees $14–$42. AE, DC, MC, V. Mon–Sat 6–9:30pm; Sun 6–9pm.

1789 ✸✸✸ AMERICAN Daniel Giusti is the latest chef in the restaurant's 47-year history to take command, and the reviews so far are good. Look for dishes like grilled wild salmon with local oysters and brioche pudding, and a thick pork chop served with pomegranate-braised onions and rapini. The menu changes daily but at least two dishes made famous by predecessor Ris Lacoste are often available (their recipes are

posted on the restaurant's website): the oyster and champagne stew with Smithfield ham and walnuts, and the roast rack of Colorado lamb with creamy feta potatoes au gratin in red-pepper-purée-infused merlot sauce.

Locals, like journalist and D.C. socialite Sally Quinn, and visiting celebrities, like Nicole Kidman and Keith Urban, love the 1789 for its romantic ambience. The five dining rooms, especially those on the first floor, are cozy dens, with a homey decor that includes historical prints on the walls, silk-shaded brass oil lamps on tables, and, come winter, fires crackling in the fireplaces. So put on your best duds and be prepared for a relaxing meal with only the food and your dinner companion to distract you. The formal but cozy restaurant occupies two floors (three, if you count the room reserved for private parties) of a Federal town house near Georgetown University.

The nightly pretheater menu, 6 to 6:45pm Monday to Friday, includes appetizer, entree, dessert, and coffee for $35. The same deal is available after 9pm Sunday through Thursday and after 10pm Friday and Saturday nights.

1226 36th St. NW. ℰ 202/965-1789. www.1789restaurant.com. Reservations recommended. Jacket required for men. Entrees $29–$38; fixed-price pretheater menu $35. AE, DC, DISC, MC, V. Mon–Thurs 6–10pm; Fri 6–11pm; Sat 5:30–11pm; Sun 5:30–10pm.

EXPENSIVE

Bistrot Lepic & Wine Bar ℰ FRENCH Bistrot Lepic is the real thing—a charming French restaurant that seems plucked right off a Parisian side street. The atmosphere is bustling and cheery, and you hear a lot of French spoken—not just by the waiters, but also by customers. The Bistrot is a neighborhood place, and you'll often see diners waving hellos across the room to each other or even table-hopping. In its 14 years, the restaurant has made some changes to accommodate its popularity, including turning the upstairs into an Asian-accented wine bar and lounge (p. 270); so if you arrive early for your reservation, you now have a place to wait. (In the past, one had to hover, hungry-eyed, at the door.) Or you can come just to hang out, sip a glass of wine, and munch on offerings from the wine bar menu, where the most expensive item is the $14 terrine of homemade foie gras, or specialties of the house from the regular menu. The wine bar hosts complimentary wine tastings every Tuesday 6 to 8pm. No need to make a reservation at the wine bar unless you plan to order dinner from the regular menu.

This is traditional French cooking, updated. The seasonal menu offers such entrees as grilled rainbow trout with tomatoes, capers, and olives; beef medallions with polenta and shiitake mushroom sauce; and sautéed sea scallops with ginger broccoli mousse. Depending on the season, specials might turn up rare tuna served on fennel with citrus vinaigrette or grouper with a mildly spicy lobster sauce upon a bed of spinach.

1736 Wisconsin Ave. NW. ℰ 202/333-0111. www.bistrotlepic.com. Reservations recommended. Lunch entrees $14–$19; 2-course ($20) and 3-course ($25) prix-fixe lunch menus also available; dinner entrees $17–$26. AE, DC, DISC, MC, V. Daily 11:30am–2:30pm; Sun–Thurs 5:30–9:30pm; Fri–Sat 5:30–10:30pm. Wine bar daily 5:30pm–midnight.

Cafe Milano ℰ ITALIAN The beautiful-people factor rises exponentially here as the night wears on. Cafe Milano has long been a magnet for Washington's famous, attractive, and powerful—and for visiting Hollywood and international celebrities. But this restaurant/nightclub/bar also serves good food. Salads are big, pasta servings are small, and fish and meat entrees are just the right size. We had the endive, radicchio, and arugula salad topped with thin sheets of Parmesan cheese; a *panzanella* salad

of tomatoes, potatoes, red onion, celery, and cucumber basking in basil a *cappellacci* (round ravioli) pockets of spinach and ricotta in cream sauce; bass on a bed of vegetables with lemon chive sauce; and the Santa Babila p has tomatoes, fresh mozzarella, oregano, and basil on a light pizza crust. All were delicious. Cafe Milano opens to a sidewalk cafe during the warm months. A bevy of good-humored waiters takes care of you. *FYI:* The Vatican chose Cafe Milano to prepare Pope Benedict's birthday meal at the Vatican Embassy when the pope visited Washington in April 2008.

3251 Prospect St. NW. ✆ 202/333-6183. www.cafemilano.net. Reservations recommended. Lunch entrees $14–$32 (most entrees are under $20); dinner entrees $15–$42. AE, DC, DISC, MC, V. Sun–Tues 11:30am–11pm (bar menu served until midnight); Wed–Sat 11:30am–midnight (bar menu served until 1am).

Hook ⭐ AMERICAN/SEAFOOD Georgetown can always use another good restaurant (as opposed to another busy bar or boutique store), so the fairly new Hook (opened mid-2007) is a welcome addition, as is its even newer sibling, Tackle Box, p. 157, which opened in April 2008. Situated near the intersection of M Street and Wisconsin Avenue, the restaurant's bar lies at the front, the spare, all-white dining room beyond that, with the semi-open kitchen pulling up the rear. Hook is committed to the "sustainable" movement, which means that the chef shops for locally farmed produce and that the menus are printed on 100% post-consumer recycled paper, to give just two examples. But Hook's real "hook" is sustainable, in-season seafood, so you can expect the blackfin tuna that arrives with the crème fraîche and potato purée on your plate to have been pulled from the water sometime within the preceding 24 hours. Get this: The chef receives a daily text message from Tobago island fishermen telling him of that day's catch, and the fish arrive within 18 to 24 hours. Be sure to order one of pastry chef Heather Chittum's lovely desserts, from warm madeleine cookies to an inventive carrot cake.

3241 M St. NW (btw. Wisconsin Ave. and 33rd St.). ✆ 202/625-4488. www.hookdc.com. Entrees $12–$24 at brunch and lunch, $22–$28 at dinner. AE, DC, DISC, MC, V. Sat–Sun 11am–2:30pm; Tues–Fri 11:30am–2:30pm; Sun–Tues 5–10pm; Wed–Sat 5–11pm.

Mendocino Grille and Wine Bar ⭐ AMERICAN As its name suggests, you should come here to enjoy West Coast wine, along with contemporary American cuisine and a California-casual ambience. Most of the 200-or-so bottles on the wine list are California vintages, with wines from Washington State and Oregon thrown in; and waiters are knowledgeable about the specifics of each, so don't hesitate to ask questions. California-casual doesn't mean cheap, though: Bottles range from $20 to $500, although most fall in the $50 to $60 range. The restaurant offers 20 wines by the glass, in different sizes, the better for tastings; and many of these run between $6 and $10 each.

Fresh ingredients predominate, whether it's an entree of olive oil–poached king salmon with sweet-and-sour red onions or South Carolina quail stuffed with pheasant sausage and accompanied by Brussels sprouts and roasted figs.

Rough-textured slate walls alternate with painted patches of Big Sur sky to suggest a West Coast winery in California's winegrowing region. The wall sconces resemble rectangles of sea glass and the dangling light fixtures look like turned-over wineglasses. It's a very pleasant place, where Georgetown neighbors tend to congregate nightly down the length of the handcrafted cherry-wood bar. Also read about Mendocino's sister restaurant, **Sonoma** (p. 122).

2917 M St. NW. ✆ 202/333-2912. www.mendocinodc.com. Reservations recommended. Dinner entrees $29–$32. AE, DC, DISC, MC, V. Sun–Thurs 5:30–10pm; Fri–Sat 5:30–11pm.

MODERATE

Clyde's of Georgetown AMERICAN Clyde's has been a favorite watering hole for an eclectic mix of Washingtonians since 1963. You'll see university students, Capitol Hill types, affluent professionals, Washington Redskins, romantic duos, and well-heeled ladies who lunch. Theme park–ish in decor, its dining areas include a cherry-paneled front room with oil paintings of sport scenes, as well as an atrium with vintage model planes dangling from the glass ceiling and a 16th-century French limestone chimney piece in the large fireplace.

Clyde's is known for its burgers, chili, and crab cake sandwiches. Appetizers are a safe bet, and Clyde's take on the classic Niçoise (chilled grilled salmon with greens, oven-roasted roma tomatoes, green beans, and grilled new potatoes in a tasty vinaigrette) is also recommended. Sunday brunch is a tradition, so popular that the brunch is offered on Saturday as well. The menu is reassuringly familiar—steak and eggs, omelets, waffles—with an assortment of sandwiches, burgers, and salads thrown in. Among bar selections are about 10 draft beers. Wines are half-price on Sundays until 10:30pm.

Clyde's inaugurated its second D.C. location (the restaurant has suburban locations, too) in late summer 2006, **Clyde's of Gallery Place**, at 707 7th St. NW (© **202/349-3700**) in the Gallery Place complex across from the Verizon Center, Penn Quarter neighborhood. See its listing in chapter 9, p. 267.

3236 M St. NW. © 202/333-9180. www.clydes.com. Reservations recommended. Lunch and brunch entrees $7.95–$18; dinner entrees $11–$26 (most under $12); burgers and sandwiches (except for crab cake sandwich) $10 or less. AE, DC, DISC, MC, V. Mon–Thurs 11:30am–midnight; Fri 11:30am–1am; Sat 10am–1am; Sun 9am–midnight (Sat–Sun brunch until 4pm).

La Chaumiere ★★ FRENCH After 32 years, La Chaumiere is still going strong. This rustically handsome dining room centers on a large hearth, which makes it an especially welcoming place in winter. Year-round, the restaurant fills up with locals who know the specials by heart; if it's Tuesday, that means "crabe en chemise" is on the menu: crepes filled with crabmeat, mushrooms, and champagne sauce. La Chaumiere prepares the full range of French classics just right, whether it's cassoulet or a chocolate soufflé. The service is warm but professional. The diners who gather here are a motley bunch, alike at least in their love of this kitchen's authentic French cooking.

2813 M St. NW (at 28th St.). © 202/338-1784. www.lachaumieredc.com. Reservations accepted. Lunch entrees $13–$18; dinner entrees $15–$30 (most are under $20). AE, MC, V. Mon–Fri 11:30am–2:30pm; Mon–Sat 5:30–10:30pm.

Leopold's Kafe & Konditorei ★ *Finds* AUSTRIAN If you find yourself at the western end of Georgetown, caught in the maze of high-end shops collectively known as Cady's Alley, you owe it to yourself to track down Leopold's and treat yourself to a delicious taste of Sacher torte or veal schnitzel. This may be the only place in Washington that serves Austrian food; it is certainly one of the most adorable eateries, with its whimsically modern furniture and bright whites punched up with orange. The customers represent a cross section of Washington, from chic to bohemian, and offer an intriguing picture to contemplate as you sip your Viennese coffee and enjoy your *apfelstrudel*. The cafe offers a full bar.

3315 Cady's Alley, no. 213 (off of M St. NW). (Find the passageway at 3318 M St., btw. 33rd and 34th sts., and walk back to Leopold's.) © 202/965-6005. www.kafeleopolds.com. No reservations. Breakfast items $1.75–$10; lunch and dinner entrees $13–$22. AE, DISC, MC, V. Sun–Tues 8am–10pm; Wed 8am–11pm; Thurs–Sat 8am–midnight.

Old Glory Barbecue *Kids* BARBECUE Raised wooden booths flank one side of the restaurant; an imposing, old-fashioned dark-wood bar with saddle-seat stools extends down the other. Background music is recorded swing music during the day, more mainstream music into the night. Old Glory boasts the city's "largest selection of single-barrel and boutique bourbons" and a rooftop deck with outdoor seating and views of Georgetown.

After 9pm or so, the two-story restaurant becomes packed with the hard-drinkin' young and restless. In early evening, though, Old Glory is prime for anyone—singles, families, or an older crowd—although it's almost always noisy. Come for the messy, tangy, delicious spareribs; hickory-smoked chicken; tender, smoked beef brisket; or marinated, wood-fired shrimp. Six sauces are on the table, the spiciest being the vinegar-based East Carolina and Lexington. The complimentary corn muffins and biscuits; side dishes of collard greens, succotash, and potato salad; and desserts like apple crisp and coconut cherry cobbler all hit the spot.

3139 M St. NW. ⓒ 202/337-3406. www.oldglorybbq.com. Reservations accepted Sun–Thurs; reservations not accepted Fri–Sat. Entrees $7.95–$25. AE, DC, DISC, MC, V. Sun 11am–2am (brunch from 11am–3pm); Mon–Thurs 11:30am–2am; Fri–Sat 11:30am–3am.

INEXPENSIVE

Ching Ching Cha *Finds* CHINESE/JAPANESE Located just below M Street, this sky-lit tearoom offers a pleasant respite from the crowds. You can sit on pillows at low tables or on chairs set at rosewood tables. Choices are simple: individual items like a tea-and-spice boiled egg, puff pastry stuffed with lotus-seed paste, or five-spice peanuts. Most typical is the $12 "tea meal," which consists of miso soup, your choice of three marinated cold vegetables, rice, and your choice of the featured meal, whether curry chicken, salmon with mustard-miso sauce, or steamed teriyaki-sauced tofu. Emphasis is really on the tea, of which there are 70 choices, including several different green, black, medicinal, and oolong teas, plus a Fujian white tea and a ginseng brew.

1063 Wisconsin Ave. NW. ⓒ 202/333-8288. www.chingchingcha.com. Reservations not accepted. All food items $4–$12; pot of tea $5–$20. AE, DISC, MC, V. Tues–Sat 11am–9pm; Sun 11am–7pm.

Tackle Box *☆* SEAFOOD What a delicious deal: your choice of crisped scallops, shrimp, calamari, clams, or oysters, or wood-grilled fresh fish, from tilapia to rainbow trout, plus two sides (whether fries, grilled asparagus, or assorted other options) for a total of $13. Tackle Box and **Hook** (p. 155), right next door, share the same eco-friendly practices and passion for top-notch food. Dine in and you'll sit at picnic benches in view and smelling range of the wood-grilling kitchen. No liquor license means you might want to do takeout to your hotel or house to enjoy your feast with a bottle of wine or beer.

3245 M St. NW. ⓒ 202/337-TBOX (8269). www.tacklebox-dc.com. All items $2–$19. AE, DC, MC, V. Daily 11am–11pm. Metro: Foggy Bottom, with a walk or ride aboard the D.C. Circulator.

Zed's ETHIOPIAN Like **Meskerem** (p. 146) in Adams-Morgan, Zed's was one of the first Ethiopian restaurants to open in D.C. And like Meskerem, its menu offers a good introduction to Ethiopian cuisine. Just ask Sen. Hillary Clinton or actor Clint Eastwood, two of the many celebrities who've sampled Zed's over the years.

Zed's is a pretty, charming little place, easy to find in Georgetown on its corner right across the street from the Four Seasons hotel. Indigenous paintings, posters, and artifacts adorn pine-paneled walls, fresh flowers grace the tables, and Ethiopian music plays in the background.

Highly recommended are the *doro watt* (chicken stewed in a tangy, hot red chili-pepper sauce), the *infillay* (strips of tender chicken breast flavored with seasoned butter and honey wine served with a delicious chopped spinach and rice side dish), flavorful lamb dishes, and the deep-fried whole fish—all scooped up with the sourdough crepelike pancake called *injera.* Consider ordering more of the garlicky chopped collard greens; red lentil purée in spicy red-pepper sauce; or a chilled purée of roasted yellow split peas mixed with onions, peppers, and garlic. There's a full bar; should you have the inclination, try the Italian pastries for dessert.

1201 28th St. NW (at M St.). ℂ 202/333-4710. www.zeds.net. Reservations accepted for 5 or more. Entrees $10–$35 (most are under $20). AE, DC, MC, V. Daily 11am–11pm.

11 Glover Park

The D.C. Circulator buses travel through Georgetown as far as Whitehaven Street, just a little bit short (south) of Glover Park; you can walk it easily, but it is all uphill. Regular Metro buses (the no. 30 series) travel to Glover Park. Perhaps the easiest thing to do is take a taxi.

MODERATE

Heritage India 🍴 INDIAN This elegant two-story dining room caters to those with sophisticated tastes for Indian food. You'll find all the standards here: tandoori dishes, lamb vindaloo, and vegetarian entrees, such as the *palak makai* (herbed spinach), and vegetable fritters, each dish carefully prepared and seasoned. Service could be better, but the overall experience is rewarding. A second Heritage India is located in the Dupont Circle neighborhood, 1337 Connecticut Ave. NW (ℂ **202/331-1414**), a "brasserie and lounge," whose menu includes contemporary Indian cuisine. Small plates of samosas, pakoras, and kabobs go down nicely with a cocktail; that's what the younger crowd comes here for, along with the dishes served at the original location and some more intriguing dishes, such as the hummus made with roasted garlic and black beans, and the tandoori-smoked mozzarella.

2400 Wisconsin Ave. NW (near Calvert St.). ℂ 202/333-3120. www.heritageindiaofgeorgetown.com. Reservations accepted. Lunch entrees $7.95–$13; dinner entrees $10–$24. AE, DC, DISC, MC, V. Daily 11:30am–2:30pm; Sun–Thurs 5:30–9:30pm; Fri–Sat 5:30–10:30pm.

Sushi-Ko 🍴 JAPANESE Sushi-Ko was Washington's first sushi bar when it opened 33 years ago, and it remains the best. The sushi chefs are fun to watch—try to sit at the sushi bar; if you do, ask chef Koji Terano to serve you his choice selections. You can expect superb sushi and sashimi standards, as well as daily specials, like a sea trout napoleon (diced sea trout layered btw. rice crackers), flounder sashimi with a black truffle sauce, and the delicately fried soft-shell crab (in season, spring and summer). Another option to capture the full range of tastes here: Order a bunch of the "small dishes," like the grilled baby octopus with mango sauce, or asparagus with smoked salmon and mustard dashi sauce. The tempuras and teriyakis are also excellent. And there's a long list of sakes, as well as burgundy wines and Japanese beer.

2309 Wisconsin Ave. NW. ℂ 202/333-4187. www.sushiko.us. Reservations recommended. Entrees $14–$24. AE, MC, V. Tues–Fri noon–2:30pm; Mon–Thurs 6–10:30pm; Fri 6–11pm; Sat 5:30–11pm; Sun 5:30–10pm.

A Seat at the Bar

Dining out in Washington can be many things: a culinary adventure, a happy pastime, a chance to transact business, a romantic interlude . . . and a competitive sport. Most restaurants require reservations, and in this cut-throat town, all the best seem always to be booked. Oh pooh! What's a hungry, reservation-less, good-food lover to do? Head to the bar, of course. In an effort to please those who haven't managed to reserve a table in their main dining rooms, but who nevertheless hope to sample some of their food, glorious food, a number of the city's top restaurants have started serving modified versions of their regular menus at the bar. The experience often proves more intimate and convivial than that in the main dining room, and here's the kicker: it's always less expensive. Consider these:

At **Palena**, 3529 Connecticut Ave. NW (© **202/537-9250**), you sit on comfy stools and in booths in the bar area at the front of the house and enjoy chef Frank Ruta's exquisitely prepared Kobe beef cheeseburger with brioche bun and *sottocenere* (a creamy Italian cheese with black truffles), Caesar salad, pastas, roasted chicken, a charcuterie plate, fried lemons (don't knock 'em 'til you try 'em) and onion rings, all perfectly done—and everything costing less than $20. This bar area is known as **Palena's Café**, to distinguish it from the formal dining room beyond. You can also choose from the main dining room menu here, but most people are happy with the cafe menu.

At **Michel Richard Citronelle**, in the Latham Hotel, 3000 M St. NW (© **202/625-2150**), the bar/lounge is located on a level just above the main dining room. There are bar stools, but also a collection of tables. The a la carte menu offers a range of items, from $12 mushroom cigars (fried mushroom duxelles with ginger sauce) to $42 duck, served medium-rare, with black cherry anise. So many people have raved about the lobster burger ($34) that Richard includes it on the menu at his new restaurant, Central (p. 128). This is Richard's award-winning cuisine, at a fraction of the cost of his tasting menus.

CityZen, in the Mandarin Oriental Hotel, 1330 Maryland Ave. SW (© **202/787-6868**), offers perhaps the most jaw-dropping bar meal: Chef Eric Ziebold's three-course tasting menu in his main dining room costs $75; at the bar, Ziebold's edited version goes for $45 to $50. The chef does not present a set bar menu but pulls one or two choices from each course on offer that night, so you can be sure you're dining on the same heavenly fare as those seated at tables: maybe a pickled shad with braised celery and potato crisps, or braised shoat shoulder with English peas. And the service is sublime.

Other bar scenes to recommend: **Marcel's** (p. 151), whose wine bar menu ranges from a gratin of endive for $13 to beef carbonade, in $15 and $28 portions (Marcel's also features live jazz in the wine bar nightly); **Bistrot Lepic** (p. 154), whose second floor is a wine bar (p. 270), offering both bar item menus and specialties of the house; and **PS7's** (p. 130), whose lounge is a cool scene and its menu even cooler—try the risotto balls, tuna sliders, and house-made half-smokes.

12 Woodley Park & Cleveland Park

VERY EXPENSIVE

Palena �übersicht CONTEMPORARY AMERICAN/FRENCH/ITALIAN One Metro stop past the Woodley Park–Zoo station takes you to the residential neighborhood of Cleveland Park, which is exploding with good restaurants. Palena is one that's worth the trip.

Palena is the creation of two former White House chefs, Executive Chef Frank Ruta and Pastry Chef Ann Amernick, who worked together at the White House in the 1980s. Ruta turns out French- and Italian-inspired dishes, such as Portuguese sardines in puff pastry, cod roasted in lavender-infused olive oil, and Dover sole filet stuffed with porcini and pan-roasted with artichokes and endive. Amernick's contributions range from complimentary caramels at dinner's conclusion, to the fresh sorbets, cheesecake, bread pudding, and other offerings on the dessert menu. This is an elegant restaurant with an old-world feel. Because of its immediate and sustained success, it's sometimes hard to get a reservation, but worth trying for. Or you can dine in the cafe/bar (see "A Seat at the Bar," above). Palena's Café, which is the name for the front of the house, is open Tuesday through Saturday and sometimes on Monday nights, serving the bar/cafe menu (diners can also choose from the main menu). Reservations are not accepted, and the place is standing room only.

3529 Connecticut Ave. NW. ⓒ 202/537-9250. www.palenarestaurant.com. Reservations recommended. Jacket and tie preferred for men. Fixed-price menus $58 (3-course), $67 (4-course), and $76 (5- to 6-course). AE, DC, DISC, MC, V. Tues–Sat 5:30–10pm. Metro: Cleveland Park (exit to the east side of Connecticut Ave.).

MODERATE

Indique 🌠 INDIAN Cleveland Park is an upscale residential community of old streets lined with towering trees and Victorian houses. A preponderance of wonks, intellects, and journalists live here with their families. It's an unlikely mecca for the wild-and-crazy 20-something crowd; but thanks to a stretch of Connecticut Avenue between Porter and Macomb streets, where a number of bars and restaurants lie, that's what it's become—a mini-mecca, let's say. In the middle of this designated hot zone lies Indique, a two-story, glass-fronted Indian restaurant. Partyers on the weekend pack the downstairs bar area, drinking pomegranate martinis. Diners without reservations, and even sometimes those with reservations, wait for tables to become available upstairs, downstairs, wherever. Indian cuisine happens to be in vogue at the moment, and Indique's is very good. Come here for the Cornish hen curry, vegetable samosas, and tandoori shrimp. Its authentic cuisine from different regions in India, from the curries and tandoori specialties of northern Italy to the appams and ishtews of southwestern India, attracts visiting dignitaries from India and Indian food-informed Washingtonians.

3512–14 Connecticut Ave. NW (btw. Porter and Ordway sts.). ⓒ 202/244-6600. www.indique.com. Reservations accepted. Lunch entrees $9–$11; dinner entrees $11–$21. AE, DC, DISC, MC, V. Daily noon–3pm; Sun–Thurs 5:30–10:30pm; Fri–Sat 5:30–11pm. Metro: Cleveland Park (exit to west side of Connecticut Ave.).

Lebanese Taverna 🌠 MIDDLE EASTERN This family-owned restaurant, which opened in 1990, gives you a taste of Lebanese culture—its cuisine, decor, and music. It's very popular, especially on weekends, so expect to stand in line. (Reservations are accepted only for seating before 6:30pm.) Diners, once seated in the courtyard-like dining room, where music plays and prayer rugs hang on the walls, hate to leave. The wood-burning oven in the back bakes the pita breads and several appetizers. What you want to order are the meze dishes: hummus, tabbouleh, baba ghanouj, stuffed grape

Chocolate Lounges

Washingtonians are all chocoholics, judging by the burst of instantly adored chocolate lounges and cafes on the dining scene. If you answer to the same calling, check out these three places:

ACKC Cocoa Gallery, at 1529C 14th St. NW (© **202/387-COCO;** www.the cocoagallery.com). Part cafe, art gallery, and artisana, ACKC is a delightful place for a chocolate break. Its eight versions of cocoa are named for some favorite femmes, including the Marilyn, Audrey, Lucy, and Liz.

CoCo. Sala, 929 F St. NW (© **202/347-4265;** www.cocosala.com). This chocolate lounge and boutique is a sweet refuge in the heart of the Penn Quarter, dispensing coffees, cocoas, and small plates of light fare throughout the day. Dessert cocktails and chocolate-spiked liqueurs are on tap into the wee hours.

Locolat Café, 1781 Florida Ave. NW (© **202/518-2570;** www.belguimlocolat. com). The Adams-Morgan-based Locolat was already a Belgian chocolate confiserie when it launched its cafe with sidewalk seating. Chocoholics can sip chocolate-enhanced coffee and hot cocoas, and savor an assortment of cakes, Belgian waffles, pastries, and created-on-the-premises chocolate bonbons.

leaves, cheese pastries, couscous, and pastry-wrapped spinach pies *(fatayer bi sabanikh),* enough for dinner for a couple or as hors d'oeuvres for more. Also consider entrees, such as the roasted half chicken wrapped in bread and served with garlic purée. The wealth of meatless dishes will delight vegetarians, while rotisserie items, especially the chicken and the chargrilled kabobs of chicken and shrimp, will please all others.

2641 Connecticut Ave. NW. © **202/265-8681.** www.lebanesetaverna.com. Reservations accepted before 6:30pm. Lunch entrees $5.95–$18; dinner entrees $8.50–$20. AE, DC, DISC, MC, V. Mon–Fri 11:30am–2:30pm; Sat noon–3pm; Mon 5:30–10pm; Tues–Thurs 5–10:30pm; Fri–Sat 5:30–11pm; Sun 4:30–9:30pm. Metro: Woodley Park–Zoo (take south exit on Connecticut Ave.).

Exploring Washington, D.C.

From the inauguration of our new president in January 2009, to the dedication of the Rev. Dr. Martin Luther King, Jr., Memorial at the end of the year, one momentous event follows another in this city built on heroic American dreams and audacious hopes.

It's a good time to visit. So much is new: the **Capitol Visitor Center** beneath the U.S. Capitol Building, the **National Museum of American History's** sensational show-off gallery for the **Star-Spangled Banner,** the fabulous **Newseum,** a second location of the **Textile Museum** on 7th Street in the Penn Quarter (no worries: the original, in Dupont Circle, is still open), and, nearly right next door on 7th Street, the **National Museum of Crime and Punishment.**

But so much remains wonderfully the same, offering visitors a menu that includes the three houses of government, scores of museums, more than 100 memorials, an abundance of historic houses and federal buildings, acres and acres of gorgeous parkland, and numerous outdoor activities.

Call Ahead

Here's a crucial piece of advice: **Call the places you plan to tour each day before you set out.** Many of Washington's government buildings, museums, memorials, and monuments are open to the general public nearly all the time—except when they're not.

Because buildings like the Capitol, the Supreme Court, and the White House are offices as well as tourist destinations, the business of the day always poses the potential for closing one of those sites, or at least sections, to sightseers. There's also the matter of maintenance. The steady stream of visitors to Washington's attractions necessitates ongoing caretaking, which may require closing an entire landmark, or part of it, to the public, or putting in place new hours of operation or procedures for visiting. (Construction of the Capitol Visitor Center is one such example.) Finally, Washington's famous museums, grand halls, and public gardens double as settings for press conferences, galas, special exhibits, festivals, and even movie sets. You might arrive at, say, the National Air and Space Museum on a Sunday afternoon, only to find some or all of its galleries off-limits because director Shawn Levy is using the museum to shoot scenes for *Night at the Museum 2: Escape from the Smithsonian.* (This really happened; look for the Air and Space Museum's star turn—with Ben Stiller—in the 2009 movie.) Want to avoid frustration and disappointment? Call ahead.

Heads Up

Eight years after September 11, 2001, Washington, D.C., has a firm handle on workable security precautions, and for visitors that means standing in line at attractions. Security clearances, no matter how efficient, do take time. At many tourist sites, like the Smithsonian's National Air and Space Museum and National Museum of Natural History, and at most government buildings, staff search handbags, briefcases, and backpacks, and, at some sites, require you to walk past metal detectors. During the busy spring and summer seasons, you may be queuing outside as you wait your turn to pass through security. So pack your patience, but otherwise carry as little as possible, and certainly no sharp objects. Museums and public buildings rarely offer the use of lockers.

Come reconnect with your inner patriot, satisfy your hunger for art, and recreate on national parkland. If you'd like some help figuring out a workable scenario, see chapter 4, "Suggested Washington, D.C., Itineraries," which offers 1-, 2-, and 3-day scenarios for tackling the town. Otherwise, peruse this chapter, see what strikes your fancy, put on some good walking shoes, and head out.

1 The Three Houses of Government

The buildings housing the executive, legislative, and judicial branches of the U.S. government remain among the most visited sites in Washington. All three—the White House, the Capitol, and the Supreme Court—are stunning to behold and experience, and offer fascinating lessons in American history and government. Although these landmarks are not as freely open to the public as they were before the terrorist attacks of September 11, 2001, all three do allow tours.

The Capitol ✦✦✦ The Capitol is as majestic up close as it is from afar. For 135 years it sheltered not only both houses of Congress, but also the Supreme Court and, for 97 years, the Library of Congress as well. When you tour the Capitol, you'll learn about America's history as you admire the place in which it unfolded. Classical architecture, interior embellishments, and hundreds of paintings, sculptures, and other artworks are integral elements of the Capitol. The 30-minute tour (see procedures below) takes you to the Crypt, the Rotunda, and National Statuary Hall. (For an in-depth description and information about the history and art of the Capitol, go to www.aoc.gov and click on the link "Visiting the Capitol.")

On the massive bronze doors leading to the **Rotunda** are portrayals of events in the life of Columbus. The Rotunda—a huge 96-foot-wide circular hall capped by a 180-foot-high dome—is the hub of the Capitol. The dome was completed, at Lincoln's direction, while the Civil War was being fought. Ten presidents have lain in state here, with former president Ronald Reagan being the most recent; when Kennedy's casket was displayed, the line of mourners stretched 40 blocks. On rare occasions, someone other than a president, military hero, or member of Congress receives this posthumous recognition. In October 2005, Congress paid tribute to Rosa Parks by allowing her body to lie in state here, the first woman to be so honored. (Parks was the black woman who in 1955 refused to relinquish her seat to a white man on a Montgomery, Alabama, bus, thereby helping to spark a civil rights movement.)

Washington, D.C., Attractions

1

2

NATIONAL ZOOLOGICAL PARK

Woodley Park-Zoo Red Line

Columbia Heights Green Line

ADAMS-MORGAN

EMBASSY ROW

ROCK CREEK PARK

3

DUMBARTON OAKS PARK

U.S. Naval Observatory

Observatory Circle

MONTROSE PARK

4

5

DUPONT CIRCLE

Dupont Circle Red Line

Georgetown University

GEORGETOWN

C & O Canal

Scott Circle

Thom. Circle

Farragut North Red Line

Washington Circle

Farragut Square

McPherson Square

Fran. Squ.

Whitehurst Fwy.

29

Francis Scott Key Bridge

Foggy Bottom-GWU Blue & Orange Lines

Farragut West Blue & Orange Lines

McPherson Square Blue & Orange Lines

George Washington University

66

Theodore Roosevelt Island

Little River

N. Lynn St.

Wilson Blvd.

Kennedy Center

10

FOGGY BOTTOM

6

7

White House

8

Rosslyn Blue & Orange Lines

11

Theodore Roosevelt Mem. Bridge

9

1 50

24

VIRGINIA

ARLINGTON

NATIONAL

CEMETERY

Arlington Cemetery Blue Line

Constitution Ave.

20

Lincoln Memorial

19

17

18

21

Washington Monument

12

Jefferson Davis Hwy.

Washington Blvd.

Arlington Mem. Bridge

50 Independence Ave.

WEST POTOMAC PARK

23

22

Potomac River

13

Tidal Basin

Cherry Trees

Ohio Dr.

West Basin Dr.

16

FDR Memorial

14

15

Jefferson Memorial

1

Anacostia Community Museum **52**
Arlington National Cemetery **12**
Arthur M. Sackler Gallery **28**
Arts and Industries Building **30**
Bureau of Engraving
 and Printing **22**
Capitol **46**
Corcoran Gallery of Art **9**
Dumbarton Oaks **3**
Enid A. Haupt Garden **29**
FDR Memorial **16**
Folger Shakespeare Library **49**
Freer Gallery of Art **27**
George Mason Memorial **14**
Hirshhorn Museum **31**
International Spy Museum **42**
Jefferson Memorial **15**
John F. Kennedy Center **10**
Korean War Veterans Memorial **18**
Library of Congress **48**
Lincoln Memorial **19**
Madame Tussauds **39**
Marian Koshland Science Museum **43**
National Air and Space Museum **32**
National Archives **36**
National Gallery of Art **34**
National Gallery of Art Sculpture
 Garden **35**
National Museum of African Art **29**
National Museum of American
 History **24**

National Museum of the American
 Indian **33**
National Museum of Crime
 and Punishment **38**
National Museum of Natural
 History **25**
National Museum of Women
 in the Arts **40**
National Postal Museum **44**
National Zoological Park **2**
Newseum **37**
Pentagon **13**
Phillips Collection **5**
Renwick Gallery **6**
Sewall-Belmont House **51**
Smithsonian American Art Museum
 and National Portrait Gallery **41**
Smithsonian Information Center **26**
Supreme Court **50**
Theodore Roosevelt Island **11**
U.S. Botanic Garden **47**
U.S. Holocaust Memorial Museum **23**
Union Station **45**
Vietnam Veterans Memorial **20**
Washington Monument **21**
Washington National Cathedral **1**
White House **7**
White House Visitor Center **8**
Woodrow Wilson House **4**
World War II Memorial **17**

Embracing the Rotunda walls are eight immense oil paintings commemorating great moments in American history, such as the presentation of the Declaration of Independence and the surrender of Cornwallis at Yorktown. In the dome is an allegorical fresco masterpiece by Constantino Brumidi, *The Apotheosis of Washington,* a symbolic portrayal of George Washington surrounded by Roman gods and goddesses watching over the progress of the nation. Brumidi was known as the "Michelangelo of the Capitol" for the many works he created throughout the building. (Take another look at the dome and find the woman directly below Washington; the triumphant *Armed Freedom* figure is said to be modeled after Lola Germon, a beautiful young actress with whom the 60-year-old Brumidi conceived a child.) Beneath the dome is a *trompe l'oeil* frieze depicting major developments in the life of America, from Columbus's landing in 1492 to the birth of the aviation age in 1903. Don't miss the sculptures in the Rotunda: a pensive Abraham Lincoln, a dignified Rev. Dr. Martin Luther King, Jr., and a ponderous trinity of suffragists Elizabeth Cady Stanton, Susan B. Anthony, and Lucretia Mott—these and others are represented here.

The **National Statuary Hall** was originally the chamber of the House of Representatives. In 1864, it became Statuary Hall, and the states were invited to send two statues each of native sons and daughters to the hall. There are 100 statues in all, New Mexico completing the collection with its contribution in 2005 of Po'Pay, a Pueblo Indian, who in 1680 led a revolt against the Spanish that helped to save Pueblo culture. (Stay tuned: The District of Columbia hopes to honor two of its own homegrown heroes with statues, despite the fact that Congress, as yet, refuses to recognize D.C. as a state.) Because of space constraints, only 38 statues reside in the Hall, with the remaining scattered throughout the corridors of the Capitol. Statues include Ethan Allen, the Revolutionary War hero who founded the state of Vermont, and Missouri's Thomas Hart Benton—not the 20th-century artist famous for his rambunctious murals, but his namesake and uncle, who was one of the first two senators from Missouri and whose antislavery stance in 1850 cost him his Senate seat. Eight women are represented, including Montana's Jeannette Rankin, the first woman to serve in Congress.

The **Crypt** of the Capitol lies directly below the Rotunda and is used mainly as an exhibit space.

Following the tour, you are allowed to linger on the first floor and to wander past the **Old Supreme Court Chamber,** which has been restored to its mid-19th-century appearance. The Supreme Court met here from 1810 to 1860. Busts of the first four chief justices are on display—John Marshall, John Rutledge, John Jay, and Oliver Ellsworth—and so are some of their desks, believed to have been purchased in the 1830s. The justices handed down a number of noteworthy decisions here, including that of Dred Scott v. Sandford, which denied the citizenship of blacks, whether slaves or free, and in so doing precipitated the nation's Civil War.

You will not see them on your tour, but the **south and north wings** of the Capitol hold the House and Senate chambers, respectively. The House of Representatives chamber is the largest legislative chamber in the world, and the setting for the president's annual State of the Union addresses. (See the information below about watching Senate and House activity.)

Procedures for Touring the Capitol: All tours of the Capitol start inside the Capitol Visitor Center (see box, above), where you obtain timed passes for the tour (if you

Capitol Hill

Capitol **1**

Folger Shakespeare Library **5**

Library of Congress:
 Thomas Jefferson Building **2**
 James Madison Building **3**
 John Adams Building **4**

National Postal Museum **8**

Supreme Court **6**

Union Station **7**

The Opening of the Capitol Visitor Center

Under construction since mid-2002, a comprehensive, underground Capitol Visitor Center finally debuted in late 2008, years behind schedule. All visitors to the Capitol now queue up inside the visitor center, which offers exhibits, 26 restrooms (compared to the 5 public restrooms the Capitol has had until now), a dining facility that seats 600, and an orientation film shown in two theaters. To find the visitor center, go to the East Front of the Capitol (along 1st St., across from the Library of Congress) and look for the signs pointing you to the entrance. As before, you and everyone in your party must have a timed pass to tour the Capitol. Best of all, though, is the fact that you can now order advance tickets online. (At the time of this writing, staff were still nailing down the exact procedure; visit www.aoc.gov for the latest information.) Whether you stand in line at the visitor center for tickets or order them online, you will receive timed tickets. During peak spring and summer sessions, you should order tickets at least 2 weeks in advance. No matter what, call ℭ 202/225-6827 in advance of your visit; that way you'll know for sure whether the Capitol is open to the public the day you wish to visit and whether touring procedures have changed.

have not already ordered them in advance online). Once you obtain your passes, you're free to tour the visitor center or leave the Capitol for touring elsewhere, returning in time for your designated tour. The guided tours are free, last 30 minutes, and are led by a Capitol Guide Service guide. The Capitol has quite a list of items it prohibits, and the recording that you listen to on the ℭ 202/225-6827 number recites them for you, everything from large bags of any kind to food and drink. Leave everything possible back at the hotel.

Procedures for Visiting the House Gallery or Senate Gallery: Try to visit when both the Senate and House are **in session** ✮✮✮. In fact, the Senate Gallery is open to visitors only when it is in session, but the House Gallery is open to visitors whether or not it is in session. (Children 5 and under are not allowed in the Senate gallery.) You must have a separate pass, one for each gallery. Once obtained, the passes are good through the remainder of the Congress. You can obtain visitor passes at the offices of your representative and senator, or in the case of District of Columbia and Puerto Rico residents, from the office of their delegate to Congress.

Congressional representatives and delegates have offices on the south side, or Independence Avenue side, of the Capitol, while senators' offices are located on the north side, or Constitution Avenue side, of the Capitol. You should be able to pick up passes to both the Senate and House galleries in one place, at either your representative's office or your senator's office. (*Note:* International visitors can obtain both House and Senate gallery passes by presenting a passport or a valid driver's license with photo ID to the Capitol Guide Service staff in the House of Representative's Gallery line, in the Capitol's South Screening Facility.)

Visit the Capitol's website, www.aoc.gov, or call your senator or congressperson's office for more exact information about obtaining passes to the House and Senate galleries, since new procedures involving the Capitol Visitor Center were yet to be defined at the time of this writing.

You'll know that the House and/or the Senate is in session if you see flags flying over their respective wings of the Capitol (*remember:* House, south side; Senate, north side), or you can check the weekday "Today in Congress" column in the *Washington Post* for details on times of the House and Senate sessions and committee hearings. This column also tells you which sessions are open to the public. Or again, access the Capitol's website, **www.aoc.gov**, which helpfully provides information about the history, art, and construction of the Capitol building; an in-depth education on the legislative process; schedules of bill debates in the House and Senate, committee markups, and meetings; and lots of other good stuff. The aoc.gov page has links to the individual Senate (www.senate.gov) and House (www.house.gov) pages, or you can go directly to those sites to connect to your Senate or House representative's page.

Capitol and Capitol Visitor Center: On East Capitol St. (at 1st St. NW). © 202/225-6827. www.aoc.gov, www.house. gov, www.senate.gov. Free admission. Year-round Mon–Sat 9am–4:30pm , with first tour starting at 9:30am and last tour starting at 3:30pm. Closed for tours Sun and Jan 1, Thanksgiving, and Dec 25. Parking at Union Station or on neighborhood streets. Metro: Union Station (Massachusetts Ave. exit) or Capitol South (to walk to the Capitol Visitor Center located on the East Front of the Capitol).

The Supreme Court of the United States ★★★ The highest tribunal in the nation, the Supreme Court is charged with the power of "judicial review": deciding whether actions of Congress, the president, the states, and lower courts, in other words, of all branches of government and government officials, are in accordance with the Constitution, and with applying the Constitution's enduring principles to novel situations and a changing country. Arguably the most powerful people in the nation, the Court's chief justice and eight associate justices hear only about 75 to 100 of the most vital cases of the 8,000 to 9,000 petitions for *writ certiorari* submitted to the Court each year. The Court's rulings are final, reversible only by an Act of Congress.

Hard to believe, but the Supreme Court—in existence since 1789—did not have its own building until 1935. The justices met in New York, Philadelphia, and assorted nooks of the Capitol (see the Capitol's write-up above) until they finally got their own place. Architect Cass Gilbert designed the stately Corinthian marble palace that houses the Court today. Best known for his skyscrapers, like New York's 761-foot-high Woolworth Building, Gilbert was an interesting choice for the Supreme Court commission in a city where Congress restricts building height to 160 feet.

You'll have plenty of time to admire the exterior of this magnificent structure if you're in town when the Court is in session and decide to try **seeing a case being argued** ★★★ because—yup, you guessed it—you have to wait in line (sometimes for

Tips **In Your Extra Time**

What to do when you've snagged a timed pass for a tour that's hours from now? A few suggestions on Capitol Hill: Visit your senator's or representative's office; wander around the Capitol Grounds and discover fine statuary, like the Garfield Monument, and private garden spots; tour the U.S. Botanic Garden (p. 219) or the National Museum of the American Indian (p. 190); or get a bite to eat, either at the American Indian museum's eatery, which everyone seems to love, or up the hill at Le Bon Café (210 2nd St. SE; © 202/547-7200), a good little sandwich place. (If you listen up when you stand in line, you're bound to overhear some juicy Capitol Hill scuttlebutt.).

hours) on the front plaza of the building. But do try! The experience is totally worth the wait. People queue in every city for tickets to concerts and sports events. But only in Washington does a wait in line grant one the privilege of watching and listening to the country's nine foremost legal experts nimbly and intensely dissect the merits of both sides of an argument, whose decisions can affect profoundly both the person and the nation. The standing-in-line itself brings with it the same sort of thrill that builds in collective anticipation of a great performance.

Here's what you need to know: Starting the first Monday in October and continuing through late April, the Court "sits" for 2 weeks out of every month to hear two to four arguments each day, Monday through Wednesday, from 10am to noon and from 1 to 2 or 3pm. You can find out the specific dates and names of arguments in advance by calling the Supreme Court (© **202/479-3211**) or by going to the website, **www. supremecourtus.gov**, where the argument calendar and the "Merits Briefs" (case descriptions) are posted.

Plan on arriving at the Supreme Court at least 90 minutes in advance of a scheduled argument during the fall and winter, and as early as 3 hours ahead in March and April, when schools are often on spring break and students lengthen the line. (Dress warmly; the stone plaza is exposed and can be witheringly cold.) Controversial cases also attract crowds; if you're not sure whether a particular case has created a stir, call the Court information line to reach someone who can tell you. The Court allots only about 150 first-come, first-served seats to the general public, but that number fluctuates from case to case, depending on the number of seats that have been reserved by the lawyers arguing the case and by the press. The Court police officers direct you into one line initially; when the doors finally open, you form a second line if you want to attend only 3 to 5 minutes of the argument.

The justices may release opinions throughout the term, on every third Monday during the Supreme Court term and on argument days (if any opinions are ready). The opinions are delivered before the arguments begin. Mid-May to late June, you can attend brief sessions (about 15 min.) at 10am on Monday, when the justices release remaining orders and opinions for the term. Again, you must stand in line on the front plaza to enter the building.

Leave your cameras, recording devices, and notebooks at your hotel; they're not allowed in the courtroom. ***Note:*** But *do* bring quarters. Security procedures require you to leave all your belongings, including outerwear, purses, books, sunglasses, and so on, in a lower-level checkroom where there are coin-operated lockers that accept only quarters.

Once inside, pay close attention to the many rituals. At 10am, the marshal announces the entrance of the justices, and all present rise and remain standing while the justices take their seats (in high-backed, cushioned swivel chairs, by the way) following the chant: "The Honorable, the Chief Justice and Associate Justices of the Supreme Court of the United States. Oyez! Oyez! Oyez! All persons having business before the Honorable, the Supreme Court of the United States, are admonished to draw near and give their attention, for the Court is now sitting. God save the United States and this Honorable Court!" Unseen by the gallery is the "conference handshake"; following a 19th-century tradition symbolizing a "harmony of aims if not views," each justice shakes hands with each of the other eight when they assemble to go to the bench. The Court has a record before it of prior proceedings and relevant briefs, so each side is allowed only a 30-minute argument.

When the Court is not in session, you can tour the building and attend a **free lecture** in the courtroom about Court procedure and the building's architecture. Lectures are given every hour on the half-hour from 9:30am to 3:30pm. After the talk, explore the Great Hall and go down a flight of steps to see the **24-minute film** on the workings of the Court. On the same floor is an exhibit highlighting the "History of High Courts Around the World," on display indefinitely. Allow about an hour to tour. A gift shop and a public cafeteria are open to the public.

One 1st St. NE (btw. E. Capitol St. and Maryland Ave. NE). ℭ 202/479-3000. www.supremecourtus.gov. Free admission. Mon–Fri 9am–4:20pm. Closed all federal holidays. Metro: Capitol South or Union Station.

The White House 🏛🏛 It's amazing when you think about it: This house has served as residence, office, reception site, and world embassy for every U.S. president since John Adams. The White House is the only private residence of a head of state that has opened its doors to the public for tours, free of charge. It was Thomas Jefferson who started this practice, which is stopped only during wartime. The war on terrorism caused the administration in 2002 to close the White House for public tours for about 2 years. Thankfully, the White House is once again open for public tours, though not walk-up tours. See the box "How to Arrange a White House Tour," below.

An Act of Congress in 1790 established the city, now known as Washington, District of Columbia, as the seat of the federal government. George Washington and city planner Pierre L'Enfant chose the site for the White House (or "President's House," as it was called before whitewashing brought the name "White House" into use) and staged a contest to find a builder. Although Washington picked the winner—Irishman James Hoban—he was the only president never to live in the White House. The structure took 8 years to build, starting in 1792, when its cornerstone was laid. Its facade is made of the same stone that was used to construct the Capitol. In 1814, during the War of 1812, the British set fire to the White House, gutting the interior; the exterior managed to endure only because a rainstorm extinguished the fire. What you see today is Hoban's basic creation: a building modeled after an Irish country house (in fact, Hoban had in mind the house of the Duke of Leinster in Dublin).

Alterations over the years have incorporated the South Portico in 1824, the North Portico in 1829, and electricity in 1891, during Benjamin Harrison's presidency. In 1902, repairs and refurnishings of the White House cost nearly $500,000. No other great change took place until Harry Truman's presidency, when the interior was completely renovated after the leg of Margaret Truman's piano cut through the dining room ceiling. The Trumans lived at Blair House across the street for nearly 4 years while the White House interior was shored up with steel girders and concrete. It's as solid as Gibraltar now.

In 1961, Jacqueline Kennedy formed a Fine Arts Committee to help restore the famous rooms to their original grandeur, ensuring treatment of the White House as a museum of American history and decorative arts. "It just seemed to me such a shame when we came here to find hardly anything of the past in the house, hardly anything before 1902," Mrs. Kennedy observed. Presidents through the years have put their own stamp on the White House, one recent example being President George W. Bush's addition of the T-ball field to the South Lawn.

Highlights of the tour include the **Gold-and-White East Room,** the scene of presidential receptions, weddings (Lynda Bird Johnson, for one), and other dazzling events. This is where the president entertains visiting heads of state and the place where seven

of the eight presidents who died in office (all but Garfield) laid in state. It was also where Nixon resigned. The room's early-18th-century style was adopted during the Theodore Roosevelt renovation of 1902; it has parquet Fontainebleau oak floors and white-painted wood walls with fluted pilasters and classical relief inserts. Note the famous Gilbert Stuart portrait of George Washington that Dolley Madison saved from the British torch during the War of 1812. The portrait is the only object to have remained continuously in the White House since 1800 (except during times of reconstruction).

You'll visit the **Green Room,** which was Thomas Jefferson's dining room but today is used as a sitting room. Mrs. Kennedy chose the green watered-silk-fabric wall covering. In the **Oval Blue Room,** decorated in the French Empire style chosen by James Monroe in 1817, presidents and first ladies have officially received guests since the Jefferson administration. It was, however, Van Buren's decor that began the "blue room" tradition. The walls, on which hang portraits of five presidents (including Rembrandt Peale's portrait of Thomas Jefferson and G. P. A. Healy's of Tyler), are covered in reproductions of early-19th-century French and American wallpaper. Grover Cleveland, the only president to wed in the White House, was married in the Blue Room. This room was also where the Reagans greeted the 52 Americans liberated after being held hostage in Iran for 444 days, and every year it's the setting for the White House Christmas tree.

The **Red Room,** with its red satin-covered walls and Empire furnishings, is used as a reception room, primarily for afternoon teas. Several portraits of past presidents and a Gilbert Stuart portrait of Dolley Madison hang here. Dolley Madison used the Red Room for her famous Wednesday-night receptions.

From the Red Room, you enter the **State Dining Room.** Modeled after late-18th-century neoclassical English houses, this room is a superb setting for state dinners and luncheons. Below G. P. A. Healy's portrait of Lincoln is an inscription written by John Adams on his second night in the White House (FDR had it carved into the mantel): "I Pray Heaven to Bestow The Best of Blessings on THIS HOUSE and on All that shall here-after Inhabit it. May none but Honest and Wise Men ever rule under this Roof."

Note: Even if you have successfully reserved a White House tour for your group, you should still call © **202/456-7041** before setting out in the morning, in case the White House is closed on short notice because of unforeseen events. If this should happen to you, you should make a point of walking by the White House anyway, since its exterior is still pretty awe-inspiring. Stroll past it on Pennsylvania Avenue, down 15th Street past the Treasury Building, and along the backside and South Lawn, on E Street.

1600 Pennsylvania Ave. NW (visitor entrance gate at E St. and E. Executive Ave.). © **202/456-7041** or 208-1631. www.whitehouse.gov. Free admission. Tours for groups of 10 or more who have arranged the tour through their congressional offices. Metro: Federal Triangle.

The White House Visitor Center

The Visitor Center opened in 1995 to provide extensive interpretive data about the White House (and to serve as a ticket-distribution center, though that function has been suspended). It is run under the auspices of the National Park Service and the staff is well-informed. A 30-minute video about the White House provides interior views of the presidential precincts (it runs continuously throughout the day). Pick up a copy of the National Park Service's brochure on the White House, which tells you a little about what you'll see in the eight or so rooms you tour and a bit about the history of the White House. The White House Historic Association runs a small shop here. Before you leave the Visitor Center, take a look at

The White House Area

Dupont Circle
Red Line

DUPONT CIRCLE

N. St.

M. St.

L. St.

Connecticut Avenue

National Geographic Society

Farragut North
Red Line

K. St.

I. St.

19th St.

18th St.

17th St.

16th St.

15th St.

Area of detail

GEORGETOWN

The White House

Union Station

ARLINGTON

U.S. Capitol

VIRGINIA

Potomac River

0 1 mi

0 1 km

Farragut West
Blue & Orange Lines

Veteran's Administration

K St.

McPherson Square
Blue & Orange Lines

14th St.

Pennsylvania Avenue

H. St.

LAFAYETTE SQUARE

New York Avenue

13th St.

Renwick Gallery

G. St.

G. St.

Executive Office Building

Treasury Department

Metro Center
Red, Blue & Orange Lines

F. St.

The White House

W. Executive Ave.

E. Executive Ave.

F. St.

General Services Administration

Octagon House

State Pl.

Treasury Pl.

Pennsylvania Avenue

Federal Triangle
Blue & Orange Lines

Corcoran Gallery of Art

South Executive Ave.

White House Visitor Center

E. St.

District Building

Interior Department

E. St.

Red Cross

Zero Milestone

Commerce Department

Ronald Reagan Building and International Trade Center

19th St.

18th St.

Constitution Hall

D St.

THE ELLIPSE

15th St.

Bureau of Indian Affairs

OAS Annex

C. St.

Organization of American States (OAS)

Labor Department

Virginia Avenue

Constitution Avenue

FOGGY BOTTOM

CONSTITUTION GARDENS

National Museum of American History

14th St.

Madison Drive

Reflecting Pool

World War II Memorial

17th St.

Washington Monument

Jefferson Drive

Sylvan Theater

John Paul Jones statue

Independence Avenue

Independence Avenue

Kutz Bridge

U.S. Holocaust Museum

15th St.

Department of Agriculture

Tidal Basin

CHERRY TREES

Bureau of Engraving and Printing

0 1/8 mile

0 100 meters

N

Tips How to Arrange a White House Tour

The White House allows groups of 10 or more to tour the White House, Tuesday through Saturday, from 7:30am to 12:30pm. Tours are self-guided and most people take no more than an hour to go through. You must have a reservation to tour the White House. At least 2 months and as far as 6 months in advance of your trip, call your senator's or representative's office with the names of the people in your group and ask for a specific tour date. The tour coordinator consults with White House on availability and, if your date is available, contacts you to obtain the names, birth dates, Social Security numbers (for those 14 and older), and other information for each of the people in your party. The Secret Service reviews the information and clears you for the tour, putting the names of the people in your group on a confirmed reservation list; you'll receive a confirmation number and the date and time of your tour usually about 1 month in advance of your trip. On the day of your tour, call ⓒ 202/456-7041 to make sure that the White House is still open that day to the public. Then off you go, to the south side of East Executive Avenue, near the Southeast Gate of the White House, with photo IDs for everyone in your party who is 15 or older.

Do not bring the following prohibited items: backpacks, book bags, handbags, or purses; food and beverages; strollers; cameras; videorecorders or any type of recording device; tobacco products; personal grooming items, from cosmetics to hairbrushes; any pointed objects, whether a pen or a knitting needle; aerosol containers; guns; ammunition; fireworks; electric stun guns; maces; martial arts weapons/devices; or knives of any description. Cellphones are okay, but not the kind that are also cameras. The White House does not have a coatcheck facility, so there is no place for you to leave your belongings while you go on the tour. There are no public restrooms or telephones in the White House, and picture taking and videotaping are prohibited. *Best advice:* Leave everything but your wallet back at the hotel.

If your party numbers fewer than 10 people, I'm afraid you're probably out of luck; though congressional offices used to try putting strangers together to make a group of 10, most congressional staff found the process unworkable. Your senator's or representative's office might be the exception, however, so go ahead and call.

the exhibits, which include information about the architectural history of the White House; portrayals by photographers, artists, journalists, and political cartoonists; anecdotes about first families (such as the time prankster Tad Lincoln stood in a window above his father and waved a Confederate flag at a military review); details about what goes on behind the scenes, focusing on the vast staff of servants, chefs, gardeners, Secret Service people, and others who maintain this institution; highlights of notable White House ceremonies and celebrations, from a Wright Brothers' aviation demonstration in 1911 to a ballet performance by Baryshnikov during the Carter administration; and photographs of the ever-changing Oval Office as decorated by administrations from Taft to Bush.

1450 Pennsylvania Ave. NW (in the Dept. of Commerce Building, btw. 14th and 15th sts.). ⓒ 202/208-1631. Free admission. Daily 7:30am–4pm. Closed Jan 1, Thanksgiving, and Dec 25. Metro: Federal Triangle.

2 The National Mall & Memorial Parks

The National Park Service refers to the national parkland that extends from the Capitol to the Potomac River, encompassing the memorials, Washington Monument, National Mall, and West and East Potomac parks as the **National Mall and Memorial Parks.** The National Mall and Memorial Parks has its own telephone number, ✆ **202/485-9880,** and website, nps.gov/nama.

THE NATIONAL MALL

As part of his vision for Washington, Pierre L'Enfant conceived of the National Mall as a bustling ceremonial avenue of embassies and other distinguished buildings. Today's 2-mile stretch of land extending westward from the Capitol reflecting pool to the Lincoln Memorial fulfills that dream to some extent. Ten Smithsonian buildings (see next section, "The Smithsonian Museums," p. 183), plus the National Gallery of Art and its Sculpture Garden, a stray government building (Dept. of Agriculture), and the U. S. Botanic Garden stake out the Mall's northern border along Constitution Avenue and southern border along Independence Avenue. Elm trees shade the pebbled walkways paralleling Jefferson and Madison drives. Tourists and locals crisscross the Mall as they visit the Smithsonian museums, hustle to work, pursue exercise, participate in whatever festival, event, or demonstration is taking place on the Mall that day, or simply go for a stroll, just as L'Enfant envisioned, perhaps.

What L'Enfant did not foresee was the toll that all of this activity might take on this piece of parkland. When you visit the Mall these days, you might be dismayed to see an expanse of browned grass instead of green, crumbling walkways, and an overall worn appearance. The National Park Service maintains the land but can't keep pace with the rate of needed repair and preservation, mostly because Congress has reduced its budget. The National Park Service is at work on a plan for the future of the National Mall (see www.nps.gov/nationalmallplan), as is the Trust for the National Mall, www.nationalmall.org, the Park Service's official fundraising partner. A third organization called the National Coalition to Save Our Mall (www.savethemall.org), made up of professional and civic groups as well as assorted concerned artists, historians, and residents, is also lobbying Congress for more support for the Mall's upkeep and improvements, including the addition of a 24/7 National Mall Welcome Center. These organizations don't necessarily agree on their visions for the Mall. Stay tuned.

THE MAJOR MEMORIALS

The National Mall and Memorial Parks' major memorials honor esteemed presidents, war veterans, founding fathers, and, by the end of 2009, a civil rights leader. On November 13, 2006, thousands attended the official groundbreaking for the National Mall's newest memorial, the **Martin Luther King, Jr., National Memorial,** with many more anticipated for the memorial's dedication in December 2009. Located on a 4-acre parcel at the intersection of West Basin Drive and Independence Avenue, adjoining the Tidal Basin and adjacent to the FDR Memorial, and positioned in a direct line with the Lincoln and Jefferson memorials, the King Memorial pays tribute to the Baptist minister. His commitment to nonviolence and direct action to force social change, and his efforts and compelling speeches profoundly moved the country toward that achievement—before he was assassinated at the age of 39 on April 4, 1968.

All of these memorials are located in picturesque **West Potomac Park** (p. 220 for full details on the park and its famous **cherry blossoms**), which lies at the western end

of the Mall, where it borders the Potomac River and encircles the Tidal Basin. Unfortunately, none of the memorials lies directly on a Metro line, so you can expect a bit of a walk from the specified station.

The easiest thing to do, if you're up to it, is to walk from one landmark to the next. I've organized just such a tour, detailed below. Or, you can go by **Tourmobile** (p. 226), which continually picks up and discharges passengers at each of these sites throughout the day and allows you to purchase a ticket in advance or as you board, whichever works for you. Still another alternative is to bike the sites. See suggested bike-rental locations listed on p. 228. Every memorial site has a bike rack.

TOURING THE MEMORIALS ON FOOT

I've designed—and tested—the following walking tour of the memorials, ordering the stops in a sequence that I believe makes most sense in terms of logistics and geography. The beauty of it is that you can easily tinker with this tour to suit your own purposes. The Washington Monument is the only site that has limited hours and requires a ticket; otherwise, the memorials are open 24 hours to the public, which means that you can follow this tour at 5am or 5pm, at 2 in the morning or 2 in the afternoon. Some believe the best time to visit the memorials is at night, when they're illuminated in all their imposing white-stone glory and the crowds have thinned. Use common sense, though. The memorials may be lit up, but not necessarily the lanes and pathways leading to them.

Before you start the tour, here's what you need to know:

- Dress for the weather: light clothing, shades, and sunscreen in summer; a hat, gloves, and warm jacket in winter. The Washington Monument and the memorials are mostly set in wide-open spaces, with little to no protection from the elements.
- The National Park Service manages all of these properties and maintains information about each of them, including upcoming events, at **www.nps.gov/nama**. Scroll down the page to click on the names of sites.
- Park rangers are on hand from 8am to 11:30pm year-round, except at the Washington Monument, which closes at 5pm.
- Restrooms are located inside the ranger lodge/ticket kiosk at the bottom of the hill from the Washington Monument; in the basements of the Jefferson and Lincoln memorials; at the back of the information and gift shop of the FDR Memorial; and in a building beyond the National World War II Memorial information lodge. Visitors to the George Mason Memorial use the restrooms at the Jefferson Memorial; visitors to the Korean War Memorial and the Vietnam Veterans War Memorial use the restrooms at the Lincoln Memorial.
- Eat well before you head off on the tour. The National Park Service prohibits food and drink inside all of the memorials and at the Washington Monument. It allows refreshment kiosks and vendors, but only at a distance. Refreshment and souvenir kiosks are located across 15th Street from the Washington Monument's ticket booth; on Daniel Chester French Drive between the Lincoln Memorial and the Korean War Memorial; on Henry Bacon Drive across the street from the Vietnam Veterans Memorial, with another on the other side of the memorial; and in front of the Jefferson Memorial. These are rudimentary services, selling beverages, sandwiches, ice cream and the like, just enough to refresh you if you're feeling faint.
- The tour will take about 3 to 4 hours and cover 3 to 4 miles.

- Best times to take the tour: weekdays and evenings to avoid crowds, early or late in summer to avoid the heat; anytime otherwise.

This tour starts at the Washington Monument on 15th Street NW and ends at the National World War II Memorial on 17th Street NW.

Starting out: Take the Metro to Metro Center (13th and G sts. exit) and walk west 2 blocks to 15th Street NW. Have breakfast, lunch, or dinner at the **Old Ebbitt Grill** (p. 135), which opens early and stays open late. Then walk about ½ mile to the Washington Monument.

Note: I've included nearest Metro information for each site, in case you choose not to walk this tour.

Washington Monument ★★★ *Kids* The idea of a tribute to George Washington first arose 16 years before his death, at the Continental Congress of 1783. But the new nation had more pressing problems and funds were not readily available. It wasn't until the early 1830s, with the 100th anniversary of Washington's birth approaching, that any action was taken.

Then there were several fiascoes. A mausoleum was provided for Washington's remains under the Capitol Rotunda, but a grandnephew, citing Washington's will, refused to allow the body to be moved from Mount Vernon. In 1830, Horatio Greenough was commissioned to create a memorial statue for the Rotunda. He came up with a bare-chested Washington, draped in classical Greek garb. A shocked public claimed he looked as if he were "entering or leaving a bath," and so the statue was relegated to the Smithsonian. Finally, in 1833, prominent citizens organized the Washington National Monument Society. Treasury Building architect Robert Mills's design was accepted.

> **Impressions**
> *May the spirit which animated the great founder of this city descend to future generations.*
> —John Adams

The cornerstone was laid on July 4, 1848; and for the next 37 years, watching the monument grow, or not grow, was a local pastime. Declining contributions and the Civil War brought construction to a halt at an awkward 150 feet (you can still see a change in the color of the stone about halfway up). The unsightly stump remained until 1876, when President Grant approved federal moneys to complete the project. Dedicated in 1885, it was opened to the public in 1888.

Visiting the Washington Monument: A series of security walls encircles the Washington Monument grounds, a barrier to vehicles but not people; the National Park Service has gone to a good bit of trouble to incorporate these 33-inch-high walls into a pleasing landscape design. Please be aware that large backpacks and open containers of food or drink are not allowed inside the monument; small sealed containers are okay. You'll need a ticket (see information below), and then you pass through a small screening facility before entering the monument's large elevator, which whisks you upward for 70 seconds.

Reaching the top, you'll be standing in the highest tip of the world's tallest freestanding work of masonry. The Washington Monument lies at the very heart of Washington, D.C., landmarks, and its 360-degree views are spectacular. Due east are the Capitol and Smithsonian buildings; due north is the White House; due west are the World War II and Lincoln memorials (with Arlington National Cemetery beyond);

due south is the Jefferson Memorial, overlooking the Tidal Basin and the Potomac River. "On a clear day, you can see west probably 60 miles, as far as the Shenandoah Mountains," says National Park Service spokesperson Bill Line. Like being at the center of a compass, the monument provides a marvelous orientation to the city.

The glass-walled elevator slows down in its descent, to allow passengers a view of some of the 192 carved stones inserted into the interior walls that are gifts from foreign countries, all 50 states, organizations, and individuals. One stone you usually get to see is the one given by the state of Alaska in 1982—it's pure jade and worth millions. There are stones from Siam (now Thailand), the Cherokee Nation, the Vatican, and the Sons of Temperance, to name just a few.

Allow half an hour here, plus time spent waiting in line. A concession stand is open at the corner of 15th Street and Madison Drive NW.

Ticket Information: Admission to the Washington Monument is free, but you still have to get a ticket. The ticket booth is located in the Monument Lodge, at the bottom of the hill from the monument, on 15th Street NW between Madison and Jefferson drives. It opens daily at 8:30am. Tickets are often gone by 9am, so plan to get there by 7:30 or 8am, especially in peak season. The tickets grant admission at half-hour intervals between the stated hours on the day you visit. If you want to get tickets in advance, call the National Park Reservation Service (✆ 877/444-6777) or go to www.recreation.gov. The tickets themselves are free, but you'll pay $1.50 per ticket, plus $2.85 for shipping and handling, if you're ordering 10 or more days in advance; otherwise, you pick up the tickets at the "will call" window at the ticket kiosk. To make sure that you get tickets for your desired date, reserve these tickets at least 2 weeks in advance. You can order up to six tickets.

Directly south of the White House, on 15th St. (btw. Madison Dr. and Constitution Ave. NW). ✆ 202/426-6841. www.nps.gov/wamo. Free admission. Daily 9am–4:45pm. Last elevators depart 15 min. before closing (arrive earlier). Closed Dec 25, open until noon July 4th. Limited parking. Metro: Smithsonian (Mall/Jefferson Dr. exit), then a 10-min. walk, or take Tourmobile or the D.C. Circulator (takes you close though not directly to it).

Return to 15th Street and head up the hill, crossing Independence Avenue SW and following the signs for the Jefferson Memorial. You'll pass the U.S. Holocaust Memorial Museum on your left, the Tidal Basin and pedal boats on your right. This will be your single longest walk on the tour—about a mile or less. Go around the bend to find the:

Jefferson Memorial 🅰🅰 President John F. Kennedy, at a 1962 dinner honoring 29 Nobel Prize winners, told his guests that they were "the most extraordinary collection of talent, of human knowledge, that has ever been gathered together at the White House, with the possible exception of when Thomas Jefferson dined alone." Jefferson penned the Declaration of Independence and served as George Washington's secretary of state, John Adams's vice president, and America's third president. He spoke out against slavery, although, like many of his countrymen, he kept slaves himself. He also established the University of Virginia and pursued wide-ranging interests, including architecture, astronomy, anthropology, music, and farming.

Franklin Delano Roosevelt, a great admirer of Jefferson, spearheaded the effort to build him a memorial, although the site choice was problematic. The Capitol, the White House, and the Mall were already located in accordance with architect Pierre L'Enfant's master plan for the city, and there was no spot for such a project that would maintain L'Enfant's symmetry. So the memorial was built on land reclaimed from the Potomac River, now known as the Tidal Basin. Roosevelt laid the cornerstone in 1939

and had all the trees between the Jefferson Memorial and the White House cut down so that he could see the memorial every morning.

The memorial is a columned rotunda in the style of the Pantheon in Rome, whose classical architecture Jefferson himself introduced to this country (he designed his home, Monticello, and the earliest University of Virginia buildings in Charlottesville). On the Tidal Basin side, the sculptural group above the entrance depicts Jefferson with Benjamin Franklin, John Adams, Roger Sherman, and Robert Livingston, all of whom worked on drafting the Declaration of Independence. The domed interior of the memorial contains the 19-foot bronze statue of Jefferson standing on a 6-foot pedestal of black Minnesota granite. The sculpture is the work of Rudolph Evans, who was chosen from more than 100 artists in a nationwide competition. Jefferson is depicted wearing a fur-collared coat given to him by his close friend, the Polish general Tadeusz Kosciuszko. If you follow Jefferson's gaze, you see that, sure enough, the Jefferson Memorial and the White House have an unimpeded view of each other.

Rangers present 20- to 30-minute programs throughout the day as time permits. Twenty to 30 minutes is sufficient time to spend here.

On Ohio Dr. SW, at the south shore of the Tidal Basin (in West Potomac Park). *C* 202/426-6841. www.nps.gov/thje. Free admission. Ranger on duty daily 9:30am–11:30pm, except Dec 25. Limited parking. Metro: Smithsonian (12th St./Independence Ave. exit), with a 20- to 30-min. walk, or take Tourmobile.

Follow the memorial's front path back out to East Basin Drive, turn right and go around the bend to the:

George Mason Memorial ✿ This memorial honors George Mason, author of the Virginia Declaration of Rights, which had much to do with the establishment of the United States Bill of Rights. Dedicated on April 9, 2002, the memorial consists of a bronze statue of Mason, set back in a landscaped grove of trees and flower beds (lots and lots of pansies), arranged in concentric circles around a pool and fountain. Mason appears in 18th-century garb, from buckled shoes to tricorn hat, seated on a marble bench, but leaning backward on one arm and gazing off in the general direction of the Washington Monument. Two stone slabs are inscribed with some of Mason's words, like these, referring to Mason's rejection of slavery, "that slow Poison, which is daily contaminating the Minds & Morals of our People." Wooden benches at the site present a pleasant opportunity to learn about Mason and take a break before moving on. *Note:* The memorial is easy to miss, since it does not lie on the Tidal Basin path. As you approach the Jefferson Memorial from the direction of the FDR Memorial, or as you approach the FDR Memorial from the direction of the Jefferson, you'll come to the bridge that arches over the inlet leading from the Tidal Basin to the Potomac River; look straight across from the bridge, and there you'll see it.

At East Basin and Ohio Dr. SW (btw. the Jefferson and FDR memorials). *C* 202/426-6841. www.nps.gov/gemm. Free admission. Always open, though rangers generally are not posted here. To find out more about George Mason, visit the Jefferson Memorial, a 5-min. walk away, across the street, on the Tidal Basin, where a park ranger is on duty 9:30am–11:30pm. Limited parking. Metro: Smithsonian (12th St./Independence Ave. exit), with a 25-min. walk, or take Tourmobile.

Recross East Basin Drive to find the opening that leads to the Tidal Basin pathway. Follow the path about 5 minutes, enjoy the spectacular view of the Tidal Basin and the capital's skyline, until you see the sign for the FDR Memorial. You'll be entering the memorial the back way, but go ahead and follow the lane and then walk all the way through to the entrance of the:

Franklin Delano Roosevelt Memorial ★★★ The FDR Memorial has proven to be one of the most popular of the presidential memorials since it opened in 1997. Its popularity has to do as much with its design as the man it honors. This 7½-acre outdoor memorial stretches out, rather than rising up, across the stone-paved floor. Granite walls define the four "galleries," each representing a different term in FDR's presidency from 1933 to 1945. Architect Lawrence Halprin's design includes waterfalls, sculptures (by Leonard Baskin, John Benson, Neil Estern, Robert Graham, Thomas Hardy, and George Segal), and Roosevelt's own words carved into the stone.

One drawback of the FDR Memorial is the noise. Planes on their way to or from nearby Reagan National Airport zoom overhead, and the many displays of cascading water can sound thunderous. When the memorial first opened, adults and children alike arrived in bathing suits and splashed around on warm days. Park rangers don't allow that anymore, but they do allow you to dip your feet in the various pools. A favorite time to visit is at night, when dramatic lighting reveals the waterfalls and statues against the dark parkland.

Conceived in 1946, the FDR Memorial had been in the works for 50 years. Part of the delay in its construction can be attributed to the president himself. FDR had told his friend Supreme Court Justice Felix Frankfurter, "If they are to put up any memorial to me, I should like it to be placed in the center of that green plot in front of the Archives Building. I should like it to consist of a block about the size [of this desk]." In fact, such a plaque sits in front of the National Archives Building. Friends and relatives struggled to honor Roosevelt's request to leave it at that, but Congress and national sentiment overrode them.

As with other presidential memorials, this one opened to some controversy. Advocates for people with disabilities were incensed that the memorial sculptures did not show the president in a wheelchair, which he used after he contracted polio. President Clinton asked Congress to allocate funding for an additional statue portraying a wheelchair-bound FDR. You will now see a small statue of FDR in a wheelchair, placed at the very front of the memorial, to the right as you approach the first gallery. Step inside the gift shop to view a replica of Roosevelt's wheelchair, as well as one of the rare photographs of the president sitting in a wheelchair. The memorial is probably the most accessible tourist attraction in the city; as at most of the National Park Service locations, wheelchairs are available for free use on-site.

If you don't see a posting of tour times, look for a ranger and request a tour; the rangers are happy to oblige. Thirty minutes is sufficient time to allot here.

On West Basin Dr., alongside the Tidal Basin in West Potomac Park (across Independence Ave. SW from the Mall). ✆ 202/426-6841. www.nps.gov/frde. Free admission. Ranger on duty daily 9:30am–11:30pm, except for Dec 25. Limited parking. Metro: Smithsonian (12th St./Independence Ave.), with a 30-min. walk, or take Tourmobile.

Return to the Tidal Basin path and turn left toward the Lincoln Memorial. As you come up to the street, you'll see the plaque, and perhaps actual construction of the memorial to the Rev. Dr. Martin Luther King, Jr., Walk to the traffic light and cross Independence Avenue. Turn right and walk a short distance to the clearing that leads you back to the DC War Memorial, which Pres. Herbert Hoover dedicated in 1931. Continue to the walkway behind the memorial and turn left to follow the main lane toward the Lincoln Memorial. But first, you'll come upon the:

Korean War Veterans Memorial ★ This privately funded memorial, founded in 1995, honors those who served in Korea, a 3-year conflict (1950–53) that produced almost as many casualties as Vietnam. It consists of a circular "Pool of Remembrance"

in a grove of trees and a triangular "Field of Service," highlighted by lifelike statues of 19 infantrymen, who appear to be trudging across fields. A 164-foot-long black-granite wall depicts the array of combat and support troops that served in Korea (nurses, chaplains, airmen, gunners, mechanics, cooks, and others); a raised granite curb lists the 22 nations that contributed to the UN's effort there; and a commemorative area honors KIAs, MIAs, and POWs. Plan to spend 15 minutes for viewing.

Southeast of the Lincoln Memorial, on the Independence Ave. SW side of the Mall. © 202/426-6841. www.nps. gov/kowa. Free admission. Ranger on duty daily 9:30am–11:30pm except Dec 25. Limited parking. Metro: Foggy Bottom, with 30-min. walk, or take Tourmobile.

Next, tour the:

Lincoln Memorial ★★★ *(Kids)* This beautiful and moving tribute to the nation's 16th president attracts millions of visitors annually. Like its fellow presidential memorials, the Lincoln was a long time in the making. Although it was planned as early as 1867—2 years after Lincoln's death—Henry Bacon's design was not completed until 1912, and the memorial was dedicated in 1922.

The neoclassical temple-like structure, similar in architectural design to the Parthenon in Greece, has 36 fluted Doric columns representing the states of the Union at the time of Lincoln's death, plus two at the entrance. On the attic parapet are 48 festoons symbolizing the number of states in 1922, when the monument was erected. Hawaii and Alaska are noted in an inscription on the terrace. Due east is the Reflecting Pool, lined with American elms and stretching 2,000 feet toward the Washington Monument and the Capitol beyond.

The memorial chamber has limestone walls inscribed with the Gettysburg Address and Lincoln's Second Inaugural Address. Two 60-foot-high murals by Jules Guerin on the north and south walls depict, allegorically, Lincoln's principles and achievements. On the south wall, an Angel of Truth freeing a slave is flanked by groups of figures representing Justice and Immortality. The north-wall mural portrays the unity of North and South and is flanked by groups of figures symbolizing Fraternity and Charity. Most powerful, however, is Daniel Chester French's 19-foot-high seated statue of Lincoln, which disappears from your sightline as you get close to the base of the memorial, then emerges slowly into view as you ascend the stairs.

Lincoln's legacy has made his memorial the site of numerous demonstrations by those seeking justice. Most notable was a peaceful demonstration of 200,000 people on August 28, 1963, at which the Rev. Dr. Martin Luther King, Jr., proclaimed, "I have a dream." Look for the words "I have a dream. Martin Luther King, Jr., The March on Washington for Jobs and Freedom, August 28, 1963," inscribed and centered on the granite step, 18 steps down from the chamber. The inscription, which the National Park Service added in July 2003, marks the precise spot where King stood to deliver his famous speech.

Rangers present 20- to 30-minute programs as time permits throughout the day. Thirty minutes is sufficient time for viewing this memorial.

On the western end of the Mall, at 23rd St. NW (btw. Constitution and Independence aves.). © 202/426-6842. www.nps.gov/linc. Free admission. Ranger on duty daily 9:30am–11:30pm except Dec 25. Limited parking. Metro: Foggy Bottom, then a 30-min. walk, or take Tourmobile, or catch the D.C. Circulator to 17th and Constitution and walk from there.

Walk from the Lincoln Memorial toward the reflecting pool, but turn left and proceed toward the information kiosk, then right, to follow the path that leads to the Vietnam Veterans Memorial. You pass first a life-size sculpture of three Vietnam soldiers by Frederick

Hart. Near the statue, a flag flies from a 60-foot staff. Another sculpture, the Vietnam Veterans Women's Memorial, *depicts three servicewomen tending a wounded soldier. Continue until you reach the:*

Vietnam Veterans Memorial ★★ The Vietnam Veterans Memorial is possibly the most poignant sight in Washington: two long, black-granite walls in the shape of a V, each inscribed with the names of the men and women who gave their lives, or remain missing, in the longest war in American history. Even if no one close to you died in Vietnam, it's wrenching to watch visitors grimly studying the directories to find out where their loved ones are listed, or rubbing pencil on paper held against a name etched into the wall. The walls list close to 60,000 people, most of whom died very young.

Because of the raging conflict over U.S. involvement in the war, Vietnam veterans had received almost no recognition of their service before the memorial was conceived by Vietnam veteran Jan Scruggs. The nonprofit Vietnam Veterans Memorial Fund raised $7 million and secured a 2-acre site in tranquil Constitution Gardens to erect a memorial that would make no political statement about the war and would harmonize with neighboring memorials. By separating the issue of the wartime service of individuals from the issue of U.S. policy in Vietnam, the VVMF hoped to begin a process of national reconciliation.

Yale senior Maya Lin's design was chosen in a national competition open to all citizens 18 and over years of age. Erected in 1982, the memorial's two walls are angled at 125 degrees to point to the Washington Monument and the Lincoln Memorial. The wall's mirror-like surface reflects surrounding trees, lawns, and monuments. The names are inscribed in chronological order, documenting an epoch in American history as a series of individual sacrifices from the date of the first casualty in 1959. The National Park Service continues to add names as Vietnam veterans die eventually of injuries sustained during the war. A movement is underway to create a visitor center for the Vietnam Veterans Memorial on the plot of land across Henry Bacon Drive from the memorial.

You should allow about 20 to 30 minutes here.

Be sure to seek out the knowledgeable park rangers if you have any questions.

Northeast of the Lincoln Memorial, east of Henry Bacon Dr. (btw. 21st and 22nd sts. NW, on the Constitution Ave. NW side of the Mall). ℭ **202/426-6841**. www.nps.gov/vive. Free admission. Ranger on duty daily 9:30am–11:30pm except Dec 25. Limited parking. Metro: Foggy Bottom, with 25-min. walk, or take Tourmobile, or catch the D.C. Circulator to 17th and Constitution and walk from there.

Now, turn back toward the reflecting pool and follow the shaded lane about half a mile east, making sure to walk as far as 17th Street, to visit the:

National World War II Memorial ★★ When this memorial was dedicated on May 29, 2004, 150,000 people attended: President Bush; members of Congress; Marine Corps General (retired) P. X. Kelley, who chaired the American Battle Monuments Commission, the group that spearheaded construction of the memorial; actor Tom Hanks and now-retired news anchor Tom Brokaw, both of whom had been active in eliciting support for the memorial; and last, but most important, thousands of World War II veterans and their families. These legions of veterans, some dressed in uniform, many wearing a cap identifying the name of the veteran's division, turned out with pride, happy to receive the nation's gratitude, 60 years in the making, expressed profoundly in this memorial.

Designed by Friedrich St. Florian and funded mostly by private donations, the memorial fits nicely into the landscape between the Washington Monument grounds to the east and the Lincoln Memorial and its reflecting pool to the west. St. Florian purposely situated the 7½-acre memorial so as not to obstruct this long view down the Mall. Fifty-six 17-foot-high granite pillars representing each state and territory stand to either side of a central plaza and the Rainbow Pool. Likewise, 24 bas-relief panels divide down the middle so that 12 line each side of the walkway leading from the entrance at 17th Street. The panels to the left, as you walk toward the center of the memorial, illustrate seminal scenes from the war years as they relate to the Pacific theater: Pearl Harbor, amphibious landing, jungle warfare, a field burial, and so on; the panels to the right are sculptured scenes of war moments related to the Atlantic theater: Rosie the Riveter, Normandy Beach landing, the Battle of the Bulge, the Russians meeting the Americans at the Elbe River. Architect and sculptor Raymond Kaskey sculpted these panels based on archival photographs.

Large open pavilions stake out the north and south axes of the memorial, and semicircular fountains create waterfalls on either side. Inscriptions at the base of each pavilion fountain mark key battles. Beyond the center Rainbow Pool is a wall of 4,000 gold stars, one star for every 100 soldiers who died in World War II. People often leave photos and mementos around the memorial, which the National Park Service gather up daily for an archive. If you are lucky, you will have the chance to talk to World War II veterans here to tour the memorial. For compelling, firsthand accounts of World War II experiences, combine your tour here with an online visit to the Library of Congress's Veterans History Project, at www.loc.gov/vets; see the Library of Congress entry later in this chapter for more information.

From the 17th Street entrance walk south around the perimeter of the memorial to reach a ranger station, where there are brochures as well as registry kiosks for looking up names of veterans. Better information and faster service is available online at www.wwiimemorial.com.

On 17th St., near Constitution Ave. NW. ℂ **800/639-4WW2** (4992) or 202/426-6841. www.nps.gov/wwii. Free admission. Ranger on duty daily 9:30am–11:30pm, except Dec 25. Limited parking. Metro: Farragut West, Federal Triangle, or Smithsonian, with a 20- to 25-min. walk, or take Tourmobile, or catch the D.C. Circulator.

Reward yourself. From here, you can catch a ride on the D.C. Circulator bus, which stops at the corner of 17th Street and Constitution Avenue NW. Take it to, say, Constitution Avenue and 7th Street NW, where it's a short walk up to Pennsylvania Avenue NW and the Penn Quarter neighborhood—and lots of restaurants.

3 The Smithsonian Museums

Our Smithsonian museums are justly famous. Collectively known as the "Smithsonian Institution," these 19 museums, nine research centers, and the National Zoological Park comprise the world's largest museum complex. Twenty-four million people visit the Smithsonians annually. The Smithsonian's collection of nearly 137 million objects spans the entire world and all of its history, its peoples and animals (past and present), and our attempts to probe into the future.

So vast is the collection that Smithsonian museums display only about 1% or 2% of the collection's holdings at any given time. Artifacts range from a 3.5-billion-year-old fossil to inaugural gowns worn by the first ladies. Thousands of scientific expeditions sponsored by the Smithsonian have pushed into remote frontiers in the deserts, mountains, polar regions, and jungles.

The Smithson Behind the Smithsonian

You must be wondering by now: How did the Smithsonian Institution come to be? It's rather an unlikely story. It's all because of the largesse of a wealthy English scientist named James Smithson (1765–1829), the illegitimate son of the duke of Northumberland. Smithson willed his vast fortune to the United States, to found "at Washington, under the name of the Smithsonian Institution, an establishment for the increase and diffusion of knowledge." Smithson never explained why he left this handsome bequest to the United States, a country he had never visited. Speculation is that he felt the new nation, lacking established cultural institutions, most needed his funds.

Smithson died in Genoa, Italy, in 1829. Congress accepted his gift in 1836; 2 years later, half a million dollars' worth of gold sovereigns (a considerable sum in the 19th c.) arrived at the U.S. Mint in Philadelphia. For the next 8 years, Congress debated the best possible use for these funds. Finally, in 1846, James Polk signed an act into law establishing the Smithsonian Institution and authorizing a board to receive "all objects of art and of foreign and curious research, and all objects of natural history, plants, and geological and mineralogical specimens . . . for research and museum purposes." In 1855, the first Smithsonian building opened on the Mall, not as a museum, but as the home of the Smithsonian Institution. The red sandstone structure suffered a fire and several reconstructions over the years, to serve today as the Smithsonian Information Center, known by all as "the Castle."

Private donations have swelled Smithson's original legacy many times over. Although the Smithsonian acquires approximately 70% of its yearly budget from congressional allocations, the institution depends quite heavily on these moneys from private donors, especially since many of the museums are undergoing or in need of renovation. In a sign of the times, and due to the need of the Smithsonian for larger contributions, the institution has imposed an admission fee for the first time ever (for one museum's exhibit only): $6 to enter the Butterfly Pavilion at the National Museum of Natural History (p. 193). General admission to the rest of the museum, and to all other Smithsonian museums, remains free.

To find out information about any of the Smithsonian museums, call ℂ 202/633-1000 or TTY 633-5285. The information specialists who answer are very professional and always helpful. The Smithsonian museums also share a website, www.si.edu, which helps get you to their individual home pages.

Individually, each museum is a powerhouse in its own field: The National Museum of Natural History is the most visited natural history museum in the world (seven million people visited in 2007, according to the latest figures available) and the most visited of the Smithsonians. The National Air and Space Museum maintains the world's largest collection of historic aircraft and spacecraft. The Smithsonian American Art Museum is the nation's first collection of American art and one of the largest in the world. And so on.

Washington lays claim to 17 Smithsonian museums and the National Zoo. (The other two museums, the Cooper-Hewitt, National Design Museum and the National Museum of the American Indian's George Gustav Heye Center, are in New York City.) Of these, 10 are on the Mall (see earlier section and map on "**The National Mall & Memorial Parks**" for more information about the Mall, p. 175.) The institution is planning to open at least one more Smithsonian museum, the National Museum of African American History and Culture, adjacent to the Washington Monument, bounded by Constitution Avenue NW, Madison Drive NW, and 14th and 15th streets NW; completion of the museum is a long way off.

Smithsonian Information Center (the "Castle")

Make this your first stop, and enter through the Enid A. Haupt Garden (see the "Parks & Gardens" section, later in this chapter) for a pleasurable experience. Built in 1855, this Norman-style red-sand-stone building, popularly known as the "Castle," is the oldest building on the Mall.

The main information area here is the Great Hall, where a 24-minute video overview of the institution runs throughout the day in two theaters. There are two large schematic models of the Mall (as well as a third in Braille), which allow visitors to locate nearly 100 popular attractions and Metro and Tourmobile stops.

The entire facility is accessible to persons with disabilities, and information is available in a number of foreign languages. The information desk's volunteer staff can answer questions and help you plan a Smithsonian sightseeing itinerary. Most of the museums are within easy walking distance of the facility.

While you're here, notice the charming vestibule, which has been restored to its turn-of-the-20th-century appearance. It was originally designed to display exhibits at a child's eye level. The gold-trimmed ceiling is decorated to represent a grape arbor with brightly plumed birds and blue sky peeking through the trellis. This is also where the Castle Cafe is located; though the items are awfully pricey, you can't beat the convenience and the fact that it's open at 8:30am. So why not grab a cup of joe and a muffin, then settle yourself outside on a bench in the Enid A. Haupt Garden with your guidebook and maps to plan your day. Ask about castle and garden tours.

1000 Jefferson Dr. SW. (✆ 202/633-1000. Daily 8:30am–5:30pm (info desk 9am–4pm). Closed Dec 25. Metro: Smithsonian (Mall exit).

Anacostia Community Museum

This museum is inconveniently located, but that's because it was initially created in 1967 as a neighborhood museum (which makes it unique among the Smithsonian branches). It's devoted to the African-American experience, focusing on Washington, D.C., and the Upper South. The permanent collection includes about 6,000 items, ranging from videotapes of African-American church services to art, sheet music, historical documents, textiles, glassware, and anthropological objects, dating from the early 1800s. In addition, the Anacostia produces a number of shows each year and offers a comprehensive schedule of free educational programs and activities in conjunction with exhibit themes. Allow about an hour here.

1901 Fort Place SE (off Martin Luther King, Jr., Ave.). (✆ 202/633-4820. http://anacostia.si.edu. Free admission. Daily 10am–5pm. Closed Dec 25. Metro: Grab a bus transfer when you enter the station and take a Green line train traveling in the direction of Anacostia; get off at the Anacostia station and head to the exit marked "Local," turn left after exiting, then take a W2 or W3 bus on Howard Rd. directly to the museum.

Arthur M. Sackler Gallery

Asian art is the focus of this museum and the neighboring Freer (together, they form the National Museum of Asian Art in the United States). The Sackler opened in 1987, thanks to Arthur M. Sackler's gift of 1,000

priceless works. Since then, the museum has received 11th- to 19th-century Persian and Indian paintings, manuscripts, calligraphies, miniatures, bookbindings from the collection of Henri Vever, and art collector Robert O. Muller's entire collection of 4,000 Japanese prints and archival materials.

Your visit begins in the entrance pavilion, where a series of rotating installations, collectively titled "Perspectives," showcases the works of contemporary artists from Asia and the Asian Diaspora. The Sackler is preparing you to appreciate the less familiar aspects of Asian art and culture.

The Sackler's permanent collection displays Khmer ceramics; ancient Chinese jades, bronzes, paintings, and lacquerware; 20th-century Japanese ceramics and works on paper; ancient Near Eastern works in silver, gold, bronze, and clay; stone and bronze sculptures from South and Southeast Asia; and a sumptuous graphic arts inventory covering a century of work by Japanese master printmakers. Supplementing the permanent collection are traveling exhibitions from major cultural institutions in Asia, Europe, and the United States. In the past, these have included such wide-ranging areas as 15th-century Persian art and culture, photographs of Asia, and art highlighting personal devotion in India. A visit here is an education in not just Asian decorative arts, but also in antiquities.

To learn more, arrive in time for a highlights tour, offered at 12:15pm most days except Wednesday. Also enlightening, and more fun, are the public programs that both the Sackler and the Freer Gallery frequently stage, such as performances of contemporary Asian music, tea ceremony demonstrations, and Iranian film screenings. All are free, but you might need tickets; for details, call the main information number or check out the website. Allow at least an hour to tour the Sackler.

The Sackler is part of a museum complex that houses the National Museum of African Art and the S. Dillon Ripley Center. It shares its staff and research facilities with the adjacent Freer Gallery, to which it is connected via an underground exhibition space.

1050 Independence Ave. SW. ⓒ 202/633-4880. www.asia.si.edu. Free admission. Daily 10am–5:30pm. Closed Dec 25. Metro: Smithsonian (the Mall/Jefferson Dr. exit).

Arts and Industries Building The building is closed for an extensive renovation. Completed in 1881 as the first U.S. National Museum, this red-brick and sandstone structure was the first Smithsonian museum on the Mall. President Garfield's Inaugural Ball took place here. (It looks quite similar to the Castle, so don't be confused; from the Mall, the Arts and Industries Building is the one on the left.) From 1976 to the mid-1990s it housed exhibits from the 1876 U.S. International Exposition in Philadelphia—a celebration of America's centennial that featured the latest advances in technology.

Weather permitting, a 19th-century **carousel** operates across the street, on the Mall. 900 Jefferson Dr. SW (on the south side of the Mall). www.si.edu/ai.

Freer Gallery of Art ⚑ Charles Lang Freer, a collector of Asian and American art from the 19th and early 20th centuries, gave the nation 9,000 of these works for his namesake gallery's 1923 opening. Freer's original interest was American art, but his good friend James McNeill Whistler encouraged him to collect Asian works as well. Eventually the latter became predominant. Freer's gift included funds to construct a museum and an endowment to add to the Asian collection, which now numbers more than 26,000 objects and spans 6,000 years. It includes Chinese and Japanese sculpture, lacquer, metalwork, and ceramics; early Christian illuminated manuscripts; Iranian

manuscripts, metalwork, and miniatures; ancient Near
Asian sculpture and paintings.

The Freer is mostly about Asian art, but it also dis
1,200 American works (the world's largest collection) b
and always on view is the famous **Harmony in Blue and**
Originally a dining room designed for the London mansi
cock Room displayed a Whistler painting called *The Prin*
lain. But after his painting was installed, Whistler was diss
setting for his work. When Leyland was away from home, ⌐⌐⌐ ⌐⌐⌐ the
very expensive leather interior and embellished it with pa⌐⌐⌐⌐⌐ or golden peacock
feathers. Not surprisingly, a rift ensued between Whistler and Leyland. After Leyland's
death, Freer purchased the room, painting and all, and had it shipped to his home in
Detroit. It is now permanently installed here. Other American painters represented in
the collections are Thomas Wilmer Dewing, Dwight William Tryon, Abbott Hander-
son Thayer, John Singer Sargent, and Childe Hassam. You could spend a happy 1 to
2 hours here.

The Freer Gallery is an oasis on the Mall, especially if you arrive here after visiting
its voluminous and crowded sisters, the Natural History and Air and Space museums.
Housed in a grand granite-and-marble building that evokes the Italian Renaissance,
the pristine Freer has lovely sky-lit galleries. The main exhibit floor galleries encircle a
beautiful landscaped courtyard, complete with loggia and central fountain. If the
weather's right, it's a pleasure to sit out here and take a break from touring. An under-
ground exhibit space connects the Freer to the neighboring Sackler Gallery, and both
museums share the **Meyer Auditorium,** which is used for free chamber music con-
certs, dance performances, Asian feature films, and other programs. Inquire about
these, as well as children's activities and free tours given daily, at the information desk.

Jefferson Dr. SW at 12th St. SW (on the south side of the Mall). ℂ 202/633-4880. www.asia.si.edu. Free admission.
Daily 10am–5:30pm. Closed Dec 25. Metro: Smithsonian (Mall/Jefferson Dr.).

Hirshhorn Museum and Sculpture Garden ✸ This museum of modern and
contemporary art is named after Latvian-born Joseph H. Hirshhorn, who, in 1966,
donated his vast collection—more than 4,000 drawings and paintings and 2,000
pieces of sculpture—to the United States "as a small repayment for what this nation
has done for me and others like me who arrived here as immigrants." The Hirshhorn
opened in 1974 to display these works, adding 5,500 more bequeathed by Hirshhorn
in 1981, upon his death. The Hirshhorn's current inventory numbers about 11,500.

Constructed 14 feet aboveground on sculptured supports, the doughnut-shaped
concrete-and-granite building stands 82 feet high and measures 231 feet in diameter.
The cylindrically shaped building encloses a hollow core, where a fountain spouts
water five stories high. The building's light and airy interior holds three levels of gal-
leries, each following a circular route that makes it easy to see every exhibit without
getting lost in a honeycomb of galleries. Natural light from floor-to-ceiling windows
makes the inner galleries the perfect venue for regarding sculpture—second only to
the beautiful tree-shaded sunken **Sculpture Garden** ✸ across the street (don't miss it).
Make your way to the third-floor oculus and you'll be rewarded with a dramatic view
of the National Mall.

A rotating show of about 600 pieces is on view at all times. The collection features
just about every well-known 20th-century artist and touches on most of the major
trends in Western art since the late 19th century, with particular emphasis on our

od. Among the best-known pieces are Rodin's *Monument to the* ...*ais* (in the Sculpture Garden), Hopper's *First Row Orchestra,* de Koon- ...*omen in the Country,* and Warhol's *Marilyn Monroe's Lips.*

...up a free calendar when you enter to find out about free films, lectures, con- ...s, and temporary exhibits. Some of these events are quite popular. For instance, the Hirshhorn hosts Hirshhorn After Hours three or four times a year, and it's always a sellout. Twenty-somethings especially love to attend the function, which takes place from 8pm to midnight and combines socializing with art, music or other perform- ance, and cocktails. The $10 tickets are available in advance online or by calling ℂ **202/633-4629.** Free tours of the collection are given daily; tours of the Sculpture Garden are offered daily in summer, weather permitting; call for information about them.

Independence Ave. at 7th St. SW (on the south side of the Mall). ℂ 202/633-4674. www.hirshhorn.si.edu. Free admission. Museum daily 10am–5:30pm. Sculpture Garden daily 7:30am–dusk. Closed Dec 25. Metro: L'Enfant Plaza (Smithsonian Museums/Maryland Ave. or Smithsonian exit).

National Air and Space Museum ★★ *Kids* With the opening of its new branch, the National Air and Space Museum has two locations. The flagship museum is this one, on the National Mall. The second facility is the Steven F. Udvar-Hazy Center, located on the grounds of Washington-Dulles International Airport.

Let's start with this one, the original, ever-popular Air and Space Museum on the Mall. The museum, now in its 33rd year, chronicles the story of the mastery of flight, from Kitty Hawk to outer space. It holds the largest collection of historic aircraft and spacecraft in the world, about 50,000—so many, in fact, that the museum is able to display only about 10% of its artifacts at any one time, hence the opening of the Udvar-Hazy Center in 2003.

During the tourist season and on holidays, arrive before 10am to make a beeline for the film ticket line when the doors open. The not-to-be-missed **IMAX films** ★ shown here are immensely popular, and tickets to most shows sell out quickly. You can pur- chase same-day tickets by phone or in person at the Lockheed Martin IMAX Theater box office on the first floor, or in advance online up to 24 hours before showtime. Sur- charges apply to phone and online orders. Two or more films play each day, most with aeronautical or space-exploration themes; *To Fly* and *3D Sun* are two that were run- ning in 2008. Tickets cost $8.50 for adults, $7 for ages 2 to 12, $7.50 for ages 60 or older; they're free for children 1 and under. You can also see IMAX films most evenings after the museum's closing; call for details (ℂ 877/932-4629).

You'll also need tickets to attend a show at the **Albert Einstein Planetarium** ★, which creates "an astronomical adventure." Projectors display space imagery upon a 70-foot-diameter dome, making you feel as if you're traveling in 3-D through the cos- mos. The planetarium's newest feature is the 23-minute **Cosmic Collisions,** which takes you on a trip through time and space, where you encounter cosmic collisions and hypersonic impacts as narrated by Robert Redford. Tickets are $8.50 for adults, $7 for ages 2 to 12, $7.50 for ages 60 or older.

Among the 22 exhibitions on display throughout the museum is one that children especially love: **How Things Fly,** which includes wind and smoke tunnels, a board- able Cessna 150 airplane, and dozens of interactive exhibits that demonstrate princi- ples of flight, aerodynamics, and propulsion. All the aircraft are originals. Kids also flock to the walk-through **Skylab orbital workshop,** part of the **Space Race** exhibi- tion on the first floor. Both children and adults stand in line to take their turn on the

museum's **Flight Simulators.** (The Udvar-Hazy Center has several, too.) You'll be strapped in and given a joystick, and for about 5 minutes you'll truly feel as if you are in the cockpit and airborne, maneuvering your craft up, down, and upside-down on a wild adventure, thanks to virtual reality images and high-tech sounds. You must pay $7 ($7.50 at the Udvar-Hazy Center) to enjoy the ride and measure at least 48 inches to go it alone. (Children under 48 in. must measure at least 42 in. and be accompanied by an adult.)

Other galleries highlight the solar system, U.S. manned spaceflights, sea-air operations, and aviation during both world wars. An important exhibit is **Beyond the Limits: Flight Enters the Computer Age,** illustrating the primary applications of computer technology to aerospace. **Explore the Universe** presents the major discoveries that have shaped the current scientific view of the universe; it illustrates how the universe is taking shape, and probes the mysteries that remain. Hundreds of space and aircraft artifacts dangle before your eyes everywhere you look, but don't miss the **1903 Flyer,** hanging in the exhibit called **The Wright Brothers and the Invention of the Aerial Age.** In late 2007, the museum debuted **America by Air,** an exhibit that covers an expanded history of commercial air travel.

The museum's cafeteria, the Wright Place, offers food from three popular American chains: McDonald's, Boston Chicken, and Donato's Pizza. Its three-level, 12,000-square-foot shop is the largest Smithsonian store.

At the Udvar-Hazy Center you'll find two hangars—one for aviation artifacts, the other for space artifacts—and a 164-foot-tall observation tower for watching planes leave and arrive at Dulles Airport. The center's James S. McDonnell Space Hangar stretches the length of three football fields and stands 10 stories high, the better to house the enormous *Enterprise,* NASA's first space shuttle; the tiny "Anita," a spider carried on Skylab inside a bottle for web formation experiments; the manned maneuvering unit used for the first untethered spacewalk; a full-scale prototype of the Mars Pathfinder Lander; and Pegasus, the first aircraft-launched rocket booster to carry satellites into space. Eventually, the gallery will hold more than 200 aircraft and 135 spacecraft. The center will also serve as the Air and Space Museum's primary restoration facility, and the public will be able to watch specialists at work. This location also shows IMAX films.

On Independence Ave. SW, btw. 4th and 7th sts. (on the south side of the Mall, with entrances on Jefferson Dr. or Independence Ave.). © **202/633-1000** (for both locations), or 877/932-4629 for IMAX ticket information. www.nasm.si.edu. Free admission. Both locations daily 10am–5:30pm. The Mall museum often stays open until 7:30pm in summer, but call to confirm. Free 1½-hr. highlight tours daily at 10:30am and 1pm. Closed Dec 25. Metro: L'Enfant Plaza (Smithsonian Museums/Maryland Ave. exit) or Smithsonian (The Mall/Jefferson Dr. exit). The Udvar-Hazy Center is located at 14390 Air and Space Museum Pkwy., Chantilly, VA.

National Museum of African Art 🅰️ Founded in 1964, and part of the Smithsonian since 1979, the National Museum of African Art moved to the Mall in 1987 to share a subterranean space with the Sackler Gallery (see above) and the Ripley Center. Its aboveground domed pavilions reflect the arch motif of the neighboring Freer Gallery of Art (see above).

The museum collects and exhibits ancient and contemporary art from the entire African continent and rotates displays of its 9,100-piece permanent collection. The museum's contemporary African art collection comprises the largest public holding in the United States. Among the museum's holdings are the **Eliot Elisofon Photographic Archives,** encompassing 80,000 photographic prints and transparencies and

120,000 feet of film on African arts and culture. A small, ongoing permanent exhibit of ceramic arts displays 14 traditional and contemporary pieces from the museum's 140-works collection. Most exciting is the Walt Disney–Tishman African Art collection, which the Walt Disney World Company donated to the museum in 2005. Its Tishman collection of 525 objects represents every area of Africa, dating from ancient to contemporary times and spanning art forms from textiles to jewelry. A rotating selection of at least 60 works are permanently on display in the museum.

Inquire at the desk about special exhibits, workshops (including excellent children's programs), storytelling, lectures, docent-led tours, films, and demonstrations. A comprehensive events schedule provides a unique opportunity to learn about the diverse cultures and visual traditions of Africa. Plan on spending a minimum of 30 minutes here.

950 Independence Ave. SW. (C) 202/633-4600. http://africa.si.edu. Free admission. Daily 10am–5:30pm. Closed Dec 25. Metro: Smithsonian.

National Museum of the American Indian ★ *Kids* The National Museum of the American Indian officially opened on September 21, 2004, having taken 5 years and $219 million to construct. Outside and in, this museum is strikingly handsome. Its burnt-sand-colored exterior of Kasota limestone wraps around the undulating walls of the museum, making the five-story building a standout among the many white-stone structures on the National Mall. Its interior design incorporates themes of nature and astronomy. For instance, the Potomac (a Piscataway word meaning "where the goods are brought in") is a rotunda that serves as the museum's main gathering place; it is also "the heart of the museum, the sun of its universe" (as noted in the museum's literature). Measuring 120 feet in diameter, with an atrium rising 120 feet to the top of the dome overhead, the Potomac is the central entryway into the museum, a venue for performances, and a hall filled with celestial references, from the equinoxes and solstices mapped on the floor beneath your feet to the sights of sky visible through the oculus in the dome above your head.

A gift shop, a theater, and the museum's excellent restaurant, Mitsitam, occupy most of the remaining space on the first floor. A second shop and the museum's main galleries lie upstairs on the second and third levels. Three permanent exhibits, "Our Universes: Traditional Knowledge Shapes Our World," "Our Peoples: Giving Voice to Our Histories," and "Our Lives: Contemporary Life and Identities," use videos, interactive technology, and displays of artifacts to help you learn about Native cosmologies, history, and contemporary cultural identity, both of Native Americans as a group and within certain individual tribes. An exhibit called "Window on the Collections: Many Hands, Many Voices" displays 3,500 objects behind glass; a computer kiosk in front of each case allows the museumgoer to zoom in and learn more about a particular item on view. These precious wood and stone carvings, masks, pottery, feather bonnets, and so on are a fraction of the 800,000 objets d'art amassed by a wealthy New Yorker named George Gustav Heye (1874–1957). Heye founded the New York Museum of the American Indian, this museum's predecessor.

The National Museum of the American Indian does not provide much direction to self-guided touring, which tends to leave visitors at a loss as to how to proceed through the museum. Faced with the vast display of objects and with galleries that have no obvious beginning or end, tourists wander around, adopting a scattershot approach to the information, emerging eventually with more of an impression than with a coherent understanding of the Indian experience, and overwhelmed by the variety and

number of artifacts and details. Perhaps that's intentional. Best advice? Stop at the Welcome Desk when you enter to sign up for a highlights tour.

4th St. and Independence Ave. SW. ℂ 202/633-1000. www.nmai.si.edu. Free admission. Daily 10am–5:30pm. Closed Dec 25. Metro: Federal Center Southwest or L'Enfant Plaza. (Smithsonian Museums/Maryland Ave. exit).

National Museum of American History ✿✿✿ *Kids* As a bastion of U.S. culture and history, this museum tells America's story in terms of everyday life. Its objects can evoke feelings of awe (the desk on which Thomas Jefferson wrote the Declaration of Independence), affection (Dorothy's ruby slippers), or connection (Julia Child's kitchen). And some things here—the museum's ultimate possession, the huge **original Star-Spangled Banner** ✿✿✿, for example—evoke all three emotions at once.

So prized is the flag that the museum's renovation showcases the 30×34-foot wool and cotton flag in a multistory gallery with floor-to-ceiling glass windows. They are designed to give visitors a sense of the same "dawn's early light" that Francis Scott Key observed the morning of September 14, 1814, when he spied this very flag waving above Fort McHenry in Baltimore's harbor, at the height of the War of 1812. Key's emotion at the sight moved him to pen the poem that, when put to music, eventually became the U.S. national anthem.

You'll notice another renovation improvement on the museum's first and second floors: the 10-foot-high "artifact walls" displaying assorted pieces from the museum's three-million-object collection.

Best to start your tour at the new Welcome Center on the second floor to figure out how you'd like to proceed. In spite of the many and much-needed architectural enhancements, like the new skylight and grand staircase, you'll find that quite a bit of the pre-renovation museum's attractions remain.

On the third floor lies the exhibit **The American Presidency: A Glorious Burden,** which explores the power and meaning of the presidency by studying those who have held the position. (There's a gift shop just for this exhibit on this floor.) Continue on this floor to the exhibit **The Price of Freedom: Americans at War,** which examines major American military events and explores the idea that America's armed forces reflect American society. Among the items on display here are George Washington's commission from Congress as commander in chief of the Continental Army and the uniform jacket that Andrew Jackson wore during the Battle of New Orleans in the War of 1812.

One of the most popular exhibits on the second floor is **First Ladies: Political Role and Public Image,** which displays the first ladies' gowns and tells you a bit about each of these women. Following that, find the exhibit called **Within These Walls . . . ,** which interprets the rich history of America by tracing the lives of the people who lived in a 200-year-old house transplanted from Ipswich, Massachusetts. If this personal approach to history appeals to you, continue on to **Field to Factory,** which tells the story of African-American migration from the South between 1915 and 1940.

First-floor exhibits explore the development of farm and power machinery. A temporary exhibit whose popularity may make it a permanent display is ***Bon Appétit!* Julia Child's Kitchen at the Smithsonian,** a presentation of the famous chef's actual kitchen from her home in Cambridge, Massachusetts. When she moved to California in late 2001, Child donated her kitchen and all that it contained (1,200 items in all) to the museum. Most of these are on display, vegetable peeler to kitchen sink. Also look here for **America on the Move,** which details the story of transportation in America since 1876: 300 artifacts displayed within period settings.

Museum Exhibits Scheduled for 2009

The following listings, though hardly comprehensive, should give you an idea about 2009's upcoming or current shows at major Washington museums. Because schedules sometimes change, it's always a good idea to call ahead. See individual entries in this chapter for phone numbers and addresses.

Anacostia Community Museum "Jubilee: African American Celebrations" (Dec 7, 2008–Oct 4, 2009). Images, traditional songs, and folklore tell the story of African-American holidays across the country.

Freer Gallery "Guests of the Hills: Travelers in Chinese Landscape Paintings," (Aug 23, 2008–Feb 22, 2009). An exhibit of paintings spanning 700 years, mid-11th to mid-18th centuries, depicting figures of recluses, recreational travelers, mountain sages, and retired gentlemen within landscapes.

Hirshhorn Museum and Sculpture Garden "Louise Bourgeois," (Feb 26–May 17). The first major survey since 1995 of this important international avant-garde artist includes sculptures, drawings, and paintings that use a wide array of images and materials.

National Gallery of Art "Looking In: Robert Frank's 'The Americans'" (Jan 18–Apr 26). Eighty-three photographs chronicle Frank's travels across the United States in 1955 and 1956.

National Museum of Natural History "Dig It! The Secrets of Soil" (Jul 19, 2008–Jan 3, 2010). Through dioramas, cultural artifacts, and interactive displays, the exhibit demonstrates the vital role that soil plays in human, agricultural, and environmental viability.

National Museum of the American Indian "Fritz Scholder: Indian/Not Indian," (Nov 1, 2008–Aug 16, 2009). One hundred and thirty-five paintings and other works celebrate Scholder's contribution to American Indian culture and art history, focusing on his 1960s-to-1970s period.

National Museum of Women in the Arts "Beyond Tradition: The Pueblo Pottery of Tammy Garcia," (Aug 22, 2008–Feb 3, 2009). A select group of Garcia's most important pots are on display.

National Portrait Gallery "Women of Our Time, Twentieth Century Photographs," (Oct 10, 2008–Feb 1, 2009). Portraits of women who have challenged America, from Georgia O'Keeffe to Gloria Steinem. This is just one exhibit of many that the gallery has on the 2009 calendar.

Sackler Gallery "Taking Shape, Ceramics in Southeast Asia" (through 2010). On exhibit are 200 diverse and visually striking ceramic vessels from Southeast Asia, from the prehistoric period to the present.

Smithsonian American Art Museum "Graphic Masters: Highlights from the Smithsonian American Art Museum," (Feb 27–Aug 30). Presents exceptional watercolors, pastels, and drawings dating from the 1860s to the 1990s of American masters from Winslow Homer to Wayne Thiebaud.

Inquire at the information desk about highlight tours, films, lectures, concerts, and hands-on activities for children and adults. Be sure to visit the museum's gift shops and dining options, also revamped during the remodeling.

On Constitution Ave. NW, btw. 12th and 14th sts. NW (on the north side of the Mall, with entrances on Constitution Ave. and Madison Dr.). © 202/633-1000. www.americanhistory.si.edu. Free admission. Daily 10am–5:30pm. Closed Dec 25. Metro: Smithsonian or Federal Triangle.

National Museum of Natural History ★★ *Kids* Stop outside first, on the 9th Street side of the building, to visit the **butterfly garden.** Four habitats—wetland, meadow, wood's edge, and urban garden—are on view, designed to beckon butterflies and visitors alike. The garden is at its best in warm weather, but it's open year-round. (And if you like that, you're going to love the museum's new Butterflies and Plants exhibit, which includes a Butterfly Pavilion—keep reading!)

Now go inside. Children often refer to this Smithsonian showcase as "the dinosaur museum," because of the dinosaur hall, or as "the elephant museum," since a huge **African bush elephant** is the first thing you see in the Rotunda when you enter from the Mall. Whatever you call it, the National Museum of Natural History is the largest of its kind in the world and one of the most visited museums in Washington. It contains more than 126 million artifacts and specimens, everything from Ice Age mammoths to the legendary Hope Diamond.

In late 2008, the museum debuted a brand-new, 22,000-square-foot **Ocean Hall,** the largest, most diverse exhibit of its kind in the world. Designed by the same firm that created the exhibits and spaces of the highly interactive International Spy Museum, the hall includes collections and state-of-the-art technology to demonstrate our oceans' essential role in life on earth. Look for a model of a 45-foot-long North American right whale and a 1,500-gallon coral reef aquarium with more than 70 live animals and 674 specimens. November 2009 brings the opening of **Origins: What Does It Mean to Be Human?** It focuses on the story of human origins and probes the ecological and genetic connection that humans have had with the natural world.

Meanwhile, the museum's long-popular exhibits continue:

If you have children, you might want to make your first stop the first-floor **Discovery Room,** which is filled with creative hands-on exhibits "for children of all ages." Call ahead or inquire at the information desk about hours. Also on this floor is the **Kenneth E. Behring Hall of Mammals.** Set in the restored west wing and boasting up-to-date lighting and sound, the Hall of Mammals features interactive dioramas that explain how mammals evolved and adapted to changes in habitat and climate over the course of millions of years. At least 274 taxidermied mammals, from polar bear to tiger, are on display, along with a dozen mammal fossils. From time to time, the hall erupts with animal sounds, all part of exhibit wizardry that helps make this a lifelike experience.

Other Rotunda-level displays include the **fossil collection,** which traces evolution back billions of years and includes a 3.5-billion-year-old stromatolite (blue-green algae clump) fossil—one of the earliest signs of life on earth—and a 70-million-year-old dinosaur egg. **Ancient Seas and Ice Age** features a 100-foot-long mural depicting primitive whales, a life-size walk-around diorama of a 230-million-year-old coral reef, and more than 2,000 fossils that chronicle the evolution of marine life. The **Dinosaur Hall** displays giant skeletons of creatures that dominated the earth for 140 million years before their extinction about 65 million years ago. Mounted throughout the Dinosaur Hall are replicas of ancient birds, including a life-size model of the *Quetzalcoatlus*

Tips Eating on the Fly

Washington has plenty of street vendors planted near various attractions, but none are remarkable for their food. Enter **On the Fly,** www.dconthefly.com, the lime-colored, eco-friendly, bug-shaped smartkarts with wings that sell fast- and fresh food prepared by locally famous eateries, like Teaism and Julia's Empanadas. Look for these zero-emission, plug-in trucks at choice locations throughout the city, including at 7th and F streets NW, near the National Portrait Gallery, and at the National Zoo. Hours vary, prices are cheap: typically $3 to $6.

northropi, which lived 70 million years ago, had a 40-foot wingspan, and was the largest flying animal ever. Also residing above this hall is the jaw of an ancient shark, the *Carcharodon megalodon,* which lived in the oceans 5 million years ago. A monstrous 40-foot-long predator with teeth 5 to 6 inches long, it could have consumed a Volkswagen Bug in one gulp. Elsewhere on this floor is **African Cultures,** which presents the people, cultures, and lives of Africa through photos, videos, and more than 400 objects.

Upstairs lies another exhibit popular among the under-10 crowd: the **O. Orkin Insect Zoo** ⍟, where kids enjoy looking at tarantulas, centipedes, and the like, and crawling through a model of an African termite mound. Right next door is the museum's newest offering, **Butterflies and Plants: Partners in Evolution** ⍟, a 4,000-square-foot exhibit that illustrates the evolving relationship between butterflies and plants over millions of years. The exhibit includes a walk-through, 1,400-square-foot Butterfly Pavilion featuring live butterflies and plants. *Note:* The museum charges a $6 fee for admission to the pavilion portion of the exhibit.

Ever a big draw is the **Janet Annenberg Hooker Hall of Geology, Gems, and Minerals** ⍟, which showcases the Hope Diamond; the 23.1-carat Burmese Carmen Lucia ruby, one of the largest and finest rubies in the world; and other treasures of the National Gem Collection. Besides staring spellbound at priceless jewelry, you can learn all you want about earth science, from volcanology to the importance of mining. Interactive computers, animated graphics, and a multimedia presentation of the "big picture" story of the earth are some of the things that have moved the exhibit and the museum a bit further into the 21st century.

Don't miss the Samuel C. Johnson **IMAX theater** with a six-story-high screen for 2-D and 3-D movies (*Sea Monsters 3D: A Prehistoric Adventure* was among those shown in 2008), a six-story Atrium Cafe with a food court, and expanded museum shops. The museum also offers the small **Fossil Café,** located within the Fossil Plants Hall on the first floor. In this 50-seat cafe, the tables' clear plastic tops are actually fossil cases that present fossilized plants and insects for your inspection as you munch away on smoked turkey sandwiches, goat-cheese quiche, and the like.

The theater box office is on the first floor of the museum; you can purchase tickets by phone (© **202/633-4629** or 877/932-4629), online, or at the box office at least 30 minutes before the screening. The box office is open daily from 9:45am to the last show. Films are shown continuously throughout the day. Ticket prices are $8.50 for adults, $7 for children (2–12), and $7.50 for seniors 60 or older. On Friday nights from 6:30 to 10pm, the theater stages live jazz starring excellent local musicians ($12

cover for the music). This is really a supper club, since a cash bar and an extensive dinner buffet are also on hand.

On Constitution Ave. NW, btw. 9th and 12th sts. (on the north side of the Mall, with entrances on Madison Dr. and Constitution Ave.). ℂ 202/633-1000, or 633-4629 for information about IMAX films. www.mnh.si.edu. Free admission. Daily 10am–5:30pm. In summer the museum often stays open until 7:30pm, but call to confirm. Closed Dec 25. Free highlight tours Feb–July Tues–Fri 10:30am and 1:30pm. Metro: Smithsonian (The Mall/Jefferson Dr. exit) or Federal Triangle.

National Postal Museum ⊀ This museum remains a hit, especially for families, but anyone might spend a pleasant hour here. Bring your address book, and you can send postcards to the folks back home through an interactive exhibit that issues a cool postcard and stamps it. That's just one feature that makes this museum visitor-friendly. Many of its exhibits involve easy-to-understand activities, like postal-themed video games.

The museum documents America's postal history from 1673 (about 170 years before the advent of stamps, envelopes, and mailboxes) to the present. (Did you know that a dog sled was used to carry mail in Alaska until 1963, when it was replaced by an airplane?) In the central gallery, suspended from the 90-foot-high atrium ceiling, are three planes that carried mail in the early decades of the 20th century. These, along with a railway mail car, an 1851 mail/passenger coach, and a replica of an airmail beacon tower, are all part of the **Moving the Mail** exhibit, recently augmented by **On the Road.** This new exhibit explores the history of such city mail vehicles as the 1931 Ford Model A mail truck on display. **Customers and Communities** traces the evolution of mail delivery as it expanded to reach growing populations in both rural areas and the cities. In **Binding the Nation,** historic correspondence illustrates how mail kept families together in the developing nation. Several exhibits deal with the famed Pony Express, a service that lasted less than 2 years but was romanticized to legendary proportions by Buffalo Bill and others. In the Civil War section you'll learn about Henry "Box" Brown, a slave who had himself "mailed" from Richmond to a Pennsylvania abolitionist in 1856. The **Art of Cards and Letters** gallery displays rotating exhibits of personal (sometimes wrenching, always interesting) correspondence taken from different periods in history, as well as greeting cards and postcards; "War Letters Lost and Found" was the theme of the letters most recently on display. In addition, the museum houses a vast research library for philatelic researchers and scholars, a stamp store, and a museum shop. Inquire about free walk-in tours at the information desk.

Opened in 1993, this off-the-Mall Smithsonian museum occupies the lower level of the palatial Beaux Arts quarters of the Old City Post Office Building, which was designed by architect Daniel Burnham and is situated next to Union Station.

2 Massachusetts Ave. NE (at 1st St.). ℂ 202/633-5555. www.si.edu/postal. Free admission. Daily 10am–5:30pm. Closed Dec 25. Metro: Union Station.

National Zoological Park ⊀⊀ *Kids* The zoo's biggest draw is the three **giant pandas:** Mei Xiang and Tian Tian and their offspring, Tai Shan, born July 9, 2005. But don't stop there.

Established in 1889, the National Zoo is home to about 400 species—some 2,400 animals—many of them rare and/or endangered. A leader in the care, breeding, and exhibition of animals, it occupies 163 beautifully landscaped and wooded acres and is one of the country's most delightful zoos. You'll see cheetahs, zebras, camels, elephants, tapirs, antelopes, brown pelicans, kangaroos, hippos, rhinos, giraffes, apes, and, of course, lions, tigers, and bears.

> **Fun Fact Early Risers?**
>
> Zoo grounds open daily at 6am, which might be too early for a lot of tourists, but not for families whose young children like to rise at the crack of dawn. You know who you are. If you find yourselves trapped and restless in the hotel room, hop on the Red Line Metro, which opens at 5am weekdays, 7am Saturday and Sunday (or drive—no problem parking at that hour), get off at the Woodley Park–Zoo station, and walk up the hill to the zoo. Lots of animals are outdoors and on view. A Starbucks, which opens at 6am Monday to Saturday and 6:30am Sunday, is directly across from the zoo's entrance on Connecticut Avenue. Good morning.

Enter the zoo at the Connecticut Avenue entrance; you'll be right by the Education Building, where you can pick up a map and find out about feeding times and any special activities. Note that from this main entrance, you're headed downhill; the return uphill walk can prove trying if you have young children and/or it's a hot day. But the zoo rents strollers, and snack bars and ice-cream kiosks are scattered throughout the park.

The zoo animals live in large, open enclosures—simulations of their natural habitats—along easy-to-follow paths. The **Olmsted Walk** winds from the zoo's Connecticut Avenue entrance all the way to the zoo's end, at Rock Creek Park. Two paths stem off the central Olmsted Walk: the **Valley Trail,** leading to seals, sea lions, beavers, the bald eagle refuge, and other North American mammals and birds; and the **Asia Trail,** which takes you past of sloth bears, frolicking giant pandas, fishing cats, clouded leopards, and Japanese salamander. You can't get lost, and it's hard to miss a thing. Be sure to catch **Amazonia,** where you can hang out for an hour peering up into the trees and still not spy the sloth. (Do yourself a favor and ask the attendant where it is.) You'll notice construction underway for the **Elephants Trails,** a new permanent exhibit that will provide an improved elephant habitat, including exercise trails; it won't be complete until 2011.

If your children are ages 3 to 8, don't miss the **Kids' Farm** at the very bottom of the zoo. Ducks, chickens, goats, cows, and miniature donkeys are among the animals kids can observe up close. Children might also enjoy the vegetable garden and pizza sculpture.

The zoo offers several dining options, including the Mane Restaurant, the Panda Café, and a number of snack stands. Other facilities include stroller-rental stations, a number of gift shops, a bookstore, and several paid-parking lots. The lots fill up quickly, especially on weekends, so arrive early or take the Metro.

3001 Connecticut Ave. NW (adjacent to Rock Creek Park). © **202/633-4800.** www.si.edu/natzoo. Free admission. Apr–Oct (weather permitting) grounds daily 6am–8pm, animal buildings daily 10am–6pm; Nov–Mar grounds daily 6am–6pm, animal buildings daily 10am–4:30pm. Closed Dec 25. Metro: Woodley Park–Zoo or Cleveland Park.

Renwick Gallery of the Smithsonian American Art Museum ★ (Finds A department of the Smithsonian American Art Museum (though located nowhere near it), the Renwick Gallery is a showcase for American creativity in crafts and decorative arts, housed in a historic mid-1800s landmark building of the French Second Empire style. It's located on the same block as the White House, just across Pennsylvania Avenue. The original home of the Corcoran Gallery (which now lies a short walk

away, down 17th Street), it was saved from demolition by First Lady Jacqueline Kennedy in 1963, when she recommended that it be renovated as part of the Lafayette Square restoration. In 1965, it became part of the Smithsonian and was renamed for its architect, James W. Renwick, Jr., who also designed the Smithsonian Castle.

On view on the first floor are temporary exhibits of American crafts and decorative arts. On the second floor, the museum's rich and diverse displays boast changing crafts exhibits and contemporary works from the museum's permanent collection, such as Larry Fuente's *Game Fish* or Wendell Castle's *Ghost Clock*. Also on the second floor is the **Victorian Grand Salon,** styled in 19th-century opulence and worth a visit on its own merits: Its 40-foot-high laylight (a skylight unexposed to the outside) and its wainscoted rose walls covered in framed paintings evoke a 19th-century picture gallery. Tour the entire gallery for about an hour, rest for a minute, and then go on to your next destination.

The Renwick offers a comprehensive schedule of crafts demonstrations, lectures, and musical performances. Also check out the museum shop near the entrance for books on crafts, design, and decorative arts, as well as craft items, many of them for children. *Note:* The main branch of the Smithsonian American Art Museum (below) is located at 8th and F streets NW, in the Penn Quarter neighborhood.

1661 Pennsylvania Ave. NW (at 17th St. NW). © 202/633-2850. http://americanart.si.edu. Free admission. Daily 10am–5:30pm. Closed Dec 25. Metro: Farragut West or Farragut North.

Smithsonian American Art Museum and National Portrait Gallery ✸✸✸

On July 1, 2006, the historic landmark building that houses both the Smithsonian American Art Museum and the National Portrait Gallery reopened after a 6-year renovation, proving to all who visit that it was well worth the wait. The structure itself is magnificent. Begun in 1836 and completed in 1868 to serve as the nation's Patent Office, it is the third-oldest federal building in the capital. With immense porticoes and columns on the outside, and colonnades, double staircases, vaulted galleries, and skylights inside, the museum captures your attention, no matter how or where you stand to look at it. The building occupies an entire city block, from 7th to 9th streets and from F to G streets.

As for the art presented throughout these three levels: It's like a shot in the arm for America. You will see here the faces of America's founding fathers and mothers, great American heroes and cultural icons, and scenes from American history and way of life, from the moment this country's story began 400 years ago. Inscribed on the walls throughout the galleries are quotes from all sorts of American artists, adding poignancy and a certain context for this grand American experience. For that is what is going on here, as you ponder here an Edward Hopper, there a Gilbert Stuart, now a portrait of Samuel Clemens (Mark Twain), and on to contemporary art by Sean Scully.

Together, the Portrait Gallery and the American Art Museum display nearly 2,000 works from their permanent collections. The galleries flow one into another, so you may not always realize that you have stepped from an American Art wing into the Portrait Gallery wing—nor is it necessary to notice. Just wander and enjoy: the folk art, introductory "American Experience" landscapes and photographs, special exhibits, American Origins portraits, and other works on the first floor; portraits of America's presidents, an exhibit on "The Presidency and the Cold War," graphic arts, and American art through 1940 on the second floor; and art since 1945 and portraits of 20th-century Americans on the third floor. Expect to be dazzled by the creations of such American masters as

Winslow Homer, Georgia O'Keeffe, David Hockney, Robert Rauschenberg, Thomas Cole, Andrew Wyeth, Mary Cassatt, and so many others. In addition, don't miss the two-level Lunder Conservation Center, where you'll be able to watch conservators working to preserve art pieces, and the Luce Foundation Center for American Art, which stores another 3,300 objects in such a way that they remain on view to the public. Finally, the museum offers a fine cafe on the third floor, sensational seating seasonally outdoors within the frame of the second level's portico, and a wonderful year-round enclosed courtyard cafe. *Please note:* The Smithsonian American Art Museum and National Portrait Gallery are located near the National Mall, but not on it; they're across from the Verizon Center in the heart of the Penn Quarter neighborhood.

8th and F sts. NW. (C) 202/633-1000. www.reynoldscenter.org. Free admission. Daily 11:30am–7pm. Closed Dec. 25. Metro: Gallery Place/Chinatown.

4 Other Attractions on or near the Mall

Bureau of Engraving & Printing This is where they will literally show you the money. A staff of 2,200 works round-the-clock, Monday through Friday, churning it out at the rate of about $750 million a day. Everyone's eyes pop as they walk past rooms overflowing with new greenbacks. But the money's not the whole story. The bureau prints security documents for other federal government agencies, including military IDs and passport pages.

Many people line up each day to get a peek at all the moola, so arrive early, especially during the peak tourist season.

To save time and avoid a line, consider securing VIP, also called "congressional," tour tickets from your senator or congressperson; write or call at least 3 months in advance for tickets. These tours take place at 8:15am and 8:45am year-round, with additional tours added in the summer.

Tickets for general-public tours are generally not required from September to February; simply find the visitors entrance at 14th and C streets. March through August, however, every person taking the tour must have a ticket. To obtain a ticket, go to the ticket booth on the Raoul Wallenberg (formerly 15th St.) side of the building and show a valid photo ID. You will receive a ticket specifying a tour time for that same day and be directed to the 14th Street entrance of the bureau. You are allowed as many as eight tickets per person. The ticket booth opens at 8am and closes when tickets sell out for the day.

The 45-minute guided tour begins with a short introductory film. Large windows allow you to see what goes into making of paper money: the inking, stacking of bills, cutting, and examination for defects. Most printing here is done from engraved steel plates in a process known as intaglio; it's the hardest to counterfeit, because the slightest alteration will cause a noticeable change in the portrait in use. Additional exhibits display bills no longer in circulation and a $100,000 bill designed for official transactions. (Since 1969, the largest denomination printed for the general public is $100.)

After you finish the tour, allow time to explore the **Visitor Center,** open from 8:30am to 3:30pm (until 7:30pm in summer), with additional exhibits and a gift shop where you can buy bags of shredded money, uncut sheets of currency in different denominations, and copies of such historic documents as the Gettysburg Address.

14th and C sts. SW. (C) 800/874-2330. www.moneyfactory.gov. Free admission. Mon–Fri 9–10:45am and 12:30–2pm (last tour begins at 1:40pm); in summer, extended hours 5–6:40pm. Closed Dec 25–Jan 1 and federal holidays. Metro: Smithsonian (Independence Ave. exit).

National Archives The Rotunda of the National Archives displays the country's most important original documents: the Declaration of Independence, the Constitution of the United States, and the Bill of Rights (collectively known as the Charters of Freedom). Until recently, however, it wasn't possible to get a very good look at these documents; and when you did, you had to view the Constitution one page at a time. A superb renovation now showcases "The National Archives Experience," whose display cases allow all visitors, but especially children and those in wheelchairs, much better viewing of the Charters. And, for the first time, you are able to see all four pages of the Constitution in one visit. Fourteen document cases trace the story of the creation of the Charters and the ongoing influence of these fundamental documents on the nation and the world. A restoration of Barry Faulkner's two larger-than-life murals brings the scenes to vivid life. One mural, titled *The Declaration of Independence,* shows Thomas Jefferson presenting a draft of the Declaration to John Hancock, the presiding officer of the Continental Congress; the other, titled *The Constitution,* shows James Madison submitting the Constitution to George Washington and the Constitutional Convention. Be sure not to miss viewing the original 1297 Magna Carta, on display as you enter the Rotunda; the document is one of only three or four known to exist, and the only original version residing permanently in the United States.

Public Vaults is an exhibit that features interactive technology and displays of documents and artifacts to explain the country's development in the use of records, from Indian treaties to presidential websites. You can listen to recorded voices of past presidents as they deliberated over pressing issues of the time, and you can scour newly declassified documents. During the day, the William C. McGowan Theater continually runs dramatic films illustrating the relationship between records and democracy in the lives of real people, and at night it serves as a premier documentary film venue for the city. The Lawrence F. O'Brien Gallery rotates exhibitions of Archives documents.

As a federal institution, the National Archives is charged with sifting through the accumulated papers of a nation's official life—billions of pieces a year—and determining what to save and what to destroy. The Archives' vast accumulation of census figures, military records, naturalization papers, immigrant passenger lists, federal documents, passport applications, ship manifests, maps, charts, photographs, and motion picture film (and that's not the half of it) spans 2 centuries. Anyone age 16 and over is welcome to use the National Archives center for genealogical research—this is where Alex Haley began his work on *Roots.* Call for details.

The National Archives building itself is worth an admiring glance. The neoclassical structure, designed by John Russell Pope (also the architect of the National Gallery of Art and the Jefferson Memorial) in the 1930s, is an impressive example of the Beaux Arts style. Seventy-two columns create a Corinthian colonnade on each of the four facades. Great bronze doors mark the Constitution Avenue entrance, and four large sculptures representing the Future, the Past, Heritage, and Guardianship sit on pedestals near the entrances. Huge pediments crown both the Pennsylvania Avenue and Connecticut Avenue entrances to the building. Allow about 90 minutes to view everything.

700 Pennsylvania Ave. NW (btw. 7th and 9th sts. NW; tourists enter on Constitution Ave., researchers on Pennsylvania Ave.). ℂ 202/357-5000. www.archives.gov. Free admission. March 15 to Labor Day daily 10am–7pm; day after Labor Day to Mar 14 daily 10am–5:30pm. Call for research hours. Closed Dec 25. Metro: Archives–Navy Memorial.

National Gallery of Art ⋆⋆⋆ This museum is such a treasure. Housing one of the world's foremost collections of Western paintings, sculpture, and graphic arts, from the Middle Ages into the 21st century, the National Gallery has a dual personality. The

original West Building, designed by John Russell Pope (architect of the Jefferson Memorial and the National Archives), is a neoclassical marble masterpiece with a domed rotunda over a colonnaded fountain and high-ceilinged corridors leading to delightful garden courts. At its completion in 1941, the building was the largest marble structure in the world. It was a gift to the nation from financier/philanthropist Andrew W. Mellon, who also contributed the nucleus of the collection, including 21 masterpieces from the Hermitage, two Raphaels among them. The modern East Building, designed by I. M. Pei and opened in 1978, is composed of two adjoining triangles with glass walls and lofty tetrahedron skylights. The pink Tennessee marble from which both buildings were constructed was taken from the same quarry; it forms an architectural link between the two structures.

Only a small percentage of the National Gallery's collection of 109,000 works is on display at one time. The Gallery's permanent collection offers reason enough to visit, but its mounted exhibitions make this museum a further must; they're always fantastic. See the box "Museum Exhibits Scheduled for 2009," earlier in this chapter, for a small preview of a coming exhibit at the Gallery.

The West Building: From the Mall entrance, you can stop first at the **Art Information Room** to design your own tour on a computer, if you like. But don't spend too much time here. Step into the gorgeous Rotunda, which leads right and left of you to light-filled halls punctuated with sculpture; off these long corridors stem intimate **painting galleries** organized by age and nationality. To your left, as you face away from the Mall, are works by the older masters, from 13th-century Italians to 16th-century Germans. To your right are their younger counterparts, from 18th- and 19th-century French and Spanish artists to later works by British and American artists. These are creations by El Greco, Bruegel, Poussin, Vermeer, Van Dyck, Rubens, Fra Angelico, Gilbert Stuart, Winslow Homer, Constable, Turner, Mary Cassatt—you name it. The only Leonardo da Vinci painting in the Western Hemisphere hangs here, his *Ginevra de' Benci,* just another masterpiece among this bevy of masterpieces.

Descend the grand marble staircase to the ground floor, where the museum's **sculpture galleries** are columned, vaulted, and filled with light. Highlights here range from Chinese porcelain to Renaissance decorative arts to 46 wax statuettes by Degas to Honoré Daumier's entire series of bronze sculptures, including all 36 of his caricatured portrait busts of French government officials.

The **National Gallery Sculpture Garden** (★, just across 7th Street from the West Wing, opened to the public in May 1999. The park takes up 2 city blocks and features open lawns; a central pool with a spouting fountain (the pool turns into an ice rink in winter); an exquisite glassed-in pavilion housing an excellent cafe; 17 sculptures by renowned artists like Roy Lichtenstein and Ellsworth Kelly (and Scott Burton, whose *Six-Part Seating* you're welcome to sit upon) and a Paris Metro sign; and informally landscaped shrubs, trees, and plants. It continues to be a hit, especially in warm weather, when people sit on the wide rim of the pool and dangle their feet in the water while they eat their lunch. Friday evenings in summer, the gallery stages live jazz performances here.

The East Building: This wing is a showcase for the museum's collection of 20th-century art, including works by Picasso, Miró, Matisse, Pollock, and Rothko; for an exhibit called **Small French Paintings,** which I love; and for the gallery's special exhibitions. But chances are, the first thing you'll notice in this wing is the famous, massive aluminum **Alexander Calder mobile** dangling in the seven-story sky-lit atrium.

And here's a tip that lots of people don't know: If you make your way to the tippy-top of the East Wing, whether by elevator or stairs, you reach a level that's actually named the "Tower," where you are rewarded with the sight of four Matisse cutouts, swirls of colorful paper creations framed against a background of white.

Altogether, you should allow at least 2 hours, but you won't see everything here.

Pick up a floor plan and calendar of events at an information desk to find out about National Gallery exhibits, films, tours, lectures, and concerts. Immensely popular is the gallery's Sunday concert series, now in its 67th year, with concerts performed most Sunday evenings, October through June, at 6:30pm in the beautiful garden court of the West Building. Admission is free and seating is on a first-come basis; my suggestion is to tour the gallery in late afternoon, lingering until 6pm, when the galleries close and the queuing begins in the Rotunda. The concerts feature chamber music, string quartets, pianists, and other forms of classical music performances. Call ℂ **202/842-6941.**

The gallery offers school tours, wide-ranging introductory tours, and tours in several languages. The gift shop is a favorite. You'll also find several pleasing dining options—among them the concourse-level Cascade Café, which has multiple food stations; the Garden Café, on the ground floor of the West Building; and best of all, the sculpture garden's Pavilion Café.

On Constitution Ave. NW btw. 3rd and 7th sts. NW (on the north side of the Mall). ℂ 202/737-4215. www.nga.gov. Free admission. Gallery: Mon–Sat 10am–5pm; Sun 11am–6pm. Sculpture Garden: late May to mid-Sept Mon–Thurs and Sat 10am–7pm, Fri 10am–9:30pm, Sun 11am–7pm; mid-Sept to late May Mon–Sat 10am–5pm, Sun 11am–6pm. Closed Jan 1 and Dec 25. Metro: Archives/Navy Memorial, or Gallery Place/Verizon Center (Arena/7th and F sts. exit).

United States Holocaust Memorial Museum ⭑⭑ Twenty-five million people from 100 different countries have visited this museum since it opened in 1993, and the museum continues to be a top draw. In the busiest months, April through July, if you arrive without a reserved ticket specifying an admission time, you'll have to wait in line to get one of the 2,000 day-of-sale tickets the museum makes available each day (see "Holocaust Museum Touring Tips," below).

Before you visit the museum, you might want to access its website, www.ushmm. org, and download copies of the Visitors Guide and the Permanent Exhibition Guide. These are also available at the museum, of course.

As you enter the museum, you may find the noise and bustle of so many visitors disconcerting, or at odds with the experience you expect is coming. But things settle down as you start the tour. When you enter, you will be issued an identity card of an actual victim of the Holocaust; at several points in the tour, you can find out the location and status of the person on your card—by 1945, 66% of those whose lives are documented on these cards were dead.

Tips **Holocaust Museum Touring Tips**

Because so many people want to visit the museum (it has hosted as many as 10,000 visitors in a single day), tickets specifying a visit time (in 15-min. intervals) are required. Reserve as many as 40 tickets in advance via Tickets.com (ℂ **800/400-9373;** www.tickets.com) for a small fee. If you order well in advance, you can have tickets mailed to you at home. You can also get as many as 20 same-day tickets (if available) at the museum beginning at 10am daily (lines form earlier, usually around 8am).

From its collection of more than 12,435 artifacts, the museum has organized some 900 items and 70 video monitors to reveal the Jewish experience in three parts: Nazi Assault, Final Solution, and Last Chapter. The tour begins on the fourth floor, where exhibits portray the events of 1933 to 1939, the years of the Nazi rise to power. On the third floor (documenting 1940–44), exhibits illustrate the narrowing choices of people caught up in the Nazi machine. You board a Polish freight car of the type used to transport Jews from the Warsaw ghetto to Treblinka and hear recordings of survivors telling what life in the camps was like.

The second floor recounts a more heartening story: It depicts how non-Jews throughout Europe, by exercising individual action and responsibility, saved Jews at great personal risk. Denmark—led by a king who swore that if any of his subjects wore a yellow star, so would he—managed to hide and save 90% of its Jews. Exhibits follow on the liberation of the camps, life in Displaced Persons camps, emigration to Israel and America, and the Nuremberg trials. At the end of the permanent exhibition is a most compelling and heartbreaking hour-long film called *Testimony,* in which Holocaust survivors tell their stories. The tour concludes in the hexagonal Hall of Remembrance, where you can meditate and light a candle for the victims. The museum notes that most people take 2 to 3 hours on their first visit; many people take longer.

In addition to its permanent and temporary exhibitions, the museum has a Resource Center for educators, which provides materials and services to Holocaust educators and students; an interactive computer learning center; and a registry of Holocaust survivors, a library, and archives, which researchers may use to retrieve historical documents, photographs, oral histories, films, and videos.

The museum recommends not bringing children 11 and under; for older children, it's advisable to prepare them for what they'll see. You can see some parts of the museum without tickets, including two special areas on the first floor and concourse: **Daniel's Story: Remember the Children** and the **Wall of Remembrance** (Children's Tile Wall), which commemorates the 1.5 million children killed in the Holocaust, and the **Wexner Learning Center.** There's a cafeteria and museum shop on the premises.

100 Raoul Wallenberg Place SW (formerly 15th St. SW; near Independence Ave., just off the Mall). ☎ 202/488-0400. www.ushmm.org. Free admission. Daily 10am–5:30pm, staying open later in peak seasons. Closed Yom Kippur and Dec 25. Metro: Smithsonian (12th St. and Independence Ave. SW exit).

5 More Museums

The Corcoran Gallery of Art ★★ This elegant art museum, a stone's throw from the White House, is a favorite party site in the city, hosting everything from inaugural balls to wedding receptions.

The first art museum in Washington, the Corcoran Gallery was housed from 1869 to 1896 in the red-brick and brownstone building that is now the Renwick. The collection outgrew its quarters and was transferred in 1897 to its present Beaux Arts building, designed by Ernest Flagg.

The collection, shown in rotating exhibits, focuses chiefly on American art. A prominent Washington banker, William Wilson Corcoran was among the first wealthy American collectors to realize the importance of encouraging and supporting this country's artists. Enhanced by further gifts and bequests, the collection comprehensively spans American art from 18th-century portraiture to 20th-century moderns like Nevelson, Warhol, and Rothko. Nineteenth-century works include Bierstadt's and Remington's imagery of the American West; Hudson River School artists; expatriates

like Whistler, Sargent, and Mary Cassatt; and two giants of the late 19th century, Homer and Eakins.

The Corcoran is not exclusively an American art museum. On the first floor is the collection from the estate of Sen. William Andrews Clark, an eclectic grouping of Dutch and Flemish masters, European painters, French Impressionists, Barbizon landscapes, Delft porcelains, a Louis XVI *salon dore* (an extravagant room with gilded ornaments and paneling) transported in toto from Paris, and more. Clark's will stated that his diverse collection, which any curator would undoubtedly want to disperse among various museum departments, must be shown as a unit. He left money for a wing to house it, and the new building opened in 1928. Don't miss the small walnut-paneled room known as "Clark Landing," which showcases 19th-century French Impressionist and American art; a room of exquisite Corot landscapes; another of medieval Renaissance tapestries; and numerous Daumier lithographs donated by Dr. Armand Hammer. Allow an hour for touring the collection.

Pick up a schedule of events or check the website for information about temporary exhibits, gallery talks, concerts, art auctions, and more. There is some street parking.

The charming Café des Artistes is open for lunch daily (except Tues) from 11:30am to 2pm, for dinner on Thursday from 5 to 8pm, and for Sunday brunch from 10:30am to 2pm (reservations accepted for parties of six or more); call © **202/639-1786** for more information. The Corcoran has a nice gift shop.

500 17th St. NW (btw. E St. and New York Ave.). © 202/639-1700. www.corcoran.org. $6 general admission; admission to special exhibits is usually $12 adults, $10 seniors and students. Always free for children 6 and under. Sun–Wed and Fri–Sat 10am–5pm; Thurs 10am–9pm. Closed Jan 1 and Dec 25. Metro: Farragut West (17th St. exit) or Farragut North (K St. exit).

Folger Shakespeare Library *Finds* "Shakespeare taught us that the little world of the heart is vaster, deeper, and richer than the spaces of astronomy," wrote Ralph Waldo Emerson in 1864. A decade later, Amherst student Henry Clay Folger was profoundly affected by a lecture Emerson gave similarly extolling the Bard. Folger purchased an inexpensive set of Shakespeare's plays and went on to amass the world's largest (by far) collection of the Bard's works, today housed in the Folger Shakespeare Library. By 1930, when Folger and his wife, Emily, laid the cornerstone of a building to house the collection, it comprised 93,000 books, 50,000 prints and engravings, and thousands of manuscripts. The Folgers gave it all as a gift to the American people. The library opened in 1932 and celebrated its 75th anniversary in 2007.

The building itself has a marble facade decorated with nine bas-relief scenes from Shakespeare's plays; it is a striking example of Art Deco classicism. A statue of Puck stands in the west garden. An **Elizabethan garden** on the east side of the building is planted with flowers and herbs of the period. Most remarkable here are eight sculptures, each depicting figures from a particular scene in a Shakespeare play. Each work is welded onto the top of a pedestal, on which are inscribed the play's lines that inspired the sculptor, Greg Wyatt. These statues are half the size of those that Wyatt created for the Great Garden at New Place in Stratford-upon-Avon, England. Inquire about guided tours scheduled at 10 and 11am on every third Saturday from April to October. The garden is also a quiet place to have a picnic.

The facility, which houses some 256,000 books, 116,000 of which are rare (pre-1801), is an important research center not only for Shakespearean scholars, but also for those studying any aspect of the English and continental Renaissance. A multimedia computer exhibition called *The Shakespeare Gallery* offers users a close-up look at

Museums of Special Interest

To the right person, with a specific interest, these lesser-known museums can be more than fascinating. Don't try to drop in without calling because most are not open daily, and some require appointments.

Anderson House, 2118 Massachusetts Ave. NW (© **202/785-2040;** www. hereditary.us/cin_anderson.htm): A century-old, 50-room mansion of amazing design and impressive art and furnishings. The mansion is headquarters for the Society of the Cincinnati, which was founded in 1783 by Continental officers (including George Washington) who had served in the American Revolution. Metro: Dupont Circle (Q St. exit).

Art Museum of the Americas, 201 18th St. NW, within the Organization of American States (© **202/458-6016;** www.museum.oas.org): From 80 to 200 works by contemporary Latin and Caribbean artists, on display from the museum's permanent collection. An Aztec garden and a second gallery in adjoining OAS building. Metro: Farragut West (17th St. exit), then walk south about 6 blocks.

Daughters of the American Revolution (DAR) Museum, 1776 D St. NW (© **202/879-3241;** www.dar.org/museum): Early American furnishings and decorative arts. Metro: Farragut West (17th St. exit), then walk south about 5 blocks.

Decatur House ⚐, 1610 H St. NW at Lafayette Park (© **202/842-0920;** www.decaturhouse.org): Historic house museum with permanent collection of Federalist and Victorian furnishings. Metro: Farragut West (17th St. exit).

Frederick Douglass National Historic Site, 1411 W St. SE (© **202/426-5961;** www.nps.gov/frdo): Last residence of the famous African-American 19th-century abolitionist. Metro: Anacostia, then catch bus no. B2, which stops by the house.

Hillwood Museum and Gardens, 4155 Linnean Ave. NW (© **202/686-5807;** www.hillwoodmuseum.org): Magnificent estate of Marjorie Merriweather Post, who collected art and artifacts of 18th-century France and Imperial Russia. Formal gardens, grand rooms, high tea. Metro: Van Ness (exit east on Connecticut Ave.).

Hillyer Art Space, 9 Hillyer Court NW (© **202/338-0680;** www.artsandartists. org/artspace.php): This new, hip little two-room gallery is an arm of International Arts & Artists and displays works of both regional and international artists in its mission to "increase cross-cultural understanding and exposure to the arts internationally." Metro: Dupont Circle (Q St. exit).

Interior Department Museum, 1849 C St. NW (© **202/208-4743;** www.doi.gov/ interiormuseum): Permanent exhibits relating to the work of agencies that fall within the Interior Department's jurisdiction: national parks, land management, Indian affairs, fish and wildlife services, environmental protection. Metro: Farragut West (18th St. exit), then walk about 6 blocks south.

Kreeger Museum, 2401 Foxhall Rd. NW (© **202/338-3050;** www.kreeger museum.org): This museum in a residential neighborhood is a treasure-trove

of art from the 1850s to the 1970s, including Impressionist paintings and the works of many American artists. No Metro; take a cab.

Mary McLeod Bethune Council House National Historic Site, 1318 Vermont Ave. NW (*(C)* 202/673-2402; www.nps.gov/mamc): Last residence of African-American activist/educator Bethune, who was a leading champion of black and women's rights during FDR's administration. Metro: McPherson Square (Franklin Sq./14th St. exit).

National Building Museum, 401 F St. NW (*(C)* 202/272-2448; www.nbm.org): Housed within a historic building is this fine museum devoted to architecture, building, and historic preservation. Metro: Judiciary Square (F St. exit).

National Geographic Museum, 17th and M streets NW. (*(C)* 202/857-7588; www.nationalgeographic.com/museum): Rotating exhibits related to exploration, adventure, and earth sciences, using interactive programs and artifacts. Metro: Farragut North (Connecticut Ave. and L St. exit).

Old Stone House, 3051 M St. NW (*(C)* 202/426-6851; www.nps.gov/olst): A 1765 structure said to be the oldest in D.C. still standing on its original foundations. Colonial appearance, English garden. Metro: Foggy Bottom, with a 15-minute walk.

Sewall-Belmont House, 144 Constitution Ave. NE (*(C)* 202/546-1210; www. sewallbelmont.org): A must for those interested in women's history, the historic house displays memorabilia of the women's suffrage movement, which got its start here. Metro: Union Station.

State Department Diplomatic Reception Rooms, 2201 D St. NW (entrance on 23rd St. NW; *(C)* 202/647-3241; https://receptiontours.state.gov): This is a fine-arts tour of rooms that serve as our country's main stage for international diplomacy. The rooms house a premier collection of Early American paintings, furniture, and decorative arts, dating from 1740. Metro: Foggy Bottom.

Textile Museum, 2320 S St. NW (*(C)* 202/667-0441; www.textilemuseum.org): Historic and contemporary handmade textile arts, housed in historic John Russell Pope mansion. Metro: Dupont Circle, Q Street exit, then walk a couple of blocks up Massachusetts Avenue until you see S Street. Second location coming in 2009 at 421 7th St. NW. Metro: Gallery Place/Verizon Center (7th and F sts. exit).

United States Navy Memorial and Naval Heritage Center, 701 Pennsylvania Ave. NW (*(C)* 202/737-2300; www.lonesailor.org): Plaza honors men and women of the U.S. Navy; museum features interactive video kiosks used to learn about Navy ships, aircraft, and history. Metro: Archives–Navy Memorial.

Woodrow Wilson House, 2340 S St. NW (*(C)* 202/387-4062; www.woodrow wilsonhouse.org): The former home of this president, preserved the way it was when he lived here in the 1920s. Docents guide visitors on hour-long tours, pointing out noteworthy objects and telling stories about the 28th president. Metro: Dupont Circle, Q Street exit, then walk a couple of blocks up Massachusetts Avenue until you reach S Street.

some of the Folgers' treasures, as well as Shakespeare's life and works. And the oak-paneled **Great Hall,** reminiscent of a Tudor long gallery, is a popular attraction for the general public. On display are rotating exhibits from the permanent collection: books, paintings, playbills, Renaissance musical instruments, and more. Plan on spending at least 30 minutes here.

At the end of the Great Hall is a theater designed to suggest an Elizabethan inn-yard where plays, concerts, readings, and Shakespeare-related events take place (see chapter 9 for details).

201 E. Capitol St. SE. © 202/544-4600. www.folger.edu. Free admission. Mon–Sat 10am–5pm. Free walk-in tours daily at 11am, with an extra tour added Sat at 1pm. Closed federal holidays. Metro: Capitol South or Union Station.

Ford's Theatre and Lincoln Museum *(Kids* **Note:** The theater and its tiny museum are closed for renovation, with the aim of reopening in time to mark Abraham Lincoln's 200th birthday on February 12, 2009. Realistically? It might not make that date. But the Petersen House across the street remains open. For background purposes, here's what you'll want to know:

On April 14, 1865, President Abraham Lincoln was in the audience at Ford's Theatre, one of the most popular playhouses in Washington. Everyone was laughing at a funny line from Tom Taylor's celebrated comedy, *Our American Cousin,* when John Wilkes Booth crept into the president's box, shot the president, and leapt to the stage, shouting, *"Sic semper tyrannis!"* ("Thus ever to tyrants!"). With his left leg broken from the vault, Booth mounted his horse in the alley and galloped off. Doctors carried Lincoln across the street to the house of William Petersen, where the president died the next morning.

The theater was closed after Lincoln's assassination and used as an office by the War Department. In 1893, 22 clerks were killed when three floors of the building collapsed. It remained in disuse until the 1960s, when it was remodeled and restored to its appearance on the night of the tragedy.

517 10th St. NW (btw. E and F sts.). © 202/426-6925. www.nps.gov/foth. Closed until winter 2009. Metro: Metro Center (11th and G sts. exit).

The House Where Lincoln Died (the Petersen House) *(Kids* After Lincoln was mortally wounded at Ford's Theatre, the doctors attending had him carried out into the street, where boarder Henry Safford, standing in the open doorway of his rooming house, gestured for them to bring the president inside. So Lincoln died in the home of William Petersen, a German-born tailor. Now furnished with period pieces, the dark, narrow town house looks much as it did on that fateful April night. It takes about 5 minutes to troop through the building. You'll see the front parlor where an anguished Mary Todd Lincoln spent the night with her son, Robert. In the back parlor, Secretary of War Edwin M. Stanton held a cabinet meeting and questioned witnesses. From this room, Stanton announced at 7:22am on April 15, 1865, "Now he belongs to the ages." Lincoln died, lying diagonally because he was so tall, on a bed the size of the one in the room. (The Chicago Historical Society owns the actual bed and other items from the room.) In 1896, the government bought the house for $30,000, and it is now maintained by the National Park Service.

516 10th St. NW. © 202/426-6924. Free admission. Daily 9am–5pm. Closed Dec 25. Metro: Metro Center.

International Spy Museum *(Kids* A visit here begins with a 5-minute briefing film, followed by a fun indoctrination into "Tricks of the Trade." Interactive monitors test one's powers of observation and teach you what to look for when it comes to

suspicious activity. In addition to surveillance games, this first section displays trick equipment (such as a shoe transmitter used by Soviets as a listening device and a single-shot pistol disguised as a lipstick tube) and runs film in which spies talk about bugging devices and locks and picks. You can watch a video that shows individuals being made up for disguise, and you can crawl on your belly through ductwork in the ceiling overhead. (The conversations you hear are taped, not floating up from the room of tourists below.)

Try to pace yourself, though, because there's still so much to see; and you can easily reach your limit before you get through the 68,000-square-foot museum. The next section covers the history of spying (the second-oldest profession) and tells about famous spy masters over time, from Moses; to Sun Tzu, the Chinese general, who wrote *The Art of War* in 400 B.C.; to George Washington, whose Revolutionary War letter of 1777 setting up a network of spies in New York is on view. Learn about the use of codes and code-breaking in spying, with one room of the museum devoted to the Enigma cipher machine used by the Germans (whose "unbreakable" codes the Allied cryptanalysts succeeded in deciphering) in World War II. An actual Enigma machine is displayed; interactive monitors allow you to simulate the experience of using an Enigma machine while learning more about its invention and inventor.

Much more follows: artifacts from all over (this is the largest collection of international espionage artifacts ever put on public display); a re-created tunnel beneath the divided city of Berlin during the Cold War; the intelligence-gathering stories of those behind enemy lines and of those involved in planning D-day in World War II; an exhibit on escape and evasion techniques in wartime; the tales of spies of recent times, told by the CIA and FBI agents involved in identifying them; and a mock-up of an intelligence agency's 21st-century operations center.

The museum's newest feature is **Operation Spy,** a 1-hour interactive immersion into espionage activities. Participants pretend to be intelligence officers and work in small teams as they conduct video surveillance of clandestine meetings, decrypt secret audio conversations, conduct polygraph tests, and so on, all in a day's work for a real-life spy. (You pay to play: a hefty $14 for those 12 and older, or $25 for combined admission to both the museum and this special feature.)

Note: Neither the main museum nor Operation Spy are recommended for children 11 and under.

You exit the museum directly to its gift shop, which leads to the Spy City Café.

While you may look with suspicion on everyone around you when you leave the museum, you can trust that what you've just learned at the museum is authoritative. The Spy Museum's executive director was with the CIA for 36 years, and his advisory board includes two former CIA directors, two former CIA disguise chiefs, and a retired KGB general.

Consider ordering advance tickets for next-day or future-date tours on the Spy Museum's website, which offers you the choice of printing your tickets at home or picking them up at the Will Call desk inside the museum. You can also purchase advance tickets, including those for tours later in the day, at the box office.

800 F St. NW (at 8th St. NW). ℓ 866/779-6873 or 202/393-7798. www.spymuseum.org. Admission $18 adults (ages 12–65), $17 for seniors, $15 for children ages 5–11. Operation Spy: $14 for ages 12 and up. Combined admission fee $25. Open daily, but hours vary; generally, the museum opens at 9am or 10am and closes most of the time at 6pm, but sometimes later, rarely earlier. Check website for details. Closed Thanksgiving, Dec 25, and Jan 1. Metro: Gallery Place/Chinatown (9th and G sts. exit) or National Archive/Navy Memorial.

Madame Tussauds Washington D.C. *(Kids)* Seven other Madame Tussauds exist, only two others are located in the U.S., and only one allows you the pleasure of sizing up George Washington, mingling with Beyoncé, or helping Tiger Woods line up his putt. Madame Tussauds is a wax museum whose life-size wax figure replicas of famous Americans and historic icons appear in one of four sections: The Spirit of Washington, D.C.; Behind the Scenes; Glamour; and Sports. Interactive displays allow visitors to step into the pictures of historic, celebrity, and sports events, whether to attend George Washington's inauguration or to hang with Julia Roberts.

1025 F St. NW (btw. 10th and 11th sts.). (C) **888/929-4632** or 202/942-7300. www.madametussaudsdc.com. Admission $19 adults, $13 children. Daily 10am–8pm. Metro: Metro Center (11th and G sts. exit).

Marian Koshland Science Museum *(★)* The National Academy of Sciences operates this small museum, which was conceived by molecular biologist Daniel Koshland, in memory of his wife, the immunologist and molecular biologist Marian Koshland, who died in 1997. The museum opened in April 2004 in the heart of downtown D.C. Recommended for children 14 and over, and especially for those with a scientific bent, the museum presents state-of-the-art exhibits that explore the complexities of science. (Do pay attention to the museum's age recommendation; I had a hard time wrapping my brain around the various exhibits, interesting though they were, and I'm a little bit older than 13.) Three exhibits currently on show are the Wonders of Science, which includes animations of groundbreaking research and an introductory film about the nature of science; Global Warming Facts and Our Future; and Infectious Disease, which covers the challenges to human health.

6th and E sts. NW. (C) **202/334-1201**. www.koshlandsciencemuseum.org. Admission $5 adults, $3 ages 5–18 and seniors (65+). Wed–Mon 10am–6pm. Closed Thanksgiving, Christmas, and New Year's Day. Metro: Gallery Place/Chinatown or Judiciary Square.

National Museum of Crime and Punishment No kidding, this museum has the feel of a haunted house, complete with dark passages, faux stone walls, a crawl space, and scary figures—mannequins dressed up as dangerous characters—placed here and there. Personally, I find it lame, but I am definitely in the minority, as you'll likely observe if you visit on a Saturday when the single-file line to get in extends out the door. Located in the heart of the Penn Quarter, the museum occupies three floors of a renovated town house, which limits the numbers of people who can shuffle through its five main chambers at any one time. Most of the museum offers a history of crime and punishment, along with tales of famous criminals, from the Middle Ages to the present.

Interactive exhibits allow visitors to place head and hands through a pillory, crack a safe, compare shooting skills to those of Old West outlaws, take a lie detector test, and simulate a police motorcycle chase. Exhibits display a hodgepodge of weapons, including hand irons and spiked chairs used to torture baddies during the Middle Ages. A replica of Wild Bill Hickock's revolver joins other sundry artifacts and objects such as sample prison garb, a re-creation of Al Capone's jail cell, John Dillinger's brilliant red 1933 Essex Terraplane car, and the getaway car used in the 1964 film, *Bonnie and Clyde*.

The last section of the museum explores crime fighting and solving, encouraging one to channel his or her inner detective to solve a case using interactive kiosks within a replica crime-scene lab. On the lower level of the museum is the *America's Most Wanted* TV studio, from which John Walsh occasionally broadcasts the show. (John

Walsh is a partner in the privately owned museum.) The museum operates a gift shop, the Cop Shop.

575 7th St. NW (at E St.). © 202/393-1099. www.crimemuseum.org. Adults $18 plus tax, seniors and children $15 plus tax; free for children 5 and under. Daily Sept–Feb 10am–6pm; Mar–Aug 9am–7pm. Metro: Gallery Place/Verizon Center (7th and F sts./Arena exit), or Archives/Navy Memorial.

National Museum of Women in the Arts This museum marked its 20th anniversary in 2007, its stunning collection still the foremost museum in the world dedicated to celebrating "the contribution of women to the history of art." Founders Wilhelmina and Wallace Holladay, who donated the core of the permanent collection—more than 250 works by women from the 16th to the 20th century—became interested in women's art in the 1960s. After discovering that no women were included in H. W. Janson's *History of Art*, a standard text (which did not address this oversight until 1986!), the Holladays began collecting art by women, and the concept of a women's art museum soon evolved.

Since its opening, the collection has grown to more than 3,000 works by more than 800 artists, including Rosa Bonheur, Frida Kahlo, Helen Frankenthaler, Barbara Hepworth, Georgia O'Keeffe, Camille Claudel, Lila Cabot Perry, Mary Cassatt, Elaine de Kooning, Käthe Kollwitz, and many other lesser-known artists from earlier centuries. You will discover here, for instance, that the famed Peale family of 19th-century portrait painters included a talented sister, Sarah Miriam Peale. The collection is complemented by an ongoing series of changing exhibits. You should allow an hour for touring.

The museum is housed in a magnificent Renaissance Revival landmark building designed in 1907 as a Masonic temple by noted architect Waddy Wood. Its sweeping marble staircase and splendid interior make it a popular choice for wedding receptions. Lunch (weekdays only) in the Mezzanine Café (© **202/628-1068**), and you'll be surrounded by works from the museum's permanent collection.

1250 New York Ave. NW (at 13th St.). © **800/222-7270** or 202/783-5000. www.nmwa.org. $10 adults, $8 students 18 and over with ID and seniors 60 and over, free for youth 18 and under. (These are general admission rates; special exhibition prices may be higher.) Mon–Sat 10am–5pm; Sun noon–5pm. Closed Jan 1, Thanksgiving, and Dec 25. Metro: Metro Center (13th St. exit).

Newseum 🎬🎬 Open since April 11, 2008, the Newseum is as much a fun house of participatory experiences and special-effects exhibits as it is a museum. In fact, the Newseum's tag line, "World's Most Interactive Museum," conveys its purpose in allowing the visitor to step into the picture: to play the reporter, TV journalist, researcher, or editor. The museum boasts 125 interactive game stations, 2 state-of-the-art broadcast studios, 14 galleries, and 15 theaters. At this particular time in history, with the business of journalism undergoing a world of change, the six-story Newseum manages to capture the magic of past, current, and future ways of covering the news.

First, take a look at the exterior, best viewed from across Pennsylvania Avenue. Covering the left side of the facade is a 75-foot-high tablet inscribed with words from the First Amendment ("Congress shall make no law . . . abridging the freedom of speech or of the press . . . "). Through its glass front, one can see (though much better at night) the huge high-definition screen hanging inside the atrium, spinning news story images. When you cross the street to enter the museum, you walk by a display of the day's front pages electronically obtained from newspapers across the country and around the world. Once inside, staff direct you first to the orientation film on the lower level (personally, I'd say skip this), then to the glass elevators that shoot you to

the sixth floor. The outdoor promenade on its own is worth the price of admission, since it offers you a breathtaking view of Pennsylvania Avenue and the Capitol. Also take time to read the fascinating history of Pennsylvania Avenue and of the city, presented in an exhibit that runs the length of the terrace.

Fifth-floor exhibits cover history. A display of "Great Books" presents 20 books and documents (originals, not copies) that are widely considered our "cornerstones of freedom." These include the 1475 printing of Thomas Aquinas's "Summa Theologica" and a 1215 edition of the Magna Carta. Next to the display is a touch screen; touch the image of the book you'd like to examine and the screen presents that book, allowing you to scroll through the first few pages. Nearby, the History Gallery showcases the Newseum's extensive collection of historic newspapers and magazines, tracing 500 years of news. Several theaters on this floor continuously play short documentaries in which esteemed journalists talk about ethics, sources, "getting it right," and other topics.

On the fourth floor, the First Amendment Gallery explores the historical contexts of the five freedoms. The 9/11 Gallery displays items recovered at the World Trade Center, images and reporting from that day, and an 11-minute film featuring personal stories by journalists who covered the attacks. While at first glance it appears to be a modern sculpture, one artifact on display here is in fact a 360-foot piece of the antenna that had stood on top of the North Tower.

On the third floor, check out the display of *New Yorker* cartoons joshing the news. In the World News Gallery, you can tune in to a current news broadcast from one of many countries (I listened briefly to a report from France on the Tour de France). The "Dateline: Danger" exhibit displays artifacts from hazardous missions that journalists have undertaken—including the laptop computer used by *Wall Street Journal* reporter Daniel Pearl before he was killed and the bloodstained notebook of *TIME* magazine reporter Michael Weisskopf, who lost his hand in an explosion in Iraq. Following that exhibit is the Journalists Memorial, a sobering display of 1,843 names written in a glass tablet to mark the deaths of those journalists who have died in pursuit of the news between 1837 and 2007. Elsewhere on this floor are several studios used by news organizations—including NPR and ABC—to broadcast programs. Visitors can sit in the audience during broadcasts or take behind-the-scenes tours when the studios are not in use.

A veritable playground for news junkies of all ages awaits on the second floor. An interactive newsroom with 48 kiosks allows you to test your skills as a photojournalist, editor, reporter, or anchor. An ethics center tests your sense of ethics. And, for a price ($8.50), you can try your hand at news anchor, reading from a teleprompter as a staff person tapes you, then watching your performance on screen.

The first floor's gallery of Pulitzer Prize photographs leaves one speechless. The gallery's database of interviews with some of the photographers, a documentary, and vignettes accompanying the photos offer fascinating context to the craft and to the stories behind the photographs.

Last but not least, return to the concourse level to view the I-Witness, a 4-D film feature that makes you feel as if you're on the scene with legends Isaiah Thomas (radical printer, not basketball legend), Nellie Bly, and Edward R. Murrow. I'm not saying another word, except: Don't miss it.

The Newseum's on-site restaurant, the Source, is already a favorite of Washingtonians. The museum has several gift shops.

555 Pennsylvania Ave. NW (at 6th St.). © 888/NEWSEUM (639-7386). www.newseum.org. $20 adults, $18 seniors 65 and older, $13 youth 7 to 12, free for children 6 and under. Daily 9am–5pm. (Closed Thanksgiving, Jan 1, and Dec 25. Metro: Judiciary Sq. (4th St. exit), Gallery Place/Verizon Center (7th and F sts./Arena exit), or Archives/Navy Memorial.

Phillips Collection ✰✰ This charming museum is even more alluring now that its expansion is complete. Its elegant 1890s Georgian Revival mansion anchors the Phillips, as it has since the gallery opened in 1921 (America's first museum of modern art). Founders Duncan and Marjorie Phillips, avid collectors and proselytizers of modernism, once lived here; now Impressionist, modernist, and American master gems from the 2,500-work permanent collection reside here. Intimate galleries retain homey features: leaded- and stained-glass windows, oak paneling, plush chairs and sofas, and individually designed fireplaces. The new wing houses the main entrance, as well as galleries devoted to special exhibits; a cafe run by a local favorite, Firehook Bakery (see "Gourmet Goodies to Go," in chapter 8, for details); a sculpture garden in the courtyard; and, most wonderfully, the Rothko Room, the small room devoted to four large, color-intense paintings by abstract expressionist Mark Rothko.

Best known for its Renoir masterpiece, *Luncheon of the Boating Party*, the Phillips boasts works by Daumier, Bonnard, Vuillard, van Gogh, Cézanne, Picasso, Degas, Klee, and Matisse. Ingres, Delacroix, Manet, El Greco, Goya, Corot, Constable, Courbet, Giorgione, and Chardin are among the premodernists represented. American notables, besides Rothko, include Dove, Hopper, Marin, Eakins, Homer, Lawrence, and O'Keeffe. You'll enjoy viewing the collection for an hour or so.

A full schedule of events includes temporary shows with loans from other museums and private collections, gallery talks, and concerts in the ornate music room. Concerts take place October to May on Sunday at 4pm; arrive early. On Thursday, the museum stays open until 8:30pm for **Artful Evenings,** usually a lecture or film screening.

Note: You may tour the permanent collection for free on weekdays. Weekends, admission is $10 per adult, $8 for seniors and students 18 and older. Special-exhibit admission prices vary, but are in effect weekdays; on weekends the regular admission price covers entry to both the permanent and special collections. The Phillips almost always has a special exhibition on view. You may order tickets in advance at the Phillips, or through Ticketmaster, online at www.ticketmaster.com, or by phone at ✆ **800/551-SEAT** (7328).

1600 21st St. NW (at Q St.). ✆ **202/387-2151.** www.phillipscollection.org. Admission: See information in the note, above. Tues–Sat 10am–5pm year-round (Thurs until 8:30pm); Sun 11am–6pm. Admission: see note, above. Call ahead for information and admission prices on special exhibits. Closed federal holidays. Metro: Dupont Circle (Q St. exit).

6 Other Attractions

John F. Kennedy Center for the Performing Arts ✰ Opened in 1971, the Kennedy Center is both the national performing arts center and a memorial to John F. Kennedy. Set on 17 acres overlooking the Potomac and designed by noted architect Edward Durell Stone, the striking facility encompasses an opera house, a concert hall, two stage theaters, a theater lab, and a theater devoted exclusively to family productions.

The best way to experience the Kennedy Center is to attend a performance. Check the website or call the toll-free number below for information about Kennedy Center happenings and prices. See chapter 9 for specifics on theater, concert, and dance offerings, including highlights of the 2008–09 season. The Center also offers free 50-minute guided tours, which include some restricted areas.

Tours depart from the parking plaza, Level A, at the Tour desk, located across from the lower-level gift shops. You tour the **Hall of Nations,** which displays the flags of all nations diplomatically recognized by the United States. Throughout the center you'll see gifts from more than 40 nations, including all the marble used in the building

(3,700 tons), which Italy donated. First stop is the **Grand Foyer,** scene of many free concerts and programs and the reception area for all three theaters on the main level; the 18 crystal chandeliers are a gift from Sweden. You'll also visit the **Israeli Lounge** (where 40 painted and gilded panels depict musical scenes from the Old Testament); the **Concert Hall,** home of the National Symphony Orchestra; the **Opera House;** the **African Lounge** (decorated with beautiful tapestries and other artwork from African nations); the **Eisenhower Theater;** the **Hall of States,** where flags of the 50 states and four territories are hung in the order in which they joined the Union; the **Performing Arts Library;** and the **Terrace Theater,** a bicentennial gift from Japan. If there's a rehearsal going on, the tour skips the visits to the theaters.

Tours are offered in English, French, German, Spanish, and Japanese. You can beat the crowds by writing in advance to a senator or congressperson for passes for a free congressional ("VIP") tour, given year-round Monday through Friday at 9:30am and 4:30pm and at 9:30am on Saturday and Sunday. Call ℂ **202/416-8340** for details.

Add another 15 minutes after the tour to walk around the building's terrace for a panoramic view of Washington.

2700 F St. NW (at New Hampshire Ave. NW and Rock Creek Pkwy.). ℂ **800/444-1324,** or 202/467-4600 for information or tickets. www.kennedy-center.org. Free admission. Daily 10am–midnight. Free guided tours Mon–Fri 10am–5pm; Sat–Sun 10am–1pm. Metro: Foggy Bottom (free shuttle service btw. the station and the center, running every 15 min. 9:45am–midnight weekdays, 10am–midnight Sat, and noon–midnight Sun). Bus: 80 from Metro Center. Parking $16.

Library of Congress ✦ The question most frequently asked by visitors to the Library of Congress is "Where are the books?" They are on the 532 miles of shelves located throughout the library's three buildings: the **Thomas Jefferson, James Madison Memorial,** and **John Adams** buildings. Established in 1800, "for the purchase of such books as may be necessary for the use of Congress," the library today serves the nation, with holdings for the visually impaired (for whom books are recorded on cassette and/or translated into Braille), research scholars, college students—and tourists. Its first collection of books was destroyed in 1814 when the British burned the Capitol (where the library was then housed) during the War of 1812. Thomas Jefferson then sold the institution his personal library of 6,487 books as a replacement, and this became the foundation of what would grow to become the world's largest library.

Today, the collection contains a mind-boggling 138 million items. Its buildings house more than 32 million cataloged books; 61 million manuscripts; millions and millions of prints and photographs, audio holdings (discs, tapes, talking books, and so on), movies, and videotapes; musical instruments from the 1700s; and the letters and papers of everyone from George Washington to Groucho Marx. Its archives also include the letters, oral histories, photographs, and other documents of war veterans from World War I to the present, all part of its **Veterans History Project;** go to www.loc.gov/vets to listen to or read some of these stories, especially if you plan on visiting the National World War II Memorial.

Just as impressive as the library's holdings is its architecture. Most magnificent is the ornate Italian Renaissance–style **Thomas Jefferson Building,** which was erected between 1888 and 1897 to hold the burgeoning collection and establish America as a cultured nation with magnificent institutions equal to anything in Europe. Fifty-two painters and sculptors worked for 8 years on its interior. There are floor mosaics of Italian marble, allegorical paintings on the overhead vaults, more than 100 murals, and numerous ornamental cornucopias, ribbons, vines, and garlands. The building's

exterior has 42 granite sculptures and yards of bas-reliefs. Especially impressive are the exquisite marble **Great Hall** and the **Main Reading Room,** the latter under a 160-foot dome. Originally intended to hold the fruits of at least 150 years of collecting, the Jefferson Building was, in fact, filled up in a mere 13 years. It is now supplemented by the James Madison Memorial Building and the John Adams Building.

In April 2008, the Library debuted its **Library of Congress Experience,** an interactive introduction to the museum and its highlights. Visitors enter into the Great Hall, proceeding to the orientation galleries in the hall for basic training in navigating the exhibits. Armed with instructions for the self-guided audio tour, visitors use touch screens and virtual interactives to zoom in on the art, architecture, and artifacts displayed within the magnificent Great Hall. Interactive features are available throughout other exhibit areas.

The Library hosts a smorgasbord of events, including a free movie and concert series. Be sure to check the LOC website before you come. Concerts take place in the Jefferson Building's elegant **Coolidge Auditorium.** The concerts are free but require tickets, which you can obtain through Ticketmaster (© **800/551-7328**). Across Independence Avenue from the Jefferson Building is the **Madison Building,** which houses the Copyright Office and the **Mary Pickford Theater,** a venue for classic film screenings.

Anyone 18 and over may use the library's collections, but first you must obtain a user card with your photo on it. Go to Reader Registration in Room LM 140 (street level of the Madison Building) and present a driver's license or passport. Then head to the Information Desk in either the Jefferson or Madison buildings to find out about the research resources available to you and how to use them. Most likely, you will be directed to the Main Reading Room. All books must be used on-site.

101 Independence Ave. SE (at 1st St. SE). © **202/707-8000.** www.loc.gov. Free admission. Madison Building Mon–Fri 8:30am–9:30pm; Sat 8:30am–6:30pm. Jefferson Building Mon–Sat 10am–5pm. Closed federal holidays. Stop at the information desk inside the Jefferson Building's west entrance on 1st St. to obtain same-day free tickets to tour the Library. Tours of the Great Hall: Mon–Fri 10:30 and 11:30am, and 1:30, 2:30, and 3:30pm; Sat 10:30 and 11:30am, and 1:30 and 2:30pm. Contact your congressional representatives to obtain tickets for congressional, or "VIP," tours, a slightly more personal tour given weekdays at 8:30am and 2pm. Metro: Capitol South.

Union Station 🎯 When you visit Union Station, you're stepping into the heart (or at least into a major artery) of everyday Washington life. Located within walking distance and full view of the Capitol, the station is a vital crossroads for locals. You'll see Hill staffers who debark the Metro's Red Line at its stop here ("Union Station" is the station name, naturally); commuters, who ride MARC and Amtrak trains from outlying cities such as Baltimore; residents who walk or Metro here to shop, work, dine, or dawdle; and travelers from all over who arrive and depart by train all day long. Paths collide, quite literally sometimes, as ambling visitors and people running to catch a train crisscross the same ground.

When it opened in 1907, this was the largest train station in the world. It was designed by noted architect Daniel H. Burnham, who modeled it after the Baths of Diocletian and Arch of Constantine in Rome. Its facade includes Ionic colonnades fashioned from white granite and 100 sculptured eagles. Graceful 50-foot Constantine arches mark the entryways, above which are poised six carved fixtures representing Fire, Electricity, Freedom, Imagination, Agriculture, and Mechanics. Inside is the **Main Hall,** a massive rectangular room with a 96-foot barrel-vaulted ceiling, an expanse of white-marble flooring, and a balcony adorned with 36 Augustus Saint-Gaudens sculptures of Roman legionnaires. Off the Main Hall is the **East Hall,** shimmering with

scagliola marble walls and columns, a gorgeous hand-stenciled skylight ceiling, and stunning murals of classical scenes inspired by ancient Pompeian art. (Today this is the station's most pleasant shopping venue: less crowded and noisy, with small vendors selling pretty jewelry and other accessories.)

In its time, this "temple of transport" has witnessed many important events. President Wilson welcomed General Pershing here in 1918 on his return from France. South Pole explorer Rear Admiral Richard Byrd was also feted at Union Station on his homecoming. And Franklin D. Roosevelt's funeral train, bearing his casket, was met here in 1945 by thousands of mourners.

But after the 1960s, with the decline of rail travel, the station fell on hard times. Rain caused parts of the roof to cave in; and the entire building—with floors buckling, rats running about, and mushrooms sprouting in damp rooms—was sealed in 1981. That same year, Congress enacted legislation to preserve and restore this national treasure, to the tune of $160 million. The remarkable restoration involved hundreds of European and American artisans who were meticulous in returning the station to its original design.

At least 25 million people come through Union Station's doors yearly. About 120 retail and food shops on three levels offer a wide array of merchandise and dining options. The sky-lit **Main Concourse,** which extends the entire length of the station, is the primary shopping area as well as a ticketing and baggage facility. A nine-screen **cinema complex** lies on the lower level, across from the Food Court. You could spend half a day here shopping or about 20 minutes touring. Stop by the visitor kiosk in the Main Hall. See chapter 8 for information about Union Station **shops.**

50 Massachusetts Ave. NE. © 202/289-1908. www.unionstationdc.com. Free admission. Daily 24 hr. Shops Mon–Sat 10am–9pm; Sun noon–6pm. Parking $6 for 1 hr. or less, up to $18 for 24 hr. Metro: Union Station.

Washington National Cathedral ⚐ Pierre L'Enfant's 1791 plan for the capital city included "a great church for national purposes." Possibly because of early America's fear of mingling church and state, more than a century elapsed before the foundation for Washington National Cathedral was laid. Its actual name is the Cathedral Church of St. Peter and St. Paul. The church is Episcopal, but it has no local congregation and seeks to serve the entire nation as a house of prayer for all people. It has been the setting for every kind of religious observance, from Jewish to Serbian Orthodox.

A church of this magnitude—it's the sixth-largest cathedral in the world, and the second-largest in the U.S.—took a long time to build. Its principal (but not original) architect, Philip Hubert Frohman, worked on the project from 1921 until his death in 1972. The foundation stone was laid in 1907 using the mallet with which George Washington set the Capitol cornerstone. Construction was interrupted by both world wars and by periods of financial difficulty. The cathedral was completed with the placement of the final stone on the west front towers on September 29, 1990, 83 years (to the day) after it was begun.

English Gothic in style (with several distinctly 20th-c. innovations, such as a stained-glass window commemorating the flight of *Apollo 11* and containing a piece of moon rock), the cathedral is built in the shape of a cross, complete with flying buttresses and 110 gargoyles. Along with the Capitol and the Washington Monument, it is one of the dominant structures on the Washington skyline. Its 57-acre landscaped grounds have two lovely gardens (the lawn is ideal for picnicking), four schools, a greenhouse, and two gift shops.

The cathedral is a truly historic place. Services to celebrate the end of World Wars I and II were held here. It was the scene of President Wilson's funeral (he and his wife are buried here), as well as President Eisenhower's. Helen Keller and her companion, Anne Sullivan, were buried in the cathedral at her request. And during the Iranian crisis, a round-the-clock prayer vigil was held in the Holy Spirit Chapel throughout the hostages' captivity. When they were released, the hostages came to a service here. President Bush's National Prayer and Remembrance service on September 14, 2001, following the cataclysm of September 11, was held here.

The best way to explore the cathedral is to take a 30-minute **guided tour;** the tours leave continually from the west end of the nave. You can also walk through on your own, using a self-guiding brochure available in several languages. Call about group and special-interest tours, both of which require reservations and fees (© **202/537-5700**). Allow additional time to tour the grounds or "close" and to visit the **Observation Gallery** 🍴, where 70 windows provide panoramic views. Tuesday- and Wednesday-afternoon tours are followed by a high tea in the Observation Gallery for $25 per person; reservations required. Call © **202/537-8993** or book online at www.visit. cathedral.org/tea.

The cathedral hosts numerous events: organ recitals; choir performances; an annual flower mart; calligraphy workshops; jazz, folk, and classical concerts; and the playing of the 53-bell carillon. Check the cathedral's website for schedules.

Massachusetts and Wisconsin aves. NW (entrance on Wisconsin Ave.). © **202/537-6200**. www.nationalcathedral. org. Donation $5 adults, $3 seniors, $15 families. Cathedral Mon–Fri 10am–5:30pm; Sat 10am–4:30pm; Sun 8am–6:30pm; May 1 to Labor Day, the nave level stays open Mon–Fri until 8pm. Gardens daily until dusk. Regular tours Mon–Sat 10–11:30am and 12:45–4pm; Sun 1–2:30pm. No tours on Palm Sunday, Easter, Thanksgiving, Dec 25, or during services. Services vary throughout the year, but you can count on a weekday Evensong service at 5:30pm, a weekday noon service, and an 11am service every Sun; call for other service times. Metro: Tenleytown, with a 20-min. walk. Bus: Any N bus up Massachusetts Ave. from Dupont Circle or any 30-series bus along Wisconsin Ave. This is a stop on the Old Town Trolley Tour. Parking garage free on Sun, flat rate of $4 on Sat, flat rate of $3 after 4pm weekdays, and $3 an hour/$12 maximum weekdays until 4pm.

7 Just Across the Potomac: Arlington National Cemetery

The land that today comprises Arlington County originally was carved out of Virginia as part of the nation's new capital district. In 1847, the land was returned to the state of Virginia. It was known as Alexandria County until 1920, when the name was changed to avoid confusion with the city of Alexandria.

The county got its name from its famous estate, Arlington House, built by a descendant of Martha Washington, George Washington Parke Custis, whose daughter married Robert E. Lee. The Lees lived in Arlington House on and off until the onset of the Civil War in 1861. After the first Battle of Bull Run, at Manassas, several Union soldiers were buried here; the beginnings of Arlington National Cemetery date from that time. The Arlington Memorial Bridge leads directly from the Lincoln Memorial to the Robert E. Lee Memorial at Arlington House, symbolically joining these two figures into one Union after the Civil War.

Arlington has long been a residential community, with most people commuting into Washington to work and play. In recent years, however, the suburb has come into its own, booming with businesses, restaurants, and nightlife, giving residents reasons to stay put and tourists more incentive to visit (see "Electric Avenues for Live-Music Lovers," in chapter 9). Here are some sites worth seeing:

Arlington National Cemetery ✦✦ Upon arrival, head over to the **Visitor Center,** where you can view exhibits, pick up a detailed map, use the restrooms (there are no others until you get to Arlington House), and purchase a **Tourmobile ticket** ($7.50 per adult, $3.75 for children 3–11), which allows you to stop at all major sites in the cemetery and then reboard whenever you like. Service is continuous and the narrated commentary is informative; this is the only guided tour of the cemetery offered. If you've got plenty of stamina, consider doing part or all of the tour on foot. Remember as you go that this is a memorial frequented not just by tourists but also by those attending burial services or visiting the graves of beloved relatives and friends who are buried here.

This shrine occupies approximately 624 acres on the high hills overlooking the capital from the west side of the Memorial Bridge. It honors many national heroes and more than 300,000 war dead, veterans, and dependents. Many graves of the famous at Arlington bear nothing more than simple markers. Five-star General John J. Pershing's is one of those. Secretary of State John Foster Dulles is buried here. So are President William Howard Taft and Supreme Court Justices Thurgood Marshall and William Brennan. Cemetery highlights include:

The **Tomb of the Unknowns,** containing the unidentified remains of service members from both world wars, the Korean War, and, until 1997, the Vietnam War. In 1997, the remains of the unknown soldier from Vietnam were identified as those of Air Force 1st Lt. Michael Blassie, whose A-37 was shot down in South Vietnam in 1962. Blassie's family, who had reason to believe that the body was their son's, had besought the Pentagon to exhume the soldier's remains and conduct DNA testing to determine if what the family suspected was true. Upon confirmation, the Blassies buried Michael in his hometown of St. Louis. The crypt honoring the dead but unidentified Vietnam War soldiers will remain empty. The entire tomb is an unembellished, massive white-marble block, moving in its simplicity. A 24-hour honor guard watches over the tomb, with the changing of the guard taking place every half-hour April to September, every hour on the hour October to March, and every hour at night year-round.

Within a 20-minute walk, all uphill, from the Visitor Center is **Arlington House** (✆ **703/235-1530;** www.nps.gov/arho), whose structure was begun in 1802, by Martha and George Washington's grandson, George Washington Parke Custis (actually, Custis was George Washington's adopted grandson). Custis's daughter, Mary Anna Randolph, inherited the estate; and she and her husband, Robert E. Lee, lived here between 1831 and 1861. When Lee headed up Virginia's army, Mary fled; and federal troops confiscated the property. A fine melding of the styles of the Greek Revival and the grand plantation houses of the early 1800s, the house has been administered by the National Park Service since 1933.

You tour the house on your own; park rangers are on-site to answer your questions. The house remains open but is likely to be unfurnished until 2010, as a renovation gets underway. Slave quarters and a small museum adjoin. Admission is free. It's open daily from 9:30am to 4:30pm, and until 5:30pm during the summer (closed Jan 1 and Dec 25).

Pierre Charles L'Enfant's grave was placed near Arlington House at a spot that is believed to offer the best view of Washington, the city he designed.

Below Arlington House is the **Gravesite of John Fitzgerald Kennedy.** John Carl Warnecke designed a low crescent wall embracing a marble terrace, inscribed with the

Arlington National Cemetery

Arlington House **4**
Gravesite of John F. Kennedy **3**
Gravesite of Pierre Charles
 L'Enfant **6**
Memorial Gate **1**
Tomb of the Unknown Civil War
 Dead **5**
Tomb of the Unknowns **7**
Women in Military Service
 for America Memorial **2**

Numbers in *italics* indicate cemetery section numbers.

35th president's most famous utterance: "And so, my fellow Americans, ask not what your country can do for you; ask what you can do for your country." Jacqueline Kennedy Onassis rests next to her husband, and Robert Kennedy is buried close by. The Kennedy graves attract streams of visitors. Arrive close to 8am to contemplate the site quietly; otherwise, it's often crowded. Looking north, there's a spectacular view of Washington.

In 1997, the **Women in Military Service for America Memorial** (© **800/222-2294** or 703/533-1155; www.womensmemorial.org) was added to Arlington Cemetery to honor the more than two million women who have served in the armed forces from the American Revolution to the present. The impressive memorial lies just beyond the gated entrance to the cemetery, a 3-minute walk from the Visitor Center. As you approach the memorial, you see a large, circular reflecting pool, perfectly placed within the curve of the granite wall rising behind it. Arched passages within the 226-foot-long wall lead to an upper terrace and dramatic views of Arlington National Cemetery and the monuments of Washington; an arc of large glass panels (which form the roof of the memorial hall) contains etched quotations from famous people about contributions made by servicewomen. Behind the wall and completely underground is the **Education Center,** housing a **Hall of Honor,** a gallery of exhibits tracing the history of women in the military, a theater, and a computer register of servicewomen,

which visitors may access for the stories and information about 250,000 individual military women, past and present. Hours are 8am to 5pm (until 7pm Apr–Sept). Stop at the reception desk for a brochure that details a self-guided tour through the memorial. The memorial is open every day but Christmas.

Plan to spend half a day at Arlington Cemetery and the Women in Military Service Memorial.

Just across the Memorial Bridge from the base of the Lincoln Memorial. © 703/607-8000. www.arlingtoncemetery.org. Free admission. Apr–Sept daily 8am–7pm; Oct–Mar daily 8am–5pm. Metro: Arlington National Cemetery. If you come by car, parking is $1.75 an hour for the 1st 3 hr., $2 an hour thereafter. The cemetery is also accessible via Tourmobile.

8 Parks & Gardens

Washington is extensively endowed with vast natural areas, all centrally located within the District. Included in all this greenery are thousands of parkland acres, two rivers, the mouth of a 185-mile-long tree-lined canalside trail, an untamed wilderness area, and a few thousand cherry trees. And there's much more just a stone's throw away.

GARDENS

Dumbarton Oaks *Finds* This 19th-century Georgetown mansion named for a Scottish castle is a research center for studies in Byzantine and pre-Columbian art and history, as well as landscape architecture. Its magical yards, which wind gently down to Rock Creek Ravine, are modeled after European gardens. The pre-Columbian museum, designed by Philip Johnson, is a small gem; and the Byzantine collection is a rich one. The mansion's **formal gardens** are a favorite of Washingtonians. The gardens include an Orangery, a Rose Garden, wisteria-covered arbors, groves of cherry trees, and magnolias. You're likely to spend as much as an hour here when everything is in bloom, but expect to share the winding paths with like-minded wanderers. You can't picnic here; instead, exit at R Street, turn left, cross an honest-to-goodness Lovers' Lane, and proceed next door to Montrose Park to hold your picnic. There is parking on the street. See box "The Roads Less Traveled: A Back-Street Tour of Historic Georgetown, with Stops at Shops," in chapter 8, which points you here and to other nearby attractions, including shops and dining.

1703 32nd St. NW (garden entrance at 31st and R sts.). © 202/339-6401. www.doaks.org. Gardens admission Mar 15–Oct 31 $8 adults, $5 children 12 and under and seniors; Nov–Mar 14 free. Museum admission free. Gardens Tues–Sun, year-round, weather permitting: 2–6pm Mar 15–Oct 31; 2–5pm Nov 1–Mar 14. Museum daily 2–5pm. Museum and gardens are closed national holidays and Dec 24.

Enid A. Haupt Garden Named for its donor, a noted supporter of horticultural projects, this stunning garden presents elaborate flower beds and borders, plant-filled turn-of-the-20th-century urns, 1870s cast-iron furnishings, and lush baskets hung from reproduction 19th-century lampposts. Although on ground level, the garden is actually on a 4¼-acre rooftop above the subterranean Ripley Center and the Sackler and African Art museums. An **"Island Garden"** near the Sackler Gallery, entered via a 9-foot moon gate, has benches backed by English boxwoods set under the canopy of weeping cherry trees.

A **"Fountain Garden"** outside the African Art Museum provides granite seating with walls overhung by hawthorn trees. Three small terraces, shaded by black sourgum trees, are located near the Arts and Industries Building. And five majestic linden trees shade a seating area around the **Downing Urn,** a memorial to American landscapist Andrew Jackson Downing, who designed the National Mall. Downing's words

are inscribed on the base of the urn: "Build halls where knowledge shall be freely diffused among men, and not shut up within the narrow walls of narrower institutions. Plant spacious parks in your cities and unclose their gates as wide as the gates of morning to the whole people." Elaborate cast-iron carriage gates made according to a 19th-century design by James Renwick, flanked by four red-sandstone pillars, are placed at the Independence Avenue entrance to the garden.

10th St. and Independence Ave. SW. ℂ 202/633-1000. Free admission. Late May to Aug daily 7am–9:15pm; Sept to mid-May daily 7am–5:45pm. Closed Dec 25. Metro: Smithsonian (12th St. and Independence Ave. exit).

United States Botanic Garden ℛ For the feel of summer in the middle of winter, for the sight of lush, breathtakingly beautiful greenery and flowers year-round, stop in at the Botanic Garden, located at the foot of the Capitol next door to the National Museum of the American Indian. The grand conservatory devotes half of its space to exhibits that focus on the importance of plants to people, and half to exhibits that focus on ecology and the evolutionary biology of plants. But those finer points may escape you as you wander through the various chambers, outdoors and indoors, upstairs and down, gazing in stupefaction at so much fauna and flora. The conservatory holds 4,000 living species (about 26,000 plants); a high-walled enclosure, called "The Jungle," of palms, ferns, and vines; an Orchid Room; a meditation garden; a primeval garden; and gardens created especially with children in mind. And there are sounds—I swear I heard a frog or two. Just outside the conservatory is the National Garden, which includes the First Ladies Water Garden, a formal rose garden, a butterfly garden, and a lawn terrace. Ask at the front desk about tours. The USBG sometimes offers entertainment and periodically publishes calendars of events.

Also visit the garden annex across the street, **Bartholdi Park.** The park is about the size of a city block, with a stunning cast-iron classical fountain created by Frédéric Auguste Bartholdi, designer of the Statue of Liberty. Charming flower gardens bloom amid tall ornamental grasses, benches are sheltered by vine-covered bowers, and a touch and fragrance garden contains such herbs as pineapple-scented sage.

100 Maryland Ave. SW (btw. 1st and 3rd sts. SW, at the foot of the Capitol on the National Mall). ℂ 202/225-8333. www.usbg.gov. Free admission. Conservatory daily 10am–5pm, National Garden 10am–7pm, Bartholdi Park dawn to dusk. Metro: Federal Center SW (Smithsonian Museums/Maryland Ave. exit).

PARKS
POTOMAC PARK

West and East Potomac parks, their 720 riverside acres divided by the Tidal Basin, are most famous for their spring display of **cherry blossoms** and all the hoopla that goes with it. So much attention is lavished on Washington's cherry blossoms that the National Park Service devotes a home page to the subject: www.nps.gov/nama/plan yourvisit/cherry-blossom-bloom.htm. (Also go to www.nationalcherryblossomfestival. org.) You can access the NPS site to find out forecasts for the blooms and assorted other details. You can also call the National Park Service (ℂ 202/426-6841) for information. In all, there are more than 3,700 cherry trees planted along the Tidal Basin in West Potomac Park, East Potomac Park, the Washington Monument grounds, and other pockets of the city.

To get to the Tidal Basin by car (*not* recommended in cherry-blossom season— actually, let me be clear: *impossible* in cherry-blossom season), you want to get on Independence Avenue and follow the signs posted near the Lincoln Memorial that show you where to turn to find parking and the FDR Memorial. If you're walking,

(Tips Cherry Night

The National Park Service offers several kinds of cherry blossom tours, but the best is the lantern walk, which takes place at night. You bring your own flashlight and a park ranger guides you beneath the canopy of cherry blossoms for 1½ miles around the Tidal Basin.

you'll want to cross Independence Avenue where it intersects with West Basin Drive (there's a stoplight and crosswalk), and follow the path to the Tidal Basin. There is no convenient Metro stop near here.

West Potomac Park encompasses Constitution Gardens; the Vietnam, Korean, Lincoln, Jefferson, World War II, and FDR memorials; a small island where ducks live; and the Reflecting Pool (see "The National Mall & Memorial Parks," p. 175, for full listings of the memorials). It has 1,678 cherry trees bordering the Tidal Basin, some of them Akebonos with delicate pink blossoms, but most Yoshinos with white, cloudlike flower clusters. The blossoming of the cherry trees is the focal point of a 2-week-long celebration, including the lighting of the 300-year-old Japanese Stone Lantern near Kutz Bridge, presented to the city by the governor of Tokyo in 1954. (This year's Cherry Blossom Festival is scheduled to run Mar 28–Apr 12, 2009.) The trees bloom for a little less than 2 weeks beginning sometime between March 20 and April 17; April 4 is the average date. Planning your trip around the blooming of the cherry blossoms is an iffy proposition, and I wouldn't advise it. All it takes is one good rain and those cherry blossoms are gone. The cherry blossoms are not illuminated at night.

East Potomac Park has 1,681 cherry trees in 10 varieties. The park also has picnic grounds, tennis courts, three golf courses, a large swimming pool, and biking and hiking paths by the water.

ROCK CREEK PARK

Created in 1890, **Rock Creek Park** ∉ (**www.nps.gov/rocr**) was purchased by Congress for its "pleasant valleys and ravines, primeval forests and open fields, its running waters, its rocks clothed with rich ferns and mosses, its repose and tranquillity, its light and shade, its ever-varying shrubbery, its beautiful and extensive views." A 1,750-acre valley within the District of Columbia, extending 12 miles from the Potomac River to the Maryland border, it's one of the biggest and finest city parks in the nation. Parts of it are still wild; coyotes have been sighted here, joining the red and gray foxes, raccoons, and beavers already resident. Most tourists encounter its southern tip, the section from the Kennedy Center to the National Zoo, but the park widens and travels much further from there.

The park's offerings include the Old Stone House in Georgetown (located on a busy street in Georgetown, outside the park but considered a park property, nonetheless), Carter Barron Amphitheater (see chapter 9), playgrounds, an extensive system of beautiful hiking and biking trails, sports facilities, remains of Civil War fortifications, and acres and acres of wooded parklands. See also p. 218 for a description of the formal gardens at **Dumbarton Oaks,** which border Rock Creek Park in upper Georgetown.

Northern Rock Creek Park Area

For full information on the wide range of park programs and activities, visit the **Rock Creek Nature Center and Planetarium,** 5200 Glover Rd. NW (☎ 202/895-6070), Wednesday through Sunday from 9am to 5pm. To get to the Nature Center by public transportation, take the Metro to Friendship Heights and transfer to bus no. E2 to Military Road and Oregon Avenue/Glover Road, then walk up the hill about 100 yards to the Nature Center. Call ☎ 202/895-6070 to request a brochure that provides details on picnic locations.

The Nature Center and Planetarium is the scene of numerous activities, including weekend planetarium shows for kids (minimum age 4) and adults; nature films; crafts demonstrations; live animal demonstrations; guided nature walks; plus a daily mix of lectures, films, and other events. Self-guided nature trails begin here. All activities are free, but for planetarium shows you need to pick up tickets a half-hour in advance. There are also nature exhibits on the premises. The Nature Center is closed on federal holidays.

Not far from the Nature Center is **Fort DeRussey,** one of 68 fortifications erected to defend the city of Washington during the Civil War. From the intersection of Military Road and Oregon Avenue, you walk a short trail through the woods to reach the fort, whose remains include high earth mounds with openings where guns were mounted, surrounded by a deep ditch/moat.

At Tilden Street and Beach Drive, you can see a water-powered 19th-century gristmill, used until not so long ago to grind corn and wheat into flour. It's called **Peirce Mill** (a man named Isaac Peirce built it), but it's currently closed for repairs.

Poetry readings and workshops are held during the summer at **Miller's Cabin,** the one-time residence of High Sierra poet Joaquin Miller, Beach Drive north of Military Road. Call (C) **202/895-6070** for information.

You'll find convenient free **parking** throughout the park.

THEODORE ROOSEVELT ISLAND PARK ★★

A serene, 91-acre wilderness preserve, Theodore Roosevelt Island is a memorial to the nation's 26th president in recognition of his contributions to conservation. During his administration, Roosevelt, an outdoor enthusiast and expert field naturalist, set aside a total of 234 million acres of public lands for forests, national parks, wildlife and bird refuges, and monuments.

Native American tribes were here first, inhabiting the island for centuries until the arrival of English explorers in the 1600s. Over the years, the island passed through many owners before becoming what it is today—an island preserve of swamp, marsh, and upland forest that's a haven for rabbits, chipmunks, great owls, foxes, muskrats, turtles, and groundhogs. It's a complex ecosystem in which cattails, arrow arum, and pickerelweed grow in the marshes, and willow, ash, and maple trees root on the mud flats. You can observe these flora and fauna in their natural environs on 2.5 miles of foot trails.

In the northern center of the island, overlooking a terrace encircled by a water-filled moat, stands a 17-foot bronze statue of Roosevelt. Four 21-foot granite tablets are inscribed with tenets of his conservation philosophy.

To drive to the island, take the George Washington Memorial Parkway exit north from the Theodore Roosevelt Bridge. The parking area is accessible only from the northbound lane; park there and cross the pedestrian bridge that connects the lot to the island. You can also rent a canoe at Thompson's Boat Center (p. 229) and paddle over, or take the pedestrian bridge at Rosslyn Circle, 2 blocks from the Rosslyn Metro station. You can picnic on the grounds near the memorial; if you do, allow about an hour here. Expect bugs in summer and muddy trails after a rain.

In the Potomac River, btw. Washington and Rosslyn, VA. See access information above. (C) 703/289-2500. www.nps. gov/this. Free admission. Daily dawn–dusk. Metro: Rosslyn, then walk 2 blocks to Rosslyn Circle and cross the pedestrian bridge to the island.

ACTIVITIES ON THE C&O CANAL

One of the great joys of living in Washington is the **C&O Canal** (**www.nps.gov/choh**) and its unspoiled 185-mile towpath. You leave urban cares and stresses behind while hiking, strolling, jogging, cycling, or boating in this lush, natural setting of ancient oaks and red maples, giant sycamores, willows, and wildflowers. But the canal wasn't always just a leisure spot for city people. It was built in the 1800s, when water routes were considered vital to transportation. Even before it was completed, though, the canal was being rendered obsolete by the B&O Railroad, which was constructed at about the same time and along the same route. Today, its role as an oasis from unrelenting urbanity is even more important.

A good source of information about the canal is the National Park Service office at **Great Falls Tavern Visitor Center,** 11710 MacArthur Blvd., Potomac, MD ((C) **301/ 767-3714**). At this 1831 tavern, you can see museum exhibits and a film about the

> **_Finds_** **Albert Einstein Memorial, 22nd Street and Constitution Avenue NW**
>
> In a grove of holly and elm trees at the southwest corner of the National Academy of Science grounds, you'll find this dear memorial displaying the slouching figure of brilliant scientist, great thinker, and peace activist Albert Einstein. He sits slightly bent and sideways, upon a granite bench, leaning on one hand and holding in the other a bronze sheet of paper on which are written mathematical equations for which he is famous. At his feet is a celestial map. His gaze looks worn and warm. The statue measures 12 feet in height and weighs 4 tons, yet children cannot resist crawling upon it and leaning up against this man.

canal; there's also a bookstore on the premises. The park charges an entrance fee, $5 per car, $3 per walker or cyclist.

In Georgetown, the **Georgetown Information Center,** 1057 Thomas Jefferson St. NW (© **202/653-5190**), can also provide maps and information.

Hiking any section of the flat dirt towpath or its more rugged side paths is a pleasure (and it's free). There are picnic tables, some with barbecue grills, about every 5 miles on the way to Cumberland, beginning at the **Boat House at Fletcher's Cove** (© **202/244-0461;** www.fletcherscove.com). It's about 3¼ miles out of Georgetown and is a good place to rent bikes or boats or to purchase bait, tackle, and a fishing license. Enter the towpath in Georgetown below M Street via Thomas Jefferson Street. If you hike 14 miles, you'll reach **Great Falls,** a point where the Potomac becomes a stunning waterfall plunging 76 feet. Or drive to Great Falls Park on the Virginia side of the Potomac.

Much less strenuous than hiking is a **mule-drawn 19th-century canalboat trip** led by Park Service rangers in period dress. They regale passengers with canal legend and lore and sing period songs. These boats depart from mid-April to mid-October. Both the Georgetown and Great Falls barge rides last about 1 hour and 10 minutes and cost $5 for everyone except children 3 and under, who ride free. Check the website, www.nps.gov/choh, for the latest schedules.

Call any of the above information numbers for details on riding, rock climbing, fishing, bird-watching, concerts, ranger-guided tours, ice-skating, camping, and other canal activities.

9 Especially for Kids

As far as I know, Pierre L'Enfant and his successors were not thinking of children when they incorporated the long, open stretch of the Mall into their design for the city. But they may as well have. This 2-mile expanse of lawn running from the Lincoln Memorial to the Capitol is a playground, really, and a backyard to the Smithsonian museums and National Gallery which border it. You can visit any of these sites assured that if one of your little darlings starts to misbehave, you'll be able to head right out the door to the National Mall, where numerous distractions await. The Mall is always busy with walkers, joggers, and bikers. Vendors sell ice cream, soft pretzels, and sodas. Festivals of all sorts take place on a regular basis, whether it's the grand Smithsonian Folklife Festival for 10 days at the end of June into July (see "Washington, D.C., Calendar of

Kids Favorite Children's Attractions

Check for special children's events at museum information desks when you enter. As noted within the listings for individual museums, some children's programs are also great fun for adults. I recommend the programs at the **Folger Shakespeare Library,** the **Phillips,** and the **Sackler Gallery** in particular. (The gift shops in most of these museums have wonderful toys and children's books.) Call ahead to find out which programs are running. Here's a rundown of big kid-pleasers in town (for details, see the full entries earlier in this chapter):

- **Madame Tussauds Washington D.C.** (p. 208): There are two kinds of people in this world: those who think wax museums are hokey, and children. Yeah, watch your offspring pretend to sing with Beyoncé, box with Evander Holyfield, stand tall next to George Washington. Maybe you'll find your inner child and start loving these wax figures, too.
- **National Museum of Crime and Punishment** (p. 208): Your little darlings can pretend to be little Dillingers and test their safecracking skills, or little Elliot Nesses as they learn how to take fingerprints and gather clues.
- **Newseum** (p. 209): Proceed directly to the interactive newsroom on the second floor, where your children will happily, endlessly play computer games while testing their news knowledge and journalism skills, and where they'll have the chance to play an on-camera reporter.
- **Lincoln Memorial** (p. 181): Kids know a lot about Lincoln and enjoy visiting his memorial. A special treat is visiting after dark.
- **National Air and Space Museum** (p. 188): Spectacular IMAX films (don't miss), thrilling flight simulators, planetarium shows, missiles, rockets, a walk-through orbital workshop, and flight simulators.
- **National Museum of the American Indian** (p. 190): Pick up a copy of the Family Guide for tips on enjoying this treasury of Native American history and culture with kids. Interesting multimedia and hands-on activities.
- **National Museum of Natural History** (p. 193): A Discovery Room just for youngsters, the new Butterfly Pavilion and exhibit, as well as the outdoor butterfly garden, an insect zoo, shrunken heads, dinosaurs, and the IMAX theater showing 2-D and 3-D films.
- **National Zoological Park** (p. 195): Pandas! Cheetahs! Kids always love a zoo, and this is an especially good one, with a Kids Farm.
- **Washington Monument** (p. 177): Spectacular 360-degree views from the center of Washington, D.C.

Events," in chapter 3), or the Kite Festival in spring. Weather permitting, a 19th-century carousel operates in front of the Arts and Industries Building on the south side of the Mall. Right across the Mall from the carousel is the children-friendly National Gallery Sculpture Garden, whose shallow pool is good for splashing one's feet in summer and for ice-skating in winter.

You don't need the excuse of recalcitrant children to enjoy the Mall, of course, though it's always good to have an escape route. The truth is, many of Washington's attractions hold various enchantments for children of all ages. It might be easier to point out which ones are not recommended for your youngest: the Supreme Court, the chambers of Congress, the U.S. Holocaust Memorial Museum, and the Marian Koshland Science Museum. The International Spy Museum is now recommending that its museum is most suitable for children 12 and over. Generally speaking, the bigger and busier the museum, the better it is for kids. On the Mall, these would be the three top draws: the National Museum of Natural History, the National Air and Space Museum, and National Museum of American History, each of which has special areas and exhibits aimed specifically at children. In late 2008 and in spring of 2009, three more attractions opened up that might have the rest beat: the **Newseum** (p. 209), **Madame Tussauds Washington D.C.** (p. 208) and the **National Museum of Crime and Punishment** (p. 208).

I have two daughters, ages 16 and 21; their favorite Washington activities over the years have included paddle-boating on the Tidal Basin (p. 229); shopping in Georgetown; attending plays at the Folger Theatre, the National Theatre, and the Kennedy Center; Wizards and Mystics basketball games at the Verizon Center (p. 255); ice-skating at the National Gallery; and visiting the National Zoo, the International Spy Museum, the National Postal Museum, the Albert Einstein Memorial (p. 223), and special exhibits at the National Gallery of Art, as long as we had something to eat at one of the cafes. (Parents, you will be happy to note that many of the museums offer food of some sort, or vendor carts at the curb.)

For more ideas, consult the Friday "Weekend" section of the *Washington Post,* which lists numerous activities (mostly free) for kids: special museum events, children's theater, storytelling programs, puppet shows, video-game competitions, and so forth. Call the Kennedy Center and the National Theatre to find out about children's shows; see chapter 9 for details.

I've noted "Family-Friendly Hotels" in chapter 5; a few, though not many, hotels have pools, and some offer little goodie packages at check-in. The "Organized Tours" and "Outdoor Activities" sections below may also be your saving grace when you've run out of steam or need a jump-start to your day.

10 Organized Tours

Enterprising individuals and organizations keep coming up with new ways to introduce the city. Go to the **Cultural Tourism D.C.** website, **www.culturaltourismdc. org**, and click on "Tours and Trails" for a longer list of organized tours. Here's a sampling of what's available.

ON FOOT

A Tour de Force (✆ **703/525-2948;** www.atourdeforce.com) is historian and raconteur Jeanne Fogel's 25-year-old company. She offers various modes of transport, from walking to bus, SUV, and limo tours. Fogel custom designs the route around the city per your request and size of group, from a romantic tour for a couple to a traditional sightseeing excursion for a convention crowd. Fogel (or her stand-in) peppers her narration with little-known anecdotes and facts about neighborhoods, historic figures, and the most visited sites. Call for rates.

Spies of Washington Walking Tours (© 703/569-1875; www.spiesofwashington tour.com) offers four walking tours that focus on espionage-related sites in Georgetown and around the White House, Pennsylvania Avenue, Capitol Hill, and the Russian Embassy areas. Carol Bessette, a retired Air Force intelligence officer, conducts the tours, which cost $12 per person. Private tours and bus tours are also available.

Anecdotal History Tours of Washington, D.C. ✦ (© 301/294-9514; www. dcsightseeing.com) offers 2-hour walks through the streets of Georgetown, Adams-Morgan, and other locations guided by author/historian Anthony S. Pitch. Inquire about private tours. Rates are $15 per person.

Segway Tours (© 877/SEG-TOUR; www.citysegwaytours.com/washington) are available March through November. Though technically they are "on foot," Segways are self-propelling scooters that operate based on "dynamic stabilization" technology, which uses your body movements. Tours last 4 hours, cost $70 per person, and include training; age 16 and up.

BY BUS

TOURMOBILE Best-known and least expensive, **Tourmobile Sightseeing** (© 888/868-7707 or 202/554-5100; www.tourmobile.com) is a good choice if you're looking for an easy-on/easy-off tour of major sites, especially since security concerns have made the already limited parking nearly nonexistent. The comfortable red, white, and blue sightseeing trams travel to as many as 24 attractions (the company changes its schedule and number of stops depending on whether sites are open for public tours), including Arlington National Cemetery. Tourmobile is the only narrated sightseeing shuttle tour authorized by the National Park Service.

The company offers a number of different tours, but the most popular is the **American Heritage Tour,** which stops at 21 sites on or near the National Mall and at 3 sites in Arlington Cemetery. (Again, the number of stops may be fewer than 21, if regularly scheduled stops are not open for public tours due to increased security.) Normally, stops include the memorials and Washington Monument, Union Station, the National Gallery, most of the Smithsonian museums (National Air and Space, National Museum of Natural History, and the Arts and Industries Building/Hirshhorn Museum), the Capitol, the White House Visitor Center, and several other locations. In Arlington Cemetery, the bus stops at the Kennedy grave sites, the Tomb of the Unknowns, and Arlington House.

You can purchase tickets at the Union Station and Washington Monument booths, or inside the Arlington National Cemetery Visitor Center, or, for a small surcharge, order your ticket in advance from Ticketmaster at © **800/551-7328** or www.ticket master.com. Or if you'd prefer, just pay your driver when you first get on the bus. Hop on a Tourmobile at any of the designated locations, then get off at any stop to visit monuments or buildings. When you finish exploring each area, just show your ticket and climb aboard the next Tourmobile that comes along. The buses travel in a loop, serving each stop about every 15 to 30 minutes. One fare allows you to use the buses all day. The charge for the American Heritage Tour is $27 for anyone 12 and older, $13 for children 3 to 11. For Arlington Cemetery only, those 12 and older pay $7.50, children $3.75. Children 2 and under ride free. Buses follow circuits from the Capitol to Arlington Cemetery and back. Well-trained and personable narrators give commentaries about sights along the route and answer questions.

The trams are heated in winter, but they're not air-conditioned in summer; and though the windows stay open, they can get hot and uncomfortable. Readers also report that Tourmobiles, being the largest trams, take a long time to load and unload passengers, which can be frustrating to those anxious to see the sights.

Tourmobiles operate 9:30am to 4:30pm, daily year-round, except Christmas. (In the busy tourist season, Tourmobile sometimes extends its hours.) Call Tourmobile or visit the website for further information about other tours and their rates.

OLD TOWN TROLLEY Old Town Trolley tours (© 202/832-9800; www.historic tours.com) offer fixed-price, on-off service as you travel in three loops around the city, with a transfer point at the Lincoln Memorial stop to go on to Arlington Cemetery and a second transfer point at Ford's Theatre to get to Georgetown and to Washington National Cathedral. Many hotels sell tickets (see chapter 5); otherwise, you can purchase tickets online or at the Old Town Trolley Tour booths at Union Station, the D.C. Visitor Center in the Ronald Reagan Building, and many other places around town. Buses operate daily from 9am to 4:30pm, extended to 5:30pm in summer. The cost is $32 for adults, $16 for children 4 to 12, free for children 3 and under. You can buy tickets online in advance and at a discount, and use those e-tickets to board at any of the stops on the route. The full tour, which is narrated, takes 2 hours (if you don't get off and tour the sites, obviously), and trolleys come by every 30 minutes or so. Old Town Trolley tours cost more than Tourmobile tours, perhaps because the buses travel to neighborhoods and attractions away from the Mall.

BY BOAT

Since Washington is a river city, why not see it by boat? Potomac cruises allow sweeping vistas of the monuments and memorials, Georgetown, the Kennedy Center, and other Washington sights. Read the information below carefully, since not all boat cruises offer guided tours. Some of the following boats leave from the Washington waterfront and some from Old Town Alexandria:

Spirit of Washington Cruises, Pier 4 at 6th and Water streets SW (© 866/302-2469 or 202/554-8000; www.spiritcruises.com; Metro: Waterfront), offers a variety of trips daily, including evening dinner, lunch, brunch, and moonlight dance cruises, as well as a half-day excursion to Mount Vernon and back. Lunch and dinner cruises include a 40-minute musical revue.

The *Spirit of Washington* is a luxury climate-controlled harbor cruise ship with carpeted decks and huge panoramic windows designed for sightseeing. There are three well-stocked bars onboard.

Potomac Party Cruises (© 703/683-6076; www.dandydinnerboat.com) operates the *Dandy* and *Nina's Dandy,* both climate-controlled, all-weather, glassed-in floating restaurants that run year-round. Lunch, evening dinner/dance, and special charter cruises are available daily. You board both vessels in Old Town Alexandria, at the Prince Street pier, between Duke and King streets. Trips range from a 2½-hour weekday lunch cruise to a 3-hour Saturday dinner cruise.

Odyssey (© 866/306-2469; www.odysseycruises.com) was designed specifically to glide under the bridges that cross the Potomac. The boat looks like a glass bullet, with its snub-nosed port and its streamlined 240-foot-long glass body. The wraparound see-through walls and ceiling allow for great views. You board the *Odyssey* at the Gangplank Marina, on Washington's waterfront at 6th and Water streets SW (Metro: Waterfront). Cruises available include lunch, Sunday brunch, and dinner excursions, with live entertainment provided during each cruise.

The **Potomac Riverboat Company** ✵ (© **877/511-2628** or 703/684-0580; www.
potomacriverboatco.com) offers three narrated tours April through October. The
Matthew Hayes and the *Miss Mallory* have a 90-minute round-trip tour past Washington
monuments and memorials; the *Admiral Tilp* is on an 80-minute round-trip tour of Old
Town Alexandria's waterfront; and the *Miss Christin* cruises to Mount Vernon, where
you hop off and reboard after you've toured the estate. You board the boats at the pier
behind the Torpedo Factory in Old Town Alexandria at the foot of King Street, or, for
the Washington monuments and memorials tour, Georgetown's Washington Harbour.
A concession stand selling light refreshments and beverages is open during the cruises.

The **Capitol River Cruise**'s *Nightingales* (© **800/405-5511** or 301/460-7447;
www.capitolrivercruises.com) are historic 65-foot steel riverboats that can accommo-
date 90 people. The *Nightingales'* narrated jaunts depart Georgetown's Washington
Harbour every hour on the hour, from noon to 9pm, April through October (the 9pm
outing is offered in summer months only). The 45-minute narrated tour travels past
the monuments and memorials to National Airport and back. A snack bar onboard
sells light refreshments, beer, wine, and sodas; you're welcome to bring your own pic-
nic aboard. To get here, take Metro to Foggy Bottom and then walk into Georgetown,
following Pennsylvania Avenue, which becomes M Street. Turn left on 31st Street NW
and follow to the Washington Harbour complex on the water.

A BOAT ON WHEELS Old Town Trolley also operates **DC Ducks** (© **202/832-
9800;** www.dcducks.com), which feature unique land and water tours of Washington
aboard the *DUKW,* an amphibious army vehicle (boat with wheels) from World War
II that accommodates 30 passengers. Ninety-minute guided tours aboard the open-air
canopied craft include a land portion taking in major sights—the Capitol, Lincoln
Memorial, Washington Monument, White House, and Smithsonian museums—and
a 30-minute Potomac cruise. Purchase tickets inside Union Station at the information
desk; board the vehicle just outside the main entrance to Union Station. Hours vary,
but departures usually follow a daily 11am, 1pm, and 3pm schedule (Mar–Oct).

BY BIKE

Bike the Sites, Inc. ✵ (© **202/842-2453;** www.bikethesites.com) offers a more
active way to see Washington, in season, from March to November. The company has
designed several different biking tours of the city, including the popular Capital Sites
Ride, which takes you past museums, memorials, the White House, Capitol, and
Supreme Court. The ride takes 3 hours, covers 7 to 8 miles, and costs $40 per adult,
$30 per child 12 and under. Bike the Sites provides you with a comfort mountain
bicycle fitted to your size, bike helmet, water bottle, light snack, and two guides to
lead the ride. All tours start from the rear plaza, 12th Street NW side of the Old Post
Office Pavilion, which is located at 1100 Pennsylvania Ave. NW (Metro: Federal Tri-
angle, on the Blue and Orange Line). Guides impart historical and anecdotal infor-
mation as you go. The company rents bikes to those who want to go their own,
unnarrated way for $7 an hour ($15 minimum) or $45 a day, including helmet, bike,
lock, and pump. It also customizes guided bike rides to suit your tour specifications.

11 Outdoor Activities

For information about spectator sports venues, including how to buy tickets and
where to go to watch **Washington Wizards** (men's) and **Mystics** (women's) basketball
games, the **Capitals** ice hockey meets, and **Nationals** baseball games, see chapter 9.

But if you prefer to work up your own honest sweat, Washington offers plenty of pleasant opportunities in many lush surroundings. See "Parks & Gardens" earlier in this chapter for complete coverage of the city's loveliest green spaces.

Joggers can enjoy a run on the Mall or along the path in Rock Creek Park.

As mentioned above, you can rent bikes from **Bike the Sites,** or from the **Boat House at Fletcher's Cove,** Reservoir and Canal roads (ℂ **202/244-0461;** www. fletcherscove.com), or **Thompson's Boat Center,** 2900 Virginia Ave. at Rock Creek Parkway NW (ℂ **202/333-4861** or 333-9543; www.thompsonboatcenter.com; Metro: Foggy Bottom, with a 10-min. walk); both Fletcher's and Thompson's rent bikes, weather permitting, from about mid-March to mid-October. At **Big Wheel Bikes,** 1034 33rd St. NW, right near the C&O Canal just below M Street (ℂ **202/ 337-0254;** www.bigwheelbikes.com), you can rent a bike year-round, Wednesday through Sunday. If you need suggested routes or want company, check out Friday's *Washington Post* "Weekend" section, which lists cycling trips. Rock Creek Park has an **11-mile paved bike route** ✸ from the Lincoln Memorial through the park into Maryland. Or you can follow the bike path from the Lincoln Memorial and go over the Memorial Bridge to pedal to Old Town Alexandria and to Mount Vernon (see chapter 10). On weekends and holidays, a large part of Rock Creek Parkway is closed to vehicular traffic. The C&O Canal and the Potomac parks, described earlier in "Parks & Gardens," also have extended bike paths. The **Capital Crescent Trail** takes you from Georgetown to the suburb of Bethesda, Maryland, following a former railroad track that parallels the Potomac River for part of the way and passes by old trestle bridges and pleasant residential neighborhoods.

Thompson's Boat Center and the **Boat House at Fletcher's Cove** (see above for both) rent boats following the same schedule as their bike-rental season, basically March to November. Thompson's has canoes, kayaks, and rowing shells (recreational and racing), and is open for boat and bike rentals daily in season from 8am to 5pm. Fletcher's is right on the C&O Canal, about 3¼ miles from Georgetown. In addition to renting bikes, canoes, and kayaks, Fletcher's also sells fishing licenses, bait, and tackle. Open 7am to 7pm daily in season, Fletcher's is accessible by car (west on M St. to Canal Rd.) and has plenty of free parking.

From mid-March to mid-October, weather permitting, you can rent **paddle boats** ✸ on the north end of the Tidal Basin off Independence Avenue (ℂ **202/479-2426;** www.tidalbasinpeddleboats.com). Four-seaters are $16 an hour; two-seaters are $8 an hour, 10am to 6pm daily mid-March to Labor Day and Wednesday to Sunday Labor Day to mid-October.

Washington has numerous **hiking paths.** The C&O Canal offers 185 miles stretching from D.C. to Cumberland, Maryland; Theodore Roosevelt Island has more than 88 wilderness acres to explore; and Rock Creek Park boasts 20 miles of hiking trails (maps are available at the Visitor Information Center or Park Headquarters).

If you're coming to Washington in winter, you can go **ice-skating** on the C&O Canal (call ℂ **301/299-3613** for information on ice conditions), as long as you bring your own skates. For a really fun experience, head to the **National Gallery Sculpture Garden Ice Rink** ✸, on the Mall at 7th Street and Constitution Avenue NW (ℂ **202/ 289-3360**), where you can rent skates, twirl in view of the sculptures, and enjoy hot chocolate and a sandwich in the Pavilion Café next to the rink. Another outdoor rink that may have reopened by the time you read this is **Pershing Park,** at 14th Street and Pennsylvania Avenue NW (ℂ **202/737-6938**).

If it's summer and your hotel doesn't have a pool, you might consider one of the neighborhood pools, including a large outdoor pool at 25th and N streets NW (© 202/727-3285) and the Georgetown outdoor pool at 34th Street and Volta Place NW (© 202/282-0381). Keep in mind that these are likely to be crowded.

Tennis lovers will have a hard time finding public courts in Washington. **East Potomac Park** (© 202/554-5962) has 24 tennis courts (10 clay, 14 hard courts), 3 illuminated at night, and 5 indoor courts; the park rents rackets as well. Fees vary with court surface and time of play. **Montrose Park,** right next to Dumbarton Oaks (p. 218) in Georgetown, has several courts available free on a first-come, first-served basis; but they're often in use.

Shopping

Let's cut to the chase: If you like to shop, you should go directly to Georgetown. Try to guess how many stores are located there. Ready? 1,078. If a new store is opening in the city, say the Denmark-based jeweler Pilgrim, or the U.K. fashion store Reiss, known for its glamorous frocks, you can bet its location will be in Georgetown. Having said that, other neighborhoods do offer certain shopping possibilities, and I point you to those, too, in this chapter.

1 The Shopping Scene

Most Washington-area stores are open from 10am to 5 or 6pm Monday through Saturday. Sunday hours tend to vary, with some stores opting not to open at all and others with shorter hours of noon to 5 or 6pm. Two neighborhoods prove the exception to these rules: Many stores in the Penn Quarter and in Georgetown keep later hours and are also open on Sunday. One example is the downtown Macy's department store (p. 249), in the heart of Penn Quarter, whose hours are noon to 6pm Sunday, 10am to 8pm Monday through Saturday. Other exceptions include suburban shopping malls, which are open late nightly, and antiques stores and art galleries, which tend to keep their own hours. Be safe and call ahead if there's a store you really want to get to.

Sales tax on merchandise is 5.75% in the District, 5% in Maryland, and 5% in Virginia. Most gift, arts, and crafts stores, including those at the Smithsonian museums, will handle shipping for you; clothing stores generally do not.

2 Great Shopping Areas

UNION STATION It's a railroad station, a historic landmark, an architectural marvel, a Metro stop, and a shopping mall. Yes, the beauteous Union Station offers some fine shopping opportunities; it's certainly the best on Capitol Hill, with more than 100 clothes and specialty shops, and more than 40 eateries. Metro: Union Station.

PENN QUARTER The area bounded east and west by 7th and 14th streets NW, and north and south by New York and Pennsylvania avenues NW, is in a frenzy of development. The latest buzz comes from the opening of a multiuse complex, **Gallery Place,** at 7th and H streets, in the heart of Chinatown, backing up to the Verizon Center and overtopping the Chinatown/Gallery Place Metro stop. Gallery Place combines condominiums, offices, a bowling alley/bar, a 14-screen theater, stores that range from Urban Outfitters to Aveda, and several restaurants. Elsewhere in the neighborhood you'll find a long list of "name" stores, such as Banana Republic, Ann Taylor, H&M, Jos. A. Bank Clothiers, and Filene's Basement; and one-of-a-kind places, such as Apartment Zero and Olsson's Books. Look for the huge Borders at 14th and F streets NW, in the grand old Garfinckel's Building. Macy's (formerly known as

Finds **The Roads Less Traveled: A Back-Street Tour of Historic Georgetown, with Stops at Shops**

Most people who visit Georgetown never get off the beaten track of the M Street/lower Wisconsin Avenue axis. Too bad for them, but good for you: While they bump into each other in the crowded bottom of Georgetown, you can tour the lovely, quiet streets in upper Georgetown, where a number of historic houses and beautiful gardens lie close to fun boutiques and delectable cafes. Consider this less traveled route. (See the color map on the last page of the color insert at the front of the book.)

Tudor Place, Dumbarton House, and the garden at Dumbarton Oaks are open for tours, but not every day, so call for hours if you want to incorporate house and garden tours in your back-street stroll; please note that all other houses on the tour are privately owned and not open to the public.

From the corner of Q Street and Wisconsin Avenue (a stop on the D.C. Circulator's Wisconsin Avenue line), walk east along Q Street to 31st Street and take a left on 31st Street to **Tudor Place** (✆ 202/965-0400), an 1816 mansion and gardens where Martha Washington's descendants lived until 1984. From Tudor Place, return to Q Street and walk farther east to no. 2715, **Dumbarton House** (✆ 202/337-2288), a Federal-style mansion built in 1805 and filled with 18th- and 19th-century furnishings and decorative arts.

Retrace your steps as far as 28th Street and proceed north on 28th Street, stopping to admire the 18th-century estate **Evermay**, built by a Scottish merchant, as you continue on your way to **Dumbarton Oaks Gardens** (p. 218; ✆ 202/339-6401) at 31st and R streets. From the gardens, walk westward on R Street to Wisconsin Avenue, passing en route **3238 R St. NW**, an early-19th-century Federal brick building once used as a summer White House by President Ulysses S. Grant—its high elevation made it cooler than 1600 Pennsylvania Ave.

You have now reached Wisconsin Avenue, just a little farther north of the hustle-bustle, but a sweet spot for shopping at one-of-a-kind shops and for enjoying a scrumptious repast. Turn south on Wisconsin Avenue to find Italian and French home and garden accessories at **A Mano** (no. 1677;

"Hecht's"), at 12th and G streets, continues as the sole department store downtown. Metro: Metro Center, Chinatown/Gallery Place, or Archives/Navy Memorial.

ADAMS-MORGAN Centered on 18th Street and Columbia Road NW, Adams-Morgan is a neighborhood of ethnic eateries and nightclubs interspersed with the odd secondhand bookshop and eclectic collectibles stores. It's a fun area for walking and shopping. Parking is possible during the day but impossible at night. For the closest Metro, you have a few choices: Woodley Park–Zoo/Adams-Morgan, then walk south on Connecticut Avenue NW until you reach Calvert Street, cross Connecticut Avenue, and follow Calvert Street across the Duke Ellington Memorial Bridge until you reach the junction of Columbia Road NW and 18th Street NW. Sunday through Friday

Ⓒ 202/298-7200), beautiful stationery at **Rooms with a View** (no. 1661; Ⓒ 202/625-0610), and a variety of women's trendy clothing boutiques at **Sugar** (no. 1633; Ⓒ 202/333-5331), **Sassanova** (no. 1641; Ⓒ 202/471-4400), **Sherman Pickey** (no. 1647; Ⓒ 202/333-4212), and **Urban Chic** (no. 1626; Ⓒ 202/338-5398). In the middle of the block is **Patisserie Poupon** (Ⓒ 202/342-3248)—I highly recommend that you pause for a ham-and-cheese sandwich and, *absolument*, for a pastry dessert: Choose from tarts, éclairs, individual little cakes, and chocolate in all its forms.

Cross Wisconsin Avenue to continue your tour on the other side. Walk south on Wisconsin Avenue to N Street and turn right, following the street to **no. 3307**, the brick town house where John and Jacqueline Kennedy lived when Kennedy was a U.S. senator. In the same block, a few houses up at **nos. 3327–3339,** are five charming houses known collectively as **"Cox's Row,"** for owner John Cox, who built the dwellings in 1817. Cox, who was the first elected mayor of Georgetown, lived at no. 3339; Revolutionary War hero the Marquis de Lafayette stayed at no. 3337 on a visit in 1824. Follow N Street to 36th Street, and turn left and again left on Prospect Street to reach **Prospect House**, at no. 3508. This restored Georgian-style house was built in 1788 by Revolutionary War hero and wealthy tobacco merchant James McCubbin Lingan; the house, like the street, was named for the views one once had here of the Potomac River. From here, it's a short stroll to **Halcyon House**, at 3400 Prospect St., whose original owner, Benjamin Stoddert, was a Revolutionary War cavalry officer and first secretary of the navy. Two hundred years ago, the Potomac River lapped right up to Stoddert's terraced garden, designed by Pierre L'Enfant.

If you still have some energy left, finish the tour by visiting a Washington hot spot, the **Cafe Milano**, 3251 Prospect St. NW (Ⓒ 202/333-6183). Then go home knowing that you've seen more of the "real" Georgetown than most Washingtonians.

evenings and all day Saturday, you can catch the no. 98 Adams-Morgan–U Street Link shuttle bus, which loops between the Woodley Park and the African-American Civil War Memorial/Cardozo (at 13th and U sts. NW) Metro stations, departing every 15 minutes from each location, traveling along 18th Street in the heart of Adams-Morgan, where you can hop off; it costs only 25¢. Second choice: Dupont Circle; exit at Q Street NW and walk up Connecticut Avenue NW to Columbia Road NW.

CONNECTICUT AVENUE/DUPONT CIRCLE Running from the mini–Wall Street that is K Street north to S Street, Connecticut Avenue NW is a main thoroughfare, where you'll find traditional clothing at Brooks Brothers, Talbots, Ann Taylor, and Burberry's; casual duds at Gap; discount items at Filene's Basement and Ann Taylor

Loft; and haute couture at Rizik's. Closer to Dupont Circle are coffee bars and neighborhood restaurants, as well as art galleries; funky boutiques; gift, stationery, book, and record shops; and stores with a gay and lesbian slant. Metro: Farragut North at one end, Dupont Circle at the other.

U STREET CORRIDOR/14TH STREET Urbanistas have been promoting this neighborhood for years, but now the number of cool shops, restaurants, and bars has hit the critical mass mark, winning the area widespread notice. If you shun brand names and box stores, you'll love the boutiques along U and 14th streets. Look for provocative handles, like Go Mama Go! and Pulp, then step inside to inspect their equally intriguing merchandise. Metro: U St./African-American Civil War Memorial/Cardozo.

GEORGETOWN Georgetown is the city's main shopping area. In the heart of the neighborhood, stores line Wisconsin Avenue and M Street NW, and they also fan out along side streets. (For a tour of Georgetown that combines historic houses, shopping, and dining, see "The Roads Less Traveled" box on p. 232.) You'll find both chain and one-of-a-kind shops, chic as well as thrift. Sidewalks and streets are almost always crowded, and parking can be tough. Weekends, especially, bring out all kinds of yahoos, who are mainly here to drink. Visit Georgetown on a weekday morning, if you can. Weeknights are another good time to visit, for dinner and strolling afterward. Metro: Foggy Bottom, then catch the D.C. Circulator bus from Washington Circle (see chapter 4 for more information). Metro buses (the no. 30 series) travel through Georgetown from different parts of the city. Otherwise, consider taking a taxi. If you drive, you'll find parking lots expensive and tickets even more so, so be careful where you plant your car.

UPPER WISCONSIN AVENUE NORTHWEST In a residential section of town known as Friendship Heights on the D.C. side and Chevy Chase on the Maryland side (7 miles north of Georgetown, straight up Wisconsin Ave.) is a quarter-mile shopping district that extends from Saks Fifth Avenue at one end to Sur La Table at the other. In between are Lord & Taylor, Neiman Marcus, Bloomingdale's, Banana Republic, Jimmy Choo, Christian Dior, Barney's Co-Op, Polo, Tiffany's, Versace, and two malls (the Mazza Gallerie and the Chevy Chase Pavilion). The street is too wide and traffic always too snarled to make this a pleasant place to stroll, although teenagers do love to loiter here. Drive if you want and park in the garages beneath the Mazza Gallerie or the Chevy Chase Pavilion. Or take the Metro; the strip is right on the Red Line, with the "Friendship Heights" exits leading directly into each of the malls and into Bloomingdale's.

OLD TOWN ALEXANDRIA Old Town, a Virginia neighborhood beyond National Airport, resembles Georgetown in its picturesque location on the Potomac, historic-home lined streets, and plentiful shops and restaurants, as well as in its less desirable aspects: heavy traffic, crowded sidewalks, difficult parking. Old Town extends from the Potomac River in the east to the King Street Metro station in the west, and from about 1st Street in the north to Green Street in the south, but the best shopping is in the center, where King and Washington streets intersect. Weekdays are a lot tamer than weekends. It's always a nice place to visit, though; the drive alone is worth the trip. See chapter 10 for full coverage of Alexandria. Metro: King Street, then take a blue and gold DASH bus (free weekends, otherwise the fare is $1) to reach the heart of Old Town.

3 Shopping A to Z

ANTIQUES

A few miles north of the city is not too far to go for the good deal or true bonanza you're likely to discover on **Antique Row.** Some 40 antiques and collectible shops line Howard Avenue, on either side of Connecticut Avenue, in Kensington, Maryland, offering every sort of item in a wide variety of styles, periods, and prices. If you don't drive or taxi, you'll have to take the Metro and two buses. From Dupont Circle, board an L2 bus and get a transfer from the driver. Ask him to tell you when you reach the transfer point for the L8 bus. Once there, board the L8 bus and ask to be let off at Connecticut and Knowles avenues. Howard Avenue is 1 block north of Knowles. For antiques in D.C. and Alexandria, try these:

Brass Knob Architectural Antiques When old homes and office buildings are demolished in the name of progress, these savvy salvage merchants spirit away salable treasures, from lots and lots of light fixtures and chandelier glass to wrought-iron fencing. 2311 18th St. NW. ℭ 202/332-3370. www.thebrassknob.com. Metro: Woodley Park or Dupont Circle. A second location near Capitol Hill stocks old house parts: the **Brass Knob's Back Doors Warehouse,** 57 N St. NW (at 1st St. NW; ℭ 202/265-0587).

Cherry This is an antiques store, all right, but as its name suggests, a little offbeat. Expect affordable eclectic furnishings and decorative arts, and lots of mirrors and sconces. 1526 Wisconsin Ave. NW. ℭ 202/342-3600. www.cherryantiques.com. Metro: Foggy Bottom, then walk or take the D.C. Circulator.

Cherub Antiques Gallery The Cherub Antiques Gallery specializes in Art Nouveau and Art Deco; signed Tiffany, Steuben, Lalique, and Gallé pieces; Liberty arts and crafts; and Louis Icart etchings. 2918 M St. NW. ℭ 202/337-2224. www.trocadero.com/cherubgallery. Metro: Foggy Bottom, then take the D.C. Circulator.

Gore-Dean This store's inventory runs from furnishings and fabrics (some American pieces, but mostly 18th- and 19th-century European furnishings) to decorative accessories, paintings, prints, and porcelains. 3214 O St. NW. ℭ 202/625-9199. www.goredean.com. Metro: Foggy Bottom, then take the D.C. Circulator.

Marston-Luce Stop in here at least to admire, if not buy, a beautiful 18th- or 19th-century French furnishing or two. 1651 Wisconsin Ave. NW. ℭ 202/333-6800. Metro: Foggy Bottom, then take the D.C. Circulator.

Millennium Decorative Arts This is antiques shopping for the TV generation, where anything made between the 1930s and the 1970s is considered collectible. The shop works with nearly a score or so of dealers; stock changes weekly. Funky wares run from Bakelite to Heywood-Wakefield blond-wood beauties to toasters to used drinking glasses. Call for hours, since the shop tends to be open only on weekends. 1528 U St. NW. ℭ 202/483-1218. www.millenniumdecorativearts.com. Metro: U St.–Cardozo (13th St. exit).

Old Print Gallery Open since 1971, this gallery carries original American and European prints from the 17th to the 19th century, including political cartoons, maps, and historical documents. It's one of the largest antique print and map shops in the United States. Prices range from $45 to $10,000. 1220 31st St. NW. ℭ 202/965-1818. www.oldprintgallery.com. Metro: Foggy Bottom, then take the D.C. Circulator.

Susquehanna Antiques This is Georgetown's largest collection of fine American, English, and European furniture, paintings, and garden items of the late 18th and

early 19th centuries. The shop is nearly 100 years old. 3216 O St. NW. © 202/333-1511. www.susquehannaantiques.com. Metro: Foggy Bottom, then take the D.C. Circulator.

ART GALLERIES

Art galleries abound in Washington, D.C., but especially in the Dupont Circle, Georgetown, and Penn Quarter neighborhoods.

DUPONT CIRCLE

For galleries listed below, the closest Metro stop is Dupont Circle. If you're in town the first Friday of the month, don't miss the Dupont Circle gallery walk, free and open to the public, 6 to 8pm. For a longer listing of Dupont Circle art galleries, access the website, www.dupontcirclegalleries.com.

David Adamson Gallery This gallery showcases digital printmaking and photography and the works of contemporary artists, like local Kevin MacDonald, as well as national and international artists Jim Dine, Chuck Close, and William Wegman. *Note:* Three other galleries are located in this same building, including **Hemphill** (© 202/234-5601; www.hemphillfinearts.com), devoted to contemporary art and exhibits of socially relevant, historically significant import. The location is actually on the very outskirts of Dupont Circle; follow P Street east about 5 blocks until you reach 14th Street. 1515 14th St. NW. © 202/232-0707. www.adamsongallery.com.

Studio Gallery This artist-owned gallery—the longest-running of its kind in the area—shows the works of some 37 local and professional artists, fine arts in all mediums. Don't miss the sculpture garden. Open Wednesday through Saturday. 2108 R St. NW. © 202/232-8734. www.studiogallerydc.com.

GEORGETOWN

For all the galleries listed below, the closest Metro stop is Foggy Bottom; from there, you can walk, hop on the D.C. Circulator bus, or transfer to a Metrobus, any of the 30 series, to get you the rest of the way.

Addison/Ripley Fine Art This gallery represents both nationally and regionally recognized artists, from the 19th century to the present; works include paintings, sculpture, photography, and fine arts. 1670 Wisconsin Ave. NW. © 202/338-5180. www.addisonripley fineart.com.

Govinda Gallery This place, a block from the campus of Georgetown University, generates a lot of media coverage because it often shows artwork created by famous names and features photographs of celebrities, also pop and contemporary art. 1227 34th St. NW. © 202/333-1180. www.govindagallery.com.

Guarisco Gallery, Ltd. Its display of 19th- and early-20th-century American and European paintings, watercolors, and sculptures by the likes of Camille Pissarro, T. Robinson, and H. Lebasque make this gallery as much a museum as a shop. 1120 22nd St. NW. © 202/333-8533. www.guariscogallery.com.

7TH STREET ARTS CORRIDOR

A couple of these galleries predate the renaissance taking place in this downtown neighborhood. To get here, take the Metro to either Archives/Navy Memorial (Blue–Orange Line) or Gallery Place/Chinatown/Verizon Center (Red–Yellow Line).

Flashpoint Flashpoint is a dance studio, theater lab, office space, and art gallery all in one. Its art gallery is dedicated to nurturing emerging local artists, who tend to use

a variety of mediums, including video, sculpture, photography, and drawings to tell their personal stories. 916 G St. NW. © 202/315-1305. www.flashpointdc.org.

Touchstone Gallery The first floor of this historic building houses Apartment Zero, a stylish contemporary furniture and design store, well worth a visit on its own merits. Then head upstairs to the second floor to find **Touchstone,** whose 16-foot-high ceilings and spacious rooms form the backdrop for a self-run co-op studio for 35 to 40 contemporary artists, each of whom has at least one work on display at all times. 406 7th St. NW (btw. D and E sts.). © 202/347-2787. www.touchsgallery.com.

Zenith Gallery Across the street from Touchstone is the 31-year-old Zenith, which exhibits diverse works by contemporary artists, most American, about half of whom are local. You can get a good deal here, paying anywhere from $50 to $50,000 for a piece. Among the things you'll find are annual humor shows, neon exhibits, realism, abstract expressionism, and landscapes. Browse the gift shop for artistic housewares and clever jewelry. 413 7th St. NW. © 202/783-2963. www.zenithgallery.com.

BEAUTY

Georgetown is the hot spot for the best hair salons and cosmetic stores, while spas are more evenly scattered throughout the city. Here's a sampling of some of the best places to go for beauty treatments and products.

Blue Mercury Half "apothecary," half spa, this chain's two D.C. locations offer a full selection of facial, massage, waxing, and makeup treatments, as well as a smorgasbord of high-end beauty products, from Acqua di Parma fragrances to Kiehl's skincare line. Very popular, so you might want to call in advance of your trip. Georgetown: 3059 M St. NW. © 202/965-1300. www.bluemercury.com. Metro: Foggy Bottom, then take the D.C. Circulator. Dupont Circle: 1619 Connecticut Ave. NW © 202/462-1300. Metro: Dupont Circle (Q St. exit).

The Grooming Lounge Not your father's barbershop. Famous for its 30-minute "hot lather shave," The Grooming Lounge also dispenses treatments with names like "The Commander in Chief" and sells beauty accessories, um, I mean, grooming tools, from nail clippers to special shaving brushes. Or you can just get a haircut. 1745 L St. NW. © 202/466-8900. www.groominglounge.com. Metro: Farragut North (L St. exit).

Okyo Beauty Salon This is probably D.C.'s most popular hair salon, known as much for its celebrity clientele as for its fantastic cuts and coloring. Expect high prices and a tight schedule. 2903 M St. NW. © 202/342-2675. www.okyosalon.com. Metro: Foggy Bottom, then take the D.C. Circulator.

SomaFit If your hotel doesn't have a fitness center or spa, visit this ultracool, one-stop-spot for a workout, massage, yoga class, pedicure, facial—whatever your little body needs or desires. This is not a membership facility, so all you have to do is call or check online for a class schedule, and just show up (only a handful of classes require that you reserve a space in advance); or call to schedule a spa treatment. 2121 Wisconsin Ave. NW. © 202/965-2121. www.somafit.com. Metro: Foggy Bottom, then take the D.C. Circulator bus.

BOOKS

Washingtonians are readers, so bookstores constantly pop up throughout the city. An increasingly competitive market means that chain bookstores do a brisk business, even though D.C. can claim more general-interest, independent bookstores than any other city. Here are some favorite bookstores in general, used, and special-interest categories.

GENERAL

Barnes & Noble This three-story shop in Georgetown is well-stocked in all genres, including sizable software, travel-book, children's-title, and music sections. The store has a cafe on the second level. 3040 M St. NW. ℂ 202/965-9880. www.bn.com. Metro: Foggy Bottom, then take the D.C. Circulator. Other area locations include 555 12th St. NW (ℂ 202/347-0176) and 4801 Bethesda Ave., in Bethesda, MD (ℂ 301/986-1761).

B. Dalton This all-purpose bookstore is heavy on the bestsellers and carries magazines, too. Union Station. ℂ 202/289-1724. www.bn.com. Metro: Union Station.

Borders With its overwhelming array of books, records, videos, and magazines, Borders competes neck and neck with Barnes & Noble. Many hardcover bestsellers are 30% off. 1801 K St. NW. ℂ 202/466-4999. www.borders.com. Metro: Farragut North (L St. exit). Other Borders stores in the District include 600 14th St. NW #100. (ℂ 202/737-1385) and 5333 Wisconsin Ave. NW (ℂ 202/686-8270), in upper-northwest D.C.

Bridge Street Books A small, serious shop specializing in politics, poetry, literature, history, philosophy, and publications you won't find elsewhere. Bestsellers and discounted books are not its specialty. 2814 Pennsylvania Ave. NW (next to the Four Seasons Hotel). ℂ 202/965-5200. Metro: Foggy Bottom, then take the DC Circulator.

Kramerbooks & Afterwords Café *Finds* Opened in 1976, Kramer's was the first bookstore/cafe in Washington, maybe in this country, and has launched countless romances. It's jammed, is often noisy, stages live music Wednesday through Saturday evenings, and is open all night weekends. Paperback fiction takes up most of its inventory, but the store carries a little of everything. 1517 Connecticut Ave. NW. ℂ 202/387-1400 or 387-3825 for information. www.kramers.com. Metro: Dupont Circle, Q St. exit.

Olsson's Books and Records This 37-year-old independent, quality bookstore chain tends toward literary tomes rather than the trashy stuff, and employs helpful staff who know what they're talking about and will order books they don't have in stock. Some discounts are given on books, tapes, and CDs, and their regular prices are pretty good, too.

Besides this 7th Street NW store, there is one other Olsson's bookstore in the District at 1307 19th St. NW (ℂ 202/785-1133). In the suburbs are four other Olsson's: in Old Town Alexandria, Virginia, at 106 S. Union St. (ℂ 703/684-0077); in Arlington, Virginia, at 2111 Wilson Blvd. (ℂ 703/525-4227) and at 2200-G Crystal Dr. (ℂ 703/413-8121); and at National Airport (ℂ 703/417-1087). The stores on 7th Street and in Alexandria each have a creditable cafe, known for its loungy atmosphere, made-in-house selections, and artistic crowd. 1307 19th St. NW. ℂ 202-785-1133. www.olssons.com. Metro: Dupont Circle (19th St./South exit).

Politics and Prose Bookstore Located a few miles north of downtown in a residential area, this much-cherished two-story shop may be worth going out of your way for. It has vast offerings in literary fiction and nonfiction alike and an excellent children's department. The store has expanded again and again over the years to accommodate its clientele's love of books; its most recent enlargement added to the travel and children's sections. The shop hosts author readings nearly every night of the year. A warm, knowledgeable staff will help you find what you need. Downstairs is a cozy coffeehouse. Staff-recommended books are 20% off; otherwise, discounts are available only to members. 5015 Connecticut Ave. NW. ℂ 202/364-1919. www.politics-prose.com. Metro: Van Ness–UDC, and walk, or transfer to an "L" bus to take you the 3/4 mile from there.

Trover Shop This family-owned and -operated shop is about 50 years old and is the only general-interest bookstore on Capitol Hill; specializations include Capitol Hill treatises (where else can you find the Directory to Congress?), political selections, magazines, and Washington Nationals merchandise. The store discounts 30% on the *Washington Post* hardcover fiction and nonfiction bestsellers. 221 Pennsylvania Ave. SE. ⓒ **202/547-BOOK** (2665). www.trover.com. Metro: Capitol South.

OLD & USED BOOKS

Second Story Books If it's old, out of print, custom bound, or a small-press publication, this is where to find it. The store also specializes in used CDs and vinyl and has an interesting collection of campaign posters. 2000 P St. NW. ⓒ **202/659-8884**. www. secondstorybooks.com. Metro: Dupont Circle (South/19th St. exit).

SPECIAL-INTEREST BOOKS

Back Stage Books and Costumes Back Stage is headquarters for Washington's theatrical community, which buys its books, scripts, trades, and sheet music here. It's also a favorite costume-rental shop. 545 8th St. SE. ⓒ **202/544-5744**. www.backstagebooks. com. Metro: Eastern Market.

Lambda Rising This gay and lesbian bookstore in the heart of the Dupont Circle neighborhood is the unofficial headquarters for the GLBT community, carrying every gay, lesbian, bisexual, and transgender book in print, as well as videos, music, and gifts. 1625 Connecticut Ave. NW. ⓒ **202/462-6969**. www.lambdarising.com. Metro: Dupont Circle, Q St. exit.

Reiter's Bookstore This independent bookstore in the middle of the George Washington University campus is one of the leading scientific, technical, medical, and professional bookshops in the area. It's a great place to stumble into, even if you're not scientifically inclined, because it also has a fine children's science section, some amusing mathematical and scientific toys, and humorous T-shirts ("Hey You, Get Out of the Gene Pool!"). 1990 K St. NW. (The entrance is on 20th St.) ⓒ **202/223-3327**. www.reiters.com. Metro: Foggy Bottom.

CAMERAS & FILM DEVELOPING

Penn Camera Exchange Penn Camera has been owned and operated by the Zweig family since 1953; its staff is quite knowledgeable, and its inventory wide-ranging. Their specialty is quality equipment and archival paper processing—not cheap, but worth it. 840 E St. NW. ⓒ **202/347-5777**. www.penncamera.com. Metro: Gallery Place (9th and G sts. exit). Also at 1015 18th St. NW (ⓒ **202/785-7366**).

Ritz Camera Centers Ritz sells camera equipment for the average photographer and offers 1-hour film processing. Call for other locations; there are many throughout the area. 1029 Connecticut Ave. NW. ⓒ **202/659-8430**. www.ritzcamera.com. Metro: Farragut North (L St. exit).

CRAFTS

A Mano Owner Adam Mahr frequently forages in Europe and returns with the unique handmade, imported French and Italian ceramics, linens, and other decorative accessories for home and garden that you'll covet here. 1677 Wisconsin Ave. NW. ⓒ **202/ 298-7200**. www.amano.bz. Metro: Foggy Bottom, then take the D.C. Circulator.

Appalachian Spring Country comes to Georgetown. This store sells pottery, jewelry, newly made pieced and appliqué quilts, stuffed dolls and animals, candles, rag

rugs, handblown glassware, an incredible collection of kaleidoscopes, glorious weavings, and wooden kitchenware. Everything is made by hand in the United States. 1415 Wisconsin Ave. NW (at P St.). ⓒ 202/337-5780. Metro: Foggy Bottom, then take the D.C. Circulator. There's another branch in Union Station (ⓒ 202/682-0505).

Go Mama Go! *Finds* Look here for Italian glassware, Dutch art, Pennsylvania tableware, Czech crystal, and original artwork. 1809 14th St. NW (at S St.). ⓒ 202/299-0850. www.gomamago.com. Metro: U St.–Cardozo (14th St. exit).

Indian Craft Shop The Indian Craft Shop has represented authentic Native American artisans since 1938, selling their hand-woven rugs and handcrafted baskets, jewelry, figurines, pottery, and other items. Since the shop is situated inside a federal government building, you must pass through security and show a photo ID to enter. Use the C Street entrance, which is the only one open to the public. The shop is open weekdays and the third Saturday of each month. Department of the Interior, 1849 C St. NW, Room 1023. ⓒ 202/208-4056. www.indiancraftshop.com. Metro: Farragut West (17th St. exit), with a bit of a walk from the station.

The Phoenix Around since 1955, the Phoenix still sells those embroidered Mexican peasant blouses popular in hippie days; high-end Mexican folk and fine art; handcrafted sterling silver jewelry from Mexico and all over the world; clothing in natural fibers from Mexican and American designers like Eileen Fisher and Flax; collectors' quality masks; and decorative doodads in tin, brass, copper, and wood. Oaxaca folk and fine art are a specialty. 1514 Wisconsin Ave. NW. ⓒ 202/338-4404. www.thephoenixdc.com. Metro: Foggy Bottom, then take the D.C. Circulator.

Torpedo Factory Art Center Once a munitions factory, this three-story building built in 1918 now houses more than 84 working studios and the works of about 165 artists, who tend to their crafts before your very eyes, pausing to explain their techniques or to sell their pieces. Artworks include paintings, sculpture, ceramics, glasswork, and textiles. 105 N. Union St., Alexandria. ⓒ 703/838-4565. www.torpedofactory.org. Metro: King St., then take the DASH bus (AT2, AT5) eastbound to the waterfront.

DISCOUNT SHOPPING

Discount shops in Washington are few and far between, with a few notable exceptions listed below. Also see the listing of flea markets, below.

Filene's Basement Its reign might be over in Boston, but Filene's is still going strong in Washington, selling designer and famous-name clothes and accessories, as well as home furnishings. 1133 Connecticut Ave. NW, Midtown. ⓒ 202/872-8430. www.filenes basement.com. Metro: Farragut North (L St. exit). Also at 529 14th St. NW, in the National Press Building (ⓒ 202/638-4110), and in the Mazza Gallerie in upper northwest Washington, 5300 Wisconsin Ave. NW (ⓒ 202/966-0208).

Potomac Mills Mall When you're stuck in the traffic that always clogs this section of I-95, you may wonder if a trip to Potomac Mills is worth it. Believe it or not, this is one of the most popular tourist attractions in the Washington area; it's one of the largest indoor outlet malls around, with more than 220 shops such as Old Navy Outlet, Nordstrom RACK, and Polo Ralph Lauren. A huge IKEA store, which used to anchor the mall, has seceded, moving to its separate location across the street from Potomac Mills. 30 miles south on I-95 in Prince William, VA. Call ⓒ 703/496-9301 for information about Potomac Mills. www.potomacmills.com. Accessible by car, or by shuttle bus (weekdays only) from the Franconia/Springfield Metro station, at the end of the Blue line in Northern Virginia.

THRIFT/CONSIGNMENT/SECONDHAND SHOPS

Christ Child Opportunity Shop Proceeds from sales go to children's charities. Here you'll find the usual thrift-shop jumble of jewelry, antiques, and collectibles—odds and ends. Most merchandise is left on consignment; if you know antiques, you might find bargains in jewelry, silver, china, quilts, and other items. 1427 Wisconsin Ave. NW (at P St.). ℭ 202/333-6635. www.christchilddc.org. Metro: Foggy Bottom, then take the D.C. Circulator.

Secondhand Rose This upscale second-floor consignment shop has been around for 30 years, specializing in designer merchandise. Creations by Chanel, Armani, Donna Karan, Calvin Klein, Yves Saint-Laurent, Ungaro, Ralph Lauren, and others are sold at about a third of the original price. A stunning Scaasi black-velvet and yellow-satin ball gown might go for $400 (from $1,200 new); Yves Saint-Laurent pumps in perfect condition can be had for as little as $45. Everything is in style, in season, and in excellent condition. Secondhand Rose is also a great place to shop for gorgeous furs, designer shoes and bags, and costume jewelry. 1516 Wisconsin Ave. NW (btw. P St. and Volta Place). ℭ 202/337-3378. Metro: Foggy Bottom, then take the D.C. Circulator.

Secondi Inc. On the second floor of a building right above Starbucks is this high-style consignment shop that sells women's clothing and accessories, including designer suits, evening wear, and more casual items—everything from Kate Spade to Chanel. 1702 Connecticut Ave. NW (btw. R St. and Florida Ave.). ℭ 202/667-1122. www.secondi.com. Metro: Dupont Circle (Q St. exit).

FARMER'S & FLEA MARKETS

Alexandria Farmers' Market The oldest continuously operating farmers' market in the country (since 1752), this market offers locally grown fruits and vegetables, along with delectable baked goods, cut flowers, and plants. Open year-round, Saturday mornings from 5 to 10am. 301 King St. (at Market Sq. in front of the city hall), in Alexandria. ℭ 703/906-1481. Metro: King St., then take the free-on-weekends DASH bus (AT2, AT5) eastbound to Market Sq.

Dupont Circle FreshFarm Market At least 30 local farmers sell their flowers, produce, eggs, and cheeses here. The market also features kids' activities and guest appearances by chefs and owners of some of Washington's best restaurants: Bis, Montmartre, and 1789. Held Sundays rain or shine, year-round, from 10am to 1pm January through March and 9am to 1pm, the rest of the year. The FreshFarm Market organization stages other farmers markets on other days around town; go to the website for locations, dates, and times. On 20th St. NW (btw. Q St. and Massachusetts Ave.), and in the adjacent Riggs Bank parking lot. ℭ 202/362-8889. www.freshfarmmarkets.org. Metro: Dupont Circle, Q St. exit.

Eastern Market A devastating fire in April 2007 gutted this Capitol Hill institution, a market that had been in continuous operation since 1873. But some vendors are operating across the street in a new, but temporary, building. Meanwhile, renovation continues on the historic market building, which is slated to reopen in late 2008 or early 2009, thanks to an intense effort by the surrounding community and the D.C. government, led by D.C. Mayor Adrian Fenty, to rebuild this essential and beloved neighborhood emporium. In fact, the outdoor farmers market stalls have remained open throughout, selling fresh produce and other goods on Saturdays and flea market items on Sundays. If Eastern Market's South Hall has been restored, you can expect to see an inside bazaar Tuesday through Sunday, where greengrocers, butchers, bakers, farmers, artists, craftspeople, florists, and other merchants sell their

wares. And if all is well, Saturday morning will once again be the best time to go to experience a D.C. tradition: blueberry pancakes at the Market Lunch counter. Saturday 7am to 6pm, Sunday 9am to 4pm (call for other days and times of operations). 225 7th St. SE (btw. North Carolina Ave. and C St. SE). www.easternmarket.net. Metro: Eastern Market.

Montgomery County Farm Woman's Cooperative Market Vendors set up inside every Wednesday, Friday, and Saturday year-round from 8am to about 4pm to sell preserves, homegrown veggies, cut flowers, slabs of bacon and sausages, and mouthwatering pies, cookies, and breads; there's an abbreviated version on Wednesday. Outside, on Saturday, Sunday, Wednesday, and Friday, from 8am to 4pm you'll find flea market vendors selling everything from rugs to tablecloths to furniture to sunglasses. 7155 Wisconsin Ave., in Bethesda. © 301/652-2291. Metro: Bethesda.

FASHION

See also "Discount Shopping," above, and "Shoes," later in this section.

CHILDREN'S CLOTHING

If your youngster has spilled grape juice all over his favorite outfit and you need a replacement, you can always head to the downtown **Macy's** (p. 249) or **H&M** (p. 243), or to the nearest **Gap Kids** in Georgetown (1267 Wisconsin Ave. NW; © 202/333-2411). Chic moms undeterred by expense shop at the Georgetown store, while practical moms shop at the midtown Kid's Closet.

Kid's Closet Now in its 26th year, Kid's Closet has seen numerous chichi children's clothing stores come and go in D.C. The secret to its staying power lies in full view: Its storefront display of affordable and practical kids' clothes are cute enough for you to imagine your child in them, but not so precious as to make you worry in advance about how you're going to remove the inevitable stains. The store is easy to find, since it stands out among the bank and restaurant facades in this downtown block. 1226 Connecticut Ave. NW. © 202/429-9247. www.kidsclosetdc.com. Metro: Dupont Circle or Farragut North.

Piccolo Piggies Here you'll love the cutie-pie children's garb, Petit Bateau to Lilly Pulitzer, for newborns up to age 14 for girls and up to age 10 for boys, as well as shoes, toys, and accessories. 1533 Wisconsin Ave. NW. © 202/333-0123. www.piccolo-piggies.com. Metro: Foggy Bottom, then take the Georgetown Metro Connection shuttle or the D.C. Circulator.

MEN'S CLOTHING

Local branches of **Banana Republic** are at Wisconsin and M streets in Georgetown (© 202/333-2554) and F and 13th streets NW (© 202/638-2724); **Gap** has several locations in Washington, including 1120 Connecticut Ave. NW (© 202/429-0691) and 1258 Wisconsin Ave. NW (© 202/333-2657).

Brooks Brothers Brooks sells traditional men's clothes, as well as the fine line of Peal & Company Collection shoes. This store made the news as the place where Monica Lewinsky bought a tie for President Clinton. It also sells an extensive line of women's clothes. 1201 Connecticut Ave. NW. © 202/659-4650. www.brooksbrothers.com. Metro: Dupont Circle (19th St./Q St. exit) or Farragut North (L St. exit). Other locations are at Potomac Mills (p. 240), at National Airport (© 703/417-1071), and at 5504 Wisconsin Ave., in Chevy Chase, MD (© 301/654-8202).

Burberry's Here you'll find those plaid-lined trench coats, of course, along with well-tailored English clothing for men and women. Hot items include cashmere sweaters and camel's hair duffel coats for men. 1155 Connecticut Ave. NW. © 202/463-3000. www.burberry.com. Metro: Farragut North (L St. exit).

Daddy & Son Camiceria Italiana This is the Italian men's store's sole retail location in the U.S. Expect to find exquisite Italian designs with fine touches, like mother-of-pearl buttons, hand-finished ties, shirts, and sweaters for boys and men. 1704 Connecticut Ave. NW. ✆ 202/462-1324. www.daddyesonusa.com. Metro: Dupont Circle (19th St./Q St. exit).

H&M This Swedish-based store sells trendy clothes for the whole family at reasonable prices. Some designer knockoffs. 1025 F St. NW. ✆ 202/347-3306. www.hm.com. Metro: Metro Center (11th St. exit). A second location, in the Shops at Georgetown Park Mall, 3222 M St. NW (✆ 202/298-6792), sells only women's and youth lines.

Jos. A. Bank Clothiers If you admire the Brooks Brothers line, but only wish it were more affordable, look here. This century-old clothier sells suits, corporate casual, weekend casual, and formal attire at prices "20% to 30% lower than competitors." Union Station. ✆ 202/289-9087. www.josbank.com. Metro: Union Station. Two other locations: Lincoln Square, 555 11th St. NW (✆ 202/393-5590) and 1200 19th St. NW (✆ 202/466-2282).

Sherman Pickey Prep to the max is this store but also a little fey: Think red corduroys. Both men's and women's clothes are on sale here, including Bill's Khakis and Barbour Outerwear for men, embroidered capris and ribbon belts for women. It's not a chain, though, so it's different in that respect. 1647 Wisconsin Ave. NW. ✆ 202/333-4212. www.shermanpickey.com. Metro: Foggy Bottom, then take the D.C. Circulator.

Thomas Pink For those who like beautifully made, bright-colored shirts, this branch of the London-based high-end establishment should please. The store also sells ties, boxer shorts, women's shirts, cuff links, and other accessories. 1127 Connecticut Ave. NW (inside the Mayflower Hotel). ✆ 202/223-5390. www.thomaspink.com. Metro: Farragut North (L St. exit).

Urban Outfitters For the latest in casual attire, from fatigue pants to tube tops. The shop has a floor of women's clothes and a floor of men's clothes, as well as apartment wares, travel books and accessories, cards, and candles. 3111 M St. NW. ✆ 202/342-1012. www.urbanoutfitters.com. Metro: Foggy Bottom, then take the D.C. Circulator. Second location: Gallery Place, 737 7th St. NW ✆ 202/737-0259. Metro: Gallery Place.

WOMEN'S CLOTHING

Washington women have many more clothing stores to choose from than men. Stores selling classic designs dominate, including **Ann Taylor,** at Union Station (✆ 202/371-8010), 1140 Connecticut Ave. NW (✆ 202/659-0120), 600 13th St. NW (✆ 202/737-0325), and Georgetown Park, 3222 M St. NW (✆ 202/337-0843); and **Talbots,** at 1122 Connecticut Ave. NW (✆ 202/887-6973), and Georgetown Park, 3222 M St. NW (✆ 202/338-3510). Beneath their modest apparel, however, Washington women like to wear racy **Victoria's Secret** lingerie—you'll find stores in Union Station (✆ 202/682-0686) and Georgetown Park (✆ 202/965-5457), as well as at Connecticut and L streets NW (✆ 202/293-7530).

See "Men's Clothing," immediately above, for locations of Banana Republic, Gap, Sherman Pickey, H&M, Brooks Brothers, and Urban Outfitters, all of which also sell women's clothes.

Hip boutiques and upscale shops proliferate as well:

Betsey Johnson New York's flamboyant flower-child designer personally decorated the bubble-gum-pink walls in her Georgetown shop. Her sexy, offbeat, play-dress-up styles are great party and club clothes for the young and the still-skinny young at heart. This is the only Betsey Johnson store in D.C. 1319 Wisconsin Ave. NW. ✆ 202/338-4090. www.betseyjohnson.com. Metro: Foggy Bottom, then take the D.C. Circulator.

Betsy Fisher A walk past the store is all it takes to know that this shop is a tad different. Its windows and racks show off whimsically feminine fashions by new American, French, and Italian designers. 1224 Connecticut Ave. NW. ℂ 202/785-1975. www. betsyfisher.com. Metro: Dupont Circle (South/19th St. exit).

French Connection This outpost of the London-based chain features clothes that are slouchy and hip, but not outrageous, for both men and women. 1229 Wisconsin Ave. NW. ℂ 202/965-4690. www.frenchconnection.com. Metro: Foggy Bottom, then take the D.C. Circulator.

Meeps Vintage Fashionette This pioneer shop opened on U Street, but has since moved around the corner to lower Adams-Morgan; its clientele and inventory remain the same: men and women urbanistas attracted to local designer ware and vintage clothes, 1930s gabardine suits to 1950s cocktail dresses to satiny lingerie. 2104 18th St. NW ℂ 202/265-6546. www.meepsdc.com. Metro: U St.–Cardozo (13th St. exit) or Woodley Park–Zoo, with a bit of a walk from either station.

Nana's Owner Jackie Flanagan left the world of advertising and publishing to open this store a couple of years ago, naming it after her fashion-wise grandmother. The shop sells new creations from independent U.S. and Canadian designs, and a small rack of vintage styles of work and play clothes, the idea being to mix old and new for a fresh look. Handbags, gifts, and bath products also on sale. 1528 U St. NW (btw. 15th and 16th sts.). ℂ 202/667-6955. www.nanadc.com. Metro: U St.-Cardozo (13th St. exit).

Reiss Washington This British import sells tailored but fun, fashion-forward but not simply trendy, clothes for both men and women. Best of all, for each design, the store sells only one item in each size, thereby narrowing the chances that you'll show up to an event wearing the same outfit as another. 1254 Wisconsin Ave. NW., Georgetown. ℂ 202/944-8566. www.reiss.co.uk.

Rizik Brothers The year 2008 marked Rizik's centennial anniversary. This downtown high-fashion store sells bridal dresses and other high-toned fashions by European and American designers such as Christian LaCroix, Brioni, and Escada Sport. 1100 Connecticut Ave. NW. ℂ 202/223-4050. www.riziks.com. Metro: Farragut North (L St. exit).

Setchi Eco-Boutique As its name indicates, Setchi is all about pesticide-free, fair-trade produced, locally made, sustainably acquired, organic products, in this case, mostly hip casual clothing for women. Designers include Sewart + Brown and Enamore. Washington's green-leaning fashionistas are beating a path to Setchi, located in upper Georgetown. 1614 Wisconsin Ave. NW. Georgetown. ℂ 202/333-5570. www.shopsetchi.com.

Wink Look for Wink beneath the Steve Madden store, and you'll discover Seven jeans and clothes by Diane von Furstenberg, Miguelina, Blue Cult, and happy women of all ages sorting through the mix. 3109 M St. NW. Lower level. ℂ 202/338-9465. www.shop winkdc.com. Metro: Foggy Bottom, then take the D.C. Circulator.

Zara This cheery store is an outpost of a popular chain started in Spain. Clothes are both dressy and casual, but all trendy. A sprinkling of coats is also found here, when the season calls for it. 1238 Wisconsin Ave. NW. ℂ 202/944-9797. www.zara.com. Metro: Foggy Bottom, then take the D.C. Circulator. Also at 1025 F St. NE. ℂ 202/393 2810.

GIFTS/SOUVENIRS

See also "Crafts," earlier in this section. Museum gift shops are also full of possibilities.

America! Stop here if you want to pick up a baseball cap with COMMANDER IN CHIEF printed across its bill, a T-shirt proclaiming I LOVE MY COUNTRY, IT'S THE GOVERNMENT

I'M AFRAID OF, White House guest towels, or other impress-the-folks-back-home items. Union Station. ✆ **202/842-0540**. www.americastore.com. Metro: Union Station. Or save your shopping for the airport; America! has at least one location at National (✆ 703/417-1782) and several at Dulles (Terminal B: ✆ 703/572-2543; Terminal C: ✆ 703/572-6033; Terminal D: ✆ 703/572-6070).

Chocolate Moose Its website welcomes browsers with the words "Serving weirdly sophisticated Washingtonians since 1978, but now attempting to reach out to the rest of you." I guess my family qualifies as weirdly sophisticated, since we're longtime fans. My husband endears himself to me and our daughters when he brings home gifts from this shop: a Wonder Woman daybook; chunky, transparent, red heart-shaped earrings; wacky cards; paperweight snow globes with figurines inside; candies; eccentric clothing; and other funny, lovely, and useful presents. 1743 L St. NW. ✆ **202/463-0992**. www.chocolatemoosedc.com. Metro: Farragut North (L St. exit).

Pulp Gifts You'll find must-have items here that you never even knew existed: a deck of slang flashcards, "Dancin' in the Streets" T-shirts, and crazy greeting cards. 1803 14th St. NW. ✆ **202/462-7857**. www.pulpdc.com. Metro: U St.–Cardozo (13th St. exit).

GOURMET GOODIES TO GO

Demanding jobs and hectic schedules leave Washingtonians less and less time to prepare their own meals. Or so they say. At any rate, a number of fine-food shops and bakeries are happy to come to the rescue. Even the busiest bureaucrat can find the time to pop into one of these gourmet shops for a movable feast.

See also "Farmer's & Flea Markets," above.

Bread Line Bread Line is wildly popular and attracts the White House crowd for lunch, with favorite sandwiches like the roast pork bun or the muffuletta; tasty soups; and desserts such as bread puddings, pear tarts, and delicious cookies. Seating is available, but most people buy carryout. The shop also sells freshly baked loaves of wheat bread, flat breads, baguettes, and more. Open weekdays 7:30am to 3:30pm. 1751 Pennsylvania Ave. NW. ✆ **202/822-8900**. www.breadlinedc.com. Metro: Farragut West or Farragut North.

Dean & Deluca This famed New York store operates this fabulous emporium in a historic Georgetown building that was once an open-air market. Though it is now closed in, this huge space still feels airy, with its high ceiling and windows on all sides. You'll pay top prices, but the quality is impressive—charcuterie, fresh fish, produce, cheeses, prepared sandwiches and cold pasta salads, hot-ticket desserts, like crème brûlée and tiramisu, and California wines. Also on sale are housewares; on-site is an espresso bar/cafe. 3276 M St. NW. ✆ **202/342-2500**. www.deandeluca.com. Metro: Foggy Bottom, then take the D.C. Circulator.

Firehook Bakery Known for its sourdough baguettes, apple-walnut bread, fresh fruit tarts, red-iced elephant and blue-iced donkey cookies, and sandwiches like smoked chicken on sesame semolina bread. Firehook now runs the cafe at the Phillips Collection (see "Views with a Meal," in chapter 6), as well as the cafe at the National Building Museum (see "Museums of Special Interest," chapter 7). 1909 Q St. NW. ✆ **202/588-9296**. www.firehook.com. Metro: Dupont Circle (Q St. exit). Also at 912 17th St. NW (✆ 202/429-2253), 3411 Connecticut Ave. NW (✆ 202/362-2253), 215 Pennsylvania Ave. SE (✆ 202/544-7003), 555 13th St. NW (✆ 202/393-0952), 441 4th St. NW (✆ 202/347-1760), and at 2 locations in Alexandria, VA.

Marvelous Market First there were the breads: sourdough, baguettes, olive, rosemary, croissants, scones. Now, there are things to spread on the bread, including

smoked salmon mousse and tapenade; pastries to die for, from gingerbread to flourless chocolate cake; and prepared foods, such as soups, empanadas, and pasta salads. The breakfast spread on Sunday mornings is sinful, and individual items, like the croissants, are tastier and less expensive here than at other bakeries. The location is grand, with 18th-century chandeliers, an antique cedar bar, and a small number of tables. 1511 Connecticut Ave. NW. (C) **202/332-3690.** www.marvelousmarket.com. Metro: Dupont Circle (Q St. exit). Also at 3217 P St. NW ((C) 202/333-2591), 5035 Connecticut Ave. NW ((C) 202/686-4040), 1800 K St. NW ((C) 202/828-0944), and 303 7th St. SE ((C) 202/544-7127).

HOME FURNISHINGS

You may not have come to Washington to shop for furniture, but step inside these beguiling shops and you may change your mind.

Apartment Zero Located on the first floor of a historic building in the delicious Penn Quarter, this sophisticated store sells hot-off-the-design-floor furnishings: Eames sofas, Zanzibar stools, "orange slice" chairs, and "petits fours" benches. The clever designers are from around the world; the prices are out of this world. Besides furniture, Apartment Zero sells everything else you need for the home, from light fixtures to bed linens. 406 7th St. NW. (C) **202/628-4067.** www.apartmentzero.com. Metro: Gallery Place/Verizon Center (Arena/7th and F sts. exit) or Archives/Navy Memorial.

Cady's Alley Cady's Alley refers not to a single store, but to the southwest pocket of Georgetown, where about 20 stores reside, in and around said alley, which dangles south of M Street. These are tony, big-name places, and include Waterworks, Thos. Moser Cabinetmakers, Baker Furniture, and European outposts, such as the high-concept designs of Ligne Roset and the hip kitchen furnishings of Bulthaup. 3318 M St. NW (btw. 33rd and 34th sts.). www.cadysalley.com. Metro: Foggy Bottom, then take the D.C. Circulator.

Home Rule Unique housewares; bath, kitchen, and office supplies; and gifts cram this tiny store. You'll see everything from French milled soap to martini glasses. 1807 14th St. NW (at S St.). (C) **202/797-5544.** www.homerule.com. Metro: U St.–Cardozo (call for specific directions from the station).

JEWELRY

Beadazzled The friendly staff demonstrates to you how to assemble your own affordable jewelry from an eye-boggling array of beads and artifacts. The store also sells textiles, woodcarvings, and other crafts from around the world. There are also classes offered to those who prefer a more hands-on experience. 1507 Connecticut Ave. NW. (C) **202/265-BEAD** (2323). www.beadazzled.net. Metro: Dupont Circle (Q St. exit).

Chas Schwartz & Son In business since 1888, Chas Schwartz specializes in diamonds and sapphires, rubies and emeralds, and is one of the few distributors of Hidalgo jewelry (enameled rings and bracelets). The professional staff also repairs watches and jewelry. 1400 F St. NW, or enter through the Willard Hotel, at 1401 Pennsylvania Ave. NW. (C) **202/737-4757.** www.chasschwartzjewelers.com. Metro: Metro Center (13th St. exit). There's another branch at the Mazza Gallerie ((C) **202/363-5432**); Metro: Friendship Heights.

Keith Lipert Gallery This decorative-arts gallery suffered a tremendous fire in January 2006 but reopened in July, to resume selling Venetian glassware, high-end costume jewelry by designers such as Oscar de la Renta, and cute little old things, like Art Deco–style handbags. The owner shops in Europe for fashion jewelry and for exquisite

gifts suitable for giving to diplomats and international business executives. 2922 M St. NW.
(C) 202/965-9736. www.keithlipertgallery.com. Metro: Foggy Bottom, then take the D.C. Circulator.

Pilgrim This Georgetown location of the Denmark-based jewelry shop is the company's first and, so far, only Pilgrim in the U.S. Pilgrim is known for fashioning jewelry out of mixed metals, mostly zinc and tin, alloyed with copper. Sunglasses and watches are a big sell. 3225 M St. NW., Georgetown. (C) 202/298-8006. www.pilgrim.us.

Tiffany & Co. Tiffany is known for exquisite diamonds and other jewelry that can cost hundreds of thousands of dollars. But you may not know that the store carries less expensive items as well, like $35 candlesticks. Tiffany will engrave, too. Other items include tabletop gifts and fancy glitz: china, crystal, flatware, and a bridal registry service. 5481 Wisconsin Ave., Chevy Chase, MD. (C) 301/657-8777. www.tiffany.com. Metro: Friendship Heights.

Tiny Jewel Box The first place Washingtonians go for estate and antique jewelry, but this six-story store next to the Mayflower Hotel also sells the pieces of many designers, from Links of London to Christian Tse, as well as crystal and other house gifts. In the month leading up to Mother's Day, the Tiny Jewel Box holds its Top-to-Bottom Sale, where you can save anywhere from 10% to 75% on most merchandise, including jewelry, handbags, and home accessories. 1147 Connecticut Ave. NW. (C) 202/393-2747. www.tinyjewelbox.com. Metro: Farragut North (L St. exit).

MALLS

If malls are your thing, D.C. has plenty for you to choose from: **Chevy Chase Pavilion,** 5335 Wisconsin Ave. NW ((C) **202/686-5335;** www.ccpavilion.com; Metro: Friendship Heights); **Gallery Place,** 7th and H sts. NW ((C) **202/624-8627;** www.galleryplace.com; Metro: Gallery Place/Verizon Center); **Mazza Gallerie,** 5300 Wisconsin Ave. NW ((C) **202/966-6114;** www.mazzagallerie.com; Metro: Friendship Heights); the **Shops at Georgetown Park,** 3222 M St. NW ((C) **202/342-8190;** www.shopsatgeorgetownpark.com; Metro: Foggy Bottom, then take the Georgetown Metro Connection shuttle or D.C. Circulator); **Tysons Corner Center,** 1961 Chain Bridge Rd., McLean, VA ((C) **703/893-9400;** www.shoptysons.com); and **Tysons Corner II, The Galleria,** 2001 International Dr., McLean, VA ((C) **703/827-7700;** www.tysonsgalleria.com). **Ronald Reagan Washington National Airport,** Arlington, VA ((C) **703/417-8600;** www.mwaa.com/national), has 100 stores to choose from, too, if you want to do some souvenir shopping on your way out of town. Also see the listing for **Potomac Mills** on p. 240.

Even if you aren't a mall rat, you might want to check out the following two establishments, which do double duty as both shopping centers and attractions:

Pavilion at the Old Post Office Not so much a mall as a tourist trap with souvenir shops and a food court. But you can ride a pair of elevators to the clock tower for a stunning view of the city. 1100 Pennsylvania Ave. NW. (C) 202/289-4224. www.oldpostofficedc.com. Metro: Federal Triangle.

Union Station One of the most popular tourist stops in Washington, Union Station boasts magnificent architecture and more than 100 shops, including Pendleton's and Appalachian Spring (p. 239). Among the places to eat are America, B. Smith, and an impressive food court. There's also a nine-screen movie-theater complex here. 50 Massachusetts Ave. NE. (C) 202/371-9441 or 202/289-1908. www.unionstationdc.com. Metro: Union Station.

MISCELLANEOUS

Fahrneys Pens, Inc. People come from all over to purchase the finest fountain pens, or to have them engraved or repaired. In business since 1929, Fahrneys is an institution, selling the best pens in the business, such as Montblanc, Cross, and Waterman. 1317 F St. NW (btw. 13th and 14th sts.). ℭ **800/624-7367** or 202/628-9525. www.fahrneyspens.com. Metro: Metro Center (13th and G sts. exit).

Ginza, "for Things Japanese" In business since 1955, Ginza sells everything Japanese, from incense to kimonos to futons to Zen rock gardens. 1721 Connecticut Ave. NW. ℭ **202/332-7000.** www.ginzaonline.com. Metro: Dupont Circle (Q St. exit).

Paper Source If you're a stationery freak like I am, you'll have to stop here to revel in the beautiful writing and wrapping papers, supplies of notebooks, journals, albums, ribbons, folders, containers, and other essentials. This store is the chain's only mid-Atlantic location. I believe it's the best stationery store in D.C. 3019 M St. NW. ℭ **202/ 298-5545.** www.paper-source.com. Metro: Foggy Bottom, with a 25-min. walk, or ride the D.C. Circulator.

MUSIC

See also the listings for **Olsson's Books and Records,** p. 238, **Barnes & Noble,** p. 238, and **Borders,** p. 238.

DJ Hut Everything for lovers of hip-hop, reggae, R&B, and go-go. 2010 P St. NW, 2nd floor. ℭ **202/659-2010.** www.djhut.com. Metro: Dupont Circle (either exit).

Melody Record Shop CDs, cassettes, and tapes, including new releases, are discounted here, plus the shop always has a table of unused but not newly released CDs that sell for about $10 each. Melody offers a wide variety of rock, classical, jazz, pop, show, and folk music, as well as a vast number of international selections. This is also a good place to shop for discounted portable electronic equipment, blank tapes, and cassettes. Its knowledgeable staff is a plus. 1623 Connecticut Ave. NW. ℭ **202/232-4002.** www.melodyrecords.com. Metro: Dupont Circle (Q St. exit).

SHOES

For men's dress shoes, try **Brooks Brothers** (p. 242). There are local outlets of **Foot Locker** at Union Station (ℭ **202/289-8364;** www.footlocker.com) and 1934 14th St. NW (ℭ **202/319-8934**). **Nine West** sells women's shoes from locations at Union Station (ℭ **202/216-9490;** www.ninewest.com), 1001 Connecticut Ave. NW (ℭ **202/ 452-9163**), and 1227 Wisconsin Ave. NW (ℭ **202/337-7256**).

Carbon "Changing D.C. from federal to funky" is this store's self-proclaimed purpose, and its merchandise is persuasive in this regard: Blackstones, Pikolinos, and Bronx are some of the names it carries in men's footwear. Carbon also carries women's shoes, and accessories and some clothes and furnishings for both sexes. 2643 Connecticut Ave. NW. ℭ **202/232-6645.** www.carbondc.com. Metro: Woodley Park–Zoo.

Comfort One Shoes Despite its unhip name, this store sells a great selection of popular styles for both men and women, including Doc Martens, Birkenstocks, and Ecco. You can always find something that looks good and actually feels comfortable. 1630 Connecticut Ave. NW. ℭ **202/328-3141.** www.comfortoneshoes.com. Metro: Dupont Circle. Also at 1607 Connecticut Ave. NW (ℭ **202/667-5300**), 3222 M St. NW (ℭ **202/333-4246**), and other locations.

Fleet Feet Though part of a national chain, this store feels decidedly part of the community, an Adams-Morgan neighborhood fixture since 1984. The couple who owns the shop, Phil and Jan Fenty, are the parents of D.C. mayor Adrian Fenty, whose

Emergency Shopping

You've just arrived in town, but your luggage hasn't—the airline lost it. Or you're about to depart for home or another destination and you notice that the zipper to your suitcase is broken. Or you've arrived at your hotel all in one piece, only to discover you've forgotten something essential: underwear, allergy medicine, an umbrella. What's a lonesome traveler to do? One of these suggestions might prove your salvation.

CVS: This is Washington's main pharmacy and essentials chain. Among the items sold at CVS stores are pantyhose, over-the-counter and prescription medicines, toys, greeting cards, wrapping paper and ribbon, magazines, film and 1-hour photo developing, batteries, candy, some refrigerated food such as milk and orange juice, and office supplies. The stores are ubiquitous, so chances are you'll find one near you. Two conveniently located 24-hour branches are at 2240 M St. NW (☎ **202/296-9877;** Metro: Gallery Place/Verizon Center) and at 6 Dupont Circle NW (☎ **202/785-1466;** Metro: Dupont Circle); www.cvs.com.

Cobbler's Bench Shoe Repair: This shop on the lower (food court) level of Union Station is open daily, Monday to Friday from 7am to 8pm, Saturday 10am to 6pm, and Sunday noon to 6pm, to come to the rescue of travelers whose shoes or luggage need mending. The cobbler also cuts keys and sells repair items. Union Station, lower level. (☎ **202/898-9009).** Metro: Union Station.

Macy's: This former Hecht's remains an old reliable and the only department store located downtown. But though it's been around a while, the store continually updates its merchandise to keep up with the times. Run here if you need cosmetics, clothes (for men, women, and children), shoes (but not for children), electronics, appliances, lingerie, luggage, raincoats, and countless other need-immediately goods. Open daily: noon to 6pm Sunday; 10am to 8pm Monday to Saturday. 1201 G St. NW. (☎ **202/628-6661).** www.macys.com. Metro: Metro Center.

Metro Stations: If it starts raining and you're scrambling to find an umbrella, look no farther than your closest Metro station, where vendors are at the ready selling umbrellas and other handy things.

brothers, if not the mayor himself, you might find racing next to you during the weekly Sunday morning 5-mile fun run that Fleet Feet launches from its doorstep at 9am. (Just show up, if you're interested.) Merchandise-wise, the store sells sports and running shoes, apparel, and accessories, and is known for its friendly staff. 1841 Columbia Rd. NW. ☎ 202/387-3888. www.fleetfeetdc.com. Metro: U St.–Cardozo (13th St. exit) or Woodley Park–Zoo, with a bit of a walk from either station.

Wild Women Wear Red Mostly funky but comfy shoes, including Mary Janes and Lisa Nadings, but also accessories, like jewelry crafted by local artists, are on sale in this boutique, whose walls are hung with images of Indira Ghandi and Rosie the Riveter. 1512 U St. NW. ☎ 202/387-5700. www.wildwomenwearred.com. Metro: U Street-Cardozo (13th St. exit).

WINE & SPIRITS

Barmy Wine and Liquor Located near the White House, this store sells it all, but with special emphasis on fine wines and rare cordials. 1912 L St. NW. ℂ 202/833-8730. Metro: Farragut North (L St. exit).

Central Liquor This is like a clearinghouse for liquor: Its great volume allows the store to offer the best prices in town on wines and liquor. The store carries more than 250 single-malt scotches. 917 F St. NW. ℂ 202/737-2800. www.centralliquors.com. Metro: Gallery Place (9th and F sts. exit).

Schneider's of Capitol Hill Two blocks south of Union Station is this family-run liquor store, in business for half a century. With a knowledgeable and enthusiastic staff, a 12,000-bottle inventory of wine, and a fine selection of spirits and beer, this shop is a find on Capitol Hill. 300 Massachusetts Ave. NE. ℂ 202/543-9300. www.cellar.com. Metro: Union Station.

Washington, D.C., After Dark

What a provocative word . . . "nightlife." Visions of drinking and dancing, rabble-rousing, flirting, and smooching come to mind. Washington offers countless opportunities for pursuing all those activities and countless more: the theater, live music concerts, comedy shows, opera, even a night out at the old ballgame. Read whatever you want into the word but definitely read this chapter to find out where you can make your own personal nightlife dream come alive.

It might help if you know a little bit about the locale. D.C.'s hip pockets include Georgetown, the U and 14th street corridors, Penn Quarter, Adams-Morgan, Barracks Row on Capitol Hill, the "Atlas District's" H Street NE (east of Union Station), Dupont Circle, and even the upper-northwest upscale residential Cleveland Park. Restaurants are often destinations in themselves, serving up a sexy lounge alongside the dining room. Bars are as much about making the scene as having a drink.

For up-to-date schedules of events—from live music and theater, to children's programs and flower shows—check the Friday "Weekend" section of the *Washington Post,* or go online, and browse the *Post's* nightlife information at **www. washingtonpost.com.** Also visit the *Washington Post Online's* "Going Out Gurus" blog, accessible from its City Guide link; the "GOGs" answer questions about nightlife live online every Thursday at 1pm, and transcripts stay posted for a time. The *City Paper,* available free at

restaurants, bookstores, and other places around town, and online at **www. washingtoncitypaper.com**, is another excellent source. Finally, check out the blog **www.dcist.com** for an irreverent inside look at what's going on around town.

TICKETS

Most performing-arts and live-music venues mentioned in this chapter require admission by tickets, which you can purchase at the venue's box office or through one of the ticket vendors listed below.

TICKETplace, Washington's only discount day-of-show ticket outlet, has one location: at 407 7th St. NW, between D and E streets (Metro: Gallery Place/Verizon Center or Archives/Navy Memorial). Call (C) **202/TIC-KETS** (842-5387) for information. The TICKETplace booth displays a chalkboard listing of those performances that still have seats available, including those at major Washington-area theaters, concert halls, opera, ballet, and other events. TICKETplace is open Tuesday through Friday from 11am to 6pm and Saturday from 10am to 5pm; half-price tickets for Sunday and Monday shows are sold on Saturday. Though tickets are half-price, you still have to pay a per-ticket service charge of 12% of the full face value of the ticket. TICKET-place accepts only credit and select debit cards.

Some TICKETplace tickets are available online at www.ticketplace.org, Tuesday through Friday, between midnight

and 4pm. Again, the tickets sold are for same-day performances, at half-price, plus the per-ticket service charge, which for online sales is 17% of the full face value of the ticket. Only MasterCard and Visa credit cards are accepted. If you've ordered tickets online, you can pick them up the at the "Will Call" booth of the venue you're attending; bring your credit card and confirmation of your purchase. TICKETplace is a project of the Cultural Alliance of Washington, in partnership with the *Washington Post*. TICKETplace also sells Ticketmaster tickets—see below.

You can buy full-price tickets for most performances in town through **Ticketmaster** (© **800/551-7328;** www.ticket master.com); expect to pay taxes, plus a service charge, an order processing fee, and a facility fee (if a particular venue tacks on that charge). Or you can visit one of Ticketmaster's numerous locations throughout the city, including TICKET-place (see information above; Macy's Department Store, at 12th and G sts. NW (Metro: Metro Center, 13th St. exit), and the D.C. Visitor Center in the Ronald Reagan Building, at 1300 Pennsylvania Ave. NW (Metro: Federal Triangle); you usually will not have to pay a convenience or order-processing fee when you purchase tickets in person. When you pay by credit card at TICKETplace and Ticketmaster, you have to show an ID to prove you are the credit card holder.

Another ticket outlet worth checking out is **Tickets.com**. While Ticketmaster has a wider selection, Tickets.com offers some performances Ticketmaster doesn't. Access its website at www.tickets.com, or visit one of its D.C. outlets, including one inside the Olsson's Bookstore at 418 7th St. NW, directly across from the TICK-ETplace office, in the Penn Quarter.

Finally, check out **InstantSeats.Com**, which bills itself as the place to go for "online ticketing for the performing arts." (I see that the site also sells tickets for river cruises on the Potomac, so perhaps the company defines "performing arts" to cover a multitude of entertainment.) This is the site that handles sales of tickets to embassy events (see box later in this chapter, "The Best of D.C.'s International Scene," for more information).

1 The Performing Arts

Washington's performing-arts scene has an international reputation. Almost anything on Broadway has either been previewed here or will eventually come here. Better yet, D.C. is home to truly excellent and renowned repertory theater troupes, and to fine ballet, opera, and symphony companies. Rock bands, headliner comedians, and jazz/folk/gospel/R&B/alternative and other musical groups make Washington a must-stop on their tours.

THE TOP THEATERS

Arena Stage Founded by the brilliant Zelda Fichandler in 1950, the Arena Stage is home to one of the oldest acting ensembles in the nation. Several works nurtured here have moved to Broadway, and many graduates have gone on to commercial stardom, including Ned Beatty, James Earl Jones, Robert Prosky, and Jane Alexander. The excellence of Arena productions has brought the theater much success, to the extent that a major expansion is underway, with 2010 the target year for opening. During the construction of the new facility, Arena is staging its 10 productions at two locations: in Crystal City, Virginia, at 1800 S. Bell St.; and at the Lincoln Theatre, 1215 U St. NW, in the U Street NW Corridor of downtown D.C.

The 2008–09 September-to-June season includes Carrie Fisher's *Outrageous Memoir, Wishful Drinking,* in which Fisher also performs; Irving Berlin's musical, *I Love a Piano;* and Edward Albee's *A Delicate Balance.*

The Arena Stage has always championed new plays and playwrights and is committed to producing works from America's diverse cultures, as well as to reinterpreting the works of past masters. Its mission during construction of its new theater is to celebrate "the rich mosaic of our nation's voices." Its main office, box office, phone number, and website remain the same: 1101 6th St. SW (at Maine Ave.). (✆ 202/488-3300. www.arenastage. org. Tickets $47–$74; discounts available for students, people with disabilities, groups, and seniors. Metro at Crystal City location: Crystal City, exiting through the underground walkway marked CRYSTAL CITY SHOPS at 2100. Metro for Lincoln Theatre: U St./Cardozo, exiting at 13th St. exit.

John F. Kennedy Center for the Performing Arts This 38-year-old theater complex strives to be not just the hub of Washington's cultural and entertainment scene, but a performing-arts theater for the nation. The center lies between the Potomac River and a crisscross of major roadways, which makes it sound like it's easily accessible when, in fact, the center remains just a bit west of the city's main action.

The Kennedy Center stages top-rated performances by the best ballet, opera, jazz, modern dance, musical, and theater companies in the world. Ticket prices vary from $15 for a family concert to $300 for a night at the opera, although most fall in the $30 to $75 range.

The Kennedy Center is committed to being a theater for the people, and toward that end, it continues to stage its **free concert series,** known as "Millennium Stage," which features daily performances by area musicians and sometimes national artists each evening at 6pm in the center's Grand Foyer. (You can check out broadcasts of the nightly performances on the Internet at www.kennedy-center.org/millennium.) The Friday "Weekend" section of the *Washington Post* lists the free performances scheduled for the coming week.

The Kennedy Center is actually made up of six different national theaters: the Opera House, the Concert Hall, the Terrace Theater, the Eisenhower Theater, the Theater Lab, and the Family Theater.

The Kennedy Center's 2008–09 season includes a wintertime festival, called **Arabesque,** which salutes the **Arts of the Arab World,** and covers all 22 Arab states. For more information, check out the Kennedy Center's online information at www. kennedy-center.org. Highlights of the Kennedy Center's 2008–09 season include the following:

- **Washington National Opera** (www.dc-opera.org) performances of Verdi's *La Traviata,* Benjamin Britten's *Peter Grimes,* and Wagner's *Siegfried,* under the artistic direction of Placido Domingo
- **National Symphony Orchestra** concerts, under the direction of Leonard Slatkin, presented in the Concert Hall from September to June
- Performances by the **New York City Ballet,** the **Joffrey Ballet,** the **American Ballet Theatre,** the **Suzanne Farrell Ballet,** and the **Kirov Ballet**
- **Broadway musicals** *Ragtime* and *Spring Awakening*
- **Kennedy Center Jazz series** performances by assorted masters, such as saxophonist Javon Jackson and pianist Les McCann
- **Family Theater** productions, like the **National Symphony Orchestra's Teddy Bear Concerts,** and
- Continuing performances of the comedy whodunit *Shear Madness,* now in its 22nd year at the Kennedy Center

Fun Fact **Longer Than the Washington Monument Is Tall**

Most Kennedy Center performances take place in theaters that lie off the Grand Foyer. But even if the one you're attending is on the Roof Terrace Level, one floor up, make sure you visit the Foyer anyway. The Grand Foyer is one of the largest rooms in the world. Measuring 630 feet long, 40 feet wide, and 60 feet high, the foyer is longer than the Washington Monument is tall (at 555⅝ ft.). Millennium Stage hosts free performances here nightly at 6pm, the famous Robert Berks sculpture of President John F. Kennedy is here, and just beyond the foyer's glass doors is the expansive terrace, which runs the length of the building and overlooks the Potomac River.

2700 F St. NW (at New Hampshire Ave. NW and Rock Creek Pkwy.). © **800/444-1324** or 202/467-4600 for tickets and information. www.kennedy-center.org. 50% discounts are offered (for select performances) to students, seniors 65 and over, people with permanent disabilities, enlisted military personnel, and persons with fixed low incomes (© **202/416-8340** for details). Garage parking $16. Metro: Foggy Bottom (though it's a fairly short walk, there's a free shuttle btw. the station and the Kennedy Center, departing every 15 min. 9:45am–midnight Mon–Fri, 10am–midnight Sat, noon–midnight Sun). Bus: 80 from Metro Center.

National Theatre The splendid Federal-style National Theatre is the oldest continuously operating theater in Washington (since 1835) and the third oldest in the nation. It's exciting just to see the stage on which Sarah Bernhardt, John Barrymore, Helen Hayes, and so many other notables have performed. The 1,672-seat National is the closest thing Washington has to a Broadway-style playhouse. The 2008 season included the musical *Mamma Mia.*

One thing that has never flagged at the National is its commitment to offering free public-service programs: Saturday-morning children's theater (puppets, clowns, magicians, dancers, and singers) and Monday-night showcases of local groups and performers September through May, plus free summer films. Call © **202/783-3372** for details. 1321 Pennsylvania Ave. NW. © **800/447-7400** or 202/628-6161 to charge tickets. www.national theatre.org. Tickets $47–$152 (most are in the $70–$80 range); discounts available for students, seniors, military personnel, and people with disabilities. Metro: Metro Center (13th and G sts. exit).

Shakespeare Theatre Company: at the Lansburgh Theatre and Sidney Harman Hall This is top-level Shakespeare, with superb acting. Try your best to get tickets; the productions are reliably outstanding. Season subscriptions claim many of the seats, and the plays often sell out; so if you're interested in attending a play here, buy your tickets now. The Shakespeare Theatre Company's productions at the Lansburgh Theatre have long been so popular that the production company has opened a second theater, the 775-seat Sidney Harman Hall, at 610 F St. NW, across the street from the Verizon Center and just around the corner from the 451-seat Lansburgh Theatre, on 7th St. NW. The 2008–09 season presents three plays at the Lansburgh, including Congreve's *The Way of the World* and Noel Coward's *Design for Living;* and four plays at Harman Hall, including *Romeo and Juliet, Twelfth Night,* and *King Lear.* Every year, the company stages a free-admission, 2-week run of a Shakespeare production at the Carter Barron Amphitheater in Rock Creek Park; *Hamlet* was the feature in 2008. Lansburgh Theatre, 450 7th St. NW (btw. D and E sts.); Sidney Harman Hall, 650 F St. NW.

ⓒ 202/547-1122. www.shakespearetheatre.org. Tickets $36–$80, $10 for standing-room tickets sold 1 hr. before sold-out performances; discounts available for students, seniors, and groups. Metro: Archives/Navy Memorial or Verizon Center/Gallery Place (7th St./Arena exit).

SMALLER THEATERS

Some of Washington's lesser-known theaters are gaining more recognition all the time. Their productions are consistently professional, and sometimes more contemporary and innovative than those you'll find in the more acclaimed theaters. These more inti-mate theaters have their own strong followings, which explains the fact that at least two, the Studio Theater and the Woolly Mammoth Theatre Company, have recently revamped and expanded their performance spaces.

Studio Theatre, 1333 P St. NW, at 14th Street (ⓒ **202/332-3300;** www.studio theatre.org), since its founding in 1978, has grown in leaps and bounds into a four-theater complex, helping to revitalize this downtown neighborhood in the process. Artistic director Joy Zinoman showcases interesting contemporary plays and nurtures Washington acting talent; the 2008–09 lineup marks the theater's 31st season. The **Woolly Mammoth Theatre Company** (ⓒ **202/393-3939;** www.woollymammoth. net) offers as many as six productions each year, specializing in new, offbeat, and quirky plays, often world premieres. The Woolly resides in a 265-seat, state-of-the-art facility, 641 D St. NW, at 7th Street NW, in the heart of the Penn Quarter.

In addition, I highly recommend productions staged at the **Folger Shakespeare Library,** 201 E. Capitol St. SE (ⓒ **202/544-7077;** www.folger.edu), which celebrated its 75th anniversary in 2007. Plays take place in the library's Elizabethan Theatre, which is styled after the inn-yard theater of Shakespeare's time. The theater is intimate and charming, the theater company is remarkably good, and an evening spent here guarantees an absolutely marvelous experience. The 2008–09 season brings to the stage Shakespeare's *Henry IV, A Winter's Tale,* and Tom Stoppard's *Arcadia.* The Eliza-bethan Theatre is also the setting for musical performances, lectures, readings, and other events.

INDOOR ARENAS & OUTDOOR PAVILIONS

When John Mayer, U2, or the Dixie Chicks come to town, they usually play at one of the huge indoor or outdoor arenas. The 20,600-seat **Verizon Center,** 601 F St. NW, where it meets 7th Street (ⓒ **202/628-3200;** www.verizoncenter.com), in the center of downtown, hosts plenty of concerts and also is Washington's premier indoor sports arena (home to the NBA Wizards, the WNBA Mystics, the NHL Capitals, and Georgetown NCAA basketball). Less convenient and smaller is the 10,000-seat **Patriot Center** at George Mason University, 4500 Patriot Circle, Fairfax, Virginia (ⓒ **703/993-3000;** www.patriotcenter.com).

During the summer, there's quality entertainment almost nightly at the **Merri-weather Post Pavilion,** 10475 Little Patuxent Pkwy., just off Route 29 in Columbia, Maryland (ⓒ **410/715-5550** for general information, 800/551-SEAT for tickets; www.merriweathermusic.com), about a 40-minute drive from downtown D.C. There's reserved seating in the open-air pavilion (overhead protection provided in case of rain) and general-admission seating on the lawn (no refunds for rain) to see such performers as Neil Young, Counting Crows, Diana Krall, the Killers, the Cure, or No Doubt. If you choose the lawn seating, bring blankets and picnic fare (beverages must be bought on the premises).

Fun Fact **The Washington Nationals Score Their Own Stadium**

Washington, D.C.'s Major League Baseball team, the **Washington Nationals,** arrived on the scene in 2005, but already have their own stadium: the newly built **Nationals Ballpark** (✆ **202/675-6287**) opened on March 30, 2008. Located in southeast Washington, the 41,000-seat stadium is bounded by South Capitol Street, N Street, 1st Street, and Potomac Avenue. The closest Metro stop is the Green line's Navy Yard station (Navy Yard West exit). For tickets, go to the website, **www.washington.nationals.mlb.com**; prices range from $5 to $75. Meanwhile, the 55,000-seat **Robert F. Kennedy Memorial Stadium** 2400 E. Capitol St. SE (✆ **202/547-9077**), where the Nationals had played their 2005–06 and 2006–07 seasons (the capital had been without a Major League Baseball team since 1971) remains the location for D.C. United (men's) and Washington Freedom (women's) soccer games, at least until these teams get their own stadium.

My favorite summer setting for music is the **Wolf Trap Farm Park for the Performing Arts,** 1551 Trap Rd., Vienna, Virginia (✆ **703/255-1868** for general information and tickets; www.wolftrap.org). The country's only national park devoted to the performing arts, Wolf Trap offers performances by the National Symphony Orchestra (it's their summer home), and has hosted Lucinda Williams, Shawn Colvin, Lyle Lovett, the Temptations, Ani DiFranco, and many others. Performances take place in the 7,000-seat Filene Center, about half of which is under the open sky. You can also buy cheaper lawn seats on the hill, which is sometimes the nicest way to go. If you do, arrive early (the lawn opens 90 min. before the performance) and bring a blanket and a picnic dinner—it's a tradition. Wolf Trap also hosts a number of very popular festivals, including the Louisiana Swamp Romp Cajun Festival in June and the International Children's Festival each September. Wolf Trap is about a 30-minute drive from D.C.; the park also runs a shuttle ($3 charge round-trip) between the West Falls Church Metro Station and the arts center.

The **Carter Barron Amphitheater,** 16th Street and Colorado Avenue NW (✆ **202/426-0486**), way out 16th Street, is in Rock Creek Park, close to the Maryland border. This is the area's smallest outdoor venue, with 4,250 seats. Summer performances include a range of gospel, blues, and classical entertainment. The shows are usually free, but tickets are required. You can always count on Shakespeare: The **Shakespeare Theatre Free For All** takes place at the Carter Barron usually for 2 weeks in late May/early June, Tuesday through Sunday evenings; the free tickets are available the day of performance only, on a first-come, first-served basis (call ✆ **202/334-4790** for details). The 2008 Free For All featured *Hamlet.*

SMALLER AUDITORIUMS

A handful of auditoriums in Washington are really fine places to catch a performance.

DAR Constitution Hall, on 18th Street NW, between C and D streets (✆ **202/628-4780;** www.dar.org), is housed within a beautiful turn-of-the-20th-century Beaux Arts building and seats 3,746. Its excellent acoustics have supported an eclectic group of performers: Sting, the Buena Vista Social Club, John Hiatt, the Count Basie Orchestra, the Los Angeles Philharmonic, Bow Wow, Ray Charles, Trisha Yearwood, the Strokes, and the *O Brother Where Art Thou?* tour.

In the heart of happening U Street, the **Lincoln Theatre,** 1215 U St. NW (© **202/ 328-6000;** www.thelincolntheatre.org), was once a movie theater, vaudeville house, and nightclub featuring black stars like Louis Armstrong and Cab Calloway. The theater closed in the 1970s and reopened in 1994 after a renovation restored it to its former elegance. Today the theater books jazz, R&B, gospel, and comedy acts, and events like the D.C. Film Festival. The theater is also staging Arena Stage productions throughout 2009, while Arena's new theater is constructed.

The **Warner Theatre,** 513 13th St. NW, between E and F streets (© **202/783-4000;** www.warnertheatre.com), opened in 1924 as the Earle Theatre (a movie/vaudeville palace) and was restored to its original, neoclassical-style appearance in 1992 at a cost of $10 million. It's worth coming by just to see its ornately detailed interior. The 2,000-seat auditorium offers year-round entertainment, alternating dance performances, like the Washington Ballet's Christmas performance of the *Nutcracker,* with comedy acts, like those of Steven Wright or Damon Wayans, with headliner entertainment (John Prine, Bob Dylan).

2 Nightclubs

If you're looking for a more interactive, tuneful night on the town, Washington offers hip jazz clubs, gay bars, warehouse ballrooms, places where you sit back and listen, places where you can get up and dance, even a roadhouse or two. If you're looking for comic relief, Washington can take care of that, too (the pickings are few but good).

Many nightspots wear multiple hats. For example, the Black Cat is a bar and a dance club, offering food and sometimes poetry readings. I've listed each nightspot according to the type of music it features. The details are in the description.

The best nightlife districts are Adams-Morgan; U and 14th streets NW between 16th and 9th streets; north and south of Dupont Circle along Connecticut Avenue; the Penn Quarter, notably 7th and 8th streets and from Pennsylvania Avenue north as far as H Street; Georgetown; and D.C.'s newest bar-and-club scene, H Street NE, between 12th and 14th streets, in the area known as the Atlas District. As a rule, while club-hopping—even in Georgetown—stick to the major thoroughfares and steer clear of deserted side streets.

As stated in the introduction to this chapter, the best sources of information about what's doing at bars and clubs are the *Washington Post*'s "Weekend" edition, online at www.washingtonpost.com, and "Going Out Gurus" blog; the fat weekly, *City Paper,* available free at bookstores, movie theaters, drugstores, and other locations, and online at www.washingtoncitypaper.com; and the blog www.dcist.com. Also check out the monthly *On Tap,* another fat freebie found mostly in bars, but whose website, www.ontaponline.com, is essential reading for carefree 20-somethings. By the way, Thursday night is "College Night" at nearly every club.

Washington's clubs and bars tend to keep their own hours; it's best to call ahead to make sure the place you're headed is open.

COMEDY

In addition to these two comedy venues, the **Warner Theatre** (see "Smaller Auditoriums," above) also features big-name comedians from time to time.

The Capitol Steps *(Moments)* This musical political satire troupe is made up of former Congressional staffers, equal-opportunity spoofers all, who poke endless fun through song and skits at politicians on both sides of the aisle and at government

goings-on in general. Washingtonians have been fans since the Steps got started in 1981. Since then, the troupe has performed more than 5,000 shows and released more than 28 albums, including the latest, "Campaign and Suffering." Shows take place in the Amphitheater, on the concourse level of the Ronald Reagan Building and International Trade Center, at 7:30pm Friday and Saturday. Order tickets from Ticketmaster (✆ **202/397-SEAT** [7328]) or in person at the Visitor Center of the Ronald Reagan Building. 1300 Pennsylvania Ave. NW (in the Ronald Reagan Building). ✆ **202/312-1555.** www.cap steps.com. Tickets $35. Metro: Federal Triangle.

The Improv The Improv features top performers on the national comedy club circuit as well as comic plays and one-person shows. *Saturday Night Live* performers David Spade, Chris Rock, and Adam Sandler have all played here, as have comedy bigs Ellen DeGeneres, Jerry Seinfeld, and Robin Williams. Shows are about 1½ hours long and include three comics (an emcee, a feature act, and a headliner). Showtimes are 8pm Sunday, 8:30pm Tuesday through Thursday, 8 and 10:30pm on Friday and Saturday. The best way to snag a good seat is to have dinner here (make reservations), which allows you to enter the club as early as 7pm Tuesday through Thursday or after 6:30pm Friday through Sunday. The Friday and Saturday 10:30pm show serves drinks and appetizers only. Dinner entrees (nothing higher than $9.95) include sandwiches and Tex-Mex fare. You must be 18 to get in. 1140 Connecticut Ave. NW (btw. L and M sts.). ✆ **202/296-7008.** www.dcimprov.com. Cover $15–$35, plus a 2-item minimum. Metro: Farragut North (L St. exit).

ROCK/INDIE/ALTERNATIVE/HIP-HOP/DJ

This category is mostly about live music clubs, but also includes a sprinkling of night-clubs known for their DJs and dance floors.

The Birchmere Music Hall and Bandstand Worth the cab fare from downtown, if you're a fan of live music by varied, stellar performers, such as Garth Brooks, Dave Matthews, Jerry Jeff Walker, Crash Test Dummies, Shawn Colvin, Joe Sample, and John Hiatt. The Birchmere is unique in the area for providing a comfortable and relatively small (500-seat) setting, where you sit and listen to the music (there's not a bad seat in the house) and order food and drinks. The Birchmere got started about 35 years ago, when it booked mostly country singers. The place has expanded over the years and so has its repertoire; there are still many country and bluegrass artists, but also folk, jazz, rock, gospel, and alternative musicians. The menu tends toward American favorites, such as nachos, burgers, and pulled-pork barbecue sandwiches. Purchase tickets at the box office or online from www.ticketmaster.com. 3701 Mount Vernon Ave., Alexandria, VA. ✆ **703/549-7500.** www.birchmere.com. Ticket prices range $17–$60. Take a taxi or drive.

Black Cat This comfortable, low-key club draws a tattooed, black-clad crowd to its concert hall, which features national, international, and local indie and alternative groups. The place is made for dancing, accommodating more than 600 people. Adjoining the hall is the Red Room Bar, a large, funky, red-walled living-roomy lounge with booths, tables, a red-leather sofa, pinball machines, a pool table, and a jukebox stocked with a really eclectic collection. A college crowd collects on weekends, but you can count on seeing a 20- to 30-something bunch here most nights, including members of various bands who like to stop in for a drink. Black Cat also hosts film screenings, poetry readings, and other quiet forms of entertainment in its ground-floor room called "Backstage," and serves vegetarian food in its smoke-free cafe. Say hello to affable owner Dante Ferrando while you're here. Black Cat is open until 2am

Finds The Best of D.C.'s International Scene

Washington is home to more than 170 embassies and international culture centers, which greatly contribute to the city's cosmopolitan flavor. There are a number of ways to soak up this international scene. First, access the website **www.embassy.org**, then click on "Embassies," which presents you with several options. If you click on "Embassy Row Tour," you'll see a detailed tour nicely outlined for you, leading you past embassies along Massachusetts and New Hampshire avenues, and including information about the neighborhoods, the embassies, and all that you see along the way. You can print the tour and take it with you as you walk.

By clicking on "Foreign Embassies of Washington, D.C.," you pull up a long list of all of the embassies in D.C., ordered alphabetically. Lots of embassies host events that are open to the public, sometimes for free, sometimes at minimal cost. In June 2008, for example, the Swedish Embassy hosted jazz on the roof of its "House of Sweden" building, located on the Georgetown waterfront overlooking the Potomac River. The cost was $25 per person; the experience was priceless.

Finally, you can buy tickets for **Embassy Series** (*(C)* 202/625-2361, www. embassyseries.com) program events. These are world-class (literally), mostly classical music performances hosted by individual embassies, held at the embassy or at the ambassador's residence. Admission tends to be pricier for these events than for those staged separately by the embassy. For instance, a performance by a Portuguese pianist and guitar player in June 2008 took place at the Portuguese ambassador's residence and cost $100 per person, which also covered a lavish buffet and drinks. But so worth it!

Sunday through Thursday, and until 3am Friday and Saturday. Concerts take place 4 or 5 nights a week, beginning at about 8:30pm (call for details). 1811 14th St. NW (btw. S and T sts.). *(C)* **202/667-7960**. www.blackcatdc.com. Cover $5–$20 for concerts; no cover in the Red Room Bar. Metro: U St.–Cardozo (13th and U sts. exit).

DC9 This medium-size venue—which holds 250—debuted in spring 2004, with a commitment to offering both live music and DJ shows. Open nightly, DC9 features both indie rock bands and DJs for dancing, including a popular Liberation Party dance event Friday nights. The two-story club includes a bar downstairs with couches, booths, bar stools, and a digital jukebox of 130,000 tunes; and the hall upstairs reserved for music. 1940 9th St. NW. *(C)* **202/483-5000**. www.dcnine.com. No cover downstairs, $5–$15 cover upstairs, depending on show. Metro: U St.–Cardozo (African American Civil War Memorial/10th St. exit).

Eighteenth Street Lounge This place maintains its "hot" status. First you have to find it, and then you have to convince the bouncer to let you in. So here's what you need to know: Look for the mattress shop south of Dupont Circle, then look up. "ESL" (as those in the know call it) sits above the shop. Wear something exotic and sexy, anything but preppy or jock-ish. If you pass inspection, you may be surprised to find yourself in a restored, century-old mansion (Teddy Roosevelt once lived here) with fireplaces, high ceilings, and a deck out back. Or maybe you'll just get right out

there on the hardwood floors to dance to acid jazz, hip-hop, reggae, or Latin jazz tunes spun by a DJ. Weekends often feature live jazz or bossa nova. 1212 18th St. NW. © 202/466-3922. www.eighteenthstreetlounge.com. Cover $10–$20 Tues–Sat. Metro: Dupont Circle (South/19th St. exit) or Farragut North (L St. exit).

kstreet Lounge You pay for the privilege of partying here: $300 to $500 will reserve you a table and bottle service. (A full bottle of your favorite liquor is delivered to your table with juices, mixes, limes, and glasses, just to make sure that the alcohol flows steadily throughout the evening.) Exclusivity is the name of the game, and if that appeals, call days ahead to book your table, especially for a Saturday romp. Even with a reservation, you might find yourself standing in line for a time. Decor is white minimalist and high-tech, with plasma TVs broadcasting VIP arrivals. Dress code is simply minimal, the tighter and littler the dress, the better, in this beauty-competitive scene. Since there's no dedicated dance floor, dancers shimmy to the DJ beats wherever they find room. Open Monday to Friday after 5pm and Saturday after 10pm. 1301 K St. NW. © 202/962-3933. www.kstreetdc.com. Cover $10 women, $20 men. Metro: McPherson Square (Franklin Sq./14th St. exit).

9:30 Club Housed in a converted warehouse, this major live-music venue hosts frequent record-company parties and features a wide range of top performers. You might catch Sheryl Crow, Simple Minds, the Clarks, Jakob Dylan, Jamie Lidell, Lucinda Williams, or even Tony Bennett. It's open only when there's a show on, which is almost every night (but call ahead), and, obviously, the crowd (as many as 1,200) varies with the performer. Best to buy tickets ($10–$50) in advance, whether at the box office or online. The sound system is state-of-the-art and the sightlines are excellent. There are four bars: two on the main dance-floor level, one in the upstairs VIP room (anyone is welcome here unless the room is being used for a private party), and another in the distressed-looking cellar. The 9:30 Club is a stand-up place, literally— there are few seats. 815 V St. NW (at Vermont Ave.). © 202/393-0930. www.930.com. Metro: U St.–Cardozo (10th St. exit).

Play Lounge For all of the Peters and Wendys out there who never wanna grow up, but who are old enough to drink. Arrive at the right time and you'll find everyone jumping up and down on the furniture. Located on the second floor of a town house in the same block of Connecticut Avenue as 1223 (see listings in "Bars & Lounges," below), Play is all about having a good time. Patrons rave about the DJ's choice of tunes, everything from '80s disco to Kanye West and the Black Eyed Peas. Those not bouncing on couches and ottomans are twirling around the stripper pole or go-go dancing on platforms set against the wall. Like all the latest clubs, Play allows you to reserve your own spot, to the tune of a $500 bar tab. Otherwise, the cover is usually $10. Open after 10pm until 2am Tuesday and Thursday and until 3am Friday and Saturday. You must be 21 and over. 1219 Connecticut Ave. NW. © 202/466-7529. www.playloungedc.com. Cover $10. Metro: Farragut North (L St. exit).

The Red & The Black Located along D.C.'s newest nightlife avenue, H Street NE, this club aims to offer an intimate setting for singer-songwriter acts, although louder indie rock bands frequently appear. The Red & The Black's owners also own the larger DC9 (see above), and it seems to catch that club's alternative sounds overflow. The two-story R&B features a New Orleans–style bar on its first level, with a tin ceiling and red-velvet drape decor, jambalaya on the menu, and Abitas listed among the beers. The music takes the stage nightly upstairs. Drive here or take a taxi. 1212 H St. NE. © 202/399-3201. www.redandblackbar.com. Cover $5–$8.

Rock and Roll Hotel On the same street as The Red & The Black, above, the R&R opened first, attracting devoted music lovers and night crawlers to come shoot pool in its second-floor pool hall, listen to live bands in its 400-person concert hall, or toss back shots in its bar. Washingtonians are loving the punk-rock decor of vintage furniture and flying guitars, but most especially the nightly acts, which range from local garage bands to national groups on tour. *FYI:* "Hotel" is just part of the name, no sleeping here. Drive here or take a taxi. 1353 H St. NE. ✆ 202/388-7625. www.rockandroll hoteldc.com. Cover $8–$15.

JAZZ & BLUES

A calendar of jazz gigs for these and other clubs is posted at **www.dcjazz.com**, although the website can be notoriously out-of-date. For instance, when last I looked, the website did not mention D.C.'s fabulous **Duke Ellington Jazz Festival.** The 2009 event will be its fifth annual. If you're a jazz fan and planning a trip to D.C. in late September/early October, check out the website, www.dejazzfest.org, for exact dates of the weeklong festival, which showcases the talents of at least 100 musicians in various venues around town, leading to a big free concert on the Mall on one of the final days.

Blues Alley Blues Alley, in Georgetown, has been Washington's top jazz club since 1965, featuring such artists as Karrin Allyson, Ahmad Jamal, Sonny Rollins, Wynton Marsalis, Rachelle Ferrell, and Maynard Ferguson. There are usually two shows nightly at 8 and 10pm; some performers also do midnight shows on weekends. Reservations are essential (call after noon); since seating is on a first-come, first-served basis, it's best to arrive no later than 7pm and have dinner. Entrees on the steak and Creole seafood menu are in the $17 to $23 range, snacks and sandwiches are $5.25 to $10, and drinks are $5.35 to $9. The decor is "classic dive": exposed-brick walls; beamed ceiling; small, candlelit tables; and a very worn look about it. Sometimes well-known visiting musicians get up and jam with performers. 1073 Wisconsin Ave. NW (in an alley below M St.). ✆ 202/337-4141. www.bluesalley.com. Cover $16–$75 (most fall in the $20–$40 range), plus a $10 per person food or drink minimum, plus $2.50 per person surcharge. Metro: Foggy Bottom, then walk or take the D.C. Circulator.

Bohemian Caverns Rising from the ashes on the very spot where jazz greats such as Duke Ellington, Billie Holiday, and so many others performed decades ago, Bohemian Caverns hopes to establish that same presence and host today's jazz stars, but has a way to go. The Caverns is actually three venues. Downstairs is the jazz club, whose decor is cavelike, as it was in the '20s. The club's performance schedule seems to fluctuate quite a bit, but when in full swing, hosts two performances nightly. At street level is Mahogany, the restaurant, whose entrees are named after jazz legends and start at about $19. The two upper floors comprise Liv, a nightclub, bar, and hip-hop lounge. 2001 11th St. NW (at U St.). ✆ 202/299-0800. www.bohemiancaverns.com. Cover $15–$22 weekends in the jazz club; $5 Fri, $20 Sat in the nightclub. Metro: U St.–Cardozo (U and 13th St. exit).

HR-57 This cool club is named for the House Resolution passed in 1987 that designated jazz "a rare and valuable national American treasure." More than a club, HR-57 is also the Center for the Preservation of Jazz and Blues. Step inside Wednesday through Saturday evenings for a jazz jam session or star performance. 1610 14th St. NW. ✆ 202/667-3700. www.hr57.org. Cover $6–$12. Metro: U St.–Cardozo (U and 13th St. exit).

Madam's Organ Restaurant and Bar *(Finds* This beloved Adams-Morgan hangout fulfills owner Bill Duggan's definition of a good bar: great sounds and sweaty people. The great sounds feature live music nightly: a funk/jazz/blues group on Sunday

and Monday; Delta bluesman Ben Andrews on Tuesday; bluegrass with Bob Perilla & the Big Hillbilly Bluegrass Band on Wednesday; and the salsa sounds of Patrick Alban or Johnny Artis on Thursday, which is also Ladies' Night. On Friday and Saturday nights, regional blues groups pack the place—hope for Bobby Parker or Cathy Ponton King. The club includes a wide-open bar decorated eclectically with an antique gilded mirror, stuffed fish and animal heads, and paintings of nudes. The second-floor bar is called Big Daddy's Love Lounge & Pick-Up Joint, which tells you everything you need to know. Keep climbing the stairs to the rooftop deck, which is now open all year; you can't hear the music up there, but you'll discover an awesome view. *Other notes:* You can play darts here, and redheads pay half-price for Rolling Rock beer. Food is served, but I'd eat elsewhere. 2461 18th St. NW. (C) 202/667-5370. www.madamsorgan. com. Cover $3–$7. Metro: U St.–Cardozo or Woodley Park–Zoo/Adams-Morgan and catch the Adams-Morgan/U St. Link Shuttle.

Mr. Henry's Capitol Hill Mr. Henry's features Milan Sweet singing standards on Thursday nights, and the Kevin Cordt Trio Friday nights at 8pm; the musicians perform on the second floor of this cozy restaurant. There's no cover, but it's expected that you'll order something off the menu (perhaps a burger or gumbo). Mr. Henry's has been around for 43 years and has always attracted a gay and lesbian clientele, though it's a comfortable place for everyone. 601 Pennsylvania Ave. SE. (C) 202/546-8412. www.mrhenrys restaurant.com. No minimum. Metro: Eastern Market.

Smithsonian Jazz Café *Value* What a treat! The museum that's a must during the day is also a must Friday evenings, 6:30 to 10pm, when the Atrium Café features performances of local jazz pros. Smaller venues, like Blues Alley and HR-57, strictly enforce the "no talking during performance" policy, but the jazz cafe, which holds upward of 300 people, is too big and laid-back for that. It feels like a supper club, complete with couples dancing in front of the stage, only it's a nightclub with no age requirements, so go on and bring the family, if you like—children 12 and under are admitted free. A cash bar and extensive buffet are available. In the National Museum of Natural History, 10th St. NW and Constitution Ave. NW. (C) 202/633-8801. www.mnh.si.edu/jazz. $12 cover, no minimum for food and drink. Metro: Federal Triangle or Smithsonian (Mall exit).

Twins Jazz This intimate, crowded, second-floor jazz club offers live music nearly every night—it's closed on Monday. On weeknights, you'll hear local artists; weekends are reserved for out-of-town acts, such as Bobby Watson, Gil Scott Heron, and James William. Musicians play two shows on Friday and Saturday nights, at 9 and 11pm. Sunday night is a weekly jam session attended by musicians from all over town. The menu features American, Ethiopian, and Caribbean dishes. The age group of the crowd varies. 1344 U St. NW. (C) 202/234-0072. www.twinsjazz.com. Cover $10–$30, with a 2-drink-per-person minimum. Metro: U St.–Cardozo (13th St. exit).

U-topia Unlike most music bars, the arty New York/SoHo–style U-topia is serious about its restaurant operation. A moderately priced international menu ($12–$21 for entrees) features vegetable couscous curry and shrimp jambalaya, not to mention pastas and filet mignon with béarnaise sauce. There's also an interesting wine list and a large selection of beers and single-malt scotches. The setting is cozy and candlelit, with walls used for a changing art gallery show. The eclectic crowd here varies with the music, ranging from early 20s to about 35, for the most part, including South Americans and Europeans. There's live music Tuesday through Sunday, with Thursday always featuring live Brazilian jazz. 1418 U St. NW (at 14th St.). (C) 202/483-7669. www.utopia indc.com. No cover, but $15 per person minimum for drink or food. Metro: U St.–Cardozo (13th St. exit).

Late-Night Bites

If your stomach is grumbling after the show is over, the dancing has ended, or the bar has closed, you can always get a meal at one of a growing number of late-night or all-night eateries.

In Georgetown, the **Bistro Francais**, 3128 M St. NW (*C* 202/338-3830), has been feeding night owls for years; it even draws some of the area's top chefs after their own establishments close. Open until 4am Friday and Saturday, until 3am every other night, the Bistro is thoroughly French, serving steak frites, omelets, and pâtés.

On U Street, **Ben's Chili Bowl** (p. 143), 1213 U St. NW (*C* 202/667-0909), serves up chili dogs, turkey subs, and cheese fries until 4am on Friday and Saturday nights.

In Adams-Morgan one all-night dining option is the **Diner,** 2453 18th St. NW (*C* 202/232-8800), which serves some typical (eggs and coffee, grilled cheese) and not-so-typical (a grilled fresh salmon club sandwich) diner grub.

Finally, in Dupont Circle, stop in at **Kramerbooks & Afterwords Café,** 1517 Connecticut Ave. NW (*C* 202/387-1400), for big servings of everything, from quesadillas to french fries to French toast. The bookstore stays open all night on weekends, and so does its kitchen.

Zoo Bar *(Value* During the day, this establishment located across the street from, you guessed it, the zoo, caters to hungry families, but Thursday through Saturday nights after 10pm, it's a blues joint. Expect a divey setting and an eclectic crowd that skews older. The quality of the music varies: Sometimes you'll stop in and find a serious bluesman from New Orleans, the next night it'll be a local boomer band fronted by a 20-something singer who can really belt it out. If you're looking for a hot club scene, this ain't it. But if you're a blues lover, the Zoo Bar's worth checking out. Plus, it's cheap—no cover—and conveniently located, right on Connecticut Avenue, a short walk from the Woodley Park–Zoo Metro stop on the Red Line. 3000 Connecticut Ave. NW (above Cathedral Ave. NW). *C* 202/232-4225. www.zoobardc.com. No cover. Metro: Woodley Park–Zoo (Woodley and Connecticut Ave. exit).

INTERNATIONAL SOUNDS

Also see Madam's Organ, Smithsonian Jazz Café, and U-topia, in preceding "Jazz & Blues" section.

Chi-Cha Lounge *(Finds* You can sit around on couches, eat Andean-inspired tapas, and listen to live Latin music, which is featured Sunday through Wednesday. (DJ plays Fri–Sat.) Or you can sit around on couches and smoke Arabic tobacco through a 3-foot-high hookah pipe. Or you can just sit around. This is a popular neighborhood place. 1624 U St. NW. *C* 202/234-8400. (Call after 5pm.) www.latinconcepts.com/chicha. No cover. Metro: U St.–Cardozo (13th St. exit).

Habana Village This three-story nightclub has a bar/restaurant on the first floor, where a band plays Latin jazz (Fri–Sat); a bar/dance floor with DJ on the second level; and a salsa-playing combo on the third floor (Fri–Sat). Salsa and merengue lessons are

given Wednesday through Saturday evenings, $10 per lesson. 1834 Columbia Rd. NW. ℭ 202/462-6310. www.habanavillage.com. Cover $6 Fri–Sat after 9:30pm (no cover for women and no cover if you've paid for dinner or dance classes). Metro: U St.–Cardozo or Woodley Park–Zoo/Adams-Morgan, and catch the Adams-Morgan/U St. Link Shuttle.

GAY CLUBS

Dupont Circle is the gay hub of Washington, D.C., with at least 10 gay bars within easy walking distance of one another. Here are three from that neighborhood.

Apex Apex (used to be called "Badlands") is an institution and still going strong as a favorite dance club for gay men. In addition to the parquet dance floor in the main room, the club has at least six bars throughout the first level. Upstairs is the Annex bar/lounge/pool hall, and a show room where karaoke performers commandeer the mic Friday night. 1415 22nd St. NW (at P St.). ℭ 202/296-0505. www.apex-dc.com. Sometimes a cover of $3–$12, depending on the event. Metro: Dupont Circle (South/19th St. exit).

Gazuza Actually, this second-story watering hole with its year-round deck overlooking Connecticut Avenue attracts straights as well as gays, couples as well as singles. Everyone wants to stand up there and survey the scene. The decor is upscale and industrial, but the glass-and-metal look is softened by candlelight and loungy sofas. D.C. doesn't offer lesbians an awful lot of club choices, but Gazuza's a good one. It's nearly right next door to the lesbian bookstore, **Lambda Rising** (p. 239), so if you meet someone there first, you can treat her to a drink just a few steps away at Gazuza. 1629 Connecticut Ave. NW (at Q St.). ℭ 202/667-5500. www.latinconcepts.com/gazuza. Metro: Dupont Circle (Q St. exit).

J.R.'s Bar and Grill This casual and intimate all-male Dupont Circle club draws a crowd that is friendly, upscale, and very attractive. The interior—not that you'll be able to see much of it, because J.R.'s is always sardine-packed—has a 20-foot-high pressed-tin ceiling and exposed-brick walls hung with neon beer signs. The big screen over the bar area is used to air music videos, showbiz singalongs, and favorite TV shows. Every night offers a special something, like the Sunday $2 Skyy Highball all night long or Thursday's Retro night theme with free shots at midnight. The balcony, with pool tables, is a little more laid-back. Food is served daily, until 5pm Sunday and until 7pm all other days. 1519 17th St. NW (btw. P and Q sts.). ℭ 202/328-0090. www.jrswdc.com. Metro: Dupont Circle (Q St. exit).

3 Bars & Lounges

Washington has a thriving and varied bar scene. But just when you think you know all the hot spots, a spate of new ones pop up. If you want to be sure to visit the latest bunch, travel to U Street NW between 9th and 18th streets, and to 14th Street, just off U Street in either direction; to H Street NE, between 12th and 14th streets; and to the Penn Quarter—these are the current favorite areas for revelry in the city. Lounges are all the rage, so be sure to stop in at restaurants such as IndeBleu, Zengo, and Rasika. (See chapter 6 for details and more suggestions.)

If you're in the mood for a sophisticated setting, seek out a bar in one of the nicer hotels, like the **Willard,** the **Sofitel Lafayette Square,** the **Ritz-Carlton Georgetown,** the **Hay-Adams,** and the **St. Regis** (see chapter 5). Otherwise, here is a range of options, from upscale to low-key, but each with its own character.

1223 At swank 1223, hipsters line up at the velvet rope, dressed to catch the eye and convince the doorman to admit them; drinks and food are outrageously high-priced; a soaring ceiling, plush couches, and crystal chandeliers create an opulent interior; and beautiful women servers purr at you, as other beautiful people mill about. Interested? 1223 Connecticut Ave. NW. © 202/822-1800. www.1223.com. Cover $10 after 10pm. Metro: Dupont Circle (South/19th St. exit) or Farragut North (L St. exit).

Big Hunt This casual and comfy Dupont Circle hangout for the 20- to 30-something crowd bills itself as a "happy hunting ground for humans" (read: meat market). It has a kind of *Raiders of the Lost Ark* jungle theme. A downstairs room (where music is the loudest) is adorned with exotic travel posters and animal skins; another area has leopard skin–patterned booths under canvas tenting. Amusing murals grace the balcony level, which adjoins a room with pool tables. The candlelit basement is the spot for quiet conversation. The menu offers typical bar food, and the bar offers close to 30 beers on tap, most of them microbrews. An outdoor patio lies off the back poolroom.
 Note: This place and the Lucky Bar might be the perfect antidotes to their exclusive neighbors down the block, the Eighteenth Street Lounge, Dragonfly, and 1223. If you're rejected there, forget about it and come here. 1345 Connecticut Ave. NW (btw. N St. and Dupont Circle). © 202/785-2333. www.thebighuntdc.com. Metro: Dupont Circle.

Blue Gin Washingtonians still marvel that this buzz-worthy bar/lounge that attracts the likes of Owen Wilson and Vince Vaughn was once the domain of rowdy jocks and Georgetown students in its life as the sports bar Champions. You find it at the back of an alley off of Wisconsin Avenue, near M Street. Downstairs maintains a party atmosphere, where everyone drinks exotic martinis and ends up dancing on tabletops. Upstairs is a laid-back lounge, where you can spy on those below by looking through the glass-inlaid floor, or sit back and watch a film. Blue Gin's a swanky place, so dress accordingly. 1206 Wisconsin Ave. NW (at M St.). © 202/965-5555. www.bluegindc.com. No cover for women, $10 for men after 10pm. Metro: Foggy Bottom, then take the D.C. Circulator, or a cab.

Bourbon *(Finds* North of Georgetown, in the homey area known as Glover Park, is this neighborhood bar that has a comfortable feel to it. The owners have invited their regulars to bring in black-and-white family photos, which they use to adorn the walls. Downstairs is a narrow room and long bar; upstairs is a dining room with leather booths. Fifty bourbons are on offer, along with many fine wines and beers, and the usual complement of bar beverages. Another plus is the rooftop deck. Bourbon has a second location in Adams-Morgan, at 2321 18th St. NW (© **202/332-0800**). 2348 Wisconsin Ave. NW. © 202/625-7770. www.bourbondc.com. Take a taxi.

Brickskeller *(Value* If you like beer and you like choices, head for the Brickskeller, which has been around for about 50 years and offers more than 1,000 beers from around the world. If you can't make up your mind, ask one of the waiters, who tend to be knowledgeable about the brews. The tavern draws students, college professors, embassy types, and people from the neighborhood. Brickskeller is a series of interconnecting rooms filled with gingham-tableclothed tables (upstairs rooms are open only weekend nights). The food is generally okay; burgers are your best bet, especially the Brickburger, topped with bacon, salami, onion, coleslaw, and cheese. 1523 22nd St. NW. © 202/293-1885. www.lovethebeer.com/brickskeller.html. Metro: Dupont Circle (either exit) or Foggy Bottom.

Value Cheap Eats: Happy Hours to Write Home About

Good-value promotions are often available at area bars and nightclubs, such as **Whitlow's on Wilson** in Arlington (see the "Electric Avenues for Live-Music Lovers" box on p. 268), where you can chow down on a half-price burger every Monday, good all day. A step above these are certain restaurants around town that set out tasty bites during happy hour, either free or for an astonishingly low price. Here are three that you might like:

In the bar area only, **McCormick & Schmick's**, 1652 K St. NW, at the corner of 17th Street NW (© 202/861-2233), not far from the White House, order a drink costing $2.50 or more, and you may select from a $1.95, $2.95, or $3.95 bar menu such tasty offerings as oyster shooters, fried calamari, quesadillas, fish tacos, and more. The offer is good Monday through Friday from 3:30 to 7:30pm.

In Georgetown, **Morton's Steakhouse**, 3251 Prospect St. NW, just off Wisconsin Ave. NW (© 202/342-6258), serves up "Power Hour" bar bites, in its Bar 12-21, Monday to Friday, 5 to 6:30pm and 9:30 to 11pm. Drinks are normal price, but the bar bites menu features a variety: cheeseburger trio, four petite filet mignon sandwiches, blue cheese french fries, and so on, each priced at $5 per plate.

In the heart of Dupont Circle neighborhood, at 1343 Connecticut Ave. NW, **Café Citron** (© 202/530-8844) has sweet deals for those with Latino tastes: a range of items, from fried plantains, to fried cheese patties, to Bolivian potato cakes stuffed with beef and cheese, priced between $3 and $7.50. Café Citron's happy hour runs Monday through Friday, 5 to 7pm, and offers special entertainment, such as the flamenco show every Monday and live Latin jazz every Tuesday.

South of Café Citron, at 1990 M St. NW, upscale restaurant **Vidalia** (© 202/659-1990) hosts a wine tasting Monday to Friday, 5:30 to 6:30pm, during which the sommelier pours complimentary sips of excellent wines, accompanied by plates of canapés whipped up by the chef.

Busboys and Poets Salon, bookstore, restaurant, performance space, lounge, bar, political activist hangout: Busboys and Poets is all these things. The name pays tribute to poet Langston Hughes, who worked as a busboy at the Wardman Park Hotel in the 1920s, writing poems on the side. Busboys has been popular right from the start, and a diverse crowd collects here day and night to peck on their laptops, plan the revolution, and listen to spoken-word performances, pausing only to take a sip of a preferred beverage, whether a Corona or champagne. Busboys' success has led owner Andy Shallal to open a second location in Arlington, Virginia (4251 Campbell Ave.; © 703/379-9756); by the time you read this, there's a good chance that Shallal will have opened a third Busboys at 5th and K sts. NW and a restaurant called Eatonville, named after the Florida town where Zora Neale Huston grew up—Eatonville will be located across the street from the original Busboys, and serve African-influenced low-country cuisine. 2021 14th St. NW (at V St.). © 202/387-POET (7638). www.busboysandpoets.com. Metro: U St/Cardozo (13th St. exit).

Clyde's of Gallery Place This enormous new Clyde's, the latest in the local empire that includes a Georgetown branch (see chapter 6), looks like Las Vegas from the outside. Inside, the two-level, 23,000-square-foot salon is filled with eye-catching oil paintings of sailing and equestrian scenes, Tiffany glass, and burnished cherry-wood furnishings. Three bars anchor the place, which is pretty much hopping every night of the week. As big as Clyde's is, it still gets crowded, especially before and after sports events at the Verizon Center, which is in the same block. Late-night prowlers will be happy to know that Clyde's stays open until 2am weekdays, 3am on weekends, with a late-night menu available daily until 1am. 707 7th St. NW (at H St.). © 202/348-3700. www.clydes.com. Metro: Gallery Place/Chinatown (H St./Chinatown exit).

The Dubliner This is your typical old Irish pub, the port you can blow into in any storm, personal or weather-related. It's got the dark-wood paneling and tables, the etched and stained-glass windows, an Irish-accented staff from time to time, and, most importantly, the Auld Dubliner Amber Ale. Most come here to imbibe, but the Dubliner is open daily from breakfast until last call; so if you're hungry, consider the burgers, grilled-chicken sandwich, or fish and chips. The Dubliner is frequented by Capitol Hill staffers and journalists who cover the Hill. Irish music groups play nightly. In the Phoenix Park Hotel, 520 N. Capitol St. NW, with its own entrance on F St. NW. © 202/737-3773. www.dublinerdc.com. Metro: Union Station.

ESPN Zone This is not a date place, unless your date happens to be Anna Kournikova. It's three levels of sports mania, in the form of interactive sports games, a restaurant, 200 televisions throughout the place tuned to sporting events, a bar area, and the most popular attraction, the Screening Room. This last venue offers a giant 16-foot video screen flanked by six 36-inch screens, each showing a different event. Seats with special headphones are arrayed in front of the screen, and you control what you listen to. ESPN Zone is also a sports bar/restaurant serving American staples: burgers, fries, huge salads, chicken tenders, and ribs. 555 12th St. NW. © 202/783-3776. www.espnzone.com/washingtondc. Metro: Metro Center (11th St. exit).

Fadó Another Irish pub, but this one is Ireland as a theme park. The odd thing about it is its location: in the heart of Chinatown. Fadó was designed and built by the Irish Pub Company of Dublin, which shipped everything—the stone for the floors, the etched glass, the milled wood—from Ireland. The pub has separate areas, including an old Irish "bookstore" alcove and a country cottage bar. Authentic Irish food, like potato pancakes, is served with your Guinness. *Fadó,* Gaelic for "long ago," accepts reservations only for large groups. The pub hosts live music performances once a week, usually Thursday nights, when it charges a cover of about $5. (Thurs is the most popular night, so get here early or else gather a group and make a reservation.) 808 7th St. NW. © 202/789-0066. www.fadoirishpub.com. Metro: Gallery Place/Chinatown (H and 7th sts. exit).

Lucky Bar Lucky Bar is a good place to kick back and relax. But, in keeping with the times, it also features free salsa dance lessons on Monday night. Sometimes the music is live, but mostly it's courtesy of a DJ. Other times the jukebox plays, but never so loud that you can't carry on a conversation. The bar has a front room overlooking Connecticut Avenue and a back room decorated with good-luck signs, couches, hanging TVs, booths, and a pool table. Lucky Bar is known in the area as a "soccer bar," with its TVs turned to soccer matches going on around the world. Also: Lucky Bar's happy hour starts at 3pm and continues until 8pm! 1221 Connecticut Ave. NW. © 202/331-3733. www.luckybardc.com. Metro: Dupont Circle (South/19th St. exit) or Farragut North (L St. exit).

Electric Avenues for Live-Music Lovers

Live music venues are ever more popular in the capital, and one neighborhood is particularly noteworthy for the sheer amount and variety of fabulous music on tap on any given night: U Street NW, between 9th and 18th streets, and its side streets. Whether you're a fan of jazz, hip-hop, indie rock, or blues, you're bound to find something to please you just by strolling along the U and 14th street corridors, especially on a Friday or Saturday evening. Bohemian Caverns, HR-57, Twins Jazz, Chi-Cha Lounge, U-Topia, the 9:30 Club, DC9, and the Black Cat are among the clubs listed in this chapter. In another part of town that's come to be known as the "Atlas District," live music venues also are springing up along H Street NE, between 12th and 14th streets (though it must be said that this locale, especially at night, is pretty iffy). Two Atlas District clubs are reviewed in this chapter: The Red & The Black, p. 260, and the Rock and Roll Hotel, p. 261. For a less urban experience, you might also check out a stretch of suburban street in Arlington, Virginia: a section of Wilson Boulevard in the Clarendon neighborhood, roughly between Highland and Edgewood roads. Arlington Row is a lot tamer and tends to attract a crowd of all ages, usually dressed for comfort. And though it's outside the District, the area is easy to reach by Metro. Streets are safer and clubs front the streets with picture windows and aren't as exclusive.

The music is live, it's outstanding (most of the time), and it's here almost nightly. So take the Metro to the Clarendon stop and walk down Wilson, or

Lucky Strike Lanes Drink up and bowl the night away at this bowling alley/lounge in the heart of the Penn Quarter, in the same block as the Verizon Center. Here you'll find a rambunctious crowd cheering, drinking, and giving the game their best shots, as a DJ plays loud hip-hop and R&B tunes. If you have to wait for a lane, which is likely if you haven't called ahead to reserve one, you can lounge on a sofa or banquette, play a game of pool, have a drink or a bite to eat at the 50-foot bar, or watch sports on one of the 10-foot projection screens. The alley opens at 10am Saturday and Sunday and closes at midnight Sunday through Thursday, 3am Friday and Saturday; ages 21 and older after 9pm. 701 7th St. NW. ✆ 202/347-1021. www.bowllucky strike.com. Metro: Gallery Place/Verizon Center (7th and H sts. exit).

Marvin Marvin opened in late 2007 and the crowds came. Downstairs is a bistro that serves Belgian specialties, like steak frites and mussels in wine and beer, and American soul-food favorites, such as shrimp and grits and fried chicken atop a waffle. The split personality derives from namesake Marvin Gaye, the late soul singer and D.C. native, who lived in Belgium for a while. The split personality applies to Marvin's function, as well, for upstairs from the restaurant is a small lounge. Intended as a neighborhood hangout, the bar/lounge is really more like a scenemaker, especially on weekends. Both bistro and lounge are usually packed, although you can at least make reservations for the dining room. DJs play nightly upstairs, mixing Motown and R&B. Fortunately, an expansive patio extends the space and offers more seating and another bar. Saturday and Sunday 10am to 3pm, Sunday to Thursday 5:30 to 11pm,

drive up Wilson from Key Bridge, turn left on Edgewood Road or another side street, and park on the street. Check out these three spots, all within walking distance of each other; all serve food:

Galaxy Hut, 2711 Wilson Blvd. (② **703/525-8646**; www.galaxyhut.com), is a comfortable bar with far-out art on the walls and a patio in the alley. Look for live alternative rock Saturday and Sunday nights; sometimes a $5 cover.

At **IOTA,** 2832 Wilson Blvd. (② **703/522-8340**; iotaclubandcafe.com), the best of the area's bands (if either Little Pink or Last Train Home is performing, go), as well as up-and-coming groups, take the stage nightly in a setting with minimal decor (cement floor, exposed-brick walls, and a wood-beamed ceiling) and a patio in back. There's live music nightly. When a cover is charged, it's usually $8 to $18.

Whitlow's on Wilson, 2854 Wilson Blvd. (② **703/276-9693**; www.whitlows. com), is the biggest spot on the block, spreading throughout four rooms, the first showcasing the music (usually blues, with anything from surfer music to rock thrown in), the other rooms holding coin-operated pool tables, dartboards, and air hockey. Two patios further enlarge Whitlow's. The place has the appearance of a diner, from Formica table-booths to a soda fountain, and serves a range of comfort food, including soul food, pastas, and hamburgers. (Mon half-price burger nights are a good deal—and very popular.). Cover is usually $3 to $5 Thursday through Saturday after 9pm.

Friday to Saturday 5:30pm to midnight. 2007 14th St. NW. ② **202/797-7171**. www.marvindc. com. No cover. Metro: U St/Carodozo (13th St. exit).

Park at 14th　This glass-fronted, four-level restaurant/lounge opened in late 2007, unabashedly promoting itself to celebrities, good-lookers, and for private parties. And it's working. Among those seen partying here have been Washington Wizards player Caron Butler, celebrating his 28th birthday, and comedian Chris Rock, who brought 10 friends with him after he finished his act at Constitution Hall. Luxury is on display, from the leather sofas, to arty glass chandeliers, to accents of mahogany and onyx. Balconies on the second and fourth floors overlook the interior action. Meanwhile, that four-story street-to-roof window front is not intended for those inside to look out, but rather to reveal the celebrating scene to wishful passersby outside. That feature and the velvet rope admission policy emphasize the exclusivity at work. The restaurant has been slow to get going, but that's all right, since for now, the Park is really about socializing. Tuesday to Friday 5pm to closing; Saturday and Sunday 9pm to closing. 920 14th St. NW. ② **202/737-7275**. www.theparkatfourteenth.com. No cover. Metro: McPherson Sq. (Franklin Sq./14th St. exit).

Pour House　This is three separate bars in one. The Pour House, on the first floor, plays on a Pittsburgh theme (honoring the owner's roots), displaying Steeler and Penguin paraphernalia, and drawing Iron City drafts from its tap and pirogi from the kitchen. Downstairs is the Scheisse Haus, a faux biergarten. The basement has pool tables, a bar, and a lounge area (behind beaded curtains); the street level has booths

Wine Bars Woo the Capital

It isn't that Washington didn't have wine bars before now, it's just that, overnight, it seems, we have so many. Pioneers Bistrot Lepic, Mendocino Grille and Wine Bar, and Sonoma, restaurants all, deserve credit for being there first, whetting locals' appetite, perhaps, for the whole idea. Now the city is home to at least 10 wine bars, most of which serve food, while still focusing on the wine. The following list directs you to some of the best:

- **Bistrot Lepic and Wine Bar,** 1736 Wisconsin Ave. NW (✆ **202/333-0111;** www.bistrotlepic.com) The Asian-accented, cozy wine bar and lounge on the second floor of its charming French restaurant offers complimentary tastings every Tuesday, 6 to 8pm. Open daily 5:30pm to midnight.
- **Veritas,** 2031 Florida Ave. NW (✆ **202/265-6270;** www.veritasdc.com) Located at the northern end of Dupont Circle, just off Connecticut Avenue, this tiny, exposed-brick-walled place holds no more than 50 people and serves 70 wines by the glass. A few nibbles are on the menu: small plates of cheeses and charcuterie, and some desserts. Open daily 5pm to closing.
- **Vinoteca Wine Bar and Bistro,** 1940 11th St. NW (✆ **202/332-WINE** [9463], www.vinotecadc.com) Like many of its neighbors in the U Street neighborhood, Vinoteca is open late—until 3am on weekends, 2am all other nights (It opens at 4:30pm.). Its town-house setting offers seating at a bar, on banquettes, in the upstairs lounge, or outside at sidewalk tables. Wine lovers can choose from 68 wines by the glass; a full menu of American cuisine is also available.
- **Cork,** 1720 14th St. NW (✆ **202/265-CORK** [2675], www.corkdc.com) Another cozy place, Cork features no American or Australian wines, choosing instead to highlight "Old World" wines. The bar offers 35 wines by the glass and a menu that serves small plates of light fare, meant for sharing (think french fries, olives, cheeses, and so on.) Wine tastings and classes are also on tap. Open Sunday, Tuesday, and Wednesday 5pm to midnight; Thursday to Saturday 5pm to 1am.

and a bar. On the top floor is "Top of the Hill," which is promoted as "hip and upscale," but it's not, really (although you will find leather chairs, art, and chandeliers here). 319 Pennsylvania Ave. SE. ✆ 202/546-7782. www.pourhouse-dc.com. Metro: Capitol South.

The Tombs Housed in a converted 19th-century Federal-style home, the Tombs, which opened in 1962, is a favorite hangout for students and faculty of nearby Georgetown University. (Bill Clinton came here during his college years.) They tend to congregate at the central bar and surrounding tables, while local residents head for "the Sweeps," the room that lies down a few steps and has red-leather banquettes.

Directly below the upscale 1789 restaurant (p. 153), the Tombs has its own chef, who serves up the usual college fare of burgers, sandwiches, and salads, as well as more serious stuff. 1226 36th St. NW. ✆ 202/337-6668. www.tombs.com. Metro: Foggy Bottom, then take the D.C. Circulator to Wisconsin Ave. and walk from there.

Tryst This is the most relaxed of Washington's lounge bars. The room is surprisingly large for Adams-Morgan, and it's jampacked with worn armchairs and couches, which are usually occupied, no matter what time of day. People come here to have coffee or a drink, get a bite to eat, read a book, or meet a friend. The place feels almost like a student lounge on a college campus, except alcohol is served. A bonus: Tryst offers free wireless Internet service. 2459 18th St. NW. © 202/232-5500. www.trystdc.com. Metro: U St.–Cardozo or Woodley Park–Zoo/Adams-Morgan and catch the Adams-Morgan/U St. Link Shuttle.

Tune Inn *(Finds)* Capitol Hill has a number of bars that qualify as institutions, but the Tune Inn is probably the most popular. Capitol Hill staffers and their bosses, apparently at ease in dive surroundings, have been coming here for cheap beer and greasy burgers since it opened in 1955. (All the longtime Capitol Hillers know that Fri is crab-cake day at the Tune Inn, and they all show up.) 331½ Pennsylvania Ave. SE. © 202/543-2725. Metro: Capitol South.

Side Trips from Washington, D.C.

There's Washington, the District of Columbia, and then there's Washington, the man for whom our nation's capital is named. It's only fitting that a visit to the city of Washington include a tour of George Washington's estate, Mount Vernon, especially since the estate is located only 16 miles south of the capital.

Plan to stop halfway in Old Town Alexandria, either en route or on your return from Mount Vernon, to round out the historical picture of what life was like here in the late 18th century, when Washington came to town to attend church, to dine, and to train his troops; and what life was like in the years that followed.

Founded in 1749, this compact, walkable, waterfront town contains cobblestone streets, Colonial and 19th-century architecture, and historic sites that are open for tours.

Old Town, you'll find, is also very much a modern town, full of of-the-moment eateries and fancy-soaps to fashion-nuts boutiques.

We in Washington tend to take for granted Old Town and Mount Vernon, but you shouldn't miss them. If you're mainly here to take in the capital but have just enough time for a day excursion, cross the Potomac River to visit Old Town Alexandria and Mount Vernon.

1 Mount Vernon

Only 16 miles south of the capital, George Washington's Southern plantation dates from a 1674 land grant to the president's great-grandfather.

ESSENTIALS

GETTING THERE If you're going by car, take any of the bridges over the Potomac River into Virginia and follow the signs pointing the way to National Airport/Mount Vernon/George Washington Memorial Parkway. Travel south on the George Washington Memorial Parkway, the river always to your left, and pass by National Airport on your right. Continue through Old Town Alexandria, where the parkway is renamed "Washington Street," and head 8 miles farther, until you reach the large circle that fronts Mount Vernon.

You might also take a bus or boat to Mount Vernon. **These bus and boat tour prices include the price of admission to Mount Vernon.**

Gray Line Buses (✆ **800/862-1400,** or at Union Station 301/386-8300; www.graylinedc.com) offers two tours daily to Mount Vernon (except Christmas, Thanksgiving, and New Year's Day). One tour lasts 6 hours and travels past Old Town Alexandria to Mount Vernon; the 10-hour tour travels through Washington, stopping at several sites along the way, including the Lincoln Memorial, before ending up at Mount Vernon. Both tours depart at 8am from the bus terminal at Union Station, the shorter tour returning by 2pm, the longer tour returning by 6pm. The ticket kiosk is

on the first level of the parking garage. The cost is $64 per adult, $32 per child for the 10-hour tour, and $45 per adult and $22 per child for the 6-hour tour. The tour is free for children 6 and under. (AAA members receive a 10% discount when they purchase tickets at the Union Station kiosk and show their membership card.) Gray Line offers several other tours, so call for further information.

The **Spirit of Washington Cruises'** (© **202/554-8000;** www.spiritcruises.com) *Spirit of Mount Vernon* leaves from Pier 4 (6th and Water sts. SW; 3 blocks from the Green Line Metro's Waterfront Station) at 8:30am, returning by 3pm, Tuesday through Sunday from March through October. The cost is $43 per adult, $35 per child (ages 6–11; free for younger children).

The **Potomac Riverboat Company's** (© **703/684-0580** or 877/511-2628; www.potomacriverboatco.com) *Miss Christin* operates Tuesday through Sunday April through August, weekends only in September and October. It departs at 10:30am for Mount Vernon from the pier adjacent to the Torpedo Factory, where Union and Cameron streets intersect, at Old Town Alexandria's waterfront. The weekday fare costs $34 per adult, $17 per child (ages 6–11; free for children 5 and under); the weekend rate is $38 per adult, $20 per child. Arrive 30 minutes ahead of time at the pier to secure a place on the boat. The narrated trip takes 90 minutes each way, stopping at Gaylord's National Harbor to pick up and discharge passengers. The boat departs Mount Vernon at 4pm to return to Old Town via Gaylord's.

If you're in the mood for exercise in a pleasant setting, rent a **bike** (see "Biking to Old Town Alexandria & Mount Vernon," on p. 282, for rental locations and other information).

Finally, it is possible to take **public transportation** to Mount Vernon by riding the Metro to the Yellow Line's Huntington Station and proceeding to the lower level, where you catch the Fairfax Connector bus (no. 101) to Mount Vernon. The connector bus departs hourly on weekends, every 30 minutes weekdays; it's a 25-minute ride and costs $1. Call © **703/339-7200** or check www.fairfaxconnector.com for schedule information.

TOURING THE ESTATE

Mount Vernon Estate and Gardens
If it's beautiful out and you have the time, you could easily spend half a day or more soaking in the life and times of George Washington at Mount Vernon. The centerpiece of a visit to this 500-acre estate is a tour through 14 rooms of the mansion, whose oldest part dates from the 1740s. The plantation was passed down from Washington's great-grandfather, who acquired the

Fun Fact **The George Washington Memorial Parkway**

Though few people realize it, the George Washington Memorial Parkway is actually a national park. The first section was completed in 1932 to honor the bicentennial of George Washington's birth. The parkway follows the Potomac River, running from Mount Vernon, past Old Town and the nation's capital, ending at Great Falls, Virginia. Today, the parkway is a major commuter route leading into and out of the city. Even the most impatient driver, however, can't help but notice the beautiful scenery and views of the Jefferson and Lincoln memorials and the Washington Monument that you pass along the way.

land in 1674, to George's half-brother, and eventually to George himself in 1754. Washington proceeded over the next 45 years to expand and fashion the home to his liking, though the American Revolution and his years as president kept Washington away from his beloved estate much of the time.

In fall 2006, the estate opened the Ford Orientation Center and the Donald W. Reynolds Museum and Education Center, which are located just inside the main gate. Much of the complex is built underground so as not to take away from the estate's pastoral setting. A 15-minute film in the orientation center fills you in on the life and character of George Washington. The education center's 25 galleries and theater presentations inform you further about Washington's military and presidential careers, rounding out the whole story of this heroic, larger-than-life man. It's especially helpful to absorb this information and gain some context for the life and times of Washington before setting off for the mansion, where tours are self-guided. Attendants stationed throughout the house and grounds do provide brief orientations and answer questions; when there's no line, a walk-through takes about 20 minutes. What you see today is a remarkable restoration of the mansion, displaying many original furnishings and objects used by the Washington family. The rooms have been repainted in the original colors favored by George and Martha.

After leaving the house, you can tour the outbuildings: the kitchen, slave quarters, storeroom, smokehouse, overseer's quarters, coach house, and stables. A 4-acre exhibit area called "George Washington, Pioneer Farmer" includes a replica of Washington's 16-sided barn and fields of crops that he grew (corn, wheat, oats, and so forth). Docents in period costumes demonstrate 18th-century farming methods. At its peak, Mount Vernon was an 8,000-acre working farm, reminding us that, more than anything, Washington considered himself first and foremost a farmer.

You'll want to walk around the grounds (especially in nice weather) and see the wharf (and take a 40-min. narrated excursion on the Potomac, offered several times a day, seasonally, Apr–Nov; $9 per adult, $5 per child ages 6–11), the slave burial ground, the greenhouse, the lawns and gardens, and the tomb containing George and Martha Washington's sarcophagi (24 other family members are also interred here). In spring 2007, Mount Vernon opened the restored distillery, located 3 miles south of the estate, next to the gristmill. Costumed staff demonstrate 18th-century techniques as they operate the gristmill and distillery, which is open April to October. Admission is $4 per adult and $2 per child, or, when combined with your Mount Vernon admission, $2 per adult and $1.50 per child (ages 6-11; kids 5 and under enter free). Celebrations are held at the estate every year on the third Monday in February, the date commemorating Washington's birthday; admission is free to anyone who shares Washington's birthday, February 22.

Mount Vernon belongs to the Mount Vernon Ladies' Association, which purchased the estate for $200,000 in 1858 from John Augustine Washington, great-grandnephew

Tips Special Activities at Mount Vernon

Events at Mount Vernon, especially in the summer, include tours on 18th-century gardens, slave life, Colonial crafts, or archaeology; and, for children, hands-on history programs and treasure hunts. Call or check the website for schedule details.

of the first president. Without the group's purchase, the estate might have crumbled and disappeared, for neither the federal government nor the Commonwealth of Virginia had wanted to buy the property when it was earlier offered for sale.

Today more than a million people tour the property annually. The best time to visit is off season; during the heavy tourist months (especially in spring), avoid weekends and holidays if possible, and arrive early year-round to beat the crowds.

Southern end of the George Washington Memorial Pkwy. (mailing address: P.O. Box 110, Mount Vernon, VA 22121). © 703/780-2000. www.mountvernon.org. Admission $13 adults, $12 seniors, $6 children 6–11, free for children 5 and under. Apr–Aug daily 8am–5pm; Mar and Sept–Oct daily 9am–5pm; Nov–Feb daily 9am–4pm.

DINING & SHOPPING

Mount Vernon's comprehensive **gift shop** offers a wide range of books, children's toys, holiday items, Mount Vernon private-labeled food and wine, and Mount Vernon licensed furnishings. A **food court** features indoor and outdoor seating and a menu of baked goods, deli sandwiches, coffee, grilled items, pizza, and Mrs. Fields cookies. Although you can't **picnic** on the grounds of Mount Vernon, you can drive a mile north on the parkway to Riverside Park, where there are tables and a lawn overlooking the Potomac. But the Mount Vernon Inn restaurant is the option I'd recommend.

Mount Vernon Inn AMERICAN TRADITIONAL Lunch or dinner at the inn is an intrinsic part of the Mount Vernon experience. It's a quaint and charming Colonial-style restaurant, complete with period furnishings and three working fireplaces. The waiters are all in 18th-century costumes. Lunch entrees range from Colonial turkey "pye" (a sort of Early American stew served in a crock with garden vegetables and a puffed pastry top) to a pulled-pork barbecue sandwich. There's a full bar, and premium wines are offered by the glass. At dinner, tablecloths and candlelight make this a more elegant setting. Choose from soups, perhaps the homemade peanut and chestnut; entrees such as roasted duck served with George Washington's favorite apricot sauce or roast venison with peppercorn sauce; and dessert, such as whiskey cake or English trifle.

Near the entrance to Mount Vernon Estate and Gardens. © 703/780-0011. www.mountvernon.org. Reservations recommended for dinner. Lunch main courses $5.50–$8.50; dinner main courses $14–$25. AE, DISC, MC, V. Daily 11am–3:30pm (11:30am–2:30pm weekdays in winter); Mon–Sat 5–9pm.

2 Alexandria

Old Town Alexandria is about 8 miles S of Washington.

The city of Washington may be named for our first president, but he never lived there. No, he called this other side of the Potomac home from the age of 11, when he joined his half-brother Lawrence, who owned Mount Vernon. Washington came to Alexandria often, helping to survey its 60 acres when he was a lad of 17, training his militia in Market Square, worshiping at Christ Church, and dining and dancing at Gadsby's Tavern.

The town of Alexandria is actually named after John Alexander, the Scot who purchased the land of the present-day town from an English ship captain for "six thousand pounds of Tobacco and Cask." Incorporated in 1749, the town soon grew into a major trading center and port, known for its handsome houses.

Today, many of those handsome houses and the places frequented by George Washington stand at the heart of Old Town, a multimillion-dollar urban renewal historic district. Market Square is the site of the oldest continuously operating farmers'

market in the country. (Go there on Sat btw. 5 and 11am, and you'll be participating in a 257-year-old tradition.) Christ Church and Gadsby's Tavern are still open and operating. Many Alexandria streets still bear their original Colonial names (King, Queen, Prince, Princess, Royal), while others, like Jefferson, Franklin, Lee, Patrick, and Henry, are obviously post-Revolutionary.

Twenty-first-century America thrives in Old Town's many shops, boutiques, art galleries, bars, and restaurants. But it's still easy to imagine yourself in Colonial times by listening for the rumbling of horse-drawn vehicles over cobblestone (portions of Prince and Oronoco streets are still paved with cobblestone); dining on Sally Lunn bread and other 18th-century grub in the centuries-old Gadsby's Tavern; and learning about the lives of the nation's forefathers during walking tours that take you in and out of their houses.

ESSENTIALS

GETTING THERE If you're driving from the District, take the Arlington Memorial or the 14th Street Bridge to the George Washington Memorial Parkway south, which becomes Washington Street in Old Town Alexandria. Washington Street intersects with King Street, Alexandria's main thoroughfare. Turn left from Washington Street onto one of the streets before or after King Street (southbound left turns are not permitted from Washington St. onto King St.), and you'll be heading toward the waterfront and the heart of Old Town. If you turn right from Washington Street onto King Street, you'll find an avenue of shops and restaurants. You can obtain a free parking permit from the Visitors Center (see information about parking in the "Visitor Information" paragraph, below), or park at meters or in garages. The town is compact, so you won't need a car.

The easiest way to make the trip is by Metro, whose Yellow and Blue line trains travel to the King Street station. From the King Street station, you can catch the free King Street Trolley, which operates daily, 10am to 10pm, making frequent stops between the Metro station and the Potomac River. The eastbound AT2 or AT5 blue-and-gold DASH bus (℘ **703/370-DASH** [3274]; www.dashbus.com) marked either OLD TOWN or BRADDOCK METRO will also take you up King Street. Ask to be dropped at the corner of Fairfax and King streets, which will put you right across the street from Ramsay House Visitors Center. The fare is $1 most of the time, but free from Friday evening to Sunday night aboard the colorfully painted Dash About buses. Or you can walk into Old Town, although it's about a mile from the station into the center of Old Town.

VISITOR INFORMATION The **Alexandria Convention and Visitors Association**'s Ramsay House Visitors Center, 221 King St., at Fairfax Street (℘ **800/388-9119** or 703/838-5005; www.funside.com), is open daily from 9am to 8pm (closed Jan 1, Thanksgiving, and Dec 25). Here you can obtain a map/self-guided walking tour and brochures about the area; learn about special events that might be scheduled during your visit and get tickets for them; and receive answers to any questions you might have about accommodations, restaurants, sights, or shopping. The center supplies materials in five languages.

If you come by car, get a free 1-day parking permit here for any 2-hour meter for up to 24 hours. When you park at the Visitors Center, be sure to put money in the meter to cover yourself until you get back outside with your permit. The permit can be renewed for a second day.

Old Town Alexandria

Alexandria Black History
and Resource Center **1**
The Athenaeum **10**
Carlyle House **6**
Christ Church **3**
Friendship Firehouse Museum **13**
Gadsby's Tavern Museum **4**
Lee-Fendall House **2**

The Lyceum **12**
Market Square **5**
Old Presbyterian Meeting House **11**
Ramsay House Visitors Bureau **7**
Stabler-Leadbeater Apothecary
Museum **9**
Torpedo Factory/Alexandria
Archaeology **8**

ORGANIZED TOURS Though it's easy to see Alexandria on your own by putting yourself in the hands of Colonial-attired guides at individual attractions, you might consider taking a comprehensive walking tour. Architectural and history tours leave from the Visitors Center garden, March through November, at least once a day Monday through Saturday, weather permitting. Tours depart at 10:30am, with additional tours added during busy seasons. These walk-up tours (no reservations needed) take 1½ hours and cost $15 per person (free for age 6 and under). You pay the guide when you arrive at the Visitors Center.

Alexandria Colonial Tours (© 703/519-1749; www.alexcolonialtours.com) conducts a number of different tours. Its Ghosts and Graveyard Tour is offered March through November (weather permitting) at 7:30 and 9pm Friday and Saturday, and 7:30pm only on Sunday. A 7:30pm tour is offered Wednesday and Thursday evenings in the summer. This 1-hour tour departs from Ramsay House and costs $10 for adults, $5 for children ages 7 to 17, and is free for children 6 and under. Reservations are recommended, though not required, for these tours; or you can purchase tickets from the guide, who will be dressed in Colonial attire and standing in front of the Visitors Center.

CITY LAYOUT Old Town is very small and laid out in an easy grid. At the center is the intersection of Washington Street and King Street. Streets change from North to South when they cross King Street. For example, North Alfred Street is the part of Alfred north of King Street. Guess where South Alfred Street is.

ALEXANDRIA CALENDAR OF EVENTS

Two organizations publish helpful calendars of key Alexandria events: the **Alexandria Convention and Visitors Association** (© 800/388-9119 or 703/838-4200; www.funside.com), which covers Alexandria at large; and the City of Alexandria's **Office of Historic Alexandria** (© 703/838-4554; www.ci.alexandria.va.us: Click on "Historic Alexandria," then "Tourism and History," then "Historic Events Calendar"), which focuses on the historic sights. You can call and ask them to mail you information, or you can access their separate and continually updated websites. Event highlights include:

February

Alexandria celebrates **George Washington's Birthday** over the course of several days, including Presidents' Weekend, which precedes the federal holiday (usually the third Mon in Feb). Festivities typically include a Colonial costume or black-tie banquet, followed by a ball at Gadsby's Tavern, a 10-kilometer race, special tours, a Revolutionary War encampment at Fort Ward Park (complete with uniformed troops engaging in skirmishes), the nation's largest George Washington Birthday Parade (50,000–75,000 people attend each year), and 18th-century comic opera performances. Most events, such

as the parade and historical reenactments, are free. The Birthnight Ball at Gadsby's Tavern requires tickets for both the banquet and the ball.

March

On the first Saturday in March, King Street is the site of a popular **St. Patrick's Day Parade.**

April

Alexandria celebrates **Historic Garden Week in Virginia** with tours of privately owned local historic homes and gardens the third Saturday of the month. Call the Visitors Center (© 703/838-5005) in early 2009 for more information about tickets and admission prices for the tour.

June

The **Red Cross Waterfront Festival,** the second or third weekend in June, honors Alexandria's historical importance as a seaport and the vitality of its Potomac shoreline today with a display of historic tall ships, ship tours, boat rides and races, nautical art exhibits, waterfront walking tours, fireworks, children's games, an arts-and-crafts show, food booths, and entertainment. Entrance fee.

July

Alexandria's birthday (its 260th in 2009) is celebrated with a concert performance by the Alexandria Symphony Orchestra, fireworks, birthday cake, and other festivities. The Saturday following the Fourth of July. All events are free.

September

Alexandria Festival of the Arts features the ceramics, sculpture, photography, and other works of more than 200 juried artists. On a Saturday and Sunday in early September. Free.

This year is the 68th Annual **Tour of Historic Alexandria Homes,** which takes you to some of the city's most beautifully restored and decorated private homes. Third Saturday in September. Tickets and information from the Visitors Center.

October

Ghost tours take place year-round but pick up around **Halloween.** A lantern-carrying guide in 18th-century costume describes Alexandria's ghosts, graveyards, legends, myths, and folklore as you tour the town and graveyards. Call the Visitors Center for information.

November

There's a **Christmas Tree Lighting** in Market Square usually the Friday after Thanksgiving. The ceremony, which includes choir singing, puppet shows, dance performances, and an appearance by Santa and his elves, begins at 7pm. The night the tree is lit, thousands of tiny lights adorning King Street trees also go on.

December

Holiday festivities continue with the **Annual Scottish Christmas Walk** on the first Saturday in December. Activities include kilted bagpipers, Highland dancers, a parade of Scottish clans (with horses and dogs), caroling, fashion shows, storytelling, booths (selling crafts, antiques, food, hot mulled punch, heather, fresh wreaths, and holly), and children's games. Admission is charged for some events.

The **Historic Alexandria Candlelight Tour,** the second week in December, visits seasonally decorated historic Alexandria homes and an 18th-century tavern. Colonial dancing, string quartets, madrigal and opera singers, and refreshments are part of the celebration. Purchase tickets at the Ramsay House Visitors Center.

There are so many **holiday-season activities** that the Visitors Association issues a special brochure about them each year. Pick one up to learn about decorations, workshops, walking tours, tree lightings, concerts, bazaars, bake sales, crafts fairs, and much more.

WHAT TO SEE & DO

Colonial and post-Revolutionary buildings are Old Town Alexandria's main attractions. My favorites are the Carlyle House and Gadsby's Tavern Museum, but they're all worth a visit.

These sites are most easily accessible via the King Street Metro station, combined with a ride on the DASH bus to the center of Old Town. The exceptions are the

Tips Planning Note

Many Alexandria attractions are closed on Monday.

Alexandria Black History and Resource Center, whose closest Metro stop is the Braddock Street station, and Fort Ward, to which you should drive or take a taxi.

Old Town is second only to Georgetown for the area's best shopping district. Brand-name stores, charming boutiques, antiques shops, art galleries, and gift shops sell everything you might desire. The Visitors Center offers brochures for specific stores as well as a general guide to shopping. Also see chapter 8, which includes some Alexandria shops.

Alexandria Black History Resource Museum In 1940, African Americans in Alexandria staged a sit-in to protest the segregation of blacks from Alexandria's main library. The community built their own public library; this 1940s building now serves as the Black History Resource Museum. The center exhibits historical objects, photographs, documents, and memorabilia relating to black citizens of Alexandria from the 18th century forward. In addition to the permanent collection, the museum presents rotating exhibits and other activities. If you're interested in further studies, check out the center's Watson Reading Room. A half-hour may be enough time to spend at the center.

The museum is actually on the outskirts of Old Town. From here, it makes sense to walk into Old Town, rather than taking the Metro or even a taxi. Have a staff person point you in the direction of Washington Street, east of the center; at Washington Street, turn right (or south) and walk 2 blocks or so to the Lee-Fendall House (p. 283) at Oronoco and Washington streets.

902 Wythe St. (at N. Alfred St.). © 703/838-4356. www.alexblackhistory.org. Free admission (donations accepted). Tues–Sat 10am–4pm. Metro: Braddock Rd. From the station, walk across the parking lot and bear right until you reach the corner of West and Wythe sts., where you'll proceed 5 blocks east along Wythe until you reach the center.

The Athenaeum This grand building, with its Greek Revival architectural style, stands out among the narrow old town houses on the cobblestone street. Built in 1851, the Athenaeum has been many things: the Bank of the Old Dominion, where Robert E. Lee kept his money prior to the Civil War; a commissary for the Union Army during the Civil War; a church; a triage center where wounded Union soldiers were treated; and a medicine warehouse. Now the hall serves as an art gallery and performance space for the Northern Virginia Fine Arts Association. Pop by to admire the Athenaeum's imposing exterior, including the four soaring Doric columns and its interior hall: 24-foot-high ceilings, enormous windows, and whatever contemporary art is on display. This won't take you more than 20 minutes, tops.

201 Prince St. (at S. Lee St.). © 703/548-0035. www.nvfaa.org. Free admission (donations accepted). Thurs–Sun noon–4pm. Closed major holidays.

Carlyle House Historic Park One of Virginia's most architecturally impressive 18th-century homes, Carlyle House also figured prominently in American history. In 1753, Scottish merchant John Carlyle completed the mansion for his bride, Sarah Fairfax of Belvoir, a daughter of one of Virginia's most prominent families. It was designed in the style of a Scottish/English manor house and lavishly furnished. Carlyle, a successful merchant, had the means to import the best furnishings and appointments available abroad for his new Alexandria home.

When it was built, Carlyle House was a waterfront property with its own wharf. A social and political center, the house was visited by the great men of the day, including George Washington. But its most important moment in history occurred in April 1755, when Maj. Gen. Edward Braddock, commander in chief of His Majesty's forces in North America, met with five Colonial governors here and asked them to tax colonists to finance a campaign against the French and Indians. Colonial legislatures refused to comply, one of the first instances of serious friction between America and Britain. Nevertheless, Braddock made Carlyle House his headquarters during the campaign, and Carlyle was less than impressed with him. He called the general "a man of weak understanding . . . very indolent . . . a slave to his passions, women and wine . . . as great an Epicure as could be in his eating, tho a brave man." Possibly these were the reasons his unfinanced campaign met with disaster. Braddock received, as Carlyle described it, "a most remarkable drubbing."

Tours are given on the hour and half-hour and take about 45 minutes; allow another 10 or 15 minutes if you plan to tour the tiered garden of brick walks and boxed parterres. Two of the original rooms, the large parlor and the dining room, have survived intact; the former, where Braddock met the governors, still retains its original fine woodwork, paneling, and pediments. The house is furnished in period pieces; however, only a few of Carlyle's possessions remain. In an upstairs room, an architecture exhibit depicts 18th-century construction methods with hand-hewn beams and hand-wrought nails.

121 N. Fairfax St. (btw. Cameron and King sts.). ℭ 703/549-2997. www.carlylehouse.org. Admission $4 adults, $2 children 12–17, free for children 11 and under. Tues–Sat 10am–4pm; Sun 1–4pm.

Christ Church This sturdy red-brick Georgian-style church would be an important national landmark even if its two most distinguished members had not been Washington and Lee. It has been in continuous use since 1773; the town of Alexandria grew up around this building that was once known as the "Church in the Woods."

Over the years, the church has undergone many changes, adding the bell tower, church bell, galleries, and organ by the early 1800s, and the "wine-glass" pulpit in 1891. For the most part, the original structure remains, including the handblown glass in the windows.

Christ Church has had its historic moments. Washington and other early church members fomented revolution in the churchyard, and Robert E. Lee met here with Richmond representatives to discuss Lee's taking command of Virginia's military forces at the beginning of the Civil War. You can sit in the pew where George and Martha sat with her two Custis grandchildren or in the Lee family pew. You might also want to walk through the graveyard and note how old the tombstones are, including the oldest stone, dated March 20, 1791.

It's traditional for U.S. presidents to attend a service here on a Sunday close to Washington's birthday and sit in his pew. One of the most memorable of these visits took place shortly after Pearl Harbor, when Franklin Delano Roosevelt attended services with Winston Churchill on the World Day of Prayer for Peace, January 1, 1942.

Of course, you're invited to attend a service (Sun at 8, 9, and 11:15am and 5pm; Mon–Fri at 7:15am, with an additional Wed service at 12:05pm). There's no admission charge, but donations are appreciated. A guide gives brief lectures to visitors. A gift shop is open Tuesday through Saturday 10am to 4pm, and Sunday 8:45am to 1pm. Twenty minutes should do it here.

118 N. Washington St. (at Cameron St.). ℭ 703/549-1450. www.historicchristchurch.org. Donations appreciated. Mon–Sat 9am–4pm; Sun 2–4pm. Closed all federal holidays.

Moments **Biking to Old Town Alexandria & Mount Vernon**

One of the nicest ways to view the Washington skyline is from across the river while biking in Virginia. Rent a bike at Thompson's Boat Center, across from the Kennedy Center and right on the bike path, or from some other location listed under "Outdoor Activities," in chapter 7. Hop on the pathway that runs along the Potomac River and head toward the monuments and the Arlington Memorial Bridge. In Washington, this is the Rock Creek Park Trail; when you cross Memorial Bridge (near the Lincoln Memorial) into Virginia, the name changes to the Mount Vernon Trail, which is, not surprisingly, a straight shot to Mount Vernon.

As you tool along, you have a breathtaking view of the Potomac and of Washington's grand landmarks: the Kennedy Center, Washington Monument, Lincoln Memorial, Jefferson Memorial, and the National Cathedral off in one direction, and the Capitol off in the other.

Of course, this mode of transportation is also a great way to see Old Town Alexandria and Mount Vernon. The trail carries you past Reagan National Airport via two pedestrian bridges that take you safely through the airport's roadway system. Continue on to Old Town, where you should lock your bike to a lamppost, walk around, tour some of the historic properties listed in this chapter, and take in some refreshment from one of the many excellent restaurants before you proceed to Mount Vernon. The section from Memorial Bridge to Mount Vernon is about 19 miles in all.

Fort Ward Museum & Historic Site *Kids* A short drive from Old Town is a 45-acre museum and park that transports you to Alexandria during the Civil War. The action here centers, as it did in the early 1860s, on an actual Union fort that Lincoln ordered erected. It was part of a system of Civil War forts called the "Defenses of Washington." About 90% of the fort's earthwork walls are preserved, and the Northwest Bastion has been restored with 6 mounted guns (originally there were 36). A model of 19th-century military engineering, the fort was never attacked by Confederate forces. Self-guided tours begin at the Fort Ward ceremonial gate.

Visitors can explore the fort and replicas of the ceremonial entrance gate and an officer's hut. A museum of Civil War artifacts on the premises features changing exhibits that focus on subjects such as Union arms and equipment, medical care of the wounded, and local war history.

There are picnic areas with barbecue grills in the park surrounding the fort. Living-history presentations take place throughout the year. This is a good stop if you have young children, in which case you could spend an hour or two here (especially if you bring a picnic).

4301 W. Braddock Rd. (btw. Rte. 7 and N. Van Dorn St.). ☎ 703/838-4848. www.fortward.org. Free admission (donations welcome). Park daily 9am–sunset. Museum Tues–Sat 9am–5pm (Nov–Mar 10am–5pm); Sun noon–5pm. Call for information regarding special holiday closings. From Old Town, follow King St. west, go right on Kenwood Ave., then left on W. Braddock Rd.; continue for ¾ mile to the entrance on the right.

Friendship Firehouse Alexandria's first firefighting organization, the Friendship Fire Company, was established in 1774. In the early days, the company met in taverns and kept its firefighting equipment in a member's barn. Its present Italianate-style brick building dates from 1855; it was erected after an earlier building was, ironically, destroyed by fire. Local tradition holds that George Washington was involved with the firehouse as a founding member, active firefighter, and purchaser of its first fire engine, although research does not confirm these stories. The museum displays an 1851 fire engine, old hoses, buckets, and other firefighting apparatus. This is a tiny place that you can easily visit in 20 minutes.

107 S. Alfred St. (btw. King and Prince sts.). (© 703/838-3891. www.oha.alexandriava.gov/friendship. Free admission. Fri–Sat 10am–4pm; Sun 1–4pm.

Gadsby's Tavern Museum ✯ Alexandria was once at the crossroads of 18th-century America. Its social center was Gadsby's Tavern, which consisted of two buildings (one Georgian, one Federal) dating from around 1785 and 1792, respectively. Innkeeper John Gadsby combined them to create "a gentleman's tavern," which he operated from 1796 to 1808; it was considered one of the finest in the country. George Washington was a frequent dinner guest; he and Martha danced in the second-floor ballroom, and it was here that Washington celebrated his last birthday. The tavern also welcomed Thomas Jefferson, James Madison, and the Marquis de Lafayette (the French soldier and statesman who served in the American army under Washington during the Revolutionary War and remained close to Washington). It was the scene of lavish parties, theatrical performances, small circuses, government meetings, and concerts. Itinerant merchants used the tavern to display their wares, and traveling doctors and dentists treated a hapless clientele (these were rudimentary professions in the 18th c.) on the premises.

The rooms have been restored to their 18th-century appearance. On the 30-minute tour, you'll get a good look at the Tap Room, a small dining room; the Assembly Room, the ballroom; typical bedrooms; and the underground icehouse, which was filled each winter from the icy river. Tours depart 15 minutes before and after the hour. Inquire about lantern tours, offered June through August on Friday nights from 7 to 10pm, admission $5, and about special living-history programs. Cap off the experience with a meal right next door, at the restored Colonial-style restaurant, **Gadsby's Tavern,** 138 N. Royal St., at Cameron Street (© **703/548-1288;** www.gadsbystavern restaurant.com).

134 N. Royal St. (at Cameron St.). (© 703/838-4242. www.gadsbystavern.org. Admission $4 adults, $2 children 11–17, free for children 10 and under. Tours Apr–Oct Tues–Sat 10am–5pm, Sun–Mon 1–5pm; Nov–Mar Wed–Sat 11am–4pm, Sun 1–4pm. Closed most federal holidays.

Lee-Fendall House Museum This handsome Greek Revival–style house is a veritable Lee family museum of furniture, heirlooms, and documents. "Light Horse Harry" Lee never actually lived here, though he was a frequent visitor, as was his good friend George Washington. He did own the original lot but sold it to Philip Richard Fendall (himself a Lee on his mother's side), who built the house in 1785.

Thirty-seven Lees occupied the house over a period of 118 years (1785–1903), and it was in this house that Harry wrote Alexandria's farewell address to George Washington, delivered when he passed through town on his way to assume the presidency. (Harry also wrote and delivered the famous funeral oration to Washington that

contained the words "First in war, first in peace, and first in the hearts of his country-men.") During the Civil War, the house was seized and used as a Union hospital.

Thirty-minute guided tours interpret the 1850s era of the home and provide insight into Victorian family life. You'll also see the Colonial garden with its magnolia and chestnut trees, roses, and boxwood-lined paths. Much of the interior woodwork and glass is original.

614 Oronoco St. (at Washington St.). ⓒ 703/548-1789. www.leefendallhouse.org. Admission $4 adults, $2 children 11–17, free for children 10 and under. Tues–Sat 10am–4pm; Sun 1–4pm. Call ahead to make sure the museum is open, since it often closes for special events. Tours on the hour 10am–3pm. Closed Thanksgiving and the month of Jan.

The Lyceum This Greek Revival building houses a museum depicting Alexandria's history from the 17th to the 20th century. It features changing exhibits and an ongoing series of lectures, concerts, and educational programs. You can obtain maps and brochures about Virginia state attractions, especially Alexandria attractions. The knowledgeable staff will be happy to answer questions.

But even without its many attractions, the brick-and-stucco Lyceum merits a visit. Built in 1839, it was designed in the Doric temple style to serve as a lecture, meeting, and concert hall. It was an important center of Alexandria's cultural life until the Civil War, when Union forces appropriated it for use as a hospital. After the war it became a private residence, and still later it was subdivided for office space. In 1969, however, the city council's use of eminent domain prevented the Lyceum from being demolished in favor of a parking lot. Allow about 20 minutes here.

201 S. Washington St. (off Prince St.). ⓒ 703/838-4994. www.alexandriahistory.org. Free admission. Mon–Sat 10am–5pm; Sun 1–5pm. Closed Jan 1, Thanksgiving, and Dec 25.

Old Presbyterian Meeting House Presbyterian congregations have worshiped in Virginia since the Rev. Alexander Whittaker converted Pocahontas in Jamestown in 1614. This brick church was built by Scottish pioneers in 1775. Although it wasn't George Washington's church, the Meeting House bell tolled continuously for 4 days after his death in December 1799, and memorial services were preached from the pulpit here by Presbyterian, Episcopal, and Methodist ministers. According to the Alexandria paper of the day, "The walking being bad to the Episcopal church the funeral sermon of George Washington will be preached at the Presbyterian Meeting House." Two months later, on Washington's birthday, Alexandria citizens marched from Market Square to the church to pay their respects.

Many famous Alexandrians are buried in the church graveyard, including John and Sarah Carlyle; Dr. James Craik (the surgeon who treated—some say killed—Washington, dressed Lafayette's wounds at Brandywine, and ministered to the dying Braddock at Monongahela); and William Hunter, Jr., founder of the St. Andrew's Society of Scottish descendants, to whom bagpipers pay homage on the first Saturday of December. It is also the site of a Tomb of an Unknown Revolutionary War Soldier. Dr. James Muir, minister between 1789 and 1820, lies beneath the sanctuary in his gown and bands.

The original Meeting House was gutted by a lightning fire in 1835, but parishioners restored it in the style of the day a few years later. The present bell, said to be recast from the metal of the old one, was hung in a newly constructed belfry in 1843; and a new organ was installed in 1849. The Meeting House closed its doors in 1889, and for 60 years was used sporadically. But in 1949 it was reborn as a living Presbyterian U.S.A. church, and today the Old Meeting House looks much as it did following its first

restoration. The original parsonage, or manse, is still intact. There's no guided tour. Allow 20 minutes for touring.

321 S. Fairfax St. (btw. Duke and Wolfe sts.). © 703/549-6670. www.opmh.org. Free admission, but you must obtain a key from the office to tour the church. Mon–Thurs 8:30am–4:30pm; Fri 8:30am–1pm. Sun services at 8:30 and 11am, except in summer, when a service is held at 10am.

Stabler-Leadbeater Apothecary Museum When its doors closed in 1933, this landmark drugstore was the second oldest in continuous operation in America. Run for five generations by the same Quaker family (beginning in 1792), the store counted Robert E. Lee (who purchased the paint for Arlington House here), George Mason, Henry Clay, John C. Calhoun, and George Washington among its famous patrons. Gothic Revival decorative elements and Victorian-style doors were added in the 1840s. Today the apothecary looks much as it did in Colonial times, its shelves lined with original handblown gold leaf–labeled bottles (the most valuable collection of antique medicinal bottles in the country), old scales stamped with the royal crown, patent medicines, and equipment for bloodletting. The clock on the rear wall, the porcelain-handled mahogany drawers, and two mortars and pestles all date from about 1790. Among the shop's documentary records is this 1802 order from Mount Vernon: "Mrs. Washington desires Mr. Stabler to send by the bearer a quart bottle of his best Castor Oil and the bill for it."

105–107 S. Fairfax St. (near King St.). © 703/838-3852. www.apothecarymuseum.org. Admission $4 adults, $2 children 11–17, free for children 10 and under. Apr–Oct Tues–Sat 10am–5pm, Sun–Mon 1–5pm; Nov–Mar Wed–Sat 11am–4pm, Sun 1–4pm. Closed major holidays.

Torpedo Factory This block-long, three-story building was built in 1918 as a torpedo shell-case factory but now accommodates some 82 artists' studios, where 165 professional artists and craftspeople create and sell their own works. Here you can see artists at work in their studios: potters, painters, printmakers, photographers, sculptors, and jewelers, as well as those who create stained-glass windows and fiber art.

On permanent display are exhibits on Alexandria history provided by Alexandria Archaeology (© **703/838-4399;** www.alexandriaarchaeology.org), which is headquartered here and engages in extensive city research. A volunteer or staff member is on hand to answer questions. Art lovers may end up browsing for an hour or two.

105 N. Union St. (btw. King and Cameron sts. on the waterfront). © 703/838-4565. www.torpedofactory.org. Free admission. Daily 10am–5pm; archaeology exhibit area Tues–Fri 10am–3pm, Sat 10am–5pm, Sun 1–5pm. Closed Easter, July 4, Thanksgiving, Dec 25, and Jan 1.

ACCOMMODATIONS

With a total of 4,200 hotel guest rooms throughout Alexandria, the city should have no trouble accommodating you, should you decide to stay overnight here. Two properties lie especially close to the heart of historic Old Town. The **Hotel Monaco Alexandria,** at 480 King St. (© **703/549-6080** or 800/KIMPTON; www.kimpton hotels.com), is a former Holiday Inn, recently converted by boutique hotel group Kimpton Hotels into a luxury property with 241 stylish rooms, a pool, health club, and chef-driven restaurant. Rates vary by season and date, but expect to pay from $159 to $179 on the weekends, $199 to $229 weekdays, for a standard double room.

If the Monaco is not available, consider another Kimpton property and standout, **Morrison House,** 116 S. Alfred St. (© **800/367-0800** or 703/838-8000; www. morrisonhouse.com). Its 45 rooms are appointed in high style with canopied

four-poster beds, mahogany armoires, decorative fireplaces, and the like. Rates can start at $175 for the smallest room off season on the weekend and at $289 for a standard room on a weekday in season. Morrison House is known for its restaurant, the **Grille,** which presents award-winning contemporary American cuisine.

For other recommendations, check the **Alexandria Convention and Visitors Association** website, **www.funside.com,** where you can book an online reservation and also read about various promotions that hotels are offering.

DINING

There are so many fine restaurants in Alexandria that Washingtonians often drive over just to dine here. Below is a mix of restaurants to suit assorted budgets, tastes, and styles, but also consider additional suggestions listed below in the box, "More Alexandria Eats."

EXPENSIVE

La Bergerie ⋆ CLASSIC FRENCH WITH BASQUE SPECIALTIES This old-school French restaurant has been here forever and is ever popular. Waiters are tuxedoed and entrees are updated traditional: escargots sprinkled with hazelnuts, smoky foie gras, lobster bisque with lobster and its coral, tournedos of beef with wild mushrooms and béarnaise sauce. La Bergerie is known for its dessert soufflés, which you must request when you order your entrees. You'll want to dress up here. And be sure to order an Irish coffee, which is prepared at your table with flourishes and drama—and it tastes great, too.

218 N. Lee St. ⓒ 703/683-1007. www.labergerie.com. Reservations required. Lunch (prix-fixe menu only) $22; dinner main courses $22–$34. AE, DC, DISC, MC, V. Mon–Sat 11:30am–2:30pm; Mon–Thurs 5:30–9:30pm; Fri–Sat 5:30–10:30pm; Sun 5–9pm.

Restaurant Eve ⋆⋆ MODERN AMERICAN Named for the first child of owners Cathal (the chef) and Meshelle Armstrong, Eve has quickly become everybody's favorite restaurant. It's as hard to book a table here as at CityZen in the District (call 2 months in advance). You choose between dining in the casual bistro and dining in the elegant tasting room, where a five-course menu ($105 per person) and a nine-course menu ($145 per person) are offered. Bistro entrees might include bouillabaisse and sirloin of veal. Tasting-menu items range from butter-poached lobster with heirloom carrots to gnocchi with spring garlic and golden beets. Available at the bar and on the five-course tasting menu is the best dessert: an old-fashioned "birthday cake," which is a mouthwatering slice of white cake layered and iced with pink frosting and sprinkles. Everything is delicious, with excellent service in truly beautiful surrounds. And be sure to read over the wine and cocktails list, since sommelier and "liquid savant" Todd Thrasher has gained such renown for his inventive concoctions—"Millions of Peaches" (peach vodka, champagne vinegar pickled peaches, and poached peaches), "Jose's Yin and Tonic" (made with house-made tonic)—that he's opened a nearby speak-easy lounge, PX, located just above Eamonn's A Dublin Chipper (see below), where he dispenses more fun drinks and good times.

110 S. Pitt St. (near King St.). ⓒ 703/706-0450. www.restauranteve.com. Reservations recommended. Bistro: Lunch items $16–$21; dinner main courses $27–$35; tasting room fixed-price 5-course dinner $105, 9-course dinner $145. Lunch menu served at the bar weekdays 11:30am–4pm for $13. AE, DC, MC, V. Bistro Mon–Fri 11:30am–2:30pm; Mon–Sat 5:30–10pm. Tasting Room Mon–Sat 5:30–9:30pm.

More Alexandria Eats

If any of the above restaurants are booked or don't appeal, consider these other options, all of which win high marks from critics:

A La Lucia, 315 Madison St., © 703/836-5123, www.alalucia.com. Southern Italian cooking in a relaxed atmosphere. This is where area CEOs go when they want to dine anonymously and happily on pizza, veal scaloppini, and the like.

Bastille, 1201 N. Royal St., © 703/519-3776, www.bastillerestaurant.com. Couples especially savor the chic atmosphere, inventive wine cocktails, and delicious French fare, like the pan-seared foie gras with Calvados sautéed apples, of this modern French bistro.

Farrah Olivia, 600 Franklin St., © 703/778-2233, www.farraholiviarestaurant. com. Iron chef contestant Morou Ouattara runs this restaurant—named after his young daughter—serving American cuisine with French, African, and Japanese touches in a setting decorated with an eye toward Ouattara's Ivory Coast background.

Overwood, 220 N. Lee St., © 703/535-3340, www.theoverwood.com. The wood-fired oven turns out fried ravioli, baby back ribs, and other good stuff for Overwood's family and sports fan clientele.

Vermilion, 1120 King St., © 703/684-9669, www.vermilionrestaurant.com. Downstairs appeals to an imbibing bar crowd. Upstairs, though also festive and relaxed, is better suited to conversation and enjoying the excellent American cuisine—try the Cobb salad, the merquez-wrapped lamb loin— prepared by chef Anthony Chittum.

MODERATE

Majestic Café ✸ MODERN/SOUTHERN AMERICAN A lively bar fronts the narrow restaurant, making a dining experience here a little noisy; that can be either annoying or festive, depending on your mood. I promise, though, that you'll enjoy the grilled calamari salad, soft-shell crabs, artichoke and fontina cheese tart, spoon bread, hush puppies, and, for dessert, German chocolate cake. The Majestic was slated to close in 2006, until that dynamic couple Meshelle and Cathal Armstrong, of Restaurant Eve, rode in to the rescue. The Majestic offers a bar lunch special Tuesday through Friday from 11:30am to 2:30pm: any lunch entree for $12; and a Sunday dinner special: $78 for four people and a set menu.

911 King St. (near Alfred St.). © 703/837-9117. www.majesticcafe.com. Reservations recommended. Lunch $11–$21; dinner $19–$26. AE, DC, DISC, MC, V. Sun 11am–3pm; Mon–Sat 11:30am–2:30pm; Mon–Thurs 5:30–10pm; Fri–Sat 5:30–10:30pm; Sun 1–9pm.

INEXPENSIVE

Eamonn's A Dublin Chipper IRISH/SEAFOOD Fish and chips and a few sides—onion rings, coleslaw—that's what we're talking here. But it's charming. Upstairs is PX, an exclusive lounge, where mixologist Todd Thrasher may be on hand

to shake the drinks he's created. This is another in the priceless strand of rare restaurant experiences that Cathal and Meshelle Armstrong are perpetrating on this side of the Potomac. The Chipper is named after their son Eamonn, **Restaurant Eve** (see above) for their firstborn daughter. The Armstrongs have a following, so expect a crowd.

728 King St. © 703/299-8384. www.eamonnsdublinchipper.com. Main courses $3.50–$8. AE, DISC, MC, V. Mon–Wed 11:30am–11pm; Thurs 11:30am–11pm; Fri–Sat 11:30am–midnight.

La Madeleine *(Kids* FRENCH CAFE It may be part of a self-service chain, but this place is charming nonetheless. Its French-country interior has a beamed ceiling, bare oak floors, a wood-burning stove, and maple hutches displaying crockery and pewter mugs. Also, the range of affordable menu items here makes this a good choice for families with finicky eaters in tow.

La Madeleine opens early—at 6:30am every day but Sunday, when it opens at 7am—so come for breakfast to feast on fresh-baked croissants, Danish, scones, muffins, and brioches, or a heartier bacon-and-eggs plate. Throughout the day, there are delicious salads (such as roasted vegetables and rigatoni), sandwiches (including a traditional croque-monsieur), and hot dishes ranging from quiche and pizza to rotisserie chicken with a Caesar salad. After 5pm, additional choices include pastas and specials such as beef tenders *en merlot* or herb-crusted pork tenderloin, both served with garlic mashed potatoes and green beans almondine. Conclude with a yummy fruit tart, or chocolate, vanilla, and praline triple-layer cheesecake with graham-cracker crust. Wine and beer are served.

500 King St. (at S. Pitt St.). © 703/739-2854. www.lamadeleine.com. Reservations not accepted. Breakfast main courses $4.50–$9; lunch and dinner main courses $7–$13. AE, DISC, MC, V. Sun 7am–10pm; Mon–Thurs 6:30am–10:30pm; Fri–Sat 6:30am–11:30pm.

Appendix:
Fast Facts, Toll-Free
Numbers & Websites

1 Fast Facts: Washington, D.C.

AMERICAN EXPRESS There's an American Express Travel Service Office at 1501 K St. NW, entrance on 15th St. NW (© **202/457-1300**).

AREA CODES Within the District of Columbia, it's 202. In Northern Virginia, it's 703. In D.C.'s Maryland suburbs, it's 301. You must use the area code when dialing any number, whether it's a local 202, 703, or 301 phone number.

ATM NETWORKS & CASHPOINTS See "Money & Costs," p. 50.

AUTOMOBILE ORGANIZATIONS Motor clubs will supply maps, suggested routes, guidebooks, accident and bail-bond insurance, and emergency road service. The **American Automobile Association (AAA)** is the major auto club in the United States. If you belong to a motor club in your home country, inquire about AAA reciprocity before you leave. You may be able to join AAA even if you're not a member of a reciprocal club; to inquire, call AAA (© **866/636-2377;** www.aaa.com). AAA has a nationwide emergency road service telephone number (© **800/AAA-HELP** [222-4357]). For travel planning, call © **800/436-4222.**

BUSINESS HOURS Offices are usually open weekdays from 9am to 5pm. Most banks are open from 9am to 3pm Monday through Thursday with some staying open until 5pm; 9am to 5pm on Friday; and sometimes Saturday mornings. Stores typically open between 9 and 10am and close between 5 and 6pm from Monday to Saturday. Stores in shopping complexes or malls tend to stay open late, until about 9pm on weekdays and weekends, and many malls and larger department stores are open on Sundays. (See chapter 8, p. 231, for more specific information about store hours.)

CAR RENTALS See "Toll-Free Numbers & Websites," p. 297.

DRINKING LAWS The legal age for purchase and consumption of alcoholic beverages is 21; proof of age is required and often requested at bars, nightclubs, and restaurants, so it's always a good idea to bring ID when you go out. Liquor stores are closed on Sunday. District gourmet grocery stores, mom-and-pop grocery stores, and 7-Eleven convenience stores often sell beer and wine, even on Sunday.

Bars and nightclubs serve liquor until 2am Sunday through Thursday and until 3am Friday and Saturday.

Do not carry open containers of alcohol in your car or in any public area that

isn't zoned for alcohol consumption. The police can fine you on the spot. And nothing will ruin your trip faster than getting a citation for DUI ("driving under the influence"), so don't even think about driving while intoxicated.

DRIVING RULES See "Getting There & Getting Around," p. 35.

ELECTRICITY Like Canada, the United States uses 110–120 volts AC (60 cycles), compared to 220–240 volts AC (50 cycles) in most of Europe, Australia, and New Zealand. Downward converters that change 220–240 volts to 110–120 volts are difficult to find in the United States, so bring one with you.

EMBASSIES & CONSULATES All embassies are located in the nation's capital, Washington, D.C. If your country isn't listed below, call for directory information in Washington, D.C. (© 202/555-1212) or check **www.embassy.org/embassies**.

The embassy of **Australia** is at 1601 Massachusetts Ave. NW, Washington, DC 20036 (© **202/797-3000;** www.austemb.org). There are consulates in New York, Honolulu, Houston, Los Angeles, and San Francisco.

The embassy of **Canada** is at 501 Pennsylvania Ave. NW, Washington, DC 20001 (© **202/682-1740;** www.canadianembassy.org). Other Canadian consulates are in Buffalo (New York), Detroit, Los Angeles, New York, and Seattle.

The embassy of **Ireland** is at 2234 Massachusetts Ave. NW, Washington, DC 20008 (© **202/462-3939;** www.irelandemb.org). Irish consulates are in Boston, Chicago, New York, San Francisco, and other cities. See website for complete listing.

The embassy of **New Zealand** is at 37 Observatory Circle NW, Washington, DC 20008 (© **202/328-4800;** www.nzembassy.com). New Zealand consulates are in Los Angeles, Salt Lake City, San Francisco, and Seattle.

The embassy of the **United Kingdom** is at 3100 Massachusetts Ave. NW, Washington, DC 20008 (© **202/588-7800;** www.britainusa.com). Other British consulates are in Atlanta, Boston, Chicago, Cleveland, Houston, Los Angeles, New York, San Francisco, and Seattle.

EMERGENCIES Call © **911** for police, fire, and medical emergencies. This is a toll-free call. (No coins are required at public telephones.)

If you encounter serious problems, contact the Travelers Aid Society International (© 202/546-1127; www.travelersaid.org.), a nationwide, nonprofit, social-service organization geared to helping travelers in difficult straits, from reuniting families separated while traveling, to providing food and/or shelter to people stranded without cash, to emotional counseling. Travelers Aid operates help desks at Washington Dulles International Airport (© 703/572-8296), Ronald Reagan Washington National Airport (© 703/417-3975), and Union Station (© 202/371-1937).

GASOLINE (PETROL) At press time, in the U.S., the cost of gasoline (also known as gas, but never petrol), is abnormally high, over $4 a gallon, and expected to remain that high or escalate even higher. Taxes are already included in the printed price. One U.S. gallon equals 3.8 liters or .85 imperial gallons. Fill-up locations are known as gas or service stations.

HOLIDAYS Banks, government offices, post offices, and many stores, restaurants, and museums are closed on the following legal national holidays: January 1 (New Year's Day), the third Monday in January (Martin Luther King, Jr., Day), the third Monday in February (Presidents' Day), the last Monday in May (Memorial Day), July 4 (Independence Day), the first Monday in September (Labor Day), the second

Monday in October (Columbus Day), November 11 (Veterans Day/Armistice Day), the fourth Thursday in November (Thanksgiving Day), and December 25 (Christmas). The Tuesday after the first Monday in November is Election Day, a federal government holiday in presidential-election years (held every 4 years, and next in 2012).

For more information on holidays, see "Washington, D.C., Calendar of Events," in chapter 3.

HOSPITALS If you don't require immediate ambulance transportation but still need emergency-room treatment, call one of the following hospitals (and be sure to get directions): Children's Hospital National Medical Center, 111 Michigan Ave. NW (© 202/476-5000); George Washington University Hospital, 900 23rd St. NW at Washington Circle (© 202/715-4000); Georgetown University Medical Center, 3800 Reservoir Rd. NW (© 202/444-2000); or Howard University Hospital, 2041 Georgia Ave. NW (© 202/865-6100). Also see the "Health" section in chapter 3.

HOT LINES To reach a 24-hour poison-control hot line, call © 800/222-1222; to reach a 24-hour crisis line, call © 202/561-7000; to reach a 24-hour rape crisis line, call © 202/333-7273 (RAPE).

INSURANCE Medical Insurance Although it's not required of travelers, health insurance is highly recommended. Most health insurance policies cover you if you get sick away from home—but check your coverage before you leave.

International visitors to the U.S. should note that unlike many European countries, the United States does not usually offer free or low-cost medical care to its citizens or visitors. Doctors and hospitals are expensive, and in most cases will require advance payment or proof of coverage before they render their services. Good policies will cover the costs of an accident, repatriation, or death. Packages such as **Europ Assistance's "Worldwide Healthcare Plan"** are sold by European automobile clubs and travel agencies at attractive rates. **Worldwide Assistance Services, Inc.** (© 800/777-8710; www.worldwideassistance.com) is the agent for Europ Assistance in the United States. Though lack of health insurance may prevent you from being admitted to a hospital in nonemergencies, don't worry about being left on a street corner to die: The American way is to fix you now and bill the daylights out of you later.

If you're ever hospitalized more than 150 miles from home, **MedjetAssist** (© 800/527-7478; www.medjetassistance.com) will pick you up and fly you to the hospital of your choice in a medically equipped and staffed aircraft 24 hours a day, 7 days a week. Annual memberships are $225 individual, $350 family; you can also purchase short-term memberships.

Canadians should check with their provincial health plan offices or call **Health Canada** (© 866/225-0709; www.hc-sc.gc.ca) to find out the extent of their coverage and what documentation and receipts they must take home in case they are treated in the United States.

Travelers from the U.K. should carry their European Health Insurance Card (EHIC), which replaced the E111 form as proof of entitlement to free/reduced cost medical treatment abroad (© 0845 606 2030; www.ehic.org.uk). *Note:* The EHIC only covers "necessary medical treatment," and for repatriation costs, lost money, baggage, or cancellation, travel insurance from a reputable company should always be sought (www.travelinsuranceweb.com).

Travel Insurance The cost of travel insurance varies widely, depending on the destination, the cost and length of your trip, your age and health, and the type of

trip you're taking, but expect to pay between 5% and 8% of the vacation itself. You can get estimates from various providers through **InsureMyTrip.com**. Enter your trip cost and dates, your age, and other information, for prices from more than a dozen companies.

U.K. citizens and their families who make more than one trip abroad per year may find an annual travel insurance policy works out cheaper. Check **www.moneysupermarket.com**, which compares prices across a wide range of providers for single and multitrip policies.

Most big travel agents offer their own insurance and will probably try to sell you their package when you book a holiday. Think before you sign. **Britain's Consumers' Association** recommends that you insist on seeing the policy and reading the fine print before buying travel insurance. The **Association of British Insurers** (© 020/7600-3333; www.abi.org.uk) gives advice by phone and publishes *Holiday Insurance*, a free guide to policy provisions and prices. You might also shop around for better deals: Try **Columbus Direct** (© 0870/033-9988; www.columbusdirect.net).

Trip Cancellation Insurance Trip-cancellation insurance will help retrieve your money if you have to back out of a trip or depart early, or if your travel supplier goes bankrupt. Trip cancellation traditionally covers such events as sickness, natural disasters, and State Department advisories. The latest news in trip-cancellation insurance is the availability of **expanded hurricane coverage** and the **"any-reason"** cancellation coverage—which costs more but covers cancellations made for any reason. You won't get back 100% of your prepaid trip cost, but you'll be refunded a substantial portion. **Travel-Safe** (© 888/885-7233; www.travelsafe.com) offers both types of coverage. Expedia also offers any-reason cancellation coverage for its air-hotel packages.

For details, contact one of the following recommended insurers: **Access America** (© 866/807-3982; www.accessamerica.com); **Travel Guard International** (© 800/826-4919; www.travelguard.com); **Travel Insured International** (© 800/243-3174; www.travelinsured.com); and **Travelex Insurance Services** (© 888/457-4602; www.travelex-insurance.com).

INTERNET ACCESS Many hotels offer guests free or inexpensive use of computers and Internet access in their business centers. If yours doesn't, find out where the nearest FedEx Kinko's is; these copy shops have computer stations with fully loaded software and Wi-Fi. In Washington's Dupont Circle neighborhood, the Kramerbooks and Afterwords bookstore, 1517 Connecticut Ave. NW (© **202/387-1400**), has one computer available for free Internet access, with a 15-minute time limit. For other listings and locations of Internet kiosks in D.C., check www.cybercaptive.com and www.cybercafe.com. Also see the "Staying Connected" section of chapter 3.

LEGAL AID If you are "pulled over" for a minor infraction (such as speeding), never attempt to pay the fine directly to a police officer; this could be construed as attempted bribery, a much more serious crime. Pay fines by mail, or directly into the hands of the clerk of the court. If accused of a more serious offense, say and do nothing before consulting a lawyer. Here the burden is on the state to prove a person's guilt beyond a reasonable doubt, and everyone has the right to remain silent, whether he or she is suspected of a crime or actually arrested. Once arrested, a person can make one telephone call to a party of his or her choice. International visitors should call your embassy or consulate.

LOST & FOUND Be sure to tell all of your credit card companies the minute you discover your wallet has been lost or

stolen and file a report at the nearest police precinct. Your credit card company or insurer may require a police report number or record of the loss. Most credit card companies have an emergency toll-free number to call if your card is lost or stolen; they may be able to wire you a cash advance immediately or deliver an emergency credit card in a day or two. Visa's U.S. emergency number is ✆ **800/847-2911** or 410/581-9994. American Express cardholders and traveler's check holders should call ✆ **800/221-7282.** MasterCard holders should call ✆ **800/307-7309** or 636/722-7111. For other credit cards, call the toll-free number directory at ✆ **800/555-1212.**

If you need emergency cash over the weekend when all banks and American Express offices are closed, you can have money wired to you via **Western Union** (✆ **800/325-6000;** www.western union.com).

MAIL At press time, domestic postage rates were 27¢ for a postcard and 42¢ for a letter. For international mail, a first-class letter of up to 1 ounce costs 94¢ (72¢ to Canada and Mexico); a first-class postcard costs the same as a letter. For more information go to **www.usps.com** and click on "Calculate Postage."

If you aren't sure what your address will be in the United States, mail can be sent to you, in your name, c/o General Delivery at the main post office of the city or region where you expect to be. (Call ✆ **800/275-8777** for information on the nearest post office.) The addressee must pick up mail in person and must produce proof of identity (driver's license, passport, and so on). Most post offices will hold your mail for up to 1 month, and are open Monday to Friday from 8am to 6pm, and Saturday from 9am to 3pm.

Always include zip codes when mailing items in the U.S. If you don't know your zip code, visit www.usps.com/zip4.

MAPS Free city maps are often available at hotels and throughout town at tourist attractions. You can also contact **Destination DC,** 901 7th St. NW, 4th Floor, Washington, DC 20001 (✆ **202/789-7000;** www.destinationdc.org).

MEDICAL CONDITIONS If you have a medical condition that requires **syringe-administered medications,** carry a valid signed prescription from your physician; syringes in carry-on baggage will be inspected. Insulin in any form should have the proper pharmaceutical documentation. If you have a disease that requires treatment with **narcotics,** you should also carry documented proof with you—smuggling narcotics aboard a plane carries severe penalties in the U.S.

For **HIV-positive visitors,** requirements for entering the United States are somewhat vague and change frequently. For up-to-the-minute information, contact **AIDSinfo** (✆ **800/448-0440** or 301/519-6616 outside the U.S.; www.aidsinfo.nih.gov) or the **Gay Men's Health Crisis** (✆ **212/367-1000;** www.gmhc.org).

NEWSPAPERS & MAGAZINES See p. 27 in chapter 3.

PASSPORTS The websites listed provide downloadable passport applications as well as the current fees for processing applications. For an up-to-date, country-by-country listing of passport requirements around the world, go to the "International Travel" tab of the U.S. State Department at **http://travel.state.gov**. International visitors to the U.S. can obtain a visa application at the same website. *Note:* Children are required to present a passport when entering the United States at airports. More information on obtaining a passport for a minor can be found at http://travel.state.gov. Allow plenty of time before your trip to apply for a passport; processing normally takes 4 to 6 weeks (3 weeks for expedited service)

but can take longer during busy periods (especially spring). And keep in mind that if you need a passport in a hurry, you'll pay a higher processing fee.

For Residents of Australia You can pick up an application from your local post office or any branch of Passports Australia, but you must schedule an interview at the passport office to present your application materials. Call the **Australian Passport Information Service** at 🄯 **131-232,** or visit the government website at www.passports.gov.au.

For Residents of Canada Passport applications are available at travel agencies throughout Canada or from the central **Passport Office,** Department of Foreign Affairs and International Trade, Ottawa, ON K1A 0G3 (🄯 **800/567-6868;** www.ppt.gc.ca). *Note:* Canadian children who travel must have their own passports. However, if you hold a valid Canadian passport issued before December 11, 2001, that bears the name of your child, the passport remains valid for you and your child until it expires.

For Residents of Ireland You can apply for a 10-year passport at the **Passport Office,** Setanta Centre, Molesworth Street, Dublin 2 (🄯 **01/671-1633;** www.irlgov.ie/iveagh). Those age 18 and under and 65 and over must apply for a 3-year passport. You can also apply at 1A South Mall, Cork (🄯 **21/494-4700**) or at most main post offices.

For Residents of New Zealand You can pick up a passport application at any New Zealand Passports Office or download it from their website. Contact the **Passports Office** at 🄯 **0800/225-050** in New Zealand or 04/474-8100, or log on to www.passports.govt.nz.

For Residents of the United Kingdom To pick up an application for a standard 10-year passport (5-year passport for children 16 and under), visit your nearest passport office, major post office, or travel agency or contact the **United Kingdom Passport Service** at 🄯 **0870/521-0410** or search its website at www.ukpa.gov.uk.

POLICE In an emergency, dial 🄯 **911.** For a nonemergency, call 🄯 **202/727-1010.**

SMOKING The District is smoke-free, meaning that the city bans smoking in restaurants, bars, and other public buildings. Smoking is permitted outdoors, unless otherwise noted.

TAXES The United States has no value-added tax (VAT) or other indirect tax at the national level. Every state, county, and city may levy its own local tax on all purchases, including hotel and restaurant checks and airline tickets. These taxes will not appear on price tags.

The sales tax on merchandise is 5.75% in the District, 6% in Maryland, and 5% in Virginia. Restaurant tax is 10% in the District, 6% in Maryland, and varied in Virginia, depending on the city and county. Hotel tax is 14.5% in the District, varied 5% to 8% in Maryland, and averages about 9.75% in Virginia.

TELEGRAPH, TELEX & FAX Telegraph and telex services are provided primarily by **Western Union** (🄯 **800/325-6000;** www.westernunion.com). You can telegraph (wire) money, or have it telegraphed to you, very quickly over the Western Union system, but this service can cost as much as 15% to 20% of the amount sent.

Most hotels have **fax machines** available for guest use (be sure to ask about the charge to use it). Many hotel rooms are wired for guests' fax machines. A less expensive way to send and receive faxes may be at stores such as the **UPS Store.**

TIME The continental United States is divided into **four time zones:** Eastern Standard Time (EST; this is Washington, D.C.'s time zone), Central Standard Time (CST), Mountain Standard Time

(MST), and Pacific Standard Time (PST). Alaska and Hawaii have their own zones. For example, when it's 9am in Los Angeles (PST), it's 7am in Honolulu (HST), 10am in Denver (MST), 11am in Chicago (CST), noon in New York City (EST), 5pm in London (GMT), and 2am the next day in Sydney.

Daylight saving time is in effect from 1am on the second Sunday in March to 1am on the first Sunday in November, except in Arizona, Hawaii, the U.S. Virgin Islands, and Puerto Rico. Daylight saving time moves the clock 1 hour ahead of standard time.

TIPPING Tips are a very important part of certain workers' income, and gratuities are the standard way of showing appreciation for services provided. (Tipping is certainly not compulsory if the service is poor!) In hotels, tip **bellhops** at least $1 per bag ($2–$3 if you have a lot of luggage) and tip the **chamber staff** $1 to $2 per day (more if you've left a disaster area for him or her to clean up). Tip the **doorman** or **concierge** only if he or she has provided you with some specific service (for example, calling a cab for you or obtaining difficult-to-get theater tickets). Tip the **valet-parking attendant** $1 every time you get your car.

In restaurants, bars, and nightclubs, tip **service staff** 15% to 20% of the check, tip **bartenders** 10% to 15%, tip **checkroom attendants** $1 per garment, and tip **valet-parking attendants** $1 per vehicle.

As for other service personnel, tip **cabdrivers** 15% of the fare; tip **skycaps** at airports at least $1 per bag ($2–$3 if you have a lot of luggage); and tip **hairdressers** and **barbers** 15% to 20%.

TOILETS You won't find public toilets or "restrooms" on the streets in most U.S. cities but they can be found in hotel lobbies, bars, restaurants, museums, department stores, railway and bus stations, and service stations. Large hotels and fast-food restaurants are often the best bet for clean facilities. Restaurants and bars in resorts or heavily visited areas may reserve their restrooms for patrons.

USEFUL PHONE NUMBERS See chapter 3 for other helpful information.

U.S. Dept. of State Travel Advisory Ⓒ **202/647-5225** (staffed 24 hr.)

U.S. Passport Agency Ⓒ **202/647-0518**

U.S. Centers for Disease Control International Traveler's Hotline: Ⓒ **404/332-4559**

VISAS For information about U.S. visas go to **http://travel.state.gov** and click on "Visas." Or go to one of the following websites:

Australian citizens can obtain up-to-date visa information from the **U.S. Embassy Canberra,** Moonah Place, Yarralumla, ACT 2600 (Ⓒ **02/6214-5600**) or by checking the U.S. Diplomatic Mission's website at **http://usembassy-australia.state.gov/consular**.

British subjects can obtain up-to-date visa information by calling the **U.S. Embassy Visa Information Line** (Ⓒ **0891/200-290**) or by visiting the "Visas to the U.S." section of the American Embassy London's website at **www.usembassy.org.uk**.

Irish citizens can obtain up-to-date visa information through the **Embassy of the USA Dublin,** 42 Elgin Rd., Dublin 4, Ireland (Ⓒ **353/1-668-8777**), or by checking the "Consular Services" section of the website at **http://dublin.us embassy.gov**.

Citizens of **New Zealand** can obtain up-to-date visa information by contacting the **U.S. Embassy New Zealand,** 29 Fitzherbert Terrace, Thorndon, Wellington (Ⓒ **644/472-2068**), or get the information directly from the website at **http://wellington.usembassy.gov**.

2 Toll-Free Numbers & Websites

MAJOR U.S. AIRLINES
(*flies internationally as well)

Alaska Airlines/Horizon Air
✆ 800/252-7522
www.alaskaair.com

American Airlines*
✆ 800/433-7300 (in U.S. and Canada)
✆ 020/7365-0777 (in U.K.)
www.aa.com

Continental Airlines*
✆ 800/523-3273 (in U.S. and Canada)
✆ 084/5607-6760 (in U.K.)
www.continental.com

Delta Air Lines*
✆ 800/221-1212 (in U.S. and Canada)
✆ 084/5600-0950 (in U.K.)
www.delta.com

Frontier Airlines
✆ 800/432-1359
www.frontierairlines.com

JetBlue Airways
✆ 800/538-2583 (in U.S.)
✆ 080/1365-2525 (in U.K. and Canada)
www.jetblue.com

Midwest Airlines
✆ 800/452-2022
www.midwestairlines.com

Northwest Airlines
✆ 800/225-2525 (in U.S.)
✆ 870/0507-4074 (in U.K.)
www.nwa.com

Sun Country Airlines
✆ 800/800-6557
www.suncountryairlines.com

United Airlines*
✆ 800/864-8331 (in U.S. and Canada)
✆ 084/5844-4777 (in U.K.)
www.united.com

US Airways*
✆ 800/428-4322 (in U.S. and Canada)
✆ 084/5600-3300 (in U.K.)
www.usairways.com

Virgin America*
✆ 877/359-8474
www.virginamerica.com

MAJOR INTERNATIONAL AIRLINES

Aer Lingus
✆ 800/474-7424 (in U.S. and Canada)
✆ 087/0876-5000 (in U.K.)
www.aerlingus.com

Aeroflot
✆ 888/686-4949
www.aeroflot.com

Air Canada
✆ 888/247-2262
www.aircanada.com

Air France
✆ 800/237-2747 (in U.S.)
✆ 800/375-8723 (in U.S. and Canada)
✆ 087/0142-4343 (in U.K.)
www.airfrance.com

Air Jamaica
✆ 800/523-5585 (in U.S. and Canada)
✆ 208/570-7999 (in Jamaica)
www.airjamaica.com

American Airlines
✆ 800/433-7300 (in U.S. and Canada)
✆ 020/7365-0777 (in U.K.)
www.aa.com

ANA
✆ 800/235-9262
www.ana.co.jp/eng

Austrian Airlines
✆ 800/843-0002
www.aua.com

British Airways
✆ 800/247-9297 (in U.S. and Canada)
✆ 087/0850-9850 (in U.K.)
www.british-airways.com

Continental Airlines
✆ 800/523-3273 (in U.S. and Canada)
✆ 084/5607-6760 (in U.K.)
www.continental.com

Copa Airlines
℃ 800/359-2672
www.copaair.com

Delta Air Lines
℃ 800/221-1212 (in U.S. and Canada)
℃ 084/5600-0950 (in U.K.)
www.delta.com

Ethiopian Airlines
℃ 800/445-2733
www.ethiopianairlines.com

Iberia Airlines
℃ 800/722-4642 (in U.S. and Canada)
℃ 087/0609-0500 (in U.K.)
www.iberia.com

KLM Royal Dutch Airlines
℃ 800/225-2525
www.klm.com

Korean Air
℃ 800/438-5000 (in U.S. and Canada)
℃ 0800/413-000 (in U.K.)
www.koreanair.com

Lufthansa
℃ 800/399-5838 (in U.S.)
℃ 800/563-5954 (in Canada)
℃ 087/0837-7747 (in U.K.)
www.lufthansa.com

Qatar Airways
℃ 877/777-2827
www.qatarairways.com

SAS
℃ 800/221-2350
www.flysas.com

Saudi Arabian Airlines
℃ 800/472-8342
www.saudiairlines.com

South African Airways
℃ 271/1978-5313 (international)
℃ 0861/FLYSAA (086/135-9722;
 in South Africa)
www.flysaa.com

TACA
℃ 800/535-8780 (in U.S.)
℃ 800/722-TACA (8222; in Canada)
℃ 087/0241-0340 (in U.K.)
℃ 503/2267-8222 (in El Salvador)
www.taca.com

United Airlines*
℃ 800/864-8331 (in U.S. and Canada)
℃ 084/5844-4777 (in U.K.)
www.united.com

US Airways*
℃ 800/428-4322 (in U.S. and Canada)
℃ 084/5600-3300 (in U.K.)
www.usairways.com

Virgin Atlantic Airways
℃ 800/821-5438 (in U.S. and Canada)
℃ 087/0574-7747 (in U.K.)
www.virgin-atlantic.com

BUDGET AIRLINES
AirTran Airways
℃ 800/247-8726
www.airtran.com

Frontier Airlines
℃ 800/432-1359
www.frontierairlines.com

JetBlue Airways
℃ 800/538-2583 (in U.S.)
℃ 801/365-2525 (in U.K. and Canada)
www.jetblue.com

Southwest Airlines
℃ 800/435-9792 (in U.S., U.K.,
 and Canada)
www.southwest.com

Spirit Airlines
℃ 800/772-7117
www.spiritair.com

Ted (part of United Airlines)
℃ 800/225-5561
www.flyted.com

USA 3000
℃ 877/872-3000
www.usa3000.com

CAR-RENTAL AGENCIES
Alamo
℃ 800/GO-ALAMO (800/462-5266)
www.alamo.com

Avis
℃ 800/331-1212 (in U.S. and Canada)
℃ 084/4581-8181 (in U.K.)
www.avis.com

Budget
℡ 800/527-0700 (in U.S.)
℡ 800/268-8900 (in Canada)
℡ 087/0156-5656 (in U.K.)
www.budget.com

Dollar
℡ 800/800-4000 (in U.S.)
℡ 800/848-8268 (in Canada)
℡ 080/8234-7524 (in U.K.)
www.dollar.com

Enterprise
℡ 800/261-7331 (in U.S.)
℡ 514/355-4028 (in Canada)
℡ 012/9360-9090 (in U.K.)
www.enterprise.com

Hertz
℡ 800/645-3131
℡ 800/654-3001 (for international reservations)
www.hertz.com

National
℡ 800/CAR-RENT (800/227-7368)
www.nationalcar.com

Rent-A-Wreck
℡ 800/535-1391
www.rentawreck.com

Thrifty
℡ 800/367-2277
℡ 918/669-2168 (international)
www.thrifty.com

MAJOR HOTEL & MOTEL CHAINS

Best Western International
℡ 800/780-7234 (in U.S. and Canada)
℡ 0800/393-130 (in U.K.)
www.bestwestern.com

Clarion Hotels
℡ 800/CLARION (800/252-7466)
or 877/424-6423 (in U.S. and Canada)
℡ 0800/444-444 (in U.K.)
www.choicehotels.com

Comfort Inn
℡ 800/228-5150
℡ 0800/444-444 (in U.K.)
www.comfortinn.com

Courtyard by Marriott
℡ 888/236-2427 (in U.S.)
℡ 0800/221-222 (in U.K.)
www.marriott.com/courtyard

Crowne Plaza Hotels
℡ 888/303-1746
www.ichotelsgroup.com/crowneplaza

Days Inn
℡ 800/329-7466 (in U.S.)
℡ 0800/280-400 (in U.K.)
www.daysinn.com

Doubletree Hotels
℡ 800/222-TREE (8733; in U.S. and Canada)
℡ 087/0590-9090 (in U.K.)
www.doubletree.com

Econo Lodge
℡ 800/55-ECONO (800/552-3666)
www.choicehotels.com

Embassy Suites
℡ 800/EMBASSY (800/362-2779)
www.embassysuites1.hilton.com

Fairfield Inn by Marriott
℡ 800/228-2800 (in U.S. and Canada)
℡ 0800/221-222 (in U.K.)
www.marriott.com/fairfieldinn

Four Seasons
℡ 800/819-5053 (in U.S. and Canada)
℡ 0800/6488-6488 (in U.K.)
www.fourseasons.com

Hampton Inn
℡ 800/HAMPTON (800/426-4766)
www.hamptoninn1.hilton.com

Hilton Hotels
℡ 800/HILTONS (800/445-8667; in U.S. and Canada)
℡ 087/0590-9090 (in U.K.)
www.hilton.com

Holiday Inn
℡ 800/315-2621 (in U.S. and Canada)
℡ 0800/405-060 (in U.K.)
www.holidayinn.com

Howard Johnson
℡ 800/446-4656 (in U.S. and Canada)
www.hojo.com

Hyatt
ⓒ 888/591-1234 (in U.S. and Canada)
ⓒ 084/5888-1234 (in U.K.)
www.hyatt.com

InterContinental Hotels & Resorts
ⓒ 800/424-6835 (in U.S. and Canada)
ⓒ 0800/1800-1800 (in U.K.)
www.ichotelsgroup.com

La Quinta Inns and Suites
ⓒ 800/642-4271 (in U.S. and Canada)
www.lq.com

Loews Hotels
ⓒ 800/23-LOEWS (5-6397)
www.loewshotels.com

Marriott
ⓒ 877/236-2427 (in U.S. and Canada)
ⓒ 0800/221-222 (in U.K.)
www.marriott.com

Motel 6
ⓒ 800/4MOTEL6 (466-8356)
www.motel6.com

Omni Hotels
ⓒ 888/444-OMNI (6664)
www.omnihotels.com

Quality
ⓒ 877/424-6423 (in U.S. and Canada)
ⓒ 0800/444-444 (in U.K.)
www.qualityinn.com

Radisson Hotels & Resorts
ⓒ 888/201-1718 (in U.S. and Canada)
ⓒ 0800/374-411 (in U.K.)
www.radisson.com

Ramada Worldwide
ⓒ 888/2-RAMADA (272-6232; in U.S. and Canada)
ⓒ 080/8100-0783 (in U.K.)
www.ramada.com

Red Carpet Inns
ⓒ 800/251-1962
www.redcarpetinns.com

Red Lion Hotels
ⓒ 800/RED-LION (733-5466)
www.redlion.rdln.com

Red Roof Inns
ⓒ 866/686-4335 (in U.S. and Canada)
ⓒ 614/601-4075 (international)
www.redroof.com

Renaissance
ⓒ 888/236-2427
www.renaissancehotels.com

Residence Inn by Marriott
ⓒ 800/331-3131 (in U.S. and Canada)
ⓒ 800/221-222 (in U.K.)
www.marriott.com/residenceinn

Rodeway Inns
ⓒ 877/424-6423
www.rodewayinn.com

Sheraton Hotels & Resorts
ⓒ 800/325-3535 (in U.S.)
ⓒ 800/543-4300 (in Canada)
ⓒ 0800/3253-5353 (in U.K.)
www.starwoodhotels.com/sheraton

Super 8 Motels
ⓒ 800/800-8000
www.super8.com

Travelodge
ⓒ 800/578-7878
www.travelodge.com

Vagabond Inns
ⓒ 800/522-1555
www.vagabondinn.com

Westin Hotels & Resorts
ⓒ 800/937-8461 (in U.S. and Canada)
ⓒ 0800/3259-5959 (in U.K.)
www.starwoodhotels.com/westin

Wyndham Hotels & Resorts
ⓒ 877/999-3223 (in U.S. and Canada)
ⓒ 050/6638-4899 (in U.K.)
www.wyndham.com

Index

See also Accommodations and Restaurant indexes, below.

FROMMER'S® PORTABLE GUIDES

Acapulco, Ixtapa & Zihuatanejo
Amsterdam
Aruba, Bonaire & Curacao
Australia's Great Barrier Reef
Bahamas
Big Island of Hawaii
Boston
California Wine Country
Cancún
Cayman Islands
Charleston
Chicago
Dominican Republic

Florence
Las Vegas
Las Vegas for Non-Gamblers
London
Maui
Nantucket & Martha's Vineyard
New Orleans
New York City
Paris
Portland
Puerto Rico
Puerto Vallarta, Manzanillo &
 Guadalajara

Rio de Janeiro
San Diego
San Francisco
Savannah
St. Martin, Sint Maarten, Anguila
 St. Bart's
Turks & Caicos
Vancouver
Venice
Virgin Islands
Washington, D.C.
Whistler

FROMMER'S® CRUISE GUIDES

Alaska Cruises & Ports of Call

Cruises & Ports of Call

European Cruises & Ports of Call

FROMMER'S® NATIONAL PARK GUIDES

Algonquin Provincial Park
Banff & Jasper
Grand Canyon

National Parks of the American West
Rocky Mountain
Yellowstone & Grand Teton

Yosemite and Sequoia & Kings
 Canyon
Zion & Bryce Canyon

FROMMER'S® WITH KIDS GUIDES

Chicago
Hawaii
Las Vegas
London

National Parks
New York City
San Francisco

Toronto
Walt Disney World® & Orlando
Washington, D.C.

FROMMER'S® PHRASEFINDER DICTIONARY GUIDES

Chinese
French

German
Italian

Japanese
Spanish

SUZY GERSHMAN'S BORN TO SHOP GUIDES

France
Hong Kong, Shanghai & Beijing
Italy

London
New York
Paris

San Francisco
Where to Buy the Best of Everythi

FROMMER'S® BEST-LOVED DRIVING TOURS

Britain
California
France
Germany

Ireland
Italy
New England
Northern Italy

Scotland
Spain
Tuscany & Umbria

THE UNOFFICIAL GUIDES®

Adventure Travel in Alaska
Beyond Disney
California with Kids
Central Italy
Chicago
Cruises
Disneyland®
England
Hawaii

Ireland
Las Vegas
London
Maui
Mexico's Best Beach Resorts
Mini Mickey
New Orleans
New York City
Paris

San Francisco
South Florida including Miami &
 the Keys
Walt Disney World®
Walt Disney World® for
 Grown-ups
Walt Disney World® with Kids
Washington, D.C.

SPECIAL-INTEREST TITLES

Athens Past & Present
Best Places to Raise Your Family
Cities Ranked & Rated
500 Places to Take Your Kids Before They Grow Up
Frommer's Best Day Trips from London
Frommer's Best RV & Tent Campgrounds in the U.S.A.

Frommer's Exploring America by RV
Frommer's NYC Free & Dirt Cheap
Frommer's Road Atlas Europe
Frommer's Road Atlas Ireland
Retirement Places Rated

Love Inspired

The Farmer's Instant Family

Jeremiah Stoltzfus hopes the Amish community of Harmony Creek will provide a fresh start… until days before closing on his new farm, he finds a beautiful trespasser. Mercy Bamberger claims the property is hers, promised by her late *grossdawdi*. Jeremiah can't turn out the single mom and her daughter, nor can he leave. His solution: temporarily sharing the farm until ownership is settled. Once a city kid adopted by a Mennonite family, Mercy yearns to make the farm a haven for unwanted children. But living beside the handsome Amish farmer has her yearning for everything that's eluded her… laughter, love and a forever family.

AMISH HEARTS:
Love comes to Lancaster County

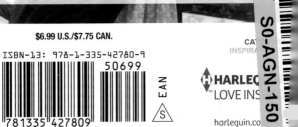

$6.99 U.S./$7.75 CAN.

ISBN-13: 978-1-335-42780-9

50699

9 781335 427809

EAN

S

S0-AGN-150

CAT
INSPIRA

HARLEQ
™ LOVE INS

harlequin.co

COMING NEXT MONTH FROM
Love Inspired®

Available January 16, 2018

A MAN FOR HONOR
The Amish Matchmaker • by Emma Miller

Luke Wheeler shows up on Honor King's doorstep determined to get the Amish widow to forgive him for leaving her at the altar—and to give him a second chance. But this time it's not just Honor he needs to win over, but her four rambunctious kids. Can Luke show Honor that he's the perfect match for her family?

A COWBOY FOR THE TWINS
Cowboys of Cedar Ridge • by Carolyne Aarsen

Looking for a fresh start, widow Shauntelle Dexter moves home with her twin daughters—and makes plans to open a restaurant. With his construction experience, cowboy Noah Cosgrove is persuaded to become Shauntelle's contractor—despite their families' tragic history. With matchmaking twins on a mission, will this be Shauntelle and Noah's chance to build a future?

HILL COUNTRY REUNION
by Myra Johnson

When Diana Matthew decides to spearhead a pets-for-therapy program at her aunt's assisted-living facility, it means joining forces with veterinarian Tripp Willoughby. Diana thought she'd marry Tripp—until he ended their relationship. Tripp is happy to be growing closer to Diana again, but will the secret he's kept all these years tear them apart once more?

HER SECRET DAUGHTER
Grace Haven • by Ruth Logan Herne

Josie Gallagher gave her daughter up for adoption years ago to a sweet couple. So why is hotel project manager—and bachelor—Jacob Weatherly the guardian to little Addie? While working together, Josie is determined to uncover the truth. What she finds is a need to become a permanent part of their family.

THE LAWMAN'S RUNAWAY BRIDE
Comfort Creek Lawmen
by Patricia Johns

Police chief Chance Morgan can't believe Comfort Creek's mayoral decree that he work with Sadie Jenkins on the town's ceremony for fallen soldiers—not when everyone knows she left his now-deceased brother at the altar. As they spend time together, will Chance's guilt over his feelings for the pretty event planner prevent him from his own happily-ever-after?

THE BACHELOR'S BABY
Liberty Creek • by Mia Ross

Desperate for a job, pregnant Lindsay Holland discovers the one open position in town is with the boyfriend she left behind years ago. Brian Calhoun is focused on making his family's blacksmith business a success. And although being near Lindsay unleashes a flood of memories, is he ready to open his heart to the woman who once broke it?

LOOK FOR THESE AND OTHER LOVE INSPIRED BOOKS WHEREVER BOOKS ARE SOLD, INCLUDING MOST BOOKSTORES, SUPERMARKETS, DISCOUNT STORES AND DRUGSTORES.

LICNM0118

ISBN-13:978-1-335-42780-9

42780

0 65373 94955 4

"I'm not going to relinquish my family's farm to you or anyone else."

"But—"

"We moved in a couple of days ago. We're not giving it up." Mercy crossed her arms over her chest. "It's our *home*."

Jeremiah had to select his words with care. He didn't know if he'd be allowed to close on the farm as scheduled. He'd never heard of a person dying before property was transferred.

Until he spoke with his real estate agent and got her advice, he didn't know what the outcome of this sticky situation would be. Mercy wasn't going to back down. That much was clear. If their situations were reversed, he suspected he'd be as unwilling to compromise. He *was* unwilling to compromise.

There wasn't room to. Either the farm was going to be his...or it wasn't.

A pleasant warmth buzzed through him again as his gaze connected with hers. He looked away. Until he knew what was going to happen with the farm, he needed to keep his distance.

Jo Ann Brown has always loved stories with happily-ever-after endings. A former military officer, she is thrilled to have the chance to write stories about people falling in love. She is also a photographer and travels with her husband of more than thirty years to places where she can snap pictures. They have three children and live in Florida. Drop her a note at joannbrownbooks.com.

Books by Jo Ann Brown

Love Inspired

Amish Hearts

Amish Homecoming
An Amish Match
His Amish Sweetheart
An Amish Reunion
A Ready-Made Amish Family
An Amish Proposal
An Amish Arrangement

Love Inspired Historical

Matchmaking Babies

Promise of a Family
Family in the Making
Her Longed-For Family

Sanctuary Bay

The Dutiful Daughter
A Hero for Christmas
A Bride for the Baron

An Amish Arrangement

Jo Ann Brown

HARLEQUIN® LOVE INSPIRED®

LOVE INSPIRED BOOKS

ISBN-13: 978-1-335-42780-9

An Amish Arrangement

www.Harlequin.com

Then the Lord put forth His hand, and touched my mouth. And the Lord said unto me, "Behold, I have put My words in thy mouth."
—*Jeremiah* 1:9

For Leon Barkley,
one of my first friends.
Together we learned softball from my dad
and basketball from your brother.
Thanks for your help with my real estate
questions and making this story possible.

A special thank-you to Tina, Melissa and Dina,
who have shared my love for the
Stoltzfus family right from the beginning
and made each book better.

Chapter One

Harmony Creek Hollow, New York

The day had started out as Jeremiah Stoltzfus had planned.

It didn't stay that way after a woman dropped into his arms.

For most men, playing the hero for a beautiful woman would have been a dream come true. But most men didn't discover that woman trespassing on a tumbledown farm in northern New York. A farm Jeremiah couldn't wait to call his own.

He'd been invited by the current owner to visit when he reached Harmony Creek. In a couple of days the farm would be his.

At dawn Jeremiah had left his family's home in Paradise Springs, Pennsylvania. He was joining others to build a new Amish settlement near the Vermont border. He'd made arrangements during

the past few months, purchasing the farm based on a few photographs sent by his Realtor. After saying goodbye to his *mamm*, brothers and sisters along with their spouses and *kinder* and knowing it was unlikely he'd see them again for a year, he'd taken a train north to Albany. There, he was met by a van, which drove him the last fifty miles to Harmony Creek Hollow.

The valley edging the creek was set outside the tiny town of Salem. Rolling hills covered with trees and meadows would support dairy farms for the Amish families moving into the area.

The owner of the sixty-acre farm he was buying, Rudy Bamberger, had invited him to stop by before the closing in two days. Jeremiah suspected the old man wanted to size him up first.

Rudy had already asked him a lot of questions through Kitty Vasic, Jeremiah's Realtor. Personal questions that Kitty told Jeremiah he didn't have to answer. However, Jeremiah had no problem with the questions, because the old man had been selling his family's farm. Jeremiah had written a long letter, explaining his background and his plans for the farm and his future. His answers must have satisfied Rudy, because the old man accepted his offer on the farm the next day.

When he'd arrived, Jeremiah had carried his two bags as he crossed the snowy yard past ne-

glected barns. No tracks had been visible. Nothing had gone in or out of the big barn since the last snowstorm. Allowing himself a quick glance at the other outbuildings, which needed, as he'd known, a lot of repairs, he'd walked through the freshly fallen snow to the main house.

The large rambling home had a porch running along the front and the side facing the barn. Through a stand of spruce trees, he could see another house, where a tenant family once would have lived. The few remaining shutters hung awkwardly at the windows, a sure sign the house was a fixer-upper, too.

He looked forward to beginning—and finishing—the tasks ahead of him as he made the farm viable again. His skills as a woodworker would be useful while renovating the barns and the sap house near the sugar bush farther up the hill.

Climbing onto the porch, he'd set down his bags before he knocked snow off his well-worn work boots. He'd gone directly to the side door. Rudy had told him to use that door when he arrived.

"Don't knock," the most recent letter had instructed him. "My ears don't work like they used to, and I don't want you standing in the cold while you bang and bang. Come in and give a shout."

He'd thrown the door open. "Rudy, are you here?"

A shriek had come from close to the ceiling.

He'd looked up to see a ladder wobbling. A dark-haired woman stood at the very top, her arms windmilling.

He leaped into the small room as she fell. After years of being tossed shocks of corn and hay bales, he caught her easily. He jumped out of the way, holding her to him as the ladder crashed to the linoleum floor. His black wool hat tumbled off his head and rolled toward the wall.

"Oh, my!" gasped the woman.

She was, he noted because her face was close to his, very pretty. Her pleated *kapp* was flat unlike the heart-shaped ones his sisters wore. Beneath it, her hair was so black it gleamed with bluish fire in the fading sunlight coming through the door and tall windows. Her brown eyes were large with shock in her warmly tanned face, where a few freckles emphasized her high cheekbones. She wore a pale pink dress with white and green flowers scattered across it in a subtle pattern. No Amish woman from Paradise Springs would use such fabric. It must be allowed in the new settlement along Harmony Creek. What else would be different here?

But first things first.

"Are you okay?" he asked, not surprised she wasn't the only one who sounded breathless. His heart had slammed against his chest when he saw her teetering. And from the moment he'd looked

into her lustrous eyes, taking a deep breath had seemed impossible.

"I'm fine. I had just a little farther to go. Just a little..." Her voice trailed away as the shuddering ladder, which had landed on its side, clattered to the floor.

Jeremiah frowned. There was nothing on the wall to prevent her from falling. He saw the ruined wallpaper and chipped crown molding along with scraps of paper she'd already pulled off were piled on the floor. Why was she tearing off wallpaper in Rudy's house?

"Who are you?" he asked at the same time she did.

"I'm Jeremiah Stoltzfus," he answered. "You are...?"

"Mercy Bamberger." Her face shifted into a polite smile, and he guessed she'd collected her wits that had been scattered by fear. "Thanks for catching me."

"Why are you here?"

Instead of answering, she said, "You can put me down."

Jeremiah was astonished his curiosity about why she was in what would be his house had let him forget—for a second—that he was still cradling her in his arms. He set her on her feet, but caught her by the elbow when she trembled like a slim branch in a thunderstorm.

Hearing uneven thumps upstairs and hoping they heralded Rudy's arrival, he steered her to the left. There, a staircase was half-hidden behind a partially closed door. Seating her on the bottom step, he picked up his hat as he asked, "Are you all right?"

"I am."

He didn't believe her, because her skin had a gray tint and her voice quivered. He wouldn't push her, because he guessed she was embarrassed by the circumstances. But one question remained: What was Mercy Bamberger doing in his house?

"Bamberger?" he asked aloud. "Like Rudy Bamberger?"

"Yes. Do you know my grandfather?"

Well, that explained who she was and why she was in the house. Glancing up the stairs, his eyes widened when he saw a shadow slip across the top. It was far too small for a grown man and appeared to have four legs.

He watched, saying nothing as he realized the silhouette belonged to a *kind*. A little girl, who looked about seven years old, had braided hair as black as Mercy's. She leaned on metal crutches with cuffs to go around her skinny arms. Her legs were encased in plastic and Velcro from the tops of her black sneakers to her knobby knees. Who was she?

As if he'd asked the question aloud, the lit-

tle girl cried, "Mommy!" Rushing at a pace that forced his heart into his throat again, because he feared she'd fall, the *kind* flung her arms around Mercy's neck. "Are you okay?"

"I'm fine," Mercy reassured her.

The *kind* glanced at him with a scowl. "I heard the ladder fall and—"

"I'm fine, Sunni." She hugged the little girl. "Jeremiah kept me from getting hurt."

"Who?"

"Jeremiah." Mercy pushed herself to her feet and swung the little girl off the steps. She kept herself between the *kind* and him, showing she didn't trust him though he'd saved her from a broken bone or worse. "He's Jeremiah." Without looking at him, she added, "Jeremiah, this is my daughter, Sunni."

Again he fought not to ask the questions battering at his lips. The *kind* was unquestionably Asian, and her eyes, like Mercy's, glistened like dark brown mud in a sun-washed puddle. She also wore plain clothing with a small print.

Comprehension struck him. Mercy and her daughter weren't Amish. They dressed like the Mennonite women who lived near Paradise Springs. He searched his mind, but couldn't recall if his Realtor had mentioned anything about Rudy living plain. He glanced up at the electric

light hanging from the ceiling. Some plain folks used electricity.

Too many questions needed answers.

Right away.

"Hi, Sunni," he said, because he didn't want to upset the little girl or her *mamm* more.

She aimed another frown at him before turning her back on him. When she didn't answer him, Mercy asked the *kind* why she'd been upstairs. He thought she was dismayed the little girl had gone on the stairs by herself until Mercy said, "Be extra careful. Don't forget the floors aren't safe."

"I stayed away from those, Mommy." Sunni raised her left crutch and tapped the floor beside her. "I do that to check before I go in." Without a pause, she asked, "Can I have a cookie?"

"One," Mercy said with a smile. "Put the bag clip on after you get your cookie."

"Okaaaay," Sunni replied in the same tone Jeremiah had used as a *kind* when his own *mamm* said something he deemed obvious.

He smiled, but again the little girl acted as if he were invisible before she drew her arms from the cuffs on the crutches. Leaning them against the wall, she hurried through a doorway to the right. He guessed it must lead to the kitchen.

His grin vanished as he glanced around the room. Rudy called it his everything room. Hooks on the wall showed where coats, hats and bonnets

could be hung. The bare floor was scraped from years of barn boots on it, and the tattered wallpaper was a grubby white. It might once have been a brighter color. The room was furnished with a rickety table and a battered sofa covered with a worn blanket. A desk had a book under one leg to keep it steady on the sloping floor. The interior of the house was in worse condition than the outside. The photographs sent by the Realtor had been misleading.

Had he failed to examine them closely enough in his eagerness to buy the farm and get started on making his dream come true? No, he'd peered at each picture through a magnifying glass to discover every detail. He knew the kitchen cabinets were painted dull brown, and there was electricity in the house. He planned to remove the latter as soon as the papers were signed.

Jeremiah picked up the ladder and raised it against the wall again. Checking it was solidly in place, he looked at Mercy. He was curious why she was peeling paper off the wall in what would be his house. He could understand if she wanted to take one of the pictures of the farm hanging on a fake brick wall behind the desk, because the farm was her *grossdawdi*'s. In the silence, the *tick-tock* of a wall clock in the kitchen was loud.

Jeremiah appraised the room again. He intended to use it for the farm's office, as he guessed Rudy

had. It was one plan among the many he had. His brothers teased him about having to have every detail set in place before he acted, but trying to find knots in a piece of wood before he began working on it had kept him from wasting time when building a piece of furniture. Being as cautious in his other endeavors seemed wise.

Though he knew, too well, the best of plans could fall apart. He'd thought his future was set with Emmarita Kramer, but she'd jumped the fence and married an *Englisch* guy she'd met at an auction Jeremiah had taken her to. She never broke the courtship off with Jeremiah, just left. He should forgive her and forget his shock, but when he hadn't been able to do either, he'd decided on a clean start in the new Harmony Creek settlement.

Hearing a throat cleared and knowing Mercy was trying to get his attention, he turned. She was shorter than he'd realized. The top of her head barely reached his shoulder. As she stuck several vagrant strands of black hair beneath her pleated *kapp*, she regarded him coolly. She was, he could tell from the set of her taut lips, as curious about him as her daughter had been.

He had a lot of things he wanted to ask her, too, but he waited for her to speak first.

She took one step, then another toward him, though she was at a disadvantage because she had to tilt her head to meet his eyes. Then, seeing the

determination in them, he wondered if she saw her height as a liability or a way to surprise those who underestimated her.

"You never answered my question," she said.

"Which one?" He couldn't remember what she'd asked him, and he refused to be put on the defensive in what would be his own home.

"The important one. What are you doing here?"

"I came to see Rudy Bamberger." He frowned. "You said he's your *grossdawdi*."

She nodded.

"Then I'm surprised he didn't tell you I'd be coming here today."

"Why?"

He didn't think she was being cagey on purpose. Until now, she'd been straightforward. "He invited me to come and look around."

She shook her head. "I don't understand why."

"Didn't he tell you he's selling me his farm?"

Mercy Bamberger was shocked speechless. Had she hit her head when she'd dropped into Jeremiah Stoltzfus's strong arms after trying to grab another strip of wall-paper? She'd made a mess of this conversation from the get-go.

With the ancient Adirondacks to the west and the gentle Green Mountains to the east, the farm had been a haven for her from the first time she'd come to visit the man she called Grandpa Rudy. It

offered the very thing she'd lost and didn't think she'd ever find again. Home. How desperate she'd been for a sanctuary! And how precious it seemed as the promise she'd held within her heart for the past decade was being fulfilled.

She couldn't mess it up. Already she'd made the mistake of not keeping a closer eye on Sunni. Her daughter had been born with a congenital curiosity not diminished by her physical challenges. Mercy's determination that the little girl should do anything a regular kid could allowed Sunni to indulge her quick and inquiring mind. Telling Sunni not to investigate the rooms upstairs because the floors were unsafe must have convinced her to find out how dangerous they were.

Mercy was letting herself get distracted by a handsome stranger who appeared to be a few years older than her twenty-five years. His bright blue eyes that had been shadowed by his black wool hat identified him as one of the Amish farmers moving into the hollow. Grandpa Rudy had told her about the new settlement in one of his letters. He'd been writing to her every week since she was eleven years old, the year she'd been adopted by his son and daughter-in-law and given a chance to have a new life and the loving family she'd feared she'd never have again.

She was startled how far up she had to look to meet Jeremiah's eyes. Few Amish men she'd met

had been as tall as he was. If his ruddy hair hadn't been cut in the plain style and he wasn't wearing a simple light blue shirt along with black suspenders and broadfall trousers beneath his black coat, she wouldn't have guessed this very good-looking man was Amish.

Scolding herself, she recalled how Graham Rapp was easy on the eyes, too, but he'd broken her heart by showing how much a "mama's boy" he was by choosing his mother when Mercy refused to be second. She must not let herself be beguiled by an attractive man again. Not when so much was on the line with her plans for the farm and the changes it could make in many young lives.

But the Amish were well-known for their honesty. So why was Jeremiah talking nonsense about Grandpa Rudy selling him the farm?

"I think you're mistaken," she said, hoping her voice didn't quake with the strong emotions rushing through her like lightning in a summer sky. "My grandfather didn't mention anything about selling Come Along Farm."

"Come Along Farm?"

"That's the name he gave the farm when I was little. He urged us to come along and keep up with him while he did chores, so we called it Come Along Farm."

"He didn't tell you he's selling me the farm?"

"No!"

"I'm sorry to take you by surprise," he said gently, "but I'll be closing the day after tomorrow."

"Impossible!" Her voice squeaked, and she took a steadying breath. Sounding as young as Sunni wouldn't help. And she didn't want her raised voice to bring her daughter from the kitchen to investigate. The little girl was upset enough already to have to leave their Mennonite community and Mercy's parents in central New York, and Mercy hadn't missed the glares Sunni had shot at Jeremiah. When she and Graham ended their ill-advised engagement, her daughter had been caught up in the aftermath and no longer trusted men she didn't know. Mercy's attempts to reassure Sunni that the little girl had nothing to do with the breakup hadn't helped.

"It's not impossible. I've got the paperwork in my suitcase on the porch. If you want to see it—"

"I don't have interest in seeing what can't be legitimate. It sounds as if someone has played a horrible prank on you, Jeremiah. I'm sorry." She was, because she guessed he'd traveled for hours or days to get there. "But the farm's not for sale."

He opened his mouth to protest, then closed it. Taking a deep breath, he released it. In a calm tone she doubted she could emulate, he said, "There's no sense in arguing. Why don't you get your *grossdawdi*, and we'll settle this?"

"I can't."

"Why not?"

She blinked on sudden tears. "Because he's dead."

When Jeremiah's face became ashen, Mercy wondered if she should tell him to take a seat. It must have been seconds, but it felt like a year before he asked, "Rudy is dead?"

"Yes." She swallowed hard past the lump in her throat.

"When?"

"Last week. It was a massive heart attack. He was buried the day before yesterday." As she spoke, she found it impossible to believe the vital, vigorous man was gone.

Rudy Bamberger had been more than a grandfather to her. He'd been her best friend, the one who had welcomed her into the family after her life had hit bottom. Rudy hadn't been a replacement for *Abuelita*, her beloved grandmother who had raised her when she was called Mercedes in a tiny apartment in the Bronx. *Abuelita* had died two weeks after Mercy's tenth birthday, and everything in Mercy's life had changed, including her name. Yet, Grandpa Rudy had made her feel as if she belonged among the people who were so different from those she'd known in the city. His love had been unconditional, and she'd returned it.

"I'm sorry," Jeremiah said with sincerity.

She wished he'd been trite instead of genuine, because one thing hadn't changed. He wanted to take away the farm that was her final gift from Grandpa Rudy. How often she'd sat on the old man's lap and talked about taking care of the apple orchard or making maple syrup as he did each spring or what color she would paint the big bedroom! He'd humored her, even when her paint choices went from pink to purple to red and black over the years.

But Jeremiah was saying her grandfather had intended to sell the farm to him.

"But Grandpa Rudy told me the farm would be mine after he passed away."

"Then why would he sign a purchase agreement with me?"

Mercy shook herself from her mental paralysis. She hated admitting she couldn't guess why her grandfather would break his promise to her.

"Mommy, what's wrong?"

Shocked she hadn't noticed Sunni in the kitchen doorway, Mercy put her arm around her daughter's narrow shoulders. "Nothing that can't be fixed," she replied with a smile.

Over the child's head, she shot Jeremiah a frown, warning him not to upset Sunni. She didn't want her daughter to feel as if her world was being taken away from her—again—as it must have when Sunni traveled from Korea to what was sup-

posed to be her forever home. It hadn't been, because her adoptive parents, who'd changed her name from Kim Sun-Hee to Sunni, couldn't handle having a daughter who wore leg braces. Sunni had been returned to social services as if she were a set of curtains that didn't match the furniture. A disrupted adoption was the name given to it. Or a failed placement. The latter fit better, because it sure felt like a failure for the child involved.

As Mercy had learned herself fifteen years ago when she'd been the one given away by what she'd thought would be her forever family. If the Bambergers hadn't been there to take her in… No, she didn't want to think of that awful time.

Again, she warned herself to focus on the present, not the past. And her and Sunni's future. She had to stop letting her emotions take over. She needed to be logical. Building Come Along Farm into a retreat for city kids would require her to face a lot of bureaucracy on local and state levels. She must be ready to stand up for what she wanted.

"Sunni, if you go and get the book we were reading, I'll meet you in the living room once I'm finished here."

The little girl looked from her to Jeremiah, then nodded. "Okay, Mommy."

Mercy said nothing as Jeremiah watched Sunni hobble away. There was no pity in his expression,

and she was grateful. Too many people felt sorry for Sunni, calling her a "poor little thing." Sunni was one of the strongest people Mercy knew and had learned to walk through perseverance and hard work. If only Mercy could help her heal from the emotional wounds she'd suffered, but those would take more time.

As soon as the little girl was out of earshot, Mercy said, "I guess I should see the purchase agreement you say my grandfather signed."

Jeremiah hooked a thumb toward the door. "Give me a minute, and I'll dig out the paperwork I've got."

She considered locking the door, but that wouldn't solve the problem. Instead, she held the door open while he brought in two scuffed duffel bags.

Closing the door, she said nothing while he opened one bag and found a manila envelope. He withdrew a sheaf of pages and sorted through them. In the middle of the stack, he pulled out several and offered them to her.

"Here's everything I got from your *grossdawdi* through my Realtor," he said without a hint of emotion.

Mercy didn't look to discover if compassion had slipped into his gaze. This time, for her. She wanted it no more than Sunni would have. When he handed her the pages, his work-roughened skin

brushed against her fingers. Sensation arced between them like electricity, and she jerked her hand away. Being attracted to the man who insisted he was buying her family's farm would be stupid.

If he had the same reaction, she couldn't tell, because she carefully kept her gaze on the papers. She scanned each page, her heart sinking lower and lower. Everything looked aboveboard, and she recognized her grandfather's scrawled signature on the bottom of each page. She didn't stop to decipher every bit of legalese, but grasped enough to know Grandpa Rudy was selling the farm to Jeremiah Stoltzfus.

Just as Jeremiah claimed.

"But my grandfather died," she whispered. "Doesn't that change things?"

"I don't know. This is the first time I've ever bought property." He gave her a lopsided grin that lifted her traitorous heart once more.

Paying it no attention, she returned the papers to him and he put them in his bag. No one could answer the question gnawing at her most. Why would her grandfather promise her the property and then decide to sell it without telling her? She'd often mentioned her plans for the farm. Hadn't he read her letters? Yes, he had, because he'd responded to things in them. But never, she realized with a jolt of dismay, had he written anything

about her intention to make Come Along Farm a sanctuary for city youngsters like the one she'd enjoyed when she was a Fresh Air kid years ago, escaping for two amazing weeks each summer from the steam bath of the Bronx.

"I'm not sure what we should do," he said when she remained silent.

"Me, either." For the first time she looked straight into his brilliantly blue eyes. He must realize what she was about to say she meant with all her heart. "However, you need to know I'm not going to relinquish my family's farm to you or anyone else."

"But—"

"We moved in a couple of days ago. We're not giving it up." She crossed her arms over her chest. "It's our *home*."

Chapter Two

Jeremiah had to select his words with care. He didn't know if he'd be allowed to close on the farm as scheduled. He'd never heard of a person dying before property was transferred, because in Paradise Springs most farms were handed down from one generation to the next.

As Mercy said Rudy had meant to do with this farm. He'd changed his mind, but why?

Until he spoke with Kitty Vasic, his Realtor, and got her advice, he didn't know what the outcome of this sticky situation would be. Mercy wasn't going to back down. That much was clear. If their situations were reversed, he suspected he'd be as unwilling to compromise. He *was* unwilling to compromise.

There wasn't room to. Either the farm was going to be his…or it wasn't.

"It's late," he said when he realized Mercy was

waiting for him to say something. "I doubt Kitty's office is open. Do you know anyone nearby who has a phone I could use?"

As if in answer to him, a faint ringing came from beyond the living room. He glanced at Mercy and saw she was as surprised as he was at the unexpected sound.

"Phone!" called Sunni. "I'll get it."

"No! I'll get it." Mercy spun on her heel and ran toward the sound.

Jeremiah followed, too curious to wait. He paid no attention to the large living room as he went after Mercy through what looked like a storage room and then into a bedroom. It was draped in shadows, but a single greenish light glared off to one side.

Mercy grabbed the cordless phone and jabbed at a button. Holding it to her ear, she asked, "Hello?"

The faint buzz of a voice reached him, but he couldn't discern words. His eyes widened when she held the phone out to him.

"It's for you," she said.

"For me?"

"Yes, unless you know another Jeremiah Stoltzfus."

He knew three others in Paradise Springs alone. Taking the phone, he said, "This is Jeremiah Stoltzfus."

"Hi, Jeremiah," replied a strained female voice.

"This is Kitty Vasic. I know Rudy invited you to the farm, so I thought I'd catch you there. We need to talk. Rudy Bamberger is dead."

"*Ja*, I know." He glanced toward Mercy, but she'd gone to stand by a window. Talking about this was uncomfortable. For him, the farm and his future were at stake, but she'd lost her *grossdawdi*. He didn't like the idea of losing his opportunity to buy this farm, but he also disliked the idea of taking Mercy's home.

"I've got something tonight I can't get out of," Kitty said. "How about I come over tomorrow afternoon?"

"Tomorrow afternoon should be fine." What else could he say?

"Good. I'll meet you at the farm around one."

He thanked her. Tilting the phone toward the faint light coming through the window, he found the button to end the call. He set it in its holder. It chirped once, and then its glow faded.

"That was my Realtor," Jeremiah said. "She's coming over tomorrow afternoon around one to discuss what happens next."

A soft click sounded in the room before a lamp came on by the side of a bed with a headboard taller than he was. It was carved with a great tree filled with birds and other beasts gathered below it. He realized the lamp must have been connected to a timer.

"I can make myself scarce," Mercy replied.

He shook his head. "Don't. You should be here so you can ask Kitty your questions. In fact, you should contact the Realtor your *grossdawdi* used and have him here."

"I have no idea who that is."

"His name is on the paperwork I signed. Why don't I get it? It might have his phone number. You can call him and get him here, too."

She rubbed her hands together. "Thank you, Jeremiah. You're being nice about this."

"Me? You didn't throw me out on my ear when I barged in."

When she smiled, it was as if another dozen lights had turned on. "I couldn't throw you out after you saved me from my own foolishness."

The pleasant warmth buzzed through him again as his gaze connected with hers. He looked away. Until he knew what was going to happen with the farm, he needed to keep his distance.

Turning on his heel, he went to where he'd left his bags. He'd get the information she needed and then…

And then what?

Tell her he'd planned to stay here tonight? He couldn't insist Mercy and her little girl find another place tonight. He wasn't sure what, under the circumstances, would happen if he left the property before the disposition of the farm was

decided. Possession being nine-tenths of the law…
or something like that.

He paused as he saw an overhead photo of the
farm. His gaze riveted on the tenant house. It was
the answer to tonight's impasse.

Digging among the stack of legal forms, he
found the purchase agreement. He paged through
it to find Rudy's Realtor's name and contact infor-
mation. There! He pulled a pencil out of his pocket
along with the small notebook that he kept handy
to take notes when someone ordered a piece of
furniture. Though he planned to concentrate on
farming, he knew he'd be doing woodworking on
the side until he could get his first crop harvested.
His hand tools and small power tools were on their
way to Harmony Creek. As he wrote the name and
number of Rudy's Realtor, he hoped he wouldn't
have to ship those heavy crates back unopened.

He handed the information to Mercy, who nod-
ded her thanks. Returning the papers in the en-
velope, he dropped it into the open bag. He drew
the strings to close it and looked at Mercy. She
was as serious as a sinner confessing in front of
the *Leit*. Maybe it was for the best she didn't smile
again. He was too fascinated by the high arch of
her cheekbones and her dark eyes.

"It's getting late," he said. "We're not going
to settle this tonight. It makes sense for you and

your little girl to stay here. I'll sleep in the tenant house."

Her eyes widened. "That's very kind, Jeremiah, but I'm not sure there's heat in the tenant house."

"I can figure out something." He glanced around the room. "Do you have blankets?"

"There are plenty upstairs. Help yourself." After she'd given him directions to the linen closet and he started for the stairs in the narrow space behind the door, she added, "Be careful. Like I told Sunni, the floors aren't as sturdy as they should be."

"I'll take my cue from her and test the floors before I step on them." He hurried upstairs before his grin popped out and betrayed how pleased he was to have an excuse to see more of the house he hoped would become his.

A pulse of guilt coursed through him, hot and powerful. The farm belonged to Mercy's family, and he'd be upset if someone came along and insisted his brother surrender his claim on the farm where Jeremiah had grown up. But if he walked away, he might not find another farm near Harmony Creek.

Leaving to live elsewhere might be the difference between the new settlement succeeding or failing. A settlement needed about a dozen families to prosper, and a single person not staying as agreed could doom it. He'd made a deal with the

other families, and he couldn't break it without trying to stay.

Following Mercy's directions to a linen closet, Jeremiah paused whenever he heard the floor creak beneath him. Each time it wasn't anything more than the sounds made by an old building. He went to the closet beside the single bathroom on the upper floor and glanced into each room as he passed. Most were empty. Remnants of wallpaper hung in loose strips, and a damp odor filled every breath. Nibbled acorns warned squirrels had invaded. He was sure they were in the attic, too. Once it was warm enough for the squirrels to go outside, he'd check the exterior and block the holes they'd made to get into the house.

If he was here then…

He sighed. "God, You've brought me here. Help me see Your plan and the way for me to be part of this new settlement."

Selecting a couple of wool blankets and guessing there would be plenty of moth holes, he grabbed two more before he went downstairs. He could get by for a single night. If it went as he hoped, by tomorrow night he'd be able to sleep in his own house.

Mercy was waiting in the exact same spot where she'd been when he'd left. Again, guilt tormented him. Part of him wanted to walk away, but he couldn't.

"Did you find enough blankets?" she asked.

"I did."

"They may not be in good condition."

"They're *gut* enough for tonight."

She rubbed her hands together as she had before, and he realized she was as torn as he was. Turning the other cheek was the Mennonites' way, too, but he'd seen how her eyes snapped when she spoke of him keeping her from making a home here for her and her *kind*.

"If it gets too cold," she said, "come back." A hint of a smile played along her lips. "You freezing to death would be a real complication."

When he chuckled, her smile broadened, revealing the gentle person she was.

"Don't worry, Mercy. I'll be fine." He hoped it wasn't a boast. The temperatures had been dropping fast when he came to the house. He headed for the door.

"Do you have anything to eat?" she asked.

Her question stopped him in his tracks. "No."

"Wait here." Mercy rushed into the kitchen. He heard cabinet doors opening and closing as well as drawers being slid in and out; then she returned with a plastic bag filled with odd shapes. "It's peanut butter and jelly and a few slices of the bread I brought with us. Also a couple of cans of orange juice. It's Sunni's favorite, so I always have a bunch on hand."

"It's my favorite, too."

The smile he hadn't guessed he'd see again spread across her face, adding an aura of light to her eyes and skin. "I'm glad!"

That pleasurable something uncurled within him once more as he gazed into her pretty eyes. A man could get lost in those eyes. He looked away. He hadn't come to Harmony Creek to get lost, but to find his dream.

Picking up his duffel bags, he opened one and stuffed the thin blankets inside. He felt like a hobo as he steered his bags and himself out of the house. By the time he'd reached the porch steps, he heard the dead bolt click closed. Mercy wasn't taking any chance he'd have second thoughts and return.

He *would* be there tomorrow, he thought as he trudged through the snow. Because he wasn't ready to give up his dream…when it was within his grasp.

The next morning Mercy surveyed the wall completely stripped of ugly, peeling wallpaper. It'd taken more effort than she'd expected to get the remaining paper off. Maybe she shouldn't have done more work until she knew for certain what was going to happen with the farm. When the clock on the mantel in the living room had chimed nine o'clock, she'd used the phone in the kitchen

and called Darren Paquette, Grandpa Rudy's Realtor. His office was in Glens Falls, more than twenty-five miles away, and she'd been grateful to catch him at his desk.

At least she had been until he told her not to do anything until she heard from him again. When she explained about the meeting that afternoon with Jeremiah and his Realtor, Mr. Paquette warned her to say nothing.

"A real estate transaction is adversarial at best," he'd said, "and this is far from the best situation."

"When can you come here?"

"Tell Kitty Vasic to call me, and we'll discuss it. There's no reason to involve you and Mr. Stoltzfus at this point."

"I'll tell her."

How could he say she and Jeremiah weren't involved in deciding the future of the farm? That was the silliest thing she'd ever heard.

"Are you okay, Mommy?" asked Sunni as she came downstairs.

Mercy smiled at her dear daughter, who looked adorable in her light green dress and with her black braids falling over her shoulders. The little girl was sensitive to everyone's moods, and Mercy didn't want her to get more upset.

"I'm fine, *eolin-i*." The phrase meaning "little one" was one of the few she knew in Korean.

"Is he coming back?"

"Jeremiah?"

"Yeah, him."

She got the broom she'd found in a kitchen closet and began sweeping the wallpaper scraps into a pile. "He's returning this afternoon with a friend of his."

"Is he going to make you sad again?"

Putting aside the broom, Mercy squatted until her eyes were level with her daughter's. "Jeremiah didn't intend to make me sad. But he talked about Grandpa Rudy, and that made me sad."

"Me, too." Her dark eyes glistened with tears. "I miss his water balloons."

"I don't miss that." Mercy forced humor into her voice. "You two made me your favorite target."

"It was fun to be splashed on a hot day."

"It was, wasn't it?" She hugged Sunni, being careful she didn't pull her daughter off balance.

Mercy started to add more, but the door opened. She gasped when Jeremiah walked in. Nobody ever knocked at her grandfather's door, but for the first time, having someone let himself in seemed like an invasion. From where she squatted, it appeared the top of his straw hat brushed the ceiling.

Telling herself not to be frivolous, she made sure Sunni was steady as she came to her own feet. Paper crunched under her sneakers when she

turned to him. "I thought you were coming this afternoon."

"It *is* afternoon."

"It is?"

He chuckled. "The hours pass swiftly when there's plenty of work, ain't so?"

Mercy warned herself to relax. His teasing was aimed at trying to make the situation as comfortable as possible. "There are never enough hours in a day."

"True." He turned to Sunni. "How are you doing today?"

"You aren't going to make my mommy sad again, are you?" her daughter shot back in a tone that warned Jeremiah he'd be sorry if he did that.

Though she wanted to remind Sunni of her manners, Mercy said nothing. How Jeremiah answered could tell her a lot about what he was planning to do next.

Taking off his hat, he held it by the brim. "I'm sorry if I made her sad before." He raised his eyes to meet Mercy's, and she saw his sincerity as he added, "And I don't want to make her or you sad."

"So you say," Sunni retorted, shocking Mercy again. Her daughter wasn't usually rude, but she seemed to have taken an instant dislike to Jeremiah. Should Mercy heed her daughter's instincts...which she now could see had been spot-on where her ex-fiancé had been concerned?

But being rude to someone in their home—or

what she hoped would be their home—wasn't acceptable. "Sunni," she interjected in a firm tone, "it's not nice to suggest Jeremiah would do something hurtful on purpose."

As it isn't kind for me to ask why Grandpa Rudy hid how he was selling the farm that he said would be mine. Why? Why would you change your mind without telling me?

"I'm sorry," Sunni said, but her obstinate frown countermanded her words.

"It's okay to ask questions," Jeremiah replied, "but my *mamm* says you can catch more flies with honey than with vinegar."

"Who wants to catch flies?" The little girl grimaced. "Gross."

Mercy struggled not to laugh as she explained the adage to her daughter. Looking at Jeremiah, she said, "It's past time for Sunni and I to have lunch, and I know how hungry she gets after doing her schoolwork. I'm homeschooling her." Realizing she was babbling, she added, "Have you eaten?"

"I had the last of the peanut butter for breakfast."

"You can join us if you don't mind leftover pizza."

"Leftover pizza sounds like manna from heaven."

Laughing, she said, "I didn't order the manna topping. I hope you like pepperoni."

A slow smile spread over Jeremiah's face, and her heart did a stutter step as his blue eyes shone like a cloudless summer sky. He'd been so serious during their previous discussions. Seeing him smile was like being confronted by a stranger.

He is *a stranger. A stranger who wants your farm.* Telling her heart to behave itself because it'd been so wrong about Graham, she led the way into the kitchen. She'd be a fool to listen to her heart that had believed Graham loved her. Fortunately, she'd realized in time she always would have been a distant second in his affections after his mother.

She'd learned her lesson. Or she should have. Maybe her brain had, but her heart had a lot to learn.

Mercy used the time while she got the pizza out of the ancient refrigerator in the off-white kitchen and began warming it in the oven to regain her equilibrium. She must not be distracted by Jeremiah's beguiling smile when the future of Come Along Farm was at stake. When she got cans of soda—a special treat for Sunni—from the fridge, she listened as Jeremiah tried to engage her daughter in conversation.

Sunni was being cautious, either not replying or giving a single-word answer. It was a reminder, though Mercy didn't need one, of how her daughter had been hurt by Graham's decision to choose someone over them and walk away without

a backward look. Too many people had done that to Sunni, and Mercy was determined her daughter wouldn't feel abandoned again.

They were finishing what was a very uncomfortable lunch when a knock came at the door. Mercy watched as the door opened and a woman stuck her head in.

"Anyone home?"

Mercy was on her feet as Jeremiah pushed back his chair. She saw him reach to assist Sunni and shook her head to halt him. Sunni needed to do everything as other kids did. If Jeremiah acted as if he thought Sunni couldn't do something, it would make the little girl dislike him more.

Jeremiah appeared taken aback, but drew aside his hands as Sunni pushed her chair out. When Mercy went to the door, he followed.

"Hi, Kitty," he said before introducing Mercy to his Realtor.

Kitty Vasic was the picture of an elegant, successful businesswoman. She wore a business suit of the brightest pink Mercy had ever seen, and her shoes had spiked heels that must be five inches high. Mercy was fascinated, because she expected the Realtor to topple on each step.

"Mr. Stoltzfus, how nice to meet you in person." Kitty held out her hand and when he took it, she pumped his hand vigorously. "And you, too, Ms. Bamberger."

"Please call me Mercy," she said at the same time Jeremiah was urging the Realtor to use his given name.

Jeremiah added, "Plain folks don't like to use titles."

"Oh, that's good to know." Kitty smiled. "With you Amish moving into southern Washington County, it's important to learn how to be good neighbors. Don't you agree?"

Mercy considered saying she wasn't Amish, but she didn't want to delay hearing what the Realtor had to say. "We appreciate you coming so we can get this unfortunate situation resolved right away."

Kitty's smile wavered. "Oh, dear! I'm sorry if I led you to believe this could be settled today."

"But I thought—" Jeremiah began.

"Let's talk, and I'll tell you what I do know." She grinned as Sunni appeared in the kitchen doorway. "Well, hello, young lady. You must be a Bamberger because I know Jeremiah doesn't have children."

"Sunni," Mercy said, "this would be a good time for you to finish the story we started last night."

The little girl glanced at Jeremiah's and Kitty's taut faces. Mercy guessed her own expression was as uneasy. With a nod, Sunni went into the dining room, where two overstuffed chairs were set by a fireplace that opened into the kitchen, as well.

It needed to be swept because ashes had tumbled onto the floor. Something else for Mercy to add to her lengthy to-do list.

Pushing aside her longing to go with her daughter and forget about these complications, Mercy squared her shoulders. "We can sit in the living room."

Behind her, the *click-click-click* of Kitty's high heels marked her steps, but Jeremiah's boot falls were surprisingly light for such a tall, muscular man. She shook those thoughts from her head. She couldn't allow herself to become distracted.

She sat in what had been her grandfather's favorite chair by the wide window offering a view of the road through the bare branches of the maple trees. Waiting until the others chose chairs, she gazed at the green tiles on the large fireplace.

"What *can* you tell us, Kitty?" she asked.

"It's unlikely the closing will go on as planned." Kitty shot an apologetic look toward Jeremiah.

His face went as blank as the wall behind him, and his gaze refused to meet hers. The pulse of sympathy surging through her was startling. If he closed on the property, her hopes for Come Along Farm would end. Yet, he had dreams for the property, too. Oh, how she wished there was a solution that could satisfy them both.

When the Realtor spoke again, Mercy focused on her. "We'll need to consult with an attorney,"

Kitty said, "to determine what New York law says. I've got to admit it's the first time I've been involved with a property transfer where one party died before closing. Mercy, I should have said this before. I'm sorry for your loss."

"Thank you."

"Your grandfather was well respected and well liked. I can't tell you how many times I enjoyed a cup of coffee with him at the Village Diner."

"Did he mention why he decided to sell?" She regretted the question. Talking about private matters when Jeremiah sat a couple of feet away was unsettling.

Kitty reached over and patted her arm. "He was selling it for you and your daughter."

"For us? But he promised…" This time she halted herself before she said too much.

"I don't know what he told you, Mercy, but Rudy mentioned that he wanted you to have a majority of the money. He hoped you'd build a nice home so you'd be close to his assisted-living apartment. He spoke often about you and your daughter and how he looked forward to spending more time with you."

"Why didn't he tell me this?"

Kitty shook her head sadly. "That's something I can't answer. I'm as perplexed as you are. I'm sure he had his reasons, but he never mentioned

them to me or Darren." Her eyes narrowed. "Have you spoken with Darren?"

"I called him this morning. He said to tell you to call him."

"I see." Her lips tightened into a straight line, an expression that said as loudly as a shout she was annoyed. "We should wait on discussing this further until Darren can be here, too, to represent Rudy's estate."

"But do *you* think the contract is valid?" Jeremiah asked.

"We should wait—"

"I think Mercy is as anxious as I am to hear your opinion. I understand we can't make decisions without Darren's input, but is the contract valid?"

"From what I've read, the answer is yes and no. In some states, the contract would be invalid upon the death of either party." She glanced from Mercy to him. "But we have leeway in New York. If the heir or heirs are willing, the contract can be completed. However, that is *my* opinion from a quick read on the internet. Until we have an opinion from an attorney, I don't think either of you should assume anything."

Jeremiah turned to Mercy. "You are your *grossdawdi*'s heir, ain't so?"

"One of them, I guess. Rudy is my father's father."

"Is your father alive?" asked Kitty.

She nodded.

"What about his brothers and sisters?"

"My father has six siblings," she replied.

Jeremiah sighed. "Kitty, when my *daed*—my dad—died, everything he had went to my mother. But if she'd died first..."

"The estate would be divided equally among his children." Kitty bit her lower lip, then said, "Unless Rudy left a written and witnessed will that specifies otherwise."

Mercy's heart sank toward her knees as she realized where the conversation was going. If Grandpa Rudy hadn't left a valid will naming her as his heir, the property would belong to her father, her four aunts and her two uncles.

"Do you have names and contact information for your father and his siblings?" asked Kitty.

"I can find them. All but one aunt have telephones."

The Realtor smiled. "I'm glad to hear that. It'll make getting in contact with them much easier. However, paperwork will have to be mailed to them for their signatures. I'm not sure, at this point, whether the signatures will have to be notarized. The probate court will let us know."

"We have to go to court?" asked Jeremiah.

Mercy heard his consternation and understood. It usually wasn't the way of plain folks to deal with courts and lawyers. Matters were settled pri-

vately and through prayer, but estate matters were different. She wondered whom her grandfather had hired to draft his will…if he had one.

She was out of her depth. Ask her about the needs of inner-city kids and the benefits of them enjoying a summer in the country, and she could expound for an hour. Since Sunni's arrival in her life, she'd learned a lot about intercountry adoption and physical therapy and the adventures of the little girl's beloved characters in her favorite books.

But she knew nothing about what would happen with the farm.

"If you agree, Jeremiah," Kitty went on, "I'll share the contract with my agency's lawyer. I'd like him to review it and give us advice to aid us in bringing the contract to a closing." She sighed. "To be honest, this won't be quick. Obtaining an agreement from seven people will take time, and we can't be certain of the outcome."

"Is there another farm for sale in the area?" Jeremiah asked.

"None that I know of. I can make inquiries, if you'd like."

"*Ja.*"

Her eyes cut toward Mercy. "I'll do what I can, Jeremiah, but I can't make promises. Not about this farm or any other."

"I know," he said again.

"And there's one other complication. Your money in escrow may be held by the probate court until there's an agreement among the heirs."

He blanched. "I can't put in another offer until the money is released."

"Yes, though if someone is eager to sell, we might be able to work something out." Kitty sighed. "However, like I said, I don't know of other farms for sale near Harmony Creek. There's one over by Scotts Lake, seven or eight miles from here."

"Too far for me to be part of this settlement."

"So I figured." She stood.

Mercy clasped her hands on her lap. If the closing went ahead, Jeremiah would own the farm. If the sale had to be approved by Grandpa Rudy's heirs, would Dad and his brothers and sisters decide to sell it to Jeremiah? Two of his siblings would be eager to use their share of the proceeds to invest in their businesses. What about the others? And how many had to say no before Jeremiah couldn't close on the farm? Was it a simple majority or could a single no vote give her the chance to buy the farm herself?

But how? The money she had was already earmarked to fix the house and the buildings to be approved for bringing children to visit. In addition, she needed to buy horses and other farm animals to give the youngsters a true farm expe-

rience. Perhaps she could convince her family to let her pay them bit by bit.

She heard Kitty say she'd contact them when she had further information. The *click-click-click* of Kitty's shoes headed toward the door, and Jeremiah went, too, talking with his Realtor.

Mercy didn't move. There had to be a solution to her dilemma, but what?

Unless Rudy left a written and witnessed will that specifies otherwise.

Kitty's words resonated in Mercy's head, and she gasped. What if she found a will? There were many rooms, and she hadn't dared to go into the ones with weak floors. What if she found her grandfather's will and it proved her assertion he wanted her to have the farm?

She got up and took a single step toward the formal staircase at the front of the house. Pausing, she looked over her shoulder when she heard Jeremiah's deep voice rumbling in the other room. If he knew of her intention to search the house, would he help her or try to halt her? Until she knew for sure, she couldn't let him know what she was doing. She didn't like secrets, but keeping this one might mean the difference between her dreams coming true and their destruction.

Chapter Three

Last night Jeremiah had discovered the tenant house was in worse condition than he'd guessed. It hadn't taken him long to explore it, using his flashlight. A tiny kitchen and a cozy living room filled the first floor. Upstairs were two cramped bedrooms and a bath. Every ceiling had brown water stains, and one wall of the entry hall was pulling away from the house. He'd been able to see light from the rising moon through the crack, and a puddle of slush was piled on the linoleum beside it.

This morning he woke to find the house cold and damp. He'd been grateful for a woodstove in the living room and a few logs stacked nearby. He'd used the rag rug by the stove as a mattress. He'd folded a blanket as a makeshift pillow. He'd told himself, though it wasn't likely it'd be com-

fortable, he'd endured worse when he'd camped in the woods when he wasn't much older than Sunni.

He'd been wrong.

Every muscle ached, and moving in the icy air seemed to make his bones creak as if he'd aged fifty years overnight. It was dark, but he guessed it was around 4:00 a.m. It was the time when he usually woke to help with chores before leaving for his woodworking shop.

His tools would be arriving today or tomorrow. He should have waited until he closed on the property before he had the crates trucked up from Paradise Springs. But how could he have imagined the debacle waiting for him in Harmony Creek?

With a groan, he pushed himself up to sit. He grimaced as the frigid air gripped him as the thick blanket fell away. Standing, he went to the stove, which was barely warm. He opened the door and saw the banked embers had burned themselves out.

Jeremiah sent up a prayer of thanks when, after he'd started a new fire in the stove, the air close to the stove warmed quickly. Something worked in the house.

After his quick inspection his first night at the house, he knew not much else did. No water had flowed into the sinks, and flushing the toilet had resulted in strange creaking sounds in the walls as if the pipes were trying to break out. The propane

tanks by the back door must be empty, because the kitchen stove had refused to light.

He hoped he would have better results this morning. He opened a door to what might have been a laundry or storage room. A rusty washer lurked beneath shelves covered with dust and droppings. In a closet, he found a lantern but no kerosene.

Brushing the kitchen table off as best he could, he grimaced when it rocked. Were the legs uneven or the floor? That answer and a whole lot more would have to wait until he could see beyond the narrow circle from his flashlight.

He made the same meal he'd eaten last night. A peanut butter and grape jelly sandwich. He thought fondly of the large meal of eggs and sausage and home fries he would have eaten at home. After he said silent grace, he ate standing up. He found a napkin Mercy had added to the bag. He sighed, wondering if it would have been much easier if she'd been rude or snarled like an angry dog. Instead, she'd made sure he had blankets to keep him warm and food to eat.

And she'd been stubborn.

Did she have ideas of her own for the farm? Most likely, as she'd started work on the house. He appreciated that, because he'd spent hours putting together his plans, something his brothers had helped him with while they teased him for trying

to look at every possible angle. Taking another bite of the sandwich, he wished his brothers were nearby. He could have used their insight.

A knock startled him. Why would someone come to a house that must have been deserted for years? Setting his sandwich down, he brushed crumbs off his hands and tossed them in the sink before he went to the door.

He opened it and saw a face he recognized. The man who had recruited others to come to Harmony Creek.

"You're Caleb Hartz, ain't so?" Jeremiah asked, remembering how Caleb had spoken at a gathering in Paradise Springs, telling about the fallow farmland on small family farms awaiting anyone who was willing to work hard to improve it.

The man nodded, then swept his too-long blond hair out of his dark green eyes. "*Ja.* I thought I'd stop by this morning to see how you're settling in." His tawny brows lowered. "I assumed you'd be at the main house, but the woman who answered the door told me I'd find you here."

"Things are a bit complicated." After he invited Caleb into the house, he gave him a quick overview of the situation.

Caleb, who would be one of his neighbors if the sale went through, listened with widening eyes. "I got to know Rudy pretty well. He was a *gut* man.

He wouldn't have signed a purchase contract with you if he didn't intend for you to buy the farm."

"Maybe he should have mentioned that to his granddaughter."

Caleb's frown deepened, drawing lines into the thin angles of his face. "It's a puzzle. I've been here a little over a month. Everyone I've talked to—both Amish and *Englisch*—has praised Rudy's honesty. He sold me a battered skid loader I'll need to move hay bales. He didn't make any bones about how much work it would need, and he sold it at a fair price."

"My dealings with him were *gut*, too. I wish I knew why he didn't let Mercy know he was selling the farm."

"I hope you won't have to leave Harmony Creek. We need every family we can convince to join us in order to make this settlement a success."

Jeremiah didn't need that reminder. From the moment he'd expressed interest in joining the Hartz family and the Waglers as well as other founding members of the Harmony Creek colony, he'd been told he must be very sure about his commitment. Each family was vital to the rest.

"I'm not leaving. I'm going to farm here." Saying the words aloud was like taking an oath in the presence of the Lord, though God was well aware of what was in Jeremiah's heart.

"Aren't you a woodworker by trade?"

"*Ja*, but farming is too much in my blood." He surprised himself by chuckling. "My late *daed* would be shocked because I hated to get out of bed to do chores."

Caleb chuckled. "My *daed* used to threaten to dump cold water on me and my brothers to get us up in the morning."

"Sounds familiar."

"I can ask around and find out if anyone is thinking about selling."

"*Danki*, but I've got to wait and hear what my Realtor learns from her attorney. As my *mamm* has said more than once, there's no need to look for trouble before it finds you."

"Sounds like something my *mamm* would have said, too."

"My brothers believe *mamms* have a special language filled with platitudes for every occasion."

Caleb laughed heartily. "Why is it dark in here?"

"I couldn't find oil for the lantern."

"The house has electricity. Rudy mentioned both houses were wired." With a wave of his hand, he added, "Let's find the fuse box and see if we can get you some light. More important is powering the well pump so you can have water."

Jeremiah followed him into the cellar. As they crossed the dirt floor to where a metal box was affixed to the wall, he wondered why he hadn't con-

sidered checking the well pump. Exhaustion could be a reason, because he felt as if he carried the house on his shoulders as he trudged after Caleb.

His neighbor whistled a single note as he popped open the door on the metal box. "A circuit breaker box. Who'd have guessed Rudy had updated his tenant house?" Reaching in, he flipped a switch.

A low rumble came from the far side of the cellar. Jeremiah aimed his flashlight in that direction and saw the well's holding tank. His fatigue fell away as he realized he could have water to brush his teeth once he'd let it run long enough to make sure any rust washed out.

"Danki," he said.

Caleb shrugged. "Glad to help. I'm sure this circuit breaker box isn't the first surprise you're going to find."

Jeremiah was tempted to say the breakers were far from the *first* surprise he'd had since his arrival, but grousing wouldn't get him anywhere. He needed to be patient until Kitty had answers for him. *That* had to be his plan. Wait and see.

A sense of calm settled over him as he realized he had a clear path…for now. He thanked God for helping him see that. He must be patient. Not an easy task when his dream was so close to realization.

Several lights were glaring against the water-

stained ceilings when he went upstairs with Caleb. He switched off everything but the fluorescent ceiling light in the kitchen, though he despised its glare.

"Let us know if you need anything before your stuff arrives," Caleb said as he reached for the doorknob. He glanced outside. "Looks like we're in for another big storm." Grimacing at the crack in the wall, he added, "We're living in the barn while we get the house repaired, and our barn is better than this. Feel free to come over if you get tired of shoveling snow out of your house."

"Danki." He knew he wouldn't abandon the house, because that might injure his fragile claim on the farm. "I appreciate it."

"We may be snowed in for a while, because we're one of the last roads plowed by the town. I don't think Rudy sold his sleigh, so if you or anyone at the main house needs something, you can use it."

"Danki." He appreciated Caleb's helpfulness, which made him more determined to be a part of the nascent community. Amish folks assisted one another. Did Mercy feel the same?

"Oh, one other thing I should let you know." Caleb turned the knob. "Wayne Flaud from the settlement north of here in Whitehall is acting as our temporary bishop. If you want me to contact him to get his thoughts on what you should do…"

"Let's see what my Realtor has to say before we bring the bishop into this. I'm sure this will work out for the best. God didn't bring me to Harmony Creek so I could turn around and leave again."

With another nod, Caleb bid him *gute mariye* and let himself out as a burst of cold and a swirl of windblown snow slipped in past him.

Jeremiah guessed Caleb believed his words. Too bad he wasn't so sure himself.

Any hopes spring might have made an early appearance overnight were dashed three days later when Mercy awoke to discover two feet of new snow. She dressed hastily, because the house was cold in the fresh light of dawn.

Peeking past Sunni's door and glad her daughter was asleep with the blankets pulled up to her chin, Mercy tiptoed down the stairs. They creaked beneath her, and she hoped Sunni wouldn't wake up until Mercy figured out what was wrong with the heat.

Despite herself, she glanced out the window that gave her a view of the trees separating them from the tenant house. She hadn't spoken to Jeremiah since he'd left after the meeting with his Realtor. She'd seen big delivery trucks in the yard the following day and watched him accept delivery of a horse, a buggy and a dozen large wooden crates, which he'd moved into an outbuilding. He'd spent

time inside, coming out with pieces of wood, so she guessed he was unpacking what he'd shipped to the farm.

That was a sign Jeremiah intended to stay.

No surprise, but if he thought she'd give up because he was making himself at home, he was in for a big surprise. She'd waited years for an opportunity to host city kids on a farm.

She'd thought her grandfather comprehended her need to pay forward the gifts she'd been given. Instantly, she was contrite. She couldn't fault Grandpa Rudy for his change of heart about what should happen with the farm after he died, but she wished he'd talked to her before signing a deal with Jeremiah.

He was as much an innocent victim of this mess as she was. Of course, if he withdrew his offer, that might make a difference for her aunts and uncles. Would they be more willing to give her time to find funds to set up the farm if they didn't have an available buyer?

Mercy had discussed that with her parents last night. Her father had sympathy for how her plans for the farm might have died along with Rudy, but he'd also emphasized that he'd go along with what his siblings decided.

"I've got to admit," Dad had told her before they'd hung up, "I'd really like to have you and Sunni closer to the rest of the family."

"But there's no place near your house where I could afford to buy land." She'd tried not to sound like a petulant child who hadn't gotten her way.

"If that's what God wants you to do, He'll help you find a way."

She agreed and was sure God had led her to Harmony Creek and the farm. Otherwise, she wouldn't have uprooted Sunni, leaving behind trusted specialists and physical therapists who worked with her daughter.

Now...

Mercy winced as she entered the kitchen and felt the cold wind that had found its way into the house. Opening the cellar door, she heard silence. Why wasn't the furnace running?

A quick check of the fuel tank gauge showed it was half-full. Next, she went to the furnace, which was raised up so high off the floor she had to stand on tiptoe to see the dials. Why wouldn't it start? She tried flipping the emergency switch at the top of the cellar steps.

Nothing.

If possible, it seemed colder when she returned to the kitchen. She needed help. She glanced at the snow sparkling as if stars had fallen along with the flakes. The road twisting through the hollow had vanished. If she called someone, how long would it take them to get to the house?

Her gaze settled on the tenant house. Should

she ask Jeremiah to check the furnace? She'd ignored him for three days, but she wasn't sure who else would be able to help them. She didn't want Sunni getting sick from the cold.

Before she could talk herself out of it, Mercy reached for the phone, an old avocado-colored unit she'd found in a drawer. She'd hung it on the wall. The long cord allowed her to walk around the kitchen while she talked. She looked at the faded numbers on the wall beside the phone and dialed the one for the tenant house.

"Hello?" Jeremiah sounded astonished to be answering a phone.

She knew many Amish didn't keep phones in their houses, but had them in the barns or a phone shack shared by multiple families.

"Jeremiah, it is Mercy. Mercy Bamberger." Who else named Mercy would know he was living at the tenant house?

"*Ja. Gute mariye*, Mercy." He sounded awkward and uncertain as he went on. "I hope my work hasn't disturbed you or Sunni. I—"

Not wanting to let the conversation drag along, she said, "I don't think my furnace is working. Will you look at it?"

She could almost see him nod before he told her he'd be over in a few minutes. Thanking him, she hung up.

Starting the coffeemaker, she sighed. If Jere-

miah took over the farm, he'd strip the electric wires out of the house. She wondered what it'd be like to live without electricity.

A knock on the door told her Jeremiah was as good as his word. Taking a steadying breath, she opened it. She forced a smile, which she hoped looked more welcoming than it felt.

Knocking snow off his boots, Jeremiah stepped inside. He unwrapped a blue-and-green scarf from around his face and let it hang over his shoulders as he unbuttoned his black wool coat. Lifting off his hat of the same fabric, he placed it on the counter near the door.

Her heart beat a bit too fast when she stood close to him again. She'd thought of him as a problem, but with him an arm's length away, she couldn't help noticing, as if for the first time, his strong jaw and the intelligence in his compelling blue eyes. As he pulled off worn work gloves, she stared at the nicks on his knuckles and stain on his fingertips. He was a man accustomed to hard work.

Graham, her former fiancé, popped into her mind. A fastidious man, his hands always looked as if he'd just had a manicure. She'd been surprised to discover he had his nails done when he took his mother to the beauty shop. When he'd told her it made Mrs. Rapp happy, Mercy had, at first, seen it as a sign of him caring deeply about

others. She hadn't guessed he'd cared more about his mother than he'd ever care for her.

"Thanks for coming over," Mercy said, holding out her hand for Jeremiah's coat.

He handed it to her, and waves of cold washed over her. It must be more frigid outside than in the house. Maybe the furnace hadn't gone out too long ago and fixing it would be easy.

"What have you done so far?" he asked, combing his fingers through his reddish hair.

"I checked the fuel oil tank." She set his coat over a kitchen chair. "There's oil in the tank, so I don't know what's wrong."

"Let me look at it."

"Thanks!" She motioned toward the cellar door. "It's down there. I'm hoping it's something simple."

"Something simple is about the extent of my skills at fixing furnaces." He gave her a grin. "Just in case, do you have the name of the person who did furnace servicing for Rudy? It's probably the same company that delivers oil."

"I probably can find it. He kept that sort of stuff in his desk." As coffee finished dripping into the clear pot, she asked, "Do you want a cup?"

"I'll have one when I'm done." Without another word, he went to the cellar door and opened it. His work boots, which were as battered as his gloves, thumped on each step.

Mercy heard Jeremiah pull on the chain to the bare bulb near the furnace. Hurrying into the room with Grandpa Rudy's desk, she grabbed a black shawl from a peg. She threw it over her shoulders, holding it close with fingers as clumsy as a collection of icicles.

The desk was heaped with papers and envelopes her grandfather must have tossed there in the days before he died. For a moment Mercy had to blink back tears. Throughout the mess of the past days, one thing hadn't changed. She missed Grandpa Rudy, the very person she wanted to turn to now.

Mercy found a receipt from the oil company and was relieved to see it had an emergency service number at the top. Putting it in the pocket of her black apron, she hurried into the kitchen to be ready to call the oil company if Jeremiah couldn't fix the furnace.

She paused when she heard uneven steps on the stairs to the second floor. Sunni was coming down the stairs without her crutches. Mercy frowned. Her daughter had promised to use them on the stairs. Worse, the little girl had wrapped herself in a blanket that threatened to trip her.

"Sunni, you need to be careful," she chided gently.

"I was afraid of turning into an ice cube if I

waited a second longer," the little girl said. "Why's it so cold, Mommy?"

"Something's wrong with the heat."

Before Mercy could say more, assertive footsteps came from the cellar steps. She turned to see Jeremiah in the doorway.

Sunni mumbled something under her breath and scowled at Jeremiah.

His gaze followed Sunni when her daughter walked into the living room, her pose beneath the blanket one of disdain. He arched his brows at Mercy.

"Were you able to see what's wrong with the furnace?" Mercy asked.

"Nothing's wrong with it." He wiped his hands on a filthy cloth he must have found in the cellar. "Your fuel oil tank is empty."

"But I checked the tank before I called you. The gauge said it was half-full."

"The gauge is broken. The tank is completely dry."

"I never considered the gauge might be wrong."

"No reason you should."

"You did." She pushed away from the stairs and flinched when the door gave a threatening creak. One disaster at a time. Reaching under her shawl, she pulled the receipt out of her pocket. "I'll call the oil company's emergency number and see if they can deliver some oil."

He glanced out the window. "They won't be able to get in until the road is plowed."

As if on cue, the rumble of a big truck could be heard coming toward the house. She saw the huge wing of the plow as it pushed snow in large, thick chunks into the yard. She shuddered, thinking of the heavy work of clearing the driveway. Her car was stored in the rickety garage, and the old-style door opened straight out, so she was going to have to clear a large area there, too.

Mercy made the call to the oil company, who assured her they'd be there before nightfall. Apparently, she wasn't the only one needing service on the cold day.

"You can't stay here with Sunni," Jeremiah said after she hung up. "The house is going to get colder and colder. The tenant house is a bit better, but you'll get so chilled going over there, it probably won't make much difference. Isn't there a fireplace in the living room?"

"Yes."

"Did Rudy use it?"

When she nodded and Jeremiah offered to start a fire, she was relieved. She found a box of matches in the kitchen junk drawer and followed him into the living room, where he checked the fireplace, looking up at the top of the firebox where the damper opened into the chimney. He drew back, wiping soot from his trousers.

While Sunni watched from the couch, as silent as she was whenever Jeremiah was near, he quickly arranged slabs of wood in the fireplace. Mercy handed him the matches and went to sit with her daughter.

He struck one match and held it to the small bits of paper he'd stuck among the wood. Small flames rose, and Mercy resisted the yearning to hold out her half-frozen hands, knowing there wouldn't be much heat yet. She needed to wait until the fire caught on the dried wood.

Suddenly, Jeremiah jumped to his feet and staggered. Thick smoke chased him toward the middle of the room.

"Get out!" he yelled.

Chapter Four

Mercy grabbed Sunni and ran toward the living room door, but paused when she heard a window slide open with the rattle of glass behind her. Jeremiah waved the smoke from the hearth out the window. Snow fell into the house, but he ignored it as he coughed. She put Sunni down and ran into the kitchen. She filled a bucket with water.

He threw the water on the hearth, where it sizzled. He stirred the ashes, making sure the fire was completely out. Then he took the glass of water she offered him. He drained it in one gulp and coughed a couple more times.

"I told you to get out," he said. "With this dried-out wallpaper, the fire could have spread fast."

"Why would I leave you here?" she asked, annoyed he treated her as if she were Sunni's age. "Once I heard you open the window, I knew the smoke would be sucked out."

"Maybe I was planning to jump out the window. Did you consider that?"

"No."

He gave her a wry grin. "Neither did I. Once I could see through the smoke, I was able to see the fire was dying out." He raised a single finger when she started to speak. "But you and Sunni should have gotten out of the house."

"To freeze in the snow?"

He sighed as fresh air poured into the room, dispersing the smoke. "I thought you said your *grossdawdi* used the fireplace."

"He did." Mercy took the glass from him.

"Recently?"

She shrugged. "I don't know. I almost always visited during the summer vacation."

"I suspect debris in the chimney has piled up over time. After it's cleaned out, there shouldn't be a problem." He grimaced. "But right now you need heat."

"I can turn on the oven and open the door."

"Gas or electric?"

"Electric. Why?"

"I don't want you to have to deal with gas fumes." He gestured toward the kitchen. "You two go into the kitchen. Shut the doors and roll up towels and put them at the bottom. That should keep the heat in as much as possible."

"How about the fireplace between the kitchen

and dining room? There are ashes on the hearth."
She glanced at the smoke stains on the ceiling.
"Do you think it'd be safe to try to light that one?"

"Let me check." He followed her and Sunni
into the kitchen.

He knelt by the hearth as she turned on the oven
and opened the door, hoping the old stove was up
to heating the kitchen. Unlike the one in the liv-
ing room, the kitchen fireplace was utilitarian. No
fancy tiles. Just plain brick turned dark after de-
cades of use. He reached in to check the damper.
Paying no attention to the ashes, he stretched out
on his back and peered into the chimney.

"It looks open." Jeremiah got up and knocked
ashes off his pants. "Let me try a small fire. Got
anything else to burn?"

She grabbed a handful of newspaper from the
pile left by her *grossdawdi*. "How about this?"

"It'll burn long enough to see if the smoke goes
up the chimney or not."

He cheered and Mercy smiled, giving Sunni's
shoulders a squeeze, when the thin wisp of smoke
was drawn up the chimney. Going into the living
room, she realized there were only a couple of
pieces of wood left. She took them into the kitchen
and handed them to Jeremiah.

"You keep the fire going, and I'll get more
wood," she said.

"Mercy, I can do that. It's cold outside." He started to stand.

She put her hand on his shoulder, the motion automatic. But her response to the strong sinews was anything but. Jerking her hand back, she wanted to shake it to stop her skin from tingling.

Somehow she was able to say, "No, you watch the fire. I'll be right back."

Racing to the door, she flung it open. She pulled on her boots before she stepped into the deep snow on the porch. Quickly closing the door, she wasn't fast enough to avoid seeing Sunni's dismay that Mercy had left her with Jeremiah.

Mercy took a steadying breath as her fingers continued to quiver from the memory of Jeremiah's shoulder beneath them. Had she lost her mind? It was a big mistake to be attracted to him. Even if he didn't want her farm, she was still reeling from a broken engagement. On top of that, her daughter didn't like him.

She hurried to the split wood that had been stored on the porch to dry. She gathered pieces in her apron and turned to go inside.

She stopped as she looked across the snowy yard. It was broken by a single set of footprints. Jeremiah's.

No, she was wrong. There were other footprints. She recognized the tiny, scampering ones of a squirrel intent on finding where it had hidden

its stash of acorns. A line near the pine trees separating the big house from the tenant house looked as if they belonged to deer. They would be having as difficult a time as squirrels in the deep snow. Once the house was warm, she needed to spread hay for the deer and strew a few handfuls of the birdseed she'd seen in a cupboard. Grandpa Rudy always had made sure his bird feeders were kept full, despite the concern of bears helping themselves to the seed.

All God's creatures need to eat, and we are His hands to take care of His creation.

How many times had she heard Grandpa Rudy say that? Oh, how she missed him!

A gust of wind swirled snow into her face, and Mercy hurried inside. As she let the wood roll onto the floor beside the hearth, Jeremiah smiled at her.

"Perfect timing," he said. "I was about to go out and make sure you hadn't frozen into a chunk of ice."

"My mommy is doing the best she can!" asserted Sunni, jutting out her tiny chin. She flounced into the dining room and hid behind a book.

Mercy started to apologize to Jeremiah for Sunni's behavior.

He motioned aside her words. "She's cold, and she's scared. I should have thought before I spoke."

"You know it doesn't have anything to do with what you said." She wouldn't sugarcoat Sunni's antipathy to him. "I'm sorry she's being bratty to you." *And I know I should be honest why, but I can't when I'm too embarrassed by what happened with Graham.*

"She's a kid. I've got enough nieces and nephews to know when they get something in their head, it's not easy to get it out."

"Do you have a lot of them?"

"More all the time, thanks to my brothers and sisters." Standing, he looked at the fire crackling contentedly on the hearth. Already warmth was pushing aside the cold. "Keep feeding it wood, and it won't go out." He hesitated, then said, "I should get going."

She asked before she could halt herself, "So how many brothers do you have?"

Jeremiah wondered why Mercy was extending the conversation when it had seemed, moments ago, she couldn't wait until he left.

"Six. Three older and three younger," he said. "And two sisters. Add in their spouses and kids, and we have a full table when everyone comes together." He couldn't halt his smile. "*Mamm* is never happier than when everyone is sitting around the table together. Do you have brothers or sisters?"

"Now, but I was an only child when I lived in the Bronx."

"I can't imagine being an only." *Or living in a big city.* "I've always been surrounded by siblings, which most of the time I appreciated."

She nodded. "I know what you mean. I've learned how siblings can be your best friends, but also they know exactly how to annoy you best."

"So your family used to live in New York City? I didn't realize Mennonites lived there."

"I wasn't Mennonite then." Before he could ask what she meant, she said, "I need to make Sunni breakfast. I promised her pancakes. Would you like some, too?"

"I had some toast when I woke up, but that was several hours ago, so I'd be grateful for a second breakfast. I've got a long day ahead of me."

"Unpacking more of those big crates?" Color rose up Mercy's cheeks, and he guessed she'd blurted out the question before thinking.

"*Ja.* I had my woodworking tools sent up from Paradise Springs before I realized..." He wasn't surprised when she went to collect the makings for breakfast. Why did she act ashamed? The situation they were in wasn't her fault. She was as much a victim of misunderstandings as he was. He hurried on to fill the abrupt silence. "I want to make sure nothing got broken between Pennsylvania and here."

"That makes sense." She took a bowl out of a glass-front hutch built into the wall opposite the fireplace. She put flour and eggs and other ingredients in the bowl and she mixed them together.

She closed the oven door and hefted a cast-iron pan out of the drawer beneath it. After heating the pan, she poured pancake batter into it.

Sunni peeked in. The frown she gave Jeremiah didn't need translation. She wished he'd go away and stay away.

Lord, help me find a way to let this kind *know I'm not her enemy. Or her* mamm*'s.*

The little girl had to be aware of the tension between Mercy and him. Sunni was old enough to understand there was a problem, but couldn't grasp the intricacies of estate law. *He* didn't get it, either, though Kitty had explained it to him. It was too bad they couldn't help each other, but his plans for the farm and Mercy's were different.

When Mercy put pancakes on a plate and set it on the kitchen table, Sunni asked, "Can I eat in the dining room?"

Mercy hesitated; then she nodded. The little girl poured herself a glass of orange juice, picked up her plate and carried her breakfast into the other room.

"I'm sorry," Mercy said as she returned to the stove.

"It won't help to force her to spend time with me," he replied.

"True." She set a stack of lightly browned pancakes in front of him. The edges of the pancakes were crisp, just as he liked them. As he started to say that, she interrupted him. "I need to explain why she's acting like this."

"Okay."

She faced the stove. "I was in a relationship that didn't work out, and she was upset when Graham and I went our separate ways after I realized I would always play second fiddle to his mother."

"*Danki.* I was beginning to think it was personal." He couldn't help being curious about how serious she and her Graham had been. He hoped not as serious as he'd been about Emmarita before she left her Amish life behind. He hoped Mercy didn't have as many regrets as he did.

"It's not. The move has upset her more than I'd guessed it would."

"And the possibility you won't be staying here isn't helping." He smothered the sting of Emmarita's betrayal by concentrating on the problem he and Mercy shared.

"Not a bit."

"Have you heard anything from your family?" he asked after he paused to say a silent grace. He

picked up his fork so he didn't have to look at her
as he waited for her answer.

"Nothing definitive. Dad said they're planning
a conference call to discuss the farm." She put a
cup of fragrant *kaffi* next to his plate before going
to the stove to make her own breakfast. "Everyone
will want to share his or her opinion."

Jeremiah waited until she brought a plate with
four pancakes to the table. She pushed two more
onto his plate before she set hers down. After get-
ting herself *kaffi* and offering him juice, which
he passed on because it would taste sour after the
syrup, she pulled out her chair and sat. She bowed
her head, and he said nothing while she thanked
the Lord for the meal.

Could she be thanking God for Jeremiah's com-
pany? Maybe she was grateful to have endured
another day with him. Was she just being more
polite than her daughter? Possibly, because she
must want to move ahead with the farm. For the
first time, he wondered if he was being short-
sighted trying to stay, but what else could he do?
Until his funds were released from escrow, he
couldn't purchase another farm. His sole choice
might be to return to Paradise Springs, and he
wasn't ready to start over at square one.

Not yet.

Jeremiah looked for a safe topic to disrupt the

silence. "You said you learned about siblings. It sounds as if you eventually had some."

"I had two brothers and a sister after I was adopted."

"Adopted?" He was glad she seemed focused on her food so she didn't see the astonishment on his face. No doubt she heard it in his voice.

"When I was eleven. That was after my *Abuelita*—my grandmother—died. She'd been raising me."

"What happened to your parents?"

She chased the syrup around her plate with a piece of pancake, but didn't lift it to her mouth. "A car accident when I was two years old. They were on their way to the hospital for the birth of their second child when they were struck by another car. *Abuelita* told me the police said they died instantly. She said I needed to be grateful they never felt any pain before they went to heaven, but I couldn't be when I was a little girl who couldn't understand why God wanted to take my mama and papa and my unborn sister away."

"Mercy, I'm so sorry." He hated the sight of tears seeping into her eyes. How many had she cried through the years as she mourned those she could barely remember?

"Thank you." She dabbed a knuckle at her eye and squared her shoulders. "*Abuelita* took me in and became more like my mother than my grand-

mother. Everything I know of my parents is from what she told me and from the picture of them on their wedding day. I don't know what happened to that photo. To be honest, Jeremiah, it seems like someone else's past. Once I was adopted by the Bambergers, my life began anew."

"Certainly you haven't forgotten the first eleven years of your life?"

"No, but I took Grandpa Rudy's advice. He urged me to treasure the memories of those who had left me behind. I have many precious ones of *Abuelita*, and I can re-create every detail of that photo. I can even recall the name of the studio where it was taken. Lincoln Photography on Fordham Road. I remember it because I thought President Lincoln had taken their picture."

"I doubt your parents would have appreciated you thinking they were that old." He chuckled. "Kids always think their parents are ancient. Sunni probably thinks you're older than the hills."

"Thanks." A grin transformed her face, and he knew he would gladly sit and look at it for hours at a time.

Shaking his head, he warned himself not to be silly. He was the only one of his siblings not married or getting ready to marry, but now was the worst time to get involved with anyone. Most especially with the woman who held the key to his future in her slender hands.

Not Mercy, his conscience argued, *but her family.*

Jeremiah pushed his plate away enough so he could fold his arms on the table. "I was nearly grown when my *daed* died, but it wasn't easy to lose him."

"No matter what anyone says, there's no good time to lose someone we love."

She didn't seem surprised that he turned the conversation to such a sad subject. In fact, she seemed grateful he was listening and wasn't trying to relieve her pain with more jests.

Quietly, she added, "Knowing they're bound for a better place is supposed to ease the loss, but it's sad to think of not seeing them for a very long time."

"A *very* long time, I hope."

She nodded, then took a sip of her orange juice. "I should have finished that before I began the pancakes." Without a pause, she went on. "Jeremiah, I know you're as eager as I am to hear from my father and his siblings. We've got to be patient."

"I'm trying."

"Me, too." She put down her glass. "It sounds as if your family lives close together."

"Except for my oldest sister, everyone lives within a mile of where we grew up."

"Not my father's family. Shortly after they were married, my parents joined others who wanted to

start a new church in western New York. That's what they told me anyhow."

"You don't believe it?"

"I'm sure they're being honest, but I think it's strange my dad's siblings moved away from Harmony Creek, and they're scattered from New York to California. I think that was one of the reasons Grandpa Rudy was glad to have me come every year. The rest of the family's visits were infrequent."

"Which explains," he said slowly, pondering the ramifications, "why nobody thought it odd Rudy was leaving the farm to you. It sounds as if none of the rest of them wanted it."

"Let's hope they still feel that way." She paused when Sunni came into the kitchen. After Mercy made more pancakes for her daughter, the little girl rushed away to the dining room as if she feared Jeremiah was infectious with a horrible disease.

He waved aside Mercy's embarrassed apology as she added another serving of pancakes to his plate. "Kids are kids. She'll accept me when she's ready."

"I pray so." As she handed him the syrup bottle, she said, "Dad hopes to get back to me in the next few days, though nothing is settled until everyone agrees. I can't imagine any of them coming here." She glanced out the window at the sparkling snow.

"But then I can't imagine why they left this beautiful hollow in the first place."

"Some people need to get out from under their family's shadow, whether it's the shadow of success or failure."

"Is that why you came here?" She put her fingers to her lips. "I'm sorry, Jeremiah. I shouldn't have asked you such a personal question."

"Why not? I've been asking you personal questions."

"I want you to know I wasn't asking why in the hope of discovering something that would give me an upper hand in claiming the farm."

He put his hand on her arm and wasn't surprised to find it trembling. What startled him was how swiftly he was suffused with warmth as if summer had arrived and flooded the house with sunshine. Knowing he should pull away, he didn't. He liked the sensation of her soft skin beneath his fingertips.

"That's not why I asked about your past, either. Mercy, we can't let this situation make us too competitive or too bitter."

"I know, but..."

He lifted his hand from her arm as she tensed beneath his fingers. "The truth of why I came here is because I wanted to start over. The woman I thought I'd marry decided to marry someone else."

"I'm sorry."

He believed her. She felt everything so deeply, and he hoped she couldn't tell he wasn't being completely honest when he said, "*Danki*, but Emmarita is in the past. I want to look to the future, so I came to Harmony Creek. Here I can be part of the building of a new settlement. It's exciting to think the steps I'm taking could lead to a place that will provide homes for Amish families for generations to come."

She didn't reply, so he pushed back his chair. With a swift prayer of gratitude for the meal, he stood.

"If you'll excuse me," he said, "I need to see if there are usable tarps in the big barn. It looks like more snow, and the roof on the barn where my tools are has more holes than an old pair of sneakers."

"Thanks for your help, Jeremiah."

"*Danki* for breakfast."

When again she remained silent, he put his hat and coat on and turned up his collar before he opened the door. A cold blast of wind sucked him out onto the porch.

He looked across the yard toward the barns. *Lord, I could use your help in seeing the way I should go. I'm here to help make this settlement a success. How can I without this farm?*

It was possible in the coming months, after they had houses fit to live in, one of the other fami-

lies might be able to offer him a place to stay. He could return to making furniture, though it would take time to establish the business, and he'd have to discover what he needed to do to open a wood-working shop in New York. Selling many of his tools in order to raise money for the farm had seemed like a *gut* choice before he found the situation was far more complicated than he'd imagined.

He did a quick inventory in his mind. He had enough tools to do simple projects. Eventually, he could buy new tools to make furniture, which would boost his profits.

But could he set aside his dream of farming? And how could he ask Mercy to put aside hers so he could have the future he wanted along Harmony Creek? He was no closer to the answer than he'd been the moment he saw her in the house.

No, he was further away because his attraction to her was sure to complicate the situation unless he was careful.

Very, very, very careful.

Chapter Five

Mercy made certain the ladder was secure against the wall before she tore off the final pieces of hideous wallpaper after lunch later that week. She was glad to toss aside the tea rose pattern and watch it flit onto the pile of scraps she'd made. If she'd had to look at the ugly wallpaper much longer, she would have had nightmares about the disgusting pink roses for a full week.

She laughed as she climbed off the ladder. Once she swept up the strips, she'd never have to see it again.

Pausing as she stepped onto the smooth wood floors, she imagined how the walls would look with a fresh coat of paint. The dark woodwork would complement it. With the variety of oak furniture in the room and forest green tiles edging the fireplace opening, the room would look invit-

ing. She wasn't sure why her grandfather hadn't changed it years ago.

Her feeling of accomplishment faded. Was it silly to do all this work? If the farm wasn't going to be hers, she was wasting her time redoing the house to make it a home for her and Sunni.

She wasn't going to sit around and wait to hear from Dad. If they agreed to let her somehow buy the farm, she'd regret the time lost. She'd already sent a copy of the approval she'd gotten as a foster parent before Sunni was placed with her as well as other forms to county and state offices to begin the approval process for turning the farm into a summer camp for underprivileged city children.

Though it was difficult to think about warm weather when it was snowing—again!—and drifts were rising over the bottom of the porch railing. It was getting so deep Sunni didn't want to go outside. And it was cold! Even with a full tank of fuel oil, the house couldn't shake its chill. No wonder Sunni had made a tent out of blankets in the dining room to give herself a warm cocoon where she could read and color.

Chafing her cold hands, Mercy decided to do something to keep her warm, too. Not sweeping up the damp wallpaper strips. She'd turn her attention to finding the will Grandpa Rudy must have left somewhere in the house.

Two hours later she was running out of places

to look on the first floor. She'd gone through the stacks of papers, mail and unread newspapers on her grandfather's desk. She'd checked every cubbyhole and drawer, including the "secret" one he'd shown her when she turned thirteen. He kept nothing in it more secret than his stash of root beer candies.

She resisted stopping to read the papers her grandfather had kept. Later…

Going to the back stairs she preferred rather than the grander front staircase, Mercy went up. The floors over the kitchen were sturdier than at the other end of the house.

Where should she begin? Where would Grandpa Rudy have put such an important document?

Mercy gnawed on her lower lip as she looked along the upper hallway. He'd told her so often that he'd made a will. Or that he was going to. If he had, wouldn't he have kept a copy somewhere in the house?

Both attorneys in nearby Salem had told her that they hadn't helped him draft a will. Why would Grandpa Rudy have been so specific about leaving her instructions on what to do after his death if he hadn't left a will somewhere? Maybe he hadn't gotten around to putting his thoughts on paper.

No, she didn't want to believe that.

Had Grandpa Rudy taken his business elsewhere? He liked to travel throughout the county as well as in the nearby hills of Vermont. His old truck had a half million miles on the odometer, proof he had friends far and wide throughout the area. Should she contact other law offices in the area?

The idea gave her a headache, because it probably would be a waste of time. Not that she didn't have time to waste. Talking to her parents last night had been as discouraging as the search for the will. Her father's siblings disagreed about what to do with the farm.

"There's no hurry," Dad had said. "Let them take the time they need to consider everything. Rushing them will annoy everyone, and making such an important decision hastily is sure to give us a reason to be sorry later."

Mercy wasn't sure if her parents were among the ones who would be irked if she pressed for an answer. She'd gently reminded them how vital it was to start the licensing procedures for the farm before she could open it to children. When her mother had expressed surprise, saying she thought Mercy's foster care license would suffice, Mercy bit back her irritation. Several times before she'd left, she'd outlined for her parents what she needed to do in preparation to make Come Along Farm possible.

"I keep my important papers in my room," Mercy said aloud, smothered by the silence. "Maybe Grandpa Rudy did, too."

Pushing on the door she hadn't opened since the funeral, she started to step into her grandfather's room, then froze in the doorway. Everything about the room was a reminder of him. At the foot of the bed was the bright red-and-green afghan he'd made when he decided learning to crochet would keep his mind sharp. Two more afghans, one black-and-white and the other a gaudy yellow, were draped over an upholstered chair whose springs were gone. The seat dropped to the floor.

A low, long dresser between the room's two windows was covered with photographs. When she'd first come to the farm, the pictures had been on a table downstairs. She'd pestered Grandpa Rudy to identify each person and tell her how they were related to her until on one visit, she discovered he'd moved them upstairs. Though he'd never complained, she guessed he'd gotten tired of sharing the same stories over and over.

She stepped back. She couldn't go in and touch his things. Not yet. Not when the pain of losing him was so fresh.

Tomorrow, she promised herself. Tomorrow she would come back if she hadn't found a will in the house. In the meantime she could look in the other rooms where the floors were solid. Perhaps up in

the attic, though she shuddered at the idea of the spiderwebs in the stairwell.

"Knock, knock," came a shout from the first floor.

Even with the voice distorted by the narrow staircase, she couldn't mistake it for another or ignore how her heart began to beat a bit faster.

Jeremiah!

Since the breakfast they'd shared the day the heat went out, she'd seen him at a distance and waved when he noticed her outside. He hadn't come to the house, though she'd heard the sound of hammering, and she guessed he was doing work on the tenant house.

Hurrying down the stairs, Mercy caught sight of Sunni slipping into the kitchen. Jeremiah either hadn't noticed her or was pretending he hadn't.

Jeremiah had taken off his black felt hat, leaving his reddish-brown hair tousled. Her fingers tingled at the thought of brushing those strands into place.

He turned to her, and her breath caught. The cold wind had burnished his face, emphasizing the strong planes that realigned when he gave her a cautious smile.

Regret slashed her. In other circumstances she and Jeremiah might have become friends, but the future of the farm remained a chasm between them. She had no idea how to cross it.

And is being friends all you aspire to become with him?

She paid no attention to the soft voice from deep within her. Instantly, she wondered if doing that was a mistake, because she hadn't heeded what it whispered when she was seeing Graham. Maybe if she'd listened then...

Jeremiah spoke, freeing her from her uneasy thoughts. "I wanted to let you know, Mercy, I've got some cattle being delivered in a couple of days."

"Cows? Here? Now?"

His face became grave. "You don't have to remind me, Mercy, how foolish I was to make these plans before the farm was officially mine. If your family decides not to sell to me, I'll have the animals removed and sold. I wanted you to know so you weren't surprised when the livestock truck backs up the drive."

"Thank you. I appreciate you letting me know." She hated how they spoke as polite strangers who intended to remain that.

"I didn't want you to think I was going behind your back."

"That never crossed my mind," she said, bowled over by his words. She'd met very few Amish people, but the ones she'd met lived a life of faith and truth.

"Gut." His smile returned. "We've got to stop

thinking the other one believes we have ulterior motives for everything we do or say."

"How do we do that?"

"By accepting whatever happens with the farm is God's will."

Mercy couldn't return his easy grin. God's will? Had it been God's will that her first placement had been disrupted by jealousy? Why would God allow her to fall for Graham so he could make her feel as if she was a second choice?

"Are you okay?" Jeremiah asked, his ruddy brows lowering.

"Fine. Or as fine as I can be, under the circumstances." That was the truth, and she wasn't going to spill why she couldn't accept God's will as easily as Jeremiah seemed to.

He scanned her face, puzzled and looking for answers. She wasn't going to share the details of her time in foster care when it'd seemed as if God had abandoned her. She'd told Graham about that, and he'd been shocked at first. Later, he'd acted as if her failed adoption was somehow all her fault.

Only much later had she realized he was repeating exactly what his mother had said. The woman had always been quick to point out what she saw as Mercy's shortcomings. Everything that went wrong, even rain on a day when they'd planned to go to an outdoor concert, was, in his mother's eyes, Mercy's fault. It made no sense, but

Mercy would have endured it if Graham had—just once—stood up for her.

He hadn't.

Not once. He quickly agreed with Mrs. Rapp, no matter how ridiculous the older woman's opinions were.

If Graham had been willing to get out from under his mother's thumb, Mercy might not have rushed to Harmony Creek before she realized Grandpa Rudy had put the farm up for sale.

Her best friend, Erika, had warned Mercy to consider Graham's proposal very, very carefully before agreeing. "If it's a choice between what his mother wants and what you want," Erika had told her more than once, "you're going to lose every time."

"But I love him," Mercy had argued, "and he loves me."

"I'm sure you're right, but he'll always side with his mother. Be careful."

She hadn't been. She'd given her heart totally, believing if she loved Graham enough, he'd change.

He hadn't. When the tough decision had to be made of where they'd live, he'd listened to Mrs. Rapp instead of doing what was best for his future wife and stepdaughter. His assumption Mercy was wrong for not understanding his mother's needs were most important hammered the final nail in

their relationship's coffin, killing hopes she'd had of a future with him.

He hadn't come to say goodbye after she'd left a message on his phone that she and Sunni were moving to Harmony Creek. He'd never returned her call, making her feel like a fool.

One thing she knew for certain. She wasn't going to be a fool for a man ever again, no matter how handsome or nice he was.

Jeremiah couldn't help being curious what Mercy was thinking. Her face was clouded with strong emotions, which he hoped had nothing to do with the arrival of the cows he'd planned to be the beginning of the farm's dairy herd. Every instinct urged him to ask her how he could help. Even more, he yearned to pull her into his arms and offer her comfort for whatever was hurting her.

He couldn't do either.

Not letting the frustrated sigh sift past his lips, he waited for Mercy to say something.

When she did, he wasn't surprised it was a lame excuse to end their conversation. His frown returned when she mentioned going into Salem to pick up groceries.

"The roads aren't plowed yet," he said.

"Oh."

Her face was so dejected he hurried to say, "You could take the sleigh."

"Sleigh?"

He nodded. "There's one in the big barn. It's half-hidden under a blanket, but other than being covered with dust, it looks in *gut* condition. The runners may have some rust. If they do, I can sand it off, and you'll be on your way as soon as we hook up Hero to the sleigh."

"Your horse's name is Hero? Isn't that an odd name for an Amish horse?"

"It's the name he had when I bought him, and he's been my hero more than once when he got me home during a storm." He grinned. "He's very even-tempered, so you shouldn't have any problem with him."

She backed away slowly. "Thanks, but I'll make up something out of whatever is in the kitchen."

He was baffled again, but comprehension burst through him like a shooting star on a summer evening. "You don't know how to drive a horse, ain't so?"

"I never have." She glanced out the window toward where her car sat beneath deep snow. "I've been able to depend on my car to get me where I need to go."

"But you want to live on a farm with horses."

"For the children to ride."

Spying her daughter, who was peeking through

the kitchen doorway, clearly eavesdropping, he acted as if he hadn't seen the *kind*. He didn't want to send her scurrying away again. "Wouldn't those *kinder* enjoy rides in a wagon, too?"

She folded her arms but laughed. "Jeremiah Stoltzfus, has anyone ever told you that once you get an idea in your head you hold on to it like a snapping turtle?"

"I'd like to think I have more sense than a turtle that won't let go even to eat." He hooked a thumb toward the door. "Might as well get started with your lessons."

"Not now."

"Why not? I've got the time, and today isn't going to be the only day you'll need the sleigh before the snow melts."

Again, she paused. Was she looking for an excuse he'd have to accept?

He realized how much he'd misconstrued her silence when she said, "I can't go outside to take driving lessons and leave Sunni alone in the house."

"Bring her along. I'll teach her, too."

"She's only seven years old."

With a laugh, he said, "I was younger than she is the first time the reins were placed in my hands." He looked straight at Sunni. "Do you want to try?" He cut his eyes to Mercy. "What do you say?"

He wasn't sure if he or Mercy was more shocked when Sunni stepped into the room and asked, "Can we, Mommy?"

Chapter Six

Mercy wanted to say no to driving lessons, but how could she when Sunni was opening up to Jeremiah for the first time? Though he might not be in their lives for long, it was good to see her daughter begin to trust another man.

But was Mercy ready to trust another man?

You're agreeing to learning to drive a sleigh, not accepting an offer to go on a date with him. That little voice was becoming more annoying, but it also was correct. *He's trying to make you less dependent on him during these storms.*

She was shocked the thought irritated her more. Poor Jeremiah! It seemed she could find an ulterior motive in whatever he did. Not his ulterior motive, but hers.

"Mommy, can we drive the sleigh?" asked Sunni, warning Mercy she'd been lost in her self-recriminating thoughts too long.

"All right." She didn't get a chance to add more before her daughter let out a cheer and began singing "Jingle Bells."

Jeremiah was grinning as broadly. "Let me get Hero hooked up to the sleigh. It may take fifteen minutes or more because I need to get the sleigh out of the barn."

"It'll give me time to make up a thermos of hot cocoa and get us bundled up," she said, excitement bursting through her. Hadn't she come to the farm to try new things? Learning to drive the sleigh would be a great place to start.

"Jingle bells, jingle bells, jingle all the way," sang Sunni at the top of her lungs as she spun about like a flat-footed ballerina.

With a wink, Jeremiah put on his hat and left. He called back that he'd pull the sleigh up to the door.

Mercy worked around her jubilant daughter and delighted in Sunni's joy. She hadn't seen her daughter so elated since before Grandpa Rudy's funeral. And Mercy was happy, too. The idea of speeding over the snow in a sleigh was exciting.

She was about to wrap a scarf around Sunni's neck when her daughter pulled away and ran to the door.

Mercy wasn't surprised to see the sleigh looked as if it'd been hit by an avalanche and buried under boulders. The paint was scraped off the dented

side, but the runners were straight, and Jeremiah's horse was pulling it without too much effort.

"Ready?" she asked Sunni as she reached for her own scarf and the thermos and trio of cups.

Sunni threw open the door, then halted. "Where are the jingle bells?"

"All I could find," Jeremiah said, "was this harness."

Sunni whirled. "But, Mommy, the song is 'Jingle Bells.' We have to have jingle bells."

Before Mercy could reply, the little girl whirled and ran up the stairs at a dangerous speed for a child wearing two leg braces.

Mercy steeled herself, praying she wouldn't hear the dreadful thump that meant Sunni had fallen on the steps.

"Are you okay?" asked Jeremiah from right behind her.

She turned to discover he'd come up on the porch. "She shouldn't go so fast up the stairs."

"Words every *mamm* has said for as long as there have been stairs. We all take a few tumbles in life and are not much the worse for it, ain't so?"

"Certainly." She appreciated how he acted as if Sunni was like every other child.

"Why does she wear those braces...if you don't mind me asking?"

"I don't." She smiled. "But I don't know. We've gotten as many different opinions as we've had

doctors for her. Most recently her pediatric orthopedist said we should worry less about what caused the weakness in her legs and concentrate on helping her walk better."

"And run."

Her smile broadened. "She's learned that well."

When Sunni came down the stairs at the same pace she'd gone up, both Jeremiah and Mercy jumped forward as the little girl stumbled three steps from the bottom. Between them, they caught her and set her on her feet.

"I know, I know," Sunni said before anyone could speak. "I need to go more slowly and use my crutches, but we have jingle bells." As she began singing the song again, she held up her right hand and shook it.

Jeremiah's eyes grew wide at the sound of bells jangling.

Taking the toy from Sunni, Mercy held it out to him. It was a wooden half circle into which was set a half dozen tiny metal bells.

"What is it?" he asked beneath the little girl's enthusiastic singing.

Mercy answered as softly, "A toy. Kids use them to make music in school. We got it as a therapy tool for Sunni last year. It helped strengthen her grip." Showing him how fingers wrapped around the wooden handle while the bells were shaken, she smiled. "I didn't realize she still had it."

Jeremiah raised his voice to include the little girl. "We've got our jingle bells and our cocoa, so let's go."

Mercy watched as he went outside. Sunni followed, and he swung her up onto the sleigh's bench. He sat beside her. They looked back in a silent urging for Mercy to hurry up.

She did and laughed as she hadn't in longer than she could remember when Jeremiah reached to assist her into the battered sleigh. At his touch, even through his thick gloves and hers, the day suddenly had seemed warmer.

When she sat beside him, he unlashed the reins from the dash and showed her how to hold them. He told her to loop the reins up between her pinkie and the next finger, grip them in her fist and let them go out between her thumb and first finger.

"That gives you the most control," he said, adjusting her hands slightly. "Hero is well trained, so call his name, and he'll go."

"And to stop him?"

"A simple 'whoa.' You don't have to tug on the reins. He'll stop right away." Again, he aligned her fingers. "There you go. Whenever you're ready."

She made the mistake of looking at him to ask another question. His face was so near to hers their misted breaths mingled in the cold air. As her gaze locked with his lustrous blue eyes, she

knew she should look away before he got the wrong idea.

Or the right one.

Even that thought couldn't convince her eyes to turn from his handsome face. As close as they sat, she could see the faint shadow of whiskers along his jaw. Her fingers tingled, teasing her to tear off her gloves and stroke that firm line. She caught a motion from the corner of her eye. His hand was rising to cup her cheek. She leaned toward it, eager to feel him against her.

"Jingle bells! Jingle bells!" sang Sunni abruptly.

The cheerful song brought Mercy to her senses. Jeremiah, too, she guessed, because he quickly slanted away from her and urged her to give the command to go.

She did, and the horse moved at a walk toward the road. Her thoughts sped far faster as she pondered what would have happened if Sunni's innocent singing hadn't intruded. Trying to convince herself it was better she didn't know, she wondered when she'd started being dishonest with herself.

"Hold that board right there," Jeremiah urged Sunni, who kept a suspicious eye on the hammer and nail he was positioning. It was the first board for the roof of a chicken coop. After finishing his barn chores, including milking and feeding the

calves delivered earlier in the week, he'd wanted time outdoors.

He smiled at Sunni. The little girl didn't trust him completely, but she didn't scurry in the opposite direction when he approached as she had before they drove the sleigh along the twisting creek that slept beneath a sheet of ice. When, during her midmorning break from her schoolwork, she'd come to watch him building the chicken coop, a simple box with a door and shelves for the hens to lay on, he'd pretended as if nothing significant had happened. Maybe if he acted as if she'd sought him out right from the beginning, he wouldn't send her fleeing again. He kept up a steady narration of everything he did, and Sunni had inched closer and closer.

Then she began asking questions, barely giving him time to answer before she fired another one— or two—at him. She asked about the coop and the chickens that would live inside. She wanted to know what color he planned to paint it and what he intended to name the chickens. He answered questions about what the chickens would eat and where they would sleep and when the rooster would crow.

Asking her to balance the board might threaten the status quo, but Jeremiah kept reminding himself with God's help, anything was possible. Even persuading a *kind* he didn't mean her ill will. He

was curious if Sunni's skittishness was for the same reason as Mercy's.

What do you know about women? he asked himself. He'd believed Emmarita when she said she was coming back. He hadn't guessed she was seeing her *Englischer* at the same time Jeremiah was escorting her home from youth events. She'd jumped the fence, and unlike two of his brothers' wives who had done the same, she hadn't returned…though he'd waited several months to make sure. When he heard she'd married her *Englischer*, he knew he needed to put the past behind him. He listened to the hopes of having a farm of his own, the hopes God had put inside him. It was easier to heed that portion of his heart when he closed off the part filled with pain at Emmarita's betrayal.

Focusing on his work, Jeremiah made sure Sunni's fingers weren't close to where he was hammering. She'd become silent, but the fact she was standing there seemed like a precious victory.

"Mommy!" Sunni suddenly shouted and released the plank.

Jeremiah grasped the board to keep it from swinging out and striking the *kind*. His heart hitched, and he knew he couldn't blame his heart's reaction totally on fright for the little girl.

His gaze riveted on Mercy as she walked toward them. Her cheeks were burnished by the cold

to the same shade as her lips, which appeared delightfully kissable. The image of his hands framing her face while he sampled her mouth was so real he lowered his eyes and swung the hammer, barely missing the nail and his thumb in his work glove. He set down the hammer, knowing, when he was that distracted, he might not miss next time.

"What are you making?" Mercy's tone hinted that she hadn't noticed how distracted he was by her.

He wasn't sure if that was *gut* or annoying.

"It's a chicken choop," Sunni answered.

"A chicken *coop*," he corrected with a smile.

"But…" Mercy looked hastily away, but not fast enough because he saw her cheeks redden more.

He wasn't going to pretend not to understand. She'd agreed on the day he taught her to drive not to look for secret intentions behind every word or deed. He wished she'd trust him.

Though he wanted to ask why she always painted him with such negative intentions, he said, "Mercy, didn't your *daed* tell you it may be several weeks before he gets an answer from his siblings?"

"He did."

"But you are working to fix up the main house. Sunni was telling me that you're painting the living room." He saw *mamm* and daughter exchange

a glance, but couldn't guess what it meant. He hoped nothing. "Like you, I don't want to wait until everything is decided. If I do and they sell me the farm, I must not be so far behind on fixing up the place I can't get a decent crop in the fields or have a place to put it when it's harvested."

"I know." She raised her eyes to meet his, and he realized he'd misjudged her reaction. She wasn't angry. She was frustrated her family hadn't made their decision. "I'm sorry this is dragging on."

Stepping around the coop so it wasn't between them, he put his hands on Mercy's shoulders. "It's not your fault."

"Thanks for saying that, but every time the phone rings, I hope it's my father with news." She grimaced. "I'm tempted to silence it and let the answering machine get the calls. That way, I'd only have to check once a day."

"Why don't you?"

Her eyes brightened. "I think I will. I'm tired of being on a ladder and having to rush down to answer it. In case it's Dad." A smile played at the corners of her mouth. "I almost tipped over the paint can yesterday. If I had, Sunni and I would be green now."

"It wouldn't be a bad color on you two," he replied in mock seriousness. "And we could use a bit more green with this snow."

The little girl giggled, and Jeremiah let his lips tilt up in a grin.

"I'll leave that to the leaves," Mercy said.

Groaning at her pun, he felt the tension dissolve around them. They might have different goals for the farm, but they were stuck in limbo together while her family debated.

"Why don't we keep doing what we've been doing?" he asked. "Any fixes we do will benefit whoever gets the farm."

"That makes sense."

"And we don't have to walk around on eggshells."

"Eggshells?" asked Sunni, looking around as if she expected to see a pile waiting to be picked up. "Where are they?"

Again, he and Mercy chuckled, and Sunni joined in.

Jeremiah rested one hand on the top of the coop. "Whether you or I or someone else ends up with the farm, me building a simple chicken coop won't make any difference. It seems strange to live on a farm without chickens."

"You can't be thinking of putting them out here now," Mercy said, wrapping her arms around herself as a frigid gust rocked the trees beyond the barn.

He shook his head. "Ordering chicks was another thing I did before I left Paradise Springs.

They'll be shipped once the weather warms up. By fall, they should be providing eggs." He gave her a wry grin. "Sorry they won't be laying in time for Easter."

"Don't worry," Mercy said. "We'll have eggs to dye for Easter."

Sunni looked relieved, but grimaced when Mercy reminded her schoolwork waited in the house.

As her daughter went inside, Mercy asked, "Do Amish kids dye eggs for Easter?"

"Some do. My *mamm* hid plastic eggs filled with jelly beans for us to find."

"I assume you have church services on Easter."

"*Ja.* Good Friday is a fast day until noon, so we can spend the morning in prayer. On Easter, we rejoice together."

"Mennonites consider it a time to be with family, and we have services on Friday and Sunday." She patted her hands together and glanced toward the house. "I should make sure Sunni is doing her schoolwork."

Gut sense told him to let her go, but he didn't want to let the moment end. "You've got a lot of questions about Amish folks."

"If I stay here, I'm going to have Amish neighbors."

He almost said if she ended up with the farm, the settlement could be in jeopardy. He needed

to stay and help it grow. There wasn't any reason to repeat what had been said already. They knew what was at stake, so why belabor it?

"Why don't you come with me to a service?" he asked. "This Sunday is a church Sunday. I think you'll get plenty of answers to your questions there."

"I didn't know your services were open to outsiders."

"They are, but few non-Amish are willing to sit on hard, backless benches for three hours to listen to sermons in High German."

"I don't understand that language."

"Visitors have someone to translate for them. I think you'd find it interesting, Mercy." *Please, God, let her say* ja. He didn't want to consider why it was suddenly so important to him that she agree, but it was.

"Thank you, Jeremiah. We'll come." Her smile banished the cold around him...and inside him.

When she walked away, he was glad she hadn't expected him to say something else. He wasn't sure what he would have said, but he was certain anything he blurted out would reveal the farm was no longer the main reason he was glad he'd come to Harmony Creek.

She was.

Chapter Seven

Jeremiah whistled one of his favorite hymns as he put the finishing touches on the chicken coop. He laughed at the sign tacked over the door.

Welkoom Hoom.

Sunni had brought it out to him right after breakfast. She'd proudly announced she'd painted it for his Amish chickens so they'd feel right at home in the coop.

It had taken every bit of restraint to keep from grinning. Not only were the words different from any he knew in *Englisch* or *Deitsch*, the everyday language of the Amish, but most of the letters had drips of green paint beneath them. He wondered if Mercy knew what her daughter had been doing.

He knew the little girl was fascinated with the idea of chickens and gathering eggs, because she'd talked of nothing else while he put the sign in place. As much as he wanted the farm to become

a part of the new Amish community, he hated the idea of Sunni not having her chance to help with the new chicks.

With each passing day, the situation was becoming more of a potential disaster, no matter which one of them ended up with the farm. Did Mercy's *onkels* and *aentis* and *daed* realize that? He doubted it. Would it do any *gut* to ask Mercy to discuss it with them?

But did he want them to announce their decision if it cost him the farm?

He no longer knew.

You know, God, he prayed, *what is to come and why. Help us to walk the path You have prepared for us, even if our hearts are broken.*

He flinched. No matter what choice the Bambergers made, his heart was going to be hurt because if he took possession of the farm, Mercy's heart—and Sunni's—would be shattered. For the first time he began to wonder if he should walk away. He could have Kitty find him another place. It might take too much time and risk the success of the settlement, but how could he stand by and watch Mercy hurt?

Help me, God, to trust You have a way to resolve the unresolvable.

When Mercy heard a knock at the door that afternoon, she made sure her kerchief was in place

before she answered it. She didn't want to meet one of her neighbors for the first time with her head not properly covered, because she knew Amish women always wore what they called prayer *kapps* or a kerchief like hers. Dust and spiderwebs didn't count as a proper covering, though she guessed there were plenty on the off-white kerchief.

A pulse of excitement caught her off guard as she wondered if Jeremiah stood on the other side of the door. What was she thinking? He'd been very kind to teach her to drive the sleigh so she could get to the village after a snowfall.

But he wanted her grandfather's farm, and if the family's decision went against her, he would do everything he could to buy it. Nothing had changed.

No, that wasn't true.

A few things had changed. She couldn't see Jeremiah as a rival trying to ruin her plans. Instead, her heart seemed to glow whenever he was around.

Throwing open the door, she was unprepared for the surge of disappointment when she realized it wasn't Jeremiah. She'd been silly to think he'd come to the front door and knock. He always walked in.

A woman, whose face was half-hidden by a garish purple and yellow crocheted scarf cover-

ing her mouth and nose, stood on the porch. From the top of her striped stocking cap to the tip of her boots topped by a ring of fake fur, she looked ready to go sledding on the hills beyond the barn.

The woman pulled aside her scarf to reveal the lower half of her face. "Are you Mercy Bamberger?"

"I am." Mercy motioned for the woman to come in.

Even if the woman was there to try to sell her something she didn't want, Mercy wasn't going to leave her out on the porch in the biting wind.

When the blonde woman set a briefcase on the floor and began to unzip her thick parka, Mercy asked, "What can I do for you?"

"I'm Whitney Albright with Washington County Children's Services." She opened a pocket on the side of the briefcase and pulled out a simple business card.

Mercy took it and glanced at it. The card confirmed what Whitney had said.

"I'd like to talk with you if you've got time," Whitney said.

"Certainly. Let's go into the living room."

Curiosity accompanied Mercy into the room, which was comfortably warm in the afternoon sunshine. She couldn't help being curious about whether Whitney thought of how the glass in the windows rattled whenever a strong gust struck the

house. Motioning for the woman to take a seat on the couch, where the cold air seeping around the sills wouldn't reach her, Mercy took a chair facing the sofa.

"I'm sorry to come unannounced," Whitney said as she sat and set her briefcase on her knees. "I did try to call. Several times yesterday. But while I got your answering machine, I didn't want to leave a message before I had a chance to talk to you. When I tried again this morning and got the machine again, I thought maybe I'd drive over and take a chance on catching you at home."

Mercy explained how she'd turned off the phone's ringer so she wasn't interrupted while she was painting. Without giving the other woman a chance to reply, she hurried on. "If this is about my daughter not being signed up to go to public school, I made arrangements to homeschool her for the rest of this year. I plan to have her go to the Son-Rise Charter School next fall."

Whitney held up her hands and shook her head. "This isn't about your daughter, Mercy, though I'll tell you I did stop at the school in Salem to find someone who knew you. They explained to me the arrangements you'd made for Sunni. You know you can get special needs services through the public school system, though she's going to the charter school, I assume."

"Yes, because we had that arrangement with our school district where we lived."

"If anyone tells you differently, call me and I'll talk to them." She smiled, but it was cool and without humor. "Some superintendents look for ways to cut costs. Not that we've had such a problem with the Salem school district, but we like to make sure none crop up."

"I appreciate that." Curious why the woman was visiting, Mercy asked if Whitney would like something hot to drink.

"That would be nice. Coffee or tea or whatever you have."

"I have green tea."

"Perfect."

Rising, Mercy went into the kitchen and put the kettle on. She glanced into the dining room and saw Sunni curled up in a chair, sound asleep. The little girl had had nightmares last night. It was good she could catch up on her sleep today, especially until Mercy discovered why a social worker had come to the house.

Whitney took an appreciative sip of the tea, but waited until Mercy was sitting again before she opened her briefcase and pulled out a laptop. "As I said, I'm not here to speak to you about Sunni. However, I'm here *because* of your daughter." The social worker looked abashed as she added, "I guess I should have told you right from the get-

go I was forwarded a copy of your files and I've read them."

"I know files are shared among social workers."

"Good." Whitney relaxed a bit as she pushed the button to activate her computer. Raising her head, she wore what Mercy called a social worker's *I hope you can get me out of a jam* face.

The first time she'd seen it was when she was in the system herself. She'd forgotten about it until another social worker spoke to her about taking in Sunni on an emergency placement. Seeing it again whetted her curiosity and her trepidation.

"You are," Whitney said, "in a somewhat unique position of having exactly the experience we need."

Mercy felt her jaw drop. Another child? Here? She thought of all she'd had to do in order to be approved as a foster parent before Sunni was placed with her. There had been more paperwork and home visits and counseling when she applied to adopt her daughter. Enough to kill off a whole forest was what Dad had said with a laugh.

Glancing around the half-painted room that opened onto another where wallpaper was peeling off a wall and the floor sloping enough to send Mercy chasing after a nail when it fell and rolled away, she looked at the social worker. Was this a joke?

"I know this is unexpected," Whitney said,

"and it may not be perfect timing, but I rarely find the time is perfect when a child's placement has been disrupted and we need to find a temporary placement."

"Oh, I'm so sorry to hear about a placement falling apart."

"I know you are."

Mercy wondered exactly how much the social worker knew about her story and Sunni's. How many files had Whitney perused before she came to Harmony Creek? No doubt, there were thick files outlining how she and Sunni had come to be part of the Bamberger family.

At the thought of her family, Mercy stiffened. What was she thinking? She needed to tell Whitney, while she understood the gravity of the situation, now was the worst time for her to consider having another child placed with her family. Even a temporary one. No, most especially a temporary one, because Sunni didn't need to deal with more change.

"I know you're not ready," Whitney said in her calm voice.

Mercy bit back a laugh. "Look around you. Come Along Farm is weeks away from being ready for me to apply for approval."

"But you are a licensed foster parent?"

"I am."

"Parker, a nine-year-old boy, needs a place-

ment." The blonde leaned forward, lowering her computer's top and putting her elbows on it. "He's a unique case because we don't get many failed international adoptions in this county. In fact, he might be the second one in sixty years. Mercy, you know how it is to be an outsider in a closed community, and your daughter was born in Korea as Parker was."

"Why does he need a placement?"

"His prospective adoptive parents can't deal with his many severe food allergies. You're raising a special needs child, so I can't imagine a better place for this boy while we look for another adoptive family than with you and Sunni."

Wanting to groan that Whitney was expecting too much of her and her daughter, Mercy said nothing. Instead, she prayed. *Lord, You don't have to tell me this is crazy. I know that, and I also know Your hand brought Whitney here. Come Along Farm is supposed to be a haven for children. How can I turn away the first one You present to me?*

A sensation of calm draped over her as she held out her hand. "Can I see his placement report?"

"It's on the computer." Whitney pressed several keys and then turned it so Mercy could read the report that wasn't so different from the one she'd been given with Sunni's other paperwork. It was from the Korean adoption agency and translated

into sometimes confusing English. The information was sparse and included his age, gender, a couple of paragraphs outlining what his Korean caretakers had observed about him, and weight and height.

"His name in Korea was Park Jae-Eun, I see," Mercy said.

"The Kentons changed it to Parker Kenton, wanting to keep part of his Korean name as part of his new name." The social worker smiled sadly. "It'll be easier for him in the States, I suppose, but his Korean name means talent and mercy."

"Mercy?"

Whitney nodded. "When I was looking for foster families with Korean-born children in the county, I saw your name, which was why I requested your file."

"He has several food allergies," Mercy said after finishing the two-page report from Korea, "but I don't see anything here."

"They apparently weren't discovered until he was here. He had no problem with Korean food, but Americans eat a wider variety of products."

Wondering why Parker's new family hadn't changed their own diets to accommodate the boy, Mercy looked at the list of Parker's allergies. Peanuts and shellfish were the first of nearly a dozen items, but it wouldn't be difficult to work around his allergies.

"Am I wrong," Whitney asked, "to think you make a lot of your meals from scratch? Parker seems to have extra trouble with prepared foods."

The social worker had an uncanny ability to guess what Mercy was thinking, or more likely, Whitney was very good at her job and had prepared herself for questions and concerns Mercy might have.

"I don't make as much from scratch as I normally would, because we don't have anything canned in the cellar." Second thoughts filled her. Sunni needed her during this difficult time, and bringing a second child into their family would curtail the time she had to work on the house. She couldn't reduce the time she spent teaching Sunni, and a nine-year-old would require homeschooling, too. So much paperwork needed to be filed, and...

"You'll want to see this." Whitney held out a small photo.

Mercy looked at it and knew her protests and logical thinking were useless. The moment she saw the proud expression on the boy's face that announced he didn't need anyone's help, she recognized a kindred spirit. Especially when she noticed how his taut shoulders revealed he was trying to hide his pain of being unwanted from the camera.

Oh, how easily she remembered those feelings! And the photographs taken against an of-

fice wall while people looked on with pitying smiles. Mercy had been older than the boy the first time she'd been subjected to the humiliation of knowing she was nobody's child. When *Abuelita* had died, Mercy's sole parent had become the state government, an indifferent guardian at best. She'd been snatched from *Abuelita*'s apartment so quickly she hadn't had time to pack the photo of her parents, her most precious possession, before being bundled up and put in a car with strangers. She'd been told her personal belongings would follow. One box had…but the photo hadn't been in it. Her other box had vanished.

A chance question when she'd asked if she would be going to her Fresh Air family had saved her from what probably would have been a life in the system. A caring social worker—Mercy couldn't remember her name—had contacted the family who'd welcomed her for the previous three summers to their farm in northern New York. But the family's agreement to take her on a trial basis hadn't been the salvation she'd expected. She hadn't been able to wait to return to the family she'd thought of constantly while she was away from it. But the fun times she'd enjoyed each summer with the two daughters had become intolerable misery when the older daughter had become wildly jealous of Mercy and the attention she'd garnered in the very conservative community.

The placement had fallen apart, and she'd found herself in a car with the social worker who'd brought her north. Returned to the city, she'd been placed with a family who used the stipend from five foster kids to help pay for their own expenses. She'd remained there, virtually ignored, for the longest four months of her life.

Then adults she hadn't known came to the house. She'd realized they were social workers, and they'd given her no warning other than she needed to pack her personal items. The other kids in the house had been told the same. Though none of them had much, they'd delayed as long as they could over the task while they'd spent time speculating about what was about to happen to them. The older children had been resigned to being put with another family in another school district, but Mercy had been terrified.

Her fear had grown when the other children were dropped off to meet other social workers so they could be introduced to their new foster families, but she'd been driven out of the city. Nobody had told her where she was going until they'd left the city behind.

She'd been taken to meet Frieda and Kevin Bamberger, a Mennonite couple whose biological children were much older than she was. When she'd reached their comfortable home, she hadn't

had high hopes. At the time it'd been another change she didn't have any say in.

But she'd been welcomed as if she'd been a part of their family her whole life. A portion of her bedtime prayers every night still included her gratitude for the two people who had stepped up to be her parents.

She had a chance to help a young child who was caught in the same trap. The Bambergers had welcomed her into their home and their hearts, giving her a new name and a new identity, though there was a remnant of Mercedes Ramirez hidden deep within her, and a family as precious to her as the one she'd shared with *Abuelita*.

"All right," Mercy whispered as she stared into the boy's face.

"All right?" repeated Whitney, astonished by Mercy's sudden about-face. "Does that mean you're willing to take Parker on a temporary basis? It could be a month or two before we find him something permanent. In the meantime, the county will provide you with an epinephrine injector in case he goes into anaphylaxis. Instructions for its use are right on the box, and you need to get familiar with them right away so you don't have to stop to read them if he has an allergy attack. Are you ready to deal with that?"

There wasn't a single doubt in her heart, though her head was blaring warnings like a fire siren. "Yes, we'll take him."

Chapter Eight

"Heard anything about what's going to happen with the farm?"

Jeremiah glanced at Caleb, who was helping him set up his woodworking equipment. For now it was a makeshift workshop, but it was in one of the sturdier outbuildings. They'd set up a portable gas generator outside to power the equipment. His neighbor had worked with him, as well, in closing up the holes in the tenant house wall so it no longer snowed indoors. In exchange, Jeremiah intended to make a few pieces for his friend's house. He'd already sketched out a large kitchen table and the benches and chairs to go with it.

"Nothing," Jeremiah said as he shifted a heavy saw a few inches to the left so there was enough space to walk past it. "I guess they're still making up their minds."

"No news is no news, ain't so?"

He grinned at his friend, who was stretched out beneath a table saw. "That's not exactly how I've heard it."

"But it's true. No news means nothing's been decided."

"You're right." Jeremiah leaned against a stack of planks as his gaze swept the workshop as if he'd entered it for the first time. He'd found the weathered boards in a small barn and brought them to his workshop. If he needed one for a project while Mercy's family discussed the farm, he'd check with her. Using Rudy's bulk tank in the barn to hold milk was one thing, but it'd be completely different to take the valuable wood without permission.

Wiping his hands on a stained cloth, Jeremiah looked out the dusty window beside him. His brows lowered at a surprising sight. He hadn't heard the late-model silver car pull into the driveway. Did Mercy have a friend visiting?

As if he'd asked the question aloud, Caleb paused in examining the underside of a piece of equipment he'd been oiling and came slowly to his feet. "What's so interesting?"

"I didn't know we had company."

Neither man spoke as a blonde *Englisch* woman came out of the house and got into the car. There was a jaunty bounce in her step.

"She sure looks happy," Caleb said. "That bolt

is not turning as smoothly as it should. Want to check it?"

"Sure." Jeremiah didn't move from beside the window. "Do you know her?"

Caleb stepped closer to the window and peered out. The car was close enough so he could get a *gut* view of the woman's face before she turned to look over her shoulder while she backed the car out.

"I've never seen her before," Caleb said. "I've met some of the *Englisch* farmers in the area, but not too many of the women. My sister said the *Englisch* women are friendly when she's gone to the store." He paused for a single heartbeat. "You seem very interested, Jeremiah. But please don't go jumping the fence after some *Englischer*. We need you to help build our settlement. We're six families since the Bowmans moved in yesterday."

Jeremiah nodded and assured Caleb that he was committed to the Harmony Creek settlement. He waited for the pain those words about jumping the fence always created. It came, but not as before. The memory of Emmarita's leaving without saying goodbye was no longer agonizing. However, Caleb's words were a reminder of what Jeremiah had tried to ignore.

Mercy was Mennonite. Getting more involved with her and her daughter would be silly. He had to ignore how his heart beat faster whenever he

thought of Mercy's black hair and eyes the color of freshly overturned earth.

Had his thoughts shown on his face? Or had he revealed the truth in other ways?

Caleb gave him a sympathetic glance. "Staying separate from the world is tougher some times than others, ain't so?"

Jeremiah must have given his friend an answer, but once it'd left his lips, he couldn't recall what it was. That Caleb gave him a companionable slap on the shoulder when he left—exactly as one of Jeremiah's brothers would have—was the proof that he'd soothed his friend's concerns.

Lingering in his shop, Jeremiah knew Caleb was worried about Jeremiah falling for a woman who should be off-limits to him. His neighbor also held the weight of the settlement's success on his broad shoulders. Adding more concern to Caleb's already overflowing plate was one of the last things Jeremiah wanted to do.

Either he or Mercy was going to be leaving the farm. Every way he looked at it, there was no future beyond friendship for them. He needed to keep that in mind.

Always.

Jeremiah's resolve lasted exactly as long as it took him to walk over to the main house.

Mercy turned from the stove as he came in. The aroma of chocolate swept through the kitchen. It

wasn't as enticing as Mercy, who had a dab of flour on one cheek and a line of chocolate beneath her other eye.

Don't think of her as enticing, he warned himself, but not being honest with himself was foolish.

"I assume the other person looks worse," he said with a wink at Sunni, whose dark braid was dusted with flour.

"What?" asked Mercy.

"You look as if someone gave you a black eye."

She glanced in the mirror over the sink where Rudy must have shaved. When she gasped and reached for a washcloth to clean her face, he and Sunni laughed. Sunni giggled harder when Mercy washed the flour out of her braid.

"Call me when the cake's ready to frost," Sunni said once the last of the white was out of her hair.

"I will. You know I depend of my best spatula cleaner." Mercy bent to kiss the top of her daughter's head.

Jeremiah couldn't keep from imagining how those lips would feel against him. He composed his expression when Sunni left the room and Mercy faced him.

Her easy smile disappeared. "I'm glad you came over, Jeremiah. I need to talk to you about something important, so you're not surprised."

"You sound like I did when I told you the cows

were being delivered. Are you having something delivered, too?"

His attempt at levity fell flat because she nodded.

"Did you see the car in the yard earlier?" she asked as she motioned for him to sit at the table.

"*Ja.* I assumed you had a friend visiting."

"Not a friend. Not yet anyhow. The woman who came here is Whitney Albright, and she's a social worker with the county."

"Oh." He wasn't sure what else to say. Had Whitney come for something to do with Sunni? But wasn't the little girl's adoption final? There shouldn't be a reason for a social worker to come to the house, unless...

Was Mercy already going ahead with her plans to get approval for Come Along Farm? Had her *daed* given her some hint to what his siblings had agreed to? She would have told him, wouldn't she?

"Whitney wanted to ask if I'd be willing to take in another child temporarily," Mercy said in not much more than a whisper.

"Are you going to?" He tried to ignore the cascade of relief as he realized, for now, she didn't know more about the future of the farm than he did.

No ulterior motives, he chided himself. She'd concurred, and he hadn't seen a sign of her reneging. He was judging her unfairly.

She wiped her hands on a towel. "As long as I've got room, I'll never turn away a child who needs a home."

When he chuckled, she frowned and asked what was so funny.

"You stating the obvious," he replied. "You want Rudy's farm so you can fill it with *kinder* every summer. It's not a big step to imagining you trying to fill this whole house with youngsters year-round."

"Not a whole houseful. Just one little nine-year-old boy who needs a home because his placement failed."

"His what failed?"

"Failed placement is a term social workers use for when a child is placed in a home with either foster parents or prospective adoptive parents and then the child needs to be removed."

"And saying it failed means the parents don't want the *kind* any longer?" He shook his head in disgust. "What were they thinking? A kid isn't something to return to the store because it's not a great fit."

Pulling out a chair, she sat facing him. "I agree, but sometimes it's for the best. If the match isn't a good one, it can be worse on the youngster than being moved somewhere else." She slid a photo toward him. "This is the boy."

Jeremiah didn't want to look. Getting more

caught up in her life and her plans would complicate their already complicated situation. As he saw the determination in her eyes, he was curious why one boy she'd never met was so important to her.

He reached for the photo.

Breathe!

Such a simple order shouldn't be difficult to follow, but Mercy found it hard to draw in a breath and release it as she waited for Jeremiah's reaction to Parker's picture.

When Jeremiah smiled, she relaxed, astonished how taut her shoulders had become.

"He looks like a normal nine-year-old." Jeremiah tapped the photo. "You can tell he doesn't want to sit still for someone to snap his picture. But why did Whitney choose you? Don't take this the wrong way, but I would have thought the state would wait until a decision is made about the farm."

Standing, she got a cloth to clean off the table. "I'm a licensed foster parent, and I've taken in other children on an emergency basis until a permanent foster home could be found."

"There must be other foster families in the area."

"There are, but Whitney liked the idea of Parker being with a family who already has an Asian child."

"Parker? That's his name?"

"Yes."

"It sounds very grown-up for a kid."

"I know. It's the name his adoptive parents gave him, but it won't be legally his name until he's adopted. Until then, he's legally Park Jae-Eun."

"That's a mouthful."

"And Jeremiah isn't?"

He smiled. "I never said it wasn't."

"I wanted to let you know there's going to be another child in the house," she said.

"Why would you take on the responsibility of another *kind* when everything about the farm is up in the air?"

"Because I know how painful a failed adoption is for a youngster."

"Sunni had a failed adoption?"

"Yes. They happen more often than you'd expect." She drew in a deep breath and released it through tight lips. "The couple who were going to adopt Sunni didn't want a daughter who depends on braces."

He flinched.

"Why are you startled?" she asked.

"Amish families consider a *kind* with physical or mental challenges a gift from God who will bring a very special love to everyone."

"Do you give them physical therapy and such?"

"Of course. We may not have doctors among

us, but we appreciate and admire the work they do to keep us healthy." When Jeremiah came to his feet, he said, "Be careful, Mercy. I admire your intentions, but…"

He didn't add more as he left the house.

She was not sure what he could have said. He was right. She needed to be careful with her heart. With the boy and with Jeremiah, who could break it easily.

Chapter Nine

On Sunday morning Jeremiah had Hero hitched to the buggy and ready to go a little before eight. They were going only a quarter of a mile, but a cold wind would make walking difficult. He hadn't hurried because they had the leisure of starting out later than he was accustomed to in Pennsylvania.

He shivered, pulling his coat's collar up to cover his nape. Slapping his hands together for what little warmth he could find, he was pleased when the door opened and Mercy and Sunni came out.

He wasn't surprised when Mercy picked up her daughter and half ran toward the buggy. Both were hidden beneath heavy coats, hats, mittens and scarves.

With a nodded greeting because his teeth were chattering too hard to speak, he handed Sunni and Mercy into the buggy. He jumped in on the

passenger side, pushing Sunni over with a laugh toward Mercy, who had to slide into the driver's position.

"I thought you'd want to drive." He held the reins out to her.

When she didn't hesitate to take them, he motioned for her to turn the buggy with care in the shoveled area of the yard. He trusted Hero to know what to do, even if Mercy wasn't sure.

"My toes are getting warm!" Sunni stared at a metal box on the buggy's floor.

"That small heater probably won't warm much more than your toes," he said. "The bishop permits their use because of the cold, cold weather in northern New York."

"The bishop is the one who makes the rules?" Mercy looked along the twisting road, then called to Hero to go.

"The *Leit* will meet to discuss and create the *Ordnung* for our district, or we will once we have enough families to be a true district. We need about a dozen."

"What's that?" Sunni asked.

"*Leit* means our people." Jeremiah was pleased the little girl was curious about Amish ways, too. "The *Ordnung* are the unwritten rules we live by. They deal with everything from how we wear our clothes to what equipment we can use. Each item is discussed, prayed about and voted on. Our

bishop helps us stick to it by defining certain aspects of life that haven't been specifically discussed. Like using small heaters in our buggies. Eventually, we'll meet to decide."

"I vote for having them," Mercy said with a laugh. "It's nice to know, even if my fingers freeze off, my toes will be safe. That is, assuming we get next door in one piece."

As they drove from sunshine to the cooler shade where thick pine trees edged the road, Jeremiah said, "You're doing *gut* with driving."

"My mommy can do anything." Sunni's tone stated he was a *dummkopf* for not already knowing that. "When I'm having trouble with my spelling, she tells me to try. She says you can't know what you can do until you try. Right, Mommy?"

Mercy didn't shift her gaze from the ruts that could catch a buggy wheel. "That's right, *eolin-i*."

"That means 'little one' in Korean," Sunni said.

"You speak Korean?" He looked at Mercy, astonished.

"A few words. I learned them from my beautiful daughter before she forgot most of her Korean as she learned English." She winked at Sunni. "I know a lot of Korean baby talk and a couple of songs. That's about it."

Smiling, Sunni began to sing a children's hymn whose tune he recognized. When she finished the

first verse, she said, "That's how Koreans sing it, Jeremiah."

"Do you know more?"

He leaned back against the seat and listened to the little girl's chirping voice singing every verse of the Korean hymn. He couldn't remember the last time he'd felt so at ease, not determined to rush off to do the next thing. It was unexpected, and he decided to enjoy the moment.

He wasn't sure when another like this one would come again.

The drive went too quickly for Mercy. She was anxious not to make a mistake and embarrass herself and Jeremiah. What if their Amish neighbors weren't pleased he'd invited her? In the weeks she'd been living on the farm, she hadn't done more than wave to her neighbors. She knew they were as busy as she was with trying to make homes out of the mostly abandoned buildings on the farms in the hollow.

Jeremiah had told her Caleb and his sister were living in one section of their main barn while they fixed up the house, which would have fallen in a few years if they hadn't come to rescue it. So she wasn't surprised when, exchanging places with Sunni and taking the reins as Hero pulled the buggy onto a farm lane, he drove to where

other buggies were parked near a barn in desperate need of paint.

Stepping out, Mercy made sure Sunni was holding her hand. A boy led Hero toward the lower portion of the barn, and Jeremiah motioned at a door on the upper level that was up a sloping concrete apron.

"Usually," he said, "we gather outside and enter in a certain order, but it's too cold for little ones and the oldsters to stay out a second longer than necessary."

"And everyone else in between," she managed to get past her teeth, which were clenched so they didn't clatter together.

Mercy didn't say anything as they entered the barn. Ropes had been hung from side to side, and bright quilts hooked to them with clothespins. It was an ingenious way to make individual rooms out of the large space. However, the center of the space was open and filled with simple benches. A dozen benches faced the other dozen, and she guessed the women sat on one side and the men on the other. It was the same in the church she attended.

About thirty people milled around, and she was amazed they made up only six Amish families. She'd known Amish parents had many children and multiple generations lived beneath a single roof, but she was overwhelmed by the number of

members attending the service. Especially when she realized most of the people were around her own age. That made sense, because it would be the young people seeking a new life by Harmony Creek.

She couldn't fail to notice the shy glances in their direction. She realized a few of the prayer coverings were quite similar to hers while the organdy on other women's heads was heart-shaped. The women must come from different church districts, maybe different states.

When a tall blonde walked toward them, Jeremiah grinned.

Mercy was shocked at the pulse of something unpleasant racing through her as the lovely woman approached. It couldn't be... No, it was impossible she was jealous of how the blonde returned Jeremiah's smile so warmly. There couldn't be any future for Mercy and Jeremiah other than as friends. She should be happy for him that a beautiful Amish woman was pleased to see him.

Lord, please keep my heart from making another mistake. I don't know if it can survive shattering again.

Jeremiah turned to her, and she schooled her face into the best imitation she could of a calm expression. His brows lowered. He was puzzled by her reaction.

So was she!

"This is Caleb's sister Miriam," he said. "She was a teacher in her old community, so I asked her to translate for you. Miriam, these are the Bambergers. Mercy and Sunni."

"We're so glad you've decided to join us for worship today." Miriam's voice was like a song, each word a pleasant note, but Mercy had noticed a flash of discomfort in her eyes when Jeremiah mentioned she'd been a teacher. Maybe she missed that job.

Mercy dampened her curiosity, knowing she couldn't pose such a personal question to someone she'd just met. Instead, she said, "Thank you. I hope I can follow along."

Miriam gave her a warm smile. "If you need help, squeeze my hand, and I'll translate or explain." She glanced at Sunni and away. "The other *kinder* are over there on the far side of the room. They're waiting for you."

Her daughter didn't need a second invitation. She crossed the space in her rolling step. Two girls close to her age met her about halfway, talking over each other in their excitement to meet her.

When it was time for the service to start, Sunni sat on one side of Mercy and Miriam on the other. Mercy tried not to stare at the massive man sitting in the first row. His gray beard reached to the center of his chest, and his deep-set eyes had an intensity that awed her.

"Is that Abraham, Mommy?" asked Sunni in a stage whisper.

Miriam had overheard Sunni's question. Her answer was serious, though Mercy saw her eyes twinkling. "That's Wayne Flaud. He's our acting bishop."

"He looks like the picture of Abraham in Mommy's Bible."

Hushing her daughter, Mercy hoped the bishop hadn't heard her daughter's comments. If he had, he didn't react as the *Leit* stood for the first hymn.

It was sung, as Jeremiah had warned her, at a very slow pace, taking two or three times longer to sing than it would have during a Mennonite service. She bowed her head and joined in the silent prayer, grateful for this opportunity to discover more about Jeremiah's world. She hoped it would help her understand him better, because he was becoming a bigger and bigger part of her and her daughter's lives.

The afternoon sun had warmed the air considerably by the time Jeremiah drove the buggy toward Rudy's farm. Sunni was asleep, her head on Mercy's lap, exhausted from playing outside with the other *kinder* after the communal luncheon in the barn.

"What did you think of the service, Mercy?"

Jeremiah asked. "Other than how uncomfortable the benches are?"

"Was I that obvious?"

He rushed to answer as he struggled to keep from laughing at her shocked and humiliated expression. "No, you weren't obvious. It's the complaint we often hear when someone who isn't Amish attends our services."

"I've got to say I missed the comfortable pews I'm accustomed to. The way you sang the hymns was amazing. The man who started each line—"

"The *vorsinger* is what he's called."

"He kept everyone together, so nobody got too far ahead or too far behind."

He turned the buggy into Rudy's drive. Drawing back on the reins, he stared at the black car parked there. A tall, balding man was stepping out. "You've got company, Mercy."

He felt her flinch. "It's Alfred, my father's oldest brother." She hesitated, then said, "I think."

"You think?"

"I haven't seen him in ten years. He lives in California, and he only comes for funerals." She sighed. "Though he didn't come for his father's."

"Was there bad blood between them?"

"My uncle doesn't get along well with anyone in the family. He thinks nobody is ever right except him."

His brows rose in astonishment. Mercy spoke

her mind and was determined to take over her *grossdawdi*'s farm, but on other subjects, she tried to look for a solution that worked for everyone involved.

Her *onkel* glanced from her to Jeremiah and Sunni, his frown deepening with each passing second, while they got out of the buggy. The little girl must have sensed the tension because she didn't say a word.

Jeremiah saw a flood of questions in the older man's expression, but her *onkel* asked, "Why is the door locked?"

Mercy took Sunni's hand before walking between the snowbanks to where her *onkel* had gone up onto the porch. She gave the cantankerous man a kiss on the cheek.

"Why didn't you let me know you were coming, Uncle Alfred?" she asked as she pulled the key out of her purse.

Instead of answering her question, he tapped his toe impatiently. Color faded from Mercy's face.

Jeremiah struggled not to frown when he realized her *onkel* saw her as a *kind*, no older or more responsible than Sunni.

"I'm tearing down wallpaper and painting," she answered, but her voice quavered, "and I didn't want someone to walk in and trip over the mess."

"You shouldn't be doing anything to the house until its future is decided."

"Dad knows I'm working on the house, and he agreed anything I do will increase the property's value."

Onkel Alfred waved aside her words. "You shouldn't lock the door. This door was never locked while my father and mother lived here."

Doubting she'd get anywhere with her *onkel*, who wasn't interested in what she had to say, Jeremiah stepped past Mercy. He opened the door and led the way into the house. He waited for the explosion he guessed would come when her *onkel* saw the changes she'd made.

Alfred began to list everything he thought Mercy was doing wrong. She seemed to shrink within herself, and Jeremiah respected how she didn't fire protests to defend herself.

Just as an Amish woman would do, whispered his own thoughts. Silencing them, he was shocked when a small hand slid into his.

He looked at Sunni's troubled face.

"I don't like that loud man," she whispered.

"He's your grandfather's brother."

"Still don't like him."

He gave her a quick smile. He didn't like Alfred Bamberger, either, though he'd barely spent two minutes in his company. Any man who bullied Mercy and acted as if he knew everything

and she knew nothing wasn't, in Jeremiah's estimation, worth getting better acquainted with.

"Mercy, have you forgotten your manners?" demanded her *onkel*, gesturing with his head toward Jeremiah.

Her cheeks became red, but she said calmly, "Uncle Alfred, I know my parents have told you about my daughter, Sunni."

The little girl greeted him with a tentative smile.

Alfred ignored her. "And who's he?"

"This is Jeremiah Stoltzfus," Mercy said, putting her arm around Sunni's shoulders. "Jeremiah, this is—"

"Are you the one who intended to buy the farm from Rudy?" asked the older man.

Jeremiah's first reaction was to laugh at the man's hypocrisy, but he hid it, because he wasn't really amused by how Alfred Bamberger dismissed Mercy. "I am."

"You're Amish, aren't you?"

"I am." He wondered if the man was always this rude. If so, he could understand why Alfred didn't get along with his siblings.

"What did you intend to do with the farm?"

"Farm it," he said in the same clipped tone the older man used. "I've got ten dairy cows in the barn. I'd arranged for their purchase before I came here, because Rudy said it was okay."

Alfred rubbed his eyes with his thumb and finger before sighing. "That sounds like my father." He grimaced. "Father hated the idea the farm might be subdivided and sold as house lots." Again, his gaze drilled Jeremiah. "He was so eager to keep the land as a farm he would have agreed to any deal."

"The price we agreed upon was fair." He wouldn't pretend not to understand what the other man was implying.

"That's yet to be seen. On behalf of my brothers and sisters, I've come to get an appraisal done on the property. An honest appraisal, not what Rudy believed it was worth to someone who said he planned to work the land."

Jeremiah didn't wince, not outwardly, as Alfred's words slashed through his tattered hopes. That the family might demand more in exchange for selling the farm wasn't something he'd considered. He and Rudy had negotiated in *gut* faith, and the Realtors involved must have agreed it was a fair deal.

Hadn't they?

"Dad didn't mention you'd be coming," Mercy said in the same deferential tone.

"He doesn't know, but he'll be grateful when he has the facts from someone who is truly part of the family, which you aren't, Mercy."

Jeremiah looked at her in horror. How could

Alfred throw in her face she hadn't been born a Bamberger? That was beyond cruel.

But Mercy motioned for him to say nothing.

Her *onkel* asked a couple more questions and walked into the living room. When they didn't follow, he bellowed Mercy's name.

Jeremiah grasped her arm as she stepped forward to follow. "He shouldn't speak to you so," he hissed, fighting to control his outrage.

"It's okay, Jeremiah." She patted his cheek gently and smiled. "I'm used to him, and it's nothing personal."

"Nothing personal? He said—"

"He's said the same thing to my sisters-in-law and my cousins' spouses. He doesn't consider anyone a true part of the family except him and his siblings, and those siblings reluctantly." Her smile broadened. "He'd prefer he was an only child."

"But—"

"Thank you, Jeremiah." She glanced at the door to the living room when her *onkel* shouted again. "But let me handle this."

She was gone before Jeremiah could agree, which was for the best, because for the next hour Alfred interrogated Mercy and him on every facet of the farm. That they could answer his questions seemed to irritate him. The man had come to the house with a chip on his shoulder. Whenever he could, Jeremiah deflected questions fired

at Mercy by answering them or turning the conversation to the land rather than the house.

Alfred left with a warning not to change another thing before the appraisal. "I'm sure the family has other plans for this property than a silly summer camp."

Jeremiah bit his lip when he saw tears blossom in Mercy's eyes. Arguing with her *onkel* could make the situation worse. When the older man shot a rancorous glance in his direction, Jeremiah knew the warning was aimed at him, as well.

When the door shut behind Alfred Bamberger, Sunni rushed to throw her arms around Mercy.

"I don't like him, Mommy," the little girl said, hiding her face in Mercy's apron. "He didn't speak to me. Not even when I said hi."

Jeremiah squatted by the *kind*. "Sunni, some people are so angry inside they can't be anything but angry on the outside. It doesn't have anything to do with you."

"That's right," Mercy said. "Uncle Alfred isn't a happy person." Helping her daughter out of her coat, she added, "I think I'll make hot chocolate for us. Do you like that idea?"

With a cheer, Sunni hugged her *mamm*, but with excitement this time. The *kind* ran into the kitchen to select the cups they'd use for the treat.

Jeremiah came to his feet as Mercy asked, "You'll stay, won't you?"

"I need to get Hero in, but then I'll come back." Putting his hands on her shoulders, he knew he might be foolish, but he couldn't let her bear the burden of her *onkel*'s threats alone. "Mercy, you can't be certain anyone else in your family will listen to what he plans."

She sighed again. "I know Uncle Alfred. That he's talking about subdividing the land to build houses means that's what he wants to do."

"It would probably bring the greatest return to your *daed* and his siblings, but only if they sell each lot themselves. A building contractor might offer less than I did because a builder would need to make a big profit in return for his investment."

She looked out the window at rolling hills set against purplish mountains reaching up into the clouds. "I can't imagine these hills covered with houses."

"Don't worry."

"How can you say that?" she asked, looking up at him.

"Because I trust in God's plan for my life."

"I wish I could, too."

At the regret in her voice, he longed to draw her into his arms and hold her until her fears vanished. It would be a mistake because he could be jeopardizing everything he was working so hard for.

Chapter Ten

After her *onkel*'s visit and his determination to squeeze every possible penny out of the property, Jeremiah wasn't sure if either of them would end up with the farm. He didn't say that to Mercy, but he guessed, by the way she evaded his eyes, she'd had similar thoughts as she threw herself into preparations for Parker Kenton's arrival, the foster *kind* being placed with her.

She and Sunni ignored her *onkel*'s edict and painted one bedroom a fresh blue for the boy. A bed was found in another room and cleaned. After a new mattress was delivered at the beginning of the week, she topped the bed with a duvet decorated with circus animals. Rudy's black-and-white afghan was draped over the footboard.

Jeremiah was asked over and over for his opinion of the room. "Because you're a boy," Sunni said each time.

Everything in the bedroom was ready by a chilly Tuesday afternoon when a silver car rolled to a stop in the yard. When the driver got out, Jeremiah recognized her as the social worker who'd come to speak with Mercy. She glanced at where he stood with Mercy and Sunni, but said nothing. She went to the passenger side and opened the door.

No one emerged.

The woman—her name was Whitney, ain't so?—bent and spoke quietly.

Sunni cut her eyes to Mercy, who was looking at the car with anticipation and anxiety.

Patting the little girl's shoulder, Jeremiah guessed Mercy was considering the changes another *kind* could make in their lives. Including his. The thought was a sure sign he was too involved with the Bambergers.

A boy oozed out of the car. The first word that came to Jeremiah's mind was sullen. The *kind* stared at the ground and didn't acknowledge them.

Parker was short for his age and skinny. He wore a new winter coat with blue jeans and stylish sneakers. His previous foster family must have provided for him well, though they weren't able to continue caring for him. When he pulled off his knit cap, his fine black hair danced with static electricity.

He glowered and licked his fingertips before

running them over his hair. Most of the strands settled, but others stood up like insane cowlicks.

Whitney put her hand on his shoulder, but he shook it off. He walked to where Jeremiah stood with Mercy and Sunni on the front porch. He didn't say a word.

Mercy opened the door and ushered everyone through the elegant front entry and into the living room.

Whitney undid her coat and motioned for Parker to do the same. He balled up his coat and threw it on a chair. The social worker started to reprimand him, but Mercy shook her head gently.

Arching her pale brows, Whitney said, "This is Mercy and her daughter, Sunni. Sunni was born in Korea as you were."

"Who cares about stupid Korea?" muttered the boy. His voice held the hint of an accent.

"And I'm Jeremiah Stoltzfus." He offered his hand to the boy as if Parker were a grown man.

For a second, the *kind*'s indifference cracked. He eyed Jeremiah up and down. He seemed to gather his defenses around himself and scorned Jeremiah's hand. "Why are you wearing a clown hat?"

Because of the *kind*'s accent, Jeremiah thought he said *crown hat*. He realized his mistake when Mercy replied.

"Jeremiah isn't a clown. He's Amish. Amish men wear black hats like that in the winter, Parker."

"My name isn't Parker."

Whitney's voice took on a stern edge. "We've talked about that, and you agreed, for now, you're going to stick with Parker."

The *kind* subsided, but crossed his arms over his chest and stood with his chin raised in defiance.

If the boy wanted another name, Jeremiah knew what it should be. Trouble. The boy was going to be trouble. Jeremiah hoped Mercy was prepared.

He wasn't sure he was.

Mercy was so proud of her daughter. Despite Parker's disdain for everything Sunni said and how often he called her silly or stupid, the little girl persisted. No doubt, Sunni remembered her own rough transition into what became her permanent family. Mercy certainly recalled her own, and she knew exactly how Parker was feeling.

Unwanted. Worthless. Determined to show the world he wasn't either.

"This is for you." Sunni placed a bright blue teddy bear in Parker's hand. Her smile wavered when he didn't say anything. "It's nice to have a special friend when you're somewhere new. Blueberry has been a good friend to me, and I hope he'll be a good friend to you."

Mercy didn't catch what Parker replied under his breath. She guessed she'd be better off not knowing.

Parker tossed the bear on the bed and then picked up his suitcase. It nearly knocked him off his feet. Jeremiah slipped a surreptitious hand under one side to help guide it onto the bed. Parker shook his head when Whitney said it was time to go downstairs, but came along reluctantly upon the social worker's insistence.

Whitney stayed for several hours, then got ready to leave to allow the family to begin to adjust to each other.

When Mercy started to make supper, she asked Jeremiah if he'd like to stay.

He heard her nervous tone, and he agreed. With two *kinder*, including one who protested over anything anyone said to him, she could use another adult there.

"I'll set the table," he said as she took hamburger and potatoes out of the refrigerator. "And keep the kids away from the stove."

"They're upstairs. Sunni knows if she wants fries, she needs to stay away while I cook them."

"She's a known quantity. The other one isn't." He paused by the table. "Where do you want these papers Whitney left with you?"

"Would you mind putting them on the desk?"

"Be glad to." He began to gather them up. His

eyes widened as he noticed the name on several of them. Mercedes R. Bamberger.

"Is your name really Mercedes?" he asked. "Like the fancy car?"

"Jeff and Pat have a Mercedes," said Parker, puffing out his chest and striding into the kitchen as if he owned the place. Jeremiah knew Jeff and Pat were the couple who were supposed to have adopted the boy. "Do you have one?"

"No, I've got that dented Ford out there." Mercy shot Jeremiah a glance, and he stepped between the boy and the stove.

The boy looked at Jeremiah, who said, "No car for me. But I've got a horse named Hero and a buggy."

Rolling his eyes, Parker opened cabinet doors and peered inside.

"So your name is really Mercedes?" Jeremiah asked.

She plucked the page out of his hand. "Yes, my name is Mercedes. It's Spanish for mercies, and it's the name I was given when I was born. The Bambergers asked if they could call me Mercy. I agreed, because I was getting a new life, so why not a new name?" She smiled coolly. "Especially when they didn't pronounce it as *Abuelita* did."

"I always wanted a shorter name like my brothers have. I liked my *daed*'s name. Paul. Nice and simple." He rubbed his chin. "*Mamm* always said

I should emulate the prophet Jeremiah and stand up and speak of the Lord."

"I didn't think the Amish evangelize."

"We don't. Or I should say, most of us don't. She meant I should proclaim God is *gut*."

"This place is ugly," Parker announced from the far corner of the kitchen.

"If you think it's ugly now," she said as she began cutting the potatoes into short lengths, "you should have seen it when I moved in here."

Mercy didn't smile when she saw the child's shock. He'd expected to annoy her with another of his insults, but she'd been a foster kid. She knew the games and the rules. Dislike everything. Push and push to see how much you could get away with.

And Parker had been yanked out of the familiar world he'd known and brought across the Pacific to a strange culture. The family that was supposed to be his forever had failed him, leaving him to be tossed into the system. Now he found himself in a plain home. That was enough to make the boy's head spin…and her heart ache.

"Can we watch TV?" the boy asked.

"We don't have one." She scraped more potatoes, figuring she'd need more than twice as many as she used when she made French fries for her and Sunni. A hardworking man and a growing boy had hearty appetites.

"How do you play video games if you don't have a TV?" His eyes widened. "Do you have a handheld?"

"No."

"Then you play on the computer."

Mercy shook her head, but Sunni, who came into the kitchen, replied, "We don't have a computer or whatever a handheld is."

Parker stared at them as if they'd crawled out of a woodchuck hole and announced they'd been hibernating. "What do you *do*?"

"Read and color," Sunni said.

"Take care of the animals and pray," Jeremiah added.

"Teach Sunni and cook." Mercy motioned to the stove.

"Build a chicken coop." Sunni giggled and glanced at Jeremiah.

"Drive the buggy," he said with a laugh, "and teach Mercy how to drive the sleigh."

Before Mercy could think of something to add to the list, Parker threw his short arms up in the air, grumbled something and stamped away. She heard his footsteps on the stairs and overhead. She looked from the heating oil to the ceiling.

"What is it?" asked Jeremiah.

"Could you do me a favor? There's the door by Parker's room that leads into the section of the

house with weak floors. I meant to lock it before he arrived."

"I'll get it."

"Be careful."

His reddish brows rose. "By that, I assume the door has to be locked from the bad side."

"Yes." She flashed him a sympathetic smile. "I've looked for the key, but I haven't found it." *Among other things, like my grandfather's will,* she wanted to say, but kept that to herself. She wasn't comfortable with Jeremiah knowing she hadn't given up the search. "Just turn the latch on the dead bolt." As he turned to go, she repeated, "Be careful."

"I'll do my best."

"I'm sure you always do."

He paused and looked at her. The kitchen seemed to telescope, the distance between them vanishing. Everything vanished, except them. A connection, invisible and powerful, matched every breath she took to his.

She wasn't sure how long they would have stood—frozen inside a splendid moment in time—if the hot oil on the stove hadn't snapped. She turned to the stove, and Jeremiah rushed away.

Steadying her breath and her heart that seemed to be beating at fast-forward, she tried to focus on cutting the fries. She patted the potatoes dry, because she didn't want the oil to splatter.

When she heard footsteps behind her, she saw her daughter standing in the doorway but not in the kitchen.

Sunni clamped her arms over her narrow chest. "He says he's not coming down for dinner."

Mercy didn't need to ask who *he* was. "Did you ask him nice?"

"Of course." Her daughter seemed insulted at the question. "But he won't open his door."

"Did he tell you why?" Infecting Sunni with Mercy's worries that the boy might try to run away would make the situation more tense.

"No! He said bad words."

Mercy turned off the burner and sent up a quick prayer of thanks the boy was still in the house. Holding out her hand, she said, "Come with me."

She didn't want Sunni to get more upset, but she wouldn't leave her daughter in the kitchen with the hot oil on the stove. When she heard Jeremiah on the front stairs, she asked him to keep an eye on the stove. He nodded, though curiosity burned in his eyes. Again, she felt the pull of the unseen contact between them. She broke it, knowing she had to find out why Parker was refusing to come and have his supper.

He must be hungry. Whitney said she'd offered to stop to get burgers, but the boy had refused. Climbing the stairs, she went to the room between Sunni's and Grandpa Rudy's.

"Parker?"

"That's not my name!" came back a snarl.

"All right, whatever your name is." Mercy kept her voice even. "It's time for supper."

"I'm not hungry."

"Yes, you are. Have you ever had French fries before?"

"Of course!" A hint of vacillation sifted into his retort.

"Homemade ones?"

For several seconds there was no answer. The door opened slowly, enough for Parker to slip through.

As he started to close it behind him, Mercy put out her hand and kept the door from shutting. He glared at her, and she met it without comment. Finally, he lowered his eyes and stepped aside.

She pushed open the door and gasped.

The room looked as if it'd been ransacked. The drawers were pulled from the dresser. The bed had been torn apart, and the pictures on the wall—at least the ones Parker could reach—were ripped down and tossed in a corner.

Sunni gave a soft cry of dismay and picked up the blue teddy bear she'd given Parker. Tears filled her eyes when she touched the stuffing peeking out of where the bear's ears had been.

"Why?" she asked.

"It's a stupid bear, and you're stupid for liking

it. Only a cripple would like something like a stupid bear." Parker crossed his arms and raised his chin, daring them to try to make him apologize.

It was at that point Mercy knew this placement was going to be harder than she'd guessed.

A lot harder.

Jeremiah had come up the stairs after making sure nothing would burn on the stove. He didn't hesitate to step into the room as Sunni ran and threw herself in Mercy's arms. He turned to the boy, who regarded them with contempt. Parker also had, Jeremiah noticed, steeled himself as if he expected to be punished harshly for what he'd done and said.

It was *gut* the *kind* understood he shouldn't have destroyed the room and the gifts Mercy and Sunni had given him. Teaching the boy to respect those who wanted to help him would be easier if Parker knew the difference between right and wrong.

Mercy started to step forward, but Jeremiah put his hand on her arm. Warmth exploded from her skin to his. For a split second, he wanted to step out into the hall with her and forget the angry boy and the hurt little girl. Just for a moment. A single moment while he gazed into Mercy's pretty eyes. If he bent forward, would she shy away from his lips?

Knowing he was being imprudent, especially when the *kinder* needed them, he said in a near whisper, "Let me, Mercy."

"Jeremiah, this isn't your problem." Her voice was as hushed as his while Parker's gaze moved from one of them to the other as if trying to read their lips.

"I know, but I can take him off your hands while you clean up this mess."

"He should help, so—"

"Look at him." He cut his eyes to the boy. "Everything about him says he's waiting for a fight or to be punished."

"I don't want to fight with him. I know he's scared."

"So let me give him something to take his mind off his fears."

For a moment, Jeremiah thought Mercy wouldn't trust him. She glanced between the boy and him.

"I'm not going to take him out behind the woodshed," he said quietly. "That wouldn't help anything."

"I know."

"Mercy, let me help. Can you hold dinner for about an hour?"

Indecision raced across her face, but then she nodded.

Thrilled by her trust in him, Jeremiah made

sure his face remained stern as he turned to the boy. "Come with me."

"I don't want to."

"I didn't ask if you wanted to. I asked you to come with me." He kept his voice steady, wondering if *Daed* had struggled, as Jeremiah was now, when he'd needed to punish one of them.

Maybe he shouldn't have volunteered to help. He didn't know a lot about kids, other than when he spent time with his nieces and nephews. But there wasn't time for second thoughts. He'd offered, and the boy needed to learn actions had consequences, whether *gut* or bad.

Jeremiah herded the boy down the stairs. He thought Parker would argue again when told to put on his coat, hat and mittens along with his boots. The boy was reluctant but he complied and rushed out the door when Jeremiah opened it.

"Whoa, there." Jeremiah caught Parker by the hood on his coat as the *kind* started to jump into a snowbank. "If you get wet, you'll be cold by the time we finish the chores."

"Chores? What are chores?"

Surprised a nine-year-old didn't know the term, Jeremiah held the coat as Parker strained against him. "Chores are what we do to earn our keep here."

"The county is paying for me."

"And how long do you think they'll do that?

A man can't depend on someone else to pay his way. Don't you want a *gut* and exciting job when you grow up?"

The boy stopped trying to pull away. Frowning, Parker said, "Sure."

"What do you want to do?"

"Be an astronaut or a fireman or maybe a policeman."

Jeremiah ignored his yearning to grin. "Those are important jobs, and they have one thing in common. They will require you to work hard to learn everything you need to know to do the job. Ever think of being a cowboy?"

"Yeah," the boy drawled, clearly suspicious.

"Here's your chance."

"Huh?"

Pretending he hadn't heard Parker's question, Jeremiah kept a hand on the boy's shoulder as they walked toward the barn. Jeremiah acted as if he didn't have a care in the world, but kept snatching glances at the *kind*'s face when they entered the barn where the cows waited to be milked.

"It smells in here," the boy said.

"It does, doesn't it?" He saw Parker's shock that Jeremiah wasn't insulted by his blunt words. "But give it a chance. Once you get used to the smell, it's kind of a nice stink."

"You're crazy!"

Jeremiah smiled. The sooner the boy learned

he couldn't get a rise out of Jeremiah, the sooner Parker might start listening to him. Really listening.

"Okay," Jeremiah said, trying to sound more certain than he felt, "I'm going to milk the cows, and you're going to clean up." He pointed at the gutter behind the cows and then handed the boy a short-handled shovel. "Pick it up and put it on that pile over there." He pointed toward a stained spot on the concrete floor near the door leading into the barnyard. "It can stay there for tonight. We'll move it outside tomorrow when it's warmer."

"You want me to shovel that—?"

"Manure? *Ja*, I do."

"That's child abuse."

"Not even close." He grinned at the boy. "Once I know you can handle that, I'll let you help me milk the cows."

"I don't want to milk old, stinky cows."

"Well, that's *gut*, because these cows are neither old nor stinky."

Again the *kind* stared at him as if Parker feared Jeremiah had lost his mind.

"B-b-but…" The boy sputtered on the single word.

"You said you wanted to be a cowboy, ain't so?"

"I did, but cowboys ride horses."

"Which need to be cleaned up after, too."

"Really?"

"*Ja*, really." Smiling, Jeremiah said, "You'd better get started."

He left the boy staring at the shovel and went to get the milking equipment out of the storage room. When he returned, Parker was poking at the gutters behind the cows. Jeremiah didn't glance at him when he heard a clang as Parker started to work.

The battle wasn't over, but Parker was willing to listen to him. Maybe Jeremiah had helped Mercy tonight. He hoped so. It felt astounding, he realized, to be on the same side for once. He prayed it wouldn't be the one and only time.

Chapter Eleven

Sunni was paging through a picture book in the living room the following week, so Mercy kept Parker in the kitchen while she washed the dinner dishes. He complained about not having TV, and he couldn't seem to find anything to do. Sleet tapped at the window, and she could scarcely make out the shape of the barn on the far side of the yard.

"Can you see where Jeremiah is?" asked Parker as he set a cup of cocoa on the table.

Mercy wasn't sure what had happened in the barn the night of Parker's arrival, but whatever Jeremiah had said or done had made a huge impression on the boy. At the same time Parker looked for any chance to spend time with Jeremiah, he resisted every request she spoke, and he treated Sunni badly, making nasty comments to

her over and over or stepping into her way when she was trying to navigate the stairs.

She recognized the pattern she'd seen in other foster kids. They'd shared stories about how they disrupted a placement on purpose. Even then, she'd understood what they hadn't said. When they had no control over their lives, being pulled from one foster home to another and maybe sent home to live with one parent for a while before being dropped back into the system, they'd decided to grab what control they could. They were determined to make sure the placement didn't work, pushing their foster parents to the edge and past it with their antics. One girl she'd shared a room with for a couple of nights had put it succinctly, "I got rid of them before they got rid of me."

However, he hung on every word Jeremiah spoke. She wondered if Parker had been close to a father figure in Korea. According to the reports Whitney had left for Mercy, Parker hadn't transferred that respect to Mr. Kenton.

Yet the child admired Jeremiah and hopped to obey any request he made. She should be grateful the boy heeded one of them. Asking Jeremiah to step in made her uncomfortable because each time was a reminder that sometime, hopefully in the near future, one of them would have the farm and the other must leave.

But she knew it was more than that. She looked

forward to every time Jeremiah came to the house or she ran into him in the yard. He'd had dinner and supper with them every day since Parker's arrival, and he'd lingered into the evening. His calm presence stopped arguments between the two children before they got heated.

"No, I don't see him," Mercy replied when the boy repeated the question. Louder this time. "He's smart enough not to work outside in a storm."

"Is he your boyfriend?"

"No." She ignored the regret that erupted in her at the simple answer.

"Why not?"

"He's Amish, and we're not." It was the easiest explanation to give the boy.

How could she explain to a nine-year-old about the feelings she didn't understand herself? The very thought of spending time with Jeremiah made her smile. When his hand brushed hers, even inadvertently, her heart thumped like hail on a roof. His kindness with the children touched her soul, for she couldn't help thinking of how Graham hadn't even wanted to discuss having a family. While Jeremiah spent time with Sunni and Parker, making them want to like him, Graham had barely tolerated her daughter.

But there was something else, something indefinable that drew her to him like a child to a cookie jar.

"You aren't Amish?" Parker asked, again interrupting her thoughts. "You wear a funny hat, too."

"It's my prayer covering." She put the last pot on the drainer and reached to let the water out of the sink. "The Bible asks women to cover their heads when they pray. As I pray throughout the day, I don't have to worry about my head being uncovered when I do."

"If you're not Amish, what are you?" He paused for a moment, then asked, "What's Amish?"

Mercy gave him a very brief answer, knowing, as a child who'd never encountered plain people, he wouldn't be able to handle too much information at once.

"Hey!" he shouted in the middle of her explanation. "There's Jeremiah." He rushed to the window that gave him the best view of the barn. "What's he doing?"

Mercy walked to stand behind him. Wiping her hands on a towel, she peered through the storm that didn't seem in a hurry to abate.

Across the yard, Jeremiah was bending over a tractor parked by the barn. She'd been surprised when he drove it out of the barn until he explained he didn't plan to use it in the fields. Instead, he wanted to use the tractor's engine as a power source.

"It looks as if he's fixing the stationary engine that runs the milking machines in the barn," she said.

Parker wore an unexpected smile. "I like helping with milking. It's fun, but I wish Jeremiah had different cows."

"What kind of cows?"

"His cows give white milk. I like chocolate milk."

She drew her bottom lip between her teeth so she didn't laugh.

"Don't you?" the boy demanded.

"Certainly I like chocolate milk."

"So why doesn't he get chocolate milk cows?"

"You'll have to check with him." Putting the towel on the counter by the sink, she said, "You can ask him tonight."

"I will!"

As the boy went to the table to finish his hot cocoa, Mercy remained by the window. She watched Jeremiah's easy, economical motions as he got the tractor's engine running. When he came inside, she'd make sure she had something warm for him to drink. She couldn't wait to tell him about chocolate milk cows.

It had been the longest conversation she'd had with Parker without him copping an attitude on her. She hoped it would be the first of many.

When Parker appeared in the barn, looking furtively over his shoulder, Jeremiah guessed the boy had snuck out of the house. He considered sending

Parker back, but Mercy would know to look first in the barn if she wanted to find the boy.

She was having a rough time with her foster *kind*. Was Parker missing his adoptive *mamm* so much he was determined not to let Mercy get close? Or was he mad at the whole world? Jeremiah tried to put himself in the *kind*'s shoes. To be yanked out of what he thought was his forever home was enough to give the boy a reason to distrust everyone.

"I didn't expect you to come out in the storm," Jeremiah said as he bent to clean a cow's udder before he attached the portable milking machine.

"You're doing your chores, so I'm here to do mine." He picked up the shovel, no longer skittish around the cows. "Besides, it's boring being stuck in the house. All they want to do is read or rip off wallpaper."

With a nod, Jeremiah wished Parker would show Mercy some respect. He couldn't force the boy to do so. All he could do was be a *gut* role model for how a man treated a woman.

"Mercy said there are cows that give chocolate milk," Parker said a few minutes later. "How come you don't have one?"

"Because I like strawberry milk better." Without batting an eye, he pointed to a ruddy Jersey cow munching hay and ignoring them. "So that's why I have a strawberry cow."

Jeremiah fought not to laugh as Parker stared in astonishment. He'd been a lot younger than the boy when his own *daed* told him the same silly story about red cows giving strawberry milk. Most likely, he'd worn the same expression of disbelief and childish yearning to believe the story was true.

"You're kidding," Parker said.

"No. The milk these cows give can be made into chocolate milk and strawberry milk and cheese and other things."

Understanding dawned on the boy's face. "So cows are pretty important."

"Ja."

"And milking them is important?"

"Very important. They depend on us to care for them, and in return they give us milk to use." He emptied the milker into a pail to carry it to the dairy tank. "We must heed what God told Adam and Eve in the Garden of Eden."

"God?"

"Ja. God told them: *Be fruitful, and multiply, and replenish the earth, and subdue it: and have dominion over the fish of the sea, and over the fowl of the air, and over every living thing that moveth upon the earth.* That means we need to take care of the animals and birds and fish that can't take care of themselves."

"Like cows?"

Jeremiah nodded. "Something every cowboy needs to know. You're well on your way to becoming one if you want."

Parker grinned. "Do I get a hat?"

Whipping off his black wool hat, Jeremiah set it on the boy's head. "There you go."

"This isn't a cowboy hat." He pulled it off with a disgusted frown.

"The very first cowboys wore hats very much like this one."

"Really?"

"Really."

The boy set the hat back on his head, paying no attention to how it dropped onto his nose. "Let's do the milking."

"Said just like a cowboy."

When Parker grinned, Jeremiah's heart swelled with happiness. He'd been curious how his brothers could welcome *kinder* into their lives, though they weren't the *kinder*'s biological *daeds*. They loved the youngsters as much as the *bopplin* born within their marriages. Admiring them, he'd wondered if he could open his heart so wide. He was beginning to believe he could.

Wide enough to let one naughty boy, one very opinionated little girl and one lovely woman into it.

If the situation with the farm was resolved...

He might as well wish for stars to dance around the sun at noon.

But with You, all things are possible. That's what Jesus taught, and what I believe. All things are possible, including finding a way out of the mess of who owns this farm. Even falling in love with the one woman standing in the way of me achieving that dream.

Jeremiah began to whistle as he carried the milk can to the dairy tank, happier than he'd been in longer than he could recall.

He was startled when he returned to clean the next cow and saw Mercy and Sunni walking into the barn.

Sunni rushed to him. "Can I help, too?"

He smiled. "Of course you can. The more hands to help the faster the job goes, but you need to ask your *mamm.*"

"Can I help, too?" Sunni asked.

Jeremiah grinned at the little girl's excitement to have a chance to spend time with him and Parker. After putting up with her foster brother's pranks and scathing comments, it was the first time since the boy's arrival she'd asked to do something when Parker was involved.

"Certainly, *eolin-i,*" Mercy said, ruffling her daughter's hair.

Parker stared at her. "I know what that means. It's Korean."

"I'm glad you remember your Korean." She gave him the warm smile that lit up the recesses of Jeremiah's heart, even when aimed at someone else. "Maybe you can teach Sunni the language. She wasn't much more than a baby when she came here, so she's lost most of what she knew."

The boy's lip curled, and Jeremiah knew he was about to say something rude. Before Parker could speak, Jeremiah said quietly, "A *gut* cowboy always helps those around him. He knows he may have to depend on others while tending the cows, so he lets others know they can depend on him."

Parker looked at him, wide-eyed, then nodded. "I'll try."

"Thank you," Mercy said. "Maybe you could help me learn, too."

"You want me to teach *you*? But you're a grown-up."

"I'm a baby when it comes to learning Korean."

The boy stared hastily at his boots, and Jeremiah would have gladly given Parker a penny—or a dollar—for his thoughts. Was Parker regretting his lack of respect toward Mercy when she treated him kindly? Or were her gentle ways tearing down the walls the boy had raised to protect himself from more hurt? Either way, Jeremiah hoped Parker realized how blessed he was to be in Mercy's care.

"Jeremiah!" Sunni's excited cry rang through the barn.

She was by the calf stall. The newest calves, four of them, had been delivered yesterday from the auction barn in Cambridge, about ten miles south. They bawled whenever he entered the barn, hoping to get his attention and something to eat.

Squatting next to Sunni, he smiled when she gazed up at him in awe.

"Look!" Her grin was almost too wide for her face. "He's sucking my fingers!"

"*She*'s hoping for milk, and she thinks your fingers might have some because they don't look much different to her than the cow's teats."

"You can't tell a girl cow," Parker taunted, "from a boy cow. You're a stupid girl."

"Enough," Jeremiah said quietly, and the boy subsided. "You were saying, Sunni?"

Her nose wrinkled, but she hurried to ask, "When does one of the cows come over to feed them?"

"The calves don't get to drink the milk from the cows. We do."

"That's not fair! She's a baby cow. She should have first dibs."

Leaning one arm on the top of the stall, Jeremiah said, "It might not sound fair to you, but what I feed the calves provides more nutrition than cow milk. They'll grow stronger much faster

with milk replacer." He motioned for Parker to join them. "Would you two like to feed them?"

Sunni cheered loudly enough so the calves jerked, staring at her with the whites of their eyes showing. Instantly, she began cooing as she tried to get them to come to her.

Parker was less enthusiastic. "You want both of us to feed them?"

"I'll help you," Jeremiah said, pretending he'd misunderstood that Parker didn't want to share the task with his foster sister.

"I don't need…" He shuffled his feet. "If you show me how to do it, I can handle baby cows."

"I'm sure you can. You, too, Sunni. That's why I asked you." Straightening, he said, "C'mon. I'll show you how I mix up the milk replacer, and we'll fill the bottles."

Within minutes the youngsters were holding the large bottles with both hands as the calves drained them so fast the milk replacer dribbled out of the sides of their mouths. Mercy took over the task of cleaning the udders before Jeremiah hooked on the milker. They worked in easy harmony as if they'd done the tasks together a hundred times before.

Mercy paused to check the *kinder* and help refill the bottles so the other two calves could have their turns. "Are you having fun?"

Jeremiah hoped Parker would reply, but Sunni

did. She nodded with a grin that revealed her loose tooth. It was her first one, and the little girl was excited about it.

Jeremiah kept hoping that while they finished the milking and other chores, Parker would say something nice to Mercy.

Nothing.

When Mercy sent the *kinder* to the house through the early evening sunshine, Parker refused to go. A single glance from Jeremiah changed the boy's mind, and he stalked out, his tightly fisted hands jammed into his coat pockets.

"Give him time," Mercy said as she wrapped a scarf around her neck.

Jeremiah reached for the light switch. "I'm trying, but how much time does he need to realize you're the best thing that could happen to him now?"

"Were you always grateful for what adults did for you? Surely you weren't that well behaved."

Closing the door behind them, he sighed as the cold scraped across his face. "I can't remember the last time I felt like a naughty kid. Not even when I was a scholar."

"That's no surprise. Were you the good boy, the one your teacher could expect to be quiet and study hard?"

"*Ja*. Sadly, I was also the one my parents sel-

dom had to scold, though I was surrounded by siblings who enjoyed pranks and jests."

"Not sadly. It's a credit to you that you were working hard for what you wanted, even when you were a child."

"What about you? Were you the *gut* little girl?"

He was surprised when she faltered a moment before saying, "Eventually."

Wanting to kick himself for forgetting she'd endured the same uncertainty and temporary homes Parker did, he wished he could see her face better in the dim light. "I'm sorry. I shouldn't have asked that, Mercy."

"Why not? Having a wonderful childhood with siblings and two parents who were always there for you isn't anything to be ashamed of. It's something to celebrate." She looked past him to the *kinder* who were almost to the house. "It's what I'd hoped to offer Sunni here. A permanent home she knew would always be there for her." Before he could reply, she waved aside his answer. "Enough of the dreary. Let's enjoy spending time with the children."

He caught her gloved hand in his own. "And each other."

"Yes, and with each other." She smiled and squeezed his fingers as they swung their hands between them on the short walk to the barn.

Again, Jeremiah's contentment was short-lived.

Sunni suddenly ran toward them. "Mommy! Mommy! We saw kittens. Can we bring them inside?"

"If you can find them," Mercy said with a chuckle.

Ten minutes later two dejected *kinder* gave up the search. The kittens seemed to have disappeared.

"Barn cats are very, very skilled at hiding," Mercy said to console them. "I used to play hide-and-seek with the kittens in the hayloft." She laughed. "They always won."

As she continued to tell the *kinder* about when she visited her *grossdawdi*, Jeremiah kept going toward the porch. But he couldn't walk away from the truth.

Mercy's connection to the farm was real and deep. Far deeper than his own.

Lord, if You've brought me here, I know You have a reason. And I also know Your reason can't be to bring Mercy unhappiness. Look at her!

He watched as she spoke with the *kinder*. Parker was acting as if he didn't need to listen, but he was as Mercy gave them ideas on how to lure the kittens to them tomorrow with fresh milk and calm voices and no quick motions.

She's a warmhearted woman, Lord, and she's eager to do whatever she can to help anyone else, even a young boy who challenges her at every

turn and other kinder *she's never met. I don't know what path You have given her to walk, but please don't let it be filled with more hurt.*

And please don't let me cause that hurt.

Chapter Twelve

Jeremiah ran his hand along the planed log. Its smooth surface would make an excellent mantel. With a few imperfections left by the growth of the tree that once had stood on the farm, the log would be the exact complement to a fieldstone fireplace. Two days ago an *Englischer* renovating a house on the road between Salem and the Vermont border had stopped by, saying he'd heard Jeremiah was a woodworker. When Jeremiah had shown him the log, the man had been skeptical…until today. After seeing the work Jeremiah had done, he'd agreed to come back tomorrow so he could get the log and have it put in place right away.

A few other commissions like that one would add to the funds Jeremiah would need to move forward with his plans to buy a farm, whether it was Rudy's or another.

The thought jolted him as he was about to pick

up another piece of wood. It was the first time he'
admitted to himself that there might be alterna
tives if Mercy's family decided not to accept th
contract he'd signed. He hadn't spoken with hi
Realtor in two weeks. Maybe Kitty had learne
about a nearby farm for sale.

He grimaced. If there was a farm availabl
along Harmony Creek, he would have heard abou
it from Caleb or one of his other neighbors.

Could he walk away after giving his word he'
help with the settlement? Maybe one of the othe
families would agree to let him live with ther
until he found a place of his own. Mercy migh
be willing to rent him some of her fields to us
as pasture and planting.

And he'd be able to see her and the *kinder.*

"You've gotten in too deep, Stoltzfus," he mut
tered to himself as he hefted the log and laid i
against the wall where it would be out of the way

The door to his workshop opened, and his hear
started doing a jig in his chest at the thought c
Mercy stepping out of his thoughts and into hi
shop.

When Parker's head appeared around the edge
Jeremiah tried to ignore the flush of disappoint
ment. He was glad to see the boy, but...

"Can I come in?" Parker asked.

"No touching the equipment," he said.

"You tell me that every time I come in." The boy pouted.

"And you still have five fingers on each hand." He winked at Parker to soften his words. "Let's keep it that way."

Parker picked up a piece of pine and pulled out a barely sharp kitchen knife. Running it down the side of the wood, he smiled. "See? I'm careful."

"I see, but you'd do better with a whittling knife than that one." He didn't ask if Mercy had given the boy permission to take it. He knew she hadn't.

"Where can I get one?"

"We can check the hardware store in the village, but first I need to see you can be trusted with it."

"I can. I can be trusted with anything."

Jeremiah simply arched his brows, and the boy got the message. No amount of bragging was allowed in the workshop.

"Can I ask you something?" Parker lowered the knife and wood onto his lap.

"What?"

"Will you help me change my name?"

He wasn't surprised. Parker had mentioned doing that several times since his arrival. "To what?"

"I haven't decided yet. Not my Korean name. Nobody can pronounce it."

"I understand," Jeremiah said, thinking of

how Mercy had said the same thing about her birth name.

"I want something other than Parker. It's a dumb name." He grimaced. "Those dumb people stuck it on me."

He frowned at the boy. "You shouldn't call the Kentons *dumm*."

"But they are. They waited and waited for a kid of their own, and then they couldn't wait to get rid of me. That's pretty dumb."

"Even so, you shouldn't call any adult *dumm*." Thinking of the names Parker had used to upset Sunni, he added quickly, "Or any *kind*, either."

"But it's okay to say Parker is a dumb name? I—Ouch!" He stared in horror at the thin red slice on his index finger. The line widened as blood ran from the cut.

Without a word as the knife clattered to the floor, Jeremiah grabbed the *kind*'s wrist. He ignored Parker's shrieks as he thrust the cut finger into a bucket of cold water he kept nearby for such emergencies. Deftly, he dabbed an antibacterial cream from his first-aid kit on the wound and bound it.

"There you go."

Tears ran down Parker's face, but he regarded his bandaged finger with as much curiosity as if it belonged to someone else. "Will I have a scar?"

He raised his eyes, which sparkled with abrupt excitement. "Like the ones you have?"

Jeremiah looked at his fingers, which showcased the long hours of hard, hands-on work he'd done since he was younger than Parker. All his knuckles, including his thumbs, bore scars, and his left palm showed where a fishhook had become embedded in it when he'd been showing off for his older brothers and their friends. Each mark told a story and evoked a memory, some *gut*, some not so *gut*, especially when he'd needed stitches on his right forefinger after being bitten by a dog shortly after he'd turned ten.

"If you end up with a scar," he said as he gathered the supplies and put them in the first-aid box, "it won't be like mine, but yours will be there to remind you to be careful as mine do."

"Will girls like my scar like Mercy does yours?"

Shocked to feel heat rising up his face, Jeremiah kept his head bent so the *kind* didn't see his reaction. "I don't think Mercy cares about my scars one way or the other."

"Sure she does." Parker climbed onto the chunk of wood, but didn't reach for his knife. "I've seen her touching them. A lot. I think she likes them. A lot."

The boy was right, Jeremiah knew. About Mercy touching him when she wanted to make a point or to console him or to make a connection.

He treasured each memory of her fingers against him, but he tried not to think of them too often. For all he knew, she might have another man in her life. Someone more important to her than he was. She seldom spoke of her life in central New York. Thinking of how she rushed to the mailbox as soon as the postal carrier drove past, he wondered—not for the first time—if she was eager to hear from someone special.

But he wasn't about to discuss his feelings for Mercy with a nine-year-old.

As he put the box on its shelf, he said, "You should tell God how grateful you are the injury isn't worse. Asking for healing wouldn't be a bad idea, either."

"You're always talking about God. Do you really believe in him?"

"Ja."

"Oh." The boy picked up the piece of wood he'd dropped and rolled it between his fingers. Staring off into the distance, he asked, "Aren't you going to ask me if I believe in God?"

"I figured you'd tell me if you wanted me to know."

The *kind* didn't answer quickly.

Jeremiah gave the boy time to think while he walked over to the plow he'd brought inside. He'd cleaned off the rust but needed to straighten it. The plow would be ready for him—or whoever

owned the farm by the time the snow melted—to work in the fields. If he was going to be able to complete the purchase of the farm, he must buy workhorses or mules. He'd need six on a team to work on the slopes, which were far steeper than in Paradise Springs.

"I'd like to believe in God," Parker said at last. "Mercy said you Amish live as you do because you want to be close to God."

"The apostle Paul wrote in Romans 12:2: *And be not conformed to this world: but be ye transformed by the renewing of your mind, that ye may prove what is that good, and acceptable, and perfect, will of God.* That's what our ministers preach and how we try to live."

"Did the Possible Paul—"

"*Apostle* Paul." He couldn't halt his grin. "An apostle is someone who teaches us about being *gut* Christians."

"Paul, huh?" The little boy started to add more, but the sound of a car pulling into the yard intruded.

Hearing a groan from Parker, Jeremiah knew it must be Whitney's. She was scheduled to come by today for a visit to check on how Parker was fitting in.

"Let's go." Jeremiah motioned with his head toward the door.

He thought Parker might protest, but the boy

walked toward the door. Every inch of the *kind* announced he wanted to go anywhere but into the house to meet with Whitney and answer her questions. Jeremiah secretly shared the boy's dislike of someone poking and prodding into his life, but the social worker needed to be sure the placement was a *gut* one for all involved.

Jeremiah's steps faltered as he was following the boy outside. This meeting could be Mercy's chance to hand the troubled *kind* over to someone else, but he couldn't imagine she would. He'd seen the pain in her eyes whenever she mentioned Parker leaving for a permanent placement. The kid might challenge her endlessly, but she wasn't ready to give up the battle to reach him.

"Hey!" called Whitney when Parker tried to sneak past her unseen.

The boy stopped, his hands behind him and his head lowered. He didn't return the greeting.

Instead, Jeremiah did as he walked toward the silver car.

With a smile, Whitney said, "Hi, Jeremiah! Has our boy been spending time with you?"

"Ja." He crooked a finger toward Parker, who reluctantly edged forward. "You'll probably want to see this right away."

The social worker's smile faded when she saw the boy's bandaged finger. "What happened to you, young man?"

Again, Parker was silent.

Whitney's gaze shot toward Jeremiah, and he realized she was waiting for an answer.

"Parker learned a *gut* lesson about using the right tool for the job," Jeremiah replied calmly. "It's a cut."

"Does he need stitches?"

Shaking his head, he said, "No. It bled a lot, but it'll heal quickly. It's not much more than a long paper cut. He can show you in the house, and I'm sure Mercy will rebandage it for him."

"I'll do that." She flashed a quick smile at the boy. "Go and let Mercy know I'm here."

Parker took off running as best he could through the piles of snow.

Once he was out of earshot, Whitney turned to Jeremiah. He told her how Parker had hurt himself.

"He won't make the same mistake again," he finished.

"Because he won't have access to knives?"

"No, because I'm going to show him the correct way to whittle once I know he's willing to be cautious."

"I don't know," she drawled.

"This is a farm, and boys on farms learn how to whittle and use a knife as a proper tool. If he's going to be here for a while, he needs to know what the other boys do, or he'll experiment on

his own. Who knows how he could hurt himself if he did that?"

Whitney nodded slowly. "I see. Does that mean you intend to remain around to teach him how to use a knife?"

He shook his head. "I honestly can't answer that. Not until Mercy's family decides what they want done with the farm."

"You know starting a children's summer camp is Mercy's dream, don't you?" Whitney asked, flashing a guilty glance at the house as if revealing an unspeakable secret.

"I know. She wants to help *kinder* enjoy getting away from the summer heat in the city."

"No, Jeremiah, it's more than that. Mercy knows her life would have been very different if she hadn't been a Fresh Air kid. She wouldn't have known the family who took her in before the Bambergers became her foster parents and then her adoptive parents. Come Along Farm is her way to repay an immeasurable debt." Whitney looked at the house again and sighed. "Will it be enough for her?"

"I don't know," he replied.

"I don't know, either, but I do know there aren't too many women her age who would have agreed to look after a very angry, very hurt, very destructive and hateful child as she has."

"Parker is a challenge, but he's not hateful."

Jeremiah thought of how the *kind* was changing...slightly.

"Parker? You don't have any idea whom I'm talking about, do you?"

"No. I thought we were talking about the boy."

"No, I'm talking about Sunni."

He couldn't hide his shock. "Sunni was destructive and hateful?"

"Yes."

"But she's such a *gut* kid."

"Now." Whitney ran her fingers lightly over the handle of her briefcase. "I've probably already said too much. If you want to know more, you'll need to ask Mercy. I wanted *you* to know, other than Sunni and the rest of her family—and I'm not too sure about her family—nothing is more important to Mercy than paying back the compassion and love she was given after her grandmother died with a bigger dose of compassion and love. Please remember that."

"I will." What else could he say as Whitney walked toward the house?

Everything and everyone kept reminding him Mercy didn't want the farm for herself. She wanted it for others.

Lord, am I being selfish to believe the farm is the only way I can help this settlement to grow and succeed? How can I stand in her way if I care for her?

And he more than cared for her, he knew. He was in danger of falling in love with her. He found it difficult to imagine a day without her being a part of it. Her smile was the last thing he thought of before falling asleep and the first thing he envisioned in the hour before dawn. The brush of her fingers set off fireworks along his skin, and the thought of kissing her left him breathless.

So how could he stand in the way of her making her dreams come true? *How, Lord?*

He turned to walk toward the barns, not sure he was ready for the answer to that question.

Mercy wasn't surprised when Jeremiah offered to help her do dishes after supper. She guessed he was curious how the meeting with Whitney had gone. She eased his concerns by telling him the social worker had been impressed with how quickly he explained what had happened to Parker's finger and why and how Jeremiah intended to prevent such things from occurring again.

"She seems very taken with you, Jeremiah," she said with a chuckle.

"I'm a very taking guy." He grimaced. "Is that even a thing?"

"Who knows? Thank you for being so up-front about Parker's injury. Once Whitney saw it was exactly as you described, she was satisfied."

"And Parker ended up with, as he described them, very cool bandages."

"Don't tell him that I bought those strips with cartoon characters for Sunni. He won't be happy then."

"I'd hoped they'd be getting along better by now."

She shrugged. "I've got to admit having him treating her badly has strengthened her." A faint smile tugged at her lips. "I suspect, in spite of my best efforts, I've babied her a bit because of her physical challenges. Parker cuts her no slack."

"That's a nice way of saying he's rude to her."

"But not to you." She smiled. "I don't know what you're doing, Jeremiah, but whatever it is, don't stop."

"I'm not planning to. By the way, I intend to start tapping the maple trees in the sugar bush tomorrow. If it's not too cold, why don't you and the *kinder* join me? I could use extra hands, and I think they'll find it fascinating. I did when I first saw sap coming out of a tree when I was a kid."

"That sounds like fun."

"It should be." He chuckled. "Do you know what Parker asked me earlier today?"

She gave a half laugh. "I don't want to try to guess. Knowing him, it could have been anything."

"He asked me if I believed in God."

Putting another stack of dirty dishes into the sink, she said, "I assume you told him you do."

"*Ja*, but I don't think he was looking for such a simple answer. He's trying to figure out why we live as we do in Harmony Creek." He picked up another plate to dry. "For a child who's so quick to anger, he can be deeply introspective when presented with a new idea. It's too bad apparently nobody has ever spoken to him about such things before he came here."

"I plan to take him to the closest Mennonite church with me on Sunday. It's about thirty miles from here." She hesitated, then asked, "Would you like to come with us?"

"You came to Sunday services with me, so I guess I should return the favor."

She faced him. "I should warn you that boys Parker's age sit with the men."

"That should make for an interesting morning, ain't so?"

Her breath grew swift as her gaze was caught by his. Strong emotions glistened in his eyes that burned a fiery blue. His fingers curved along her cheek, the warmth of his palm caressing her skin. As he stepped closer to her, he gently tilted her face toward him.

He was going to kiss her! Every nerve went on alert, and she was aware of him as she'd never been, the scent of the soap he used, the rough tex-

ture of his arms beneath her fingertips, the way his hair fell forward over his eyes as he bent to bring her lips to his.

A loud cry came from the mudroom, and Mercy yanked herself away from him. Shoving the dishrag that had been dripping unnoticed on the floor into Jeremiah's hands, she ran to referee the latest argument between the two children. She sent Sunni to the dining room and Parker into the living room, telling them to cool off.

From behind her as she stood in the middle of the empty room, she heard Jeremiah say, "*Ja*, I think it's going to be very interesting at church." He went into the kitchen.

She was about to follow, then paused. The moment between them was gone, and she would be wise not to let it happen again. She wasn't sure she could step away without kissing him next time.

Chapter Thirteen

Mercy wasn't sure who was more excited when the next day dawned with a cloudless sky and temperatures that should rise above freezing by midday. The kids were thrilled when they heard Jeremiah's invitation to help him with tapping the maple trees. She was just as excited, praying she'd have the chance to discover if he'd truly intended to kiss her.

She had to insist the children eat a hearty breakfast. They wanted to rush out and get to work right away. She also made them show her what they were wearing. She told Parker to zip his coat and wrap a scarf around his neck. When Sunni protested wearing her snow pants, Mercy refused to let her daughter draw her into an argument. If she didn't wear them, she wasn't going.

Seeing a hastily hidden smirk on Parker's face, Mercy wanted to ask what he'd said to persuade

Sunni to go out without proper clothing. She didn't. Later, when she had a chance to speak to her daughter alone, she'd find out. Why Sunni listened to him when he said such things was a mystery to Mercy, but her own siblings were so much older than she was, so they hadn't shared growing up years with her.

Mercy found a new problem when they went outside. The snow was melting, and walking through the high piles was as difficult as slogging through knee-deep mud. Watching Sunni, she wasn't sure the little girl could trudge up the hill and into the woods.

"Who wants a ride?" asked Jeremiah as he appeared around the house with an ancient toboggan topped with buckets and spiles to use to tap the trees.

The toboggan's front was scraped as if it'd hit bushes or caromed off a tree. No cushions eased the hard seats, but he connected a new nylon rope to it.

Not waiting for an answer to his question, he bowed. "Young ladies first."

His words earned a giggle from Sunni as she climbed on, and a mouthed "Thank you" from Mercy. She was grateful for how he didn't act as if Sunni was incapable.

At first, Parker was going to ride, but he changed his mind when Jeremiah asked him to help carry

the battery-operated drill he'd use to make the holes for the sap. Jeremiah grabbed two handfuls of buckets off the toboggan, leaving plenty of room for Sunni.

When Mercy urged Jeremiah and Parker to go ahead, the boy followed him toward the clump of trees halfway up the hill behind the barn. She pulled Sunni on the toboggan, following the path Jeremiah and Parker had made. It was a beautiful day, cold but the sunshine glistened on the unbroken snow. She pointed to animal tracks and had Sunni guess which animal might have made them. Crows sang their raucous songs as they wheeled overhead, and Sunni giggled with delight at the ride through the snow.

"Just like when we went in the sleigh, Mommy!" she called out.

"Except I'm playing the horse's part."

That brought more laughter from her daughter, and Mercy's footsteps grew lighter, even as the wet snow tried to hold her back.

Jeremiah paused and let Mercy catch up. "Do you want me to take the toboggan?"

"No, I'm fine."

"That you are." He gave her a wink that made her heart dance with delight.

He went to a tree and walked around it. Looking up at the sky, he shifted partway around again. "Okay, here's the southeast side of the tree."

"Is that important?" Parker asked.

"It is. The southeast side gets sunshine first in the late winter." He held out his hand for the drill. "Stay back."

Sunni clambered off the toboggan so she could watch as the drill whirred, sending pieces of wood flying in every direction. Her eyes were wide as she leaned closer.

Mercy put her hands on her daughter's shoulders, drawing her back slightly. She didn't want the little girl hit by the debris.

Picking up a thin twig, Jeremiah showed Parker how to clean the shavings out of the hole. "This way, they won't get in the sap." He hammered a spile into the tree.

"Will the tree be okay?" Sunni asked with sudden concern. "You're not hurting it, are you?"

"It'll be fine." Jeremiah gave her a gentle smile. "We won't be greedy, so the tree will have plenty of sap to carry up its branches to grow leaves. This is a grown-up tree." He pointed to the trunk at chest height. "Once a tree is ten inches around at this height, it can share its sap with us."

He showed Mercy how to place the bucket on the hook built into the tap so it would catch the drippings. He warned her to be careful the bucket's handle wasn't in the way. When the first drop fell with a ping into the bucket, Mercy was as enthralled as the children. While Jeremiah helped

Sunni set the metal "roof" over the bucket, he explained the folded piece would prevent windblown leaves and other debris from falling into the sap. Some would find their way into the bucket, but not as much as if the bucket was left open.

"It looks like it's wearing a hat," Sunni said with a grin.

Motioning for them to follow, Jeremiah began drilling another hole in the tree. He did three in the smaller trees and four in the massive ones. Each of the others had their tasks. Mercy waited while Parker cleared the hole, leaving tiny specks of wood on the snow at his feet. She and Sunni set the bucket and cover in place.

They fell into an easy rhythm as they moved from one tree to the next. After drilling holes in twenty-five trees, Jeremiah called a halt.

"If we do more," he said, "I won't have time to collect the sap, make the syrup and milk the cows." He ruffled the top of Parker's hat, leaving it askew. "Even with my *gut* assistant here."

The boy grinned. "Can I help make syrup, too?"

"*Ja.* I'll need everyone to pitch in." He stepped aside to let Parker clear out the hole. "Wait a moment, Mercy, before you put the bucket on. Do you *kinder* want to try a sample of the sap?"

This time, Parker went first. He bent and stuck out his tongue beneath the hole exactly as Jeremiah instructed. The boy waited and waited, then

frowned at Jeremiah, as if he thought the man was playing a trick on him.

"You've got to be patient," Jeremiah said with a laugh. "Sap comes out one drip at a time, and it's pretty chilly, so it's moving slowly."

"Let her try." He pointed to Sunni and stepped back, disgruntled.

"All right. Sunni, you want to have a taste?"

Mercy smiled as Sunni stepped forward to take her turn. She stood as Parker had. Silence, except for the rustle of birds in the higher branches, settled on them as she waited with her tongue poised near the hole. When she yelped in excitement, Mercy knew a drop had finally emerged.

"It's sweet!" Sunni's face glowed with happiness.

"Wait till you taste how sweet the syrup will be." Jeremiah turned to Parker as Mercy gave her daughter a hug. "You want to try again?"

"Yeah." His surly tone surprised Mercy because he hadn't used it with Jeremiah since the day of his arrival. He stepped forward, elbowing Sunni aside. As she fell into the snow, he ordered, "Get out of my way, cripple!"

Hearing Mercy's dismayed gasp, Jeremiah grabbed the boy by his shoulders and pulled him away from the tree. Anger blared through Jeremiah, and he wasn't sure he could quiet it. Mer-

cy's face was as pale as the snow as she lifted her daughter to her feet, and fat tears showered Sunni's cheeks. He wasn't sure if she was physically hurt or wounded by the cruel words.

"Mercy, will you and Sunni finish putting the bucket on there? We'll meet you at the house." Without another word, Jeremiah walked away, tugging Parker with him.

The boy started to speak several times as they went toward the tenant house. Each time, Jeremiah cut him off sharply.

Steering him inside, Jeremiah motioned for Parker to take a seat at the kitchen table. He half expected the boy to make a snide remark about the state of the house, but Parker stared at the floor.

"Why would you say something horrible to Sunni?" Jeremiah asked, not wanting to beat around the bush.

"I dunno," he muttered.

"I think you do. You treat Sunni and Mercy as if they're manure on the bottom of your boots."

The boy clamped his lips closed.

Knowing he needed to take another tack, Jeremiah forced his voice to be calm. The boy wasn't going to respond to anger. Parker would get defensive and close up.

Quietly, Jeremiah sighed.

The boy looked up, startled.

"Parker, I thought you wanted to be here working with me."

"I do." The boy bumped his toe against an uneven floorboard and again didn't meet Jeremiah's gaze.

"I can't work with someone who says bad things to other people."

"People say bad things to me."

He sat on a chair beside the *kind*'s. "I'm sorry to hear that, Parker. People used to say bad things about me, too."

"You?" The boy's head jerked up, revealing his shock. It made him look younger than his nine years and vulnerable. "But everyone says what a nice guy you are. When we went to the hardware store last week, I heard a man say he wouldn't be as willing as you are to wait to get what he'd signed papers for." Puzzlement threaded his brow. "What papers?"

Not wanting to be distracted from the issue at hand, Jeremiah said, "Business stuff. Nothing important now." He was astonished to realize how true his words were. As much as he wanted to own the farm, at that moment his whole attention was on the *kind*.

"What did they say about you?" Parker asked.

"I was too short. I was too chubby. I was stupid because I had a hard time alphabetizing my spelling words."

The boy's nose wrinkled. "I hate alphabetizing my spelling words, too."

"I couldn't see the point of doing it when I could be in the barn working with the cows or whittling. The cows and that stick of wood didn't care if I knew which word should come first." He leaned toward Parker. "And they didn't care what anyone else said about me. They didn't care about anything other than I did my chores and took care of them. So that's what I did."

"Me, too."

"But as much as you and I are alike, there's one way we're different. I try never to say anything hurtful to someone else. Jesus asked us to treat everyone else the way we want to be treated."

"That's what I'm doing."

Jeremiah caught and held the boy's gaze. "Do you really want Sunni to say such nasty things to you?"

Parker's shoulders sagged. "No."

"Then why do you say them to her?"

"Sometimes I get mad."

"I know how that is."

The boy stiffened. "Do you? Sometimes I get so mad I want to hit someone."

"I know."

He frowned. "I thought Amish guys didn't fight."

"We shouldn't, but once, when I was about your

age, I thought about hitting the bully who said bad things about me. I didn't."

"Why not?"

"Because I knew I was loved the way I was."

Parker shook his head. "Good for you. Nobody wants me."

"No? Mercy opened her home to you. Sunni includes you in everything she does. Don't you realize she thinks you're someone special? Haven't you noticed how she was eager to help in the barn because you were helping there?"

He shrugged, not wanting to be swayed by Jeremiah's words. "Maybe she thought she was missing out on something."

"Maybe she did, but she didn't realize it until you showed her how much fun chores can be. She never was interested before you came here."

Tears bubbled out of the boy's eyes, and Jeremiah had to resist his immediate impulse to put his arms around Parker and comfort him. The *kind* needed to realize his mistakes and decide to change.

"I'm sorry, Jeremiah. Don't hate me, too."

"I don't hate you. Nobody on the farm hates you."

"Sunni does." He wiped his nose with his arm. "She has to. I hate me."

"If she hated you, she wouldn't want to spend time with you. And she does."

Parker dashed away more tears. "She's a silly little girl."

"Maybe, but that silly little girl doesn't hate you. I don't hate you, and Mercy doesn't." He put a hand on the boy's shoulder. "Let me tell you one more very important thing. God loves you."

"How do you know that?"

"Because His son told us so." He gave the boy a gentle smile. "He loves all his *kinder*, including when we make mistakes. I've made plenty." The image of Emmarita's face flashed through his mind, but he easily ignored it. "God chose for me to be exactly like I am, so He must love what I am. Just as he loves you. Believe it." He tapped Parker's chest. "Right here, believe it. Next time you feel angry, give that anger over to God. He doesn't mind, and He'll ease the pain in your heart."

"He will?"

"*Ja.*" Coming to his feet, Jeremiah said, "I think you know what you need to do."

"Apologize to Sunni?" He got up. "Will you come with me?"

"Of course."

A few minutes later Jeremiah stood beside the boy while Parker asked Sunni to forgive him. When the little girl did with a sincerity Jeremiah found endearing, he saw gratitude in Mercy's eyes. He put his arms around all of them, pulling them into a hug. Feeling Mercy's soft hand on his

back, he knew he'd lost the battle to stop himself from loving her.

That made everything more difficult, and he needed to figure out what to do about it. But right now he was going to enjoy holding her—and the *kinder*—close.

Chapter Fourteen

The interior of the church could have belonged to the one Mercy had attended with her parents in central New York. Plain, whitewashed walls and simple benches. A trio of windows on either side of the pews had no stained glass like other churches in the village.

Adjusting her prayer covering, she walked with Sunni to a bench on the women's side. She glanced at where Parker sat next to Jeremiah. The boy's legs swung as he waited for the service to start. When Jeremiah bent to whisper something in his ear, Parker gave him a big grin.

How she wished she could get such a response from the boy, but he refused to trust her. She kept telling herself not to take it personally. He didn't trust any woman as far as she could see, and he had good cause. Not only had he been abandoned by his mother in Korea, left at a grocery store ac-

cording to his records, but Pat Kenton had let him love her and then turned her back on him, as well.

Someday, sometime in the future when Parker was old enough to understand, she hoped she could tell him how much she empathized with his fear of loving again. Mrs. Kenton had chosen her other life over her son's, as Graham had chosen his mother over Mercy…and her Fresh Air family had chosen their older daughter's lies over Mercy's and their younger daughter's protestations of truth.

Life wasn't fair, but it was good.

She wasn't sure who'd said that first, but she believed it with every ounce of her being. If Parker would let her closer, she might be able to convince him she knew his sense of betrayal. Maybe someday…but not today because he'd ignored Sunni and her, talking only to Jeremiah in the car. Even so, she longed to see the boy smile at something she said or did with as much joy as he did when he was with Jeremiah.

Jeremiah… Did he suspect she'd invited him to the Mennonite service hoping he'd feel comfortable enough that he'd consider putting aside his Amish life to join the Mennonites? It wouldn't be so different for him.

Except he wouldn't be part of the new community on the banks of Harmony Creek.

Praying about what to do so they could have a

future together hadn't brought her any answers. Few people joined the Amish, and fewer stayed. The dedication to community and to a life separate from the rest of the world was too much for most people who hadn't been raised in it.

As well, there was the issue of Come Along Farm. Opening a summer camp for children probably wouldn't fit with the Amish ideas of staying separate. She glanced at Sunni, who was looking everywhere but at Parker on the other side of the aisle. From Whitney, she'd learned Amish might adopt, but it was usually an internal matter. A baby born to an Amish girl who couldn't rear it would be given to another family.

But if I can't become Amish and he won't become Mennonite, there's no future for us.

That thought echoed through Mercy's head as she listened to the service but kept glancing over to where Parker sat beside Jeremiah. When the boy yawned, Jeremiah put his arm around the child and leaned Parker against him. She smiled gently before Sunni nestled against her. Pushing her worries from her mind, she gave herself over to the peace filling the sanctuary.

Mercy was smiling when, after the service, she led Sunni to where Jeremiah and Parker were waiting by her car. Urging them to get in out of the windy day, she slid behind the wheel. She turned the key to start the car and twisted the dial

so the heat would fill the space. Other cars were backing up and pulling out of the parking lot, so she waited.

After turning to check both children wore their seat belts, she asked the question that weighed so heavily on her mind. "So what did you think of the service, Jeremiah?"

"The harmony when you sing the hymns is pretty. Four-part harmony, ain't so?"

"Yes, and we sing the hymns at a quicker tempo than you do. I hope that didn't trip you up."

"I was able to keep up." He gave her a smile, which did delightful things to her middle.

"You know that's not what I meant."

"Maybe I did. Maybe I didn't." He winked at the children.

Sunni began to giggle, but Parker looked baffled as if he couldn't figure out why someone would find the conversation amusing.

"I've made up my mind," he said abruptly.

"About what?" Mercy asked.

"My name."

"Is that so?" she asked, careful to make her voice sound calm. "What other name have you decided on? Or do you want to keep the one you've got?"

"Not Parker." His nose wrinkled. "I sound like someone working in a parking lot."

Jeremiah chuckled. "I had the same thought when I first heard it."

The boy remained serious. "I thought about Jerry because it's like your name, Jeremiah, but you might think Mercy is scolding you when I do something wrong."

Again, Jeremiah laughed, but Mercy could see how deeply touched he was by the child's desire to be connected to him. Her eyes were awash in tears she didn't want to let fall because the boy might think she was upset.

"So tell us your name!" Sunni leaned toward him, excited.

"I want to be Paul." He looked at Jeremiah. "I remember hearing you say the day I arrived Paul was your dad's name. That's right, ain't so? And, if I'm Paul, you won't get confused when Mercy's talking to us."

When Jeremiah nodded, Mercy realized he was so overcome with emotion he was unable to speak. Not only was the boy picking up his way of speaking, but Parker had also chosen a name that meant so much to Jeremiah.

Clearing his throat, Jeremiah said, "You're right. Paul was my *daed*'s name, and I think he would have been happy to share it with you."

"All right. Call me Paul." Without a pause, he asked what was for lunch.

"Would you like to stop somewhere to eat?"

Mercy was no longer surprised by she needed to remember to call hi Whitney know about the change sure the boy wouldn't pick a diffe morrow. She was not surprised by Paul's focus on his next meal. The boy seemed endlessly hungry. "There's a nice diner between here and the farm. Grandpa Rudy used to take me there once or twice each summer when I visited him. You'll get so much to eat you'll feel like a stuffed turkey at Thanksgiving."

That brought cheers of excitement from the back seat. When she glanced at Jeremiah, he smiled.

"How could I say no when I'm outnumbered?" he asked with a chuckle.

She backed the car out, determined to enjoy the day and the company the Lord had given her.

Jeremiah wasn't surprised when Mercy walked beside him as the *kinder* raced toward the diner's door.

Slanting her head toward him, she murmured, "You do realize the importance of the name he picked, right? It's his way of telling you he wants to be a family with you."

"It's pretty overwhelming."

"It is, isn't it?" She squeezed his arm and smiled. "You've worked wonders with him, and

ows that, though he can't—or won't—say
. Are you truly okay with him using your fa-
ther's name?"

He nodded, and unabashed tears gleamed in
his eyes. "My *daed* used to say that he wanted a
dozen *kinder*. He and *Mamm* were blessed with
the nine of us, but it feels now as if he's one more
kid closer to his goal."

When she gave him a lovely smile, he wasn't
sure how the day could get better. He thought
about taking her hand, but they'd reached the door
where Sunni and *Paul* were waiting impatiently.
He opened the door and ushered them inside.

The diner was long and narrow. A single line of
booths edged the windows overlooking the park-
ing lot. Cutting the building down the middle was
a curved counter. The stools were repaired with
black electrical tape. However, everything was
sparkling clean.

When Mercy led the way to the booth she called
her favorite, he followed the *kinder*. He couldn't
fail to notice the glances in their directions. They
were the only plain folk in the diner.

A waitress in a simple white shirt and black
pants beneath her red-checkered apron took their
orders. Fortunately, the menu for *kinder* was lim-
ited, so Sunni and Paul selected quickly. Chicken
nuggets for Sunni and spaghetti for Paul. After
checking that none of the boy's allergies would be

triggered by what he'd ordered, Mercy asked for an open-faced hot turkey sandwich. Glad the others had ordered first, Jeremiah debated between two favorites and settled on chicken Parmesan.

The servings were as huge as Mercy recalled and as delicious. The children wasted no time cleaning their plates, their eyes continuously shifting toward the pie trolley on top of the gray counter.

When the waitress came to remove their plates, she asked if they wanted dessert. The enthusiastic response came from Jeremiah as well as the children.

The waitress smiled. "Just so you know, we get our pies from an Amish woman."

"Do you have *snitz* pie?" he asked.

"We do."

"Then two adult-size servings and two kid-size ones. Two cups of *kaffi*—coffee—and two glasses of milk."

"Chocolate?" interjected Paul.

She nodded. "Chocolate it'll be."

As she walked away, Sunni asked, "What is *snitz*?"

"Wait and see." He winked at Mercy as the kids wiggled with anticipation.

The waitress returned with their drinks before going to the counter to cut four slices of pie. She smiled as she set the plates on the table.

Paul wrinkled his nose as he looked at the dark brown filling in his serving. "What is it?"

"Is it chocolate?" asked Sunni, peering at her slice from every direction.

"It's *snitz* pie." Jeremiah grinned. "If you don't want it, I'll eat it." He held out his hand. "I never pass up a piece of *snitz* pie, especially my *mamm*'s. Ask anyone, and they'll tell you Wanda Lapp makes the best *snitz* pie in Lancaster County. Maybe the whole world."

"Why isn't her name Wanda Stoltzfus?" asked Sunni, ever the one to try to nail down every detail.

"Because she got remarried after my *daed* died."

"My father is dead, too." The little girl's lower lip began to tremble. "And my mommy." Her gaze darted to Mercy. "Not this mommy, my before mommy."

"My whole family is dead," stated Paul, not to be outdone. As he began to tell an outrageous tale that sounded as if it'd come from a television show too violent for a child his age, he must have seen the adults weren't buying his story. "It's true!"

"But it's not *gut* conversation for the dinner table." Jeremiah caught the boy's eyes and tilted his head toward where Mercy and Sunni sat. "The ladies, you know. They don't like rough talk like cowmen use. That's very important, ain't so?"

Mercy picked up her cup of coffee and took a sip so the boy didn't see her lips twitching with a smile. When Paul agreed with Jeremiah, she guessed the child had no idea what Jeremiah meant, but he wasn't going to let anyone see that.

"But what is it?" persisted Paul.

Mercy decided Jeremiah had teased the children long enough. "Apple pie."

Paul shook his head. "It looks strange."

"Because it's made with dried apples." She looked at the boy, who was clearly torn between standing firm so he didn't look as if he was giving in to her and his obvious longing to give in to the temptation to try the pie.

"It tastes like apple butter."

"Yummy!" announced Sunni and dove into her dessert.

Not to be outdone, Paul broke off the tiniest piece with his fork and stared at it. "It's polite to eat what's put in front of me," he said, obviously repeating something he'd heard at his previous home.

Mercy exchanged a glance with Jeremiah as she wondered how many times Paul's prospective mother had uttered those words. Her sorrow at what the boy had experienced vanished when Paul's eyes lit up as he tasted the pie.

"Can we have seconds?" he asked as he jabbed his fork into the pie for another bite.

They laughed, and Mercy savored the chance to look at each of them as they all smiled at the same time. It hadn't happened often. She hoped it would more often from this point forward.

"Mommy! Stop! Now!"

When Sunni screamed, Mercy looked in the rearview mirror and saw her daughter's terror. They'd just driven out of the diner's parking lot.

Jeremiah swung around. "Mercy, pull over!"

She twisted the wheel. The car behind her honked in annoyance, but she ignored it as she jammed the shifting lever into Park. As their car rocked to an abrupt stop, she jumped out at the same time Jeremiah did.

He tore open the door on his side and leaned over Paul, who was straining to breathe. The boy's lips were already turning blue, and his face was swollen with hives.

Grabbing her purse, she pulled out the epinephrine injector she'd been carrying since Paul joined their family. She ran around the car, pushed Jeremiah aside and flipped the top off the injector. She gripped it tightly before grabbing the fleshy part of the boy's thigh. She pressed the injector against his pants. Hearing a click, she counted off ten seconds.

"We passed an urgent care just before we pulled into the diner," Jeremiah said.

"Can you drive a car?"

He nodded. "But I haven't in a while."

"Get in and drive." She climbed between the two children, keeping her eyes on the wheezing boy. "Go!"

Jeremiah jumped behind the wheel and jammed the shift into Drive. They were thrown back against the seats as the tires squealed when he rammed the gas pedal to the floor.

"You're going to be okay," she said as she brushed Paul's bangs from his brow that was covered with cold sweat.

She heard Jeremiah praying and added her own prayers that they'd reach the urgent care quickly and—as another car blared its horn at them—without an accident.

Hours later, when Mercy sat across from Jeremiah at the kitchen table having a calming cup of tea while he drank coffee, she strained her ears to listen for footsteps upstairs. The children had been worn out by the day's exciting events.

"A single piece of candy with a single peanut in it." Mercy shook her head. "He didn't realize he'd grabbed one with a peanut from the bowl by the cash register. Not until it was in his mouth."

"But he's all right."

"I'd like to say my nerves are all right, too."

Jeremiah laughed quietly. "Maybe yours are.

I think mine will calm down in a month or so. You were *wunderbaar*, Mercy. You didn't stop to think. You did what you had to do."

"You would have done the same."

"I'd like to think so, but I was shocked when his condition was getting more dire by the second."

Letting her shoulders sag and wincing at the ache from holding them taut for so long, she said, "Thank God it turned out all right."

"*Ja*, we must most definitely thank God. He was with us, protecting us."

"Especially when you were driving." She allowed herself a smile. "I didn't realize your previous driving experience was as a race driver."

Again, he chuckled. "Just so you know, I was praying as fast as I was driving." He sipped his coffee. His hands remained unsteady.

Just like hers. *Thank You, God, for watching over Paul today and guiding us to get help for him.*

"I hope you enjoyed the Mennonite service," Mercy said, needing to talk about something other than Paul's close brush with death.

"It was interesting. Like an Amish one, but yet not like it." He gave her a weary smile. "And I don't mean just the pace of the singing."

"If you'd like to come with us again, you're welcome." Wishing she could come out and ask him what she really wanted to know—would he ever

consider becoming a Mennonite?—she couldn't. If he said no, then that ended any hopes for them to have a future together.

You're getting ahead of yourself, her conscience whispered. *He hasn't said anything about the future other than his plans for the farm. Can't you see what comes first?*

Pain twisted in her stomach. Jeremiah had been honest about the fact his dreams were his number one priority. If Graham had been so forthcoming, it would have saved them a lot of hurt.

"*Danki,*" he replied, "but I may be doing some traveling."

"Really?"

"Caleb mentioned that he may need me to help him find other families for the settlement." He didn't add more, but she understood what he wasn't saying. If it wasn't God's will for him to have the farm, recruiting others to come to the Harmony Creek settlement might be the best way for him to help it thrive.

"When would you be leaving?"

"Most likely soon. Once spring comes, there won't be time for anything but fieldwork and chores." He gave her a weak smile. "Caleb suggested I go to central New York. Actually not far from where your family lives."

"You should stop in and see them if you do."

His brows lowered. "You don't think I'd try to influence them into selling me the farm?"

"I thought we weren't going to look for hidden motives." She didn't say the words harshly, because the thought had slipped through her mind, as well. "My parents would be glad to offer you a place to stay because you're my friend."

Did she see him flinch at *friend*? Or was she hoping he had? Could he feel about her as she did about him?

Her hopes he might faded when he asked, "Would there be anyone else you'd like me to take a message to? Did you leave someone special behind in central New York?"

She snorted. "How many men do you know who'd be willing to date a woman with a child, especially one with special medical needs? I could count them on the number of hairs on a bald man's head!"

"My brother Daniel married his wife, who was responsible for a *kind* with Down syndrome and her *grossmammi* Ella, who has Alzheimer's."

"Maybe so, but he's one of a kind."

He folded his arms on the table and shook his head. "Actually not. When my brothers—and sisters—have fallen in love, they haven't cared about the complications of *kinder*. Our family has grown very quickly in the past couple of years with additions, *bopplin* and older kids."

"Then your whole family is one of a kind. Most men I've met head in the other direction once they find out I have a child."

"Two."

"But for how long?" She raised her eyes toward the ceiling where the children should be asleep.

"What do you mean?"

"How long will Paul be here? There are so many reasons he could leave, some having to do with the social services. Others to..."

When her voice faded, he put his hand over her fingers on the table. "Others having to do with who ends up owning the farm? Is that what you were going to say?"

"I'm sorry, Jeremiah." She gazed at his hand on hers, confused. On one hand, she thrilled in his touch. On the other, she struggled to trust him. She knew he wasn't Graham, but her heart bore the scars of that betrayal.

"Mercy, you must realize if your family decides to sell me the farm, I'm not planning on throwing you and the kids out ten seconds later."

"I know, but you've got your plans for the farm." She slid her hand out from beneath his. Thinking clearly when his rough palm burnished her fingers was impossible.

Standing, she went to where she could look at the first stars poking through the crisp winter night. When Jeremiah moved behind her, he

didn't touch her, but she was as much aware of hi breathing as hers. In the silence she could hear hi heartbeat matching her own. If she leaned back even an inch, her head would be against him.

"Mercy, will you look at me?" His voice was n more than a whisper, but she could hear sorrov in it. "Tell me what you're thinking."

Facing him, she stared at the top button on hi shirt. Meeting his gaze when she was so unsettled might be foolish.

"Why is it taking so long?" Not giving him a chance to answer, she added, "You've got to be asking that yourself."

"Some people need time to make an importan decision. My family teases me because sometime I'm the last one to make up my mind, but I've go to look at the decision from every angle so I know I've made the right one."

In spite of herself, she raised her eyes toward his. "Did it take you a long time to decide to buy this farm?"

"It took me a long time to realize I was happie farming than doing anything else. I immediately started looking for a *gut* place to go because knew there weren't any farms I could afford nea Paradise Springs. I wasn't sure where I'd go unti Caleb talked to me about Harmony Creek. Coming here seemed the perfect answer."

"Until you got here and found us."

He arched his brows, and she saw a hint of his smile before it swiftly vanished. "I don't blame you."

"You should, you know."

"No, I shouldn't. For a reason neither of us can guess, God brought us together like this. He knows the future. We can't do anything but believe His reasons are for our *gut*, and if we continue forward toward what He has planned for us, we'll know His blessings."

"So we wait."

He shrugged, and his smile reappeared. "I don't see any alternative."

"I know." She clasped her hands behind her so she didn't reach out to throw her arms around him and beg him to hold her. "And every day we don't hear is another day Paul can stay here." She allowed herself a faint grin. "Not that any day is easy with him."

"Eventually, he'll realize what a blessing you and Sunni are for him." He went toward the door.

Had her face betrayed her longing to be in his arms? "And you. He wants your respect more than anything else now."

"Learning to respect you and Sunni would go a long way toward earning that."

"But he'd have to share you with us, and he's made it clear he doesn't want to."

He sighed and pulled his coat off the peg by the door. "He's a confused *kind*."

"I agree."

"So what can I do to help?" He reached for his scarf.

"Keep doing whatever you've been doing. I can see so many changes in him when he's with you. He listens to you."

"Sometimes."

"Which is a lot more than he listens to me. I know he craves action. That's one of the reasons he likes doing chores with you. Painting doesn't interest him."

He put his hand on the doorknob, but didn't turn it. "I'll be collecting sap and starting the evaporator to make syrup in the morning. Paul can help me."

"That should definitely keep him busy."

"Oh, I'll find lots for him to do." His eyes twinkled and then grew serious again. "He truly is blessed to have you care about him so much. Just as I am." He bent and kissed her cheek. "Sleep well, Mercy."

He was gone before she could reply. Raising her fingers to the place where his lips had grazed her face, she stared at the closed door.

He'd kissed her.

True, it'd been as chaste as a kiss he'd give the children, but he'd kissed her.

She wished she knew what it meant.

Chapter Fifteen

❧

"Cool! Hey, Sunni! Come and see this."

Shocked by Paul's eager invitation to Sunni, whom he didn't want hanging around him, and not sure what the boy was up to, Mercy jumped up from where she was mending yet another rip in the knees of Paul's trousers. She ran to where the cellar door was open.

He stood a couple of steps below her on the stairs and looked at her with an excited grin. "Why didn't you tell me you were putting a pool in the cellar? This is the coolest house ever!"

"Pool?" She edged past him. She halted when she heard the unmistakable sound of moving water. In fact, if she hadn't known better, she would have guessed there was a waterfall in the cellar.

"How big is it? I wanna see." The boy reached for the switch to turn on the lights.

She grabbed his wrist, not wanting to risk him getting a shock.

"Go!" she cried. "Get Jeremiah. Tell him we've got a flooded basement." Looking over her shoulder, she repeated her order.

As Paul started to go, there was a pop. Lights went out, leaving the house in a dusky twilight, and Sunni squealed from upstairs.

Mercy went up and into the kitchen. She grabbed a flashlight from the junk drawer. When she sprayed the light, she saw the water was halfway up the stairs. High enough to have flooded the electrical box and shorted it out. Boxes and other items bobbed on the rising water. She was tempted to try to snag them, but didn't want to fall into the filthy water topped by what looked like an oil slick.

It seemed forever before Paul returned with Jeremiah. When she heard Jeremiah calling, she wanted to sag with relief.

Instead, she shouted, "In the cellar!"

He hurried toward her and whistled. "I thought Paul was exaggerating. There really is a swimming pool here."

"It's rising fast."

"The snow is melting quickly, and the ground is frozen, so the water must have found its way through the foundation." He paused. "Sounds like it's pouring in over behind the fuel tank." As he

started up the stairs, he said, "Let me get the generator from my workshop. We'll hook it to a pump. Rudy must have one around here."

"I'll look for it after I open the bulkhead."

"*Gut* idea. That'll give the water an exit out of the cellar."

Warning both children to stay away from the cellar steps, Mercy didn't pause to grab a coat. She stuck her feet into boots and rushed out into the evening dusk. Glancing at the workshop where Jeremiah was unplugging the generator as fast as he could, she ran through the slushy snow and deep puddles beginning to ice over again. The cold should stop the flood.

She put her foot against one side of the double doors and pulled the other. It moved with the protest of rusty hinges. She groaned when she saw another door at the base of the stairs. Water was seeping out, reaching the top of the first step even as she watched in shock.

Hurrying to where Jeremiah pushed the generator across the yard while he balanced hoses over his shoulder, she told him about the door. "If we open it, we'll get washed away."

"Look for a pump while I get the generator ready to go. You know what one looks like?"

She nodded and ran toward the garage. Her grandfather had kept a small pump on a shelf when she was a kid. Was it still there?

Finding it, her next question was if it worked. There was no way to find out without hooking it up. She handed it to Jeremiah. He deftly connected the pump to hoses and then to the generator. Yanking on the starter cord, he bent to push open one of the cellar windows. He shoved one hose inside, then started the pump.

Water whooshed out, spraying them. He switched off the pump, grabbed the hose that had showered them with dirty water and tossed it in the direction of the road. When he restarted the pump, water erupted in a geyser again, but fell harmlessly into a snowbank.

Once assured the pump was working, Mercy followed Jeremiah into the house. He told her he had enough gasoline to keep the generator running for the next twenty-four hours.

"By then, the weather will probably have turned cold again." He sighed. "I hope so, because if it stays this warm, the sap will run too fast and won't be *gut* for syrup."

Throughout the evening, Jeremiah checked on the level of the water in the cellar. It didn't begin to lower until it was time for the children to go to bed, unhappy they'd had cold sandwiches for supper.

"Now you know how it is to live like the Amish do," Jeremiah said with a chuckle as they started up the stairs.

He got peeved looks in return, but, by the time they went upstairs, he'd brought kerosene lanterns from the tenant house and barn. Mercy helped Sunni and Paul brush their teeth, making sure they skimped on water. Until the well pump was running again, they had to conserve what was in the tank. Paul perked up, glad to skip his bath.

Mercy was relieved when Sunni and Paul went to sleep quickly. She'd piled her grandfather's crocheted afghans on top of their beds, hoping to keep them warm until morning. If it was too cold when she went upstairs, she'd carry them into her bed, where they would keep each other from freezing.

When she came into the living room, she sat on the sofa where she'd been working what seemed like days ago. A kerosene lamp gave off more light than she'd expected. She picked up Paul's pants. She'd gotten the patch sewn on one knee and needed to finish one on the other knee.

"I don't know how he can rip out the knees of his trousers when there's a couple of feet of snow on the ground," she said wryly.

Jeremiah closed the woodworking supply catalog he'd been looking at and set it on the table beside the other end of the sofa. "The boy has a rare talent for such things."

"Another week is almost over." Her needle darted

in and out of the denim, jabbing with her frustration as she added, "And nothing has changed."

"I don't want to talk about the farm and your family tonight."

"Neither do I, but the delay in getting an answer has been much on my mind, especially with the flooded cellar."

He gave her a cockeyed grin. "Me, too. That's why I don't want to talk about it. Why don't we talk about something we haven't talked about?"

"What's that?"

"Rudy." He shifted so he could look at her, leaving himself mostly in silhouette. "I never met the man, though everyone tells me about him. Everyone but you."

She frowned. "I talk about my grandfather all the time."

"Bits and pieces. Tell me about the Rudy you knew."

For a moment she was silent. Not because she wasn't sure what to tell him. She wasn't sure what to tell him *first*. So many memories were layered on top of each other, images as clear in her mind as the photo of her parents in *Abuelita*'s apartment.

How could she explain to Jeremiah how important Grandpa Rudy had been to her? Not once had he made her feel like she was different from his other grandchildren. He didn't care she'd had

other parents before the Bambergers. She was his granddaughter, and that was all that mattered.

"He loved to laugh," she said. "Apparently, he was a prankster his whole life. Any tin can could contain a fake snake. Any glass could be a dribble one, and I quickly learned to look before I sat. He really loved whoopie cushions."

"He sounds like fun."

"He was, and what he liked was for someone to play a trick on him. I spent hours before each visit trying to come up with something to surprise him and make him laugh."

"And did you?"

"I don't know if I ever surprised him, but he always laughed. He found much joy in everything. He considered everything he could see and hear and touch a gift from God, and he was thankful every day of his life." Lowering her mending to her lap, she gazed out the window toward the dark backyard. "He grew rows of rhubarb behind the house, though he was allergic to it. Touching it gave him hives, but he made sure the rhubarb grew every year and invited the neighbors to pick it."

"Why?"

"Because his wife loved rhubarb, and he'd loved her. She died quite young, so I never met her." She blinked back sudden tears. "I don't think I'd ever been so proud than when he told me, though

I looked like my mother, I reminded him of his late wife." She felt her cheeks heat. "I'm sorry. I know you Amish think pride is wrong."

"I think there are exceptions to everything, even *hochmut*. It sounds as if that compliment was one." He reached across the cushion between them and took her hand. "*Danki* for sharing your love for Rudy with me, Mercy. I've known from the beginning how important the farm is to you, but I thought it was only because of your hope of helping *kinder*. I see you want the farm to be a tribute to your *grossdawdi*, who helped you find the family you thought you'd lost."

"I never thought of it that way."

When he didn't reply immediately, she realized he was giving her the chance to consider his words. And she did. Was building the farm into something special important because it symbolized what she'd found after losing everything and everyone important to her?

He shifted again, closer to her. She could see his intense expression. She dampened her lips, and his eyes followed the motion. Quickly, she looked down.

His fingers beneath her chin brought her face up. She shivered as a powerful warmth sliced through her, radiating from where his fingertips touched her. When he tilted her mouth toward his, she wondered why she was fighting what

she yearned for. His face, which was rough with a day's growth of whiskers, brushed against her when he lightly kissed her right cheek.

Her breath caught. Was another chaste kiss all he wanted? It was so sweet, but when he moved to kiss her other cheek, she caught his face between her palms. His eyes burned like the heart of a fire, sparks glinting through their shadowed depths.

"Kiss me," she whispered softly.

"I am kissing you."

"Kiss my lips."

"I want that more than you can know, *liebling*."

The gentleness of his lips mesmerized her, and she deepened the kiss. When he started to lift his mouth away, she steered it back to hers.

With a chuckle, he pulled her closer as he captured her lips again. His kiss was a delicious confirmation of the feelings she'd prayed he shared with her. She shouldn't be falling in love with him, not when he wanted to take her farm from her, but she wouldn't lie to herself or to him. Being in his arms was what she wanted right now and for the rest of…

She drew back. When he arched a brow at her, she realized he knew the course of her thoughts. Were they similar to his own?

Then she realized she didn't care. Sliding her hands up to his shoulders, she leaned forward once more. This time when he kissed her, thoughts of

pulling away vanished. For one special moment, the past and the future didn't exist. Only now. The worries would return, but for now she wanted to relish his kisses.

"Danki," Jeremiah said when Mercy slid another slice of French toast onto his plate. She'd started the gas stove with a match, enabling her to make them a warm breakfast.

"You're welcome."

That was the longest sentence she'd spoken to him since Paul had insisted Jeremiah join the rest of them for breakfast. Mercy was quiet, not teasing either Sunni or Paul. Was she thinking, as he was, of the kisses they'd shared last night? She hadn't met his eyes since he came in.

He understood too well. Sleep had been elusive last night. Lying awake, he'd stared at the water-stained ceiling in the tenant house. The shadows of bare branches had rocked in the moonlight as wind groaned beneath the eaves. He'd fallen asleep a couple of times, but something jerked him awake. Finally, he realized he wanted to avoid dreaming about having Mercy in his arms.

It couldn't happen again. Well, it easily could, but he needed to make sure it didn't. Their kiss hadn't changed anything. They remained rivals for the farm, and, more important, she wasn't Amish.

If she was willing to try...

He didn't allow the thought to form. He'd seen others try, drawn by what they saw as a bucolic life. Few of them lasted more than a couple of months. Though he had no doubts Mercy could do whatever she put her mind to, her yearning to build Come Along Farm and help city kids wouldn't fit into an Amish life.

Would they?

He honestly didn't know how strict the *Ordnung* would be for the settlement because they hadn't begun discussing it yet. So far, each family was living by the rules established in their home district, and that served them well.

"Can I have more?" Paul held his syrupy plate up for another piece, too.

"You've got a hollow leg," Jeremiah said with a chuckle.

The joke fell flat when nobody else laughed.

Though he knew the French toast must be delicious, it tasted like sawdust in his mouth. He ate and then waited while the *kinder* went into the other room to do their schoolwork.

"Finished?" Mercy asked as she reached for his plate. She was stacking the dishes by the sink, planning to wash them once the electricity was on and the well pump was working again.

"Ja." He needed to build a solar setup to power the well pump so he didn't have to be dependent on the grid. He could have his younger brother

come up and put a couple panels on the roof. But first he needed to check if the rafters could support the weight.

Telling Mercy why he was going up in the attic, he took the flashlight from the drawer and left the kitchen. Her urging to be careful with the weak floors sounded automatic. She said the same words each time one of the *kinder* went upstairs alone.

Floorboards creaked as Jeremiah crossed the second floor to get to the attic door. When he opened it, he heard water dripping. He wasn't surprised there were holes in the roof. Everything about the house needed repairs.

He switched on the flashlight and aimed it at the rafters. He didn't need to test the rafters with a nail to see if there was dry rot. Several of them were bowing and one was broken. It'd dropped across the attic, crushing boxes stored there.

A scan of the boxes showed him that the contents had probably been ruined before the rafter collapsed. He calculated what the cost of replacing the broken rafter would be. Once it was in place, the other rafters should straighten. The roof could then support two solar panels.

As he started toward the stairs, the flashlight's beam flickered on a box set off by itself. It was on its side, and he guessed it had been pushed aside when the rafter broke. He froze as the light

showcased the words: *Personal items of Mercedes Ramirez.*

He picked up the box, shifting it carefully so he didn't break anything in it. Or anything else, he realized when he heard the tinkle of broken glass.

Closing the attic door behind him, he took care as he crossed the creaking second floor. He rushed into the kitchen.

Mercy looked over her shoulder, and her eyes widened. "What do you have there?"

"Something you've been looking for."

She put the measuring cup she held on the counter. When he set the box on the table, he turned it so she could see the words.

She gasped and pressed her fingers to her lips. "Mercedes Ramirez? This box has to be from before I was adopted."

"My guess is it's from when you first were put into the state's care."

"How do you figure that?"

He answered her question with a question. "Remember what you said last night?"

Her flush deepened, and he knew she was blushing at the thought of what had been said with words *and* kisses.

Tapping her cheek, he said, "This is charming." He didn't give her a chance to reply as he went on, "I remember how you said Rudy told you that

while you resembled your *grossmammi* in temperament, you looked like your *mamm*."

"He mentioned that several times through the years."

"Don't you see what it means, Mercy? Rudy saw your *mamm*, and the only way he could have done that was by seeing the photo of your parents. The one you remember from when you were a kid." He patted the box. "It could be in here. Can I open it?"

She nodded, her teeth clamped on her lower lip.

Unfolding the flaps, he lifted out the topmost item. A stuffed rabbit made like a crazy quilt in the brightest colors he could imagine.

Mercy took it carefully. "I remember this. *Abuelita* made it for me for my fifth birthday." She touched the ears, which once had been a brilliant white and now were a sad and stained brown. "What's it doing here?"

"I don't know." He picked up a *kind*'s heavily embroidered dress. "Do you recognize this?"

"Yes," she whispered. "*Abuelita* made matching ones for me and her for a block party when I was six or seven. She said it would give her practice for when she made my *Quinceañera* gown when I turned fifteen."

"What kind of gown?"

Running her fingers along the flowers and birds stitched into the small dress, she said, "It's

a Hispanic custom for a girl's fifteenth birthday. There's a big party, and she dresses like a princess in the fanciest dress you can imagine. Of course, I never had a *Quinceañera* because, by the time I was fifteen, I was living a Mennonite life."

He dug a couple of damp picture books out of the box, but they fell apart in his hands. With care, he reached for the final item in the box. It was surrounded by shards of glass. He lifted it out and discovered it was a picture encased in a cheap metal frame. The glass that once had been inserted in it was broken.

Handing it to Mercy, he said nothing.

She stared at the picture that was black with mold. Half of it had been gnawed away. Whoever or whatever was depicted in it had become an indistinct blur.

"Maybe it's not the right picture," Jeremiah said softly. "Maybe we can find the picture of your parents somewhere else upstairs."

"It's the right one." She cradled the ruined picture as if it were a *boppli*. "Look! You can make out the word 'Lincoln' on the bottom. Lincoln Photography is where the picture was taken."

"I'm sorry, Mercy. I wish we could have found it before damp and mice got to it."

Lowering the frame to her lap, she touched her chest right over her heart. "I keep my birth parents right here. Nothing's ever changed about that."

When tears flooded along her cheeks, he started to apologize.

"Thank you, Jeremiah," she said. "You've cleared up a mystery that's bothered me for years."

"I wonder why it was here."

"I don't know, but knowing the picture wasn't thrown away is a weight off my heart." She reached up and ran her fingers along his jaw.

When she guided his mouth to hers, he could think of a dozen different reasons he shouldn't kiss her. He could think of only one reason why he should. He loved her. Later he would think of the complications. Now he savored the sweet caress of her lips.

Chapter Sixteen

Jeremiah drew in a deep breath of the moist air in the sap house the next morning. The small outbuilding was barely large enough for the evaporator, the stack of wood that heated it and shelves where he'd put empty bottles and his tools. It took several hours every other day to cook the sap into syrup because he was making small batches. The sap needed to go past water's boiling point by ten degrees before it started to cook into golden maple syrup. Once it did, he filled bottles and set them on a shelf to cool.

Bending, he checked the fire under the evaporator. He shoved a couple more pieces of split wood in so the heat stayed steady. If he stayed on the farm, he would like to tap more trees. He could buy a gas-powered evaporator and make enough syrup to sell at the farmer's market in Salem. Several of the other families were already planning

to set up tables once spring came, selling every-thing from freshly made bread to goat milk soap to eggs and dried herbs.

If Mercy's family decided to sell him the farm. If they didn't increase the price beyond what he could afford. If he was able to make a success of the property.

Why was it easier to think about the farm than Mercy's eager response to his kisses? Each time the memories tried to assert themselves, he si-lenced them. They were a reminder of how wit-less he was. He'd known right from the beginning Mercy was Mennonite. She'd invited him to her church and hadn't hid how much she hoped he'd consider being baptized as a Mennonite. The pic-ture of her family, though it'd been ruined, was another indication she was definitely *Englisch*.

God, how have I failed to see I'm making the same mistake again? Show me a way to fix this without ruining everything.

He snorted. What made him think God was going to bail him out of this predicament? Jere-miah had gone in with his eyes open, but should have kept his heart closed. He had to find the words to tell Mercy though she was *wunderbaar* in his arms, he was committed to helping the Amish community.

For what purpose? That vexing voice was back demanding he be honest with himself. *What pur-*

pose do you have for building a home in Harmony Creek if you're not going to share it with the woman you love?

"Jeremiah?"

He looked up, startled to discover Sunni standing in the sap house's doorway. He'd been so lost in his thoughts he hadn't heard the door open.

The little girl was bundled up in her winter coat and snow pants and boots. Her steps were stiff as she came in. Her motions reminded him instantly of Mercy's when she was nervous.

He wanted to put the *kind* at ease, but he couldn't when he didn't know why Sunni was there. Apparently alone, because she closed the door behind her.

"Hi, Sunni!" he said with a smile.

The little girl was adorable in her winter clothes that left only her nose and dark eyes visible between her scarf and the hood of her coat. She looked as round as she was tall. When she pulled her scarf off, she wore the most somber expression he'd ever seen on her young face.

"Are you okay?" he asked.

She nodded as she edged around the evaporator, gazing up at the steam rising into the vent and outside.

"Do you want something?" A stupid question. She wouldn't have taken the long walk from the house unless she had a reason.

He pulled a bench from beneath the shelves and motioned for her to take a seat.

She did as she loosened her coat and pulled off her mittens, shoving them into her pockets.

"Is the syrup done?" she asked.

"Another fifteen minutes should do it." He squatted in front of her. "Sunni, you look like a gal with something on your mind. Why don't you spit it out?"

Opening her mouth, she hastily closed it.

"Sometimes," he said, "the most difficult words are the first ones. Push them out, and the others will follow."

Sunni swallowed hard. "Do you like my mommy?"

"*Ja.* Your *mamm* is a nice person. I think everyone around here likes her."

The little girl shifted to perch on the very edge of the bench. "I don't mean that kind of like. I mean do you *like* her?"

"Ah…" He understood what the child was asking, but he also knew whatever he said might be repeated to Mercy once Sunni returned to the farmhouse. "I think that topic should be discussed by your *mamm* and me. Don't you think so?"

Sunni slowly nodded.

"*Gut.*" He came to his feet. "Do you want to stay until the syrup is ready?"

"Will you promise me one thing?" she asked instead of answering his question.

"Amish don't make promises. We trust our word is as *gut* as a promise."

She stared at him, baffled. Her lips moved as she repeated his words as she tried to make sense of them. The moment when she got the meaning was obvious because the lines threading her forehead vanished.

"All right. I believe you," she said.

"Danki." He was amused by her stern composure. It wouldn't have been out of place for a bishop. "What did you want to ask me?"

"Please don't hurt my mommy."

He flinched at the words the *kind* spoke with a yearning from the little girl's heart. "That's the last thing I'd ever want to do, Sunni. Your *mamm* is a kind and generous woman, and I admire how hard she works."

"I know Mommy is kind, but I don't want you to hurt her."

"How do you think I'd hurt her? By buying the farm?"

Sunni shook her head. "Not that. I don't want you to hurt her like Graham did. He said he loved her and asked her to marry him. I'd hoped she'd say no, but she said yes, and then he made her cry and cry when he always did what his mother wanted. Not just once, but a lot of times because

his mother didn't like Mommy. That old lady was mean to Mommy and to me."

He realized the little girl was speaking of Mercy's former boyfriend. No, Graham actually had been her fiancé. Had he missed that fact, or had she failed to mention it? Not that it mattered. From Sunni's sorrowful words, it was clear whatever had been between Mercy and Graham was over. All that remained was a little girl determined to protect her *mamm*.

He folded Sunni's small hands between his much larger ones and held her gaze. "I don't ever intend to hurt your *mamm*. I don't want to see her cry, either."

She regarded him dubiously. "Graham said that, too. More than once I heard him say that, but then Mommy cried over and over again for months. She tried to make it work because she thinks I need a daddy."

"What do you think?"

Again, the little girl took time to ponder before she answered. He wondered if she'd always been such a deep-thinking *kind*, or if her experience in leaving Korea and coming to a new family only to have them discard her had made her question every aspect of everything around her. In so many ways, she seemed too old for such a young *kind*.

"I thought our family was perfect. Me an

Mommy and Grandma and Grandpa and the rest of the family."

"Especially Grandpa Rudy?"

"Uh-huh." Sunni's eyes grew luminous with tears, and he realized he'd never given thought to how the old man's death had affected this little girl. "When Mommy told me she was going to marry Graham and he'd be my new daddy, I tried to be happy, but I didn't like him."

"For the same reason you didn't like me at first?"

"No, I didn't like him. I didn't know then how someone could be so mean and make my mommy cry. I know that now."

Jeremiah sought words to soothe the *kind*'s pain, but anything he could come up with seemed trite. He wondered if Mercy knew how badly her broken engagement had both relieved and hurt her daughter.

Sunni didn't seem to notice he hadn't answered. "But then Paul came along, and he's part of our family." Her mouth twisted. "Lots of the time, I don't like him, especially when he says bad things about me or Mommy, but I could get used to him being my brother." She sighed. "So many people come and go. I think that's what makes Mommy sad. It makes me sad, too, when people can't stay." Again, she sounded far older than her few years, but her voice cracked when she added, "Especially people like you, Jeremiah."

She jumped to her feet and left the sap house, the door slamming in her wake.

He wanted to give chase, but he couldn't leave the evaporator. Or maybe that was an excuse, because what could he have said to the little girl?

He stared at the evaporator as an unexpected thought burst into his head. Should he leave the Amish before being baptized? Could he? Until he'd met Mercy, he'd never considered he'd ever make such a choice.

He laughed at the irony. When Emmarita had jumped the fence, he'd assumed it'd been a rash decision made to please her *Englischer*. Maybe it had been, but as he wrestled with the choice himself, he suspected she hadn't left her family and friends behind easily.

Or him.

It's long past time to forgive her. The whisper of his conscience seemed loud in the quiet. He forgave her as he comprehended what Emmarita had faced as she made her decision to leave. He knew, as he hadn't before, the choice hadn't been easy for her.

But Emmarita had made her choice. He now must, too.

Mercy picked her way through the icy patches on her way to the mailbox. She'd be so glad when spring arrived, and the last of the snow was gone.

An electrician had fixed the circuit breaker box and gotten the furnace started so they had light and heat in the house. Even so, the generator sat nearby, ready to pump out water if it seeped into the cellar again. The next time she spoke with her father, she would ask him if he knew of a way to seal the rock foundation to keep water out.

She opened the metal mailbox that still had Rudy's name on the side. Pulling out the stack of mail inside, she smiled when she saw a folded copy of the latest edition of *The Budget*. She looked at the index on the left side, and her smile broadened when she saw a listing for the Mennonite church they used to attend. Sunni enjoyed hearing news from there because sometimes her friends' names were mentioned by the correspondent. When Paul was at his worst and made fun of the names or what her friends were doing, Sunni ignored him.

That was the only time.

With a sigh, Mercy closed the box. She'd hoped by now the two children would have gotten over their obvious distaste for each other. Should she say something to Whitney? Disrupting Paul with another placement wouldn't help him, but Mercy didn't like her daughter being the target of his cruel teasing. Sunni was too young to understand why Paul was acting out, and Mercy was running out of ideas for how to bridge the gap between the two of them.

Riffling through the envelopes, she halted and stared at the return address on the bottommost one. Tucking the newspaper under her arm and the rest of the mail in her coat pocket, she ran up the slushy driveway. Mud splashed on the hem of her coat and her dress as she sped across the yard, hitting many of the puddles hidden beneath the grass that had been matted by the winter's heavy snow.

Pausing at the door of Jeremiah's shop, she peered inside. It was empty. Where was he? His buggy was in the yard, and it was too early to start the milking.

Mercy heard a thud, then a crack. He must be splitting wood on the far side of the house for use in making the last of the maple syrup. He mentioned at breakfast the wood box was empty. As she rounded the porch, she saw him with his ax raised before he brought it down in a quick, smooth arc. The blade cut into the chunk of wood on top of a stump. Two pieces of wood tumbled to the ground.

As he bent to pick them up, he must have seen her, because he halted and called a greeting.

She didn't slow until she reached where he stood. Her face must have revealed her thoughts, because he asked what was wrong. She tried to answer, but had to take a moment to regain her breath. He waited with more patience than she would have if their situations were reversed.

Holding out the letter, she said, "It's from my family's lawyer." Her voice cracked in spite of her efforts to hide her trepidation.

"What does it say?"

"I don't know. It's addressed to you."

When he set aside the ax, leaning it against the woodpile, he took the envelope. He pulled off one work glove, then the other before he took a knife out of his pocket and slit the top of the envelope open.

She held her breath as he drew out a single sheet of paper. She couldn't guess if such a short missive was good news for her or bad.

He read it fast, then read it again.

"What does it say?" she asked as he had.

He swallowed hard. "Your family has come to a consensus about the future of the farm."

"They've decided to sell it to you, haven't they?" She didn't know why she'd bothered to make it a question. His hesitation had told her the truth.

"I think maybe, but I'm not sure with the fancy lawyer language. Why don't you read it and tell me what you think?"

She took the letter and had to puzzle through the meaning of a couple of the long, elaborate sentences. The beginning of one seemed to contradict its ending, but she understood enough to know why the letter had been addressed to him.

Her father and his siblings intended to honor the purchase contract Jeremiah had signed.

"Congratulations, Jeremiah," she said as she returned the letter. She wished she could show more enthusiasm, but how could she when she was numb? "It's okay. You can celebrate if you want."

"How can I celebrate when I know what this decision means to you and the summer camp you wanted to have for city *kinder*?" He folded the letter and put it in the envelope.

"You're going to make your dream of having your own farm come true, Jeremiah. I'm happy for you." She blinked on hot tears. "Despite what I may look like, I'm happy for you."

"You look lovely."

"I wasn't fishing for a compliment."

"I know, but I wanted to give you one I should have said long ago." When she didn't answer, he asked, "What will you do?"

"I want to build a summer camp for city kids." Her gaze swept the place that soon wouldn't be her home. "It'll have to be somewhere else. I owe a great debt to the people who run the Fresh Air program. It's my mission. I know you may not understand because Amish don't do mission work."

"Some do."

"Not many."

He sighed. "You're right. Not many do."

"You probably want to tell Caleb you'll be stay

ing here." She took a step back. "I need to check on the kids." Her breath caught sharply. "Paul!"

"Won't Whitney let him stay with you?"

"I don't know." Her voice broke as she added, "I don't know about anything." She raised her chin. "Congratulations, Jeremiah. I know Grandpa Rudy would be thrilled to know the plans he made with you are going to work out."

Turning on her heel, she raced around the side of the house. She heard Jeremiah call after her, but she didn't slow. She wasn't sure how much longer she could pretend she was okay with her best chance to make her dream come true being dashed.

Chapter Seventeen

Putting the last dish in the cupboard, Mercy draped the damp dish towel over the rod hanging off a cabinet. She glanced at the clock. She'd finished exactly two minutes before Whitney was supposed to arrive. Yesterday, after the letter came from the family's lawyer, Mercy had called the social worker and explained what had happened.

"Don't worry, Mercy," she'd said. "Things can be worked out in situations like this."

Mercy had prayed Whitney was right. She'd planned on talking to the social worker on her next visit about when Paul would be free to be adopted. She wanted to get her name at the top of the list of potential adoptive parents.

The crunch of tires on frozen mud in the drive way announced the social worker was punctual as always. Opening the side door, Mercy motione

for Whitney to hurry in. The day was as cold as if the thaw had never happened.

A motion in the yard caught her eyes. Jeremiah strode toward the house, and she was relieved he was going to be with her when she spoke to Whitney about Paul's future.

"Brrr," said the blonde as she unzipped her coat. "I don't think this winter is ever going to end."

"It seems that way."

"Hi, Jeremiah. Good to see you again." She pulled off her coat and looked around. "Where are the children?"

"Upstairs." Mercy took a step toward the staircase. "I can get them."

"No!" The social worker's voice was startlingly sharp. "I need to speak to you without the children first."

Mercy motioned for them to come into the kitchen. What was bothering Whitney? The blonde was usually calm, even when Paul snarled at her.

Jeremiah's brows lowered, a sure sign he was puzzled by Whitney's odd behavior, too. He sat at the head of the table, but didn't say anything.

"Want coffee, Whitney?" she asked, reaching for the pot.

"No, thank you." Putting her briefcase on the chair, Whitney stood behind it. "I think what I have to say is best said quickly."

"What's wrong?" She couldn't keep from

glancing at Jeremiah, who was watching the social worker.

"The Kentons have been in contact with us for the past two weeks. Their social worker has spent time with them. She believes they're sincere in wanting their son returned to them."

Mercy stared at Whitney, sure she'd heard her wrong. Somehow, she pushed out a question. "They want him back?"

"Yes."

"Can they do that?" Mercy answered her own question before the social worker could. "I mean, I know they can ask, but why are you agreeing?"

"Parker—"

Jeremiah said with quiet dignity, "He calls himself Paul now."

"I know, but the Kentons still want to call him Parker." Whitney sighed. "I'll let them know again that he prefers the other name. Mercy, Jeremiah, I know you're attached to the boy, but he was with the Kentons for more than six months, and, though they were overwhelmed and needed a break, they've put together a support network they—and we—think will make the placement a success."

"Does he have input into the decision?" Jeremiah asked.

"He's a child." She cut her eyes to Mercy. "You

know children aren't in any position to judge what's best for them in the long run."

Mercy lowered herself to a chair and clasped her hands in her lap. "I know the hurt jerking a child around can create. I had two placements before I came to the Bambergers, and I was a very angry child who didn't trust anyone." She stared at the table crisscrossed with nicks and gouges, the sign of long use. "If it hadn't been for Grandpa Rudy, I don't know if I ever would have trusted again."

When Jeremiah's hand covered hers, she knew he was offering what comfort he could.

"I understand," Whitney said as she looked from Mercy to Jeremiah.

"So do I," Mercy replied with a sigh.

Jeremiah erupted from his chair. "And that's it? You aren't going to give us time to say goodbye?"

"Of course you'll have time." Whitney sighed. "I'm not heartless, but I've got to think what's best for him."

"Staying here is best for him." Jeremiah's scowl deepened.

Mercy put her hand on Jeremiah's arm. She'd never seen him so furious and knew he was fighting to keep his temper under control. "Getting angry won't help."

"So you're going to let him go?" He snapped his fingers. "Just like that?"

"Please don't make it harder," she said.

"I don't know how it could be." Hurt blazed in his eyes as they locked with Mercy's. "Why can't he stay here with Mercy so she can adopt him?"

"We have a two-parent family who wants him," Whitney replied. "Our first choice for a child is always to have two parents."

"But they didn't want him, and Mercy does."

Knowing it was Jeremiah's grief speaking, Mercy interjected, "Whitney, will you excuse us?"

"I'll wait in the living room." She glanced at her watch. "I can give you twenty minutes. No more."

Once the social worker left the kitchen, Jeremiah came around the table so he stood beside Mercy. "I love that boy. I don't want to lose him."

"I know. I love him, too, but he has a chance for a home with two parents who love him."

"Two parents who tossed him aside like an unwanted puppy."

Wondering how she could reach through his hurt to help him understand, she knew the only way was to be honest. "Jeremiah, I don't like this any more than you do, but—"

"What if they decide they don't want him again?" He flung out his hands. "Will they throw him away again?"

"We have to pray they won't."

His shoulders dropped, and she knew she'd fi

nally gotten him to understand. Paul's life, like theirs, was in God's hand. They had to trust God would watch over the boy.

Going to the base of the stairs, she shouted for the children. She frowned when she got no response. Paul... She'd just gotten used to calling him that, and now she had to remember to address him as Parker. He might refuse to answer her, but Sunni always came when Mercy called.

"Are you up here?" she tried again.

She heard Whitney coming from the living room and Jeremiah from the kitchen, but she ran up the stairs. Why weren't the children answering?

Jeremiah exchanged a glance with Whitney as Mercy's voice drifted to them. Before he could speak, Mercy rushed down the stairs. Her face was a sick shade.

"What's wrong?" he asked.

"Sunni and Parker have disappeared." She looked at the shocked social worker. "They aren't here."

"Let me find them," he said. "They couldn't have gone far."

"If they heard us..." Whitney choked out.

Shoving his black hat on his head, he ran out of the house. Ten minutes later he'd searched the outbuildings and the tenant house. Fruitlessly.

Mercy was waiting on the porch when he returned to the house. "Whitney wants to call the police."

"Not yet," he said. "I'll get our neighbors to help find them."

The social worker opened the door. "No, Jeremiah. The boy is my responsibility. We have to call the police before he runs away too far."

"We don't know if they've run away. They may have slipped out before you got here. I'm going to check with the neighbors. Someone must have seen them."

Whitney started to protest, but Mercy silenced her by touching her arm.

"Let Jeremiah try. Give him an hour."

"Two," he insisted. "That's enough time to check every place along the creek."

"Give him two hours," Mercy pleaded. "If the kids see policemen, they may hide instead of coming out of wherever they are."

"An hour. No longer, and it's against my better judgment." Whitney wrapped her arms around herself. "I'm risking my job on this."

"We know, and we appreciate it." Mercy kept talking to the blonde as she steered Whitney into the house. Looking back before she closed the door, she mouthed, "Find them. Fast."

Jeremiah loped along the drive and toward Caleb's farm. As the word spread through the ho-

low, more and more people joined the hunt for the *kinder*. He asked everyone to check their own outbuildings and then the woods on both sides of the creek. He hoped Sunni and Paul hadn't tried to cross it because the ice was no longer thick enough to hold them.

Time sped past too fast. Ever conscious of how little time they had to search so many acres and buildings, his hope the youngsters could be found before the police were called began to fade. Leaving Caleb to direct the search as the hour elapsed, Jeremiah hurried to where Mercy and the social worker waited.

Whitney was on her cell phone as he came in. When Mercy looked at him, he shook his head, sick at heart for failing her. She'd trusted him, and he'd let her down. He thought of what Sunni had told him about Mercy's ex-fiancé not being there for her. He hadn't wanted to do the same.

She offered him a cup of cocoa, and he took it gratefully. His toes felt like a quintet of frozen blocks of ice in each of his boots. As he raised the cup to his lips, a motion outside caught his eye.

Smoke coming from the sap house? He hadn't left a fire in there after he finished the latest batch of maple syrup.

"Mercy, I think I know where they are."

"Where?" asked both women at the same time.

He pointed out the window toward the sap

house. Setting down his untasted cocoa, he grabbed Mercy's coat and thrust it into her hands. She was pulling it on as she followed him out of the house. Behind them, Whitney yelled for them to wait up. They kept going.

The ice sent Mercy skidding into him. He grabbed her hand as they climbed the hill to the small building.

When he threw open the door, heat struck his face. He stepped inside and called, "*Komm* out! know you're in here."

Sunni peeked around the side of the evaporator. "Jeremiah!" Looking back, she motioned. "It' okay, Paul. Jeremiah will make it okay."

Mercy saw the pain on Jeremiah's face and knew he wished desperately Sunni was right. She stepped into the sap house, but halted Whitney from pushing past her.

"Let us talk to them," she said, "while you ca the police and let them know the kids have bee found."

For a second she thought the social worke would insist, but then Whitney nodded. "I'll mee you at the house in ten minutes."

"It may take a bit longer."

"I can't give you more time, Mercy. We're a ready late meeting the Kentons."

Nodding, Mercy headed for the far end of th

sap house. She doubted her feet touched the floor more than twice as she bounded forward to sweep the children into her arms. Sunni clung to her, and Parker did, too. When Jeremiah put his arms around them, they stood in silence for the length of two heartbeats.

Sunni and Parker began explaining how they'd started a fire beneath the evaporator to stay warm.

"While we waited for that woman to go away." Parker shivered.

Mercy put her arm around him and gave him a comforting squeeze, knowing he wasn't cold, but scared. When Jeremiah drew the boy away and bent so his eyes were even with Parker's, she draped her arms over her daughter, clasping her hands in front of Sunni.

"If we hid, that lady couldn't take Paul away," her daughter said.

"Whitney wants the best for him," Jeremiah said.

"We're the best for him." Her daughter looked up at her. "Isn't that right, Mommy?"

"She wants to take me back to people who don't want me," the little boy insisted. "I don't want to go!"

"Would you try spending a weekend with the Lentons?" Mercy asked.

The boy and the man wore identical expres-

sions of dismay, but understanding lit Jeremiah's eyes and he nodded.

"Just a weekend?" Parker asked, suspiciously.

"Yes, for now. Maybe it won't be as bad as you think it'll be."

"Maybe."

"You know you won't be going alone," she said softly as she reached out to take the boy's right hand. "God will be with you whether you are here or somewhere else."

"I know." He looked at Jeremiah, who took his other hand. "I can lay my bad feelings at His feet, and He'll sweep them away with His toes."

Mercy didn't try to restrain her smile. "That's right. You're a smart boy to figure that out."

"I didn't figure it out. Jeremiah told me."

Jeremiah winked at him. "I'm glad you listened I need to go and let the searchers know the kids have been found. I'll meet you at the house, okay? I'll be back as fast as I can."

Mercy nodded, knowing he hoped Parker would be there when he returned. She smiled. She wasn' sure how, but she'd find a way to persuade Whit ney to wait.

Her concerns were needless because when she and the children entered the house, Whitney too' her aside and said the Kentons had called and ar ranged to meet Parker the next afternoon.

"So he can stay here until then?" Mercy asked

"If you make sure he's here when I come back."

"I'll do my best. I won't let either of them out of my sight until then."

Parker stared, openmouthed, when Whitney said he could stay overnight. He stammered out his thanks as Sunni squealed with excitement.

"Why are you sounding like a pig?" Parker asked. "Is it because you look like one?"

"Mommy!" cried Sunni. "Tell him I'm not a pig."

Knowing the kids' temporary truce was broken, Mercy herded them into the kitchen and sat them at the table once Whitney left. But she couldn't keep from smiling as they bickered. Even that annoying sound was precious while she spent these last hours with Parker.

Somehow, she managed to keep her tears hidden and her voice cheerful while they had supper and she tucked the children into bed. She kissed their freshly washed faces and wished them pleasant dreams. As she went down the stairs, she heard hushed voices and footsteps. She looked back to discover Sunni sneaking into Parker's room. She suspected when she checked later, she'd find them curled together like the litter of kittens in the barn.

Jeremiah was waiting at the bottom of the stairs. Crooking a finger, he walked into the living room. She caught up with him and put her

arms around him, leaning her face against his strong back.

"Thank you," she whispered. "Thank you for finding them."

Facing her, he said, "I've been thinking, Mercy. Whitney said a two-parent family is always the best choice for a *kind*. Do you know Sunni believes you agreed to marry Graham because you wanted her to have a *daed*?"

"No." Shock raced through her. "I didn't know she knew that."

"So you were marrying him to give her a *daed*?"

"It's embarrassing to admit, but it's partly true. I did think I loved Graham."

He took her hands and led her to the sofa. Sitting beside her, he asked, "You *thought* you loved him?"

"Yes, until I realized what love really is. You taught me that."

"As you've taught me." He brushed his lip against hers. "I need to ask you something. Would you consider staying here on the farm as my wife?"

"So we can try to adopt Parker if things don't work out with the Kentons?"

"In part, but I'm asking because I love you and I can't endure the thought of losing you." He smoothed loose strands from her face. "I thought

couldn't hurt worse than when the woman I loved jumped the fence and married an *Englischer*. But the idea of being without you is torture. Marry me, Mercy."

"Does that mean you're willing to become a Mennonite?"

"I'd hoped you would consider being baptized Amish, Mercy. You've seen how we live, and you seem comfortable with it."

She wasn't surprised at his request. And he was right. During the days when they were without electricity, she'd learned to manage the household and keep them fed. "I want to tell you yes, but I told God I'd repay the kindnesses done to me when I was little. Won't that be impossible if I became Amish?"

"I don't know, but I can present your idea for Come Along Farm to our bishop."

"But what about your plans for the farm?"

"We're two smart people. I'm sure we can figure out a way to make both our dreams come true on this farm."

"Assuming the bishop is okay with it?"

"*Ja.* I must get his opinion if it's permissible for an Amish woman to oversee a summer camp."

"Do you think he'll agree?" she asked as her heart danced within her.

"I don't know Wayne well enough to be sure, but I know he'll listen and pray for guidance."

"I have information I'd put together earlier, if you want to give it to him."

"Let's pray there will be an easy way to resolve this. If Wayne says he's okay with your plans for a summer program, we can—"

Her finger against his lips halted him. "One problem at a time, Jeremiah."

"I don't consider getting you to agree to marry me a problem." Folding her hands between his, he asked, "If we can work this out, will you marry me?"

She gave him her answer with a kiss that told him far better than words how much she loved him and wanted to be his wife.

Chapter Eighteen

The candles had been blown out, and the chocolate cake was gone except for a few crumbs on the platter. Outside the cozy kitchen, a chilly October wind whistled at the eaves.

As Mercy looked around the kitchen, she had to smile. The house didn't look different, but in the past months, it had gone through as many changes as she had. Wayne Flaud had been hesitant about Mercy being baptized. He refused to start baptism classes with her until she lived a full Amish life for six months.

She'd agreed and, with Jeremiah's assistance as well as her neighbors', complied. She attended baptism classes with the bishop, a process that took longer than usual because of the distances involved. Instead of meeting weekly with him, they met twice a month when he came to join the *Leit* for services.

And last month, at her final session with the bishop, whom she discovered wasn't as rigid and imposing as his appearance had suggested, Wayne had told her after hours of prayer and long correspondence with other bishops, he couldn't see how it would be a problem for her to bring in Fresh Air kids for two weeks each summer. It was, he told her, no different from Amish families who took in *Englischers* in a farm-stay bed-and-breakfast for them to discover what an Amish farm was like. She'd wanted to throw her arms around him and hug him, but she'd simply said, "*Danki*, Wayne."

Mercy yawned as Jeremiah entered the kitchen. She wouldn't ever get tired of looking at the sparkle of happiness in his eyes when his gaze shifted to her.

Picking up the last of the dishes, she put them in the sink. "Next time I'm not going to plan a wedding the day after you throw a birthday party for me."

"I'd rather hoped you wouldn't ever be planning another wedding." He gave her one of the scintillating smiles she adored.

"Sunni will marry someday."

He chuckled. "Let me enjoy her being a *kind* before I think of her marrying and making me a *grossdawdi*. Now admit it. You had a *wunderbaar* time at the party."

"I enjoyed every moment of it, but the idea of another huge party tomorrow is overwhelming."

"Be grateful you're here instead of the tenant house." Jeremiah slid his arm around her waist, but kept his other hand behind his back. Was he hiding something? "I think every corner is covered with food to be served tomorrow. *Mamm* and my sisters-in-law cooked as if there were forty families here instead of seven. I don't know if they've left me a place to sleep."

"Most of my relatives will be coming in the morning. They kindly found places to stay in the villages around here, so the house won't be filled to capacity before the ceremony begins." Her eyes widened as she recalled the service would be in High German, a language she was struggling to learn. She recognized more words every church Sunday. "Jeremiah, did you ask—?"

He tapped her nose. "All my siblings, except Isaiah who, as an ordained minister, will be helping with the service, and their spouses have offered to translate portions of the ceremony not in English as well as the songs."

"My family will know most of them, I'm sure." She smiled. "I've already warned them not to harmonize and to sing really, really, really slow."

"Look what I found!" called an excited voice from the stairs.

Sunni and the boy they again called Paul ran

into the kitchen, sliding to a stop inches from Mercy. Jeremiah smiled at them. Sunni would become his daughter after tomorrow. Paul would be their son as soon as the adoption paperwork was completed in the coming weeks.

It was as if Paul had been with them his whole life. When he'd returned to the Kentons for the planned visit, Whitney returned with him only a few hours later.

"The Kentons changed their minds yet again," the social worker had said with an outraged frown. "I can assure you they won't have another chance. As you said, Mercy, jerking a child around is cruel."

Paul shoved an envelope into Mercy's hand.

"What's that?" she asked.

He shrugged. "I found it in the back of the top drawer in my dresser when I was trying to find clean socks." The boy's room continued to look as if a gale swept through it twice a day. "It's got your name on it."

Mercy gasped when she recognized Grandpa Rudy's handwriting on the envelope. Could it be the will she'd searched in vain for? She hoped not, because that could complicate Jeremiah's ownership of the farm he'd closed on four months ago.

Pulling out the single sheet with quivering fingers, she read aloud:

"My dear Mercy,

"I hope you and your darling daughter have found the perfect home for yourselves with the proceeds from the farm. I know you wanted the farm to make a camp for city children, but my farm needs too much work for you and Sunni to handle alone.

"I have enclosed a copy of the deed for fifteen acres across the road from the farm. It's big enough for you to build a house, a barn and riding area for your summer kids."

"Fifteen acres?" Jeremiah glanced at the surprisingly flat fields edged by Harmony Creek. "Why didn't we see your *grossdawdi*'s name as a neighboring landowner on the deed for this property when I closed on this farm?"

"I don't know." She continued reading.

"Ask Jeremiah Stoltzfus for his help. He seems like a good man, for my farm and for you."

She smiled at Jeremiah, who was shaking his head in amazement.

"I never guessed," he said, "why he asked me so many questions before he agreed to sell me the farm. Your *grossdawdi* was a matchmaker, Mercy."

"He knew a good thing when he saw it." She

gave him a quick kiss before continuing to read Grandpa Rudy's letter.

"The land has been held in trust for you. Make your difference, Mercy, in other lives. But remember you don't carry a debt for how your life has turned out. You may think you are beholden to us for you being a part of the family. You aren't. You weren't an obligation. You were a blessing, a gift to all of us."

It was signed "your loving grandpa."

She pressed the letter to her heart as she whispered, "I love you, too, Grandpa Rudy." Raising her eyes to Jeremiah's, she said, "We have Wayne's approval, and we can have Come Along Farm and your farm. What an amazing birthday gift!"

"Would you like another?" Sunni asked. "It's time, Jeremiah."

"Time for what?" Mercy saw the ill-concealed grins on the children's—no, she needed to use her *Deitsch*—the *kinder*'s faces.

Jeremiah took her hand and sat her at the table. "Before anything else, I want to tell you I've solved another mystery for you. When I spoke with your parents during their visit here last month, they were as surprised as you were to learn the box of possessions from *Abuelita*'s apartment ended

up in Rudy's attic. They did know about the box, because your social worker mentioned it. Apparently, your parents were in the middle of a move because your *daed* was changing jobs around the time you came to them. Your *mamm* assumes they gave your social worker this address to make sure the box was safely delivered." He drew his hand from behind his back and handed her a manila envelope. "Open it."

The envelope wasn't thick, so there couldn't be anything more than a page or two inside. Was it something to do with Paul's adoption? No, Whitney had said they'd filled out all the necessary forms, though there would be more to sign the day Paul's adoption became final.

"Open it!" Sunni urged.

"Open it!" shouted Paul, and the two *kinder* began to repeat the words over and over.

Mercy did and reached inside. She pulled out a single slick piece of paper. It was blank, so she turned it over.

"Oh, my!" she whispered as she stared at the photograph. The woman's face matched the shape of hers, and the man's eyes crinkled as hers did when she smiled. Her parents! It was the photo she'd last seen whole the day *Abuelita* died. "But how…?" She couldn't finish the question because words refused to push past the thick lump in her throat.

Jeremiah sat beside her and leaned her head against his shoulder so they looked at the picture together. "I found an address on the framed photograph. I wrote to the photography studio and asked if they were still in business. I heard from the wife of the man who'd taken that picture. He's passed away, and their son is running the business. They searched the old files and found the negative for the picture of your parents. I had them make you a new print."

"Look!" She motioned for the children to come closer. "These are your grandparents. Gilberto and Amada Ramirez. They—" She sat up straight "But I'm Amish since I was baptized last month, and the Amish don't like photographs."

He gave her a gentle smile. "We don't like photos taken of us. Your parents weren't Amish, so there's no problem with you having it."

"Danki," she whispered as she wept.

"Are you sad, Mommy?" asked Sunni.

"We want you to be happy," Paul quickly added

"I'm happy. Happier than I've ever been." She hugged each of them.

Jeremiah said, "I wanted your family to be as complete as possible on our wedding day."

Holding the picture over her heart, she put her other arm around Paul and Sunni. As Jeremiah drew them closer, she said, "You've given m

what I wanted my whole life. A family that's all my own."

"And my own, too," he said.

"And my own," repeated the *kinder* together.

They all laughed in the moment before Jeremiah captured her lips that would be his for the rest of their lives.

* * * * *

Don't miss these other
AMISH HEARTS *stories*
from Jo Ann Brown:

AMISH HOMECOMING
AN AMISH MATCH
HIS AMISH SWEETHEART
AN AMISH REUNION
A READY-MADE AMISH FAMILY
AN AMISH PROPOSAL

Find more great reads at
www.LoveInspired.com

Dear Reader,

All of us face disappointment at some time in our lives, especially when something gets in the way of our dreams. Both Jeremiah and Mercy had big dreams for themselves and for ways they could help others. When those dreams are in danger of being thwarted, they have to work together to remember a very basic lesson. God has a plan for each of us, and we need to understand that sometimes the answer to a prayer is "No" or "Not now." The important thing, I've learned as a writer and as a human, is to keep going and have faith so can discover the wonderful things God has waiting for me.

Visit me at *www.joannbrownbooks.com*. Look for my next story coming soon from Harlequin Love Inspired, the first in a new series set in Harmony Creek Hollow.

Wishing you many blessings,
Jo Ann Brown

Get 2 Free Books, <u>Plus</u> 2 Free Gifts—
just for trying the Reader Service!

Get 2 Free Books,
Plus 2 Free Gifts—
just for trying the Reader Service!

HOMETOWN HEARTS ♥

YES! Please send me **The Hometown Hearts Collection** in Larger Print. This collection begins with 3 FREE books and 2 FREE gifts in the first shipment. Along with my 3 free books, I'll also get the next 4 books from the Hometown Hearts Collection, in LARGER PRINT, which I may either return and owe nothing, or keep for the low price of $4.99 U.S./ $5.89 CDN each plus $2.99 for shipping and handling per shipment*. If I decide to continue, about once a month for 8 months I will get 6 or 7 more books, but will only need to pay for 4. That means 2 or 3 books in every shipment will be FREE! If I decide to keep the entire collection, I'll have paid for only 32 books because 19 books are FREE! I understand that accepting the 3 free books and gifts places me under no obligation to buy anything. I can always return a shipment and cancel at any time. My free books and gifts are mine to keep no matter what I decide.

262 HCN 3432 462 HCN 3432

Name	(PLEASE PRINT)	
Address		Apt. #
City	State/Prov.	Zip/Postal Code
Signature (if under 18, a parent or guardian must sign)		

Mail to the **Reader Service:**

IN U.S.A.: P.O. Box 1867, Buffalo, NY. 14240-1867
IN CANADA: P.O. Box 609, Fort Erie, Ontario L2A 5X3

HHBPA17

READERSERVICE.COM

Manage your account online!

- Review your order history
- Manage your payments
- Update your address

We've designed the Reader Service website just for you.

Enjoy all the features!

- Discover new series available to you, and read excerpts from any series.
- Respond to mailings and special monthly offers.
- Browse the Bonus Bucks catalog and online-only exclusives.
- Share your feedback.

Visit us at:
ReaderService.com